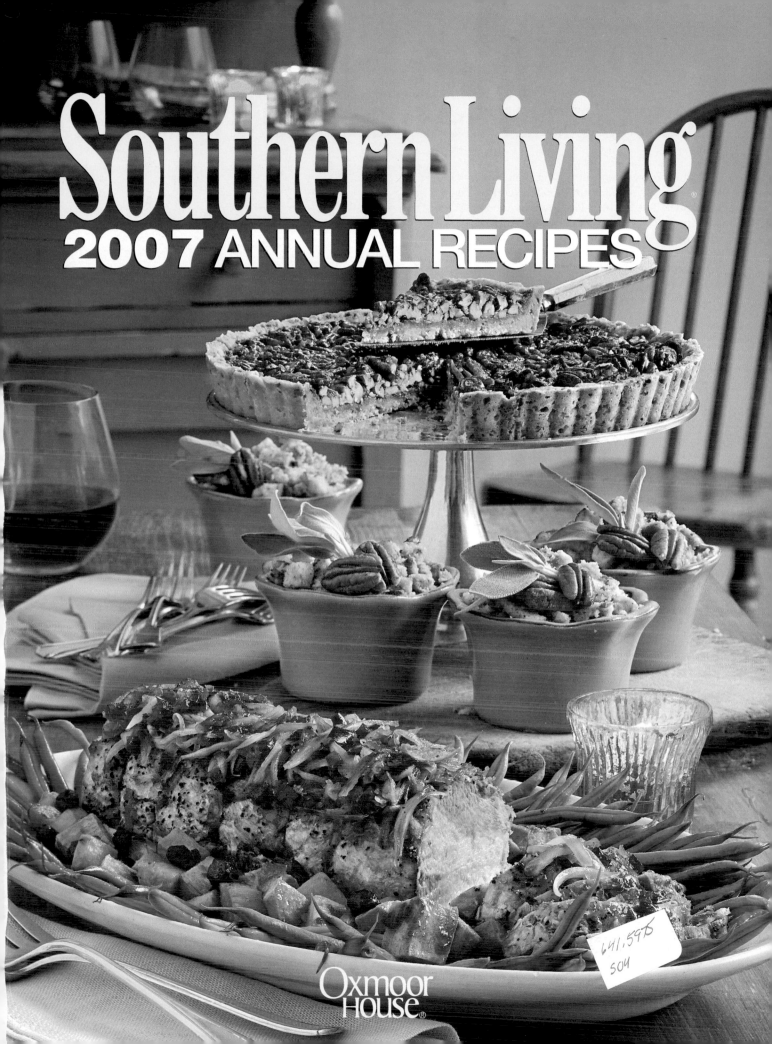

Southern Living
2007 ANNUAL RECIPES

Oxmoor
House

best recipes of 2007

No one knows the South better than *Southern Living*, and no one knows food better than the magazine's Test Kitchens Professionals and Foods Editors. Each year our staff evaluates thousands of recipes, allowing only the best-of-the-best onto the pages of the magazine. Many recipes receive two, three, or even four tests to ensure that they are tasty, easy to prepare, and that they also offer the "wow" factor, that standout quality that gets cooks big compliments. Evaluating these scrumptious recipes was a tough, but mouthwatering job—and here we share this year's favorites.

Orange Rolls *(page 50)* ▶
Make these melt-in-your-mouth treats with Honey Topping and Fresh Orange Glaze and you might get the same result we did—the whole batch will be gone in a matter of minutes.

▼ **Graduation Cake With Cream Cheese Frosting** *(page 109)* Fresh lemon juice is the secret ingredient in this easy-to-make celebration cake and icing.

◄ **Spiced Pecans** *(page 83)*
Sugar, cinnamon, and cayenne
pepper add a sweet, spicy, and
hot flavor to these crunchy
treats. Here, the nuts are used as
a salad topping with leafy
greens, mango slices, strawberries, asparagus, and zucchini
ribbons. Drizzled with a vinaigrette dressed up with fresh
lemon juice and grated lemon
rind and sprinkled with feta
cheese, the salad is perfect
served alongside grilled chicken.

▼ **Grilled Shrimp-and-Green
Bean Salad** *(page 102)* The
garden and the grill come
together in this savory combo.

▲ **Banana Pudding Pie** *(page 46)* Layers of bananas and a scrumptious Vanilla Cream Filling atop a crisp cookie-crumb crust make this Southern favorite absolutely irresistible.

Chocolate Chunk-Mocha Cookies *(page 87)* With two types of chocolate on the inside and a luscious Mocha Frosting, it's impossible to resist the rich taste of these treats.

▲ **Grilled Chicken With White Barbecue Sauce** *(page 98)* Several robust ingredients flavor this versatile mayonnaise-based barbecue sauce. It pairs perfectly with tender, juicy chicken thighs flavored with a tasty rub.

◄ **Italian Cheese Bites** *(page 36)* Thick, crusty bread slices coated with a buttery Parmesan cheese spread encrust melted provolone cheese for a gooey little sandwich that's the ultimate comfort food.

▲ **Fluffy Buttermilk Biscuits** *(page 120)* We went against the norm by kneading this biscuit dough more than normal and by cranking up the oven temperature for these mouthwatering morsels.

Mango-Papaya Daiquiri *(page 139)* Summer cocktails don't get much better than a slushy cooler that mixes the great taste of fresh and frozen fruits with some fruit juice and coconut rum.

◄ **Mississippi Mud Cake** *(page 194)* Toasted pecans add a flavorful crunch to this ooey, gooey chocolate dessert that's a surefire crowd-pleaser.

Nectarine-and-Toasted Almond Blend *(page 143)* Personalize basic vanilla ice cream with a refreshing five-ingredient combination of nectarine slices, sugar, butter, almonds, and salt.

Tomato-Watermelon Sorbet *(page 136)* Colorful and delicious, this is one of the coolest concoctions we've seen in a while. ▼

▲ **Gingerbread Cake With Stout Buttercream** *(page 224)* Beer adds to the old-fashioned flavor of this super-moist dessert that starts with a cake mix.

Cinnamon Rolls With Cream Cheese Icing *(page 287)* ▶ After following our foolproof instructions for these delicate rolls with gooey frosting, you'll never want storebought again. Try our variations of Apple-Cinnamon Rolls, Chocolate-Cinnamon Rolls, and Cranberry-Cinnamon Rolls.

Thanksgiving Sparkler *(page 261)* A spiced syrup adds a kick to this three-ingredient cocktail.

Dark Chocolate Bundt Cake *(page 278)* You won't believe how simple it is to make this good-to-the-last-crumb treat that's sure to dazzle your guests.

▼ **Caramel-Pecan Tart** *(page 262)* This combination of toasted pecans mixed with a buttery-rich brown sugar-and-honey topping created a sensation in our kitchens.

Caramel-Pecan Bars *(page 262)* This bite-size version of the Caramel-Pecan Tart makes the perfect addition to any occasion.

Buttermilk Biscuits
(page 263) ▶
Discover the unique dough-folding method that we used to make these melt-in-your-mouth perfect. Don't miss our tasty variations of this Southern classic.

Pecan Divinity Cake
(page 252) Tender layers of sour cream cake hide beneath fluffy divinity-inspired frosting. You won't believe this impressive cake starts with a mix.

▼ **Pecan Cheesecake Pie**
(page 263) This scrumptious dessert boasts a creamy bottom layer of batter that rises to the top of the crust during baking.

▲ **Red Velvet-Peppermint Cake** *(page 250)* A holiday twist on those chocolate-swirled marble cakes, this recipe uses two mixes but delivers made-from-scratch flavor.

Fresh Orange Italian Cream Cake *(page 253)* Sweet orange curd sandwiched between tender cake layers makes this spectacular dessert a standout.

Praline-Pecan Cakes *(page 256)* Perfect for holiday gift giving, this recipe yields 9 (5-inch) loaves that can be frozen up to a month.

▲ **Roasted Banana Ice Cream With Warm Peanut Butter Sauce** *(page 300)* A warm peanut sauce drizzled over a flavorful banana ice cream was the $100,000 grand prize winner in our cook-off.

Tequila-Flambéed Bananas With Coconut Ice Cream *(page 301)* It takes less than 30 minutes to whip up this company-worthy dessert.

Coconut-Cream Bread Pudding *(page 301)* A caramelized sugar sauce and crispy coconut, pecan, and butter topping adds a unique twist to this Southern classic.

Hazelnut Chocolate Biscotti *(page 308)* Two types of chocolate candy bars mixed with a hazelnut liqueur make this a melt-in-your-mouth treat.

▼ **Decadent S'mores Tiramisù** *(page 307)* The creativity of this dish helped make this a $10,000 Your Best Recipe category cook-off winner.

Apple Jack Pork Burgers With Apple-Fennel Marmalade *(page 308)* A sweet marmalade and spicy mayonnaise mixture combine for a one-of-a-kind burger.

Coconut Macadamia Shrimp With Warm Tropical Salsa *(page 302)* ▶ A crunchy coating of coconut and macadamia nuts pairs nicely with a refreshing fruity salsa.

California Sushi Bites *(page 302)* This colorful appetizer makes enough to serve a large crowd.

Curried Beef Kabobs With Jade Sauce *(page 303)* Toasted coconut combined with a minty, sweet and spicy sauce flavors a flat iron steak.

Pork Pad Thai *(page 304)* A spicy peanut butter sauce tops this stir-fried dish.

▼ **Tuscan Catfish With Sun-dried Tomato Aïoli** *(page 304)* A pita chip crust coats this Southern-fried specialty that garnered $10,000 as the Quick Weeknight Favorites cook-off winner.

▲ **Peanut Shrimp Salad With Basil-Lime Dressing** (page 305) Bright and refreshing, this Good-For-You category cook-off winner makes an easy one-dish meal.

Szechwan Burgers With Cilantro Slaw (page 305) This Asian-inspired dish takes just 20 minutes of prep time.

Mole Rubbed Chicken With Confetti Corn Relish (page 306) Brown sugar, unsweetened cocoa, and a few spices provide a unique rub for this main-dish favorite.

Chili-and-Lime Grilled Shrimp With Seasoned White Beans (page 306) Your family will love this one-dish meal that's quick to make.

meet the *Southern Living* foods staff

For over 40 years, the *Southern Living* Foods Staff has been the trusted source of Southern cuisine. These dedicated professionals bring to their readers the benefit of more than 200 years of combined experience. On these pages, we invite you to match the names and faces of the people who test, photograph, and write about our favorites (left to right unless otherwise noted).

▲ (seated) SCOTT JONES, *Executive Editor;* SHANNON SLITER SATTERWHITE, *Foods Editor;* (standing) LYDA JONES BURNETTE, *Test Kitchens Director;* PAT YORK, *Editorial Assistant;* SANDRA J. THOMAS, *Administrative Assistant*

◀ (seated) KRISTI MICHELE CROWE *and* ANGELA SELLERS, *Test Kitchens Professionals;* (standing) PAM LOLLEY, *Test Kitchens Professional;* REBECCA KRACKE GORDON, *Assistant Test Kitchens Director*

(standing) ▶
ASHLEY LEATH, *Assistant Recipe Editor;*
MARY ALLEN PERRY, *Associate Foods Editor;*
JAMES SCHEND, *Assistant Foods Editor;*
KATE NICHOLSON, SHIRLEY HARRINGTON, *and* VICKI A. POELLNITZ, *Associate Foods Editors;*
(seated) CHARLA DRAPER, *Associate Foods Editor;*
ANDRIA SCOTT HURST, *Senior Writer;*
NATALIE KELLY BROWN *and* MARION McGAHEY, *Assistant Foods Editors;*
DONNA FLORIO, *Senior Writer*

our year at
Southern Living.

Dear Food Friends,

The 29th volume of *Southern Living* Annual Recipes is loaded with tempting recipes and helpful cooking tips. It's all here in one dynamic and beautifully illustrated cookbook. The variety of recipes we highlight each year is truly astounding. From quick and easy weeknight suppers to spectacular appetizers to stunning desserts, these recipes reflect what our readers are cooking in kitchens across the South.

Be sure to reference the Test Kitchens Notebook tips scattered throughout the chapters. You'll uncover our top secrets for success and learn everything you need to know to get these irresistible recipes just right. One of my favorite sections is Slow-Cooker Favorites, which offers more than recipes for main dishes; it also has appetizers, sides, and desserts. It's the perfect companion for planning supper or your next get-together.

> **"This year, please allow us to set the *Southern Living* table with you in mind."**

This year, please allow us to set the *Southern Living* table with you in mind. We'd love for you to share your favorite recipes with us for possible publication. We're looking for everything from simple meals to special entertaining. We'd also like to know what you're doing to make meals fit into your healthy lifestyle. For each recipe we use, we'll send you $20 when the recipe is published and a copy of the *Southern Living* Annual Recipes cookbook the following January. Please e-mail recipes to sl_foodedit@timeinc.com.

Thanks for inviting us into your homes. I look forward to hearing from you and seeing more of your recipes soon.

Sincerely,

Scott Jones
Executive Editor

© 2007 by Oxmoor House, Inc.
Book Division of Southern Progress Corporation
P.O. Box 2262, Birmingham, Alabama 35201-2262

Southern Living®, *Summer Living*®, *Christmas All Through the House*®, and *Holiday Dinners*® are federally registered trademarks of Southern Living, Inc.

ISBN-13: 978-0-8487-3155-7
ISBN-10: 0-8487-3155-7

Printed in the United States of America
First printing 2007

To order additional publications, call 1-800-765-6400.

For more books to enrich your life, visit **oxmoorhouse.com**

To search, savor, and share thousands of recipes, visit
myrecipes.com

Cover: Vanilla Butter Cake, page 278

Page 1: Holiday Pork Loin Roast (page 272) with Cranberry Sweet Potatoes (page 265), and steamed green beans. Serve your favorite dressing in individual baking dishes, and finish with Pecan Cheesecake Pie (page 263).

Southern Living®

Executive Editor: Scott Jones
Foods Editor: Shannon Sliter Satterwhite
Senior Writers: Donna Florio, Andria Scott Hurst
Associate Foods Editors: Charla Draper, Shirley Harrington, Kate Nicholson, Mary Allen Perry, Vicki A. Poellnitz
Assistant Foods Editors: Natalie Kelly Brown, Marion McGahey, James Schend
Assistant Recipe Editor: Ashley Leath
Test Kitchens Director: Lyda Jones Burnette
Assistant Test Kitchens Director: Rebecca Kracke Gordon
Test Kitchens Specialist/Food Styling: Vanessa McNeil Rocchio
Test Kitchens Professionals: Marian Cooper Cairns, Kristi Michele Crowe, Norman King, Pam Lolley, Angela Sellers
Editorial Assistant: Pat York
Administrative Assistant: Catherine K. Russell
Production and Color Quality Manager: Katie Terrell Morrow
Creative Director: Jon Thompson
Design Director: Howard Greenberg
Copy Chief: Paula Hunt Hughes
Copy Editor: Cindy Riegle
Senior Foods Photographer: Jennifer Davick
Photographers: Ralph Anderson, William Dickey, Beth Dreiling Hontzas
Senior Photo Stylist: Buffy Hargett
Photo Stylists: Rose Nguyen, Lisa Powell Bailey
Photo Production Manager: Larry Hunter
Photo Services Manager: Tracy Duncan
Photo Services: Catherine Carr
Assistant Production Manager: Jamie Barnhart
Production Coordinators: Christy Coleman, Paula Dennis

Oxmoor House, Inc.

Editor in Chief: Nancy Fitzpatrick Wyatt
Executive Editor: Susan Carlisle Payne
Art Director: Keith McPherson
Managing Editor: Allison Long Lowery

Southern Living® ***2007 Annual Recipes***

Editor: Susan Hernandez Ray
Copy Chief: L. Amanda Owens
Copy Editor: Donna Baldone
Editorial Assistant: Amelia Heying
Director of Production: Laura Lockhart
Senior Production Manager: Greg A. Amason
Production Assistant: Faye Porter Bonner

Contributors

Designer: Nancy Johnson
Indexer: Mary Ann Laurens
Editorial Consultant: Jean Wickstrom Liles
Editorial Intern: Tracey Apperson
Proofreader: Dolores Hydock, Leah Marlett

contents

favorite columns at a glance

Each month we focus on topics that are important to our readers—
from Southern classics to fast dinners to delicious menus.

>> top-rated recipes

■ Enjoy a year of health and prosperity with a **New Year's Day Meal** featuring Classic Barbecue Ribs, Hearty Black-eyed Peas, and Turnip Greens Stew (page 28).

■ **Start With Tex-Mex** for your first meal of the day. Eye-pleasing, appetite-satisfying Southwest Eggs Benedict delivers big taste alongside a refreshing Pineapple-Grapefruit Spritzer (page 67).

■ Garlic Flank Steak, Dill Rice, Grilled Vegetables With Pesto, and Creamy Lemonade Pie (page 96) make a **Surefire Meal** that takes advantage of the late spring's beautiful grilling weather (page 113).

■ Relax and have some fun with a **Pack-and-Go Picnic,** which includes a mega Turkey, Bacon, and Havarti Sandwich, Sour Cream Coleslaw, and Fresh-Squeezed Lemonade (page 121).

■ An up-to-date cooking method gives an amazing taste to **Sweet-Hot Baby Back Ribs** basted in a "wow" sauce (page 152).

■ Dazzle guests with a dinner based around standout sides like **Warm Goat Cheese Salad** and **Grilled Romaine Salad With Buttermilk-Chive Dressing** (page 205).

■ Take advantage of the Halloween festivities and host a **Ghoulish Gathering** with nibbles like Monster Eyes and Green Dip With Spooky Chips (page 234).

>> taste of the south

■ **Red Rice** (page 28) This tangy Lowcountry favorite starts with bacon drippings for sautéing onions, and then welcomes a tomato paste-chicken broth mixture that simmers with long-grain rice.

■ **Golden Oyster Stew** (page 47) With its base of potato soup and chunks of celery, onion, and mushroom, this stew is a heartier version of the Southern classic.

■ **Guacamole** (page101) Fresh avocados and lime juice are the essential ingredients in this Tex-Mex specialty.

■ **Fluffy Buttermilk Biscuits** (page 120) Discover our unique tricks for making melt-in-your-mouth biscuits from scratch that are worth every delicious bite.

■ **Best Boiled Peanuts** (page 199) Southerners frequently pick up a bag of these salty snacks on the way to the beach or a sporting event. But the nibbles are very easy to make at home.

>> quick & easy

■ Discover what a lifesaver having cooked chicken on hand can be (page 53).

■ Start with frozen green beans for side dishes that deliver mighty taste in minimum time (page 62).

■ Rejuvenate your supper with these mustard-enhanced recipes (page 107).

■ Serve shrimp in a snap with these two dishes that are simple enough for weeknights and scrumptious enough for guests (page 121).

■ Fast and simple, pasta is just right for those nights when you're in a hurry. While the pasta boils, chop the vegetables, open a jar or can, stir it all together, and cook until heated (page 134).

■ For the best of both worlds, enjoy a main-dish salad for supper—quick prep, and even faster cleanup (page 157).

■ Stir-frying lets you whip up a good-for-you meal with unexpected and delicious flavors (page 206).

■ Purchase a rotisserie chicken, and discover that a speedy dinner is as close as your grocery store's deli (page 232).

■ Start supper with this collection of 30-minute meals from *Southern Living* staffers (page 264).

■ Add a breath of fresh air to your meal planning with these six-ingredient (or less) sides (page 282).

>> what's for supper?

■ Let the slow-cooker handle the main dish roast for this busy-day dinner. Fill in with a a few quick sides for a comfy family supper (page 38).

■ For a quick supper that uses on-hand ingredients, try serving breakfast (page 45).

■ When you need to get in and out of the kitchen in a hurry, try our Chicken-and-Two Plate dinner (page 63).

■ Combine leftover ham and a few fresh ingredients for a quick, one-dish meal that pairs nicely with a simple Caesar salad (page 88).

■ Time-saving items available at most grocery stores let you start dinner with most of the cooking already done (page 104).

■ Prepare the side dishes for this quick weeknight menu while the chicken bakes to a golden crunch in the oven (page 122).

■ An herb marinade jazzes up a turkey burger and grilled onion rings—a combo that beats the drive-through any day of the week (page 146).

■ Spice up dinnertime with an easy enchilada you can make ahead casserole and refried beans that take just 10 minutes to get ready for the oven (page 193).

■ Pan-fry ham steak while you roast seasonal vegetables for a speedy weeknight meal (page 204).

■ Get the whole family in the kitchen to create this Tex-Mex twist on lasagna. Pair it with an easy-to-make Southwestern salad (page 230).

■ Take a break, and stir up a wholesome vegetable-filled chowder alongside a salad and some toasty bread for a stress-free and comforting meal (page 267).

>> healthy foods

♥ These nutrient-packed dishes each cook or bake in just 10 minutes or less (page 54).

♥ Choose a warm, gooey sandwich or hearty, stuffed pita to match with a fresh, flavorful soup for a combo that's sure to wow your taste buds (page 64).

♥ Good-for you fruits and vegetables add color to your plate while also boosting your health and well-being (page 99).

♥ Tea creates an exciting blend of flavors in these fragrant, delicious dishes (page 136).

♥ Four tasty recipes showcase how you can improve your body's overall health. Rich in antioxidants, they're a simple way to add healthful foods to your diet (page 155).

♥ Satisfy your sweet craving with these tempting desserts made with wholesome fruits, grains, and dairy (page 209).

♥ One of the leanest—and tastiest—meats around, pork tenderloin makes busy weeknights a breeze (page 266).

♥ Discover why cranberries aren't just a condiment for your holiday turkey. Enjoy some re-invented ways to use this winter fruit in these fabulous appetizers, main dishes, and desserts (page 284).

cook's chat

Our readers chat online about what they think about our recipes and how they use them. Here they brag about some of their favorites.

>> appetizers

Tropical Guacamole, page 101—"This recipe has a delicious combination of sweet, crunchy, creamy that is great with salty tortilla chips or served alongside chicken. It's easy to make half for a smaller group."

Spicy Southwestern Deviled Eggs, page 125—"What an appetizer hit! The crowd devoured them in record time. Good thing I made two batches. This recipe is quick and easy to prepare. Great tip about purchasing eggs 10 days prior. They peeled like a dream. I took the seeds out of the peppers prior to dicing them, which makes them not quite as hot. I highly recommend this crowd-pleasing recipe."

Brown Sugar Fruit Dip, page 139—"This dip is amazing. It's so light, but with just the right amount of sweetness. It tastes great with fresh summer fruits."

>> soups and stews

30-Minute Chili, page 31—"This chili is fabulous. I have made it several times for my family. They all like it, and I love it because it is so easy to make. I have made it with red beans as the recipe suggests, which is fine, but we really liked it with organic chili beans too. I have served it plain and also over rice. Both ways are delicious. It is the perfect weeknight meal in our busy house."

Cantaloupe Soup, page 159—"I served this soup to some friends for lunch with some chicken salad sandwiches. What a fabulous meal for a hot day! The cantaloupe was even better for lunch the next day."

Beef Vegetable Soup, page 227—"Hearty, satisfying, richly flavored. After browning the beef, I added a little more oil and sautéed the onion and celery until translucent. Then I added the garlic and the rest of the ingredients. The sweetness of ketchup is a nice balance to the acidity of the other tomato products. I chose to use beef flavor base instead of chicken bouillon cubes. Test the potatoes to avoid overcooking. My husband and I had this as a main course with salad and crackers. We'll find out how well it freezes."

>> entrées

Peanut-Chicken Stir-fry, page 34—"This is so easy and so tasty—you don't have to love peanut butter to love this! It's enough for almost two meals for two adults. This dish has the nicest flavor! I highly recommend this recipe."

Grilled Lamb Chops With Lemon-Tarragon Aïoli and Orange Gremolata, page 77—"The very best lamp chop recipe I've ever used—and my husband and I love lamp chops. I served it for some guests and they said the recipe rivaled any they had tasted at the five-star restaurant where they often eat. Kudos, *Southern Living*, for having the recipe and making me a star! I used all the ingredients mentioned in recipe, which is very simple. I served it with grilled vegetables like squash, radishes, asparagus, and baby portobello mushrooms."

Ham-and-Tomato Pie, page 88—"I made this for a late breakfast for guests and served it with cheese grits. We all loved it. I was glad I had the foresight to double the recipe and make two pies! Quick, easy, and tasty—a terrific combination!"

Grilled Chicken With White Barbecue Sauce, page 98—"My husband and I have an addition to our favorite grill recipes! This was easy and great! Only change was that we went back and added a touch more vinegar to the white sauce to thin it out more and give it more tang. We cannot wait to cook these for guests! "

Almond-Crusted Tilapia, page 94—"This a wonderful recipe. I'm not really a fish lover, but this recipe is really delicious. I've made it several times for company and they always ask for the recipe. In addition to being delicious it's also easy and quick. Enjoy."

Beach Shrimp, page 122—"This recipe was delicious! My husband and I loved it. It made a great summertime meal. I cut the amount of butter in half, and it was still great. This was so quick and easy it would be great for cookout or family gatherings."

Sweet-Hot Baby Back Ribs, page 152— "These are the best ribs I have ever made. I used the stack method to cook them and they turned out perfect. This is the only way I'll be cooking ribs from now on. The only recommendation I have is to cut the sauce recipe in half. The full recipe is way more than you need for 3 racks."

Honey Mustard Grilled Chicken, page 203—"Home run! Easy, flavorful, delicious! Slather one side, put it grill side down, then slather the other side while it is face up cooking. Manage your fire control, as the sauce likes to flare up fires. Next time I'd reserve a little sauce for some toasted buns as a sandwich."

» sandwiches

Pesto-Crusted Grilled Cheese, page 36— "This is the best grilled cheese I have ever put in my mouth! The presentation is fabulous. The pesto/mayo combination browns exceptionally well. My son is a chef at an exclusive country club and I passed this recipe onto him. He served it as a special and everyone loved it! I used English Muffin bread rather than sourdough, though either would work."

Slow-cooker Sloppy Joes, page 90— "Excellent. My family really enjoyed the Sloppy Joes and they were really great with baked beans. I would recommend this dish for a casual gathering as well as weeknight dinner."

Turkey, Bacon, and Havarti Sandwich, page 121—"This sandwich is fabulous! Definitely use a crusty sourdough bread—it doesn't get soggy that way. I made this and put it in the fridge overnight. We cut it, wrapped it, and took it to the beach. Great gourmet sandwich!"

Tasty Turkey Burgers, page 146— "Excellent! These were my first attempt at turkey burgers, and they did not disappoint. My husband said they were easier to grill than beef burgers because of fewer flare-ups. We will definitely keep this recipe!"

Lightened Hot Browns, page 228—"Living in Kentucky, hot browns are a regular on restaurant menus. I was thrilled to see a light version in *Southern Living* because their recipes are always right on target. Well, we weren't disappointed! This is a great recipe for any time because the ingredients can already be found in your pantry and fridge. I served this with a side of steamed broccoli and fresh corn. This recipe got a thumbs up from the whole family! Thank you!"

» salads

Grilled Chicken-and-Artichoke Salad, page 102—" We have really enjoyed this salad. It is great on a hot day. I usually use less chicken or double the artichokes."

Cha-Cha Chicken Salad, page 119—"I loved this recipe! I loved the curry flavor mixed with the pineapple and the subtle orange taste from the cranberries. It is very easy to make and would be perfect for an elegant garden party or a casual picnic. I plan on making this again in the very near future."

Tomato-and-Watermelon Salad, page 135—"Admit it . . . the ingredients are probably the most unusual grouping I've ever come across. But let me assure you that the watermelon and tomato, chilled overnight, and then served over romaine salad, was delightful! Teenagers who don't like salads or tomatoes almost pulled their deck chairs up to the serving table to be able to get at it. The seedless watermelon that I bought wasn't as sweet as anticipated, so I increased the sweetener. We served this for dinner with steak kabobs, some sweet pork kabobs, corn on the cob, and roasted vegetables. The family birthday celebration was a grand success, and recipes requested all around!"

Warm Goat Cheese Salad, page 205—"I thought the fried goat cheese medallions were superb. I think the goat cheese would be wonderful served with some gourmet crackers or baguettes."

>> sides

Stuffed Cherry Tomatoes, page 40—"This recipe is easy, quick and delicious! I made it for a party—it disappeared quickly and I had numerous people ask me for the recipe. I added the salt and pepper to the avocado mixture rather than adding it at the end. Also, I used a melon baller to clean out the tomatoes and it worked great! I'll definitely make this again! "

Tomato Florentine, page 59—"This was delicious and colorful. The tomatoes need to be drained really well, as the tomatoes give off some more liquid when baking. Next time, I think I'll toss in some toasted pine nuts for another texture."

Tomato-Zucchini Tart, page 155—"This was so good! I didn't even use the pie crust, just started with the layer of zucchini in the bottom of a greased pan. It was so good."

Summer Squash Casserole, page 157—"Outstanding. Wouldn't change a thing. The best part is that the entire dish cooks in the microwave!"

>> breads

Fluffy Buttermilk Biscuits, page 120—"Excellent choice for buttermilk biscuits. Really easy to refrigerate unused portion of dough and have 'fresh' biscuits every night. Also good for breakfast sandwiches."

Banana Breakfast Bread, page 159—"This recipe is very good and easy to make. It makes a denser bread compared with other banana bread recipes, which is not normally my style. However, everybody in the house really liked the bread, from our two-year-old all the way through to my mother. A rare endorsement from all six of us."

>> desserts

Blackberry Dumpling Cobbler, page 30—"I've tried a lot of cobbler recipes and this is definitely the best. I like that it has both a bottom and top crust, which helps it stay together better than others with a top crust alone. A teaspoon of cinnamon and pinch of nutmeg were nice additions. For the health-conscious, it has fiber from the uncooked oats as well as the fruit. You could even kick up the health index with some wheat germ!"

Banana Pudding Pie, page 46—"This is an excellent recipe! Very simple, quick to put together, and it looked as perfect as the picture. It was a major hit, immediately securing its place at all future family gatherings. Not an easy feat in a Southern family with very high food expectations! Next time I will make it a day in advance, as the flavor was significantly better the second day. Thank you, *Southern Living*, for another fabulous recipe!"

Creamy Lemonade Pie, page 96—"Yum! This is the perfect summer dessert. It's easy and elegant. I made it for my son's graduation party. I used all national name brand products, and it was really delicious. My lemonade concentrate was completely thawed and it worked fine. Make sure you get the large 9 oz. crust that's called for—not the usual size. This one's a keeper!"

Oatmeal-Raisin Bars, page 110—"This is delicious, and the applesauce helps to bind the bars together. The taste is outstanding and they do well to chill overnight. My husband devoured it for breakfast!"

Blond Texas Sheet Cake, page 145—"Good alternative to a chocolate dessert; everyone loved it. Easy to transport. I made it in a sheet cake pan with a cover and cut in squares to serve. It's good with vanilla ice cream on the side."

Mississippi Mud Cake, page 154—"I loved this recipe. It totally satisfies the chocolate crave. The cake was quick and easy to make. I love to bake, love chocolate, and I give this five stars!"

Lemon-Coconut Cake, page 256—"I made this cake for my mom's 91st birthday. This cake was a great big hit. Everybody (9 people) loved it. The night before I squeezed the lemons to make ⅓ cup and measured all my dry ingredients and put them together. It made things easier having the dry ingredients already measured out and put together. I even measured the powdered sugar and sifted it the day before. I also measured out the dry ingredients in the filling and put them together. The only thing I changed in the cake is I added 1 tsp. coconut extract along with 1 tsp. pure vanilla. I would for sure make this cake again. It's really a good feeling when everybody brags about what you have made."

january

Celebration Feast

A year's worth of good fortune never tasted so good.

New Year's Day Meal

Serves 4 to 6

Classic Barbecue Ribs

Hearty Black-eyed Peas

Turnip Greens Stew

Cornbread

Good luck is said to be the reward for eating black-eyed peas on New Year's Day. So if you partake of the little legumes just in case, try our Hearty Black-eyed Peas.

Some folks also say health and prosperity will be yours when you eat pork and greens with the peas. Here we offer some simple, succulent barbecue ribs and Turnip Greens Stew.

Classic Barbecue Ribs
make ahead
PREP: 15 MIN., COOK: 7 HR.
Put these on before you leave for work, or cook them overnight and refrigerate until dinnertime. If you make this recipe a day ahead, refrigerate overnight and remove fat from the sauce before reheating. If you reheat in the microwave, use 50% power.

4 lb. bone-in country-style pork ribs
2 tsp. salt, divided
1 medium onion, chopped
1 cup firmly packed light brown sugar
1 cup apple butter
1 cup ketchup
½ cup lemon juice
½ cup orange juice
1 Tbsp. steak sauce
1 tsp. coarse ground pepper
1 tsp. minced garlic
½ tsp. Worcestershire sauce
Garnish: chopped fresh parsley

1. Cut ribs apart, if necessary, and trim excess fat; sprinkle 1 tsp. salt evenly over ribs.
2. Stir together remaining 1 tsp. salt, onion, and next 9 ingredients until blended. Pour half of onion mixture into a 5-qt. slow cooker. Place ribs in slow cooker, and pour remaining mixture over ribs.
3. Cover and cook on HIGH 6 to 7 hours or until ribs are tender. Garnish, if desired. **Makes** 4 to 6 servings.

Note: For testing purposes only, we used A.1. Steak Sauce.

Hearty Black-eyed Peas
PREP: 10 MIN.; COOK: 1 HR., 35 MIN.
Be sure to pick up a package of the peas long before the approaching holiday when there is an ample supply.

3 cups low-sodium chicken broth
1 medium onion, chopped
1 smoked ham hock
1 bay leaf
½ tsp. pepper
4 whole jalapeño peppers (optional)
1 (16-oz.) package dried black-eyed peas
1 tsp. salt

1. Bring first 5 ingredients, 3 cups water, and, if desired, jalapeños to a boil in a Dutch oven; cover, reduce heat, and simmer 30 minutes.
2. Rinse and sort peas according to package directions. Add peas and ½ tsp. salt to Dutch oven; cook, covered, 1 hour or until tender. If desired, remove meat from ham hock, finely chop, and return to Dutch oven. Season with remaining ½ tsp. salt or to taste. Discard bay leaf. **Makes** 4 to 6 servings.

Turnip Greens Stew
PREP: 5 MIN., COOK: 30 MIN.
According to another old Southern belief, a side dish of greens promises you a year full of dollar bills in your pocket.

2 cups chopped cooked ham
1 Tbsp. vegetable oil
3 cups chicken broth
2 (16-oz.) packages frozen chopped turnip greens
1 (10-oz.) package frozen diced onion, red and green bell peppers, and celery
1 tsp. sugar
1 tsp. seasoned pepper

1. Sauté ham in hot oil in a Dutch oven over medium-high heat 5 minutes or until lightly browned. Add broth and remaining ingredients; bring to a boil. Cover, reduce heat to low, and simmer, stirring occasionally, 25 minutes. **Makes** 6 to 8 servings.

taste of the south
Lowcountry Red Rice

This tangy recipe ranks high in everyday Lowcountry cooking. It starts with bacon drippings for sautéing onions, and then comes a tomato paste-chicken broth mixture that simmers with long-grain rice.

Steaming is the preferred method for making this South Carolina specialty because the tomato paste tends to scorch over direct heat. Still, occasional stirring (about every 15 minutes) is a must.

Purchase a traditional cooktop steamer at Charleston Hardware ([843] 556-0220) for about $30 or an electric rice cooker (prices vary) at your local superstore. You can also try our oven-baked method. For those who don't have a rice steamer, we adapted this recipe from a local cookbook, Bishop England High School's *Gracious Goodness. . .Charleston!* (Sandlapper Publishing, 1991).

Red Rice

PREP: 15 MIN.; COOK: 1 HR., 30 MIN.

9 bacon slices
1 small onion, chopped
1 (12-oz.) can tomato paste
3½ cups chicken broth
2 tsp. sugar
1 tsp. salt
½ tsp. pepper
2 cups uncooked long-grain rice

1. Cook bacon slices in a large skillet over medium-high heat until crisp. Remove bacon, and drain on paper towels, reserving 2 Tbsp. drippings in skillet. Crumble bacon, and set aside.
2. Sauté chopped onion in hot drippings in skillet over medium-high heat 3 minutes or until tender.
3. Add tomato paste to skillet, stirring until mixture is smooth. Gradually stir in 3½ cups chicken broth, stirring to loosen particles from bottom of skillet. Stir in sugar, salt, and pepper. Bring to a boil; reduce heat, and simmer, stirring occasionally, 10 minutes.
4. Combine tomato mixture and 2 cups uncooked long-grain rice in top portion of a cooktop rice steamer. Stir in crumbled bacon. Add water to bottom of steamer, and bring to a boil over high heat. (We used 4½ cups water, but water amounts may vary with different steamers. Follow manufacturer's instructions.) Place the top of steamer over boiling water. Reduce heat to medium-high; cover and cook 1 hour or until rice is tender, stirring every 15 minutes. **Makes** 6 to 8 servings.

Note: For testing purposes only, we used a 5½-qt. Metro cooktop rice steamer.

Oven Method: Prepare recipe as directed through Step 3. Stir 2 cups uncooked long-grain rice into tomato mixture in skillet, and bring to a boil. Stir in bacon pieces. Pour mixture into a lightly greased ovenproof Dutch oven; bake, covered, at 350° for 1 hour or until rice is tender.

Appetizers Done Right

Serve good eats from kickoff till the clock winds down.

Make your house bowl-game-day headquarters. Treat guests to three new appetizers to perk up the usual spread of chips and dips. You can assemble the Bacon-Wrapped Almond-Stuffed Apricots and Louisiana Poppers up to a day ahead; then bake when ready to serve. The party will be a big win, no matter the final score.

Bacon-Wrapped Almond-Stuffed Apricots

make ahead

PREP: 10 MIN., BAKE: 25 MIN.
A sweet and salty dipping sauce pairs deliciously with an appetizer of crunchy almonds nestled inside sweet apricots wrapped with bacon.

24 dried apricot halves
24 whole almonds, lightly toasted
8 bacon slices, cut into thirds
¾ cup apricot preserves
2 Tbsp. soy sauce
⅛ tsp. pepper

1. Fold each apricot half around 1 whole almond. Wrap 1 bacon piece around each stuffed apricot. Secure with wooden picks. Place stuffed apricots on a wire rack in an aluminum foil-lined jelly-roll pan.
2. Bake at 375° for 20 to 25 minutes or until bacon is crisp, turning once.
3. Microwave preserves, soy sauce, and pepper in a small microwave-safe bowl at MEDIUM (50% power) 1 minute or until preserves are melted. Serve dipping sauce with stuffed apricots. **Makes** 8 appetizer servings (24 pieces).

MARGIE TYLER
MURFREESBORO, TENNESSEE

Louisiana Poppers

make ahead

PREP: 10 MIN., BAKE: 30 MIN.
These can be made in advance. After covering the poppers in sausage, chill in the fridge. Just before baking, roll poppers in cracker crumbs.

1 (1-lb.) package ground pork sausage
1 (8-oz.) package frozen cream cheese jalapeño poppers
1 sleeve round buttery crackers, crushed

1. Divide sausage into 10 equal portions; press 1 portion around each popper, covering completely. Roll in cracker crumbs. Place on a wire rack in a jelly-roll pan.
2. Bake at 375° for 30 minutes or until thoroughly cooked. Drain briefly on paper towels. Cut in half before serving. **Makes** 20 pieces.

Homemade Variation: Substitute 2 (7-oz.) cans pickled whole jalapeño peppers, drained, for frozen poppers. Cut stem ends off each jalapeño pepper. Remove and discard seeds and membranes. Place ½ (8-oz.) package cream cheese, softened, in a zip-top plastic bag. Seal bag, and snip a small hole in 1 corner of bag. Pipe cream cheese into hollowed peppers. Cover stuffed peppers with sausage as directed, making sure each pepper is completely covered by sausage so that cheese is sealed inside. Continue preparing and baking stuffed peppers as directed in Steps 1 and 2.

Note: For testing purposes only, we used Poppers Cream Cheese Jalapeños and La Costeña Green Pickled Jalapeño Peppers.

DAWN BOYTER
DOYLINE, LOUISIANA

One-Dish Goodness

Grab a spoon, and dig in for a taste of delicious home-cooked flavor.

Everyone will want second helpings of these fast-to-fix family favorites. Each recipe is ready for the oven in less than 30 minutes, and most of the ingredients can be kept on hand in the pantry or freezer.

Roasted Chicken Drumettes

PREP: 15 MIN., BAKE: 45 MIN.

This oven-baked appetizer with a lemon-mustard glaze is a finger-licking crowd-pleaser.

24 chicken drumettes
2 Tbsp. olive oil
2 tsp. sugar
1 tsp. salt
1 tsp. garlic powder
¼ tsp. pepper
⅓ cup Dijon mustard
3 Tbsp. fresh lemon juice
1 tsp. dried oregano

1. Rinse chicken with cold water, and pat dry.
2. Stir together oil and next 4 ingredients in a large bowl. Add chicken, tossing to coat. Arrange chicken in a single layer on a wire rack in an aluminum foil-lined jelly-roll pan.
3. Bake at 450° for 30 to 35 minutes.
4. Combine mustard, lemon juice, and oregano in a large bowl. Remove pan from oven, and carefully add hot chicken to mustard mixture. Toss to coat. Drain and discard any accumulated fat from pan. Place mustard-coated chicken in a single layer on wire rack in jelly-roll pan.
5. Bake at 450° for 8 to 10 more minutes or until done. **Makes** 8 appetizer servings (24 pieces).

Maw-Maw's Chicken Pie

family favorite

PREP: 15 MIN., BAKE: 40 MIN.

This simple recipe gives rise to a golden, cakelike crust that won rave reviews at the tasting table. Try replacing a portion of the chicken with an equal amount of frozen, thawed vegetables, or stir a cup of shredded cheese into the soup mixture. We especially enjoyed the pie with broccoli and Cheddar cheese.

4 cups chopped cooked chicken
1 (10¾-oz.) can cream of chicken soup
1½ cups chicken broth
2 Tbsp. cornstarch
1½ cups self-rising flour
1 cup buttermilk
½ cup butter, melted

1. Place chopped chicken in a lightly greased 12- x 8-inch baking dish. Whisk together soup, broth, and cornstarch; pour mixture evenly over chicken.
2. Whisk together flour, buttermilk, and butter; spoon batter evenly over chicken mixture.
3. Bake at 400° for 40 minutes or until crust is golden brown. **Makes** 8 servings.

DOROTHY J. SWEAT
CHILDERSBURG, ALABAMA

Blackberry Dumpling Cobbler

family favorite

PREP: 15 MIN., COOK: 5 MIN., BAKE: 35 MIN.

This is just as tasty prepared with frozen peaches or cherries. Serve with a dollop of sweetened whipped cream and a sprig of fresh mint.

2 (16-oz.) packages frozen blackberries
2 cups sugar, divided
¼ cup butter
3 (8-oz.) packages ⅓-less-fat cream cheese, softened
⅔ cup fat-free milk
2¼ cups all-purpose baking mix
¾ cup uncooked oats

1. Bring blackberries, 1⅓ cups sugar, and butter to a boil in a large saucepan over medium heat, stirring gently until butter is melted and sugar dissolves; remove blackberry mixture from heat.
2. Beat cream cheese and remaining ⅔ cup sugar at medium speed with an electric mixer until fluffy; add ⅔ cup milk, and beat until smooth. Stir in baking mix and uncooked oats. Spread two-thirds of cream cheese mixture (about 3 cups) onto bottom of a lightly greased 13- x 9-inch baking dish; spoon blackberry mixture evenly over cream cheese mixture. Dollop remaining cream cheese mixture evenly over blackberry mixture.
3. Bake at 350° for 35 minutes or until golden brown. **Makes** 12 servings.

Note: For testing purposes only, we used Bisquick All-Purpose Baking Mix.

DEBRA K. ARTHUR
MOUNT STERLING, KENTUCKY

Warm Up With Chili

Here's a hearty dish that just about everyone enjoys. Whether chili is served solo in a bowl or atop grits, spaghetti noodles, baked potatoes, or hot dogs, most folks agree it's a great pick to warm up a winter evening.

We've developed four recipes that share one seasoning mix. Once it's blended, store it in an airtight container on the shelf with your other herbs and spices, and you're ready to stir up a batch of chili in no time.

Chili Seasoning Mix
fast fixin's
PREP: 5 MIN.
This versatile mix yields big dividends in time-saving suppers. Loaded with flavor, it pairs perfectly with beef, pork, poultry, or seafood.

¾ cup chili powder
2 Tbsp. ground cumin
2 Tbsp. dried oregano
2 Tbsp. dried minced onion
2 Tbsp. seasoned salt
2 Tbsp. sugar
2 tsp. dried minced garlic

1. Stir together all ingredients. Store seasoning mix in an airtight container up to 4 months at room temperature. Shake or stir well before using. **Makes** about 1⅓ cups.

Shrimp-and-Poblano Chili
PREP: 10 MIN., COOK: 25 MIN.

2 poblano chile peppers, diced
1 Tbsp. olive oil
4 (16-oz.) cans navy beans, undrained
4 cups frozen whole kernel corn
1 cup chicken broth
2 Tbsp. Chili Seasoning Mix
2 lb. peeled, medium-size raw shrimp

1. Sauté diced chile peppers in 1 Tbsp. hot oil in a Dutch oven over medium-high heat 2 minutes. Stir in navy beans and next 3 ingredients; bring to a boil over medium-high heat, stirring occasionally. Cover, reduce heat to low, and simmer, stirring occasionally, 15 minutes. Stir in peeled shrimp, and cook, uncovered, 5 minutes. Serve with desired toppings. (See "Toppings for Chili" below.) **Makes** 8 servings.

Barbecue Chili
fast fixin's
PREP: 5 MIN., COOK: 20 MIN.
Pick up shredded pork from your favorite restaurant, or use one of the ready-to-serve products from your supermarket. The flavor of commercial barbecue sauce can range from sweet to smoky, so use whichever brand you prefer.

1½ lb. shredded barbecue pork
2 (14.5-oz.) cans diced tomatoes with green pepper, celery, and onion
1 (8-oz.) can tomato sauce
1 cup barbecue sauce
⅓ cup Chili Seasoning Mix

1. Stir together all ingredients in a Dutch oven; bring to a boil over medium-high heat, stirring occasionally. Cover, reduce heat to low, and simmer, stirring occasionally, 15 minutes. Serve with desired toppings. (See "Toppings for Chili" below.) **Makes** 8 servings.

30-Minute Chili
fast fixin's
PREP: 5 MIN., COOK: 25 MIN.
(Pictured on page 161)

2 lb. lean ground beef
⅓ cup Chili Seasoning Mix
2 (14.5-oz.) cans diced tomatoes with green pepper, celery, and onion
2 (8-oz.) cans tomato sauce
1 (16-oz.) can black beans, undrained
1 (15.5-oz.) can small red beans, undrained

1. Brown beef in a Dutch oven over medium-high heat, stirring often, 4 to 5 minutes or until beef crumbles and is no longer pink; drain well. Return beef to Dutch oven; sprinkle evenly with seasoning mix, and sauté 1 minute over medium-high heat.
2. Stir in diced tomatoes and remaining ingredients, and bring to a boil over medium-high heat, stirring occasionally. Cover, reduce heat to low, and simmer, stirring occasionally, 15 minutes. **Makes** 8 servings.

Italian-Style Chili: Substitute 1 lb. Italian pork sausage and 1 lb. lean ground beef for 2 lb. lean ground beef. Remove casings from sausage, and discard; brown sausage and ground beef together as directed. Omit beans, and stir in 1 small onion, diced; 1 green bell pepper, diced; 2 small zucchini, diced; and remaining ingredients. Proceed with recipe as directed. Serve chili over hot cooked noodles tossed with olive oil and chopped fresh cilantro. **Makes** 6 to 8 servings. Prep: 10 min., Cook: 25 min.

Toppings for Chili

Good choices to add to your bowl include sour cream, salsa, diced plum tomatoes (they have a meatier texture and are easy to find in winter), shredded lettuce or spinach, shredded cheese, diced onion, sliced green onions, chopped cilantro, chopped avocado, sliced jalapeño peppers, cornbread croutons, and tortilla chips.

Just before serving Shrimp-and-Poblano Chili, add a splash of flavor to each bowl with fresh lime juice and a sprinkling of chopped cilantro.

Healthy Living®

Easy, positive changes add up to big results for good health.
Check out our delicious recipes and tips for living well.

Easy Family Meal

Gather in the kitchen to cook up this healthful supper.

It's no secret that exercise and good eating habits go hand in hand, so an active lifestyle and nutritious choices are top priorities for one Georgia family. Billy and Kerri Ray of Alpharetta—along with their two girls, Tori (12) and Katie (10)—are always on the go. But that doesn't stop them from coming together to prepare Kerri's favorite weeknight recipes. We lightened some of the dishes and added a few wholesome ingredients. Try them, and put a healthier plan into action.

Oven-fried Chicken
family favorite • fast fixin's
PREP: 10 MIN., BAKE: 15 MIN.

¼ cup fat-free mayonnaise
1 Tbsp. Dijon mustard
1 tsp. dried parsley flakes
¼ tsp. garlic powder
¼ tsp. salt
¼ tsp. pepper
1 cup multigrain cracker crumbs (about 20 crackers)
¼ cup freshly grated Parmesan cheese
1¼ lb. chicken breast strips

1. Stir together first 6 ingredients in a medium bowl. Combine multigrain cracker crumbs and Parmesan cheese in a shallow bowl. Brush chicken evenly with mayonnaise mixture; dredge in cracker crumb mixture. Place chicken on an aluminum foil-lined baking sheet.
2. Bake at 400° for 15 minutes or until golden and chicken is done. **Makes** 4 servings.

Per serving: Calories 117; Fat 4.5g (sat 1.2g, mono 0.2g, poly 0.1g); Protein 6.1g; Carb 12.7g; Fiber 1.4g; Chol 12mg; Iron 0.3mg; Sodium 640mg; Calc 109mg

Creamy Macaroni and Cheese
family favorite
PREP: 10 MIN., COOK: 15 MIN., BAKE: 20 MIN., STAND: 5 MIN.
A Southern favorite gets a healthy makeover.

½ (16-oz.) package multigrain penne pasta
1 Tbsp. butter
3 Tbsp. all-purpose flour
3 cups fat-free milk
½ tsp. salt
½ tsp. dry mustard
1 (8-oz.) block 2% reduced-fat sharp Cheddar cheese, shredded and divided
Vegetable cooking spray

1. Cook pasta according to package directions; drain.
2. Melt butter in a large saucepan over medium heat. Whisk in flour, and cook, whisking constantly, 2 minutes. Gradually whisk in milk, salt, and dry mustard; cook, whisking constantly, 5 minutes or until slightly thickened. Remove from heat.
3. Add 1½ cups cheese, stirring until cheese melts and mixture is smooth. Stir in pasta until well combined.
4. Spoon mixture into an 8-inch square baking dish coated with cooking spray. Sprinkle evenly with remaining ½ cup cheese.
5. Bake at 375° for 20 minutes or until golden and bubbly. Let stand 5 minutes before serving. **Makes** about 6 servings.

Per serving: Calories 332; Fat 10.7g (sat 6.6g, mono 0.6g, poly 0.3g); Protein 21.1g; Carb 36.5g; Fiber 2.8g; Chol 33mg; Iron 1.4mg; Sodium 609mg; Calc 407mg

Test Kitchen *Notebook*

Family Meals Facts

Conversation at suppertime can improve your child's vocabulary and draw family members closer. Here are some great dinnertime discussions.

• Ask everyone at the table to talk about their day.

• Take the opportunity to share your favorite childhood stories.

• Plan a family vacation or other special outing that you can do together.

• Talk about a book they're reading, a recent movie they've seen, or a favorite television show. Just be sure to keep the television off during dinnertime to keep the conversation flowing.

Shannon Sliter Satterwhite
FOODS EDITOR

Green Beans, Corn, and Pea Salad
family favorite • make ahead
PREP: 10 MIN., CHILL: 2 HR.
Serve this bright and colorful salad in individual glass bowls.

½ cup white wine vinegar
¼ cup sugar
¼ cup vegetable oil
¼ tsp. salt
¼ tsp. pepper
1 medium-size red bell pepper, chopped
1 (16-oz.) package frozen white corn, thawed
1 (16-oz.) package frozen French-cut green beans, thawed
1 (16-oz.) package frozen small baby green peas, thawed

1. Whisk together first 5 ingredients in a large bowl. Add red bell pepper and remaining ingredients; toss to coat. Cover and chill at least 2 hours or up to 8 hours. Stir before serving with a slotted spoon. **Makes** 8 cups.

MARLISA GRADY
ALPHARETTA, GEORGIA

Per 1-cup serving: Calories 210; Fat 8g (sat 0.8g, mono 3g, poly 3.1g); Protein 5.9g; Carb 31.1g; Fiber 5.8g; Chol 0mg; Iron 1.5mg; Sodium 139mg; Calc 40mg

Ham-and-Broccoli Muffins
freezeable • make ahead
PREP: 15 MIN., BAKE: 18 MIN., STAND: 3 MIN.
Store muffins in zip-top freezer bags for up to one month. For a quick snack, thaw the muffins at room temperature, or microwave them in damp paper towels at HIGH for 10 to 15 seconds or until thawed.

1½ cups reduced-fat all-purpose baking mix
1 cup finely chopped cooked ham or Canadian bacon
2 cups (8 oz.) shredded 2% reduced-fat Cheddar cheese, divided
1 (10-oz.) package frozen chopped broccoli, thawed and well drained
½ cup fat-free milk
1 Tbsp. butter, melted
1 large egg, lightly beaten
Vegetable cooking spray

1. Combine baking mix, chopped ham, 1¾ cups shredded cheese, and broccoli in a large bowl; make a well in center of mixture.
2. Stir together fat-free milk, melted butter, and lightly beaten egg until well blended; add to cheese mixture, stirring just until moistened. Place paper baking cups in muffin pans, and coat with cooking spray. Spoon batter into paper baking cups, filling three-fourths full. Sprinkle tops evenly with remaining ¼ cup cheese.
3. Bake at 425° for 18 minutes or until golden. Let stand 2 to 3 minutes before removing from pans. **Makes** 1 dozen.

Note: Substitute miniature muffin pans for regular pans, if desired. Bake at 425° for 14 minutes or until golden. Makes 2½ dozen miniature muffins.

Per muffin: Calories 166; Fat 7.5g (sat 4g, mono 0.9g, poly 0.2g); Protein 10.8g; Carb 13g; Fiber 0.9g; Chol 44.3mg; Iron 0.9mg; Sodium 364mg; Calc 171mg

Healthy Benefits

■ Cooking together teaches teamwork, organization, and an appreciation for new foods.
■ Girls and women who play sports have more positive body images, higher self-esteem, and better success in school and the workplace.

Good-for-You Fats

Believe it or not, a little fat can be beneficial—
if you choose the right type. Try these
flavorful recipes low in saturated fat.

Guess what? Our bodies need fat. It helps in the performance of vital functions, such as transporting vitamins, protecting organs, and maintaining healthy skin and hair. Too much of it, however, isn't good. The key is eating the right fats in moderation.

We don't have to give up the richness of butter or ice cream to stay healthy, but we do need to limit the amount of artery-clogging saturated fats we eat. Monounsaturated and polyunsaturated cooking oils, lean meats, low-fat dairy, and heart-healthy seafood can provide lots of flavor and great benefits.

Taste these dishes, and enjoy healthful food choices. You'll agree that fat-smart is the best way to live.

A Healthy Change

Notice anything different about the nutritional analysis that appears below our lighter recipes? It has to do with fat—"% calories from fat," to be exact. We took it out of our calculations because the number can be easily misinterpreted.

Take Lemon Vinaigrette (opposite page), for example. If we told you that the calories from fat percentage is about 98%, you might avoid it, thinking it's too high in fat. You might also believe that it's in violation of the 30% daily recommendation for fat calories, right? Wrong. The percentage we're omitting (98%) is merely a proportion of fat calories in that particular recipe; it's not a daily value.

The truth is, Lemon Vinaigrette is actually very good for you, with only 85 calories per serving, and it's rich in healthful monounsaturated fat from olive oil. So forget percentages. Here's what you should know.

- Balance your daily calorie intake with physical activity.
- Eat fiber-rich carbs (including whole grains, fruits, and vegetables), unsaturated fats, and lean meats.
- Increase your calcium intake to 1,000mg to 1,200mg a day (for adults) to keep your bones strong and help prevent osteoporosis.
- Try to keep your sodium intake below 2,300mg per day.

Peanut-Chicken Stir-fry
PREP: 15 MIN., COOK: 30 MIN.

1 cup uncooked jasmine rice
2 skinned and boned chicken breasts, cubed
¾ tsp. salt, divided
1 cup reduced-sodium fat-free chicken broth
1 Tbsp. light brown sugar
½ tsp. cornstarch
2 Tbsp. lime juice
2 Tbsp. sweet chili sauce
2 Tbsp. creamy peanut butter
1 tsp. grated fresh ginger
1 Tbsp. lite soy sauce
1 tsp. dark sesame oil
1 Tbsp. peanut or vegetable oil
1½ cups fresh sugar snap peas, trimmed
1 red bell pepper, cut into thin strips
Garnish: chopped dry-roasted peanuts

1. Cook rice according to package directions.
2. Sprinkle chicken with ½ tsp. salt.
3. Whisk together chicken broth and next 7 ingredients. Set aside.
4. Heat oils in a large nonstick skillet or wok over high heat 1 to 2 minutes or until hot. Add chicken, and stir-fry 5 minutes or until chicken pieces are browned and no longer pink inside.
5. Add peas, bell pepper, and remaining ¼ tsp. salt; cook 2 minutes, stirring often. Stir chicken broth mixture, and add to skillet; bring to a boil. Cook, stirring constantly, 2 minutes or until thickened. Serve over rice; garnish, if desired. **Makes** 4 servings.

Note: For testing purposes only, we used Maggi Taste of Asia Sweet Chili Sauce found in the Asian section of large supermarkets.

Per serving (not including garnish): Calories 310; Fat 11g (sat 2.3g, mono 4.2g, poly 2.6g); Protein 20g; Carb 35g; Fiber 2.5g; Chol 38mg; Iron 1.5mg; Sodium 747mg; Calc 55mg

Herb Flounder With Lemon Vinaigrette
fast fixin's
PREP: 15 MIN., BROIL: 12 MIN.

1 tsp. salt
1 tsp. dried thyme
1 tsp. dried rosemary
1 tsp. dried basil
1 tsp. freshly ground black pepper
¼ tsp. ground red pepper
2 lb. flounder or tilapia fillets
2 garlic cloves, minced
2 lemons, thinly sliced
Lemon Vinaigrette

1. Combine first 6 ingredients; sprinkle evenly over both sides of fillets. Arrange fish on a lightly greased rack in a broiler pan. Sprinkle evenly with garlic. Arrange lemon slices over fish.
2. Broil 6 inches from heat 10 to 12 minutes or until fish flakes with a fork. Drizzle with Lemon Vinaigrette. **Makes** 6 servings.

Per serving (not including vinaigrette): Calories 190; Fat 2.5g (sat 0.6g, mono 0.4g, poly 1g); Protein 38g; Carb 1.4g; Fiber 0.6g; Chol 106mg; Iron 1mg; Sodium 746mg; Calc 47mg

Lemon Vinaigrette:
fast fixin's
PREP. 10 MIN.

½ tsp. grated lemon rind
1½ Tbsp. fresh lemon juice
¼ tsp. salt
¼ tsp. dried basil
¼ tsp. pepper
¼ cup olive oil

1. Whisk together all ingredients. **Makes** about ⅓ cup.

Per serving (about 1 Tbsp.): Calories 85; Fat 9.3g (sat 1.3g, mono 7.2g, poly 0.8g); Protein 0g; Carb 0.4g; Fiber 0g; Chol 0mg; Iron 0mg; Sodium 97 mg; Calc 1.6mg

Peanut Butter Dip
family favorite • fast fixin's
PREP: 5 MIN.
Serve this luscious dip with fresh fruit or vegetable slices for a healthy snack.

1. Stir together 1½ cups plain low-fat yogurt, ½ cup creamy peanut butter, and ¼ cup maple syrup. **Makes** about 2 cups.

ADELYNE SMITH
DUNNVILLE, KENTUCKY

Per ¼-cup serving: Calories 150; Fat 8.9g (sat 2.1g, mono 4g, poly 2.2g); Protein 6.5g; Carb 13g; Fiber 0.9g; Chol 2.8mg; Iron 0.5mg; Sodium 108mg; Calc. 97mg

Healthy Benefits

■ A diet moderate in fat provides a sense of fullness—or satiety—after meals, which helps prevent overeating.
■ Three servings per day of low-fat dairy, including yogurt, milk, and cheese, can actually help your body burn fat.

Test Kitchen *Notebook*

Facts About Fats

With all the confusing hype about what to eat (or what not to eat), it's hard to know what to do. Make better choices with this helpful guide.

• **Monounsaturated fat:** Found in certain cooking oils, such as olive, peanut, and canola, this heart-healthy fat may help reduce "bad" cholesterol levels and lower the risk of heart disease. Other sources include avocados and most nuts.

• **Polyunsaturated fat:** Good sources include vegetable, safflower, corn, sunflower, soy, and cottonseed oils. Health benefits are similar to those of monounsaturated fat.

• **Omega-3 fatty acids:** These polyunsaturated fats are mostly found in seafood, such as salmon, mackerel, tuna, and herring. Walnuts and flaxseeds also contain omega-3 fatty acids. Eating fish regularly may help reduce the risk of coronary artery disease by 50%.

• **Saturated fat:** This solid fat is mostly found in animal products, such as beef, poultry, pork, butter, and whole milk. Other sources include tropical oils, such as coconut and palm oils. Too much may increase bad cholesterol, raising the risk of heart disease and stroke. Limit your intake to less than 10% of your total daily calories.

• **Trans fat:** Also known as hydrogenated fat, trans fat is commonly found in vegetable shortening, some margarines, and commercial baked goods. Because it has health risks similar to saturated fat, keep your intake as low as possible.

Shannon Sliter Satterwhite

FOODS EDITOR

Grilled Cheese

Need we say more?

A gooey grilled cheese sandwich is quite possibly the quickest comfort food.

Italian Cheese Bites

PREP: 15 MIN., COOK: 6 MIN. PER BATCH
We visited our supermarket bakery for a presliced Italian bread loaf. (Pictured on page 7)

½ cup butter, softened
½ cup freshly grated Parmesan cheese
16 Italian bread slices
16 provolone cheese slices
Marinara sauce

1. Stir together butter and Parmesan cheese; spread on 1 side of each bread slice. Place 8 bread slices, buttered sides down, on wax paper.
2. Layer each of 8 bread slices on wax paper with 2 provolone cheese slices, and top with remaining bread slices, buttered sides up.
3. Cook sandwiches, in batches, on a hot griddle or in a nonstick skillet over medium heat, gently pressing with a spatula, 3 minutes on each side or until golden brown and cheese melts. Cut each sandwich into fourths, and serve with marinara sauce for dipping. **Makes** 8 appetizer servings.

KATHLEEN LOCKWOOD
SIMI VALLEY, CALIFORNIA

Pesto-Crusted Grilled Cheese

PREP: 15 MIN., COOK: 6 MIN. PER BATCH

⅓ cup mayonnaise
2 Tbsp. jarred pesto sauce
8 sourdough bread slices
4 (1-oz.) fontina cheese slices*
1 (12-oz.) jar roasted red bell peppers, drained and chopped
4 (1-oz.) Cheddar cheese slices

1. Stir together mayonnaise and pesto sauce. Spread evenly on 1 side of each sourdough bread slice. Place 4 bread slices, pesto sides down, on wax paper.
2. Layer 4 bread slices on wax paper each with 1 fontina cheese slice, bell peppers, and 1 Cheddar cheese slice; top with remaining bread slices, pesto sides up.
3. Cook sandwiches, in batches, on a hot griddle or in a nonstick skillet over medium heat, gently pressing with a spatula, 3 minutes on each side or until golden brown and cheese melts. **Makes** 4 servings.

*Substitute provolone or mozzarella cheese, if desired.
MELISSA QUIÑONES
EUSTIS, FLORIDA

Hot Buttery Brie Melts
fast fixin's
PREP: 10 MIN., COOK: 3 MIN. PER BATCH
If you don't have a panini press, place sandwiches in a hot skillet over medium heat. Press sandwiches with a cast-iron skillet or other heavy weight, and cook 3 minutes on each side or until golden brown.

1 (8-oz.) Brie round or wedge
1 (12-oz.) French baguette
½ cup jalapeño jelly
1 Tbsp. chopped fresh cilantro

1. Trim and discard rind from Brie. Cut Brie into ¼-inch-thick slices, and set aside.
2. Cut baguette into 4 equal pieces; halve pieces lengthwise.
3. Heat jelly in a microwave-safe bowl at HIGH 2 minutes. Stir in cilantro. Spread mixture evenly on cut sides of each bread slice. Layer 4 bread slices, jelly sides up, evenly with Brie; top with remaining bread slices, jelly sides down.
4. Cook sandwiches, in batches, in a preheated panini press 3 minutes or until grill marks appear and cheese melts. **Makes** 4 servings.

AMOREENA SHENEFELT
ATLANTA, GEORGIA

Grilled Pimiento Cheese
family favorite
PREP: 25 MIN., COOK: 6 MIN. PER BATCH
To save time, purchase prepared pimiento cheese.

¾ cup mayonnaise, divided
1 (2-oz.) jar diced pimiento, drained
½ tsp. Worcestershire sauce
⅛ tsp. Cajun seasoning
Pinch of granulated garlic
⅛ tsp. ground black pepper
¼ tsp. hot sauce
1 (10-oz.) block Cheddar cheese, shredded
8 slices whole grain white bread

1. Stir together ½ cup mayonnaise and next 6 ingredients; gently stir in cheese. Cover and chill up to 3 days, if desired.

Grill It Up Golden

An electric griddle allows you to cook several sandwiches at a time. Test Kitchens Professional Angela Sellers says, "The secret is to preheat your griddle or skillet to a medium temperature." The results are perfectly melted cheese and crispy, golden crusts every time.

2. Spread remaining ¼ cup mayonnaise evenly on 1 side of each bread slice. Place 4 bread slices, mayonnaise sides down, on wax paper.

3. Spread cheese mixture evenly on top of 4 bread slices on wax paper; top with remaining bread slices, mayonnaise sides up.

4. Cook sandwiches, in batches, on a hot griddle or in a large nonstick skillet over medium heat 3 minutes on each side or until golden brown and cheese melts. **Makes** 4 servings.

Note: For testing purposes only, we used Sara Lee Whole Grain White Bread.

Cuban Grills
family favorite
PREP: 15 MIN., COOK: 8 MIN. PER BATCH
This twist on the classic Cuban sandwich uses corn tortillas instead of crusty bread. Look for thinly sliced roasted pork in the deli section of your grocery store.

8 (5-inch) corn tortillas
1 Tbsp. butter, melted
2 Tbsp. honey mustard
8 baby Swiss cheese slices
8 thin slices deli ham
8 thin slices deli roasted pork
12 dill pickle chips
2 Tbsp. hot mustard

1. Brush 1 side of each tortilla with melted butter. Place 4 tortillas, buttered sides down, on wax paper.

2. Spread honey mustard evenly over 4 tortillas on wax paper. Layer each tortilla with 1 cheese slice, 2 ham slices, and 2 pork slices; top with 3 pickle chips and 1 cheese slice. Spread hot mustard evenly on 1 side of 4 remaining tortillas, and place, mustard sides down, over layered tortillas.

3. Cook sandwiches, in batches, on a hot griddle or in a nonstick skillet over medium heat, gently pressing with a spatula, 4 minutes on each side or until golden brown and cheese melts. **Makes** 4 servings.
VALERIE HOLT
CARTERSVILLE, GEORGIA

Peanut Butter Cookies

Cookies equal comfort. Easiest Peanut Butter Cookies are one of our favorites. The dough freezes well, so keep a batch on hand to bake whenever you need a pick-me-up.

Easiest Peanut Butter Cookies
freezeable
PREP: 20 MIN., BAKE: 15 MIN. PER BATCH

1 cup peanut butter
1 cup sugar
1 large egg
1 tsp. vanilla extract

1. Stir together all ingredients in a large bowl until combined; shape dough into 1-inch balls. Place balls 1 inch apart on ungreased baking sheets, and flatten gently with tines of a fork. Bake at 325° for 15 minutes or until golden brown. Remove to wire racks to cool. **Makes** about 30 cookies.
STEVENY MCCALLA
MARION, ILLINOIS

Variations: Evenly press 1 cup of your desired addition (for example, chocolate morsels, chocolate-coated toffee bits, and chopped peanuts) onto the top of prepared cookie dough on baking sheets; bake as directed.

Peanut Butter-and-Chocolate Cookies: Divide peanut butter cookie dough in half. Stir 2 melted semisweet chocolate baking squares into half of dough. Shape doughs into 30 (1-inch) half peanut butter, half chocolate-peanut butter balls. Flatten gently with a spoon. Proceed as directed.

Creamy Peanut Butter Jammies
family favorite
PREP: 30 MIN., BAKE: 45 MIN., COOL: 1 HR., CHILL: 30 MIN.

1 (16.5-oz.) package refrigerated peanut butter cookie dough
1 (8-oz.) package cream cheese, softened
½ cup sugar
1 large egg
1 tsp. vanilla extract
⅓ cup seedless strawberry jam
⅓ cup chunky peanut butter
⅓ cup chopped roasted peanuts

1. Line bottom and sides of an 11- x 7-inch baking dish with aluminum foil, allowing edges to overhang 2 to 3 inches. Lightly grease the foil. Press two-thirds cookie dough evenly onto bottom.

2. Beat cream cheese and next 3 ingredients at medium speed with an electric mixer until smooth; spread evenly over cookie dough.

3. Stir together jam and peanut butter using a fork; dollop evenly over cream cheese mixture, being sure to include corners of pan. Gently swirl jam mixture and cream cheese mixture with a knife; crumble remaining cookie dough evenly over filling. Sprinkle with peanuts.

4. Bake at 325° for 40 to 45 minutes or until cream cheese layer is set and a wooden pick inserted in center comes out clean. Cool in pan on a wire rack 1 hour; chill in pan at least 30 minutes. Lift edges of foil, and remove from pan; gently peel off foil. Cut into 24 squares. Store in the refrigerator. Remove from refrigerator 1 hour before serving. **Makes** 24 squares.
CAROLYN NOWELL
MARIETTA, GEORGIA

Cook While You're Out

A slow cooker is the answer to your dinner dilemma. And cleanup is a breeze!

A Comfy Busy-Day Dinner

Serves 6

Slow-cooker Roast and Gravy

Noodles, mashed potatoes, or rice

Sautéed Broccoli Spears

Italian-seasoned cloverleaf rolls
(Tip: Find these rolls alongside other frozen bread and biscuit products.)

Blackberry Dumpling Cobbler (page 30)

Slow-cooker Roast and Gravy

make ahead

PREP: 10 MIN., COOK: 8 HR.

Remember, don't lift the lid. Each time you do, heat is lost, and you'll need to cook 20 to 30 more minutes.

1 (10¾-oz.) can cream of mushroom with roasted garlic soup
1 (10½-oz.) can condensed beef broth
1 (1-oz.) envelope dry onion-mushroom soup mix
1 (3½- to 4-lb.) eye of round roast, trimmed
2 Tbsp. all-purpose flour
1 tsp. salt
½ tsp. pepper
2 Tbsp. vegetable oil

1. Stir together first 3 ingredients in a 5½-qt. slow cooker.

2. Sprinkle roast evenly with flour, salt, and pepper. Brown roast on all sides in hot oil in a large Dutch oven over medium-high heat. Transfer roast to slow cooker.

3. Cover and cook on LOW 8 hours.

4. Remove roast from slow cooker; slice to serve. Skim fat from gravy in slow cooker, if desired. Whisk gravy; serve over roast. **Makes** 6 servings.

SHARRON WRIGHT
AUSTELL, GEORGIA

Sautéed Broccoli Spears

fast fixin's

PREP: 10 MIN., COOK: 10 MIN.

One (16-oz.) package frozen broccoli spears may be substituted for fresh in this recipe— you don't even have to thaw or change the cook time.

1 lb. fresh broccoli crowns, cut into spears
2 Tbsp. butter
2 tsp. fresh lemon juice
½ tsp. salt
¼ tsp. pepper
1 (2-oz.) jar diced pimiento, drained (optional)

1. Cook broccoli spears in boiling water to cover 4 to 6 minutes or until crisp-tender. Plunge broccoli into ice water to stop the cooking process, and drain.
2. Melt 2 Tbsp. butter in a large non-stick skillet over medium-high heat; stir in broccoli spears, and sauté 2 minutes. Stir in fresh lemon juice, salt, pepper, and, if desired, diced pimiento; sauté 1 minute. Serve immediately. **Makes** 6 servings.

A Colorful Side

Broccoli is Associate Foods Editor Shirley Harrington's favorite vegetable. She buys it in cuts called crowns, which have the woody stalk removed. Separate the crown into spears with a paring knife. For more tender cooked stalks, remove the thin peel with a vegetable peeler.

february

Gather 'Round the Table

Surprise your family any night of the week with a doable menu from one of our past Cook-Off winners.

Memorable Menu

Serves 6

Stuffed Cherry Tomatoes

Mixed Greens Salad With Apple Cider Vinaigrette

Marinated Flank Steak

Roasted Garlic Smashed Potatoes

Spinach-and-Red Pepper Sauté

Chocolate Chimichangas With Raspberry Sauce

Keeping food simple—yet making it look good and taste great—paid off for Susan Rotter when she entered the *Southern Living* Cook-Off in 2003. Southern-Fried Stuffed Chicken With Roasted Red Pepper-and-Vidalia Onion Gravy was so good it earned Susan the $100,000 grand prize. Here Susan divulges her tricks for exceptional everyday food.

Stuffed Cherry Tomatoes

make ahead

PREP: 25 MIN., DRAIN: 15 MIN., CHILL: 1 HR.
(Pictured on page 163)

2 pt. cherry tomatoes
1 avocado, peeled and diced
1 tsp. lemon juice
¼ cup mayonnaise
8 cooked bacon slices, crumbled
2 green onions, finely chopped
Salt and pepper to taste

1. Cut a small slice from the top of each tomato; scoop out pulp with a small spoon or melon baller, and discard pulp. Place tomatoes, cut sides down, on paper towels, and let drain 15 minutes.
2. Meanwhile, combine avocado and lemon juice in a small bowl, stirring gently; drain. Stir together mayonnaise, bacon, and green onions; add avocado mixture, and stir gently until combined.
3. Spoon avocado mixture evenly into tomato shells. Cover with plastic wrap, and chill 1 hour. Sprinkle with salt and pepper to taste just before serving. **Makes** 8 servings.

Mixed Greens Salad With Apple Cider Vinaigrette

fast fixin's

PREP: 5 MIN., BAKE: 15 MIN.

½ cup chopped pecans
2 (5-oz.) bags mixed baby salad greens, thoroughly washed
1 (4-oz.) package crumbled feta cheese
¾ cup dried cranberries
Apple Cider Vinaigrette

1. Place pecans in an even layer in a shallow pan.
2. Bake pecans at 350° for 15 minutes or until toasted, stirring once.
3. Place greens in a large bowl. Top with cheese, cranberries, and toasted pecans. Drizzle with Apple Cider Vinaigrette just before serving. **Makes** 8 servings.

Apple Cider Vinaigrette:

fast fixin's • make ahead
PREP: 5 MIN., COOK: 3 MIN.

2 Tbsp. sesame seeds
½ cup cider vinegar
⅓ cup sugar
½ cup olive oil
2 tsp. minced onion
¼ tsp. paprika
1 Tbsp. poppy seeds (optional)

1. Heat sesame seeds in a small skillet over medium-high heat, stirring constantly, 3 minutes or just until toasted.
2. Microwave vinegar in a medium-size, microwave-safe glass bowl at HIGH 1 minute or just until hot. Add sugar, and whisk until dissolved. Add next 3 ingredients, toasted sesame seeds, and, if desired, poppy seeds; whisk until blended. Store in refrigerator up to 1 week. **Makes** 1¼ cups.

Marinated Flank Steak

PREP: 10 MIN., CHILL: 1 HR., GRILL: 10 MIN., STAND: 10 MIN.

1 (2-lb.) flank steak
1 cup soy sauce
1 cup pineapple juice
2 garlic cloves, minced
½ cup firmly packed brown sugar
5 Tbsp. sesame oil
2 Tbsp. jerk seasoning

1. Place steak in a large zip-top plastic freezer bag.
2. Combine 1 cup soy sauce, pineapple juice, and next 4 ingredients, stirring until sugar dissolves; pour over steak. Seal bag, and chill at least 1 hour or up to 8 hours, turning occasionally. Remove steak from marinade; discard marinade.
3. Grill steak, covered with grill lid, over medium-high heat (350° to 400°) 5 minutes on each side or to desired degree of doneness. Let stand 10 minutes before slicing; cut steak diagonally across the grain. **Makes** 6 servings.

Note: For testing purposes only, we used McCormick Caribbean Jerk Seasoning.

Roasted Garlic Smashed Potatoes

family favorite • make ahead

PREP: 15 MIN., BAKE: 1 HR., COOK: 25 MIN.

The garlic can be roasted and stored in the refrigerator up to one day ahead.

1 large or 2 small garlic bulbs
1 Tbsp. olive oil
4 lb. red potatoes, peeled and
    quartered
1 (8-oz.) package cream cheese,
    softened
1 cup sour cream
½ cup butter
¼ cup milk
¾ tsp. salt
¼ tsp. pepper
Garnish: chopped fresh chives

1. Cut off pointed end of garlic bulb; place garlic on a piece of aluminum foil, and drizzle with oil. Fold foil to seal.
2. Bake at 350° for 1 hour; cool. Squeeze pulp from garlic; set aside.
3. Cook potatoes in a Dutch oven in boiling salted water to cover 20 to 25 minutes or until tender; drain and place in a large bowl.
4. Mash potatoes with roasted garlic pulp, cream cheese, and next 5 ingredients in bowl until smooth. Garnish, if desired. **Makes** 6 to 8 servings.

Spinach-and-Red Pepper Sauté

fast fixin's

PREP: 10 MIN., COOK: 10 MIN.

3 (10-oz.) packages fresh spinach,
    thoroughly washed and torn
2 garlic cloves, pressed
1 Tbsp. olive oil
½ (12-oz.) jar roasted red bell peppers,
    drained and chopped
½ tsp. salt
¼ tsp. pepper

1. Sauté spinach and garlic in 1 Tbsp. hot oil in a nonstick skillet over medium-high heat 8 to 10 minutes or until spinach wilts. Drain well. Stir in remaining ingredients. **Makes** 6 servings.

Spinach-and-Red Pepper Sauté With Toasted Pine Nuts: Sauté ¼ cup pine nuts in 1 Tbsp. hot oil in a nonstick skillet over medium-high heat 4 minutes or until golden. Remove from skillet. Sauté spinach and garlic in same skillet over medium-high heat 8 to 10 minutes or until spinach wilts. Drain well. Stir in pine nuts and remaining ingredients. **Makes** 6 servings. Prep: 10 min., Cook: 14 min.

Chocolate Chimichangas With Raspberry Sauce

freezeable • make ahead

PREP: 15 MIN., FREEZE: 20 MIN., FRY: 18 MIN.

Chocolate Chimichangas, really just sweet fried burritos, are a cinch to make and pair perfectly with five-ingredient Raspberry Sauce. For a different flavor, serve them with your favorite bottled praline sauce instead. To save time, assemble the chimichangas up to one week ahead. Place in a zip-top plastic freezer bag, and store in the freezer. (Pictured on page 163)

6 (1.55-oz.) milk chocolate candy bars
6 (10-inch) burrito-size flour tortillas
Vegetable oil
Raspberry Sauce
Vanilla ice cream
Garnishes: shaved chocolate, mint sprigs

1. Place 1 candy bar just below center of 1 tortilla. Fold bottom of tortilla up and over candy bar just until partially covered. Fold left and right sides of tortilla over; roll up, and place, seam side down, on a baking sheet. Repeat procedure with remaining candy bars and tortillas. Freeze 20 minutes.
2. Pour oil to depth of 1 inch into a large skillet; heat to 375°. Place 2 tortillas, seam sides down, in hot oil, gently pressing with tongs for a few seconds to seal. Fry tortillas 2 to 3 minutes on each side or until golden brown. Repeat procedure with remaining tortillas. Drain on paper towels. Serve with Raspberry Sauce and vanilla ice cream. Garnish, if desired. **Makes** 6 servings.

Raspberry Sauce:

fast fixin's • make ahead

PREP: 3 MIN., COOK: 10 MIN.

1 (10-oz.) package frozen raspberries,
    thawed
½ cup sugar
3 Tbsp. lemon juice
1 Tbsp. orange liqueur (optional)
1 tsp. cornstarch

1. Combine first 3 ingredients and, if desired, orange liqueur, in a large saucepan. Bring to a boil; reduce heat, and simmer, uncovered, 5 minutes or just until raspberry mixture starts to thicken. Remove from heat, and let cool completely.
2. Press raspberry mixture through a wire-mesh strainer into a small saucepan, using the back of a spoon to squeeze out juice. Discard pulp and seeds. Whisk in 1 tsp. cornstarch. Bring to a boil, and cook 1 to 2 minutes or until thickened. Store in refrigerator up to 3 days. **Makes** about 1 cup.

Place chimichangas, seam sides down, into hot oil; then press down gently with tongs for a few seconds to ensure a tight seal.

Shortcuts to Supper

Jump-start hearty casseroles by prepping and freezing the main ingredients ahead.

Stock your freezer with cooked ground meats, cubed chicken or turkey, and shredded cheese, and you can assemble family-pleasing main dishes in a snap. In fact, if your freezer is stocked, our recipes boast prep times of only 15 minutes.

(Look for more great recipes on opposite page.) Add a tossed salad and bread, and you have an impressive menu. And as a handy guide to some sure shortcuts, see "Easy Measuring, Easy Freezing," below—then enjoy your time to unwind.

Easy Measuring, Easy Freezing

■ 1 to 1¼ lb. uncooked lean ground beef, turkey, or sausage = about 2½ to 3 cups cooked and crumbled

■ 1¼ to 1½ lb. uncooked chicken breasts = about 3 cups cubed and cooked

■ Preshredded cheeses are convenient and freeze great but can be costly. Consider grating your own (2 [8-oz.] blocks of cheese, shredded = about 4 cups). Partially freezing the block, especially softer cheeses such as Swiss and Monterey Jack, makes grating a breeze.

■ Pint- to gallon-size, zip-top plastic freezer bags are excellent choices for storing food items. (A pint-size zip-top plastic freezer bag is perfect for 1 cup cubed cooked chicken breasts.)

Also check out the great plastic freezer container choices that go from freezer to microwave to dishwasher. They come in several sizes, including 3 cups. Whichever you choose, make sure you purchase good-quality bags and containers that are designed for the freezer.

■ Label your items for freezing, including the amount and date. If properly stored, shredded cheeses and cooked meats can be frozen up to three months.

■ Chopped onions show up as an ingredient in lots of recipes. You can freeze them after chopping, but freeze them raw.

Chicken 'n' Spinach Pasta Bake
freezeable • make ahead
PREP: 15 MIN., BAKE: 1 HR.

You'll find this dish perfect for company, but also speedy enough for weeknight meals. (Pictured on page 162)

8 oz. uncooked rigatoni
1 Tbsp. olive oil
1 cup finely chopped onion (about 1 medium)
1 (10-oz.) package frozen chopped spinach, thawed
3 cups cubed cooked chicken breasts
1 (14.5-oz.) can Italian-style diced tomatoes
1 (8-oz.) container chive-and-onion cream cheese
½ tsp. salt
½ tsp. pepper
1½ cups (6 oz.) shredded mozzarella cheese

1. Prepare rigatoni according to package directions.
2. Meanwhile, spread oil on bottom of an 11- x 7-inch baking dish; add onion in a single layer.
3. Bake at 375° for 15 minutes or just until tender. Transfer onion to a large bowl, and set aside.
4. Drain chopped spinach well, pressing between layers of paper towels.
5. Stir rigatoni, spinach, chicken, and next 4 ingredients into onion in bowl. Spoon mixture into baking dish, and sprinkle evenly with shredded mozzarella cheese.
6. Bake, covered, at 375° for 30 minutes; uncover and bake 15 more minutes or until bubbly. **Makes** 4 to 6 servings.

Sausage 'n' Spinach Pasta Bake: Substitute 3 cups cooked, crumbled hot Italian sausage for 3 cups cubed cooked chicken breasts. Reduce salt to ¼ tsp., and omit ½ tsp. pepper. Proceed with recipe as directed.
SUSAN RUNKLE
WALTON, KENTUCKY

Be Casserole Ready

Let us help you put together a delicious meal on the run.

Cooked and ready-to-go main ingredients in the freezer are like money in the bank. If you keep basic pantry items (such as pastas and canned tomatoes) and frozen items (such as mashed potatoes and veggies) on hand, you'll be able to have a super dinner on the table in just about no time at all. See opposite page for more great recipes and information.

Loaded Barbecue Baked Potato Casserole
family favorite

PREP: 15 MIN., COOK: 10 MIN., BAKE: 45 MIN., STAND: 10 MIN.

We streamlined Linda Wells's luscious casserole with frozen mashed potatoes and barbecue pork from the supermarket to make it more weeknight friendly.

6 bacon slices
1 (22-oz.) package frozen mashed potatoes
2 cups milk
1 cup (4 oz.) shredded Monterey Jack cheese with peppers
½ (8-oz.) package ⅓-less-fat cream cheese, cut into cubes
½ tsp. salt
½ tsp. pepper
3 cups (12 oz.) shredded Cheddar cheese, divided
1 (8-oz.) container light sour cream
1 (4-oz.) can chopped green chiles, drained
3 cups shredded barbecue pork or beef
¾ cup barbecue sauce
Garnish: chopped fresh parsley

1. Cook bacon in a large skillet over medium-high heat 8 to 10 minutes or until crisp; remove bacon, and drain on paper towels, reserving 2 Tbsp. drippings. Crumble bacon; set aside.
2. Stir together reserved bacon drippings, potatoes, next 5 ingredients, and 2 cups Cheddar cheese in a large microwave-safe bowl. Microwave at HIGH 4 minutes. Stir in sour cream and chiles until well blended.
3. Spoon potato mixture into a lightly greased 13- x 9-inch baking dish. Sprinkle evenly with bacon and remaining 1 cup Cheddar cheese. Arrange pork evenly over cheese. Drizzle barbecue sauce evenly over pork.
4. Bake at 350° for 45 minutes. Let stand 10 minutes before serving. Garnish, if desired. **Makes** 8 servings.

LINDA WELLS
CALERA, ALABAMA

Freeze Frame

If using frozen cooked ingredients, add 15 minutes to your bake time. If the recipe is covered during the first part of baking (Chicken 'n' Spinach Pasta Bake [opposite page] and Easy Beef Lasagna), then you'll add the 15 minutes to the covered baking time.

Easy Beef Lasagna
family favorite

PREP: 15 MIN.; BAKE: 1 HR., 15 MIN.; STAND: 10 MIN.

Fire-roasted tomatoes in the pasta sauce add robust flavor, but your favorite sauce will work just fine.

3 cups cooked lean ground beef
1 (26-oz.) jar fire-roasted tomato-and-garlic pasta sauce
1 (15-oz.) container ricotta cheese
½ cup shredded Parmesan cheese
6 no-cook lasagna noodles
2 cups (8 oz.) shredded mozzarella cheese

1. Stir together ground beef and pasta sauce. Stir together ricotta cheese and Parmesan cheese.
2. Spread one-third of meat sauce in a lightly greased 11- x 7-inch baking dish; layer with 3 lasagna noodles and half each of ricotta cheese mixture and shredded mozzarella cheese. Repeat procedure once. Spread remaining one-third of meat sauce over mozzarella cheese.
3. Bake, covered, at 375° for 1 hour; uncover and bake 15 more minutes. Let stand 10 minutes before serving. **Makes** 6 to 8 servings.

WENDY GAULE
DALLAS, TEXAS

Note: For testing purposes only, we used Classico Fire Roasted Tomato & Garlic pasta sauce and Barilla Oven Ready Lasagne.

Easy Turkey Lasagna: Substitute 3 cups cooked ground turkey for 3 cups cooked lean ground beef, and proceed as directed.

Six-Ingredient Entrées

These easy recipes deliver big taste.

It just doesn't get better than this—four entrées with only six or less ingredients. So when you have company coming, simply select one of these delicious main dishes, and then add your favorite sides. Each recipe is ready to bake in no time at all, leaving you plenty of time to prepare for your guests.

Saucy Beef Brisket

PREP: 20 MIN.; BAKE: 3 HR., 30 MIN.;
STAND: 20 MIN.

1 (5-lb.) beef brisket, trimmed
1½ cups ginger ale
1½ cups ketchup
½ cup teriyaki sauce
1 (1-lb.) package baby carrots
6 small red potatoes, quartered

1. Place brisket, fat side up, in an aluminum foil-lined roasting pan.
2. Stir together ginger ale, ketchup, and teriyaki sauce; pour over brisket.
3. Bake, covered, at 350° for 3 hours. Add carrots and potatoes. Cover and cook 30 more minutes or until brisket and vegetables are tender.
4. Remove brisket and vegetables from pan, reserving sauce mixture in pan; let stand 20 minutes. Cut brisket across the grain into thin slices using a sharp knife. Pour sauce over sliced brisket and vegetables to keep moist. **Makes** 8 servings.

Note: For testing purposes only, we used Kikkoman Marinade & Teriyaki Sauce.
CYNDIE FOGARTY
MEMPHIS, TENNESSEE

Dijon Pork Loin

PREP: 10 MIN.; BAKE: 1 HR., 15 MIN.;
STAND: 15 MIN.
It takes just 10 minutes to get this tasty entrée ready for the oven.

4 Tbsp. steak seasoning
2 Tbsp. all-purpose flour
¼ cup butter, melted
2 Tbsp. Dijon mustard
1 (3½- to 4-lb.) boneless pork loin roast, trimmed
Garnishes: fresh basil leaves, cherry tomatoes

1. Combine first 4 ingredients in a small bowl. Rub mustard mixture evenly over roast. Place roast on an aluminum foiled-lined broiler pan.
2. Bake at 475° for 20 minutes. Reduce heat to 350°, and bake 50 to 55 more minutes or until a meat thermometer inserted in thickest portion registers 155°. Remove from oven, and let stand 15 minutes or until thermometer reaches 160° before slicing. Garnish, if desired. **Makes** 6 to 8 servings.

Note: For testing purposes only, we used McCormick Grill Mates Montreal Steak Seasoning.
MYRTLE JONSON
METTER, GEORGIA

Poppy Seed Chicken
family favorite
PREP: 10 MIN., BAKE: 40 MIN.
This creamy chicken casserole with a buttery cracker crust tastes great over rice; just add a side salad for an easy weeknight meal.

3 cups chopped cooked chicken
1 (10¾-oz.) can cream of chicken soup
1 (16-oz.) container sour cream
3 tsp. poppy seeds
31 round buttery crackers, crushed
¼ cup butter, melted

1. Combine first 4 ingredients. Spoon mixture into a lightly greased 11- x 7-inch baking dish.
2. Stir together cracker crumbs and melted butter; sprinkle evenly over casserole.
3. Bake at 350° for 35 to 40 minutes or until hot and bubbly. **Makes** 6 servings.

Note: For testing purposes only, we used Keebler Town House crackers.
KELLY SKINNER
ALPHARETTA, GEORGIA

Catfish Jezebel
fast fixin's
PREP: 5 MIN., BAKE: 20 MIN.

¼ cup orange marmalade
¼ cup ketchup
1 Tbsp. horseradish sauce
1 tsp. spicy brown mustard
1 Tbsp. Creole seasoning
4 (6-oz.) catfish fillets

1. Stir together first 4 ingredients, and set aside.
2. Sprinkle Creole seasoning evenly over catfish. Place fish in an aluminum foil-lined roasting pan.
3. Bake at 425° for 20 minutes or until fish flakes with a fork. Serve with marmalade mixture. **Makes** 4 servings.
PATRICIA HORAK
OVERLAND PARK, KANSAS

what's for supper?

Breakfast Tonight

One Swift Dinner

Serves 4

Smoked Chops-and-Cheese Omelet

Tangelo segments dipped in vanilla yogurt or a green salad with Ranch dressing

Sparkly Cranberry Scones, frozen biscuits with raspberry jam, or garlic toast

Iced coffee or tea

With omelets you have an easy meal in your hip pocket. You can even customize the filling. Substitute leftover rotisserie chicken or roast beef and almost any cheese—Cheddar, Swiss, or mozzarella—you have on hand. Add a side or bread, and dinner is ready.

Smoked Chops-and-Cheese Omelet

PREP: 10 MIN., COOK: 15 MIN.

Use a heat-resistant spatula to flip the omelet over to cook on the second side. Keep cooked omelets warm on an ovenproof platter in a 250° oven.

1¼ cups chopped smoked pork chops
  (about 1 lb.)
2 small plum tomatoes, chopped
2 Tbsp. finely chopped onion
6 large eggs
1 Tbsp. chopped fresh parsley
¼ tsp. salt
¼ tsp. pepper
4 tsp. butter, divided
⅔ cup shredded Gouda cheese

1. Cook chopped pork in an 8-inch nonstick omelet pan or heavy skillet with sloped sides over medium-low heat 5 minutes or until thoroughly heated. Add tomatoes and onion, and cook, stirring often, until onion is tender. Remove pork mixture from pan; set aside. Wipe skillet clean with paper towels.
2. Whisk together eggs and next 3 ingredients.
3. Melt 1 tsp. butter in skillet over medium heat. Pour one-fourth egg mixture into skillet. As egg mixture starts to cook, gently lift edges of omelet with a spatula, and  tilt pan so uncooked portion flows underneath. Cook 1 to 2 minutes or until almost set. Flip omelet over.
4. Sprinkle 1 side of omelet with one-fourth each of cheese and reserved chopped pork mixture. Cook 1 minute or until cheese begins to melt. Slide filled side of  omelet onto a plate, flipping remaining side of omelet over filling. Repeat procedure 3 times with remaining butter, egg mixture, cheese, and pork mixture. Serve immediately. **Makes** 4 servings.

Note: For testing purposes only, we used Smithfield Smoked Pork Chops.

You can substitute 1 (15-oz.) carton garden vegetable flavor egg substitute for eggs, parsley, salt, and pepper.

Sparkly Cranberry Scones
fast fixin's
PREP: 10 MIN., BAKE: 20 MIN.
Shortly after Christmas, teenager Madeline Unger was challenged by her parents to "use up the leftover cranberries." This delectable breakfast treat was the result.

2 cups all-purpose flour
½ cup granulated sugar
2 tsp. baking powder
½ tsp. salt
1 cup fresh or frozen cranberries,
  thawed
½ cup butter, melted
½ cup milk
2 large eggs
1 Tbsp. milk
2 Tbsp. sparkling sugar ✱

1. Stir together first 4 ingredients in a large bowl; stir in cranberries.
2. Whisk together butter, ½ cup milk, and 1 egg; add to flour mixture, stirring just until dry ingredients are moistened and dough forms. Drop dough by ⅓ cupfuls onto a lightly greased baking sheet. Whisk together remaining 1 egg and 1 Tbsp. milk. Brush tops of dough with egg mixture, and sprinkle evenly with sparkling sugar.
3. Bake at 400° for 20 minutes or until golden brown. **Makes** 9 scones.

Note: Purchase sparkling sugar at crafts stores or supercenters with cake-decorating supplies.

✱Substitute granulated sugar, if desired.

Banana Pudding Pie

Layers of flavor in a crisp cookie-crumb crust make this Southern favorite irresistible.

Pie just doesn't get much easier or better than this tasty twist on banana pudding. Chilling the pie after it cools at room temperature further sets the filling and makes for perfect slices.

Test Kitchen Notebook

To prevent meringue from shrinking as it bakes, spread it to the very edge of the crust. Make sure the meringue completely covers the hot filling, touching the crust all the way around the pie.

Mary Allen Perry
ASSOCIATE FOODS EDITOR

Banana Pudding Pie

PREP: 20 MIN.; BAKE: 24 MIN.;
COOL: 1 HR., 30 MIN.; CHILL: 4 HR.

Hang onto your egg yolks—you'll be using them in the Vanilla Cream Filling. Also if you're a big fan of vanilla wafers, pick up an extra box, and tuck some into the edges of the meringue before baking. They will add a decorative look to your pie. (Pictured on page 4)

1 (12-oz.) box vanilla wafers, divided
½ cup butter, melted
2 large bananas, sliced
Vanilla Cream Filling
4 egg whites
½ cup sugar

1. Set aside 30 wafers; pulse remaining vanilla wafers in a food processor 8 to 10 times or until coarsely crushed. (Yield should be about 2½ cups.) Stir together crushed vanilla wafers and butter until blended. Firmly press on bottom, up sides, and onto lip of a 9-inch pieplate.
2. Bake at 350° for 10 to 12 minutes or until lightly browned. Remove to a wire rack, and let cool 30 minutes or until completely cool.
3. Arrange half of banana slices over bottom of crust. Prepare Vanilla Cream Filling, and spread ¾ cup hot filling over bananas; top with 20 vanilla wafers. Spread ¾ cup hot filling over vanilla wafers, and top with remaining half of banana slices. Spread remaining hot filling (about 1 cup) over banana slices. (Filling will be about ¼ inch higher than top edge of crust.)
4. Beat egg whites at high speed with an electric mixer until foamy. Add sugar, 1 Tbsp. at a time, beating until stiff peaks form and sugar dissolves. Spread meringue evenly over hot filling, sealing the edges.
5. Bake at 350° for 10 to 12 minutes or until golden brown. Remove from oven, and let cool 1 hour on a wire rack or until completely cool. Coarsely crush remaining 10 vanilla wafers, and sprinkle evenly over top of pie. Chill 4 hours. **Makes** 8 servings.

Note: For testing purposes only, we used Nabisco Nilla Wafers.

Crumb Crust Perfection

Pressing the crumb mixture partially up the pieplate sides creates a thick, uneven crust that is too shallow to hold the filling.

Pressing the crumb mixture up the sides and over the pieplate lip creates the perfect crust.

Vanilla Cream Filling:
fast fixin's
PREP: 5 MIN., COOK: 10 MIN.

¾ cup sugar
⅓ cup all-purpose flour
2 large eggs
4 egg yolks
2 cups milk
2 tsp. vanilla extract

1. Whisk together first 5 ingredients in a heavy saucepan. Cook over medium-low heat, whisking constantly, 8 to 10 minutes or until it reaches the thickness of chilled pudding. (Mixture will just begin to bubble and will be thick enough to hold soft peaks when whisk is lifted.) Remove from heat, and stir in vanilla. Use immediately. **Makes** 2½ cups.

Cook's Notes

■ If you don't have a food processor, place the cookies in a large zip-top plastic bag, and gently crush with a rolling pin or mallet.
■ The slightest hint of grease can ruin beaten egg whites. Before making meringue, be sure the bowl and beaters are super clean and completely dry.
■ To neatly cut a meringue pie, dip the knife blade in cold water or lightly coat with vegetable cooking spray.

---

taste of the south
Oyster Stew

Stew is one of the pleasures of cold weather, especially when oysters are in season. Winter oysters tend to be fatter and larger than fall oysters. While the winter ones are not as economical as those harvested early in the season, they are both equally as good in the stew pot.

Classic oyster stew is simplicity itself—oysters, cream, salt, pepper, and perhaps a touch of butter for richness and onion to boost the briny flavor of the mollusks. But for our taste, it's a little, well, bland. Golden Oyster Stew, with its base of potato soup and chunks of celery, onion, and mushroom, is heartier and better fits the definition of a stew. This recipe received an enthusiastic welcome at the tasting table, so stir up a potful to enjoy the praise of your own tasters.

When you find shucked oysters at a good price, buy several containers and freeze them for up to six weeks. Thaw them overnight in the refrigerator for fresh flavor all season long.

Golden Oyster Stew
freezeable • make ahead
PREP: 15 MIN., COOK: 25 MIN.
Oyster liquor is the liquid found in the container with shucked oysters (or inside the shell of whole oysters).

2 Tbsp. butter
½ cup chopped onion
½ cup sliced celery
1 (8-oz.) package sliced fresh
  mushrooms
2 Tbsp. all-purpose flour
2 cups milk
1 cup (4 oz.) shredded sharp Cheddar
  cheese
1 (10¾-oz.) can cream of potato soup
1 (2-oz.) jar diced pimiento, undrained
¼ tsp. salt
¼ tsp. pepper
¼ tsp. hot sauce
1 (12-oz.) container standard oysters,
  undrained
Saltines or oyster crackers
  (optional)

1. Melt butter in a Dutch oven over medium heat; add onion and celery, and cook, stirring occasionally, 8 minutes or until tender. Add mushrooms, and cook, stirring occasionally, 5 minutes. Add flour, and cook, stirring constantly, 1 minute.
2. Gradually stir in 2 cups milk; cook, stirring often, 5 minutes or until mixture is thickened and bubbly.
3. Reduce heat to low, and stir in cheese

---

and next 5 ingredients. Cook, stirring often, 3 minutes or until cheese melts and mixture is hot.
4. Add oysters and oyster liquor, and simmer 3 minutes or just until edges of oysters begin to curl. Serve with crackers, if desired. **Makes** 6 servings.

Note: To make ahead, prepare the stew through Step 3. Freeze the mixture in a large zip-top plastic freezer bag for up to 2 months. Thaw in the refrigerator overnight. Heat in a Dutch oven over medium-low heat 10 minutes or until thoroughly heated. Proceed with recipe as directed in Step 4.

Choosing the Best

Fresh shucked oysters are found in the seafood department of supermarkets or at seafood markets. We don't recommend substituting canned oysters in this recipe. Fresh oysters come in 12-oz. containers and range in size from standards (the smallest) to counts (the largest). Standards and selects are the most economical and are the best choices for oyster stew.

Drain the oysters before cooking so you can pick out bits of shell before adding the mollusks to your recipe. If the liquor seems especially gritty, line the colander with a coffee filter.

Living in the Kitchen

Today's special: Three clever kitchens with delicious recipes on the side.

Sunny Space

With a designated area for baking, super storage ideas, and a cabinet full of kids-only pots and pans, the Austin, Texas, kitchen of Susannah and Jase Auby combines food and fun in stylish ways. Like sunshine breaking through clouds of gray, yellow cabinets are a cheery choice against a pewter background. The bright shade is just right for a space focused on family life. With an emphasis on organization and convenience, it's perfect for an on-the-go mom.

The baking zone is an added luxury. At least once a week, Susannah and the kids bake a cake, cookies, or some other dessert. With its own sink, oven, and microwave, the area is efficient and convenient.

Chocolate-Chocolate Cupcakes With White Frosting
family favorite

PREP: 15 MIN., BAKE: 30 MIN., COOL: 35 MIN.

Although most cupcake recipes say to fill the baking cups only two-thirds full, you can fill these all the way to the top. The batter is thick enough to form a nice dome when baked.

¾ cup unsweetened cocoa
¾ cup all-purpose flour
½ tsp. baking powder
½ tsp. salt
½ cup unsalted butter, softened
1 cup sugar
3 large eggs, at room temperature
1 tsp. vanilla extract
½ cup sour cream
1½ cups milk chocolate morsels
White Frosting

1. Sift together first 4 ingredients in a medium bowl; set aside.
2. Beat butter and sugar at medium speed with an electric mixer until light and fluffy. Add eggs, 1 at a time, beating until well blended after each addition. Stir in vanilla.
3. Add cocoa mixture to butter mixture alternately with sour cream, beginning and ending with cocoa mixture. Beat at low speed until blended after each addition. Stir in morsels.
4. Place 12 paper baking cups in a muffin pan; spoon batter evenly into cups, filling completely full.
5. Bake at 350° for 25 to 30 minutes or until a wooden pick inserted in center comes out clean. Cool in pan 5 minutes; transfer to a wire rack, and cool 30 minutes or until completely cool. Spread cupcakes evenly with White Frosting. **Makes** 1 dozen.

White Frosting:
fast fixin's

PREP: 10 MIN.

½ cup unsalted butter, softened
3 cups powdered sugar
1 tsp. vanilla extract
2 to 3 Tbsp. milk

1. Beat butter with an electric mixer at medium-high speed until creamy. Gradually beat in sugar until smooth. Beat in vanilla and 2 Tbsp. milk, adding additional milk, if necessary, for desired consistency. **Makes** about 2½ cups.

Savvy Storage Solutions

1 Knives are kept beneath the cutting board. Everything in the kitchen is stored close to where it will be used.

2 A drawer beside the dishwasher provides the perfect home for sippy cups used by the Auby children.

3 Olive oil and other bottled ingredients are easy to find inside a low drawer with divided sections.

Cool Looks, Smart Spending

Some kitchens are best made from scratch. When Donnajean Ward launched a remodeling crusade on her row house in Washington, D.C., she converted a bedroom off her living room into a dream-come-true cooking space.

Donnajean loves having friends over for meals, but without a lot of space in her old kitchen, seating was a challenge. So she cooked up a solution with architect Chris Landis. A central island with a butcher-block top is big enough to allow five guests to pull up seats. The substantial island has several deep cupboards and drawers, which help "squeeze in as much storage as I can get," says Donnajean.

To capture a clean, contemporary style, Donnajean opted for stainless steel appliances that look outstanding next to the original wood floors and exposed redbrick wall. "Now I have that faux loft feel in a Victorian row house," says Donnajean.

Mimosa Gelée
make ahead

PREP: 5 MIN., COOK: 3 MIN., CHILL: 3 HR
These may be made up to a day ahead. Keep chilled and tightly covered with plastic wrap, and garnish just before serving.

1½ cups chilled Champagne or
    sparkling wine
2 (¼-oz.) envelopes unflavored gelatin
2½ cups orange juice
1 (8-oz.) jar orange blossom honey
Garnishes: orange segments, mint sprigs

1. Pour Champagne into a large bowl. Sprinkle gelatin over Champagne. Set aside.
2. Heat orange juice and honey in a small saucepan over medium-high heat 3 minutes or until well blended and thoroughly heated.
3. Add hot juice mixture to Champagne mixture, and stir 5 minutes or until gelatin dissolves. Pour mixture evenly into

8 Champagne flutes, and chill 3 hours or until set. Garnish, if desired. **Makes** about 4 cups.

Orange Honey-Ade: Combine 2 cups orange juice, 1½ cups water, and ⅓ cup orange blossom honey in a large pitcher. Chill 2 hours. Serve over crushed ice. Prep: 5 min., Chill: 2 hr.

Baked Oatmeal

PREP: 10 MIN., BAKE: 50 MIN.
Here, Donnajean shares her recipe for Baked Oatmeal—delicious on a chilly winter morning. Round out the menu with fresh fruit, muffins and croissants, and flavored coffee.

2 cups frozen blueberries
2 Tbsp. fresh lemon juice, divided
1 (18-oz.) container regular oats
3 large eggs, beaten
1 cup firmly packed brown sugar
1 cup unsweetened applesauce
1 Tbsp. ground cinnamon
4 tsp. baking powder
1 tsp. salt
1¼ cups water
1 cup milk
¼ cup melted butter

1. Toss 2 cups blueberries in 1 Tbsp. lemon juice, and spread evenly on bottom of a lightly greased 13- x 9-inch baking dish.
2. Combine oats, next 9 ingredients, and remaining 1 Tbsp. lemon juice in a large bowl, stirring until well blended. Pour oat mixture evenly over blueberries.
3. Bake, covered, at 350° for 30 minutes; uncover and bake 20 more minutes or until golden brown and set. **Makes** 8 to 10 servings.

Apple-Pecan Baked Oatmeal: Place ½ cup chopped pecans in a single layer on a baking sheet. Bake at 350° for 15 minutes or until toasted, stirring once. Omit blueberries and lemon juice. Peel and chop 5 Granny Smith apples. Spread on bottom of a lightly greased 13- x 9-inch baking dish. Sprinkle toasted pecans over apples. Prepare oat mixture as directed, and pour evenly over apples and pecans. Bake as directed.

Totally Cottage

Homeowners Marnie and Jamie Gray of Homewood, Alabama, turned a dated split-level ranch house into an updated English-style cottage, and their fabulous kitchen is the star. The new space benefits their passions for cooking and entertaining. When it comes to preparing meals for family and friends, this is a perfectly planned room.

They created a kitchen island for serving when the family entertains. Topped with an African wood called iroko, it's also designed to be the ultimate storage unit. Iroko is highly resistant to moisture and is easy to maintain. Scratches can be buffed out with fine steel wool and finished with an oil stain. Each cabinet in the island is designed for full use from front to back—that means no wasted space. Pullout shelving and drawer units make this possible, plus the island limits the need for upper cabinets.

Mustard Baked Chicken

PREP: 10 MIN., CHILL: 30 MIN., BAKE: 50 MIN., STAND: 15 MIN.

1 (4-lb.) whole chicken
1 Tbsp. paprika
1½ tsp. dry mustard
1 tsp. salt
1 tsp. pepper
2 Tbsp. Worcestershire sauce
1 Tbsp. olive oil

1. Remove giblets and neck, and rinse chicken with cold water; pat dry. Place chicken in a large zip-top plastic freezer bag. Stir together paprika and next 5 ingredients until well blended; rub over chicken, coating evenly. Seal and chill at least 30 minutes or up to 8 hours, turning occasionally. Remove from marinade, discarding marinade. Place chicken in a roasting pan.
2. Bake at 425° for 50 minutes or until a meat thermometer inserted in thickest portion registers 170°. Let stand, covered, 15 minutes before slicing. **Makes** 8 servings.

Our Favorite Sweet Rolls

The time invested is worth every incredible bite.

Between forkfuls, the fun started flying as our Foods staff taste-tested these amazing rolls. Body language spoke loudly. We leaned towards the rolls like magnets pulled by metal, and we all thought the same thing: "How can I steal the whole pan with all these people watching?" Yes, they are that good, so make them, and let us know the response at your home.

Orange Rolls
family favorite
PREP: 30 MIN., STAND: 5 MIN., RISE: 3 HR., BAKE: 22 MIN., COOL: 2 MIN.
The rolls need rising time, so plan this recipe for a weekend or day off. (Pictured on page 2)

1 (¼-oz.) envelope active dry yeast
1 tsp. sugar
¼ cup warm water (100° to 110°)
½ cup butter, softened
½ cup sugar
1 tsp. salt
2 large eggs, lightly beaten
1 cup milk
1 Tbsp. fresh lemon juice
4½ cups bread flour
¼ tsp. ground nutmeg
¼ to ½ cup bread flour
Honey Topping
1 cup coarsely chopped pecans (optional)
Fresh Orange Glaze

1. Combine first 3 ingredients in a 1-cup glass measuring cup; let stand 5 minutes.
2. Beat butter at medium speed with a heavy-duty electric stand mixer, using the paddle attachment, until creamy. Gradually add ½ cup sugar and salt, beating at medium speed until light and fluffy. Add eggs, milk, and lemon juice, beating until blended. Stir in yeast mixture.
3. Combine 4½ cups bread flour and nutmeg. Gradually add to butter mixture, beating at low speed 2 minutes or until well blended.
4. Turn dough out onto a surface floured with about ¼ cup bread flour; knead for 5 minutes, adding additional bread flour as needed. Place dough in a lightly greased large bowl, turning to grease top of dough. Cover and let rise in a warm place (85°), free from drafts, 1½ to 2 hours or until doubled in bulk.
5. Punch dough down; turn out onto a lightly floured surface. Divide dough in half. Divide 1 dough half into 12 equal pieces, and shape each piece, rolling between hands, into a 7- to 8-inch-long rope. Wrap each rope into a coil, firmly pinching end to seal. Place rolls in a lightly greased 10-inch round cake pan. Repeat procedure with remaining dough half. Drizzle Honey Topping evenly over each pan of rolls.
6. Let rise, covered, in a warm place (85°), free from drafts, 1 hour or until doubled in size. Top evenly with pecans, if desired.
7. Bake at 350° for 20 to 22 minutes or until rolls are lightly browned. Cool rolls 2 minutes in pans. Spoon Fresh Orange Glaze evenly over each pan of warm rolls, and serve immediately. **Makes** 24 servings.

Honey Topping:
fast fixin's
PREP: 5 MIN.

1⅓ cups powdered sugar
½ cup butter, melted
¼ cup honey
2 egg whites

1. Stir together all ingredients until smooth. **Makes** 1⅓ cups.

Fresh Orange Glaze:
fast fixin's
PREP: 10 MIN.

2 cups powdered sugar
2 Tbsp. butter, softened
2 tsp. grated orange rind
3 Tbsp. fresh orange juice
1 Tbsp. fresh lemon juice

1. Beat powdered sugar and butter at medium speed with an electric mixer until blended. Add remaining ingredients, and beat until smooth. **Makes** ¾ cup.

To easily form the coils, wrap ropes of dough around a finger.

Satisfying Sippers

The next time friends come over, serve them one of these tasty beverages. If you need to warm up, try Orange Spiced Cider. Creamy Mocha Latte is delectable enough to be dessert. You can't go wrong with either choice.

Orange Spiced Cider

PREP: 10 MIN., COOK: 30 MIN.
Omit rum for a kid-friendly treat.

1 (64-oz.) bottle apple cider
¼ cup firmly packed brown sugar
1 orange, cut into wedges
2 (3-inch) cinnamon sticks
1 tsp. whole cloves
1 tsp. whole allspice
Dash of ground nutmeg
½ cup dark rum (optional)
Garnishes: cinnamon sticks, dried
    persimmon slices

1. Bring first 7 ingredients to a boil in a Dutch oven. Reduce heat, and simmer 30 minutes. Pour mixture through a wire-mesh strainer into a container, discarding solids. Stir in rum, if desired. Garnish, if desired, and serve warm. **Makes** 8 cups.

DANIELLE MCINERNEY
TUSCALOOSA, ALABAMA

Creamy Mocha Latte

PREP: 10 MIN., FREEZE: 2 HR.

¾ cup hot water
½ cup instant cappuccino drink mix
2 cups milk
1 (14-oz.) can sweetened condensed
    milk
1 pt. coffee ice cream, softened

1. Stir together ¾ cup hot water and ½ cup cappuccino drink mix in a bowl. Pour into ice cube trays, and freeze 2 hours.
2. Process half each of milk, sweetened condensed milk, ice cream, and cappuccino ice cubes in a blender until smooth, stopping to scrape down sides. Repeat procedure with remaining half of ingredients, and serve immediately. **Makes** 8 cups.

Note: For testing purposes only, we used General Foods International Coffees Italian Cappuccino mix.

Start With Pancake Mix

Combine four staple ingredients to make batter for pancakes and frying.

Save money and add extra goodness to weekend breakfasts by making your own pancake mix. The recipe goes together in a snap and stays fresh for up to six weeks. Use it in a variety of preparations, from Banana-Pecan Pancakes to Big Fat Onion Rings. Once you try this simple recipe, you'll be reminded that homemade doesn't have to be hard.

Pancake Mix

fast fixin's • make ahead
PREP: 10 MIN.

6 cups all-purpose flour
3 Tbsp. baking powder
2 tsp. baking soda
2 tsp. salt

1. Stir together all ingredients in a large bowl; store in a zip-top plastic bag up to 6 weeks. **Makes** 6 cups.

Basic Pancakes

family favorite • make ahead
PREP: 10 MIN., COOK: 8 MIN.
Don't head to a restaurant for breakfast: Basic Pancakes are tender and easy to make.

1½ cups Pancake Mix
1 Tbsp. sugar
1½ cups buttermilk
1 large egg, lightly beaten
1 Tbsp. vegetable oil

1. Combine Pancake Mix and sugar in a medium bowl.
2. Whisk together 1½ cups buttermilk, egg, and oil; add to dry ingredients, whisking just until lumps disappear.

3. Pour about ¼ cup batter for each pancake onto a hot, lightly greased griddle or large nonstick skillet. Cook pancakes 2 minutes or until tops are covered with bubbles and edges begin to look cooked; turn and cook 2 more minutes or until done. **Makes** 4 servings (about 15 pancakes).

SUZAN L. WIENER
SPRING HILL, FLORIDA

Banana-Pecan Pancakes: Stir 1 chopped banana and ¼ cup toasted chopped pecans into batter; proceed as directed.

Test Kitchen Notebook

Pretty pancakes: For nice, evenly shaped pancakes, mix the batter in a large (pint or quart) measuring cup. Pour the same amount of batter onto the griddle for each pancake. If you have children and want to make shaped pancakes, use a bulb baster; it allows you to be creative, but also control the amount of batter that's released.

Donna Florio
SENIOR WRITER

Big Fat Onion Rings
family favorite
PREP: 25 MIN., COOK: 4 MIN. PER BATCH

1 medium-size yellow onion
1 medium-size red onion
1¾ cups Pancake Mix, divided (recipe on previous page)
1 Tbsp. sugar
½ cup buttermilk
½ cup beer
Peanut oil

1. Cut onions into ½-inch slices, and separate into rings. Set aside.
2. Combine 1¼ cups Pancake Mix and sugar. Stir together buttermilk and beer; whisk into sugar mixture until smooth. Set aside.
3. Place onion rings and remaining ½ cup Pancake Mix in a large zip-top plastic freezer bag. Seal and shake to coat.
4. Pour oil to a depth of 2 inches into a Dutch oven; heat to 370°.
5. Dip onion rings, 1 at a time, in batter, coating well. Fry, in batches, 4 minutes or until golden, turning occasionally; drain on paper towels. Serve immediately. **Makes** 8 servings.

Kitchen Express: Substitute 1¾ cups all-purpose baking mix for 1¾ cups Pancake Mix, and omit sugar. Proceed as directed, reducing frying time for each batch to 2 minutes.

Use Pancake Mix to stir up batter for Big Fat Onion Rings. Coat the rings with dry mix first to help the batter stick, and then dip them in the wet mixture.

Comfort on the Side

Round out your meal with these delicious, timeless side dishes featuring super-quick prep times.

Tasty, budget-stretching side dishes that can be easily pulled together are a must for any busy family. Keep these recipes on hand for a weeknight meal or even for a last-minute dinner party. The best part is they all have prep times of 15 minutes or less.

For Baked Winter Squash, choose smaller butternut squash (around 1 lb.). They're more tender and less stringy, giving you wonderful results every time.

Classic Baked Macaroni and Cheese gets a pop of flavor from sharp Cheddar cheese and a touch of ground red pepper. We even offer a lightened version of this recipe as well as a one-pot version that omits the baking.

Baked Winter Squash
family favorite
PREP: 10 MIN., BAKE: 45 MIN.
This cooking method works well for all types of winter squash. Adding water to the baking dish prevents the bottom of the squash from burning. Substitute sorghum or maple syrup for the honey, if desired.

2 small butternut squash (about 1 lb. each)
¼ cup butter
4 tsp. honey
¼ tsp. salt
¼ tsp. pepper

1. Cut squash in half lengthwise; remove and discard seeds. Place squash, skin sides down, in a 13- x 9-inch baking dish. Place 1 Tbsp. butter and 1 tsp. honey in the cavity of each squash half; sprinkle squash evenly with salt and pepper. Add water to baking dish to a depth of ¼ inch.
2. Bake, covered, at 400° for 30 minutes; uncover and bake 15 more minutes or until squash is tender. **Makes** 4 servings.

ADELYNE SMITH
DUNNVILLE, KENTUCKY

Classic Baked Macaroni and Cheese

family favorite

PREP: 15 MIN., COOK: 7 MIN., BAKE: 20 MIN., STAND: 10 MIN.

Shredding a block of cheese adds a little more prep time, but the smooth and creamy results are worth it.

1 (8-oz.) package elbow macaroni
2 Tbsp. butter
2 Tbsp. all-purpose flour
2 cups milk
½ tsp. salt
½ tsp. freshly ground black pepper
¼ tsp. ground red pepper
1 (8-oz.) block sharp Cheddar cheese, shredded and divided

1. Prepare pasta according to package directions. Keep warm.
2. Melt butter in a large saucepan or Dutch oven over medium-low heat; whisk in flour until smooth. Cook, whisking constantly, 2 minutes. Gradually whisk in milk, and cook, whisking constantly, 5 minutes or until thickened. Remove from heat. Stir in salt, black and red pepper, 1 cup shredded cheese, and cooked pasta.
3. Spoon pasta mixture into a lightly greased 2-qt. baking dish; top with remaining 1 cup cheese.
4. Bake at 400° for 20 minutes or until bubbly. Let stand 10 minutes before serving. **Makes** 2 to 3 main-dish or 4 to 6 side-dish servings.

Note: For testing purposes only, we used Kraft Sharp Cheddar Cheese. To lighten, 2% reduced-fat milk and reduced-fat cheese may be substituted.

One-Pot Macaroni and Cheese: Prepare recipe as directed, stirring all grated Cheddar cheese into thickened milk mixture until melted. Add cooked pasta, and serve immediately. Prep: 10 min., Cook: 7 min.

STEWART GORDON
CHARLESTON, SOUTH CAROLINA

quick & easy

Start With Cooked Chicken

Having chopped or shredded cooked chicken on hand is a lifesaver. You'll save both time and money. Watch for sales on chicken to get the lowest prices; then cook, package, and freeze bags of it. Supper will be ready to serve much faster. And, in a pinch, you can always use a rotisserie chicken from the deli.

Chicken-and-Sausage Creole

family favorite

PREP: 15 MIN., COOK: 30 MIN.

1 cup uncooked long-grain rice
2 (14-oz.) cans low-sodium fat-free chicken broth, divided
½ lb. smoked sausage, cut into ½-inch rounds
1 medium-size yellow onion, chopped (about 2 cups)
1 cup chopped celery
1 green bell pepper, chopped
2 garlic cloves, minced
3 cups chopped cooked chicken
1 (14½-oz.) can diced tomatoes
2 tsp. chopped fresh parsley
1 tsp. salt
⅛ tsp. ground red pepper
2 bay leaves

1. Prepare rice according to package directions, substituting 2 cups broth for water.
2. Meanwhile, sauté sausage and next 4 ingredients in a lightly greased Dutch oven over medium-high heat 5 minutes or until vegetables are tender. Stir in remaining broth, chicken, and next 5 ingredients. Bring to a boil over medium-high heat. Reduce heat to low; simmer, stirring occasionally, 20 minutes. Remove and discard bay leaves. Serve chicken mixture over hot cooked rice. **Makes** 6 servings.

DOREN CLARK
MCDONOUGH, GEORGIA

One-Dish Wonder

We enjoy the simplicity of Creamy Chicken and Noodles (page 54), but when you have a good thing, sometimes it's hard to leave it alone. Our staff is always full of suggestions to dress up recipes with ingredients that add additional flavor. Here are a few stir-in variations to enjoy.

Chopped Ham and Peas: Stir in 8 oz. diced ham and 1 cup thawed frozen peas.

Southwestern Style: Omit Italian dressing and Parmesan cheese. Stir in 1 (10-oz.) can diced tomatoes and green chiles and ½ cup (2 oz.) shredded Mexican four-cheese blend.

Italian Style: Add ¼ cup diced sun-dried tomatoes and 1 cup turkey pepperoni slices.

Creamy Chicken and Noodles

family favorite • fast fixin's

PREP: 10 MIN., COOK: 15 MIN.

Creamy Chicken and Noodles is a 25-minute, one-pan main dish. Round out the meal with a green vegetable, salad, or fresh fruit. Soft rolls are excellent to help savor all the richness by sopping the bowl clean.

1 (0.6-oz.) envelope Italian dressing mix
1 (8-oz.) package wide egg noodles
2 Tbsp. butter, softened
3 cups chopped cooked chicken
1 cup whipping cream
¼ cup freshly grated Parmesan cheese
2 Tbsp. chopped fresh parsley

1. Remove 1 Tbsp. Italian dressing mix from envelope, and set aside; reserve remaining mix for another use.
2. Cook noodles according to package directions; drain well, and return noodles to pan.
3. Stir in 2 Tbsp. butter, and toss to coat. Stir in chopped chicken, next 3 ingredients, and 1 Tbsp. dressing mix. Cook mixture over medium-high heat, tossing to coat evenly, 5 minutes or until thoroughly heated. Serve immediately. **Makes** 6 servings.

KIM MORTON
BIRMINGHAM, ALABAMA

Test Kitchen *Notebook*

Here are 2 different methods for cooking chicken.

Grilled Chicken:

6   skinned and boned chicken breasts (about 2½ lb.)
1   tsp. salt
½   tsp. pepper

Sprinkle chicken evenly with salt and pepper or desired seasoning. Grill, covered with grill lid, over medium-high heat (350° to 400°) about 6 to 7 minutes on each side or until done. Cool chicken slightly; chop chicken, and store in airtight containers in freezer up to 3 months. **Makes** 6 cups.

Basic Baked Chicken:

4   celery ribs with leaves, cut into 4-inch pieces
2   carrots, sliced
2   medium onions, sliced
6   bone-in chicken breasts (about 4 lb.)
½   tsp. salt
¼   tsp. pepper

Arrange celery, carrots, and onions in a lightly greased 15- x 12-inch roasting pan. Top with chicken; sprinkle with salt and pepper. Bake, covered, at 350° for 1 hour or until chicken is done. Uncover and let cool 20 minutes; remove and discard skin and bones. Chop chicken, and store in airtight containers in freezer up to 3 months. **Makes** 8 cups.

Vicki A. Poellnitz
ASSOCIATE FOODS EDITOR

healthy foods
Fast and Fresh

These quick, healthful dishes will have you feeling great about feeding your family. Best of all, they cook or bake in 10 minutes or less. Try some of our favorites. Salmon fillets are packed with good fats and are ready in only 6 minutes, while whole wheat couscous, which is rich in fiber and whole grains, fluffs up in just 10 minutes.

Almond-Crusted Chicken

family favorite • fast fixin's

PREP: 10 MIN., COOK: 8 MIN.

Jamaican jerk seasoning offers the sweet-spicy flavors of thyme, allspice, and crushed red pepper.

¼ cup almonds, coarsely chopped
½ cup fine, dry breadcrumbs
2 tsp. Jamaican jerk seasoning
¼ tsp. kosher salt
1 tsp. grated lime rind
1½ lb. skinned and boned chicken breast cutlets
1 Tbsp. olive oil, divided

1. Process first 5 ingredients in a food processor or blender 45 seconds or until finely ground. Place almond mixture in a shallow bowl.
2. Brush chicken evenly with ½ Tbsp. olive oil. Dredge chicken in almond mixture.
3. Cook chicken in remaining ½ Tbsp. hot olive oil in a nonstick skillet over medium-high heat 4 minutes on each side or until done. **Makes** 5 servings.

Per serving: Calories 245; Fat 7.7g (sat 1g, mono 4.1g, poly 1.3g); Protein 33.8g; Carb 8.7g; Fiber 1.1g; Chol 79mg; Iron 1.7mg; Sodium 402mg; Calc 53mg

Super-Fast Foods

Each of these items is guaranteed to help you have dinner on the table quickly. Plus, they're loaded with good-for-you nutrients.

- whole wheat couscous
- instant brown rice (box, bag, or pouch variety)
- fresh fish fillets such as salmon or tuna
- canned beans (rinsed and drained)
- boneless, skinless chicken breast cutlets
- eggs or egg substitute
- fresh, frozen, or canned vegetables
- fresh, frozen, or canned fruit
- leafy greens such as spinach, kale, or collard greens
- lean ground beef or ground turkey breast
- lean pork cutlets, trimmed

Warm Cinnamon Apples

family favorite • fast fixin's
PREP: 10 MIN., COOK: 10 MIN.

If you can't find McIntosh apples, substitute another baking apple such as Rome or Gala, or try a crisp, tart green apple such as Granny Smith.

4 McIntosh apples, peeled and sliced
    (about 2 lb.)
½ cup firmly packed light brown
    sugar
1 tsp. ground cinnamon
¼ tsp. ground nutmeg
2 Tbsp. water
1 Tbsp. butter

1. Toss together first 4 ingredients in a large zip-top plastic bag, tossing to coat apples.

2. Cook apple mixture, 2 Tbsp. water, and 1 Tbsp. butter in a medium saucepan over medium heat, stirring occasionally, 8 to 10 minutes or until apples are tender. **Makes** 6 servings.

BETTY ADAMS
FORT PAYNE, ALABAMA

Per (½-cup) serving: Calories 128; Fat 2g (sat 1.2g, mono 0.5g, poly 0.1g); Protein 0.3g; Carb 29.2g; Fiber 1.3g; Chol 5mg; Iron 0.6mg; Sodium 21mg; Calc 25mg

Mediterranean Salmon With White Beans

PREP: 15 MIN., COOK: 10 MIN.

Salmon is packed with heart-healthy omega-3 fats, but any fish fillet may be substituted for the salmon. (Pictured on page 175)

1 medium onion, coarsely chopped
2 Tbsp. olive oil, divided
1 (15-oz.) can cannellini beans, rinsed
    and drained
½ cup chopped pitted kalamata olives
1 cup halved grape tomatoes
2 Tbsp. chopped fresh basil
4 (6-oz.) salmon fillets
½ tsp. salt
½ tsp. pepper
Garnish: fresh parsley sprigs

1. Sauté onion in 1 Tbsp. hot oil in a saucepan over medium heat 2 minutes or until slightly softened. Add beans, olives, and tomatoes; cook over medium heat, stirring occasionally, 2 minutes or until thoroughly heated. Remove from heat, and stir in basil.

2. Sprinkle salmon fillets evenly with salt and pepper. Cook salmon in a large nonstick skillet in remaining 1 Tbsp. hot oil over medium-high heat 3 minutes on each side or until fish flakes easily. Spoon bean mixture onto a serving platter, and top with fillets; serve immediately. Garnish, if desired. **Makes** 4 servings.

JANICE ELDER
CHARLOTTE, NORTH CAROLINA

Per serving: Calories 375; Fat 16.4g (sat 2.4g, mono 7.4g, poly 5.2g); Protein 37.8g; Carb 17.3g; Fiber 4.8g; Chol 94mg; Iron 3.4mg; Sodium 683mg; Calc 74mg

Mango Couscous

PREP: 20 MIN., BAKE: 10 MIN., STAND: 5 MIN.

Whole wheat couscous is actually the same thing as whole wheat pasta, so look for it on the same grocery aisle. Because couscous is so tiny, it cooks in a fraction of the time. Find dried mangoes with other dried fruit and mango nectar with the fruit juices.

¼ cup chopped macadamia nuts ✱
1¼ cups low-sodium fat-free chicken
    broth
¼ cup mango nectar
1½ cups whole wheat couscous
¾ cup chopped dried mango
1 tsp. grated lime rind
2 tsp. fresh lime juice
2 Tbsp. chopped fresh cilantro
1 Tbsp. chopped fresh mint

1. Place macadamia nuts in an even layer in a shallow pan.

2. Bake at 350° for 10 minutes or until lightly toasted, stirring occasionally.

3. Meanwhile, microwave broth and mango nectar in a medium-size microwave-safe bowl at HIGH 3 to 5 minutes or until mixture begins to boil. Place couscous and dried mango in a large bowl, and stir in broth mixture. Cover and let stand 5 minutes.

4. Fluff couscous with a fork, and stir in toasted macadamia nuts, lime rind, and next 3 ingredients. Serve warm or at room temperature. **Makes** 5 servings.

✱Substitute ¼ cup chopped walnuts or almonds, if desired.

Note: Reheat leftover couscous in the microwave, stirring in a small amount of low-sodium fat-free chicken broth as needed to moisten.

Per (1-cup) serving: Calories 256; Fat 6.1g (sat 1g, mono 4.1g, poly 0.2g); Protein 6.6g; Carb 46.2g; Fiber 5.4g; Chol 0mg; Iron 1.6mg; Sodium 46mg; Calc 58mg

from our kitchen

Flavors You'll Love

Dried beans and peas are the best food value anywhere. Not only are they tasty, but add rice or cornbread and you have a hearty main dish. Beans add body and texture to a wide array of dishes as well. We enjoy peas in Hoppin' John, a Lowcountry South Carolina rice dish, while red beans and rice help New Orleanians make it through Mondays. You'll likely agree that beans are also a robust addition to chili (unless, of course, you're a Texan).

Beans are amazingly nutritious as well. They're full of proteins, fiber, vitamins, and micronutrients and are low in fat and surprisingly low in calories. Experts believe that a diet rich in legumes can help prevent cancer, heart disease, and diabetes. You can buy all this good health and great taste for as little as $1 for a bag of beans that will feed six to eight people.

So keep some of your favorites in the pantry. Lentils and split peas don't need to soak, but larger beans do. Soak them overnight, or use this quick-soak method if you're in a hurry: Place the beans and water to cover by 2 inches in a Dutch oven, and bring to a boil. Boil 1 minute, cover, and remove from heat. Let stand 1 hour, and drain. Then add desired ingredients, and cook as directed.

Acid and salt can prevent beans from getting tender, so it's best to let them cook a while before adding salt or tomato and other acidic ingredients. Cooked beans also freeze well.

To Skim or Not to Skim?

Once beans start to boil, a layer of scum bubbles up to the surface. While this is mostly soluble protein, it may also include impurities and bits of skin from the beans. Most members of our Foods staff remove the scum, but a few don't bother. While it won't hurt to leave it, you'll get a clearer broth by skimming the top of the mixture. Simply remove the scum with a spoon, drop it into a cup or small bowl on the counter, and then discard it when you're done.

30 Minutes to a Super Bowl Party

You don't have to spend hours in the kitchen preparing food to celebrate the year's biggest sports event. These six-ingredient sweet-and-spicy sausages take only 5 minutes to prepare, with another 20 minutes on the stove, so you can be ready for a gathering with short notice. Serve Spicy Chipotle Barbecue Sausage Bites in a slow cooker, and enjoy them throughout the game.

While the sausages are heating, take time to root for your team.

Spicy Chipotle Barbecue Sausage Bites
PREP: 5 MIN., COOK: 20 MIN.

1 (28-oz.) bottle barbecue sauce
1 (18-oz.) jar cherry preserves
3 chopped canned chipotle peppers in adobo sauce
½ cup water
1 Tbsp. adobo sauce from can
2 (16-oz.) packages cocktail-size smoked sausages

1. Whisk together barbecue sauce, cherry preserves, and next 3 ingredients in a Dutch oven over medium-high heat; bring to a boil. Add smoked sausages, and return to a boil. Reduce heat to medium, and simmer, stirring occasionally, 15 minutes. **Makes** 12 to 14 servings.

Note: To serve, keep warm in a slow cooker on LOW, if desired. Serve with miniature rolls, if desired.

march

Supper's on Hand

This busy dad proves that the key to great family fare is as close as your pantry and freezer.

Family Friendly Dinner

Serves 8

Juiced-up Roast Pork

Edamame Succotash

Cauliflower-Leek Puree

Tomato Florentine
(double recipe)

Berry Cobbler

"I'm all about cooking with kids," Marvin Woods says enthusiastically. "It feeds their natural curiosity and gets them excited about trying different foods." This renowned chef, popular television personality, and cookbook author has legions of fans, but to 2-year-old Madison, who follows him around the kitchen, he's just "Poppi."

He's a master of lively flavors and family-friendly dishes. "Just because an ingredient is out-of-season doesn't mean you have to do without," he says. Here he demonstrates how bright, easygoing recipes can come from frozen fruits and vegetables and other items you have on hand.

Juiced-up Roast Pork

family favorite

PREP: 15 MIN.; CHILL: 4 HR.;
BAKE: 4 HR., 30 MIN.; STAND: 10 MIN.
(Pictured on page 166)

2 cups orange juice
½ cup firmly packed dark brown sugar
¼ cup loosely packed fresh oregano leaves
¼ cup loosely packed fresh sage leaves
1 Tbsp. salt
1 Tbsp. garlic powder
1 Tbsp. paprika
1½ tsp. onion powder
1 tsp. ground chipotle chile powder
1 (5- to 6-lb.) boneless pork shoulder roast (Boston butt)

1. Process first 9 ingredients in a blender until smooth.
2. Pierce roast with a sharp knife at 2-inch intervals. Place roast in a large zip-top plastic freezer bag; pour orange juice mixture over roast, turning to coat. Seal and chill at least 4 hours or up to 8 hours, turning occasionally.
3. Remove roast from marinade, reserving marinade. Place roast on a wire rack in an aluminum foil-lined roasting pan.
4. Bake at 450° for 30 minutes. Reduce oven temperature to 300°, and bake 4 more hours or until a meat thermometer inserted into thickest portion of roast registers 150°, basting with reserved marinade every 30 minutes during first 3 hours of baking time. Let roast stand 10 minutes before slicing. **Makes** 8 servings.

Edamame Succotash

PREP: 20 MIN., COOK: 15 MIN.
Edamame is just a fancy word for heart-healthy soybeans—used here in place of traditional lima beans. Look for them in the frozen vegetable case. (Pictured on page 166)

1 medium onion, chopped
2 Tbsp. canola oil
1 medium-size orange bell pepper, seeded and diced
1 medium-size red bell pepper, seeded and diced
1 medium-size yellow bell pepper, seeded and diced
2½ cups frozen whole kernel corn
½ cup chicken broth
1 (16-oz.) package frozen edamame, thawed
1 Tbsp. butter
1 Tbsp. chopped fresh mint
Salt and pepper to taste

1. Sauté onion in hot oil in a large skillet over medium heat 3 minutes or until tender. Add bell peppers and corn, and cook 5 more minutes or until tender.
2. Stir in chicken broth, and bring to a boil over medium-high heat; reduce heat to low. Stir in edamame; cook 3 minutes. Stir in butter until melted. Remove from heat, and stir in mint and salt and pepper to taste. Serve immediately. **Makes** 8 servings.

Cauliflower-Leek Puree

fast fixin's

PREP: 10 MIN., COOK: 10 MIN.
This low-fat dish is a terrific substitute for mashed potatoes. Marvin enjoys cooking this dish with his family. (Pictured on page 166)

1 leek
1 (2-lb.) head cauliflower, cut into florets
¼ cup plain yogurt
2 Tbsp. chopped fresh parsley
¼ tsp. salt
⅛ tsp. ground nutmeg
⅛ tsp. pepper

1. Remove root, tough outer leaves, and tops from leek, leaving 1 inch of dark leaves. Cut into quarters lengthwise. Thinly slice leek; rinse well, and drain.

2. Cook leek and cauliflower florets in boiling water to cover in a large saucepan 10 minutes or until tender; drain. Return vegetables to saucepan, and toss in pan over high heat to remove any excess moisture. Remove from heat.

3. Process vegetables with ¼ cup yogurt, in 2 batches, in a food processor until smooth, stopping to scrape down sides as needed. Stir in chopped parsley and next 3 ingredients; transfer puree to a serving bowl. Serve immediately. **Makes** 6 to 8 servings.

Tomato Florentine
PREP: 10 MIN., COOK: 8 MIN., BAKE: 25 MIN.
Use kitchen shears to chop tomatoes right in the can.

1 (10-oz.) package frozen chopped
   spinach, thawed
¼ cup (1 oz.) grated Parmesan cheese
2 Tbsp. olive oil, divided
2 Tbsp. Japanese breadcrumbs (panko)
   or dry breadcrumbs
1 medium onion, chopped
4 garlic cloves, finely chopped
¼ tsp. salt
¼ tsp. pepper
⅛ tsp. ground nutmeg
2 (28-oz.) cans whole tomatoes, drained
   and coarsely chopped

1. Drain spinach well, pressing between paper towels.

2. Combine Parmesan cheese, 1 Tbsp. olive oil, and 2 Tbsp. breadcrumbs in a small bowl.

3. Cook onion in remaining 1 Tbsp. hot oil in a medium skillet over medium heat 5 minutes or until tender. Add garlic, and cook 1 more minute. Stir in spinach, and cook 2 minutes or until thoroughly heated. Remove from heat, and stir in salt, pepper, and nutmeg.

4. Place tomatoes in a 9-inch square baking dish. Spoon spinach mixture evenly over tomatoes; sprinkle with breadcrumb mixture.

5. Bake at 400° for 25 minutes or until golden brown. Serve immediately. **Makes** 4 servings.

Berry Cobbler
family favorite
PREP: 20 MIN., BAKE: 1 HR., STAND: 10 MIN.
Use the fresh or frozen berries of your choice in this no-fuss dessert; bring the skillet right to the table for serving.

4 Tbsp. unsalted butter
2 (12-oz.) packages frozen raspberries ✱
1 cup sugar, divided
1½ cups all-purpose flour
2 tsp. baking powder
½ tsp. salt
1 cup milk
1½ tsp. vanilla extract
Vanilla ice cream (optional)
Garnish: fresh mint sprigs

1. Place 4 Tbsp. butter in a 10-inch cast-iron skillet, and put skillet in a 350° oven 10 minutes or until butter is melted.

2. Meanwhile, toss raspberries with ¾ cup sugar in a large bowl.

3. Sift together 1½ cups flour, baking powder, and salt in a medium bowl. Stir in milk, vanilla, and remaining ¼ cup sugar.

4. Add hot melted butter to flour mixture, and stir until blended. Pour batter evenly into skillet. Pour berry mixture into center of batter.

5. Bake at 350° for 50 minutes or until top is golden brown and a wooden pick inserted in crust comes out clean. Let stand 10 minutes. Serve with vanilla ice cream, if desired. Garnish, if desired. **Makes** 8 servings.

✱Substitute 2 (12-oz.) packages frozen mixed berries for frozen raspberries, if desired.

Our Favorite Shortcut

We often receive phone calls asking what is "all-purpose baking mix." You probably know it by brand names such as Bisquick or Pioneer. It's a combination of flour, baking soda, salt, sugar, and shortening that saves you prep time.

French Onion Biscuits
fast fixin's
PREP: 5 MIN., BAKE: 8 MIN., STAND: 5 MIN.
Once you open the all-purpose baking mix, transfer it to an airtight container, and store in a cool, dry place such as the pantry.

1 (8-oz.) carton French onion dip
¼ cup milk
1 Tbsp. finely chopped fresh parsley
2 cups all-purpose baking mix
1 Tbsp. butter, melted
Garnish: fresh parsley sprigs

1. Whisk together first 3 ingredients until smooth. Stir in baking mix until well blended. Divide dough into 12 equal portions, and arrange on a lightly greased baking sheet. Brush tops of dough with melted butter.

2. Bake at 450° for 7 to 8 minutes or until lightly golden. Let stand 5 minutes before serving. Garnish, if desired. **Makes** 1 dozen.

CAROL MACRITCHIE
HOLLAND, OHIO

Note: For testing purposes only, we used Bisquick All-Purpose Baking Mix.

Ranch Biscuits: Substitute 1 (8-oz.) carton Ranch dip for French onion dip. Prepare recipe as directed.

Appetizers in a Snap

Bite-size foods never looked and tasted so good.
They're so easy, you'll make them again and again.

S howcase the South's finest ingredients—in miniature—at your next gathering. These mouthwatering appetizers featuring catfish, okra, black-eyed peas, dried figs, and pecans are sure to draw a crowd. A novel crostini bar, which takes only a few minutes to assemble, offers guests a chance to experiment. With our make-ahead and serve-with instructions, you'll be ready to host a great party with time to spare.

Spicy Olive Shortbread
freezeable • make ahead
PREP: 20 MIN., FREEZE: 1 HR.,
BAKE: 18 MIN. PER BATCH, COOL: 35 MIN.
Purchase prepared olive tapenade in the specialty cheese case in the deli at your supermarket. Once baked, store shortbreads up to three days in an airtight container. Bake stored shortbreads at 350° for 3 to 4 minutes to make them crispy again.

¾ cup butter, softened
2½ cups all-purpose flour
½ tsp. salt
¾ tsp. ground red pepper
1 (8-oz.) block sharp Cheddar cheese, shredded
⅓ cup refrigerated olive tapenade, drained well

1. Beat butter at medium speed with a heavy-duty stand mixer until fluffy. Gradually add flour, salt, and red pepper, beating just until combined. (Mixture will be crumbly.) Add cheese and tapenade, beating at low speed just until combined.

2. Roll dough into 2 (10-inch) logs, using plastic wrap to shape dough. Wrap each in plastic wrap, and freeze at least 1 hour. Cut each log into ¼-inch-thick slices, and place on parchment paper-lined baking sheets.

3. Bake at 350° for 15 to 18 minutes or until lightly browned. Cool 5 minutes on pan; remove from pan to a wire rack, and cool 30 minutes or until completely cool. **Makes** about 6 dozen.

Note: Shortbread dough can be frozen up to 1 week; just allow it to stand at room temperature 5 to 10 minutes before slicing.

Mini Catfish Cakes
make ahead
PREP: 20 MIN., COOK: 8 MIN. PER BATCH
Make the catfish mixture up to one day ahead before forming into patties, if desired. Find panko on the Asian product aisle of your supermarket.

1 lb. catfish fillets
1¼ cups Japanese breadcrumbs (panko) *
3 green onions, minced
2 large eggs, beaten
½ cup finely chopped red bell pepper
½ tsp. salt
¼ tsp. freshly cracked black pepper
¼ cup vegetable oil
Garnishes: Caper-Dill Sour Cream (recipe on opposite page), fresh dill sprigs

1. Chop catfish into ¼-inch pieces. Combine catfish, ¾ cup breadcrumbs, and next 5 ingredients; gently stir until well blended. Shape mixture into 12 patties (about ¼ cup each). Dredge patties in remaining ½ cup breadcrumbs.

2. Cook patties, in batches, in hot oil in a large nonstick skillet over medium heat 3 to 4 minutes on each side or until golden; drain on paper towels. Garnish, if desired. **Makes** 6 appetizer servings.

* Substitute 1¼ cups fresh breadcrumbs, if desired. KEDRON HAY
WINDSOR, NEW YORK

Prosciutto-Wrapped Figs With Blue Cheese
fast fixin's • make ahead
PREP: 15 MIN., BAKE: 10 MIN., BROIL: 3 MIN.
Depending on brand and size, some figs may already have slits. Assemble these a few hours ahead, and broil them once guests arrive.

16 whole almonds
4 thin slices prosciutto *
16 dried mission figs, trimmed
½ (4-oz.) package blue cheese, cut into 16 pieces
1 Tbsp. extra virgin olive oil
¼ tsp. pepper
⅛ tsp. salt

1. Place almonds in a shallow pan.
2. Bake at 350° for 10 minutes or until lightly toasted, stirring occasionally.
3. Cut each prosciutto slice lengthwise into 4 thin strips. If necessary, make a small slit in center of each fig. Stuff each fig with 1 piece of blue cheese and 1 almond. Wrap 1 prosciutto slice around each fig, pressing to seal. Toss wrapped figs with oil, pepper, and salt; arrange in a single layer on a baking sheet.
4. Broil figs 3 inches from heat 3 minutes or until prosciutto begins to crisp. Serve immediately. **Makes** 8 servings.

* Substitute 4 thin slices deli ham, if desired. JENNIFER CAIRN
ALABASTER, ALABAMA

Black-eyed Pea-and-Ham Dip

make ahead

PREP: 20 MIN., COOK: 13 MIN.

½ cup diced country ham
2 (15.8-oz.) cans black-eyed peas, rinsed
    and drained
¾ cup water
1 large tomato, finely chopped
2 green onions, sliced
1 celery rib, finely chopped
¼ cup chopped fresh parsley
2 Tbsp. olive oil
1 to 2 Tbsp. apple cider vinegar
Cornbread crackers

1. Sauté ham in a lightly greased large nonstick skillet over medium-high heat 3 to 5 minutes or until lightly browned; stir in black-eyed peas and ¾ cup water. Reduce heat to medium, and simmer 8 minutes or until liquid is reduced by three-fourths. Partially mash beans with back of a spoon to desired consistency.

2. Stir together tomato and next 5 ingredients. Spoon warm bean mixture into a serving dish, and top with tomato mixture. Serve with crackers. **Makes** 12 appetizer servings.

Note: Prepare dip 24 hours in advance, if desired; then reheat before serving.

Mini Bacon, Tomato, and Basil Sandwiches

fast fixin's

PREP: 15 MIN.

Sandwiches can be assembled up to two hours ahead. Simply cover with a damp paper towel to keep bread from drying out.

9 slices ready-to-serve bacon,
    halved
½ cup shredded Parmesan cheese
⅓ cup mayonnaise
1 garlic clove, minced
9 slices extra-thin white bread slices
3 plum tomatoes, sliced
12 fresh basil leaves

1. Heat bacon according to package directions until crisp.
2. Stir together cheese, mayonnaise, and garlic. Spread mayonnaise mixture evenly onto 1 side of each bread slice. Layer 3 bread slices, mayonnaise sides up, with 3 bacon slices each. Top bacon evenly with 1 bread slice, tomato slices, and basil. Top each with remaining bread slices, mayonnaise sides down. Cut each sandwich into quarters. **Makes** 12 appetizer servings.

JANET SOESMAN
CLOVIS, CALIFORNIA

Stir in Flavor

Begin with sour cream, and add in the following ingredients to make irresistible dips or toppings. Each variation yields about 1 cup and can be made up to two days in advance.

Caper-Dill Sour Cream: Stir together 1 (8-oz.) container sour cream; 3 Tbsp. chopped, drained capers; 1 Tbsp. chopped fresh dill; 2 tsp. lemon juice; and salt and pepper to taste. Serve with sliced cucumbers, pita chips, or Mini Catfish Cakes (on opposite page).

Roasted Red Bell Pepper-Basil Sour Cream: Stir together 1 (8-oz.) container sour cream; ½ cup finely chopped jarred roasted red peppers; 2 Tbsp. chopped fresh basil; and salt and pepper to taste. Serve with thin breadsticks or Fried Pecan Okra (recipe on following page).

Smoky Chipotle-Lime Sour Cream: Stir together 1 (8-oz.) container sour cream; 1 Tbsp. finely chopped canned chipotle peppers in adobo sauce; 1 tsp. adobo sauce from can; 1 tsp. lime rind; 2 tsp. lime juice; and salt and pepper to taste. Serve with potato chips or quesadillas.

Avocado-Cumin Sour Cream: Stir together 1 (8-oz.) container sour cream; 1 avocado, mashed; ¼ cup chopped fresh cilantro; 1 Tbsp. lime juice; ½ tsp. ground cumin; and salt and pepper to taste. Serve with tortilla chips, vegetable chips, or cherry tomatoes.

Build-Your-Own Crostini

Cut 1 (8.5- to 12-oz.) French bread baguette into ¼-inch-thick slices (yields around 50 slices). Top each bread slice with your favorite soft cheese, preserve, and toasted nut. For small get-togethers, offer one or two selections from each category; for larger parties, offer three or four.

Pick a cheese:
- goat cheese
- blue cheese
- Brie
- cream cheese

Pick a preserve:
- apricot
- fig
- raspberry
- red pepper jelly

Pick a toasted nut:
- pecan halves
- almonds
- hazelnuts
- walnuts

Fried Pecan Okra

family favorite

PREP: 10 MIN., BAKE: 10 MIN.,
FRY: 6 MIN. PER BATCH

1 cup pecans
1½ cups all-purpose baking mix
1 tsp. salt
½ tsp. pepper
2 (10-oz.) packages frozen whole okra, thawed*
Peanut oil

1. Place pecans in an even layer in a shallow pan.
2. Bake at 350° for 10 minutes or until lightly toasted, stirring occasionally.
3. Process pecans, baking mix, and next 2 ingredients in a food processor until pecans are finely ground. Place pecan mixture in a large bowl. Add okra, tossing to coat. Gently press pecan mixture into okra.
4. Pour oil to a depth of 2 inches into a Dutch oven or cast-iron skillet; heat to 350°. Fry okra, in batches, turning once, 5 to 6 minutes or until golden; drain on paper towels. **Makes** 6 to 8 appetizer servings.

*Substitute 1 (16-oz.) package frozen cut okra, thawed, if desired.

Note: For testing purposes only, we used Bisquick All-Purpose Baking Mix.

quick & easy
Fantastic Green Beans

These three delicious recipes start with frozen green beans and all have prep times of 10 minutes or less. Frozen vegetables have a fresher flavor, crisper texture, and brighter color than canned. On the day you plan to serve them, place the beans in the refrigerator to thaw that morning, and they'll be ready to cook for supper. You may substitute an equal amount of fresh beans in all of these recipes, but you'll have additional prep time for trimming them. So follow our lead, and head for the freezer.

Green Beans Provençal

fast fixin's • make ahead

PREP: 10 MIN., COOK: 4 MIN.

This tasty veggie combination features trademark ingredients of Provence, France. If you chill this recipe longer than four hours, the bright color of the green beans will start to fade. To make ahead, prepare the beans and vinaigrette separately; cover each, and chill. Toss together right before serving.

1 (16-oz.) package frozen cut green beans, thawed
½ pt. grape tomatoes, halved
3 Tbsp. minced red onion
2 Tbsp. white wine vinegar
2 Tbsp. water
2 tsp. olive oil
1 Tbsp. grated Parmesan cheese
¼ tsp. salt
¼ tsp. dried thyme
¼ tsp. pepper
1 garlic clove, minced

1. Cook green beans in boiling salted water to cover 3 to 4 minutes or until crisp-tender; drain well.
2. Combine beans, tomatoes, and onion; toss gently. Whisk together vinegar and next 7 ingredients until well combined. Pour over bean mixture; toss to coat. Serve at room temperature, or cover and chill until ready to serve. **Makes** 4 to 6 servings.

Green Beans Amandine

fast fixin's

PREP: 5 MIN., COOK: 12 MIN.

Browning the butter and almonds gives this dish an extra-nutty flavor.

1 (16-oz.) package frozen French-cut green beans, thawed
¼ to ⅓ cup butter
½ cup sliced almonds
1 Tbsp. lemon juice
1 tsp. salt
¼ tsp. pepper

1. Cook green beans in boiling salted water to cover in a Dutch oven 4 minutes or until tender; drain well. Rinse Dutch oven well, and dry.
2. Melt butter in Dutch oven; add almonds, and sauté over medium heat 6 minutes or until butter and almonds are golden brown. Stir in green beans, 1 Tbsp. lemon juice, 1 tsp. salt, and ¼ tsp. pepper, tossing to coat. Serve immediately. **Makes** 4 to 6 servings.

Green Beans With Shallots and Red Pepper

fast fixin's

PREP: 10 MIN., COOK: 10 MIN.

2 (16-oz.) packages frozen whole green beans, thawed
¼ cup butter
3 large shallots, thinly sliced*
1 large red bell pepper, cut into thin strips
1 tsp. kosher salt**
½ tsp. pepper
½ tsp. garlic powder

1. Cook green beans in boiling salted water to cover 3 to 4 minutes or until crisp-tender; drain well.
2. Melt butter in a large skillet over medium-high heat; add sliced shallots and bell pepper, and sauté 4 minutes or until tender. Add green beans, salt, pepper, and garlic powder, and toss to combine. **Makes** 8 to 10 servings.

*Substitute ½ small sweet onion, thinly sliced, if desired.

**Substitute ½ tsp. regular salt, if desired.

Superfast Chicken

Everyone needs a couple of quick, go-to recipes for supper. Just ask our Editor in Chief, John Floyd, and his wife, Pam. They handed over their family's best 10-minute-prep chicken recipes to share with you.

A Chicken-and-Two Plate

Serves 6

Sun-dried Tomato Chicken or Crispy Seasoned Chicken Cutlets

Hash browns or rice

Apple-Pear Salad With Lemon-Poppy Seed Dressing (page 70)

Vanilla Ice Milk

Crispy Seasoned Chicken Cutlets

fast fixin's

PREP: 10 MIN., COOK: 6 MIN. PER BATCH

Cutlets may cost more, but they save you the time of pounding skinned and boned chicken breasts.

½ tsp. salt
8 chicken breast cutlets (about 2 lb.)
⅓ cup yellow cornmeal
1 (1-oz.) envelope Ranch dressing mix
2 Tbsp. all-purpose flour
1 Tbsp. paprika
3 Tbsp. olive oil

1. Sprinkle salt evenly over cutlets.
2. Stir together cornmeal and next 3 ingredients in a shallow dish or pieplate. Dredge cutlets in cornmeal mixture, coating both sides.
3. Cook cutlets, in batches, in hot oil in a large nonstick skillet over medium heat 3 minutes on each side or until golden brown and done. Serve immediately. **Makes** 6 to 8 servings.

Sun-dried Tomato Chicken

PREP: 10 MIN., BAKE: 1 HR.

The toppings of sun-dried tomatoes and sliced fresh basil add more flavor and a pretty appearance. Here's the trick to softening the texture of sun-dried tomatoes: Buy them packed in oil, and then drain and rinse in hot water to remove oil. Chop tomatoes with a knife, or snip them into smaller pieces with kitchen shears.

1 (4-lb.) package chicken pieces
   (3 breasts, 4 thighs, 3 legs)
1 cup sun-dried tomato vinaigrette with
   roasted red pepper dressing
½ tsp. coarsely ground pepper
Toppings: chopped sun-dried tomatoes,
   sliced fresh basil

1. Arrange chicken pieces in a single layer in a lightly greased 13- x 9-inch baking dish. Pour dressing evenly over chicken pieces, and sprinkle with ground pepper.
2. Bake, uncovered, at 400° for 1 hour or until done, basting every 15 minutes. Sprinkle baked chicken with desired toppings. **Makes** 6 servings.

Note: For testing purposes only, we used Good Seasons Sun Dried Tomato Vinaigrette With Roasted Red Pepper dressing.

Sun-dried Tomato Chicken Breasts: Substitute 6 skinned and boned chicken breasts for chicken pieces. Prepare recipe as directed, decreasing bake time to 30 minutes.

Vanilla Ice Milk

PREP: 10 MIN., FREEZE: 20 MIN.

John likes to add fruit such as chopped strawberries or blueberries to the mixture.

½ cup sugar
2½ Tbsp. fat-free, sugar-free vanilla
   instant pudding mix
2 cups 2% reduced-fat milk
1 (12-oz.) can evaporated fat-free milk
½ cup egg substitute
2 tsp. vanilla extract

1. Combine sugar and pudding mix in a large bowl. Gradually whisk in milk and remaining ingredients.

2. Pour milk mixture into freezer container of a 1½-qt. electric ice-cream maker, and freeze according to manufacturer's instructions. (Instructions and times will vary.) **Makes** about 12 (½-cup) servings.

Anytime Smoothie

This great-tasting pick-me-up is packed with vitamins and tastes as rich as a milk shake.

Morning Energizer Smoothie

fast fixin's

PREP: 10 MIN.

As bananas ripen and brown, they actually become sweeter. Instead of throwing them away, slice and place in a zip-top plastic freezer bag. Simply toss the frozen slices directly into the blender.

1 cup vanilla frozen yogurt
¾ cup orange juice
¾ cup fresh pineapple chunks
¾ cup sliced fresh strawberries
¾ cup fresh raspberries
1 large banana, sliced

1. Process all ingredients in a blender until smooth, stopping to scrape down sides as needed. Serve immediately. **Makes** 3 to 4 servings.

WENDY BRAKE
SAN ANTONIO, TEXAS

Ready When You Are

You might not have to do any grocery shopping for this delicious treat. Check your freezer, fridge, and pantry first. You can make a smoothie with virtually any of your favorite fruits, including frozen, bottled, and canned produce.

Sensational Soups and Sandwiches

Make a meal of these nutritious recipes that is sure to wow your taste buds. Transform a standard grilled ham-and-cheese sandwich into a warm, gooey Monte Cristo in just a few quick steps. For a light supper, use leftover chicken breast to stuff Peanut Chicken Pitas, and heat make-ahead dumplings in broth for Pork Dumpling Soup. These combos are so good that they'll soon become your new standbys.

Healthy Benefits

- Curb your appetite and consume fewer calories throughout your meal by starting with a small cup of low-calorie, low-fat soup.
- Kids are more likely to eat their vegetables when you puree them in a soup.

Monte Cristo Sandwiches
fast fixin's
PREP: 10 MIN., COOK: 6 MIN. PER BATCH

3 Tbsp. whole grain mustard
8 (1-oz.) whole wheat bread slices
8 oz. thinly sliced smoked deli ham
4 (1-oz.) reduced-fat Swiss cheese slices
⅓ cup egg substitute
⅓ cup fat-free milk
Vegetable cooking spray
4 Tbsp. tomato chutney
2 Tbsp. powdered sugar (optional)

1. Spread mustard evenly over 1 side of each bread slice. Layer each of 4 bread slices, mustard sides up, with 2 oz. ham and 1 cheese slice. Top with remaining bread slices, mustard sides down.
2. Whisk together egg substitute and milk in a shallow dish. Dip both sides of each sandwich into egg mixture.
3. Cook, in batches, in a large nonstick skillet coated with cooking spray over medium heat 3 minutes on each side or until lightly browned. Top each sandwich with 1 Tbsp. chutney, and, if desired, dust with powdered sugar. **Makes** 4 servings.

Per serving: Calories 325; Fat 9.5g (sat 3.2g, mono 0.2g, poly 0.4g); Protein 31.9g; Carb 30.6g; Fiber 6.7g; Chol 41mg; Iron 2.5mg; Sodium 982mg; Calc 429mg

Peanut Chicken Pitas
fast fixin's
PREP: 15 MIN.

1 romaine lettuce heart, chopped
1¼ cups chopped cooked chicken breast
¾ cup frozen snow peas, thawed and trimmed
¼ cup shredded carrot
¼ cup chopped roasted lightly salted peanuts
½ cup light sesame-ginger dressing
8 (1-oz.) mini whole wheat pita rounds, halved

1. Combine first 5 ingredients in a large bowl. Drizzle with sesame-ginger dressing; toss to combine. Fill each pita half evenly with mixture. **Makes** 8 servings.

Note: For testing purposes only, we used Newman's Own Low Fat Sesame Ginger Dressing and Toufayan Bakeries Hearth Baked Whole Wheat Pitettes Pita Bread.
REBECCA BOURGEOIS
NEW YORK, NEW YORK

Per serving: Calories 166; Fat 4g (sat 0.6g, mono 1.4g, poly 1g); Protein 11.9g; Carb 22g; Fiber 3.2g; Chol 19mg; Iron 2mg; Sodium 383mg; Calc 47mg

Fresh Asparagus Soup
freezeable • make ahead
PREP: 15 MIN., COOK: 25 MIN., STAND: 10 MIN.

1 lb. fresh asparagus
2 cups low-sodium fat-free chicken broth
½ cup chopped onion
1 garlic clove, chopped
¾ tsp. fresh thyme, divided
1 Tbsp. all-purpose flour
2 cups 1% low-fat milk
2 tsp. butter
½ tsp. salt
½ tsp. grated lemon rind, divided
½ cup reduced-fat sour cream
1 Tbsp. fresh lemon juice
Garnish: fresh thyme sprig

1. Snap off and discard tough ends of asparagus. Cut into 2-inch pieces.
2. Combine asparagus, chicken broth, onion, garlic, and ½ tsp. thyme in a large saucepan over medium-high heat;

bring mixture to a boil. Reduce heat to medium-low; cover and simmer 10 minutes. Remove from heat; let mixture stand 10 minutes.

3. Process asparagus mixture, in batches, in a blender or food processor until smooth. Return to pan.

4. Whisk together flour and milk until smooth. Gradually add flour mixture to asparagus mixture, whisking until blended. Bring to a boil, stirring constantly. Reduce heat; simmer, stirring constantly, 5 minutes. Remove from heat; stir in butter, salt, ¼ tsp. lemon rind, and remaining ¼ tsp. thyme.

5. Combine sour cream, lemon juice, and remaining ¼ tsp. lemon rind. Top each serving with about 5 tsp. sour cream mixture. Garnish, if desired. **Makes** 4 servings.

Note: Freeze soup after Step 3 for up to 1 month. When ready to serve, thaw, reheat, and continue with Step 4.

Per serving (1¼ cups soup and 5 tsp. sour cream mixture): Calories 163; Fat 6.1g (sat 3.8g, mono 1.2g, poly 0.4g); Protein 10.4g; Carb 19.8g; Fiber 2.8g; Chol 20mg; Iron 2.9mg; Sodium 439mg; Calc 190mg

Pork Dumpling Soup
freezeable • make ahead
PREP: 30 MIN., COOK: 20 MIN.

½ lb. lean ground pork
1 Tbsp. minced fresh ginger
3 Tbsp. chopped fresh cilantro
3 Tbsp. hoisin sauce, divided
15 won ton wrappers
3 (14-oz.) cans low-sodium fat-free
   chicken broth
½ cup sliced fresh mushrooms
¼ cup sliced green onions
Garnish: cilantro sprigs

1. Brown pork with ginger in a nonstick skillet over medium-high heat, stirring often, 5 minutes or until meat crumbles and is no longer pink.

2. Combine pork mixture, cilantro, and 2 Tbsp. hoisin sauce in a medium bowl.

3. Arrange 1 won ton wrapper on a clean, flat surface. (Cover remaining wrappers with a damp towel to prevent drying out.) Moisten edges of wrapper with water (photo 1). Spoon about 1 Tbsp. pork mixture in center of wrapper (photo 2); fold 2 opposite

corners together over pork mixture, forming a triangle. Press edges together to seal (photo 3). Cover with a damp cloth. Repeat procedure with remaining wrappers and pork mixture.

4. Bring broth and remaining 1 Tbsp. hoisin sauce to a light boil in a Dutch oven over medium heat; gently stir in 8 dumplings. Cook 4 to 5 minutes or until dumplings float to top. Place dumplings in 5 individual serving bowls. Repeat procedure with remaining 7 dumplings.

5. Add mushrooms and onions to simmering broth; cook 1 minute. Ladle 1 cup broth mixture over dumplings in bowls. Garnish, if desired. Serve immediately. **Makes** 5 servings.

Note: To freeze dumplings, assemble as directed, and place in a single layer in a large zip-top plastic freezer bag. Freeze up to 3 months. Cook as directed.

Per serving (3 dumplings and 1 cup broth mixture): Calories 206; Fat 6.3g (sat 2.1g, mono 0.7g, poly 0.5g); Protein 16.7g; Carb 21.8g; Fiber 0.7g; Chol 36mg; Iron 1.4mg; Sodium 384mg; Calc 25mg

Quick-and-Easy Dumplings

Use fingertip to moisten the edges of won ton wrapper with water.

Spoon about 1 Tbsp. pork mixture into center of wrapper.

Fold two opposite corners together to form a triangle. Press edges together to seal.

Pretty, Luscious Cupcakes

Bake up from-scratch flavor with cake-mix recipes and basic frostings.

Whether you prefer white cake, chocolate cake, or both, these recipes will please. Their charm lies in their petite size. Who can resist a handheld cake swathed in creamy frosting? Both cakes are made from box mixes enriched with buttermilk or sour cream and butter, so the batter bakes up melt-in-your-mouth moist every time. Best of all, you don't even have to pull out the mixer. Stirring them together by hand creates a tender texture. Freeze the cakes for up to a month, tightly wrapped in foil and stored in a zip-top plastic freezer bag; thaw them at room temperature.

The addition of cream cheese stabilizes the delectable buttercream frostings. With just a few extra ingredients, you can easily create a range of flavors from coconut to chocolate. Pair one of these with the cake of your choice for a sweetly satisfying creation.

Pull a vegetable peeler along the edge of a thin chocolate mint to make a garnish on the Chocolate-Mint Cupcakes.

Moist Chocolate Cupcakes
family favorite • freezeable
PREP: 10 MIN.; BAKE: 25 MIN.;
COOL: 1 HR., 10 MIN.

1 (18.25-oz.) package German chocolate cake mix
1 (16-oz.) container sour cream
¼ cup butter, melted
2 large eggs
1 tsp. vanilla extract
Vegetable cooking spray

1. Beat first 5 ingredients at low speed with an electric mixer just until dry ingredients are moistened. Increase speed to medium, and beat 3 to 4 minutes or until smooth, stopping to scrape bowl as needed.
2. Place paper baking cups in muffin pans, and coat with cooking spray; spoon batter evenly into baking cups, filling each two-thirds full.
3. Bake at 350° for 25 minutes or until a wooden pick inserted in center comes out clean. Cool in pans on wire racks 10 minutes; remove cupcakes from pans to wire racks, and cool 1 hour or until completely cool. **Makes** 2 dozen.

Chocolate-Mint Cupcakes: *(Pictured on page 165)* Prepare Moist Chocolate Cupcakes as directed. Prepare Chocolate Buttercream as directed, stirring in ¼ cup finely chopped thin crème de menthe chocolate mints. Spread cupcakes evenly with Chocolate Buttercream. Garnish with shaved or chopped thin crème de menthe chocolate mints, if desired.
Note: For testing purposes only, we used Andes Crème de Menthe Thins.

Basic White Cupcakes
family favorite • freezeable
PREP: 15 MIN.; BAKE: 25 MIN.;
COOL: 1 HR., 10 MIN.
We call for using a mixer, but you can stir together by hand with great results. Because the mixer adds more air to the batter, you'll end up with 17 cakes rather than 24 when you stir them by hand.

1 (18.25-oz.) package white cake mix with pudding
1¼ cups buttermilk
¼ cup butter, melted
2 large eggs
2 tsp. vanilla extract
½ tsp. almond extract
Vegetable cooking spray

1. Beat first 6 ingredients at low speed with an electric mixer just until dry ingredients are moistened. Increase speed to medium, and beat 2 minutes or until batter is smooth, stopping to scrape bowl as needed.
2. Place paper baking cups in muffin pans, and coat with cooking spray; spoon batter evenly into baking cups, filling each two-thirds full.
3. Bake at 350° for 25 minutes or until a wooden pick inserted in center comes out clean. Cool in pans on wire racks 10 minutes; remove cupcakes from pans to wire racks, and cool 1 hour or until completely cool. **Makes** 2 dozen.

Note: For testing purposes only, we used Pillsbury Moist Supreme Classic White Cake Mix.

Coconut Cupcakes: *(Pictured on page 165)* Prepare Basic White Cupcakes as directed. Spread evenly with Coconut Buttercream (on opposite page), and sprinkle with sweetened flaked coconut.

Vanilla Buttercream
fast fixin's
PREP: 10 MIN.
Don't limit yourself to just one; try each delicious flavor with a different cake.

½ cup butter, softened
1 (3-oz.) package cream cheese
1 (16-oz.) package powdered sugar
¼ cup milk
1 tsp. vanilla extract

1. Beat butter and cream cheese at medium speed with an electric mixer until creamy. Gradually add powdered sugar, beating at low speed until blended. Increase speed to medium, and slowly add milk and vanilla, beating until smooth. **Makes** 3 cups.

Chocolate Buttercream: Prepare Vanilla Buttercream as directed. Microwave 1 cup (6 oz.) dark chocolate morsels in a microwave-safe bowl at MEDIUM (50% power) 1½ to 2 minutes or until melted and smooth, stirring at 30-second intervals. Gradually add melted chocolate to Vanilla Buttercream; beat until blended and smooth.
Note: For testing purposes only, we used Nestlé Chocolatier Dark Chocolate Morsels.

Coconut Buttercream: Prepare Vanilla Buttercream as directed, substituting ¼ cup cream of coconut for ¼ cup milk.

top-rated menu
Spice Up a Breakfast Classic

Don't neglect your first meal of the day. Try these eye-pleasing, appetite-satisfying recipes that deliver big taste. Follow our simple instructions for poaching eggs, and you'll be on your way to enjoying Southwest Eggs Benedict. Lastly, serve Pineapple-Grapefruit Spritzer in stemmed glasses for a festive touch.

Start With Tex-Mex
Serves 8

Southwest Eggs Benedict with Chipotle Hollandaise Sauce
Creamy grits
Pineapple-Grapefruit Spritzer

Southwest Eggs Benedict
PREP: 10 MIN., FRY: 4 MIN. PER BATCH,
COOK: 15 MIN.
Crisp corn tortillas replace English muffins in Southwest Eggs Benedict. Chipotle Hollandaise Sauce is a tasty twist too.

8 (5-inch) fajita-size corn tortillas
¼ cup vegetable oil
1 cup (4 oz.) shredded Monterey Jack cheese with peppers
½ tsp. white vinegar
8 large eggs
Chipotle Hollandaise Sauce
1 cup salsa
Garnish: fresh cilantro sprigs

1. Fry tortillas, in batches, in hot oil in a medium skillet 1 to 2 minutes on each side or until crisp. Top each tortilla evenly with shredded cheese. Keep warm.
2. Add water to a depth of 3 inches to a large Dutch oven. Bring to a boil; reduce heat, and maintain a light simmer. Add vinegar. Break 4 eggs, and slip into water, 1 at a time, as close as possible to surface. Simmer 3 to 5 minutes or to desired degree of doneness. Remove with a slotted spoon. Trim edges, if desired. Repeat procedure with remaining 4 eggs.
3. Top each warm tortilla with a poached egg, Chipotle Hollandaise Sauce, and 2 Tbsp. salsa. Garnish, if desired. Serve immediately. **Makes** 8 servings.

Chipotle Hollandaise Sauce:
fast fixin's
PREP: 10 MIN.

⅓ cup egg substitute
¼ tsp. salt
¼ tsp. pepper
1 cup butter, melted and slightly cooled
1 Tbsp. minced fresh cilantro
3 to 4 canned chipotle peppers in adobo sauce, pureed (about 4 tsp.)
2 Tbsp. fresh lime juice

1. Process ⅓ cup egg substitute, salt, and pepper in a blender or food processor on high 1 minute; reduce to low speed. With blender running, pour in melted butter in a slow, steady stream. Add minced cilantro, pureed chipotle peppers, and lime juice; process until smooth. Microwave sauce at HIGH 10 to 15 seconds before serving, if desired. **Makes** 1½ cups.

Note: Chipotle peppers in adobo sauce may be found in the international foods section of your supermarket or in Latin grocery stores.

Pineapple-Grapefruit Spritzer
make ahead
PREP: 10 MIN., CHILL: 1 HR.
For an equally refreshing, alcohol-free drink, use chilled ginger ale instead of wine.

2 cups pineapple juice
1 cup pink grapefruit juice
2 Tbsp. honey
1 Tbsp. minced fresh ginger
1 (750-milliliter) bottle sparkling white wine, chilled

1. Stir together first 4 ingredients in a large container; cover and chill 1 hour.
2. Pour through a fine wire-mesh strainer into a pitcher, discarding solids. Stir in wine just before serving. Serve over ice. **Makes** 6 to 8 servings.

Spaghetti Two Ways

Try something new with this affordable pantry staple.

Before you cook that skinny package of spaghetti, here are some tips. Boil in lots of salted water. Follow package directions for cook times, using the shorter amount if the recipe calls for added baking time.

Chili-Style Spaghetti and Meatballs
freezeable

PREP: 20 MIN., BAKE: 15 MIN., COOK: 20 MIN.
If desired, freeze leftovers in single servings—spaghetti, three meatballs, and sauce.

1½ lb. ground round
1 Tbsp. grated onion
1 tsp. salt
1 tsp. ground cumin
12 oz. uncooked spaghetti
1 Tbsp. chili powder
2 tsp. olive oil
1 (14½-oz.) can diced tomatoes, undrained
1 (14-oz.) can beef broth
1 (6-oz.) can tomato paste
1 (4-oz.) can chopped green chiles
1 (15-oz.) can black beans, rinsed and drained
Toppings: shredded Cheddar cheese, sour cream, chopped red onion

1. Combine first 4 ingredients in a large bowl just until blended. Gently shape mixture into 18 (1½-inch) balls.
2. Place a lightly greased rack in an aluminum foil-lined broiler pan. Arrange meatballs on rack.
3. Bake at 350° for 15 minutes or until browned. (Centers will be slightly pink.)
4. Prepare pasta according to package directions. Keep warm.
5. Cook chili powder in hot oil in a Dutch oven over medium heat, stirring constantly, 2 minutes. Stir in tomatoes and next 3 ingredients. Gently stir meatballs into tomato mixture. Bring to a boil; cover, reduce heat, and simmer, stirring occasionally, 10 minutes. Gently stir in beans, and cook 3 more minutes. Serve immediately with spaghetti and desired toppings. **Makes** 6 servings.

M.B. QUESENBERRY
DUGSPUR, VIRGINIA

Pizza Spaghetti Casserole
freezeable • make ahead

PREP: 15 MIN., COOK: 15 MIN., BAKE: 40 MIN.
We preferred turkey pepperoni so you don't get a greasy appearance. Freeze the unbaked casserole up to one month. Thaw overnight in the refrigerator; let stand 30 minutes at room temperature, and bake as directed.

12 oz. uncooked spaghetti
½ tsp. salt
1 (1-lb.) package mild ground pork sausage
2 oz. turkey pepperoni slices (about 30), cut in half
1 (26-oz.) jar tomato-and-basil pasta sauce
¼ cup grated Parmesan cheese
1 (8-oz.) package shredded Italian three-cheese blend

1. Cook spaghetti with ½ tsp. salt according to package directions. Drain well, and place in a lightly greased 13- x 9-inch baking dish.
2. Brown sausage in a large skillet over medium-high heat, stirring occasionally, 5 minutes or until meat crumbles and is no longer pink. Drain and set aside. Wipe skillet clean. Add pepperoni, and cook over medium-high heat, stirring occasionally, 4 minutes or until slightly crisp.
3. Top spaghetti in baking dish with sausage; pour pasta sauce over sausage. Arrange half of pepperoni slices evenly over pasta sauce. Sprinkle evenly with cheeses. Arrange remaining half of pepperoni slices evenly over cheese. Cover with nonstick or lightly greased aluminum foil.
4. Bake at 350° for 30 minutes; remove foil, and bake 10 more minutes or until cheese is melted and just begins to brown. **Makes** 6 servings.

PAM TODD
BIRMINGHAM, ALABAMA

Cook's Note

Labeling on spaghetti packages can be confusing. Spaghetti labeled "thick" is bigger around than normal spaghetti, while vermicelli, thin spaghetti, and spaghettini are thinner. Use regular spaghetti in casseroles, and serve any thickness with meatballs and sauce. Try the thinner pastas with lightweight stir-ins such as fresh tomato sauce or olive oil.

Try Corned Beef at Home

We know that many of our readers enjoy corned beef, but we're also pretty sure most have never really considered making it themselves. Take it from us—now's the time to discover just how easy it is to prepare.

Corned Beef With Marmalade-Mustard Glaze

PREP: 5 MIN., BAKE: 35 MIN.

This is a great make-ahead dish. Follow the package directions to cook the corned beef the day before, and refrigerate. Use our glaze for even more flavor, and just pop it in the oven.

1. Stir together ½ cup orange marmalade and 2 Tbsp. stone-ground mustard. Brush 1 (3- to 3½-lb.) corned beef brisket, fully cooked, with half of marmalade mixture, and place in a lightly greased jelly-roll pan. Bake at 425° for 30 to 35 minutes or until golden brown, basting with remaining half of marmalade mixture every 10 minutes. Serve corned beef with cooked cabbage. **Makes** 6 to 8 servings.

Carolyn's Corned Beef and Cabbage

PREP: 15 MIN.; COOK: 3 HR., 15 MIN.

1 (3- to 3½-lb.) package corned beef brisket with spice packet
1 large head cabbage (about 2½ lb.), coarsely chopped
Creamy Lemon Horseradish Sauce

1. Place corned beef, fat side up, and contents of spice packet in a large Dutch oven; cover with water, and bring to a boil over medium-high heat. Cover, reduce heat, and simmer 2 hours and 45 minutes or until fork-tender.
2. Skim and remove fat from surface; add cabbage, and return to a boil over medium-high heat. Reduce heat; simmer 15 more minutes or just until cabbage is tender. Serve with Creamy Lemon Horseradish Sauce. **Makes** 6 to 8 servings.

Corned Beef, Cabbage, Potatoes, and Carrots: Simmer corned beef as directed in Step 1. Skim fat, and add 1 lb. small red potatoes, halved, and 8 oz. baby carrots. Bring to a boil over medium-high heat; reduce heat, and simmer 10 minutes. Add 1 lb. cabbage, coarsely chopped, and simmer 15 more minutes or until vegetables are tender. Prep: 20 min.; Cook: 3 hr., 30 min.

KATHERINE FLOURNOY
BATON ROUGE, LOUISIANA

Creamy Lemon Horseradish Sauce:

PREP: 5 MIN.

1 (8-oz.) container sour cream
6 Tbsp. mayonnaise
3 Tbsp. prepared horseradish
1 tsp. grated lemon rind
1 tsp. fresh lemon juice

1. Stir together all ingredients until blended. Chill until ready to serve. Sauce can be stored in an airtight container in the refrigerator up to 1 month. **Makes** about 1½ cups.

Celebrate the Season

Any of these refreshing drinks will bring pleasure to your day. Keep a pitcherful of your favorite in the refrigerator. You never know when something will need celebrating.

Iced Mint Tea

PREP: 10 MIN., COOK: 5 MIN., STAND: 1 HR., CHILL: 1 HR.

4 cups water
1 cup sugar
⅓ cup lemon juice
2 family-size tea bags
1 cup loosely packed fresh mint leaves
4 cups cold water
Ice cubes

1. Bring 4 cups water to a boil over medium-high heat. Stir in 1 cup sugar; cook, stirring constantly, 1 minute or until sugar dissolves. Remove from heat. Stir in ⅓ cup lemon juice, tea bags, and mint leaves. Cover and let stand 1 hour.
2. Remove tea bags from water, squeezing gently; discard tea bags. Pour mixture through a wire-mesh strainer into a 2-qt. pitcher, discarding mint leaves. Stir in 4 cups cold water. Cover and chill at least 1 hour. Serve over ice. **Makes** 8½ cups.

JOHNSIE FORD
ROCKINGHAM, NORTH CAROLINA

Raspberry-Orange-Mint Cooler

family favorite • fast fixin's

PREP: 10 MIN.

This alcohol-free drink boasts rich color and flavor. It's a great choice for the whole family.

¼ cup packed fresh mint leaves
¼ cup honey
2 Tbsp. fresh lemon juice
6 cups pulp-free orange juice, chilled
1½ cups frozen raspberries, thawed
Ice cubes
Garnish: fresh raspberries

1. Process mint leaves, honey, and lemon juice in a blender until mint leaves are finely chopped (about 30 seconds); pour into a pitcher. Add 2 cups orange juice and 1½ cups raspberries to a blender, and process until smooth, stopping to scrape down sides as needed. Pour raspberry mixture through a wire-mesh strainer into pitcher, discarding seeds. Stir in remaining 4 cups orange juice; serve over ice. Garnish, if desired. **Makes** about 7 cups.

Pineapple-Ginger-Limeade Cooler

PREP: 10 MIN., COOK. 12 MIN., STAND: 1 HR.

No need to peel the ginger—it will be strained out of the mixture before serving.

1 (46-oz.) can unsweetened pineapple juice
1½ cups sugar
1½ cups water
1¼ cups fresh lime juice
1 (3-inch) piece fresh ginger, chopped
1½ tsp. grated lime rind
2 cups light rum (optional)
Crushed ice

1. Bring first 5 ingredients to a boil, stirring until sugar dissolves. Reduce heat, and simmer 8 minutes. Remove from heat; let stand 1 hour.
2. Pour pineapple juice mixture through a wire-mesh strainer into a large pitcher, discarding ginger. Stir in lime rind, and, if desired, rum. Serve over crushed ice. **Makes** about 12 cups.

SHARON D. GREEN
ATLANTA, GEORGIA

Fresh Ideas for Salads

An assortment of fruit adds sweetness to these quick-fix recipes.

Summer tomatoes may be months away, but you can still toss together a great-tasting salad. Leafy greens topped with crumbled goat cheese, grapes, and asparagus make Spring Salad the perfect side dish. The salty crunch of roasted cashews and colorful dried cranberries turn Apple-Pear Salad With Lemon-Poppy Seed Dressing into company fare. Enhance the flavor and texture of dried fruits by soaking them in boiling water to cover for 10 to 15 minutes; drain well before adding to salads. Pair these no-fuss salads with grilled beef, pork, or chicken for an elegant menu that's easy enough to serve anytime.

Apple-Pear Salad With Lemon-Poppy Seed Dressing
fast fixin's
PREP: 10 MIN.
A vegetable peeler quickly cuts paper-thin slices of Swiss cheese. If desired, an equal amount of shredded Swiss cheese may be substituted for shaved. (Pictured on page 167)

1 (16-oz.) package romaine lettuce, thoroughly washed
1 (6-oz.) block Swiss cheese, shaved
1 cup roasted, salted cashews
½ cup sweetened dried cranberries
1 large apple, thinly sliced
1 large pear, thinly sliced
Lemon-Poppy Seed Dressing

1. Toss together first 6 ingredients in a large bowl; serve with Lemon-Poppy Seed Dressing. **Makes** 6 to 8 servings.

Lemon-Poppy Seed Dressing:
fast fixin's • make ahead
PREP: 10 MIN.

⅔ cup light olive oil
½ cup sugar
⅓ cup fresh lemon juice
1½ Tbsp. poppy seeds
2 tsp. finely chopped onion
1 tsp. Dijon mustard
½ tsp. salt

1. Process all ingredients in a blender until smooth. Store in an airtight container in the refrigerator up to 1 week; serve at room temperature. **Makes** 1¼ cups.

LORI MANRY
ROCHESTER HILLS, MICHIGAN

Spring Salad
fast fixin's
PREP: 20 MIN., COOK: 4 MIN.
Use your favorite brand of bottled balsamic vinaigrette, or make one from scratch (see "From Our Kitchen" on page 74).

1 lb. fresh asparagus
8 cups baby salad greens, thoroughly washed
2 cups seedless red grapes
8 cooked bacon slices, crumbled
1 (4-oz.) package goat cheese, crumbled
4 green onions, sliced
¼ cup pine nuts
Balsamic vinaigrette

1. Snap off and discard tough ends of asparagus; arrange asparagus in a steamer basket over boiling water. Cover and steam 2 to 4 minutes or until asparagus is crisp-tender. Plunge asparagus into ice water to stop the cooking process; drain and cut into 1-inch pieces.
2. Arrange salad greens on a serving platter; top evenly with asparagus, grapes, and next 4 ingredients. Serve with vinaigrette. **Makes** 4 servings.

VERONICA CASSONE
HOBE SOUND, FLORIDA

Orange, Radish, and Cucumber Salad
fast fixin's
PREP: 15 MIN.

3 large navel oranges
1 small bunch radishes, thinly sliced
½ large seedless cucumber, thinly sliced
1 Tbsp. finely chopped fresh mint
1 tsp. olive oil
Salt and freshly ground black pepper to taste

1. Peel oranges; remove and discard white pith. Separate oranges over a bowl into sections, reserving juice (see photo below). Place orange sections and 2 Tbsp. juice in a serving bowl; gently stir in radishes and next 3 ingredients. Sprinkle with salt and freshly ground black pepper to taste. **Makes** 4 servings.

CAROLINE W. KENNEDY
COVINGTON, GEORGIA

Springtime Pasta Toss

It takes only a few simple ingredients and a little imagination to create pasta salads everyone will love.

Greek Pasta Salad

fast fixin's • make ahead
PREP: 15 MIN.

Make a meal out of this salad by adding grilled chicken, baked ham, or smoked turkey.

1 (12-oz.) package angel hair pasta
1 (6-oz.) package feta cheese, crumbled
1 (4-oz.) jar diced pimientos, drained
1 (2½-oz.) can sliced black olives, drained
6 green onions, thinly sliced
Fresh Citrus Salad Dressing

1. Prepare pasta according to package directions. Toss pasta with remaining ingredients. Serve immediately, or cover and chill up to 2 days. **Makes** 6 to 8 servings.

BARBARA SHERRER
BAY CITY, TEXAS

Shrimp-and-Pasta Salad

fast fixin's • make ahead
PREP: 15 MIN.

12 oz. uncooked small pasta shells
2 lb. peeled cooked shrimp
6 green onions, thinly sliced
½ cup chopped fresh basil
1 Tbsp. grated lemon rind
1½ tsp. crushed red pepper flakes
Fresh Citrus Salad Dressing

1. Prepare pasta according to package directions. Toss pasta with remaining ingredients. Serve immediately, or cover and chill up to 2 days. **Makes** 6 to 8 servings.

Fresh Citrus Salad Dressing: Whisk together ½ cup light olive oil, 3 Tbsp. Greek seasoning, 3 Tbsp. fresh lemon juice, and 3 Tbsp. mayonnaise. **Makes** about ¾ cup.

No-Fuss Fix

A make-your-own pasta bar is an easy solution for dinner.

We used a tsp. or two of grated lemon rind to brighten the flavor of bottled vinaigrette. A variety of pasta shapes with similar cooking times adds texture and eye appeal. Peppery watercress offers a spicy bite and pairs well with the sweet, nutty flavor of edamame (green soybeans, found shelled and fully cooked in the freezer section). Crumbled feta cheese with sun-dried tomatoes and basil, blanched asparagus, and diced yellow bell pepper are other optional stir-ins.

Flavorful Green Onions

They are among the most overlooked produce of spring. Though available in supermarkets year-round, these immature onions are at their peak at this time.

Beef-and-Green Onion Stir-fry

fast fixin's
PREP: 15 MIN., COOK: 10 MIN.

You can substitute presliced steak for the sirloin. Look for it in the meat department of your grocery store. Serve the stir-fry over hot cooked rice, if desired.

1½ bunches green onions
1 lb. top round steak **∗**
3 Tbsp. cornstarch, divided
3 Tbsp. lite soy sauce
1 medium-size red bell pepper, thinly sliced
2 Tbsp. vegetable oil
1 tsp. sesame oil (optional)
1 cup beef broth
2 Tbsp. rice wine vinegar
¼ to ½ tsp. crushed red pepper flakes
Peanuts (optional)

1. Thoroughly wash green onions. Remove root ends and tips of onions; cut into 2-inch pieces. Place pieces in a large bowl.
2. Cut steak across the grain into thin slices, and add to green onions in bowl. Sprinkle with 2 Tbsp. cornstarch and soy sauce, tossing to coat.
3. Sauté beef mixture and red bell pepper, in 2 batches, in hot vegetable oil and, if desired, sesame oil in a large nonstick skillet over medium-high heat 3 minutes or until beef is done and bell pepper is crisp-tender. Whisk together beef broth, vinegar, red pepper flakes, and remaining 1 Tbsp. cornstarch. Add to beef mixture in skillet, and bring to a boil. Cook 1 minute or until thickened. Top with peanuts, if desired. **Makes** 4 servings.

∗Substitute 1 lb. skinned and boned chicken breasts, if desired.

Homemade Delights

Don't bother with takeout; these recipes are better.

A few pantry basics are all you need to enjoy dishes such as sesame chicken and egg rolls. Pick up egg roll wrappers in the produce section, where you can also grab a bag of shredded cabbage.

Easy Egg Rolls With Sweet-and-Sour Orange Dipping Sauce

PREP: 30 MIN., COOK: 15 MIN.,
STAND: 30 MIN., FRY: 3 MIN. PER BATCH
Test Kitchens Professional Rebecca Kracke Gordon added the quick-stir sauce.

1 lb. hot ground pork sausage
1½ Tbsp. grated fresh ginger
2 garlic cloves, pressed
1 (10-oz.) bag shredded coleslaw mix
1 (16-oz.) package egg roll wrappers
Vegetable oil
Sweet-and-Sour Orange Dipping Sauce

1. Brown sausage in a large nonstick skillet over medium-high heat, stirring until it crumbles and is no longer pink. Drain excess grease, and pat dry with paper towels, if necessary.
2. Return sausage to skillet. Stir in ginger and garlic; cook 1 minute. Add coleslaw mix, and cook, stirring occasionally, 3 minutes or until coleslaw mix is tender; let stand 30 minutes to cool.
3. Spoon ¼ cup sausage mixture in center of each egg roll wrapper. Fold top corner of each wrapper over filling (photo 1); fold left and right corners over filling (photo 2). Lightly brush remaining corner with water; tightly roll filled end toward remaining corner, and gently press to seal (photo 3).
4. Pour vegetable oil to a depth of 2 inches into a wok or Dutch oven; heat to 375°. Fry, in batches, 2 to 3 minutes or until golden, turning once; drain on paper towels. **Makes** 15 egg rolls.

Note: Egg rolls can be assembled up to a day ahead. Place them in a single layer on a baking sheet, cover tightly with plastic wrap, and chill. Fry according to recipe instructions. Do not fry them ahead of time or fry and freeze. We weren't happy with the results.

ELLEN RYAN
MAUMEE, OHIO

Sweet-and-Sour Orange Dipping Sauce:
make ahead
PREP: 5 MIN., COOK: 5 MIN., STAND: 30 MIN.

1 (18-oz.) jar orange marmalade
½ cup white vinegar
2 Tbsp. sugar
1 Tbsp. soy sauce

1. Bring all ingredients to a boil in a small saucepan over medium heat. Cook 2 to 3 minutes or until marmalade melts. Remove from heat, and let stand 30 minutes. Serve at room temperature. Cover and store in refrigerator up to 1 week. **Makes** 2 cups.

Quick-and-Easy Egg Rolls

1 Fold the top corner of the wrapper over filling.

2 Fold the left and right corners over filling. Lightly brush remaining corner with water; tightly roll filled end toward remaining corner, and gently press to seal.

3 Tightly roll filled end toward remaining corner, and gently press to seal.

Sweet Sesame Chicken

PREP: 15 MIN., COOK: 25 MIN.

1 cup uncooked rice
2 Tbsp. sesame seeds
2 lb. skinned and boned chicken breasts
2 Tbsp. cornstarch
1 Tbsp. olive oil
½ cup pineapple juice
¼ cup honey
3 Tbsp. lite soy sauce
2 Tbsp. grated fresh ginger
2 green onions, chopped

1. Prepare rice according to package directions; keep warm.
2. Place a large skillet over medium-high heat until hot; add 2 Tbsp. sesame seeds, and cook, stirring constantly, 3 to 4 minutes or until seeds are toasted. Remove seeds from skillet.
3. Cut chicken into 1-inch pieces. Combine chicken and cornstarch, tossing to coat.
4. Heat 1 Tbsp. olive oil in skillet over medium-high heat. Cook chicken pieces about 5 minutes on each side or until done. Reduce heat to medium, and stir in ½ cup pineapple juice and next 3 ingredients. Bring to a boil, and cook, stirring occasionally, 1 minute or until thickened. Remove skillet from heat.
5. Remove chicken mixture to a serving platter. Sprinkle with toasted sesame seeds and chopped green onions. Serve with warm rice. **Makes** 4 servings.

ZITA WILENSKY
NORTH MIAMI, FLORIDA

taste of the south
Have Some Hearty Jambalaya

Chances are, you already have most of the ingredients needed for a bowl of this tasty comfort food. The common denominator among all jambalayas is rice. After that, anything goes. Shrimp, chicken, and ham are used in this recipe adapted from *Eula Mae's Cajun Kitchen: Cooking Through the Seasons on Avery Island* (The Harvard Common Press, 2002), but you can incorporate smoked sausage, pork, oysters, or whatever you have on hand. For extra Cajun kick, add a dash of hot sauce to your bowl.

Chicken, Shrimp, and Ham Jambalaya

PREP: 45 MIN.; COOK: 1 HR., 50 MIN.

2 lb. unpeeled, medium-size raw shrimp
1½ lb. skinned and boned chicken thighs, cut into 1-inch cubes
1 tsp. salt
⅛ tsp. freshly ground black pepper
⅛ tsp. ground red pepper
2 Tbsp. vegetable oil
½ lb. cooked ham, cut into ½-inch cubes
4 garlic cloves, chopped
2 medium-size yellow onions, chopped (2 cups)
2 celery ribs, chopped (1 cup)
1 medium-size green bell pepper, chopped (1 cup)
3 cups chicken broth
1 (14.5-oz.) can diced tomatoes
3 green onions, chopped (½ cup)
2 Tbsp. chopped fresh parsley
2 cups uncooked long-grain rice
1 tsp. hot sauce

1. Peel shrimp; devein, if desired.
2. Sprinkle chicken evenly with salt, black pepper, and red pepper.
3. Heat oil in a Dutch oven over medium heat. Add chicken, and cook, stirring constantly, 8 to 10 minutes or until browned on all sides. Remove chicken using a slotted spoon.
4. Add ham to Dutch oven, and cook, stirring constantly, 5 minutes or until lightly browned. Remove ham using a slotted spoon.
5. Add garlic and next 3 ingredients to Dutch oven; stir to loosen particles from bottom. Stir in ham and chicken. Cover, reduce heat to low, and cook, stirring occasionally, 20 minutes.
6. Add chicken broth. Bring to a boil over medium-high heat; cover, reduce heat to low, and simmer 35 minutes. Add tomatoes and next 3 ingredients. Bring to a boil over medium-high heat; cover, reduce heat to medium-low, and simmer 20 minutes. Stir in shrimp and hot sauce; cook, covered, 10 more minutes or until liquid is absorbed and rice is tender. **Makes** 6 to 8 servings.

Supermarket Express

If you're pressed for time, try a commercial jambalaya mix. Just cook according to package directions, and then stir in leftover meat. Here are a couple of brands worth trying.
■ Zatarain's New Orleans Style Ready-to-Serve Jambalaya Rice (microwaves in 60 seconds)
■ Vigo Authentic Jambalaya Cajun Rice Mix

Deveining shrimp is easy. Use a small paring knife to cut a slit across the top of each shrimp, and simply remove the vein. We prefer fresh shrimp, but you can also use frozen raw, deveined shrimp to save time.

from our kitchen

Standout Salad Dressings

Homemade salad dressing is one of those small touches that makes a meal special. The flavor is generally lighter and cleaner than that of purchased dressings, and it's much cheaper to make your own. Best of all, in five minutes flat you can whisk together a batch of delicious vinaigrette that can be stored in the refrigerator for up to 3 to 5 days.

■ All you need is oil, vinegar, salt, pepper, and a jar with a tight-fitting lid. Balsamic vinegar and olive oil is our preferred combination, though cider vinegar, canola oil, and flavored oils such as hazelnut or walnut work well too. Light olive oil offers a milder taste than olive oil but has the same amount of calories. Because balsamic is a sweeter tasting vinegar, we like the ratio of 1 part vinegar to 2 parts oil. (The standard ratio for other vinegars is 1 part vinegar to 3 parts oil.) Put these in the jar with the salt and pepper, shake well, and you're done.

■ You can also make dressing right in the measuring cup. Measure ⅔ cup oil, and then add the balsamic up to the 1-cup line. Add the seasonings, and beat the mixture with a fork or a whisk. Dressing made this way separates after a few minutes, so if you prefer yours emulsified, whisk the oil slowly into the vinegar. Combine the mixture in a blender for a dressing that will stay together for days. The addition of mustard, dry mustard, or preserves will also help blend ingredients.

■ For a lower fat dressing, substitute water, chicken broth, apple juice, or orange juice for some of the oil. This tends to make a thinner dressing, so frequent shaking or whisking will be required.

Table Talk

Whenever we sample a dish at the tasting table that seems a bit bland, we often add a little citric acid. Lemon or lime juice or grated rind adds a touch of brightness that turns a recipe from good to great, as in Smoky Chipotle-Lime Sour Cream on page 61. Vinegar is another sound choice to add a tangy kick. It provides a savory spark in this month's Beef-and-Green Onion Stir-fry (page 71) and Black-eyed Pea-and-Ham Dip (page 61). So if you have a dish that's lacking flavor, consider a small sprinkle of tartness.

Cupcakes on the Move

These treats are terrific for taking to a family reunion or covered-dish dinner or packing in a lunchbox. We found two new inventions that allow cupcakes to arrive intact.

The Cup-a-Cake Holder is just right for transporting a single cake. The holders come in a variety of fun colors. You can buy them at **www.cupacake.com,** in The Baker's Catalogue, or at The Container Store.

If you need to carry cupcakes for a crowd, Martha Stewart Everyday 3-Tier Cupcake Carrier will get treats to a party with ease. This handy device holds up to 27 cupcakes. Buy one at Kmart.

april

Four Special Entrées

We've made these recipes doable, and they're sure to be the center of attention at your next gathering.

Get ready for a feast. These ham, chicken, beef, and lamb recipes are good-looking and easy. They're ideal for a Sunday lunch, Easter dinner, or casual weekend gathering. Each one is home-cook friendly: Three are baked in the oven, while the fourth is quick to grill.

Take your pick based on the flavors you crave. We've seasoned, sauced, and spiced with fresh herbs, citrus, plum preserves, ginger, and even barbecue sauce. Must-know tips for success and simple garnish ideas are included too. Serve any one of our impressive entrées to your friends and family, and you'll want to try the others soon.

Sweet-Hot Plum-Glazed Ham
family favorite
PREP: 15 MIN.; COOK: 8 MIN.;
BAKE: 3 HR., 15 MIN.; STAND: 15 MIN.
(Pictured on page 170)

1 cup plum preserves
½ cup orange juice
2 Tbsp. lime juice
1 Tbsp. yellow mustard
1 Tbsp. honey
2 tsp. minced fresh ginger
½ tsp. dried crushed red pepper
1 (7-lb.) smoked fully cooked, bone-in ham
Garnishes: pineapple, kiwifruit, green onions, black sesame seeds

1. Stir together first 7 ingredients in a saucepan over medium-high heat; bring to a boil, stirring constantly. Reduce heat to medium-low; simmer, stirring constantly, 5 minutes or until preserves are melted and mixture is blended. Pour half of plum preserve mixture into a microwave-safe bowl.
2. Trim excess fat on ham to ⅛-inch thickness. If desired, make long, shallow cuts (about 1/16 inch deep) over entire ham, forming diamond patterns. Place ham on a wire rack in an aluminum foil-lined roasting pan. Brush ham with a portion of plum preserve mixture in saucepan.
3. Bake ham, uncovered, at 350° on lower oven rack 1 hour and 30 minutes, basting with remaining plum preserve mixture in saucepan every 30 minutes. Loosely cover with aluminum foil, and bake 1 hour and 45 minutes or until a meat thermometer inserted into thickest portion registers 140°, basting every 30 minutes. Let ham stand 15 minutes before slicing. Garnish, if desired.
4. Microwave plum preserve mixture in bowl at HIGH 1 minute or until thoroughly heated. Serve ham with warm mixture. **Makes** 10 servings.

Ginger Ale-Can Chicken
family favorite
PREP: 10 MIN.; CHILL: 8 HR.;
BAKE: 1 HR., 40 MIN.; STAND: 10 MIN.
Use oven mitts or a towel to hold and gently slide chickens off the hot cans. Buy reduced-sodium liquid steak seasoning if you're watching your salt intake.(Pictured on page 171)

2 (3-lb.) whole chickens
¼ cup vegetable oil
½ cup liquid steak seasoning
1 Tbsp. salt
1 Tbsp. chopped fresh rosemary
2 tsp. minced garlic
1 tsp. pepper
2 (12-oz.) cans ginger ale
Garnishes: red leaf lettuce, green grapes, rosemary sprigs

1. Remove giblets and necks, if necessary. Rinse chickens with cold water; pat dry. Place each chicken in a large zip-top plastic freezer bag.
2. Whisk together oil and next 5 ingredients. Pour evenly over chickens. Seal bags, and chill, turning occasionally, 8 hours. Remove chickens from marinade, discarding marinade.
3. Using a can opener, carefully remove lids from cans of ginger ale. Remove one-fourth ginger ale from each can, and reserve for another use, leaving remaining ginger ale in can. Place cans in a lightly greased large roasting pan. Place each chicken upright onto a ginger ale can, fitting can into cavity. Pull legs forward to form a tripod, allowing chickens to stand upright.
4. Bake, uncovered, at 325° for 1 hour and 40 minutes or until a meat

---

Plan for Ham

- Clear space in the fridge to store this large cut of meat.
- To cook, move one oven rack to the lowest position; remove the second rack. If you don't have a double oven, plan side dishes that are served cold or prepared on the cooktop or in the microwave. Pop rolls in the oven while the baked ham rests before slicing.
- Store leftovers tightly covered or sealed in zip-top plastic bags up to three days. Well-wrapped ham can be frozen up to one month. The meat may dry out, so use it in casseroles or our Ham-and-Tomato Pie on page 88.
- If you're watching your salt intake, buy a reduced-sodium ham. A serving will have one-fourth to one-third less sodium, depending on the brand, than traditional ham. You'll prep and bake both types the same way.

thermometer inserted into thigh registers 170° and chickens are golden brown. Let stand 10 minutes; carefully remove cans before serving. Garnish, if desired. **Makes** 8 servings.

Note: For testing purposes only, we used Dale's liquid steak seasoning.

PEGGY RAY
STURGIS, MISSISSIPPI

How to Cook a Juicy Chicken

■ Don't just pop the tops on the ginger ale cans; rather, remove the entire lid with a can opener. Pour about one-fourth of the ginger ale out of each can before sliding chickens onto cans. In the hot oven, the ginger ale steams, keeping the chicken moist.
■ This vertical roasting method allows fat to drip through and around chicken, giving it rich roasted flavor and beautiful browning.

Get to Know Lamb

■ Excellent quality lamb is available year-round now, not just in the spring. It's produced in America and also imported from Australia and New Zealand.
■ Our recipe calls for loin chops (photo 1), but rib chops (photo 2) may be substituted. Both are very tender cuts of meat. Expect to pay anywhere from $6 per lb. from a wholesale club to $13 from a butcher.
■ Lamb is sold packaged fresh in a meat tray with a plastic overwrap. Use within 4 days of purchase, or freeze up to 4 months. It is also sold vacuum-sealed in heavy plastic wrapping. Store in the fridge up to two weeks, or freeze. When you open a vacuum-sealed package you may detect a slight, unusual smell. This is normal and will dissipate in a few minutes.
■ Thaw lamb as you would other frozen meats—overnight in the fridge. This method preserves juiciness, texture, and flavor.

Grilled Lamb Chops With Lemon-Tarragon Aïoli and Orange Gremolata

PREP: 10 MIN., STAND: 20 MIN., GRILL: 14 MIN.
At medium-rare, the meat will feel soft and slightly springy when pressed with tongs or your finger. Medium lamb will be slightly firm and springy. Lamb chops cooked beyond medium doneness may be tough and dry. Remember, the meat will continue to cook during the five-minute standing time.

8 (1½- to 2-inch-thick) lamb loin chops (about 2½ lb.)
2 Tbsp. olive oil
1 tsp. salt
½ tsp. freshly ground pepper
1 navel orange
Lemon-Tarragon Aïoli
Orange Gremolata

1. Trim fat from edges of lamb chops to ⅛-inch thickness. Brush both sides of lamb evenly with olive oil. Sprinkle evenly with salt and pepper. Let stand 15 minutes.
2. Grill lamb chops, covered with grill lid, over medium-high heat (350° to 400°) 4 to 5 minutes on each side (medium-rare) or to desired degree of doneness. Transfer lamb chops to a serving platter; cover loosely with aluminum foil, and let stand 5 minutes.
3. Cut orange into 8 wedges. Grill orange wedges, covered with grill lid, over medium-high heat (350° to 400°) 1 to 2 minutes on each side or until grill marks appear. Serve lamb chops with grilled orange wedges, Lemon-Tarragon Aïoli, and Orange Gremolata. **Makes** 4 servings.

Lemon-Tarragon Aïoli:
make ahead
PREP: 10 MIN., CHILL: 30 MIN.
A basic aïoli (ay-OH-lee) is a garlic-flavored mayonnaise. Try this lemon-and-tarragon version with grilled steak or chicken breast as well.

1 shallot, chopped
¾ cup mayonnaise
2 Tbsp. chopped fresh tarragon
2 Tbsp. fresh lemon juice
1 tsp. fresh minced garlic
1½ tsp. Dijon mustard

1. Process all ingredients in a blender until smooth; transfer to a small bowl. Cover and chill at least 30 minutes or up to 3 days. **Makes** about 1 cup.

Orange Gremolata:
fast fixin's • make ahead
PREP: 10 MIN.
A typical gremolata (greh-moh-LAH-tah) is a finely chopped, flavorful garnish of parsley, lemon rind, and garlic. We like this twist of using orange rind instead of lemon.

½ cup minced fresh flat-leaf parsley
2 tsp. grated orange rind
2 tsp. minced fresh garlic
⅛ tsp. salt
Pinch of pepper

1. Combine all ingredients. Serve immediately, or cover and chill up to 3 days. **Makes** about ½ cup.

JAMIE MILLER
MAPLE GROVE, MINNESOTA

Grandmother's Texas Barbecued Brisket

PREP: 15 MIN., CHILL: 8 HR., BAKE: 5 HR., STAND: 10 MIN.

The brisket is baked at a low oven temperature for five hours in order to tenderize this lean cut of meat.

1 (3- to 4-lb.) beef brisket
1 tsp. celery salt
1 tsp. garlic powder
1 tsp. onion salt
½ cup barbecue sauce
2 Tbsp. ketchup
2 Tbsp. Worcestershire sauce
½ tsp. liquid smoke
Garnish: fresh parsley sprigs

1. Trim fat from brisket to ⅛-inch thickness. Combine celery salt, garlic powder, and onion salt. Sprinkle brisket evenly with mixture; rub thoroughly into meat.
2. Stir together barbecue sauce and next 3 ingredients until blended. Brush barbecue sauce mixture evenly onto brisket. Wrap brisket in heavy-duty aluminum foil; place in a roasting pan. Chill 8 hours.
3. Bake at 300° for 5 hours or until a meat thermometer inserted in thickest portion registers 190°. Let stand 10 minutes. Cut brisket across the grain into thin slices. Garnish, if desired. **Makes** 8 servings.

JULIE GRIMES BOTTCHER
TABLES OF CONTENT: SERVICE, SETTINGS, AND SUPPER
JUNIOR LEAGUE OF BIRMINGHAM, ALABAMA

Dinner in One Dish

Casseroles are time-savers for busy families and a popular choice for potluck gatherings. They're also great ways to welcome new neighbors and comfort sick friends. Make it easy on everyone, and bake the ones to go in disposable pans. We hope you'll add these to your list of favorites.

Shrimp Casserole

family favorite

PREP: 30 MIN., COOK: 17 MIN., BAKE: 25 MIN.

1½ cups uncooked long-grain rice
1½ lb. unpeeled, medium-size raw shrimp
½ cup butter
1 green bell pepper, chopped
1 onion, chopped
3 celery ribs, chopped
2 garlic cloves, minced
4 green onions, chopped
2 (10¾-oz.) cans cream of shrimp soup *
¼ tsp. salt
¼ tsp. freshly ground pepper
1 cup (4 oz.) shredded Cheddar-colby cheese blend
¼ cup fine, dry breadcrumbs

1. Prepare rice according to package directions.
2. Peel shrimp, and devein, if desired.
3. Melt butter in a large skillet over medium heat; add bell pepper and next 4 ingredients, and sauté 10 to 12 minutes or until tender. Stir in soup, shrimp, salt, and pepper; cook 3 minutes or just until shrimp turn pink. (Do not overcook.)
4. Combine shrimp mixture and rice. Pour mixture into a lightly greased 13- x 9-inch baking dish. Sprinkle evenly with 1 cup shredded cheese and ¼ cup breadcrumbs.
5. Bake at 350° for 25 minutes or until cheese is melted. **Makes** 8 servings.

*Substitute 2 (10¾-oz.) cans cream of celery soup if desired.

Chicken-and-Rice Casserole: Substitute 3 cups chopped cooked chicken for shrimp and 2 (10¾-oz.) cans cream of chicken soup for cream of shrimp soup. Proceed with recipe as directed.

CAROL DODD
ARLEY, ALABAMA

Sausage-and-Wild Rice Casserole

make ahead

PREP: 20 MIN., COOK: 30 MIN., BAKE: 1 HR., STAND: 5 MIN.

You can assemble this dish the night before through Step 4 (do not add broth), and refrigerate. Stir in broth just before baking.

½ cup chopped pecans
1 (1-lb.) package sage ground pork sausage
1 Tbsp. butter
1 large onion, chopped
1 cup chopped celery
2 (6-oz.) packages long-grain and wild rice mix
2 Tbsp. chopped fresh flat-leaf parsley
1 Tbsp. chopped fresh or 1 tsp. dried rubbed sage
½ tsp. freshly ground pepper
3½ cups low-sodium chicken broth

1. Heat ½ cup chopped pecans in a large nonstick skillet over medium-low heat, stirring often, 5 minutes or until toasted. Remove toasted pecans from skillet.

2. Brown sausage in same skillet over medium-high heat, stirring often, 10 minutes or until meat crumbles and is no longer pink. Remove sausage from skillet using a slotted spoon; reserve drippings in skillet.

3. Melt butter in hot drippings over medium heat. Add onion and celery, and sauté 10 to 15 minutes or until celery is tender.

4. Remove 1 seasoning packet from rice mixes; reserve for another use. Combine sausage, vegetable mixture, remaining seasoning packet, rice, and next 3 ingredients in a lightly greased 13- x 9-inch baking dish. Stir in chicken broth until well blended.

5. Bake, covered, at 325° for 1 hour or until liquid is almost absorbed. Let stand 5 minutes. Sprinkle chopped pecans on top. **Makes** 8 to 10 servings.

CAROLINE HARRIS
LEXINGTON, GEORGIA

quick & easy
Pasta to the Rescue

These suppers are a great solution as your schedule picks up with the longer days. All the recipes here are ready to serve in about 30 minutes. For heartier versions, stir in chopped, cooked chicken or leftover diced ham.

Garlic-Herb Pasta
PREP: 10 MIN., COOK: 18 MIN.

8 oz. uncooked thin spaghetti
5 garlic cloves, minced
2 Tbsp. olive oil
2 lb. plum tomatoes, cut into eighths
3 Tbsp. minced fresh parsley
3 Tbsp. thinly sliced or chopped
   fresh basil (see box at right)
1 tsp. salt
¼ tsp. freshly ground pepper
Freshly grated Parmesan cheese

1. Cook pasta according to package directions; drain. Place pasta in a serving bowl, and keep warm.

2. Sauté garlic in hot oil in a large skillet over medium heat 1 minute. Stir in tomatoes and next 4 ingredients. Cook, stirring occasionally, 5 minutes or until thoroughly heated and tomatoes release juices. Pour over pasta; toss to combine. Sprinkle with Parmesan cheese. **Makes** 4 servings.

BRENDA RUSSELL
SIGNAL MOUNTAIN, TENNESSEE

Bacon Bow Tie Pasta
PREP: 10 MIN., COOK: 25 MIN.

½ (16-oz.) package bow tie
   pasta
½ lb. bacon
1 (8-oz.) package cream cheese,
   softened
¼ cup butter, softened
1½ tsp. Italian seasoning
⅔ cup milk
½ cup grated Parmesan cheese

1. Cook pasta according to package directions; drain. Keep warm.

2. Cook bacon according to package directions; drain well, and crumble.

3. Beat cream cheese, butter, and Italian seasoning in a medium-size microwave-safe bowl at low speed with an electric mixer until smooth. Gradually add milk, beating until mixture is smooth.

4. Microwave cream cheese mixture at HIGH 3 minutes or until thoroughly heated, whisking every 30 seconds. Pour cream cheese mixture over warm pasta, tossing to coat. Top with crumbled bacon and ½ cup grated Parmesan cheese. **Makes** 4 servings.

Lightened Bacon Bow Tie Pasta: Substitute reduced-fat or turkey bacon, ⅓-less-fat cream cheese, and 2% reduced-fat milk. Proceed as directed.

GAIL CARTER
IRMO, SOUTH CAROLINA

Herbs How-to

Chiffonade (shihf-uh-NAHD): This French term means "made of rags." In the kitchen, it describes lettuces or fresh herbs, such as basil and sage, which are cut into thin strips or shreds. The slender pieces are perfect for tossing into salads and pasta dishes such as Garlic-Herb Pasta. They also make an impressive garnish.

■ If stirring chiffonade into a dish without cooking, wait until the last minute to cut, as the edges will quickly darken.

■ Use a sharp knife for clean cuts. A dull blade will only mash and tear the herb.

■ Wash basil, and pat dry with paper towels. Remove and discard stems. Stack leaves, starting with larger ones on the bottom. If using really big leaves, cut into strips lengthwise and stack. Tightly roll up, cigar style. Roll lengthwise for shorter shreds and from the stem end to the tip for longer pieces.

■ Using a rocking motion, start with the tip of the knife on the cutting board, and cut all the way through the herb roll each time. The closer together your cuts, the finer your chiffonade will be. Separate the strips using your fingers.

Simple Food, Fresh Style

Update these Southern favorites with our easy tips.

Create a snappy but casual feel at your next get-together with our fresh ideas. We've given Southern favorites such as chicken salad, egg salad, and pimiento cheese some unexpected flavors and presentations full of no-fuss flair. Mix and match these delicious, short recipes, and use our helpful tabletop tips for your own fabulous affair.

Spicy Roasted Red Bell Pepper Pimiento Cheese

fast fixin's • make ahead

PREP: 25 MIN.

Use the largest holes on a box grater to shred cheese in a snap.

1¼ cups mayonnaise
½ (12-oz.) jar roasted red bell peppers, drained and chopped
2 tsp. finely grated onion
2 tsp. coarse-ground mustard
½ tsp. ground red pepper
2 (10-oz.) blocks sharp white Cheddar cheese, shredded
Freshly ground black pepper to taste
Assorted crackers

1. Stir together first 5 ingredients until well blended; stir in cheese and black pepper to taste. Serve with assorted crackers. Store in the refrigerator in an airtight container up to 4 days. **Makes** 4 cups.

Cream Cheese-Olive Spread

make ahead

PREP: 10 MIN., CHILL: 30 MIN., BAKE: 8 MIN., COOL: 30 MIN. *(Pictured on page 173)*

1 (8-oz.) package cream cheese, softened
½ cup finely chopped pimiento-stuffed Spanish olives
1 Tbsp. mayonnaise
½ cup chopped pecans
¼ cup chopped fresh chives

1. Stir together first 3 ingredients. Shape cream cheese mixture into 2 (6-inch) logs; wrap in plastic wrap, and chill at least 30 minutes, or store in the refrigerator in an airtight container up to 2 days.
2. Place pecans in a single layer in a shallow pan.
3. Bake pecans at 350° for 8 minutes or until lightly toasted, stirring occasionally. Let cool 30 minutes or until completely cool.
4. Roll cream cheese logs in chopped chives and toasted pecans just before serving. **Makes** about 1½ cups.

Lemon-Dill Chicken Salad-Stuffed Eggs

make ahead

PREP: 30 MIN.; GRILL: 16 MIN.;
STAND: 15 MIN.; CHILL: 1 HR., 30 MIN.

Grilling the chicken adds a smoky flavor to such a simple recipe; however, 5 cups shredded cooked chicken can be substituted. Lemon-Dill Chicken Salad can be stored in the refrigerator in an airtight container up to three days. See page 91 for quick hard-cooked eggs. (Pictured on page 173)

2¼ lb. skinned and boned chicken breasts
1½ tsp. salt, divided
½ tsp. freshly ground pepper
24 large hard-cooked eggs, peeled
1 cup mayonnaise
2 green onions, finely chopped
1 Tbsp. chopped fresh parsley
1 Tbsp. chopped fresh dill
2 Tbsp. fresh lemon juice

1. Sprinkle chicken evenly with 1 tsp. salt and ½ tsp. pepper. Grill, covered with grill lid, over high heat (400° to 500°) 6 to 8 minutes on each side or until done. Let stand 15 minutes; cover and chill at least 30 minutes.
2. Slice hard-cooked eggs in half lengthwise; carefully remove yolks, keeping egg white halves intact. Reserve yolks for another use.
3. Stir together mayonnaise, next 4 ingredients, and remaining ½ tsp. salt in a large bowl.
4. Pulse chicken, in batches, in a food processor 3 or 4 times or until shredded; stir into mayonnaise mixture until blended. Spoon mixture evenly into egg white halves. Cover and chill at least 1 hour. **Makes** 48 appetizer servings.

Test Kitchen *Notebook*

Tabletop Tips
• Fold, iron, and layer an inexpensive bedsheet from a discount store for a no-sew, carefree table runner.
• Pep up place settings by tucking napkins between salad and dinner plates to add depth and instant style.
• Tuck pansies into pots or containers for an effortless smart table arrangement. Streamline the look, keeping the color palette in the same hue. Plant the pansies outdoors when blooms begin to fade.

Lisa Powell Bailey
PHOTO STYLIST

Sparkling Punch
make ahead
PREP: 10 MIN., CHILL: 1 HR.
Serve this refreshing beverage in martini glasses.

2 (46-oz.) cans pineapple juice
1 (12-oz.) can frozen pink lemonade
   concentrate, thawed
1 (10-oz.) can frozen strawberry
   daiquiri mix concentrate, thawed
2 (1-liter) bottles ginger ale
Garnish: lemon slices

1. Stir together first 3 ingredients. Cover and chill 1 hour. Stir in ginger ale just before serving. Garnish, if desired. **Makes** about 1½ gal.

NORA HENSHAW
OKEMAH, OKLAHOMA

Easy Egg Salad Crostini
make ahead
PREP: 20 MIN., BAKE: 12 MIN.,
STAND: 20 MIN., CHILL: 15 MIN.

1 (20-oz.) French bread baguette,
   thinly sliced
3 Tbsp. melted butter
1 garlic clove, pressed
8 large hard-cooked eggs, grated
½ cup mayonnaise
⅓ tsp. sugar
¼ tsp. salt
¼ tsp. freshly ground pepper

1. Arrange baguette slices on a baking sheet. Stir together butter and garlic; brush evenly on tops of baguette slices.
2. Bake at 350° for 10 to 12 minutes. Let stand 20 minutes.
3. Meanwhile, combine hard-cooked eggs and next 4 ingredients in a large bowl. Cover and chill at least 15 minutes or up to 2 days.
4. Spoon egg mixture evenly on toasted baguette slices. **Makes** about 3 dozen.

Bacon-Blue Cheese Salad With White Wine Vinaigrette
PREP: 35 MIN., BAKE: 8 MIN., COOL: 30 MIN.
Serving this salad in cucumber rings (see steps below) makes it extra special. (Pictured on page 172)

2 Tbsp. chopped pecans
2 medium cucumbers, peeled
3 cups mixed baby greens
2 cooked thick-cut bacon slices, halved
⅓ cup shredded or matchstick carrots
¼ cup crumbled blue cheese
Salt and freshly ground pepper to taste
White Wine Vinaigrette

1. Place chopped pecans in a single layer in a shallow pan.
2. Bake at 350° for 8 minutes or until lightly toasted, stirring occasionally. Let pecans cool 30 minutes or until completely cool.
3. Using a Y-shaped vegetable peeler, cut cucumbers lengthwise into very thin strips just until seeds are visible (photo 1). Discard cucumber core.
4. Shape largest cucumber slices into 4 (2½- to 2¾-inch-wide) rings. Wrap evenly with remaining cucumber slices (photo 2). Stand rings upright on 4 serving plates.
5. Fill each cucumber ring evenly with mixed greens, next 3 ingredients, and toasted pecans. Sprinkle with salt and pepper to taste. Drizzle each salad with 1 Tbsp. White Wine Vinaigrette, and serve with remaining vinaigrette. **Makes** 4 servings.

Note: Y-shaped vegetable peelers can be found at most kitchen, home goods, and discount stores from $6.99 to $19.95.

White Wine Vinaigrette:
fast fixin's • make ahead
PREP: 5 MIN.

¼ cup white wine vinegar
1 Tbsp. Dijon mustard
1 garlic clove, minced
1 tsp. sugar
½ cup olive oil
Salt and freshly ground pepper to taste

1. Whisk together first 4 ingredients until blended. Add oil in a slow, steady stream, whisking constantly until smooth. Whisk in salt and pepper to taste. Store in the refrigerator in an airtight container up to 1 week. **Makes** about ⅔ cup.

Cucumber Rings

Impress guests by serving the Bacon-Blue Cheese Salad With White Wine Vinaigrette in these clever containers.

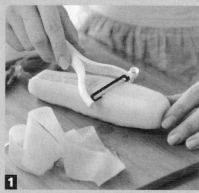

1 Use a Y-shaped vegetable peeler to cut cucumbers into long, thin strips.

2 Shape the largest cucumber slices into 4 rings. Wrap them evenly with remaining cucumber slices.

Healthy Living®

Experience the joy of the season with family and friends through happy moments and scrumptious recipes.

Fabulous for You

Enhance your healthy lifestyle with these nutrient-packed foods.

Peach-Oat Muffins
freezeable • make ahead
PREP: 15 MIN., BAKE: 20 MIN.

These muffins are loaded with many of the components of a well-rounded breakfast: fiber and whole grains from oats and bran cereal, good fats from pecans and canola oil, dairy from nonfat buttermilk, and fruit from dried peaches.

¼ cup chopped pecans
1¾ cups uncooked regular oats
1 cup sugar
½ cup canola oil
2 large eggs
1¼ cups all-purpose flour
1 tsp. baking soda
½ tsp. salt
1 cup peach nectar
1 cup nonfat buttermilk
5 cups wheat bran cereal
⅓ cup chopped dried peaches

1. Heat pecans in a small nonstick skillet over medium-low heat, stirring often, 2 to 4 minutes or until toasted.
2. Process oats in a food processor or blender about 45 seconds or until finely ground.

3. Beat sugar and oil at medium speed with an electric mixer 1 minute. Add eggs, 1 at a time, beating until blended after each addition. (Mixture will be light yellow.)
4. Combine ground oats, flour, baking soda, and salt in a small bowl. Stir together peach nectar and buttermilk in a small bowl. Add oat mixture to sugar mixture alternately with peach nectar mixture, beginning and ending with oat mixture. Stir until blended after each addition. Gently stir in bran flakes, dried peaches, and toasted pecans. Spoon batter into lightly greased muffin cups, filling three-fourths full.
5. Bake at 375° for 20 minutes or until golden brown. **Makes** 24 muffins.

Note: Muffins may be frozen for up to 1 month. Heat in toaster oven or microwave at HIGH 30 seconds. For testing purposes only, we used Post Premium Bran Flakes cereal.

DONNA HAYES
JONESBOROUGH, TENNESSEE

Per muffin: Calories 176; Fat 6.6g (sat 0.6g, mono 3.6g, poly 1.8g); Protein 3.5g; Carb 27.5g; Fiber 2.5g; Chol 18mg; Iron 3mg; Sodium 180mg; Calc 21mg

Blueberry Soy Shakes
fast fixin's
PREP: 10 MIN.

You can use soy milk in place of milk in coffee; when preparing hot or cold cereal; when making creamy soups, casseroles, or smoothies; and in mixes for pancakes or muffins.

2 cups frozen unsweetened blueberries
1 cup soy vanilla yogurt, softened *
1½ cups low-fat soy milk *

1. Process all ingredients in a blender or food processor until smooth, stopping to scrape down sides. Serve immediately. **Makes** 3 servings.

Note: We prefer frozen blueberries over fresh in this recipe because they yield a brighter color and smoother texture.

* Substitute 1% low-fat yogurt or milk, if desired.

Per 1½-cup serving: Calories 175; Fat 2.6g (sat 0.1g, mono 0.4g, poly 0.9g); Protein 4.4g; Carb 35.6g; Fiber 5.5g; Chol 0mg; Iron 1.1mg; Sodium 55mg; Calc 334mg

Healthy Benefits

■ Stave off heart disease, certain cancers, and diabetes with wholesome super foods.
■ Soy provides isoflavones that reduce the risk of cardiovascular disease and certain cancers, enhance bone health, and decrease menopause symptoms.

Homemade Takeout

Make your own fast-food favorites.

Spiced Pecans

freezeable • make ahead

PREP: 10 MIN., BAKE: 20 MIN., COOL: 30 MIN.

1 egg white
4 cups pecan halves (about 1 lb.)
½ cup sugar
1 tsp. ground cinnamon
1 tsp. ground ginger
¼ to ½ tsp. ground red pepper
¼ tsp. salt

1. Whisk egg white in a large bowl until foamy. Add pecans, and stir until evenly coated with egg white.
2. Stir together sugar and next 4 ingredients until blended. Sprinkle sugar mixture evenly over pecans; stir gently until pecans are evenly coated. Spread pecans in a single layer in a lightly greased aluminum foil-lined 15- x 10-inch jelly-roll pan.
3. Bake at 350° for 18 to 20 minutes or until pecans are toasted and dry, stirring once after 10 minutes. Remove from oven, and let cool 30 minutes or until completely cool. **Makes** about 5 cups.

Note: Store pecans in a zip-top plastic freezer bag at room temperature up to 3 days, or freeze up to 3 weeks.

Per (2-Tbsp.) serving: Calories 85; Fat 7.8g (sat 0.7g, mono 4.4g, poly 2.3g); Protein 1.1g; Carb 4.1g; Fiber 1.1g; Chol 0mg; Iron 0.3mg; Sodium 16mg; Calc 8mg

Simple Super Salad

Choose your favorite combination of fruits and vegetables to toss with leafy salad greens. Add fresh mango slices and strawberries for a vitamin C boost. Their acidity increases iron absorption from the salad greens. Try asparagus spears, zucchini ribbons, and Spiced Pecans for crunch. For added convenience, use bottled vinaigrette dressed up with fresh lemon juice and grated lemon rind. Sprinkle salad with feta cheese, and serve alongside grilled chicken, pork, or seafood.

Skip the drive-through, and prepare these yummy and affordable meals at home.

Turkey Cheeseburgers With Rosemary Onions

family favorite

PREP: 10 MIN., CHILL: 30 MIN.,
COOK: 25 MIN., BROIL: 5 MIN.

Serve this burger with frozen oven-baked fries. The Test Kitchens staff and Foods editors sampled several varieties to determine the tastiest and best for you. We discovered that the healthiest fries (lowest in calories, fat, and sodium) avoided "homestyle," "extra crispy," and "seasoned" in the name. We especially liked the taste of Ore-Ida Golden Fries and Alexia Oven Fries—Olive Oil, Rosemary, and Garlic. (Pictured on page 168)

1 (20-oz.) package lean ground turkey breast
1 large egg, lightly beaten
1 tsp. salt
½ tsp. freshly ground pepper
1½ Tbsp. butter, divided
1 large sweet onion, halved and sliced
1 tsp. chopped fresh or dried rosemary
Vegetable cooking spray
1 (4-oz.) package goat cheese, sliced*
6 (1.5-oz.) whole grain white hamburger buns
Toppings: lettuce leaves, Dijon mustard, tomato slices

1. Gently combine first 4 ingredients. Shape mixture into 6 thin patties; cover and chill 30 minutes.

2. Melt 1 Tbsp. butter in a nonstick skillet over medium-high heat; add onion and rosemary, and sauté 10 minutes or until onion is tender and golden. Remove onion mixture from skillet.
3. Melt remaining ½ Tbsp. butter in same skillet over medium heat. Cook patties 6 minutes on each side or until no longer pink in center. Place on an aluminum foil-lined baking sheet or broiler pan coated with cooking spray.
4. Top each patty evenly with onion mixture and 1 cheese slice. Broil 6 inches from heat 3 to 5 minutes or until cheese is lightly browned. Serve on hamburger buns with desired toppings. **Makes** 6 servings.

*Substitute 4 oz. blue cheese, Gorgonzola cheese, or Swiss cheese, if desired.

SUSAN KIRILL
RICHMOND, VIRGINIA

Per serving (not including toppings): Calories 320; Fat 10.5g (sat 5.7g, mono 2g, poly 0.8g); Protein 30.8g; Carb 25g; Fiber 1.4g; Chol 89mg; Iron 2.3mg; Sodium 783mg; Calc 138mg

Healthy Benefits

■ Meals prepared at home are usually more nutritious than takeout because they contain more fruits, vegetables, and dairy products and have less oil and salt.
■ Restaurant portions are often twice as large as what people prepare at home.

Veggie Fried Rice
fast fixin's

PREP: 10 MIN., COOK: 10 MIN.

Try this dish for a tasty vegeterian side or light supper. Toss in leftover chicken, ham, or shrimp, and you'll have a superfast meal packed with whole grains. (Pictured on page 169)

1 (5.3-oz.) bag quick-cooking brown rice
1 (8-oz.) package fresh sugar snap peas
4 green onions, cut into 2-inch pieces
½ cup matchstick-cut carrots
Vegetable cooking spray
1 Tbsp. grated fresh ginger
2 garlic cloves, minced
2 large eggs, lightly beaten
3 Tbsp. lite soy sauce
2 tsp. dark sesame oil

1. Cook rice according to package directions; drain well.
2. Sauté peas, green onions, and carrots in a large nonstick skillet coated with cooking spray over medium-high heat 3 minutes or until crisp-tender. Add ginger and garlic; sauté 1 minute. Add rice, and cook 2 minutes or until thoroughly heated. Push rice mixture to sides of pan, making a well in center of mixture.
3. Add eggs to center of mixture, and cook, stirring occasionally, 1 to 2 minutes or until set. Stir eggs into rice mixture. Stir in soy sauce and sesame oil. **Makes** 4 servings.

Per (1¼-cup) serving: Calories 240; Fat 5.8g (sat 1.1g, mono 1g, poly 0.4g); Protein 9.6g; Carb 38.7g; Fiber 4g; Chol 106mg; Iron 2.2mg; Sodium 439mg; Calc 92mg

Crispy Oven-Fried Drumsticks
family favorite

PREP: 15 MIN., BAKE: 30 MIN.

No frying necessary: Cornflake cereal gives this recipe a crunchy coating. We loved these drumsticks with ½ tsp. red pepper. Use ¼ tsp. for kids. (Pictured on page 169)

3 cups cornflake cereal, crushed
⅓ cup grated Parmesan cheese
½ tsp. salt
¼ to ½ tsp. ground red pepper
¼ tsp. freshly ground black pepper
¾ cup fat-free buttermilk
8 chicken drumsticks (about 2 lb.), skinned
Vegetable cooking spray

1. Combine first 5 ingredients in a large zip-top plastic freezer bag; seal and shake well to combine.
2. Pour buttermilk into a shallow bowl. Dip 2 drumsticks in buttermilk, and place in bag. Seal and shake well, coating drumsticks completely. Place drumsticks on an aluminum foil-lined baking sheet coated with cooking spray. Repeat procedure with remaining drumsticks. Sprinkle remaining cornflake mixture evenly over drumsticks on baking sheet. Lightly coat with cooking spray.
3. Bake at 425° for 25 to 30 minutes or until drumsticks are well browned and done. Serve immediately. **Makes** 4 servings.

KATIE MCCANN
ORLANDO, FLORIDA

Per serving (2 drumsticks): Calories 324; Fat 7.8g (sat 2.6g, mono 2.4g, poly 1.5g); Protein 40.7g; Carb 21.3g; Fiber 1g; Chol 137mg; Iron 5.9mg; Sodium 790mg; Calc 150mg

Pepperoni Pizza
family favorite • fast fixin's

PREP: 5 MIN., BAKE: 12 MIN.

Bake the crust as directed on the oven rack for a crisp texture. Place the pizza on a baking sheet for a softer crust. (Pictured on page 169)

1 cup tomato-and-basil pasta sauce
1 (10-oz.) package prebaked whole wheat thin Italian pizza crust
¼ cup turkey pepperoni slices (about 24)
1½ cups (6 oz.) part-skim mozzarella cheese

1. Spoon tomato-and-basil pasta sauce evenly over crust, leaving a 1-inch border around edges. Top with half of pepperoni slices. Sprinkle with cheese. Top with remaining pepperoni.
2. Bake pizza at 450° directly on oven rack 11 to 12 minutes or until crust is golden and cheese is melted. Cut into 6 slices, and serve immediately. **Makes** 6 servings.

Note: For testing purposes only, we used Boboli 100% Whole Wheat Thin Pizza Crust and Classico Tomato & Basil Pasta Sauce.

Per serving (1 slice): Calories 260; Fat 9.5g (sat 3.9g, mono 2.1g, poly 0.7g); Protein 19.2g; Carb 26.9g; Fiber 4g; Chol 40mg; Iron 2mg; Sodium 861mg; Calc 280mg

Test Kitchen Notebook

If you're not a pepperoni fan, consider substituting other healthy pizza toppings like ground turkey sausage or Canadian bacon. You can also load your pizza with your favorite veggies.

Holley Johnson
ASSOCIATE FOODS EDITOR

Greet Spring With Asparagus

The slim green spears on display in the produce aisle are a sure sign of spring. Asparagus is value-priced during its peak season from February to June. Delicate flavor and easy preparation make this vegetable a natural addition to menus right now.

You can grill, roast, steam, or microwave asparagus (our recipes and tip box include how-tos for each method). The key to success is not overcooking the stalks. You can check for doneness by piercing them with a knife or fork to make sure they are tender.

These recipes give you a couple of great options for taking advantage of this vegetable's wonderful flavor. Enjoy some asparagus soon.

Grilled Asparagus With Parmesan Salsa
fast fixin's • make ahead
PREP: 15 MIN., GRILL: 10 MIN.
You can make this recipe a day early and serve it chilled.

1 lb. fresh asparagus
1 Tbsp. vegetable oil
1 garlic clove, minced
⅛ tsp. salt
1 (½-inch-thick) sweet onion slice
1 tsp. vegetable oil
1 small tomato, finely chopped (about ½ cup)
¼ cup shredded Parmesan cheese
Dash of salt
Dash of pepper

1. Snap off and discard tough ends of asparagus; remove scales with a vegetable peeler, if desired.
2. Stir together 1 Tbsp. vegetable oil and garlic. Combine asparagus with vegetable oil mixture in a large bowl, tossing to coat. Sprinkle evenly with ⅛ tsp. salt.
3. Brush sweet onion slice evenly on both sides with 1 tsp. vegetable oil.
4. Grill onion slice and asparagus, without grill lid, over medium heat (300° to 350°). Grill onion 4 to 5 minutes on each side or until tender. Grill asparagus 2 to 3 minutes on each side or until tender.
5. Finely chop onion. Stir together onion, tomato, and next 3 ingredients. Serve salsa with warm asparagus. **Makes** 4 to 6 servings.

MYRA WHITTEMORE
WADMALAW ISLAND, SOUTH CAROLINA

Asparagus With Citrus Sauce
make ahead
PREP: 10 MIN., CHILL: 1 HR., STEAM: 7 MIN.
This flavorful appetizer is a great addition to any buffet. You can trim last-minute prep time by making the sauce, cooking the asparagus, and refrigerating them in a serving dish the day before you're planning to serve them.

½ cup light mayonnaise
½ cup plain yogurt or light sour cream
1 Tbsp. minced fresh chives
1 tsp. grated orange rind
2 tsp. fresh orange juice
¼ tsp. Dijon mustard
⅛ tsp. salt
⅛ tsp. freshly ground pepper
2 lb. fresh asparagus
Garnish: chopped fresh chives

1. Stir together first 8 ingredients. Cover citrus sauce, and chill 1 hour.
2. Snap off and discard tough ends of asparagus; remove scales with a vegetable peeler, if desired.
3. Fill an asparagus steamer with 2 inches water, and bring to a boil over medium-high heat. Place asparagus, cut ends down, in steamer basket; place basket in steamer. Cover, and steam 6 to 7 minutes or just until asparagus spears are tender.
4. Plunge asparagus into ice water to stop the cooking process; drain.
5. Arrange asparagus spears on serving platter. Garnish citrus sauce, if desired, and serve with asparagus. **Makes** 6 to 8 servings.

Asparagus Pointers

■ Look for firm, bright green spears with tightly closed leaves.
■ Thinner asparagus spears are usually more tender. We found thin asparagus in the local market when testing these recipes. If you find asparagus with larger, thicker stalks, add 2 to 3 extra minutes to the cooking time.
■ One lb. equals about 16 to 20 spears or 2 cups chopped.
■ Store unwashed stalks upright in a tall, heavy glass of water in the refrigerator, and cover them loosely with a zip-top plastic bag. Change the water daily to keep them in the best condition, or wrap stems in a damp paper towel and seal the asparagus in a zip-top plastic bag.
■ To microwave, place asparagus in an 11- x 7-inch dish. Cover tightly with heavy-duty plastic wrap, and fold back a small corner to allow the steam to escape. Microwave at HIGH 6 to 7 minutes or until crisp-tender, giving the dish a half-turn after 3 minutes.
■ To roast, place asparagus on a lightly greased baking sheet. Bake at 425° for 13 to 15 minutes or to desired degree of tenderness.
■ To steam, we used an asparagus steamer (photo below). If you don't have one, bring 2 inches water to a boil in a large skillet. Place asparagus in water; cover and boil 6 to 7 minutes or just until tender.

Dreamy Chocolate

Go ahead, indulge. Tempting treats will satisfy your inner chocoholic.

It's an ingredient that immediately brings to mind mouthwatering desserts. We love chocolate in anything sweet—cookies, cakes, pies, ice creams, and beverages. For the most intense flavor, look for chocolate with a higher cocoa content. These luscious recipes will give you new ways to enjoy this favorite treat.

Buttermilk-Mexican Chocolate Pound Cake

PREP: 15 MIN.; BAKE: 1 HR., 10 MIN.; COOL: 1 HR., 45 MIN.

Instead of using Mexican chocolate in this recipe, we developed the same flavor profile using more common ingredients—semisweet chocolate and cinnamon. If you prefer to use Mexican chocolate, look for it with the hot drink mixes or on the Hispanic food aisle.

1 (8-oz.) package semisweet chocolate baking squares, chopped*
1 cup butter, softened
1½ cups sugar
4 large eggs
½ cup chocolate syrup
2 tsp. vanilla extract
2½ cups all-purpose flour
2 tsp. ground cinnamon
¼ tsp. baking soda
⅛ tsp. salt
1 cup buttermilk
Garnish: powdered sugar

1. Microwave chocolate baking squares in a microwave-safe bowl at HIGH 1 minute and 15 seconds or until chocolate is melted and smooth, stirring every 15 seconds.

2. Beat butter at medium speed with an electric mixer 2 minutes or until creamy. Gradually add sugar, beating 5 to 7 minutes or until light and fluffy. Add eggs, 1 at a time, beating just until yellow disappears after each addition. Stir in melted chocolate, chocolate syrup, and vanilla until smooth.

3. Combine flour and next 3 ingredients; add to butter mixture alternately with buttermilk, beginning and ending with flour mixture. Beat at low speed just until blended after each addition. Pour batter into a greased and floured 10-inch tube pan or 12-cup Bundt pan.

4. Bake at 325° for 1 hour and 10 minutes or until a long wooden pick inserted in center of cake comes out clean. Cool in pan on a wire rack 10 to 15 minutes; remove from pan to a wire rack, and let cool 1 hour and 30 minutes or until completely cool. Garnish, if desired. **Makes** 12 servings.

*Substitute 2 (4.4-oz.) packages Mexican chocolate, chopped, for semisweet chocolate baking squares, if desired. Omit ground cinnamon, and proceed with recipe as directed.

Note: For testing purposes only, we used Nestlé Abuelita Mexican Chocolate.

Fudgy Cookie Bars
freezeable • make ahead
PREP: 15 MIN., BAKE: 35 MIN., COOK: 5 MIN., COOL: 1 HR.

1¾ cups all-purpose flour
¾ cup powdered sugar
¼ cup unsweetened cocoa
1 cup cold butter, cut into pieces
1 (14-oz.) can sweetened condensed milk
1 tsp. vanilla extract
1 (12-oz.) package semisweet chocolate morsels
1 cup chopped pecans or walnuts

1. Combine first 3 ingredients in a large bowl; cut in cold butter pieces with a pastry blender or 2 forks until crumbly. Press mixture onto bottom of a 13- x 9-inch pan.

2. Bake at 350° for 15 minutes. Remove pan, and place on a wire rack.

3. Stir together condensed milk, vanilla, and 1 cup chocolate morsels in a small saucepan over medium heat, stirring occasionally, 5 minutes or until smooth. Pour mixture evenly over prepared crust, spreading to edges of the pan. Sprinkle with chopped pecans or walnuts and remaining chocolate morsels.

4. Bake at 350° for 20 minutes. Cool in pan on a wire rack 1 hour or until completely cool. Cut into 48 (1½-inch) bars. **Makes** 48 bars.

Note: Store bars in airtight containers up to 1 week. You can also freeze the bars up to 1 month. GLORIA ADAMS
BECKVILLE, TEXAS

White Chocolate Panna Cotta With Dark Chocolate Sauce
make ahead

PREP: 10 MIN., STAND: 5 MIN., COOK: 4 MIN., CHILL: 24 HR.

Panna cotta is a delicate eggless custard. Serve this dessert in stemmed glasses or classically molded ramekins for a fun, updated presentation.

1 (¼-oz.) envelope unflavored gelatin
1½ cups cold milk, divided
1 cup whipping cream
½ cup white chocolate morsels
¼ cup sugar
Dark Chocolate Sauce
Garnishes: fresh mint sprigs, chocolate shavings

1. Sprinkle gelatin over ¼ cup milk in a small bowl; stir until moistened. Let stand 5 minutes. (Mixture will be lumpy.)

2. Cook whipping cream, chocolate morsels, and sugar in a saucepan over medium-low heat, stirring occasionally, 4 minutes or until morsels are melted and sugar is dissolved. Remove from heat, and add gelatin mixture, stirring until mixture is dissolved. Stir in remaining 1¼ cups milk.

3. Pour mixture evenly into 4 to 6 stemmed glasses or 6 (8-oz.) ramekins. Cover and chill 24 hours. Serve with Dark Chocolate Sauce. Garnish, if desired. **Makes** 4 to 6 servings.

SUELLEN CALHOUN
DES MOINES, IOWA

Dark Chocolate Sauce:
fast fixin's

PREP: 5 MIN.

1 (3-oz.) dark chocolate baking bar, chopped
¾ cup heavy cream

1. Microwave chocolate and cream in a small microwave-safe bowl at HIGH 1½ minutes or until melted and smooth, stirring every 30 seconds. **Makes** about 1 cup.

Chocolate Chunk-Mocha Cookies
freezeable • make ahead

PREP: 25 MIN., BAKE: 12 MIN. PER BATCH, COOL: 32 MIN.

These amazing frosted cookies received our highest rating.

2¼ cups all-purpose flour
⅔ cup unsweetened cocoa
1 tsp. baking soda
¼ tsp. salt
1 cup butter, softened
¾ cup granulated sugar
⅔ cup firmly packed brown sugar
1 tsp. vanilla extract
2 large eggs
1 (11.5-oz.) package semisweet chocolate chunks
Mocha Frosting
Powdered sugar (optional)

1. Combine first 4 ingredients in a bowl.

2. Beat butter and next 3 ingredients at medium speed with an electric mixer until creamy. Add eggs, 1 at a time, beating just until blended after each addition. Gradually add flour mixture, beating at low speed until blended. Stir in chocolate chunks.

3. Drop dough by heaping tablespoonfuls onto parchment paper-lined baking sheets.

4. Bake at 350° for 10 to 12 minutes or until puffy. Cool on baking sheets 2 minutes; remove to wire racks, and let cool 30 minutes or until completely cool. Spread cookies with Mocha Frosting. Dust evenly with powdered sugar, if desired. **Makes** 3 dozen.

Note: Dough may be frozen up to 1 month or refrigerated up to 2 days. Let stand at room temperature before baking as directed.

Mocha Frosting:
fast fixin's

PREP: 10 MIN.

¼ cup unsweetened cocoa
¼ cup hot strong brewed coffee
¼ cup butter, melted
1 tsp. vanilla extract
3½ cups powdered sugar, sifted

1. Stir together first 4 ingredients until smooth. Gradually add powdered sugar, stirring until creamy. **Makes** about 3 cups.

Good News

Chocolate can actually be good for you. Here's a sampling of chocolate's other good stuff.
• Calories: A typical dark chocolate bar contains significantly fewer calories and carbs than milk chocolate.
• Fat: Although it contains saturated fat that's believed to increase LDL, or "bad" cholesterol, new studies reveal that dark chocolate doesn't raise LDL levels. Its high stearic acid content is actually thought to lower serum cholesterol levels.
• Magnesium: Dark chocolate contains magnesium, known to regulate blood pressure, reducing the risk of heart disease. Magnesium also helps to metabolize the sugar in chocolate—a good double whammy.
• Antioxidants: Cacao beans (from which chocolate is made) have the highest levels of antioxidants.

Tasty Menu Anytime

Fill Your Plate With Flavor

Serves 4 to 6

Ham-and-Tomato Pie

Caesar-Style Salad or Caesar salad kit

French bread or crescent rolls

S'more Puffs

Gather around the table to enjoy a nice meal any day of the week. Ham-and-Tomato Pie is a comfy main dish you can prepare with packaged chopped ham or leftover ham. Toss together the Caesar-Style Salad in minutes (the dressing can be made the day before), and wrap up the meal with bread and dessert.

Ham-and-Tomato Pie

PREP: 20 MIN., COOK: 5 MIN., BAKE: 23 MIN., COOL: 20 MIN.

We don't suggest using deli ham due to the moisture content. Use a traditional 9-inch pie shell, not a deep-dish. There's no need to thaw the crust before assembling.

1 (8-oz.) package diced cooked ham
½ cup sliced green onions (about 4 onions)
1 (9-inch) frozen unbaked pie shell
1 Tbsp. Dijon mustard
1 cup (4 oz.) shredded mozzarella cheese, divided
2 medium plum tomatoes, thinly sliced
1 large egg
⅓ cup half-and-half
1 Tbsp. chopped fresh basil
⅛ tsp. pepper
Garnishes: fresh basil sprigs, tomato slices

1. Sauté ham and green onions in a large nonstick skillet over medium heat 5 minutes or until ham is brown and any liquid evaporates.
2. Brush bottom of pie shell evenly with mustard; sprinkle with ½ cup mozzarella cheese. Spoon ham mixture evenly over cheese, and top with single layer of sliced tomatoes.
3. Beat egg and half-and-half with a fork until blended; pour over tomatoes. Sprinkle evenly with basil, pepper, and remaining ½ cup cheese.
4. Bake on lowest oven rack at 425° for 20 to 23 minutes or until lightly browned and set. Cool on a wire rack 20 minutes. Cut into wedges to serve; garnish, if desired. **Makes** 4 to 6 servings.

Caesar-Style Salad

fast fixin's

PREP: 15 MIN.

For another night's meal, make the salad, and toss in cooked cheese tortellini, or top with grilled chicken or shrimp.

½ cup olive oil
⅓ cup fresh lemon juice
2 garlic cloves, pressed
1 tsp. Worcestershire sauce
¾ tsp. kosher salt
½ tsp. freshly ground pepper
1 head romaine lettuce, torn
½ cup freshly grated or shredded Parmesan cheese
1 cup large plain croutons

1. Whisk together first 6 ingredients.
2. Place lettuce in a large bowl. Pour olive oil mixture over lettuce, and toss. Sprinkle with cheese, tossing to combine. Top with croutons, and serve immediately. **Makes** 6 servings.

Note: Olive oil mixture may be prepared up to 24 hours ahead. Cover and store in refrigerator until ready to serve. Whisk before serving.

ELIZABETH STEWART
DALLAS, TEXAS

S'more Puffs

family favorite • fast fixin's

PREP. 5 MIN., BAKE: 8 MIN., COOL: 5 MIN.

Line the baking sheet with aluminum foil for easy cleanup. Watch the little ones—the center of the marshmallow will still be warm after the 5-minute cooling time. Chocolate kisses will soften but not melt.

12 round buttery crackers
12 milk chocolate kisses
6 large marshmallows, cut in half

1. Place crackers on a baking sheet. Top each with 1 milk chocolate kiss and 1 marshmallow half, cut side down.
2. Bake at 350° for 8 minutes or just until marshmallows begin to melt. Let cool on a wire rack 5 minutes. **Makes** 12 puffs.

Flavorful Sampler

Everyone loves great food, regardless of its heritage. Jewish culture in the South has put its spin on the region's cuisine. Marcie Cohen Ferris explains these traditions in her book, *Matzoh Ball Gumbo: Culinary Tales of the Jewish South* (The University of North Carolina Press, 2005), from which these superb dishes are adapted. Give them a try; we think you'll find the only culture that matters here is the one of good taste.

Crunchy Fried Green Tomatoes

PREP: 25 MIN., FRY: 8 MIN. PER BATCH

This recipe makes a tasty use of produce just now showing up in stores. A coating of matzo meal, which is made from unleavened flour and water, gives this classic dish extra crunch. Look for matzo in the kosher section.

½ cup matzo meal
1 tsp. kosher salt
½ tsp. ground red pepper
⅛ tsp. sugar
4 to 5 large green tomatoes (about 2 lb.), cut into ½-inch-thick slices
2 large eggs, lightly beaten
Vegetable oil
Kosher salt (optional)

1. Combine first 4 ingredients in a shallow dish.
2. Dip tomatoes into eggs, allowing excess to drip off. Dredge in matzo mixture, pressing it into the surfaces. Place on a wax paper-lined baking sheet.
3. Pour oil to a depth of ½ inch into a large, deep cast-iron or heavy skillet; heat over medium heat to 360°. Fry tomatoes, in batches, 3 to 4 minutes on each side or until golden. Drain on paper towels. Sprinkle with additional salt, if desired. Serve immediately. **Makes** 4 to 6 servings.

MILDRED LUBRITZ COVERT
NEW ORLEANS, LOUISIANA

Fruit Compote

make ahead

PREP: 20 MIN., STAND: 10 MIN., COOK: 15 MIN.

Prepare this up to a day ahead, and store, covered, in the refrigerator. The amount of lemon juice you use will depend on the sweetness of the fruit.

3 ripe Granny Smith apples
3 ripe Bartlett pears
½ cup sugar
2 to 3 Tbsp. fresh lemon juice
¾ tsp. ground cinnamon
1 cup sliced fresh plums (2 plums)
½ tsp. vanilla extract

1. Place whole apples and pears in a large heat-resistant bowl, and cover with boiling water. Let stand 10 minutes, turning fruit a few times. Drain; peel fruit, and cut into chunks.
2. Stir together apples, pears, sugar, 2 Tbsp. lemon juice, and cinnamon in a 3½-qt. saucepan. Bring to a boil over high heat, stirring often. Cover, reduce heat to low, and simmer, stirring occasionally, 8 minutes or until fruit is tender.
3. Gently stir in plums, and cook 2 to 3 minutes or until plums are tender. Remove from heat; stir in vanilla, and, if desired, an additional 1 Tbsp. lemon juice. Serve warm or cold. **Makes** 8 servings.

HUDDY HOROWITZ COHEN
CHAPEL HILL, NORTH CAROLINA

Mississippi Praline Macaroons

make ahead

PREP: 20 MIN., BAKE: 40 MIN., COOL: 21 MIN.

1 cup coarsely chopped pecans
3 egg whites, at room temperature
¼ tsp. cream of tartar
Pinch of salt
1 cup firmly packed light brown sugar
36 pecan halves

1. Place chopped pecans in a single layer in a shallow pan.
2. Bake at 350° for 7 minutes or until pecans are lightly toasted, stirring occasionally.
3. Beat egg whites, cream of tartar, and salt at medium speed with a heavy-duty electric stand mixer until frothy; increase speed to high, and gradually add brown sugar, beating until stiff peaks form. Gently fold in toasted chopped pecans.
4. Drop batter by heaping teaspoonfuls 1 inch apart onto lightly greased aluminum foil-lined baking sheets. Press 1 pecan half into each cookie, flattening slightly.
5. Bake at 325° for 33 minutes or until pecan halves are toasted and cookies are lightly golden. Let cool on baking sheets 1 minute. Transfer to wire racks; let cool 20 minutes. (Cookies will crisp while cooling.) Store in airtight containers up to 1 week. **Makes** about 3 dozen.

ANN GRUNDFEST GERACHE
VICKSBURG, MISSISSIPPI

Sloppy Joes and More

Yummy, fast-to-fix offerings are sure to score big at the weeknight dinner table.

Sloppy Joe Supper

Serves 8

Slow-cooker Sloppy Joes

Chive 'n' Onion Potato Chips

Easy Coleslaw

Ice cream sandwiches

You can always use an easy menu with great standby choices suitable for any casual gathering. Look no farther than this terrific group of recipes to satisfy hungry appetites. Convenience products make the sides a cinch to fix, while the main attraction, Slow-cooker Sloppy Joes, can also be prepared on the cooktop. The meat mixture can even be made ahead and frozen for later.

Slow-Cooker Sloppy Joes
freezeable • make ahead
PREP: 15 MIN.; COOK: 4 HR., 10 MIN.

1½ lb. lean ground beef
1 (16-oz.) package ground pork
    sausage
1 small onion, chopped
½ medium-size green bell pepper,
    chopped
1 (8-oz.) can tomato sauce
½ cup ketchup
¼ cup firmly packed brown sugar
2 Tbsp. cider vinegar
2 Tbsp. yellow mustard
1 Tbsp. chili powder
1 Tbsp. Worcestershire sauce
½ tsp. salt
¼ cup all-purpose flour
8 hamburger buns, toasted

1. Brown beef and sausage with onion and bell pepper in a large Dutch oven over medium-high heat, stirring 10 minutes or until beef and sausage crumble and are no longer pink. Drain well.
2. Place beef mixture in a 4½-qt. slow cooker. Stir in tomato sauce, next 8 ingredients, and ½ cup water. Cover and cook on HIGH 4 hours. Serve on hamburger buns. **Makes** 8 servings.

Note: To freeze leftover Sloppy Joe mixture, let cool completely. Place in zip-top plastic freezer bags; lay bags flat, and stack in freezer. Freeze up to 1 month. Thaw overnight in the fridge, or defrost in the microwave.

Cooktop Method: Proceed with recipe as directed in Step 1, returning drained beef mixture to Dutch oven. Stir in tomato sauce, next 7 ingredients, and ½ cup water, omitting flour. Bring mixture to a boil over medium-high heat. Cover, reduce heat to medium, and simmer, stirring occasionally, 30 minutes. Prep: 15 min., Cook: 45 min.

MANDY FUGATE
ORANGE CITY, FLORIDA

Chive 'n' Onion Potato Chips
family favorite
PREP: 10 MIN., BAKE: 22 MIN.

1. Divide 1 (26-oz.) bag frozen potato oven chips between 2 lightly greased jelly-roll pans, spreading chips in single layers in pans. Sprinkle potatoes evenly with 2 Tbsp. dried chives, 1 tsp. onion powder, ½ tsp. garlic powder, and, if desired, ¼ tsp. salt. Bake at 450° for 20 to 22 minutes or until potatoes are golden brown and crisp. **Makes** 8 servings.

Note: For testing purposes only, we used Ore-Ida Oven Chips (Crispy, Battered, Skin-On Potato Slices).

Easy Coleslaw
make ahead
PREP: 10 MIN., CHILL: 1 HR.
Reader Nora Henshaw adds crunch to her coleslaw with a toasted peanut variation.

6 fully cooked bacon slices
¾ cup mayonnaise
1 Tbsp. sugar
2 Tbsp. cider vinegar
1 (16-oz.) package coleslaw mix
Salt and pepper to taste

1. Crisp bacon slices according to package directions.

2. Whisk together mayonnaise, sugar, and vinegar in a large bowl. Crumble bacon, and add to mayonnaise mixture in bowl. Add coleslaw mix and salt and pepper to taste; toss to coat. Cover and chill at least 1 hour or up to 8 hours. Serve with a slotted spoon. **Makes** 8 to 10 servings.

Note: For testing purposes only, we used Hormel Fully Cooked Bacon.

Creamy-Crunchy Coleslaw: Heat ¼ cup chopped lightly salted peanuts in a small skillet over medium-high heat, stirring often, 2 minutes or until lightly toasted. Let cool 15 minutes. Prepare recipe as directed, adding peanuts before chilling. Prep: 15 min., Cook: 2 min., Cool: 15 min., Chill: 1 hr.

NORA HENSHAW
OKEMAH, OKLAHOMA

Perfect Hard-cooked Eggs

There's more than one way to hard cook an egg, but we think this is the fastest for achieving perfect yolks. The secret is to not keep the water at a rolling boil the whole time.

See the box below for our quick cooking-and-cooling method. Then, crack and peel the shells under cold running water.

Know Your Yolks

undercooked
a soft center

perfectly cooked
a firm yolk

overcooked
a dark ring around the yolk

South-of-the-Border Deviled Eggs
make ahead
PREP: 25 MIN., CHILL: 1 HR.

1 dozen large hard-cooked eggs, peeled
1 small ripe avocado, peeled and coarsely chopped
2 green onions, finely chopped
2 Tbsp. sweet pickle juice
2 Tbsp. mayonnaise
1 Tbsp. dry Ranch dressing mix
½ tsp. chili powder (optional)
½ cup mild salsa

1. Slice eggs in half lengthwise; carefully remove yolks, keeping egg white halves intact.

2. Mash together yolks and avocado in a medium bowl. Stir in green onions and next 3 ingredients until smooth. Spoon yolk mixture evenly into egg white halves. Sprinkle evenly with chili powder, if desired. Cover and chill at least 1 hour or up to 24 hours. Dollop with salsa just before serving. **Makes** 12 servings.

CATHY DODSON
KNOXVILLE, TENNESSEE

12-Minute Eggs

1. Place eggs in a single layer in a stainless steel saucepan. (Do not use nonstick.) Add water to a depth of 3 inches, and bring to a rolling boil.

2. When the water boils, cover pan with lid, and remove from heat. Let eggs stand for 12 minutes.

3. Drain and return eggs to pan. Fill it with cold water and ice, and let eggs stand for a few minutes to cool. Then, crack shells on all sides on your countertop or other work surface. Peel eggs under cold running water, starting at the large end.

from our kitchen

Grind for Goodness

A superb cup of coffee is the perfect accompaniment with warm, buttery rolls or a rich dessert. For the very best taste, that means freshly ground beans and boiling water. Ground coffee loses flavor quickly, especially once it's exposed to air, so even the tastiest brands go stale shortly after opening. Grinding right before brewing is absolutely the best method. But when this isn't possible, grind a two- or three-day supply, and keep it in a tightly sealed container.

For short-term storage (two weeks or less), place coffee beans in an airtight bag or container in the pantry or other dry place. If you have extra you want to keep longer, you can freeze coffee beans for up to two months by storing them in two layers of plastic freezer bags to keep stray flavors from getting in.

Burr grinders offer the most even texture but are more expensive and require more maintenance than a simple blade grinder. Shaking a blade grinder several times during processing helps produce an even grind.

Try These Tips

Tender green spears of asparagus are phenomenal when they have been properly prepared. To avoid tough, stringy asparagus, try the suggestions in "Asparagus Pointers" on page 85. Before you begin cooking this fresh springtime treat, however, you will want to follow a couple of simple steps that will make it the perfect side dish.

■ Use a vegetable peeler to remove the tough outer portion of the stalk.

■ Snap off the tougher portion of the asparagus stem by hand. Just grip the vegetable 1 to 1½ inches from the stem end and bend it slightly; it will break right off.

Hot and Crusty Chicken Salad
Here's an easy and novel way to serve chicken salad: Bake it in a crescent. "These rolls offer a nice, economical way to serve chicken salad," says Associate Foods Editor Mary Allen Perry. "One cup of the mixture will fill an 8-oz. can of crescents. Use finely chopped chicken salad that has only a small amount of mayonnaise for best results. You can flavor it with curry or even add raisins or pecans, if you prefer." Mary Allen likes serving these rolls with a green salad.

Chicken Salad Crescent Rolls: Unroll 1 (8-oz.) can refrigerated crescent rolls; separate each dough portion along center and diagonal perforations, forming 8 triangles. Spoon 2 Tbsp. of your favorite chicken salad on the wide end of each triangle. Starting at the wide end of each triangle, roll dough over chicken salad, pinching edges to seal. Place rolls, seam sides down, on a lightly greased baking sheet. Sprinkle tops of rolls evenly with 2 Tbsp. poppy seeds. (Seeds will stick to rolls without a binder; you don't need to brush with egg.) Bake at 375° for 10 to 12 minutes or until golden brown.

may

Delicious Fish at Home

Let us show you just how fast and easy it can be.

Cooking fish is easy. Senior Foods Writer Donna Florio knows, because in 20 years as a seafood marketing expert, she cooked an ocean of it. Along the way, she landed basic knowledge that will help anyone cook fish confidently. Here are her top three tips.

1. Be sure the fish you buy is in premium condition. (See "Quality Counts" below.) Frozen fish that's carefully thawed can be excellent, just as poorly handled fresh fish can be awful. Unless you live on the coast or in a large city, most seafood (except salmon) will have been frozen. But even if you live in a tiny town, good fish can be as close as your supermarket or wholesale club.

Here's the secret: If you're not happy with the fish in the seafood case, ask for some that is still frozen. Or purchase bags of individually quick frozen (IQF) fillets. Thaw as many as you need in the refrigerator overnight or in a tightly sealed plastic bag under cold running water if you're in a hurry. It is best to cook fish the day you bring it home, but you can refrigerate it (on ice) for up to 48 hours.

2. Don't overcook. When you insert a fork in the thickest part, the flesh should be opaque nearly all the way through. A tiny streak of pink in the center is okay; the fish will continue cooking off the heat. Ten minutes of cooking time per inch of thickness is the rule of thumb, but start checking at eight minutes just in case.

3. Keep it simple. It's hard to beat perfectly sautéed, baked, or grilled fish paired with a simple sauce or topping. (And because most of us will be doing our own cooking, that's a good thing.)

Quality Counts

The longer the fish is out of water, the more it deteriorates, a process slowed by freezing. When shopping, select fish that is firm and glossy, with a bright red bloodline. Fish that is soft, and its line is brown, is not very fresh. The longer blood is exposed to air, the browner it becomes. Because most fish is displayed bloodline side down, ask the seafood salesperson to turn the fillet over if you're in doubt about the freshness.

Almond-Crusted Tilapia

fast fixin's

PREP: 15 MIN., COOK: 9 MIN.

If you don't have a skillet large enough to hold all the fillets comfortably, we recommend cooking them in batches. You can substitute catfish, flounder, or orange roughy for tilapia.

1 cup sliced almonds, divided
¼ cup all-purpose flour
4 (6-oz.) tilapia fillets
½ tsp. salt
2 Tbsp. butter
2 Tbsp. olive oil

1. Process ½ cup almonds in a food processor until finely chopped, and combine with ¼ cup flour in a shallow bowl.
2. Sprinkle fish evenly with salt; dredge in almond mixture.
3. Melt butter with olive oil in a large heavy skillet over medium heat; add fish, and cook 4 minutes on each side or until golden. Remove fillets to a serving plate.
4. Add remaining ½ cup almonds to skillet, and cook, stirring often, 1 minute or until golden. Remove almonds with a slotted spoon, and sprinkle over fish. **Makes** 4 servings.

LYNN PEON
ATLANTA, GEORGIA

Grilled Salmon With Herb Vinaigrette

fast fixin's

PREP: 10 MIN., COOK: 5 MIN., GRILL: 14 MIN.

You can substitute grouper, redfish, or tuna for salmon.

4 (8-oz.) salmon fillets
1 tsp. salt, divided
½ tsp. pepper
2 shallots, minced
½ cup olive oil, divided
2 Tbsp. white wine vinegar
1 Tbsp. Dijon mustard
¼ tsp. sugar
1 Tbsp. each chopped fresh chives, parsley, and tarragon
⅛ tsp. dried crushed red pepper (optional)
Vegetable cooking spray

1. Sprinkle salmon evenly with ¾ tsp. salt and ½ tsp. pepper.
2. Sauté shallots in 1 Tbsp. hot oil over medium heat 5 minutes or until golden. Remove from heat.
3. Whisk together vinegar and mustard in a small bowl; whisk in remaining oil in a slow, steady stream until mixture is thickened and blended. Stir in shallots, remaining ¼ tsp. salt, sugar, herbs, and, if desired, crushed red pepper.
4. Coat cold cooking grate with cooking spray; place on grill over high heat (400° to 500°). Place salmon on cooking grate, and grill 5 to 7 minutes on each side or to desired degree of doneness. Serve with vinaigrette. **Makes** 4 servings.

CAROL S. NOBLE
BURGAW, NORTH CAROLINA

Pan-Seared Trout With Italian-Style Salsa

chef recipe • fast fixin's
PREP: 5 MIN., COOK: 4 MIN. PER BATCH
You can substitute catfish, salmon, tuna, or tilapia for trout.

6 (6-oz.) trout fillets
¾ tsp. salt
½ tsp. freshly ground pepper
4 Tbsp. olive oil
Italian-Style Salsa
Garnish: lemon slices

1. Sprinkle fillets with salt and pepper.
2. Cook 3 fillets in 2 Tbsp. hot oil in a large nonstick skillet over medium-high heat 1 to 2 minutes on each side or until fish flakes with a fork. Repeat with remaining fillets and oil. Top fish with salsa. Garnish, if desired, and serve immediately. **Makes** 6 servings.

Italian-Style Salsa:
chef recipe • make ahead
PREP: 10 MIN.
Make this salsa up to one day ahead, but stir in the feta just before serving.

4 plum tomatoes, chopped
½ small red onion, finely chopped
12 kalamata olives, pitted and chopped
2 garlic cloves, minced
2 Tbsp. chopped fresh parsley
1 Tbsp. balsamic vinegar
1 Tbsp. olive oil
2 tsp. drained capers
¼ tsp. salt
¼ tsp. freshly ground pepper
¼ cup crumbled feta cheese (optional)

1. Stir together first 10 ingredients, and, if desired, feta cheese, in a medium bowl. Cover and chill until ready to serve. **Makes** 2 cups.

CHEF ROBERT STRICKLIN
BIG CEDAR LODGE
RIDGEDALE, MISSOURI

Crispy Baked Cod
fast fixin's
PREP: 10 MIN., BAKE: 17 MIN.
You can substitute mahi mahi, grouper, catfish, salmon, or tilapia for cod.

1 cup Japanese breadcrumbs (panko) ✱
2 Tbsp. chopped fresh parsley
2 tsp. grated lemon rind
1 tsp. minced garlic
6 (6-oz.) cod fillets
1 tsp. salt
2 Tbsp. butter, melted

1. Combine first 4 ingredients in a small bowl.
2. Place fillets on a lightly greased wire rack in a pan; sprinkle evenly with salt. Spoon breadcrumb mixture evenly onto fillets, pressing down gently. Drizzle evenly with 2 Tbsp. melted butter.
3. Bake at 400° for 17 minutes or until breadcrumbs are golden and fish flakes with a fork. **Makes** 6 servings.

✱Substitute 1 cup fine, dry breadcrumbs, if desired.

Cut meaty fish such as grouper, wreckfish, and snapper into strips for easier cooking.

Here's to Your Health

Two servings of fish a week offer tremendous health benefits. Fish is low in cholesterol and has modest amounts of fat. Salmon and mackerel offer omega-3 fatty acids, which help stave off heart disease and arthritis and are great for brain function. But large fish can have high mercury contents due to pollution. Even small quantities of mercury can be harmful to pregnant women and small children. Avoid shark, swordfish, king mackerel, and tilefish, all of which are high in mercury. Even canned albacore has more mercury than light tuna. To learn more about mercury content and the benefits of seafood, visit **www.mayoclinic.com.**

No-Cook Lemonade Pies

Stir, freeze, done. It doesn't get any easier than that.

When we say these recipes are easy, we mean you can practically make them with your eyes closed. Better still, they look and taste good enough to serve at your fanciest gathering.

Both pies have a prep time of 10 minutes or less, use no more than 6 ingredients, and start with thawed frozen lemonade concentrate and a ready-made pie crust. Just be sure to let the cream cheese soften and to thaw the frozen whipped topping and frozen lemonade concentrate before you start preparing the recipes. Then enjoy these cool, creamy pies.

Creamy Lemonade Pie
freezeable • make ahead
PREP: 10 MIN., FREEZE: 4 HR.
Lemon-flavored instant pudding mix and softened cream cheese add extra richness to this tangy dessert. (Pictured on page 177)

2 (5-oz.) cans evaporated milk
2 (3.4-oz.) packages lemon instant pudding mix
2 (8-oz.) packages cream cheese, softened
2 (3-oz.) packages cream cheese, softened
1 (12-oz.) can frozen lemonade concentrate, partially thawed
1 (9-oz.) ready-made prepared graham cracker crust
Garnishes: whipped cream, fresh mint sprigs, lemon slices

1. Whisk together evaporated milk and pudding mix in a bowl 2 minutes or until thickened.
2. Beat cream cheeses at medium speed with an electric mixer, using whisk attachment, until fluffy. Add lemonade concentrate, beating until blended; add pudding mixture, and beat until blended.
3. Pour into crust; freeze 4 hours or until firm. Garnish, if desired. **Makes** 8 servings.

JEAN VOAN
SHEPHERD, TEXAS

Lemon Pie Dip
family favorite • make ahead
PREP: 5 MIN., CHILL: 2 HR.
Serve this treat as a finger-friendly snack or casual dessert. Simply hollow out lemon halves for a fun presentation.

1 (14-oz.) can sweetened condensed milk
½ cup fresh lemon juice
Graham cracker sticks

1. Whisk together condensed milk and lemon juice in a bowl until blended, and chill 2 hours. Serve with graham cracker sticks. **Makes** 8 to 10 servings.

Note: For testing purposes only, we used Honey Maid Grahams Cinnamon Sticks.

Serve Lemon Pie Dip in hollowed-out lemons.

Raspberry-Lemonade Pie
family favorite • make ahead
PREP: 10 MIN., FREEZE: 4 HR.

1 (14-oz.) can sweetened condensed milk
1 (6-oz.) can frozen lemonade concentrate, partially thawed
3 Tbsp. seedless raspberry preserves
1 (8-oz.) container frozen whipped topping, thawed
1 (6-oz.) ready-made prepared graham cracker crust
Garnishes: fresh raspberries, fresh mint sprigs

1. Whisk together first 3 ingredients in a large bowl until smooth. Fold in whipped topping.
2. Pour into crust; freeze 4 hours or until firm. Garnish, if desired. **Makes** 8 servings.

LIZA HAMMONS
JACKSON, MISSISSIPPI

Pink Lemonade Pie: Substitute pink lemonade concentrate for lemonade concentrate and omit raspberry preserves. Prepare as directed.

Seedless raspberry preserves are the secret to Raspberry-Lemonade Pie.

Frosty Treats

There's nothing old-fashioned about these beverages.

Scoop your favorite ice cream in a blender, pour in some milk, and whip up a luscious milk shake.

Brandy Alexander Milk Shake
PREP: 10 MIN.

½ cup whipping cream
2 tsp. powdered sugar
1 pt. vanilla ice cream
½ cup milk
¼ cup brandy
1 Tbsp. dark crème de cacao
Freshly ground nutmeg (optional)

1. Beat whipping cream at high speed with an electric mixer until foamy; gradually add powdered sugar, beating until soft peaks form.
2. Process ice cream and next 3 ingredients in a blender until smooth, stopping to scrape down sides.
3. Pour ice-cream mixture evenly into 4 serving glasses; spoon whipped cream mixture on top of each serving. Sprinkle with freshly ground nutmeg, if desired. Serve immediately. **Makes** 4 servings.

Note: For testing purposes only, we used Häagen-Dazs Vanilla Ice Cream.

Lemon-Blueberry Cheesecake Shake
PREP: 10 MIN.

1 (3-oz.) package cream cheese
1 pt. vanilla ice cream
1 cup fresh or frozen blueberries
½ cup milk
¼ cup sugar
2 tsp. grated lemon rind
1 tsp. vanilla extract

1. Microwave cream cheese in a small microwave-safe bowl at HIGH 30 seconds; stir until smooth.
2. Process melted cream cheese, ice cream, blueberries, and remaining ingredients in a blender until smooth, stopping to scrape down sides. Serve immediately. **Makes** 4 servings.

Note: For testing purposes only, we used Häagen-Dazs Vanilla Ice Cream.

Coconut-Orange Delight Shake
PREP: 10 MIN.

1 pt. vanilla ice cream
½ cup cream of coconut
½ cup milk
2 Tbsp. thawed orange juice concentrate
1½ tsp. grated orange rind

1. Process all ingredients in a blender until desired consistency, stopping to scrape down sides. Serve immediately. **Makes** 4 servings.

Note: For testing purposes only, we used Häagen-Dazs Vanilla Ice Cream and Coco López Cream of Coconut.

Dulce de Leche Coffee Shake
PREP: 5 MIN.

1 cup dulce de leche ice cream
1 cup coffee ice cream
½ cup milk
1 Tbsp. coffee liqueur (optional)

1. Process first 3 ingredients, and, if desired, 1 Tbsp. coffee liqueur in a blender until smooth, stopping to scrape down sides. Serve immediately. **Makes** 4 servings.

Note: For testing purposes only, we used Häagen-Dazs Dulce de Leche and Coffee Ice Creams and Kahlúa coffee liqueur.

Hot Fudge Sundae Shake
PREP: 10 MIN.

Pick up your favorite bakery brownies to make this frosty refresher. Microwave caramel and fudge toppings according to package directions. (Pictured on page 164)

1 pt. vanilla bean ice cream
½ cup milk
8 Tbsp. hot fudge topping, warmed
8 Tbsp. caramel topping, warmed
1 (8.5-oz.) can refrigerated instant whipped cream
¼ cup crumbled brownies, divided
4 maraschino cherries (with stems)

1. Process ice cream and milk in a blender until smooth, stopping to scrape down sides.
2. Divide half of ice-cream mixture evenly among 4 (8-oz.) glasses. Top each with 1 Tbsp. fudge topping and 1 Tbsp. caramel topping. Repeat layers with remaining ice-cream mixture and fudge and caramel toppings.
3. Top each with instant whipped cream; sprinkle with 1 Tbsp. crumbled brownies, and top with a cherry. Serve immediately. **Makes** 4 servings.

Note: For testing purposes only, we used Häagen-Dazs Vanilla Bean Ice Cream and Smucker's Hot Fudge and Caramel Flavored Toppings.

Cook's Notes

Use these tips to customize a milk shake that works for you.
■ If you're lactose intolerant, whip up a shake using bananas as a thickener paired with soy milk and your favorite fruit.
■ You can reduce calories by substituting skim milk and your favorite low-fat ice cream.
■ Use less milk if you want a thicker shake.
■ Before serving, chill glasses in freezer until frosty.
■ Serve the Brandy Alexander Milk Shake in a martini glass or brandy snifter for an elegant look.

Great on the Grill

Chicken thighs give you tender, juicy results on a dime.

They are probably the moistest and most flavorful parts of the bird. While skin-on, bone-in pieces are the least expensive, boneless, skinless chicken thighs are also easy on the budget. Look for large resealable bags of individually quick-frozen thighs; you can thaw and cook only as many as you need.

Grilled Chicken With White Barbecue Sauce
PREP: 15 MIN., CHILL: 4 HR., GRILL: 20 MIN.
(Pictured on page 5)

1 Tbsp. dried thyme
1 Tbsp. dried oregano
1 Tbsp. ground cumin
1 Tbsp. paprika
1 tsp. onion powder
½ tsp. salt
½ tsp. pepper
10 chicken thighs (about 3 lb.) *
White Barbecue Sauce

1. Combine first 7 ingredients. Rinse chicken, and pat dry; rub mixture evenly over chicken. Place chicken in a zip-top plastic freezer bag. Seal and chill 4 hours. Remove chicken from bag, discarding bag.
2. Grill chicken, covered with grill lid, over medium-high heat (350° to 400°) 8 to 10 minutes on each side or until a meat thermometer inserted into thickest portion registers 180°. Serve chicken with White Barbecue Sauce. **Makes** 5 servings.

*Substitute 4 chicken leg quarters (about 3 lb.) for chicken thighs, if desired. Increase cooking time to 20 to 25 minutes on each side.

White Barbecue Sauce:
make ahead
PREP: 10 MIN.
Developed by Test Kitchens Professional Pam Lolley, this versatile sauce received our highest rating and is also good over baked potatoes or as a condiment for burgers.

1½ cups mayonnaise
¼ cup white wine vinegar
1 garlic clove, minced
1 Tbsp. coarsely ground pepper
1 Tbsp. spicy brown mustard
1 tsp. sugar
1 tsp. salt
2 tsp. horseradish

1. Stir together all ingredients until well blended. Store in an airtight container in refrigerator up to 1 week. **Makes** 1¾ cups.

Grilled Chicken With Orange-Jalapeño Glaze
family favorite
PREP: 15 MIN., GRILL: 20 MIN.
Boneless chicken thighs may be used; grill about 4 to 5 minutes on each side.

Orange-Jalapeño Glaze
10 skinned chicken thighs
    (about 3 lb.)
½ tsp. salt
½ tsp. pepper

1. Remove and reserve 1 cup Orange-Jalapeño Glaze.
2. Rinse chicken, and pat dry. Sprinkle evenly with salt and pepper. Brush chicken lightly with remaining ⅔ cup Orange-Jalapeño Glaze.

3. Grill, covered with grill lid, over medium-high heat (350° to 400°) 8 to 10 minutes on each side or until a meat thermometer inserted into thickest portion registers 180°, basting each side with reserved 1 cup glaze during last few minutes. **Makes** 5 servings.

Orange-Jalapeño Glaze:
PREP: 15 MIN., COOK: 20 MIN.

2 cups orange juice
3 medium jalapeño peppers, seeded and
    finely chopped
4 garlic cloves, minced
3 Tbsp. grated orange rind
1 Tbsp. olive oil
3 Tbsp. maple syrup
1 tsp. salt
½ tsp. ground ginger
½ tsp. pepper

1. Stir together all ingredients in a medium saucepan, and bring to a boil over medium-high heat. Reduce heat to medium, and cook, stirring often, 15 minutes or until reduced by half. **Makes** 1⅔ cups.
MEG JERNIGAN
SHREVEPORT, LOUISIANA

Is It Done Yet?

We recommend an instant-read thermometer to accurately test the doneness of poultry. For safety, do not depend on touch or visual cues. A dark brown exterior doesn't necessarily indicate that chicken is thoroughly cooked.

Once an internal temperature of 180° is reached, remove pieces from grill, and cover them so they stay moist.

---

healthy foods
Good-for-You Color

Fruits and vegetables rich in color not only add brightness to your plate, but they are also great ways to boost your health and well-being. These nutrient-dense foods have disease-fighting capabilities and are loaded with antioxidants and phytochemicals. Read on for more reasons to enjoy beneficial produce, and sample Minted Fruit Salsa for a tasty variety of fruits.

Nutrition Update

The Centers for Disease Control and Prevention and the Produce for Better Health Foundation recently replaced the 5 A Day campaign with the new slogan *Fruits & Veggies—More Matters.*

Minted Fruit Salsa
make ahead
PREP: 10 MIN., CHILL: 2 HR

Top angel food cake, vanilla fat-free frozen yogurt, or pancakes with this sweet salsa, or serve it with baked cinnamon pita chips. Make the salsa up to four hours ahead, and chill. (Pictured on page 177)

1 cup diced strawberries
1 cup diced Granny Smith apples
1 cup diced mango
1½ Tbsp. chopped fresh mint
1 Tbsp. fresh lime juice
2 Tbsp. orange marmalade
1 tsp. minced fresh ginger
Garnish: fresh mint sprigs

1. Stir together first 7 ingredients in a bowl; cover and chill 2 hours. Garnish, if desired. **Makes** 4 servings.

PETER HALFERTY
CORPUS CHRISTI, TEXAS

Per ¾-cup serving: Calories 69; Fat 0.2g (sat 0g, mono 0.1g, poly 0.1g); Protein 0.5g; Carb 18.4g; Fiber 1.8g; Chol 0mg; Iron 0.3mg; Sodium 7mg; Calc 15mg

---

Lime-Raspberry Bites
fast fixin's
PREP: 15 MIN.

1 (8-oz.) container soft light cream cheese
½ cup powdered sugar
1 tsp. grated lime rind
1 Tbsp. fresh lime juice
2 (2.1-oz.) packages frozen mini-phyllo pastry shells, thawed
28 fresh raspberries
1 tsp. powdered sugar

1. Stir together first 4 ingredients in a small bowl. Spoon cream cheese mixture evenly into pastry shells. Top each with 1 raspberry. Dust evenly with 1 tsp. powdered sugar just before serving. **Makes** 28 tartlets.

ROBBI ANNE ADAMSON
MEMPHIS, TENNESSEE

Orange-Raspberry Bites: Substitute equal amounts orange rind and orange juice for lime rind and lime juice. Prepare recipe as directed.

Per 1 lime or orange tartlet: Calories 47; Fat 2.3g (sat 0.9g, mono 0.6g, poly 0.2g); Protein 0.8g; Carb 5.5g; Fiber 0.3g; Chol 3.8mg; Iron 0.2mg; Sodium 51mg; Calc 11mg

---

Toasted Pecan-and-Broccoli Salad
make ahead
PREP: 15 MIN., BAKE: 8 MIN., CHILL: 2 HR.

Serve this yummy salad alongside beef or chicken for a sweet and tangy side.

⅓ cup chopped pecans
1 cup light mayonnaise
⅓ cup sugar
2 Tbsp. cider vinegar
1½ lb. fresh broccoli florets, chopped*
¼ cup chopped red onion
⅓ cup sweetened dried cranberries or raisins
4 cooked reduced-fat bacon slices, crumbled

1. Place chopped pecans in a single layer in a shallow pan.
2. Bake at 350° for 6 to 8 minutes or until lightly toasted, stirring occasionally.
3. Stir together mayonnaise, sugar, and vinegar in a large bowl; add broccoli,

---

onion, and cranberries, gently tossing to coat. Cover and chill 2 hours. Sprinkle with bacon and pecans just before serving. **Makes** 10 servings.

*Substitute 2 (12-oz.) packages fresh broccoli slaw, if desired.

Per ¾-cup serving: Calories 175; Fat 11g (sat 1.5g, mono 5.6g, poly 3.3g); Protein 3.8g; Carb 16.5g; Fiber 2.6g; Chol 12mg; Iron 0.8mg; Sodium 266mg; Calc 38mg

---

Eggplant-Squash-Tomato Sauté
PREP: 20 MIN., COOK: 20 MIN.

1 medium onion, chopped
1 Tbsp. olive oil
1 lb. eggplant, peeled and cubed
1 lb. yellow squash, halved lengthwise and diced
1 lb. plum tomatoes, chopped
1 Tbsp. fresh oregano, chopped
1 tsp. salt
½ tsp. minced garlic
¼ tsp. ground red pepper

1. Sauté onion in hot oil in a large non-stick skillet over medium-high heat 5 minutes or until crisp-tender. Add eggplant and squash. Cover and cook, stirring occasionally, 10 minutes or until eggplant begins to soften. Stir in tomatoes and remaining ingredients. Cover and cook 5 more minutes. **Makes** 8 servings.

PAT RUSH BENIGNO
VICKSBURG, MISSISSIPPI

Per 1-cup serving: Calories 55; Fat 2.1g (sat 0.3g, mono 1.3g, poly 0.3g); Protein 1.9g; Carb 8.8g; Fiber 3g; Chol 0mg; Iron 0.6mg; Sodium 303mg; Calc 22mg

---

Healthy Benefits

■ Steaming, stir-frying, or microwaving veggies in a small amount of water preserves nutrients.
■ Mayonnaise is a heart-healthy condiment loaded with vitamin E. But it is a calorie-dense food, so use it in moderation.

Three-Ingredient Appetizers

These bite-size nibbles are simple, tasty, and, best of all, affordable.

Throw an incredible party with these 14 speedy recipes. They require little preparation and, with the exception of salt, pepper, cooking spray, and water, use only three ingredients.

Green Olive Poppers ■ ● ▲ ◆

Whisk together 1 egg and 2 Tbsp. water. Cut 1 frozen puff pastry sheet, thawed, into 15 (¾-inch) strips. Cut strips into fourths. Brush 1 side of pastry strip with egg mixture, and wrap around 1 small green olive, pressing edges to seal. Repeat with remaining pastry and olives. Arrange, seam sides down, on a lightly greased baking sheet; brush with egg mixture, and sprinkle with pepper. Bake at 400° for 10 to 12 minutes or until golden. **Makes** 60 poppers. Prep: 20 min., Bake: 12 min.

Pizza Sticks ■ ● ▲

Top 1 (12-oz.) refrigerated thin pizza crust with 1 (10.5-oz.) container tomato bruschetta topping. Sprinkle evenly with 1 cup (4 oz.) shredded Italian cheese blend. Bake at 450°, directly on oven rack, 12 minutes or until crust is golden and cheese is bubbly. Cut pizza in half, and cut each half lengthwise into 2-inch strips. **Makes** about 12 strips. Prep: 5 min., Bake: 12 min.
Note: For testing purposes only, we used Buitoni Classic Bruschetta.

Gazpacho Shooters ■

Stir together 1 (16-oz.) container refrigerated mild salsa, 1 cup Bloody Mary mix, ¾ cup finely chopped seedless cucumber, and ½ cup water. Cover and chill until ready to serve. Serve gazpacho in 2- to 4-oz. shot glasses. Garnish with cucumber sticks, if desired. **Makes** about 4 cups. Prep: 10 min.

Pecan-Stuffed Dates With Bacon ● ▲ ✳

Heat 15 pecan halves in a small nonstick skillet over medium-low heat, stirring often, 2 to 3 minutes or until toasted. Cut a lengthwise slit down the center of 15 seedless dates. Stuff 1 pecan half in each date, and wrap each with 1 slice ready-to-serve bacon. Bake at 425° for 8 minutes or until bacon is crisp. **Makes** 15 stuffed dates. Prep: 10 min., Cook: 3 min., Bake: 8 min.

Apricot-Chicken Salad Tarts ● ✳

Stir together 1 cup deli chicken salad and ⅓ cup chopped dried apricots. Spoon evenly into 15 mini-phyllo pastry shells. Bake at 350° for 8 minutes or until thoroughly heated. **Makes** 15 tarts. Prep: 10 min., Bake: 8 min.

Queso Verde ■

Tear 1 lb. white American cheese slices into large pieces; combine with 1 cup salsa verde and 1 (7-oz.) can chopped green chiles in a microwave-safe bowl. Microwave at HIGH, stirring at 1-minute intervals, 5 minutes or until cheese is melted and mixture is smooth. **Makes** 3 cups. Prep: 10 min.

Swiss-and-Walnut Pears ● ▲ ✳

Heat ⅓ cup finely chopped walnuts in a small nonstick skillet over medium-low heat, stirring often, 2 to 3 minutes or until toasted. Cut 1 Bosc or Bartlett pear into about 20 equal slices. Stir together 3 (¾-oz.) wedges Swiss spreadable cheese. Spread bottom half of 1 side of each pear slice evenly with cheese. Sprinkle with walnuts. **Makes** about 20 pieces. Prep: 15 min., Cook: 3 min.
Note: For testing purposes only, we used The Laughing Cow Original Creamy Swiss spreadable cheese.

Prosciutto-Wrapped Melon ● ▲ ✳

Cut half of a cantaloupe into bite-size pieces. Wrap each piece with 1 (½-inch-wide) strip of thinly sliced prosciutto; secure with a wooden pick. Drizzle with 1 Tbsp. extra virgin olive oil. Sprinkle with freshly cracked pepper. **Makes** 8 servings. Prep: 10 min.

Spicy Grilled Chicken Wings ■ ✳

Combine 1½ cups barbecue sauce and ¾ cup hot sauce in a large zip-top plastic bag; remove and reserve ¾ cup sauce. Add 1 (40-oz.) package frozen chicken wing sections, thawed, to bag. Seal and chill at least 3 hours or up to 24 hours. Remove chicken from marinade, discarding marinade. Grill chicken, covered with grill lid, over medium-high heat (350° to 400°) 20 minutes or until done, turning occasionally. Toss wings with reserved ¾ cup sauce. **Makes** 6 servings. Prep: 10 min., Chill: 3 hr., Grill: 20 min.

Banana Bread Bruschetta ● ✳

Slice 1 (4- x 5½-inch) loaf bakery banana bread into (½-inch-thick) slices (about 10 slices). Cut each slice in half, and arrange on a baking sheet. Broil 6 inches from heat 2 to 3 minutes. Spread each slice evenly with 2 tsp. goat cheese and ½ tsp. apricot or pear preserves. Top with freshly ground black pepper. **Makes** 10 servings. Prep: 10 min., Broil: 3 min.

Chutney-Topped Brie ● ▲ ◆

Trim and discard rind from top of an 8-oz. Brie round, leaving a ¼-inch border. Place Brie in an ovenproof serving dish; top with ¼ cup apricot chutney. Bake at 400° for 10 minutes or until cheese is melted. Heat 2 Tbsp. chopped almonds in a small nonstick skillet over medium-low heat, stirring often, 2 to 3 minutes or until toasted. Sprinkle Brie with almonds. **Makes** 6 to 8 servings. Prep: 10 min., Bake: 10 min., Cook: 3 min.

Parmesan-Pesto Breadsticks ● ▲ ◆

Unroll 1 (11-oz.) can refrigerated soft breadstick dough. Spread ¼ cup pesto evenly over dough. Sprinkle with ¼ cup (1 oz.) shredded Parmesan cheese. Separate dough at perforations. Stretch dough into 10-inch-long strips; twist strips, and place on a lightly greased baking sheet. Bake at 375° for 13 minutes or until golden brown. **Makes** 12 breadsticks. Prep: 10 min., Bake: 13 min.

Roasted Garlic Spread ● ▲ ◆

Cut off pointed end of 5 large garlic bulbs. Place garlic bulbs on a piece of aluminum foil, and drizzle with 1 Tbsp. olive oil. Fold foil to seal. Bake at 400° for 1 hour. Squeeze pulp from garlic into a small bowl. Stir in 2 Tbsp. olive oil, ½ tsp. chopped fresh thyme, and salt and pepper to taste. Serve with toasted bread slices, if desired. **Makes** about ⅔ cup. Prep: 5 min., Bake: 1 hr.

Salmon-and-Herb Cheese Bites ▲ ◆

Arrange ½ (4-oz.) package sliced smoked salmon evenly on 18 (¼-inch-thick) cucumber slices. Place ⅓ cup garlic-and-herb spreadable cheese in a small zip-top plastic bag. Snip 1 corner of bag to make a small hole, and pipe cheese evenly onto salmon. **Makes** 18 pieces. Prep: 15 min.

Note: For testing purposes only, we used Alouette Garlic & Herbs Spreadable Cheese.

taste of the south
Our Favorite Guacamole

This tasty delight has become one of our most preferred staples in Tex-Mex cuisine. Fresh avocado and lime juice are essential to guacamole. Other ingredients vary by recipe. Onions, chiles, garlic, tomatoes, and cilantro are most commonly included. But you can create your own delicious combination.

You can actually freeze mashed, fresh avocado to keep on hand for an "emergency" guacamole. Just add ½ tsp. of lime or lemon juice per avocado, mix well, and store in a zip-top plastic freezer bag, making sure to remove all the air before sealing. Thaw in the refrigerator or in a bowl of cool water.

Guacamole

PREP: 10 MIN., STAND: 30 MIN.

To keep guacamole from changing color when stored in the refrigerator, place a layer of plastic wrap directly on its surface.

5 ripe avocados
2 Tbsp. finely chopped red onion
2 Tbsp. fresh lime juice
½ medium jalapeño pepper, seeded and chopped
1 garlic clove, pressed
¾ tsp. salt
Tortilla chips

1. Cut avocados in half. Scoop pulp into a bowl, and mash with a potato masher or fork until slightly chunky. Stir in red onion and next 4 ingredients. Cover with plastic wrap, allowing wrap to touch mixture, and let stand at room temperature 30 minutes. Serve guacamole with tortilla chips. **Makes** 3½ cups.

Cilantro Guacamole: Mash avocado, and stir in ingredients as directed. Stir in 3 Tbsp. chopped fresh cilantro and an additional 1 Tbsp. lime juice. Cover mixture, and let stand at room temperature 30 minutes.

Tropical Guacamole
chef recipe
PREP: 20 MIN.

Chef Zurita often serves this flavorful recipe over grilled fish.

2 ripe avocados
1 large ripe mango, peeled and diced
1 cup peeled and diced jicama (about ½ small jicama)
¼ cup chopped sweet onion
2 Tbsp. lime juice
½ tsp. salt
¼ tsp. minced garlic
¼ tsp. pepper
Tortilla chips

1. Cut 1 avocado in half. Scoop pulp into a bowl; mash with a potato masher or fork until slightly chunky. Cut remaining avocado in half. Peel and dice.
2. Stir mango and next 6 ingredients gently into mashed avocado until combined. Add diced avocado, and gently stir until combined. Serve with tortilla chips. **Makes** 2⅓ cups.

CHEF RICARDO MUÑOZ ZURITA
MEXICO CITY, MEXICO

Get It Ripe

A perfect avocado should have clean, unblemished skin. Ripe avocados should yield slightly when gently squeezed. Store unripe avocados at room temperature until ripe, or place in a loosely closed brown paper bag to accelerate the ripening process.

Amazing Salads

The best of the garden and grill come together in these savory combos.

These salads are perfect for busy week-nights or casual get-togethers. The shrimp, chicken, or pork can be grilled up to a day ahead. Store the prepared dressings in the fridge for up to a week; return to room temperature just before tossing with the salads.

Grilled Pork Salad With Spicy Peanut Dressing
make ahead
PREP: 20 MIN., GRILL: 20 MIN.,
STAND: 15 MIN., COOK: 1 MIN.
Fresh peaches or nectarines make a great substitution for mangoes in this recipe.

⅓ cup ketchup
3 Tbsp. firmly packed brown sugar
1 Tbsp. cider vinegar
¾ tsp. garlic salt
¾ tsp. chile powder
1 (1½-lb.) package pork tenderloins
½ lb. sugar snap peas, trimmed
8 cups mixed salad greens
2 mangoes, peeled and sliced
½ cup roasted, unsalted peanuts
Spicy Peanut Dressing

1. Stir together first 5 ingredients until blended; brush evenly over pork.
2. Grill pork, covered with grill lid, over medium-high heat (350° to 400°) 10 minutes on each side or until a meat thermometer inserted in thickest portion of tenderloins registers 155°. Remove from grill; let stand 15 minutes before slicing.
3. Cook sugar snap peas in boiling salted water to cover 1 minute or until crisp-tender; drain. Plunge into ice water to stop the cooking process; drain and pat dry.
4. Arrange salad greens on a large serving platter; top evenly with sugar snap peas, mangoes, sliced pork, and peanuts. Serve with Spicy Peanut Dressing. **Makes** 6 servings.

Spicy Peanut Dressing:
fast fixin's • make ahead
PREP: 5 MIN.

¾ cup creamy peanut butter
1 Tbsp. brown sugar
3 Tbsp. soy sauce
1½ Tbsp. fresh lemon juice
½ tsp. crushed red pepper flakes

1. Whisk together all ingredients and ¾ cup water in a large bowl until smooth. **Makes** about 1¾ cups.   LINDA MORTEN
KATY, TEXAS

Grilled Chicken-and-Artichoke Salad
make ahead
PREP: 20 MIN., CHILL: 2 HR., GRILL: 14 MIN.,
STAND: 15 MIN., COOK: 4 MIN.

1½ lb. skinned and boned chicken
    breasts
½ cup light Italian dressing
2 Tbsp. sesame seeds
1 (14-oz.) can artichoke hearts, drained
    and quartered
⅓ cup mayonnaise
2 Tbsp. chopped fresh basil
2 Tbsp. sesame oil
½ tsp. salt

1. Place chicken and dressing in a zip-top plastic freezer bag; seal and chill 2 hours, turning occasionally. Remove chicken from marinade, discarding marinade.
2. Grill chicken, covered with grill lid, over medium-high heat (350° to 400°) 5 to 7 minutes on each side or until done. Remove from grill, and let stand 15 minutes; coarsely chop.
3. Heat sesame seeds in a small nonstick skillet over medium-low heat, stirring often, 4 minutes or until toasted.
4. Stir together grilled chicken, sesame seeds, artichoke hearts, and remaining ingredients in a large bowl just until blended. **Makes** 4 servings.

BETH MOORE
GERMANTOWN, TENNESSEE

Grilled Shrimp-and-Green Bean Salad
make ahead
PREP: 30 MIN., SOAK: 30 MIN., COOK: 4 MIN.,
CHILL: 15 MIN., GRILL: 4 MIN.
Tuck a piece of toasted cornbread beneath this delicious salad for a layer of crouton-like crispness. (Pictured on page 3)

8 (12-inch) wooden skewers
1½ lb. fresh green beans, trimmed
2 lb. peeled, medium-size raw shrimp
Basil Vinaigrette, divided
6 cooked bacon slices, crumbled
1⅓ cups shredded Parmesan cheese
¾ cup chopped roasted, salted almonds
Cornbread (optional)

1. Soak wooden skewers in water to cover 30 minutes.
2. Cook green beans in boiling salted water to cover 4 minutes or until crisp-tender; drain. Plunge into ice water to stop the cooking process; drain, pat dry, and place in a large bowl.
3. Combine shrimp and ¾ cup Basil Vinaigrette in a large zip-top plastic freezer bag; seal and chill 15 minutes, turning occasionally. Remove shrimp from marinade, discarding marinade. Thread shrimp onto skewers.
4. Grill shrimp, covered with grill lid, over medium-high heat (350° to 400°) 2 minutes on each side or just until shrimp turn pink. Remove shrimp from skewers; toss with green beans, bacon, cheese, almonds, and remaining ¾ cup Basil Vinaigrette. Serve over hot cornbread, if desired. **Makes** 4 to 6 servings.

Basil Vinaigrette:
fast fixin's • make ahead
PREP: 10 MIN.

½ cup balsamic vinegar
½ cup chopped fresh basil
4 large shallots, minced
3 garlic cloves, minced
1 Tbsp. brown sugar
1 tsp. seasoned pepper
½ tsp. salt
1 cup olive oil

1. Whisk together first 7 ingredients in a small bowl until blended; gradually add olive oil, whisking constantly until blended. **Makes** about 1½ cups.

SHELLY KING
ST. PETERSBURG, FLORIDA

Note: 1 cup packed fresh basil leaves yields about ½ cup chopped.

Test Kitchen *Notebook*

Much of the preparation for these salads can be done ahead. Cook vegetables such as green beans and sugar snap peas in advance, and refrigerate in separate airtight containers or zip-top plastic bags until ready to serve. Store the prepared salad dressings in the refrigerator up to one week, and return to room temperature just before tossing with the salad ingredients.

Mary Allen Perry
ASSOCIATE FOODS EDITOR

Skillet Pasta in a Flash

We've found some quick pasta dishes that will have supper on the table in about 45 minutes or less. Keep essential staple items, such as pasta, spices, and jarred or canned tomato sauces, on hand. All you need to add is your favorite protein and vegetable to the skillet for an easy meal solution.

Hearty Beef-and-Tortellini Supper
PREP: 15 MIN., COOK: 33 MIN.
Save money by purchasing ground beef on sale. Cook beef, and divide it for freezing to have on hand when you need it.

1 (13-oz.) package cheese- and spinach-filled tortellini *
1 lb. lean ground beef
2 medium onions, chopped
½ cup freshly grated Parmesan cheese, divided
1 (28-oz.) can tomato puree
⅓ cup dry red wine **
1½ tsp. dried basil
¾ tsp. salt
½ tsp. pepper

1. Prepare pasta according to package directions.
2. Brown beef and onions in a large skillet over medium-high heat 10 minutes, stirring until meat crumbles and is no longer pink and onions are tender.
3. Add ¼ cup grated Parmesan cheese, tomato puree, and next 4 ingredients to beef mixture in skillet. Bring mixture to a boil over medium-high heat; reduce heat to medium-low, and simmer, stirring occasionally, 20 minutes.
4. Add prepared tortellini to skillet, tossing to coat. Sprinkle mixture with remaining ¼ cup grated Parmesan cheese, and serve immediately. **Makes** 4 servings.

*Substitute 1 (19-oz.) package frozen cheese-filled tortellini, if desired.

**Substitute beef broth, if desired.

Note: For testing purposes only, we used Barilla Cheese & Spinach Tortellini.

GILDA LESTER
WILMINGTON, NORTH CAROLINA

Hearty Turkey-and-Tortellini Supper: Substitute ground turkey for ground beef. Proceed as directed.

Cajun Chicken Pasta
PREP: 15 MIN., COOK: 20 MIN.

12 oz. uncooked linguine
2 lb. chicken breast strips
1 Tbsp. Cajun seasoning
1¼ tsp. salt, divided
¼ cup butter
1 small red bell pepper, thinly sliced *
1 small green bell pepper, thinly sliced *
1 (8-oz.) package fresh mushrooms
2 green onions (white and light green parts only), sliced *
1½ cups half-and-half
¼ tsp. lemon pepper
¼ tsp. dried basil
¼ tsp. garlic powder
Garnish: chopped green onions

1. Prepare pasta according to package directions.
2. Sprinkle chicken with Cajun seasoning and 1 tsp. salt. Melt ¼ cup butter in a large nonstick skillet over medium-high heat; add chicken, and sauté 5 to 6 minutes or until done. Remove chicken.
3. Add bell peppers, mushrooms, and green onions to skillet, and sauté 9 to 10 minutes or until vegetables are tender and liquid evaporates.
4. Return chicken to skillet; stir in half-and-half, next 3 ingredients, and remaining ¼ tsp. salt. Cook, stirring often, over medium-low heat 3 to 4 minutes or until thoroughly heated. Add pasta; toss to coat. Garnish, if desired; serve immediately. **Makes** 4 servings.

*Substitute ½ (16-oz.) bag frozen sliced green, red, and yellow bell peppers and onion, if desired. For testing purposes only, we used Birds Eye Pepper Stir-Fry.

LILANN HUNTER TAYLOR
SAVANNAH, GEORGIA

Fast Weeknight Meal

Our insider secrets will show you how.

Spanish Supper

Serves 4

Cuban-Style Shredded Pork over
Black Beans 'n' Spuds

Weeknight Fondue

Start your next dinner with most of the cooking done using three time-saving items available at most grocery stores: a fully cooked pork roast, refrigerated mashed potatoes, and a bagged salad.

Cuban-Style Shredded Pork

PREP: 10 MIN., COOK: 5 MIN.
Mojo criollo Spanish marinating sauce is found on the international foods aisle. Or make your own by using our Quick Spanish Marinating Sauce. The pork mixture is also great for sandwiches.

1 (17-oz.) package fully cooked pork roast au jus
½ cup chopped onion
1 Tbsp. olive oil
7 Tbsp. mojo criollo Spanish marinating sauce
Black Beans 'n' Spuds
Garnishes: fresh cilantro sprigs, dill pickle stacker slices

1. Remove pork roast from package, and rinse with warm water; drain and pat dry with paper towels. Using two forks, break pork roast into chunks.

2. Sauté onion in hot oil in a large skillet over medium-high heat 3 minutes or until tender. Stir in mojo criollo sauce and roast. Cook 1 to 2 minutes or until thoroughly heated. Serve over Black Beans 'n' Spuds. Garnish, if desired. **Makes** 4 servings.

Cook's Note

If you can't find mojo criollo sauce at your grocery store, use this homemade alternative.

Quick Spanish Marinating Sauce

fast fixin's
PREP: 5 MIN., COOK: 1 MIN.

Sauté ½ tsp. bottled minced garlic, ½ tsp. ground oregano, and ¼ tsp. ground cumin in 1 tsp. olive oil in a small saucepan over medium heat 1 minute. Stir in ¼ cup fresh orange juice, 2 Tbsp. fresh lemon juice, and 1 Tbsp. fresh lime juice. **Makes** about 7 Tbsp.

Black Beans 'n' Spuds

fast fixin's
PREP: 10 MIN.
Black beans add extra protein and fiber to this meal. We think it is a fun, creative way to dress up potatoes. If the kids wonder about the black spots (the beans), call 'em polka-dot potatoes.

1 (24-oz.) package refrigerated mashed potatoes
1 (15-oz.) can black beans, rinsed and drained
1 Tbsp. butter
1 Tbsp. chopped fresh cilantro

1. Microwave potatoes according to package directions.
2. Stir together potatoes, black beans, and butter in a large microwave-safe bowl. Cover with plastic wrap; fold back a small edge to allow steam to escape. Microwave at HIGH 1 to 2 minutes or until hot. Stir in cilantro. Serve immediately. **Makes** 4 servings.

Note: For testing purposes only, we used Diner's Choice Country Style Mashed Potatoes. You can substitute 4 cups of your favorite hot mashed potatoes.

Weeknight Fondue

fast fixin's
PREP: 10 MIN.
Use 6- or 12-inch wooden skewers to spear the fruit for dipping.

½ cup dark chocolate syrup
¼ cup powdered sugar
¼ tsp. vanilla extract
Assorted fruit (strawberries, pineapple chunks, kiwifuit chunks, banana slices), cookies, marshmallows

1. Whisk together first 3 ingredients in a medium bowl until smooth. Serve with fruit, cookies, and marshmallows. **Makes** 4 servings.

Natural Sweetness

We love honey not only for its sweet flavor and golden color but also for its ability to absorb and retain moisture. This is especially helpful for keeping your baked goods moist for longer periods of time. Raw honey is also loaded with vitamins, minerals, and antioxidants, making this natural source of energy a healthful alternative to sugar.

Nectar from flower blossoms influences the flavor and color of honey. The darker the color, the stronger the flavor. Orange blossom, tupelo, and sourwood are favored Southern varieties, all light colored and relatively mild in flavor.

Honey Yeast Rolls

freezeable • make ahead

PREP: 30 MIN.; STAND: 1 HR., 5 MIN.;
COOK: 5 MIN.; RISE: 2 HR.; BAKE: 12 MIN.

Tender, delectable Honey Yeast Rolls are best served warm from the oven and slathered with sweet honey butter.

¼ cup warm water (100° to 110°)
1 (¼-oz.) envelope active dry yeast
1 tsp. honey
1¾ cups milk
2 large eggs, at room temperature
½ cup butter, melted and
    cooled
⅓ cup honey
3 tsp. salt
6½ cups all-purpose flour, divided
½ cup butter, softened
¼ cup honey

1. Combine first 3 ingredients in a small bowl, and let stand 5 minutes or until mixture bubbles.
2. Meanwhile, heat milk in a saucepan over medium heat 3 to 5 minutes or until 100° to 110°.
3. Stir together warm milk, eggs, and next 3 ingredients in a bowl of a heavy-duty electric stand mixer, blending well. Add yeast mixture, stirring to combine. Gradually add 5 cups flour, beating at medium speed, using paddle attachment. Beat 3 minutes. Cover with plastic wrap, and let stand 1 hour.
4. Uncover dough, and add remaining 1½ cups flour, beating at medium speed 5 minutes. (Dough will be sticky.) Transfer to a lightly greased large bowl. Cover with plastic wrap, and let rise in a warm place (85°), free from drafts, 1 hour or until doubled in bulk.
5. Punch down dough. Turn dough out on a well-floured surface, and roll into 28 (2½-inch) balls (about ¼ cup dough per ball). Place balls in 4 lightly greased 9-inch pans (7 balls per pan). Cover and let rise in a warm place (85°), free from drafts, 1 hour or until doubled in bulk.
6. Stir together ½ cup softened butter and ¼ cup honey.
7. Bake rolls at 400° for 10 to 12 minutes or until golden brown. Brush tops with honey butter. Serve with remaining honey butter. **Makes** 28 rolls.

JANE AND CLINT WALKER
ROGERS, TEXAS

Note: To freeze, place baked rolls in zip-top plastic freezer bags, and freeze up to 2 months. Let thaw at room temperature. Reheat, if desired.

Honey-Peanut-Glazed Pork Loin

PREP: 15 MIN., BAKE: 50 MIN., STAND: 10 MIN.

It takes just 15 minutes to get this tender entrée ready for the oven.

1 (2-lb.) boneless pork loin roast,
    trimmed
2 garlic cloves, pressed
1½ tsp. salt
1 tsp. pepper
1 small red onion, sliced
Honey-Peanut Glaze

1. Rub roast evenly with garlic, salt, and pepper. Place roast in a lightly greased 13- x 9-inch pan. Arrange onion slices on and around roast. Cover pan tightly with aluminum foil, sealing edges.
2. Bake, covered, at 325° for 30 minutes. Remove from oven, and discard foil. Remove onions from pan. Pour Honey-Peanut Glaze evenly over roast, and bake, uncovered, 20 more minutes or until a meat thermometer inserted in thickest portion registers 150°. Let roast stand 10 minutes before slicing. Serve with onion slices and pan juices. **Makes** 6 servings.

Honey-Peanut Glaze:
fast fixin's • make ahead
PREP: 5 MIN.

⅓ cup dry-roasted peanuts, finely
    chopped
½ cup honey
2 Tbsp. orange marmalade
1 Tbsp. whole grain mustard
½ tsp. horseradish

1. Stir together all ingredients. Cover and chill up to 2 hours, if desired. **Makes** 1 cup.

MARTHA RUTLEDGE
MOBILE, ALABAMA

Honey How-tos

When substituting honey for sugar in a recipe, reduce any liquid by ¼ cup and add a tsp. of baking soda for each cup of honey used. Also reduce oven temperature by 25° to prevent overbrowning. Coat your measuring cups and spoons with vegetable cooking spray to make it easy for honey to slide out when pouring. Store honey at room temperature. If it crystallizes, remove lid, and place in a container of hot water until crystals dissolve.

A Taste of Louisiana

Sample some of Lafayette's excellent comfort food.

The more than 200 pages of *Something to Talk About* (Junior League of Lafayette, Louisiana, 2005) hold a wealth of top-notch South Louisiana recipes. This Junior League of Lafayette gem is the fourth in the *Talk About Good!* cookbook series. It's filled with plenty of bayou dishes, including gumbo, oyster pie, and bread pudding, along with weeknight favorites such as chicken lasagna. Try these two selections soon.

Red Beans and Sausage

PREP: 15 MIN., COOK: 2 HR.

Cooking red beans and rice on wash day Mondays is an old Louisiana custom. Families would simmer a pot of beans all day while they did laundry. We tasted this dish after just 1 hour of the 1½ hour simmering time and loved it. Cook the full time for a darker sauce and mellower flavor.

2 lb. hot hickory-smoked sausage, sliced
1 red bell pepper, finely chopped
1 green bell pepper, finely chopped
3 celery ribs, finely chopped
1 cup chopped onion
4 garlic cloves, minced
3 (15-oz.) cans red beans, drained
1 (15-oz.) can tomato sauce
3 Tbsp. sweet pepper sauce
1 Tbsp. Worcestershire sauce
2 tsp. hot sauce
1½ cups uncooked long-grain rice

1. Cook sausage in a Dutch oven over medium-high heat about 5 minutes, stirring until sausage is brown. Remove sausage, and drain on paper towels, reserving 1 Tbsp. drippings in Dutch oven. Sauté bell peppers and next 3 ingredients in hot drippings 5 minutes or until tender.
2. Stir in red beans, next 4 ingredients, and 1⅔ cups water. Bring to a boil; reduce heat, and simmer 15 minutes. Stir in sausage. Simmer, covered, 1½ hours.
3. Prepare rice according to package directions. Serve Red Beans and Sausage over hot cooked rice. **Makes** 6 servings.

Note: For testing purposes only, we used Bush's Red Beans and Pickapeppa Sauce for sweet pepper sauce.

Puddin Place Eggs

PREP: 10 MIN., BAKE: 25 MIN.

Put this indulgent dish on your weekend to-do list. Elizabeth Picard, whose aunt owned Puddin Place Bed and Breakfast in Oxford, Mississippi, contributed this recipe to the book.

6 Canadian bacon slices
1½ cups (6 oz.) shredded mozzarella cheese
6 large eggs
½ tsp. salt
½ tsp. coarsely ground pepper
¾ cup whipping cream
¼ tsp. paprika
3 English muffins, split and toasted (optional)

1. Place 1 slice each of Canadian bacon on bottom of 6 (6-oz.) lightly greased ramekins or custard cups. Sprinkle ¼ cup cheese on top of bacon in each ramekin, and push cheese against sides of ramekin, making a well in center of cheese. Break 1 egg into center of each well. Sprinkle evenly with salt and pepper. Pour 2 Tbsp. whipping cream over top of each egg. Sprinkle each evenly with paprika. Place ramekins on a baking sheet.
2. Bake at 350° for 20 to 25 minutes or until egg is cooked to desired degree of doneness. Serve with toasted English muffin halves, if desired. **Makes** 6 servings.

Freshen Up Your Plate

We mixed Southern staples such as cornmeal and grits with some popular ingredients to stir up tasty side dishes.

Skillet Grits With Seasoned Vegetables

fast fixin's • make ahead
PREP: 10 MIN., COOK: 20 MIN.

You can make the vegetables a day ahead; just cook them a few minutes less to ensure they don't overcook when they're reheated.

1 (32-oz.) container chicken broth
3 Tbsp. butter
1 tsp. salt
1½ cups uncooked regular grits
1 cup (4 oz.) shredded Cheddar cheese
⅓ cup (1.5 oz.) shredded Parmesan cheese
½ tsp. pepper
Seasoned Vegetables

1. Bring first 3 ingredients to a boil in a large saucepan over medium-high heat. Gradually whisk in grits; return to a boil. Reduce heat to medium-low, and simmer, stirring occasionally, 10 to 12 minutes or until thickened.

2. Whisk in cheeses and pepper until cheeses are melted. Spoon Seasoned Vegetables evenly over grits, and serve immediately. **Makes** 6 to 8 servings.

Seasoned Vegetables:

PREP: 20 MIN., COOK: 35 MIN.

This recipe is similar to a ragoût—a thick, well-seasoned stew. We served the richly flavored vegetables over grits; you can also try them over rice or egg noodles.

1 medium onion, chopped
2 garlic cloves, minced
2 Tbsp. olive oil
4 carrots, chopped
3 small red potatoes, diced
2 small turnips (about ½ lb.), peeled and chopped
2 celery ribs, diced
1 medium zucchini, chopped
1 (14-oz.) can chicken broth
1 tsp. salt
1 tsp. dried thyme
½ tsp. pepper
1 tsp. cornstarch

1. Sauté onion and garlic in hot oil in a large skillet over medium heat 5 minutes or until caramelized. Add carrots and next 4 ingredients, and sauté 12 to 15 minutes or until vegetables are tender. Increase heat to medium-high; stir in chicken broth and next 3 ingredients. Bring to a boil. Reduce heat to medium-low, and simmer, stirring occasionally, 5 minutes.

2. Whisk together cornstarch and 1 Tbsp. water until smooth. Whisk into vegetable mixture in skillet, and cook, stirring constantly, 3 to 5 minutes or until thickened. **Makes** 6 to 8 servings.

Chile-Corn Griddle Cakes

PREP: 10 MIN., COOK: 8 MIN. PER BATCH

Liven up time-tested hoe cakes with green chiles and corn. These cakes stir up in 10 minutes. Golden brown and hot off the griddle, they can be served with butter or syrup.

1 cup frozen corn niblets, thawed
1 cup cornmeal mix
½ cup buttermilk
½ cup boiling water
1 (4.5-oz.) can chopped green chiles, undrained
1 Tbsp. vegetable oil
¼ tsp. ground cumin
Butter

1. Whisk together first 7 ingredients, whisking just until dry ingredients are moistened. (Batter will be thin.)

2. Spoon batter by level ¼ cupfuls onto a hot (375°) greased griddle or a greased nonstick skillet over medium-high heat. Cook, in batches, 3 to 4 minutes or until tops are covered with bubbles and edges look slightly dry and cooked; turn and cook until done. Serve with butter. **Makes** 10 (4-inch) cakes.

quick & easy
Squeeze on Flavor

Let these mustard-enhanced recipes rejuvenate your supper.

No-Cook Mustard Sauce

make ahead

PREP: 5 MIN., CHILL: 24 HR.

This sauce has a kick when first prepared. A little time in the refrigerator will soften the bite by allowing the flavors to meld and mellow a little. Find dry mustard on the spice aisle of the supermarket.

1 cup pineapple preserves
1 cup apple jelly
½ cup firmly packed brown sugar
1 (2-oz.) tin dry mustard
3 Tbsp. horseradish
Freshly ground pepper to taste

1. Stir together first 5 ingredients. Add pepper to taste. Cover and chill at least 24 hours or up to 2 weeks. **Makes** about 2½ cups.

NORA HENSHAW
OKEMAH, OKLAHOMA

Mustard Pork Chops: Brush 1 cup No-Cook Mustard Sauce evenly over 4 (¾-inch-thick) bone-in pork chops. Grill, covered with grill lid, over medium heat (300° to 350°) 6 to 7 minutes on each side or until a meat thermometer inserted in thickest portion registers 155°. Let stand 5 minutes or until thermometer registers 160°. **Makes** 4 servings. Prep: 10 min., Grill: 14 min., Stand: 5 min.

Horseradish-Dijon Sauce

PREP: 5 MIN.

Dish it up with a grilled steak or on a roast beef sandwich.

¼ cup mayonnaise
¼ cup low-fat sour cream
2 Tbsp. chopped green onions
1 Tbsp. horseradish
2 tsp. Dijon mustard
Freshly ground pepper to taste

1. Stir together first 5 ingredients. Add pepper to taste. Serve immediately, or cover and chill up to 1 week. **Makes** ⅔ cup.

Horseradish-Dijon Potato Salad: Cook 6 to 8 medium potatoes (about 3 lb.), cubed, in boiling water to cover in a Dutch oven over medium heat 15 to 18 minutes or until tender. Drain and let cool slightly. Toss with ⅔ cup Horseradish-Dijon Sauce. Serve immediately, or cover and chill until ready to serve. **Makes** 6 servings. Prep: 10 min., Cook: 18 min.

LINDA LEFLER
HIGH POINT, NORTH CAROLINA

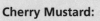

stir ins

Combine equal parts mustard and jelly or jam for effortless sauces to pair with grilled sausages, chicken, fish, or pork chops. You can also serve them as dips for chicken strips, ham strips, or sausage biscuits.

Plum Mustard
PREP: 5 MIN.

½ cup plum preserves
½ cup yellow mustard

1. Stir together both ingredients. Cover and chill until ready to serve. **Makes** 1 cup.

Mango Mustard:
Substitute mango chutney for plum preserves.

Cherry Mustard:
Substitute cherry preserves for plum preserves.

Orange Mustard:
Substitute orange marmalade for plum preserves.

Host a Special Gathering

A terrific celebration cake tops off a fun outdoor menu.

Festive Food

Serves 24

Dressed-Up Burger Wraps (make 4 recipes)

Horseradish-Dijon Potato Salad
(make 4 recipes; see previous page)

Store-bought baked beans

Graduation Cake With Cream Cheese Frosting or
Memorial Day Cupcakes With Cream Cheese Frosting

Warm weather is the perfect reason to take your party outside. We have just the menu—it even includes an easy-to-make cake. If cupcakes are your preference, we have that covered with a recipe using the same batter and frosting. We're betting you'll be so inspired you'll be thinking of ways to decorate a cake for Mother's Day, a birthday, or whatever suits your next party.

Dressed-Up Burger Wraps
fast fixin's
PREP: 10 MIN., GRILL: 18 MIN.
Ground beef and pork sausage pair up for great burgers.

1 lb. lean ground beef
1 lb. hot ground pork sausage
¼ tsp. salt
6 mozzarella cheese slices
1 (11.2-oz.) package flat bread
Basil Mayonnaise
Toppings: green leaf lettuce, tomato slices

1. Combine first 3 ingredients. Shape into 6 (5-inch-long) oval patties.

2. Grill patties, covered with grill lid, over medium-high heat (350° to 400°) 7 to 8 minutes on each side or until centers are no longer pink. Top each patty with 1 cheese slice, and grill 2 minutes or until cheese is melted.
3. Serve cooked patties wrapped in flat bread with Basil Mayonnaise and desired toppings. **Makes** 6 servings.

Note: For testing purposes only, we used Flatout Original Wraps.

Basil Mayonnaise:
fast fixin's • make ahead
PREP: 5 MIN.

½ cup mayonnaise
2 Tbsp. chopped fresh basil
1½ tsp. fresh lemon juice

1. Stir together all ingredients. Cover and chill until ready to serve. Store in an airtight container in the refrigerator up to 1 month. **Makes** about ½ cup.

CINDY BLEDSOE CROSBY
PLANO, TEXAS

Graduation Cake With Cream Cheese Frosting
family favorite • make ahead
PREP: 25 MIN., BAKE: 35 MIN., COOL: 55 MIN., FREEZE: 30 MIN.
(Pictured on page 2)

2 cups sugar
1 cup butter
2 large eggs
2 tsp. fresh lemon juice
1 tsp. vanilla
2½ cups cake flour
½ tsp. baking soda
1 cup buttermilk
Cream Cheese Frosting
Graduation Cake Decorations (see tip box below)

1. Beat sugar and butter at medium speed with an electric mixer until creamy. Add eggs, 1 at a time, beating until yellow disappears after each addition. Beat in lemon juice and vanilla.
2. Combine flour and baking soda in a small bowl; add to sugar mixture alternately with buttermilk, beginning and ending with flour mixture. Beat at medium speed just until blended after each addition. Pour batter into a greased and floured 13- x 9-inch pan.
3. Bake at 350° for 30 to 35 minutes or until a wooden pick inserted in center comes out clean. Cool in pan on a wire rack 10 minutes. Remove cake from pan to wire rack, and cool 45 minutes or until completely cool. Wrap in plastic wrap, and freeze 30 minutes. Place cake on a serving platter. Remove and reserve ¼ cup Cream Cheese Frosting for decorations, and spread top and sides of cake evenly with remaining Cream Cheese Frosting. Top cake with Graduation Cake Decorations. **Makes** 24 servings.

Graduation Cake Decorations

½ (12-oz.) box chocolate-coated malted milk balls
1 (4.75-oz.) box chocolate-covered mint-filled candies
Chocolate sprinkles
Blue gourmet jelly beans
Blue food coloring gel
4 mint-filled chocolate squares
1 (4-inch) piece thin ribbon
1 rolled vanilla cookie

■ Remove and reserve ¼ cup Cream Cheese Frosting before frosting cake. Spread remaining Cream Cheese Frosting evenly on top and sides of cake. Press chocolate-coated malted milk balls and chocolate-covered mint-filled candies alternately around bottom edges of frosted cake. Arrange chocolate sprinkles and blue jelly beans around outside top edges of cake, forming a 1-inch border.
■ Tint reserved ¼ cup Cream Cheese Frosting with food coloring gel, stirring to achieve desired color, and place in a zip-top plastic freezer bag. Snip 1 corner of bag to make a small hole, and pipe a number corresponding with the graduation year on each mint-filled chocolate square. Arrange chocolate squares on center of cake, pressing gently to secure.
■ Diploma: Tie ribbon around rolled vanilla cookie. Press cookie diploma into Cream Cheese Frosting in top left corner of cake.
■ For testing purposes only, we used Whoppers for chocolate-coated malted milk balls, Junior Mints for chocolate-covered mint-filled candies, Ghirardelli Dark Chocolate with Mint Filling Squares for mint-filled chocolate squares, Jelly Belly for gourmet jelly beans, and DeBeukelaer Pirouluxe Belgian Rolled Butter Vanilla Cookies for rolled vanilla cookie.

Cream Cheese Frosting:
fast fixin's
PREP: 5 MIN.

½ cup butter, softened
1 (8-oz.) package cream cheese, softened
1 (3-oz.) package cream cheese, softened
1 (16-oz.) box powdered sugar
2 tsp. fresh lemon juice

1. Beat all ingredients at medium speed with an electric mixer until fluffy. **Makes** 3½ cups.

Memorial Day Cupcakes With Cream Cheese Frosting
make ahead
PREP: 25 MIN., BAKE: 22 MIN., COOL: 55 MIN.
Spreading frosting on cupcakes can be time-consuming. You'll love our quick-and-easy way using a zip-top plastic freezer bag.

1. Place 24 paper baking cups in muffin pans. Prepare Graduation Cake batter as directed, and spoon into baking cups, filling two-thirds full.
2. Bake at 350° for 18 to 22 minutes or until a wooden pick inserted in center of cupcake comes out clean. Cool in pans on wire racks 10 minutes. Remove cupcakes from pans to wire racks, and cool 45 minutes or until completely cool.
3. Place all of Cream Cheese Frosting in a zip-top plastic freezer bag. Cut off 1 corner of bag to make a hole (about 1 inch in diameter). Squeeze a small amount of frosting on top of each cupcake. Sprinkle each frosted cupcake with red-, white-, and blue-colored sprinkles, or top each with 1 red, 1 white, and 1 blue jelly bean. **Makes** 24 cupcakes.

Note: To make ahead, bake and cool cake layers or cupcakes as directed. Do not frost and decorate. Double wrap in plastic wrap and heavy-duty aluminum foil or place in airtight containers, and freeze up to 1 month.

Irresistible Oatmeal Bars

Add a selection of flavors to create crowd-pleasing treats.

When you're in the mood for cookies, try one of these fiber-rich offerings. They are easy to make, especially with the head start of a cake mix. Serve with a glass of cold milk, and you'll agree that they are very good! And because of the quick-cooking oats in each, you'll want to use a light-colored baking pan since a dark one can cause the bars to brown.

Caramel-Pecan Oatmeal Bars

family favorite

PREP: 15 MIN., BAKE: 35 MIN., COOL: 1 HR.

These tasty bites start with the convenience of cake mix. We then added nuts, chocolate morsels, and caramel.

1 cup chopped pecans
1 (18.25-oz.) package yellow cake mix
2½ cups uncooked quick-cooking oats
¾ cup butter, melted
1 (11.5-oz.) package milk chocolate morsels or 1 (12-oz.) package semisweet chocolate morsels
25 caramels

1. Place pecans in a single layer in a 13- x 9-inch (light-colored) pan.
2. Bake at 350° for 4 to 5 minutes or until toasted, stirring occasionally. Remove nuts from pan.
3. Line bottom and sides of pan with aluminum foil, allowing 2 to 3 inches to extend over sides; lightly grease foil.
4. Stir together cake mix and oats in a large bowl. Stir in butter with a fork until mixture is crumbly and dry ingredients are moistened. Press half of oat mixture evenly onto bottom of prepared pan. Sprinkle chocolate morsels and toasted pecans evenly over oat mixture in pan. Sprinkle with remaining oat mixture.
5. Bake at 375° for 30 minutes or until top is golden brown.
6. Microwave caramels and 1 Tbsp. water in a microwave-safe bowl at HIGH 1 minute or until caramels are melted. Drizzle evenly over warm bars in pan. Let cool on a wire rack 1 hour or until completely cool.
7. Lift baked bars from pan, using foil sides as handles. Place on a cutting board, and cut into 24 bars. **Makes** 2 dozen.

Oatmeal-Raisin Bars

family favorite

PREP: 15 MIN., BAKE: 30 MIN., COOL: 1 HR.

1 (18.25-oz.) package yellow cake mix
2 cups uncooked quick-cooking oats
½ cup raisins
¾ cup butter, melted
1 cup chunky applesauce
¼ tsp. apple pie spice
¼ tsp. grated lemon rind

1. Line bottom and sides of a 13- x 9-inch (light-colored) pan with aluminum foil, allowing 2 to 3 inches to extend over sides; lightly grease foil.
2. Stir together cake mix, oats, and raisins in a large bowl. Stir in butter with a fork until mixture is crumbly and dry ingredients are moistened. Press half of oat mixture onto bottom of prepared pan.
3. Stir together applesauce, apple pie spice, and lemon rind. Gently spread over oat mixture in pan. Sprinkle evenly with remaining oat mixture.
4. Bake at 375° for 30 minutes or until top is golden brown. Let cool in pan on a wire rack 1 hour or until completely cool.
5. Lift baked bars from pan, using foil sides as handles. Place on a cutting board, and cut into 24 bars. **Makes** 2 dozen.

Peanut Butter-and-Jam Oatmeal Bars

family favorite

PREP: 15 MIN., BAKE: 30 MIN., COOL: 1 HR.

1 (18.25-oz.) package yellow cake mix
2½ cups uncooked quick-cooking oats
¾ cup butter, melted
½ cup creamy peanut butter
½ cup strawberry preserves
½ cup chopped roasted peanuts

1. Line bottom and sides of a 13- x 9-inch (light-colored) pan with aluminum foil, allowing 2 to 3 inches to extend over sides; lightly grease foil.
2. Stir together cake mix and oats in a large bowl. Stir in butter with a fork until mixture is crumbly and dry ingredients are moistened. Press half of oat mixture onto bottom of prepared pan.
3. Stir together peanut butter and preserves in a medium bowl. Gently spread peanut butter mixture evenly over oat mixture in pan. Sprinkle peanuts and remaining half of oat mixture evenly over peanut butter mixture.
4. Bake at 375° for 30 minutes or until top is golden brown. Let cool in pan on a wire rack 1 hour or until completely cool.
5. Lift baked bars from pan, using foil sides as handles. Place on a cutting board, and cut into 24 bars. **Makes** 2 dozen.

Baking Secret

For testing purposes only, we used Pillsbury Moist Supreme Classic Yellow Premium Cake Mix for all these recipes. Don't substitute margarine for the butter in these recipes.

Nothing-to-It Jams

Jam with no cooking? Yep. You simply crush the fruit, stir in freezer jam pectin, spoon into decorative canning jars, and freeze—it couldn't be easier. These spreads are some of the finest we've ever tasted.

Jam or jelly will keep in the freezer for up to one year or in the refrigerator for three weeks. And you really can freeze it in a jar—a proper jar, that is. For safety purposes and to avoid a mess in the freezer, just be sure to use jars specifically made and labeled for food preservation. Canning jars or plastic freezer jars work fine for any of these recipes. You can find them at the supermarket, large discount retailers, or even your local hardware store.

Take advantage of fruit at its peak to prepare these jams for enjoying at home and gift giving year-round. If you happen to miss your favorite fresh fruit in season, we've tested a version using frozen fruit with the same highly rated results.

Double Berry Freezer Jam

freezeable • make ahead

PREP: 10 MIN., STAND: 20 MIN.

Other seasonal berries may be substituted.

4 cups fresh whole blueberries
3 cups fresh strawberries
1½ cups sugar
1 (1.59-oz.) envelope freezer jam pectin

1. Pulse blueberries in a food processor 2 to 4 times or until finely chopped, stopping to scrape down sides. Place in a medium bowl. Pulse strawberries in food processor 8 to 10 times or until finely chopped, stopping to scrape down sides. Add to blueberries in bowl. Stir in sugar, and let stand 15 minutes.
2. Gradually stir in pectin. Stir for 3 minutes; let stand 5 minutes.
3. Spoon mixture into sterilized canning jars, filling to ½ inch from top; wipe jar rims clean. Cover with metal lids, and screw on bands. Place in freezer. **Makes** about 5 cups.

New plastic jars made for food preservation are foolproof for freezer jellies and jams.

Frozen Strawberry Freezer Jam

freezeable • make ahead

PREP: 15 MIN., CHILL: 4 HR., STAND: 45 MIN.

Check the jam pectin envelope for more information on using frozen fruits.

6 cups frozen strawberries
1½ cups sugar
1 (1.59-oz.) envelope freezer jam pectin

1. Place frozen strawberries in refrigerator 4 hours or until partially thawed. (Some ice crystals should be visible.)
2. Pulse strawberries in a food processor 8 to 12 times or until slightly chunky, stopping to scrape down sides. Place mixture in a medium bowl; stir in sugar, and let stand 15 minutes.
3. Gradually stir in pectin. Stir for 3 minutes, and let stand 30 minutes.
4. Spoon fruit mixture into 1-cup plastic freezer jars, filling to fill line (about ¾ inch from top); wipe jar rims clean. Twist on lids, and place in refrigerator or freezer. **Makes** about 5 cups.

Note: For testing purposes only, we used Ball Freezer Jars.

Jammin' Tip

For testing purposes only, we used Ball Fruit Jell Freezer Jam Pectin in each of these recipes.

Granny Smith Apple Freezer Jam

freezeable • make ahead

PREP: 15 MIN., STAND: 20 MIN.

Pair this jam with some peanut butter for a mighty fine sandwich.

5 cups coarsely chopped, unpeeled Granny Smith apples (about 5 medium apples or 1½ lb.)
1 cup sugar
½ cup pasteurized apple juice
1 (1.59-oz.) envelope freezer jam pectin

1. Pulse chopped apples in food processor 10 times or until finely chopped. Place in a medium bowl. Stir in sugar and juice; let stand 15 minutes.
2. Gradually stir in pectin. Stir for 3 minutes; let stand 5 minutes.
3. Spoon fruit mixture into sterilized canning jars, filling to ½ inch from top; wipe jar rims clean. Cover with metal lids, and screw on bands. Place in freezer. **Makes** about 3½ cups.

Pomegranate Freezer Jelly

freezeable • make ahead

PREP: 10 MIN., STAND: 20 MIN.

When making jelly using only juice, the pectin must be doubled. This recipe requires two packages of pectin, while the others only need one.

3 cups pomegranate juice
1½ cups sugar
2 (1.59-oz.) envelopes freezer jam pectin

1. Stir together pomegranate juice and sugar in a medium bowl; let stand 15 minutes.
2. Gradually stir in pectin. Stir for 3 minutes; let stand 5 minutes.
3. Spoon juice mixture into sterilized canning jars, filling to ½ inch from top; wipe jar rims clean. Cover with metal lids, and screw on bands. Place in freezer. **Makes** about 4 cups.

Note: For testing purposes only, we used refrigerated POM Wonderful Pomegranate Juice.

Jazzy Thirst Quenchers

Turn everyday sippers into something impressive.

Give flair to a tall glass of lemonade or iced tea with our host of easy ideas. Citrus fruit ice cubes or flavored syrup are just a couple of quick ways to give one of these drinks a special twist.

Lime Ice Cubes
freezeable • make ahead
PREP: 10 MIN., FREEZE: 8 HR.
We tested this recipe with limes and lemons. You may substitute an equal amount of lemons and lemon juice.

2 medium limes
1 qt. cold water
¼ cup fresh lime juice

1. Cut each lime into ¼-inch-thick slices; cut each slice into 4 wedges.
2. Stir together 1 qt. cold water and ¼ cup lime juice. Fill each compartment of 3 ice cube trays evenly with lime juice mixture. Place 1 lime wedge in each ice cube compartment. Freeze 8 hours or until firm. **Makes** 42 ice cubes.

Very Refreshing Iced Tea
fast fixin's
PREP: 5 MIN., COOK: 5 MIN., STEEP: 5 MIN.
To make this version sweet, stir ¼ to ½ cup sugar into the hot tea, stirring until dissolved. This recipe is unsweetened so you can try our delicious herb-flavored syrups and sweeten to your taste.

2 family-size tea bags
Ice cubes
Garnish: halved lemon and lime slices

1. Bring 3 cups water to a boil in a medium saucepan; add 2 family-size tea bags, and remove mixture from heat. Steep 5 minutes. Remove and discard tea bags.
2. Pour tea into a ½-gal. heatproof container, and add ice cubes to fill; stir. Serve over additional ice, and garnish, if desired. **Makes** 2 qt.

PRISCILLA KENDRICK
HENDERSONVILLE, NORTH CAROLINA

Lemonade
fast fixin's
PREP: 10 MIN., COOK: 5 MIN.
Use one cup of sugar if you plan to serve lemonade with a simple syrup. To extract the most juice from lemons, microwave them at HIGH for about 15 seconds before juicing.

1 to 1½ cups sugar
1 Tbsp. grated lemon rind (about 2 lemons)
1½ cups fresh lemon juice (about 13 lemons)
7 cups ice water

1. Bring ½ cup water to a boil in a medium saucepan. Stir in sugar and grated lemon rind, stirring until sugar is dissolved; remove from heat. Stir in lemon juice and ice water. **Makes** 2½ qt.

Limeade: Substitute 1 Tbsp. grated lime rind for lemon rind and 1½ cups fresh lime juice for lemon juice, and proceed with recipe as directed.

Basil Simple Syrup
fast fixin's • make ahead
PREP: 5 MIN., COOK: 5 MIN., STAND: 30 MIN., CHILL: 4 HR.
Stir two to three Tbsp. of this tasty syrup into Very Refreshing Iced Tea or Lemonade.

1 cup sugar ✱
1 cup loosely packed fresh basil
Garnish: fresh basil sprigs

1. Stir together sugar, basil, and 1 cup water in a medium saucepan over medium-high heat. Bring to a boil, stirring occasionally, and boil 1 minute or until sugar is dissolved. Remove from heat, and let stand 30 minutes. Pour liquid through a wire-mesh strainer into a cruet or airtight container, discarding basil. Cover and chill 4 hours. Garnish, if desired. Syrup may be stored in refrigerator up to 1 month. **Makes** about 1½ cups.

✱Substitute ¾ cup sugar/no-calorie sweetener, if desired. For testing purposes only, we used Splenda Sugar Blend for Baking.

Lemon Balm Simple Syrup: Substitute 1 cup loosely packed fresh lemon balm leaves for fresh basil. Prepare recipe as directed. Garnish with fresh lemon balm leaves, if desired.

Mint Simple Syrup: Substitute 1 cup loosely packed fresh mint leaves for fresh basil. Prepare recipe as directed. Garnish with fresh mint leaves, if desired.

Rosemary Simple Syrup: Substitute 4 fresh rosemary sprigs for fresh basil. Prepare recipe as directed. Garnish with fresh rosemary sprigs, if desired.

Surefire Meal

Serves 4

Garlic Flank Steak

Dill Rice

Grilled Vegetables With Pesto

Creamy Lemonade Pie (page 96)

Here's a budget-friendly menu that you can cook and eat outside. These sizzling recipes take advantage of this month's beautiful grilling weather. Dill Rice is a tasty alternative to potatoes and can be made a day ahead. It is the perfect complement to flavorful Garlic Flank Steak and Grilled Vegetables With Pesto. Savor the evening's end with a piece of Creamy Lemonade Pie.

Garlic Flank Steak
PREP: 10 MIN., CHILL: 3 HR., GRILL: 20 MIN., STAND: 10 MIN.

1 Tbsp. olive or vegetable oil
1 tsp. salt
1 tsp. coarsely ground pepper
3 garlic cloves, pressed
2 lb. flank steak

1. Stir together first 4 ingredients in a small bowl. Rub mixture evenly over flank steak; place steak in a shallow dish. Cover and chill 3 hours.
2. Grill steak, covered with grill lid, over medium-high heat (350° to 400°) 8 to 10 minutes on each side or to desired degree of doneness. Let steak stand 10 minutes before slicing. Cut diagonally across the grain into thin strips. **Makes** 4 servings.

Dill Rice
PREP: 10 MIN., COOK: 20 MIN., COOL: 20 MIN.
Brown rice or orzo are good substitutions for the long-grain rice.

1 cup uncooked long-grain rice
1 (14-oz.) can quartered artichoke hearts, drained
½ cup sliced green onions
3 Tbsp. chopped fresh dill *
1½ tsp. grated lime rind
3 Tbsp. fresh lime juice
2 Tbsp. olive oil
½ tsp. salt
¼ tsp. pepper

1. Cook rice according to package directions; cool 20 minutes.
2. Stir together rice, artichoke hearts, and remaining ingredients. **Makes** 4 servings.

* Substitute 1½ Tbsp. dried dill for fresh, if desired.

Grilled Vegetables With Pesto
fast fixin's
PREP: 15 MIN., GRILL: 6 MIN.

2 medium-size yellow squash
2 medium zucchini
1 medium-size red bell pepper
3 Tbsp. refrigerated pesto
Salt and pepper to taste

1. Cut squash and zucchini lengthwise into ¼ inch-thick slices. Cut bell pepper into ½-inch-thick strips.
2. Grill vegetables, covered with grill lid, over medium-high heat (350° to 400°) 2 to 3 minutes on each side or until tender.
3. Toss hot vegetables with pesto. Sprinkle with salt and pepper to taste, and serve immediately. **Makes** 4 servings.

Note: For testing purposes only, we used Buitoni Pesto With Basil.

from our kitchen

One Great Marinade

This recipe for Orange-Soy-Ginger Marinade tastes wonderful on grilled beef as well as tuna, chicken, and pork. Such a find is too good to keep a secret, so we thought we'd share it with you, along with a recipe for using it on a flank steak.

Very Clean Veggies

You may have noticed that our recipes utilizing bagged salad greens call for them to be "thoroughly washed." We added this phrase to our editing style after outbreaks of E. coli in spinach and salad. While rinsing under running water offers some protection against unsafe bacteria, Test Kitchens Food Scientist Kristi Michele Crowe, PhD, offers some better suggestions.

"Make a solution of 1⅓ cups 3% hydrogen peroxide and 2⅔ cups distilled water, and keep it in a spray bottle in the kitchen," Kristi advises. "Spritz the greens with the solution, rinse with running water, and then spin or pat them dry. Replace the solution once a week. It is an effective, budget-friendly solution to both expensive vegetable cleaners and to bleach, which the processors use."

The peroxide solution works well on other vegetables, too, but Kristi says a good old-fashioned vegetable brush (used only for cleaning produce) and distilled water are good weapons against harmful bacteria.

Orange-Soy-Ginger Marinade
fast fixin's • make ahead
PREP: 15 MIN.

¼ cup soy sauce
¼ cup dry sherry *
¼ cup olive oil
2 Tbsp. grated orange rind
¼ cup fresh orange juice
2 garlic cloves, chopped
1 Tbsp. minced fresh ginger

1. Stir together all ingredients. Use immediately, or cover and chill up to 1 week. **Makes** about 1 cup.

*Substitute ¼ cup orange juice, if desired.

Marinated Flank Steak
family favorite
PREP: 5 MIN., CHILL: 2 HR., COOK: 5 MIN., GRILL: 18 MIN.

2 lb. flank steak
Orange-Soy-Ginger Marinade
2 tsp. brown sugar
Vegetable cooking spray

1. Place flank steak in a shallow dish; pour marinade over steak. Cover and chill at least 2 hours or up to 8 hours. Remove steak from marinade, and pour marinade into a small saucepan. Stir in brown sugar.
2. Bring marinade to a boil over medium-high heat. Reduce heat to medium, and simmer, stirring often, 3 to 4 minutes or until slightly thickened. Remove from heat.
3. Coat cold cooking grate with cooking spray, and place on grill over medium heat (300° to 350°). Place steak on cooking grate, and grill 10 minutes; turn and grill 8 more minutes or to desired degree of doneness. Serve with marinade. **Makes** 4 servings.

Hot Grilling Tips
Whatever you're grilling will taste better and stick less if you cook it on a clean, well-oiled grill grate. Spraying the grate with vegetable cooking spray is a good method—as long as the grill is cold and unlit or you use a special spray made for grilling. Spraying a hot grate over flames is not a smart plan. So if your grill is hot before you remember to lubricate it, try this method: Fold a paper towel or an old, clean dish towel, and moisten it with vegetable oil. Using tongs, rub the oily towel over the hot grill. It works like a charm and prevents possible flare-ups.

For a superclean grill, lay aluminum foil, shiny side down, on the grill rack. Fire up the grill, close the lid, and let the grill burn until the rack is covered with ash. Remove the foil, and brush the rack with a wire grill brush. Then the grate will be ready for oiling and cooking.

june

Sundown in The Delta

Start the weekend with good friends and good eats from Shrimp Shooters to Dixie Caviar.

Easygoing Entertaining Menu

Serves 8

Delta Tamales

Dixie Caviar

Shrimp Shooters

Lemon Squares

Beer, wine, and soft drinks

Hospitality in The Delta is legendary. Jamie and Jenny Smith of Merigold, Mississippi, personalize their entertaining by focusing on the beauty of a summer sunset. The couple's roots go deep into the clay of this area: They are part of the McCarty family, whose pottery is internationally renowned.

At the end of a day spent molding clay, the best elixir for unwinding is to gather with friends. The Smiths' menu showcases regional foods and is stocked with make-ahead recipes. In fact, this easygoing repast needs just a few last-minute touches. Once everyone serves up a plate of tempting favorites, they're ready to toast the gorgeous sun as it slips away over the flat and fertile land.

Delta Tamales
freezeable • make ahead
PREP: 45 MIN.; SOAK: 1 HR.;
COOK: 3 HR., 15 MIN.

We call for using an entire package of corn husks in this recipe because some of them will be torn or split; use the larger whole ones. Tamales can be assembled a day ahead and refrigerated until you're ready to cook them.

1 (6-oz.) package dried corn husks
Cornmeal Dough
Meat Filling
2 (15-oz.) cans tomato sauce
2 tsp. chili powder
2 tsp. ground cumin
Toppings: diced red onion, sliced
   jalapeño peppers

1. Soak corn husks in hot water 1 hour or until softened. Drain husks, and pat dry.
2. Spread 3 Tbsp. Cornmeal Dough into a 3- x 3½-inch rectangle in center of 1 husk. Spoon 1 heaping Tbsp. Meat Filling down center of Cornmeal Dough rectangle.
3. Fold long sides of husk over, enclosing filling completely with Cornmeal Dough; fold bottom of husk over folded sides (leave top end open). Repeat procedure using remaining husks, Cornmeal Dough, and Meat Filling.
4. Place a 1-cup ovenproof glass measuring cup upside down in center of a Dutch oven. Stir together tomato sauce, chili powder, cumin, and 4 cups water. Pour tomato sauce mixture around measuring cup in Dutch oven.
5. Stand tamales, open end up, around measuring cup. Bring to a boil over medium-high heat. Cover, reduce heat to low, and simmer 3 hours. Using tongs, remove tamales to a serving plate. Remove measuring cup. Cook tomato mixture over medium-high heat 10 minutes or until thickened. Serve tamales with sauce and desired toppings. **Makes** about 24 tamales.

Note: After cooking, the tamales with the sauce can be frozen up to 1 month. Thaw overnight in refrigerator. Microwave thawed tamales in sauce in a single layer at HIGH in 45-second intervals until hot.

Cornmeal Dough:
fast fixin's
PREP: 10 MIN.

1¼ cups shortening
4 cups instant corn masa mix or yellow
   cornmeal
1¾ cups warm chicken broth
1 Tbsp. salt
2 tsp. paprika

1. Beat shortening at medium speed with an electric mixer 2 to 3 minutes or until creamy.
2. Stir together corn masa mix and next 3 ingredients in a medium bowl until well blended. Gradually add corn masa mixture to shortening, beating at medium speed just until blended after each addition. Cover dough with plastic wrap until ready to use. **Makes** 4½ cups.

Meat Filling:
fast fixin's
PREP: 10 MIN.

1 (17-oz.) package fully cooked pork roast au jus
1 (10-oz.) can mild diced tomatoes and green chiles, drained
¾ cup barbecue sauce
1 tsp. garlic powder
1 tsp. onion powder
1 tsp. chili powder
½ tsp. ground red pepper
¼ tsp. salt

1. Rinse and drain au jus from pork roast. Shred and chop pork.
2. Stir together pork and remaining ingredients until blended. **Makes** about 2 cups.

Dixie Caviar
make ahead
PREP: 15 MIN., CHILL: 24 HR.

2 (15.8-oz.) cans black-eyed peas, rinsed and drained
2 cups frozen whole kernel corn
2 medium tomatoes, finely chopped
1 medium-size green bell pepper, finely chopped
1 small sweet onion, finely chopped
4 green onions, sliced
1 to 2 jalapeño peppers, seeded and minced
1 to 2 garlic cloves, minced
1 cup Italian dressing
¼ cup chopped fresh cilantro
½ cup sour cream
Tortilla chips
Garnish: cilantro sprig

1. Combine first 9 ingredients in a large zip-top plastic freezer bag. Seal and chill 24 hours; drain.
2. Spoon mixture into a serving bowl. Stir in cilantro, and top with sour cream. Serve with tortilla chips. Garnish, if desired. **Makes** 6 cups.

CAMILLE WARLICK
MERIGOLD, MISSISSIPPI

Shrimp Shooters
chef recipe • make ahead
PREP: 15 MIN., CHILL: 8 HR.
This refreshing appetizer, inspired by a recipe from chef Robert St. John's book A Southern Palate *(Purple Parrot Co., Inc., 2002), showcases Gulf Coast shrimp. Offer this dish in juice or cocktail glasses to give the Gulf Coast favorite a fresh look. Place glasses inside a serving dish filled with ice to keep everything cool.*

⅔ cup olive oil
½ cup white balsamic vinegar
1 Tbsp. chopped fresh cilantro
2 Tbsp. grated lemon rind
1 tsp. salt
1 tsp. freshly ground pepper
1 tsp. hot sauce
1½ lb. peeled, large cooked shrimp
Romaine lettuce heart leaves

1. Whisk together first 7 ingredients in a large bowl.
2. Place cooked shrimp and vinaigrette mixture in a large zip-top plastic freezer bag. Seal and chill at least 8 hours or up to 24 hours, turning bag occasionally.
3. Arrange lettuce leaves in 8 (6- to 8-oz.) glasses. Spoon shrimp mixture evenly into glasses. **Makes** 8 servings.

Note: Vinaigrette may be prepared ahead and stored in an airtight container in the refrigerator up to 1 week. Let vinaigrette come to room temperature, and whisk before adding cooked shrimp.

Lemon Squares
make ahead
PREP: 20 MIN., BAKE: 40 MIN., COOL: 2 HR.
Whipped cream and crushed lemon drops update this sweet-tart dessert.

2¼ cups all-purpose flour, divided
½ cup powdered sugar
¾ cup chilled butter, cut into pieces
4 large eggs
1½ cups granulated sugar
2 Tbsp. grated lemon rind (about 5 lemons)
½ cup fresh lemon juice (about 6 lemons)
1 tsp. baking powder
¼ tsp. salt
Garnishes: whipped cream, crushed lemon drop candies

1. Pulse 2 cups flour, ½ cup powdered sugar, and ¾ cup butter in a food processor 6 times or until mixture is crumbly. Press mixture into a lightly greased 13- x 9-inch pan.
2. Bake at 350° for 15 to 20 minutes or until lightly golden.
3. Whisk together eggs and next 3 ingredients. Combine baking powder, salt, and remaining ¼ cup flour; whisk into egg mixture. Pour batter into prepared crust.
4. Bake at 350° for 20 minutes or until set. Cool lemon squares on a wire rack 2 hours or until completely cool. Cut into squares. Garnish, if desired. **Makes** 24 squares.

JAMIE SMITH
MERIGOLD, MISSISSIPPI

Favorites for the Grill

Our resident foodies raided their recipe boxes to share their top picks with you. Get the fire started!

Steak Dinner

Serves 4

Strip Steak With Rosemary Butter

Steak Fries

Grilled Okra and Tomatoes

Cucumber Salad

Cream-Filled Grilled Pound Cake

Serve sizzling steaks, vegetables, and even dessert in short order with these favorite recipes from the Foods staff. First, make Associate Foods Editor Charla Draper's Cucumber Salad and Assistant Foods Editor Natalie Brown's Rosemary Butter a day ahead. Then one hour before dinner, rub steaks and assemble pound cake sandwiches.

Most of us prefer the flavor a charcoal fire delivers, but we're also spoiled by the speed of gas. The choice is up to you. On most grills, you can place the small okra and tomatoes directly on the rack. If the spaces between the grates are too wide, use a grill basket or wok. (If you don't have a basket or wok, it's no problem. Just place a wire rack across the cooking grate to keep small items from falling through.)

Kids will love the flavor of Senior Writer Andrea Scott Hurst's Steak Fries, and the whole family will thank you for Associate Foods Editor Mary Allen Perry's Cream-Filled Grilled Pound Cake.

Strip Steak With Rosemary Butter

PREP: 15 MIN., CHILL: 1 HR., GRILL: 8 MIN. *(Pictured on page 179)*

½ cup butter, softened
1 Tbsp. fresh rosemary
2 tsp. grated lemon rind, divided
Salt and pepper to taste
1 Tbsp. dried Italian seasoning
1½ Tbsp. olive oil
2 garlic cloves, minced
1 tsp. pepper
½ tsp. salt
4 (6-oz.) beef strip steaks (½ inch thick)

1. Stir together butter, rosemary, 1 tsp. grated lemon rind, and salt and pepper to taste. Cover and chill until ready to serve.
2. Combine Italian seasoning and next 4 ingredients in a small bowl. Stir in remaining 1 tsp. lemon rind. Rub mixture over steaks. Cover and chill 1 hour.
3. Grill steaks, covered with grill lid, over medium-high heat (350° to 400°) 3 to 4 minutes on each side or to desired degree of doneness. Serve with butter. **Makes** 4 servings.

Steak Fries

PREP: 5 MIN., GRILL: 12 MIN. *(Pictured on page 179)*

1 (28-oz.) bag frozen steak fries
Salt and pepper to taste

1. Grill steak fries, covered with grill lid, over medium-high heat (350° to 400°) 4 to 6 minutes on each side or until browned and crisp. Sprinkle grilled steak fries evenly with salt and pepper to taste. **Makes** 4 servings.

Grilled Okra and Tomatoes
fast fixin's
PREP: 10 MIN., GRILL: 6 MIN. *(Pictured on page 179)*

1 lb. fresh okra, trimmed
1 pt. cherry tomatoes
2 Tbsp. olive oil
½ tsp. salt
½ tsp. pepper
2 Tbsp. chopped fresh basil

1. Combine first 5 ingredients in a large bowl.
2. Place mixture on cooking grate, and grill, covered with grill lid, over medium-high heat (350° to 400°). Grill tomatoes 3 minutes or just until they begin to pop. Turn okra, and grill, covered with grill lid, 2 to 3 more minutes or until tender.
3. Transfer okra and tomatoes to a serving dish, and sprinkle with basil. Serve immediately. **Makes** 4 servings.

Cucumber Salad
make ahead
PREP: 15 MIN., STAND: 2 HR., COOK: 3 MIN., CHILL: 2 HR. *(Pictured on page 179)*

3 large seedless cucumbers, thinly sliced
2 celery ribs, thinly sliced
1 small green bell pepper, thinly sliced
1 small red bell pepper, thinly sliced
1 large red onion, thinly sliced
1½ Tbsp. salt
1 cup sugar
1 cup white vinegar
1 tsp. celery seeds
½ tsp. mustard seeds

1. Combine first 6 ingredients in a large glass bowl; let stand at room temperature, stirring occasionally, 1 hour. Drain.
2. Bring sugar and next 3 ingredients to a boil in a medium saucepan over medium-high heat. Boil, stirring constantly, 1 minute or until sugar dissolves. Let stand 1 hour. Pour over vegetables. Cover and chill 2 hours. **Makes** 12 servings.

Cream-Filled Grilled Pound Cake
family favorite • fast fixin's
PREP: 5 MIN., GRILL: 6 MIN.
We didn't think pound cake could get any better until Mary Allen suggested we grill it. Choose homemade, frozen, or fresh store-bought cake. (Pictured on page 178)

4 Tbsp. pineapple cream cheese
8 (½-inch-thick) slices pound cake
Sweetened whipped cream
Fresh strawberries and blueberries

1. Spread pineapple cream cheese evenly over 1 side of 4 pound cake slices. Top with remaining 4 pound cake slices.
2. Grill, covered with grill lid, over medium-high heat (350° to 400°) 2 to 3 minutes on each side. Remove from heat. Top with whipped cream and berries. Serve immediately. **Makes** 4 servings.

Keep the Grill Ready

A clean grill invites spur-of-the-moment use. We suggest you clean it immediately after each use. It's a lot easier task at this point and requires less elbow grease to get the job done.
■ Remove racks from grill, and scrape off stuck-on particles using a stiff grill brush or scouring pad. Racks may still be slightly warm.
■ Clean racks with hot soapy water; rinse and dry thoroughly.
■ Coat racks with vegetable cooking spray or oil.
■ Clean out firebox.
■ Replace racks; cover with grill lid.

Creative Chicken Salads

A make-ahead recipe for great chicken salad is perfect for a refreshing luncheon entrée or a crowd-pleasing appetizer.

Produce markets are loaded with fresh ways to garnish these creations. And you don't need fancy serving pieces. Clear glass bowls, platters, and cake stands shine when paired with colorful fruits or table linens.

Cream cheese helps Cha-Cha Chicken Salad hold its shape overnight. However, when you're short on time, almost any chicken salad that is tightly bound with mayonnaise can be placed on a platter and decoratively shaped by smoothing the top and sides with a cake-frosting spatula.

Cha-Cha Chicken Salad
make ahead
PREP: 20 MIN., CHILL: 8 HR. *(Pictured on page 176)*

1 (8-oz.) package cream cheese, softened
1 cup mayonnaise
2 tsp. curry powder
1 tsp. salt
6 cups chopped cooked chicken
1 (8-oz.) can crushed pineapple
⅔ cup orange-flavored sweetened dried cranberries
1 cup chopped roasted, salted almonds
Garnishes: fresh herbs, blackberries, raspberries, sliced peaches

1. Whisk together first 4 ingredients in a large bowl; stir in chicken, pineapple, and cranberries just until blended.
2. If desired, spoon mixture into a plastic wrap-lined 8-inch round cake pan; cover and chill at least 8 hours or up to 24 hours. Invert chicken salad onto a cake stand, and remove plastic wrap. Gently press chopped almonds onto sides of chicken salad. Garnish, if desired. **Makes** 6 to 8 servings.

PATRICIA GREENE
MURFREESBORO, TENNESSEE

Lemon-Tarragon Chicken Salad
make ahead
PREP: 20 MIN., BAKE: 7 MIN., COOL: 15 MIN.
When fresh tarragon isn't available, substitute 1½ tsp. dried crushed tarragon.

½ cup chopped pecans
¾ cup mayonnaise
1 Tbsp. chopped fresh tarragon
1 tsp. grated lemon rind
1 Tbsp. fresh lemon juice
1 tsp. salt
½ tsp. freshly ground pepper
3 cups chopped cooked chicken
2 celery ribs, finely chopped
½ small sweet onion, finely chopped
2 cups seedless red grapes, cut in half (optional)
Garnish: halved lemon slices

1. Arrange pecans in a single layer on a baking sheet.
2. Bake at 350° for 5 to 7 minutes or until lightly toasted. Cool pecans on a wire rack 15 minutes or until completely cool.
3. Whisk together mayonnaise and next 5 ingredients in a large bowl; stir in pecans, chicken, celery, and onion just until blended. Stir in grape halves, if desired. Garnish, if desired. **Makes** 4 to 6 servings.

NANCY MARSH
GEORGETOWN, TEXAS

Curried Chicken Salad
fast fixin's • make ahead
PREP: 15 MIN.

½ cup mayonnaise
¼ cup orange marmalade
1 Tbsp. fresh lemon juice
1 tsp. curry powder
¼ tsp. salt
¼ tsp. pepper
3 cups chopped cooked chicken
3 green onions, finely chopped

1. Whisk together first 6 ingredients in a medium bowl; stir in chopped chicken and green onions just until blended. **Makes** 4 servings.

APRIL WILLIAMS
WINTER PARK, FLORIDA

taste of the south
Divine, Fluffy Biscuits

Here's your chance to make melt-in-your-mouth biscuits from scratch that are worth every bite. Experienced cooks may be surprised by this unique recipe. We went against the norm of handling the dough with kid gloves and actually kneaded it 20 to 25 times. Plus, we cranked up the oven to 500°, instead of the usual 375° to 425° range, to bake them. Get the perfect texture for these biscuits by taking time to cut shortening and butter into the flour mixture until crumbles are evenly sized. See what you think.

Steps to Success

We share all our tricks to making the best biscuits.

1. The dough will be very soft out of the bowl. Generously sprinkle dough and work surface with self-rising flour to get started. Flour your hands too.

2. To knead, fold 1 side of dough over, push away, turn dough, and repeat 20 to 25 times (not minutes). Work in self-rising flour as needed to prevent dough from sticking to countertop or hands.

3. Stop a couple of times during kneading to press the dough with your finger. When it springs back—stop kneading. Use fingers to pat dough into an 8½-inch circle.

4. A bench scraper makes fast work of transferring biscuits to ungreased baking sheets. You can reroll the scraps (foreground) once, and cut 6 additional biscuits. By the way, make sure to cut biscuits straight down. Twisting the cutter will seal the edges of the biscuit, reduce the rise, and cause them to bake lopsided rather than straight and tall. We discovered that cutting biscuits with a glass sealed the edges and reduced the amount of rise as well. (You need both ends of the cutter to be open to allow air to exit as you press down.) Biscuit cutters are sold at grocery stores.

Fluffy Buttermilk Biscuits
family favorite
PREP: 20 MIN., BAKE: 11 MIN.
We preferred this half shortening-half butter combination, but all of one (even margarine) works well too. If using margarine, use the higher fat varieties or ones labeled "for baking." Shake the carton of buttermilk before measuring. (Pictured on page 6)

3½ cups self-rising soft wheat flour
2¼ tsp. baking powder
2¼ tsp. sugar
¼ cup shortening
¼ cup butter, chilled and cut into pieces
1½ cups buttermilk
½ to 1 cup self-rising soft wheat flour
1 Tbsp. butter, melted

1. Combine first 3 ingredients in a bowl until well blended. Cut in shortening and chilled butter with a pastry blender or a fork until crumbly. Add buttermilk, stirring just until dry ingredients are moistened.
2. Turn dough out onto a well-floured surface; sprinkle with ½ cup self-rising flour. Knead 20 to 25 times, adding up to ½ cup additional flour until dough is smooth and springy to touch.
3. Pat dough into a ¾-inch-thick circle (about 8½ inches round). Cut dough with a well-floured 2-inch round cutter, making 12 biscuits. Place on ungreased baking sheets. Knead remaining dough together 3 or 4 times; repeat procedure, making 6 more biscuits. Lightly brush tops with melted butter.
4. Bake at 500° for 9 to 11 minutes or until golden. **Makes** about 18 biscuits.

Note: For testing purposes only, we used White Lily Self-Rising Soft Wheat Flour.

Rosemary Biscuits: Stir 2 to 3 tsp. chopped fresh rosemary into dry ingredients. Proceed as directed.

Parmesan-Pepper Biscuits: Stir ½ cup (2 oz.) grated Parmesan cheese and 2 tsp. coarsely ground pepper into dry ingredients. (Less flour will be required while kneading.) Proceed as directed.

Pack-and-Go Picnic

Food seems to taste better at a picnic. Make our menu, which includes a mega sandwich that feeds four and transports with ease, and fill in with goodies you buy along the way (see our list below).

Laid-Back Menu

Serves 4

Turkey, Bacon, and Havarti Sandwich

Sour Cream Coleslaw

Fresh-Squeezed Lemonade

Turkey, Bacon, and Havarti Sandwich

make ahead

PREP: 20 MIN., CHILL: 1 HR.

Havarti is a semisoft Danish cheese with small irregular holes and a mild flavor; substitute Muenster or Swiss if you can't find Havarti.

1 (7-inch) round sourdough bread loaf
¼ cup balsamic vinaigrette
½ lb. thinly sliced smoked deli turkey
6 (1-oz.) Havarti cheese slices
1 (12-oz.) jar roasted red bell peppers, drained and sliced
4 fully cooked bacon slices

1. Cut top 2 inches off sourdough loaf, reserving top; hollow out loaf, leaving a 1-inch-thick shell. (Reserve center of bread loaf for other uses, if desired.)
2. Drizzle 2 Tbsp. vinaigrette evenly in bottom bread shell; layer with half each of turkey, cheese, and peppers. Repeat layers with remaining turkey, cheese, and peppers, and top with bacon. Drizzle evenly with remaining 2 Tbsp. vinaigrette, and cover with reserved bread top; press down firmly.
3. Wrap in plastic wrap, and chill at least 1 hour or up to 8 hours before serving. Cut into 4 wedges. **Makes** 4 servings.

Sour Cream Coleslaw

make ahead

PREP: 15 MIN., CHILL: 2 HR.

1 (8-oz.) container sour cream
1 Tbsp. sugar
1 Tbsp. white vinegar
2 tsp. caraway or celery seeds
½ tsp. salt
1 (10-oz.) package finely shredded cabbage
½ cup diced green bell pepper
1½ Tbsp. minced red onion

1. Stir together first 5 ingredients in a large bowl; add shredded cabbage, bell pepper, and onion, tossing well. Cover and chill at least 2 hours or up to 8 hours. Toss coleslaw before serving. **Makes** 11 cups.

Fresh-Squeezed Lemonade

PREP: 20 MIN.

1½ cups sugar
½ cup boiling water
1 Tbsp. grated lemon rind
1½ cups fresh lemon juice (8 large lemons)

1. Stir together 1½ cups sugar and ½ cup boiling water until sugar is dissolved. Stir in lemon rind, lemon juice, and 5 cups water. Cover and chill. Serve over ice. **Makes** 8 cups.

Pick Ups

Here's what you may want to buy on the way to your picnic spot.
- fried chicken
- barbecue
- fresh salsa and chips
- hummus or spinach dip
- cut raw vegetables
- chicken salad
- pimiento cheese
- brownies or cookies

Serve the food on brightly colored paper and plastic products, which are pretty, sturdy, and inexpensive. You can even find plastic flatware that looks just like stainless.

Shrimp in a Snap

Serve the South's favorite seafood in record time with these highly rated recipes. They are simple enough for weeknights and scrumptious enough for guests. If fresh shrimp are not available, don't hesitate to use frozen. We tested these dishes both ways with great results.

Cajun Sautéed Shrimp

PREP: 20 MIN., COOK: 12 MIN.

Reader Richard Galloway serves this over toasted garlic bread slices with a tossed green salad for a relaxed supper. If six servings are too many for your family, dish up leftovers over plain grits.

2 lb. unpeeled, large raw shrimp*****
2 Tbsp. butter
½ sweet onion, diced
1 Tbsp. chopped fresh or 1 tsp. dried basil
1 Tbsp. chopped fresh or 1 tsp. dried oregano
1 bay leaf
½ tsp. salt
¼ to ½ tsp. ground red pepper
1 garlic clove, chopped

1. Peel shrimp, and, if desired, devein.
2. Melt butter in a large skillet over medium-high heat; add onion and next 5 ingredients, and sauté 5 minutes or until onion is tender. Stir in garlic, and sauté 1 more minute.
3. Stir in shrimp, and cook, stirring occasionally, 6 minutes or just until shrimp turn pink. Remove and discard bay leaf. **Makes** 6 servings.

*Substitute 2 lb. frozen peeled, large raw shrimp, thawed according to package directions, if desired.

RICHARD GALLOWAY
POPLARVILLE, MISSISSIPPI

Beach Shrimp

PREP: 10 MIN., BAKE: 25 MIN.

Serve with toasty French bread to sop up the sauce. To bake this when you are on vacation at the beach, purchase a large disposable roasting pan for easy cleanup.

3 lb. unpeeled, large raw shrimp*
1 (16-oz.) bottle Italian dressing
1½ Tbsp. freshly ground pepper
2 garlic cloves, pressed
2 lemons, halved
¼ cup chopped fresh parsley
½ cup butter, cut up

1. Place first 4 ingredients in a 13- x 9-inch baking dish, tossing to coat. Squeeze juice from lemons over shrimp mixture, and stir. Add lemon halves to baking dish. Sprinkle with parsley; dot with butter.
2. Bake at 375° for 25 minutes, stirring after 15 minutes. Serve in baking dish. **Makes** 6 to 8 servings.

*Substitute 3 lb. frozen peeled, large raw shrimp, thawed according to package directions, if desired. Prepare recipe as directed, reducing pepper to ½ tsp.

DEBBIE CANTIENY
MOUNTAIN BROOK, ALABAMA

Seafood Facts

■ Shrimp is the most popular seafood in the United States. Southerners consume about 50% of the total 200 million lb. of fresh shrimp harvested from our Atlantic and Gulf coastal waters each year.
■ Most shrimp are flash frozen right on the boats, so unless you're on the coast, fresh shrimp sold in grocery stores are usually "previously frozen." They should be labeled as such. Don't be afraid to ask.
■ Mandatory country of origin labeling laws for seafood went into effect in 2004 for seafood markets, grocery stores, and restaurants. Ask if you don't see the information listed and want to know.
■ The "count" is the number of shrimp per lb. This can vary somewhat, but these are the approximate numbers: large—20 to 30; medium—30 to 40.

what's for supper?
An All-star Combo

Meal With Pizzazz

Serves 4

Peanut-Baked Chicken

Sesame-Ginger Rice

Steamed broccoli

Orange sherbet

For a change of pace from frying, try crunchy Peanut-Baked Chicken. Marinate the chicken while you make the toasted peanut coating. Once the chicken is in the oven, you can focus on the rest of the menu.

Peanut-Baked Chicken

freezeable • make ahead

PREP: 15 MIN., CHILL: 30 MIN., BAKE: 35 MIN.

4 chicken legs (about 1½ lb.)
4 chicken thighs (about 1 lb.)
½ cup creamy peanut butter
2 Tbsp. lite soy sauce
2 Tbsp. honey
1 Tbsp. grated lemon rind
1 Tbsp. fresh lemon juice
½ cup honey-roasted peanuts
½ cup fine, dry breadcrumbs
2 garlic cloves, minced
1 tsp. salt
¼ tsp. ground red pepper

1. Place chicken legs and thighs in a gallon-size zip-top plastic freezer bag.
2. Microwave peanut butter and next 4 ingredients in a microwave-safe bowl at HIGH 1 to 2 minutes, stirring until smooth. (Mixture will appear broken at first.) Spoon mixture over chicken in bag, and seal. Using hands, work peanut butter mixture onto chicken until evenly coated. Chill 30 minutes, turning occasionally. Remove chicken from peanut butter mixture, discarding mixture.

3. Process peanuts and next 4 ingredients in a food processor until peanuts are finely ground. Place crumbs in a large zip-top plastic freezer bag, and add chicken; seal. Shake to coat. Place chicken on a lightly greased wire rack in an aluminum foil-lined broiler pan.
4. Bake at 375° for 35 minutes or until a meat thermometer inserted in thickest portion of thigh registers 170°. **Makes** 4 servings.

Note: Baked chicken may be frozen in a zip-top plastic freezer bag up to 3 months. Let thaw in refrigerator overnight. To reheat, place chicken on a wire rack in an aluminum foil-lined broiler pan. Bake at 375° for 15 to 20 minutes or until thoroughly heated.

Sesame-Ginger Rice

PREP: 15 MIN., COOK: 30 MIN.

2 Tbsp. butter
1 cup uncooked long-grain rice
1 tsp. sesame seeds
2 cups chicken broth
½ tsp. salt
½ tsp. ground ginger
¼ tsp. ground pepper
2 Tbsp. chopped fresh parsley*
Garnish: fresh lime wedges

1. Melt butter in a 3½-qt. saucepan over medium-high heat. Stir in rice, and sauté 2 minutes or until rice turns opaque. Stir in sesame seeds. Add chicken broth and next 3 ingredients; bring to a boil.
2. Cover, reduce heat to low, and cook mixture 20 to 25 minutes or until liquid is absorbed and rice is tender; fluff with a fork. Stir in 2 Tbsp. chopped parsley. Garnish, if desired. **Makes** 4 servings.

ELENA COLEMAN
ORANGE PARK, FLORIDA

Note: To make rice in the oven instead of on the cooktop, prepare recipe as directed through Step 1, using an oven-proof saucepan. Bake, covered, at 350° for 20 to 25 minutes or until liquid is absorbed and rice is tender. Proceed with recipe as directed.

*Substitute 2 Tbsp. chopped fresh cilantro, if desired.

Let's Have a Party

Celebrate a wedding, anniversary, or birthday with make-ahead recipes.

Hosting a brunch is always fun, and this midmorning meal continues to be a favorite among Southerners. Most of the recipes can be prepared in advance.

Blushing Mimosas

fast fixin's
PREP: 5 MIN.
The classic mimosa is equal parts orange juice and Champagne. In this recipe, pineapple juice and grenadine add a twist of flavor and color.

2 cups orange juice (not from concentrate)
1 cup pineapple juice, chilled
2 Tbsp. grenadine
1 (750-milliliter) bottle Champagne or sparkling wine, chilled *

1. Stir together first 3 ingredients.
2. Pour equal parts orange juice mixture and Champagne into Champagne flutes. **Makes** 6 cups.

MELANIE BACON
SHREVEPORT, LOUISIANA

Note: For testing purposes only, we used Simply Orange 100% Orange Juice.

*Substitute 2 (12-oz.) cans ginger ale or lemon-lime soda, if desired.

Brie-and-Veggie Breakfast Strata

make ahead • vegetarian
PREP: 30 MIN., COOK: 12 MIN., CHILL: 8 HR., BAKE: 50 MIN.

1 large sweet onion, halved and thinly sliced
1 large red bell pepper, diced
1 large Yukon gold potato, peeled and diced
2 Tbsp. olive oil
1 (8-oz.) Brie round *
1 (12-oz.) package sourdough bread loaf, cubed
1 cup (4 oz.) shredded Parmesan cheese
8 large eggs
3 cups milk
2 Tbsp. Dijon mustard
1 tsp. seasoned salt
1 tsp. pepper

1. Sauté first 3 ingredients in hot oil 10 to 12 minutes or just until vegetables are tender and onion slices begin to turn golden.
2. Trim and discard rind from Brie. Cut cheese into ½-inch cubes.
3. Layer a lightly greased 13- x 9-inch baking dish with half each of bread cubes, onion mixture, Brie cubes, and Parmesan cheese.
4. Whisk together eggs and next 4 ingredients; pour half of egg mixture over cheeses. Repeat layers once. Cover and chill at least 8 hours or up to 24 hours.
5. Bake at 350° for 45 to 50 minutes or until lightly browned on top and set in center. **Makes** 8 to 10 servings.

DEBBIE TYE
MEQUON, WISCONSIN

*Substitute 2 cups (8 oz.) shredded Swiss cheese, if desired.

Sweet 'n' Spicy Sausage

PREP: 15 MIN., COOK: 30 MIN.

2 (12-oz.) packages pork sausage links
1 (10.5-oz.) jar hot pepper jelly

1. Cook sausage, in 2 batches, in a large skillet according to package directions. Drain on paper towels.
2. Wipe skillet clean; spoon pepper jelly into skillet, and cook, stirring often, 3 to 4 minutes or until melted and smooth. Return sausage to skillet; cook, gently stirring, 2 to 3 minutes or until sausage is thoroughly heated and coated. **Makes** 8 to 10 servings.

Note: For testing purposes only, we used Braswell's Hot Pepper Jelly.

Minted Mixed Fruit

make ahead
PREP: 15 MIN., CHILL: 2 HR.

1 qt. strawberries, halved (about 3 cups)
3 cups fresh pineapple chunks
4 kiwifruit, peeled and sliced
1 cup sugar
½ cup pineapple juice
½ cup ginger ale
¼ cup chopped fresh mint

1. Place fruit in a shallow serving bowl. Whisk together sugar, juice, and ginger ale until sugar is dissolved; gently stir in mint, and pour over fruit. Cover and chill 2 hours before serving. **Makes** 8 to 10 servings.

Heart-Shaped Cookies
freezeable • make ahead
PREP: 30 MIN., CHILL: 2 HR.,
BAKE: 9 MIN. PER BATCH, COOL: 22 MIN.

½ cup butter, softened
¼ cup shortening
1¼ cups sugar
2 large eggs
⅓ cup milk
3 cups all-purpose flour
1 tsp. baking powder
½ tsp. baking soda
½ tsp. salt
1 tsp. grated lemon rind
2 tsp. fresh lemon juice
Icing
Green and orange liquid food
    colorings

1. Beat butter and shortening at medium speed with an electric mixer until creamy. Gradually add sugar, beating well. Add eggs and milk, beating until blended.
2. Combine flour and next 3 ingredients. Add to butter mixture, beating at low speed just until blended; stir in lemon rind and juice. Divide dough into 4 equal portions; wrap each in plastic wrap, and chill at least 2 hours or up to 6 hours.
3. Roll 1 dough portion to a ¼-inch thickness on a lightly floured surface. Cut with a 3-inch heart-shaped cookie cutter, and place on lightly greased baking sheets. Repeat procedure with remaining dough portions.
4. Bake at 350° for 8 to 9 minutes or until lightly browned on bottoms. Let cool on baking sheets 2 minutes; remove to wire racks, and cool 20 minutes or until completely cool.
5. Remove and reserve about ¼ cup Icing. Tint remaining Icing with green food coloring. Spread green-tinted icing on tops of cookies. Tint reserved ¼ cup Icing with orange food coloring, and spoon into a zip-top plastic bag. Snip 1 corner to make a small hole; pipe dots on cookies. **Makes** 4½ dozen.

Note: To make ahead, bake and cool cookies as directed. Do not frost. Place in airtight containers, and freeze up to 1 month. Thaw and frost as directed.

Icing:
fast fixin's
PREP: 10 MIN.
To keep the icing soft, cover the bowl with a damp paper towel.

2 cups powdered sugar
¼ cup butter, softened
6 to 8 tsp. fresh lemon juice

1. Beat together powdered sugar, butter, and 6 tsp. lemon juice at medium speed with an electric mixer 1 to 2 minutes or until spreading consistency, adding up to 2 tsp. lemon juice, ½ tsp. at a time, if necessary. **Makes** 1 cup.

ELVIRA SCHNEIDER
NEW BRAUNFELS, TEXAS

Last-Minute Pizza

You don't need a lot of fancy ingredients—or time—to serve homemade pizza. Follow the lead of Test Kitchens Professional Marian Cooper Cairns' fun combinations to get you started, or use whatever you have to create a one-of-a-kind specialty.

Greek Pizza
fast fixin's
PREP: 15 MIN., BAKE: 14 MIN.

1 (12-inch) prebaked pizza crust
1 cup deli hummus
1 cup grape tomatoes, halved
½ cup pitted kalamata olives, coarsely chopped
½ small green bell pepper, thinly sliced
½ cup chopped red onion
¾ cup crumbled feta cheese
2 Tbsp. olive oil (optional)

1. Spread crust with hummus. Arrange grape tomatoes and next 3 ingredients over pizza. Sprinkle with feta cheese.
2. Bake at 450° for 12 to 14 minutes or until cheese is lightly browned. Drizzle with olive oil, if desired. **Makes** 4 servings.

Antipasto Pizza
fast fixin's
PREP: 10 MIN., BAKE: 14 MIN.
Roasted or marinated vegetables, such as red bell peppers, assorted olives, or pickled okra, would also taste great on this zesty pie.

1 (12-inch) prebaked pizza crust
¼ cup refrigerated pesto
¾ cup chopped artichoke hearts
½ cup diced salami or deli ham
¼ cup sliced banana peppers
¼ cup sliced black olives
¼ cup sun-dried tomatoes in oil, drained and chopped
1½ cups shredded mozzarella cheese

1. Spread pizza crust evenly with ¼ cup pesto. Sprinkle evenly with remaining ingredients.
2. Bake at 450° for 12 to 14 minutes or until cheese is melted. **Makes** 4 servings.

Barbecue Pizza
fast fixin's
PREP: 10 MIN., BAKE: 14 MIN.
Chowchow gives this pizza pizzazz. You can substitute a vinegar-based coleslaw.

1 (12-inch) prebaked pizza crust
1 cup chowchow
½ lb. shredded or chopped barbecue pork
1½ cups (6 oz.) shredded Monterey Jack cheese
½ cup warm barbecue sauce

1. Spread crust evenly with chowchow; top with pork and cheese.
2. Bake at 450° for 12 to 14 minutes or until cheese is melted. Drizzle with warm barbecue sauce. **Makes** 4 servings.

Tasty Tips

After the pizza is out of the oven, add a few teaspoons of crushed red pepper flakes, Italian seasoning, grated Parmesan, or hot sauce to taste. Fresh oregano, rosemary, and basil pair well with most any pizza; just be sure to add them right before serving for best flavor and color.

Ultimate Cheese Pizza

family favorite • fast fixin's

PREP: 10 MIN., BAKE: 14 MIN.

Combine any leftover bits of cheese you find in the fridge for this simple pie. To avoid having to get out the cutting board, you can crush whole tomatoes with clean hands instead of chopping them.

1 (14.5-oz.) can whole tomatoes, drained and chopped
1 tsp. bottled minced garlic
1 (12-inch) prebaked pizza crust
2 cups (8 oz.) mixed shredded cheese

1. Stir together tomatoes and garlic. Spread crust evenly with tomato mixture, and sprinkle with cheese.
2. Bake at 450° for 12 to 14 minutes or until cheese is melted. **Makes** 4 servings.

Ultimate Cheeseburger Pizza: Substitute 1½ cups shredded Cheddar cheese for 2 cups mixed shredded cheese. Prepare Ultimate Cheese Pizza as directed, sprinkling 1½ cups cooked and crumbled ground beef (about ½ lb.), ¼ cup chopped green onions, and ½ tsp. salt over tomato mixture. Bake as directed. Serve with pickles, if desired. Prep: 15 min., Bake: 14 min.

Ultimate Veggie Pizza: Prepare Ultimate Cheese Pizza as directed, arranging 2 cups roasted or grilled vegetables over tomato mixture. Bake as directed. Prep: 10 min., Bake: 14 min.

Southwest Pizza

PREP: 10 MIN., BAKE: 14 MIN.

Add a sprinkle of Mexican-style chili powder or ground red pepper before baking for extra flavor. Serve sour cream, guacamole, or Ranch dressing on the side for dipping.

1 (12-inch) prebaked pizza crust
1 cup picante sauce
1 (15-oz.) can seasoned black beans, drained
½ cup canned corn, drained
¼ cup pickled jalapeño peppers (optional)
1½ cups shredded Mexican four-cheese blend*
¼ cup chopped fresh cilantro

1. Spread crust with picante sauce. Sprinkle with beans, corn, and, if desired, jalapeño peppers. Sprinkle with cheese.
2. Bake at 450° for 12 to 14 minutes or until cheese is melted and bubbly. Sprinkle evenly with cilantro. **Makes** 4 servings.

*Substitute 1 (7-oz.) package shredded chipotle Cheddar cheese, if desired.

Bring a Fabulous Dish

We found a couple of great reunion dishes that will have the group clamoring for second and third helpings.

Macaroni-Ham Salad

make ahead

PREP: 20 MIN., CHILL: 2 HR.

3 cups uncooked elbow macaroni
1 cup chopped cooked ham
1 cucumber, peeled, seeded, and diced
1 tomato, seeded and diced
1 small red bell pepper, diced
1 small yellow bell pepper, diced
1 small green bell pepper, diced
1¼ cups mayonnaise
1½ tsp. Cajun seasoning
2 tsp. lemon juice
Salt to taste

1. Prepare macaroni according to package directions. Drain and rinse with cold water until cool.
2. Combine macaroni and next 9 ingredients until blended. Add salt. Cover and chill at least 2 hours. **Makes** 8 to 10 servings.

KEVA COLSTON
BATON ROUGE, LOUISIANA

Spicy Southwestern Deviled Eggs

PREP: 15 MIN., CHILL: 1 HR.

The fresher the eggs, the more difficult they can be to peel. For ease of peeling, buy and refrigerate eggs 7 to 10 days before using. For more tips on hard-cooked eggs, see page 91.

1 dozen large eggs, hard-cooked and peeled
6 Tbsp. mayonnaise
2 to 4 Tbsp. pickled sliced jalapeño peppers, minced
1 Tbsp. yellow mustard
½ tsp. ground cumin
⅛ tsp. salt
Garnish: chopped fresh cilantro

1. Cut eggs in half lengthwise, and carefully remove yolks. Mash yolks; stir in mayonnaise and next 4 ingredients. Spoon or pipe egg yolk mixture into egg halves. Cover and chill at least 1 hour or until ready to serve. Garnish, if desired. **Makes** 2 dozen.

EDIE BULLARD
DETROIT, MICHIGAN

Healthy Living.

Fill your summer days with happy get-togethers and tasty recipes.

Light-and-Flavorful Backyard Feast

Share these good-for-you recipes at your next family gathering.

Take supper outside with a delicious menu that promises great tastes and easy prep for any casual get-together. You won't miss the fat or the calories in these scrumptious recipes.

Summertime Feast

Serves 6

Grilled Pork Tenderloin Sandwiches

Grilled Summer Veggies

Succotash Salad

Fresh Peach-Basil Vinaigrette over tomatoes

Cheesecake Tarts

Grilled Pork Tenderloin Sandwiches
family favorite
PREP: 10 MIN., GRILL: 24 MIN., STAND: 10 MIN.
Add vitamin-rich leafy greens, such as romaine lettuce, Bibb lettuce, or peppery arugula to these great sandwiches.

1 tsp. garlic powder
1 tsp. salt
1 tsp. dry mustard
½ tsp. coarsely ground pepper
2 (¾-lb.) pork tenderloins
Vegetable cooking spray
6 whole wheat hamburger buns
6 Tbsp. Vidalia Onion Barbecue Sauce

1. Stir together first 4 ingredients; rub pork tenderloins evenly with seasoning mixture. Lightly coat pork with vegetable cooking spray.

2. Grill, covered with grill lid, over medium-high heat (350° to 400°) 10 to 12 minutes on each side or until a meat thermometer inserted into thickest portions registers 155°. Remove from grill, and let stand 10 minutes. Chop or slice, and serve on hamburger buns. Drizzle each sandwich with 1 Tbsp. Vidalia Onion Barbecue Sauce. **Makes** 6 servings.
SHARON GRAY
MOUNT JULIET, TENNESSEE

Per serving (including 1 Tbsp. barbecue sauce): Calories 264; Fat 6.4g (sat 1.8g, mono 2.3g, poly 1.3g); Protein 26.6g; Carb 25.5g; Fiber 3.4g; Chol 63mg; Iron 2.4mg; Sodium 743mg; Calc 57mg

Vidalia Onion Barbecue Sauce:
make ahead
PREP: 10 MIN., COOK: 25 MIN.

1 medium-size sweet onion, finely chopped
1 cup ketchup
2 Tbsp. firmly packed brown sugar
2 Tbsp. fresh lemon juice
2 Tbsp. apple cider vinegar
2 Tbsp. Worcestershire sauce
1 Tbsp. olive oil
1 garlic clove, minced
½ tsp. salt
½ tsp. pepper

1. Stir together all ingredients and ½ cup water in a large saucepan; bring to a boil over medium heat. Reduce heat to low, and simmer, stirring occasionally, 20 minutes. **Makes** about 2½ cups.
BETTE BOUCK
MARSHALL, MICHIGAN

Per Tbsp.: Calories 15; Fat 0.4g (sat 0.1g, mono 0.3g, poly 0.1g); Protein 0.2g; Carb 3g; Fiber 0.1g; Chol 0mg; Iron 0.1mg; Sodium 105mg; Calc 4mg

Grilled Summer Veggies
fast fixin's
PREP: 10 MIN., GRILL: 10 MIN.

2 medium-size red bell peppers
3 medium-size yellow squash
3 small zucchini
2 medium-size sweet onions
Vegetable cooking spray
½ tsp. salt
½ tsp. pepper

1. Cut bell peppers into 1-inch-wide strips. Cut squash and zucchini lengthwise into ¼-inch-thick slices. Cut onions into ½-inch-thick slices. Lightly coat vegetables evenly with cooking spray.
2. Grill vegetables, covered with grill lid, over medium-high heat (350° to 400°) 3 to 5 minutes on each side or until tender. Remove from grill, and sprinkle evenly with salt and pepper. **Makes** 6 servings.

Per serving: Calories 60; Fat 0.8g (sat 0.1g, mono 0g, poly 0.1g); Protein 2.5g; Carb 12.2g; Fiber 4g; Chol 0mg; Iron 1mg; Sodium 202mg; Calc 40mg

Succotash Salad
make ahead
PREP: 20 MIN., COOK: 23 MIN.

1 cup fresh butter beans
2 cups fresh corn kernels (3 large ears)
3 Tbsp. canola oil, divided
2 Tbsp. fresh lemon juice
3 Tbsp. chopped fresh chives
½ tsp. hot sauce
¼ tsp. salt
¼ tsp. pepper

1. Cook butter beans in boiling salted water to cover 20 minutes or until tender; drain.
2. Sauté corn in 1 Tbsp. hot oil in a small skillet over medium-high heat 2 to 3 minutes or until crisp-tender.
3. Whisk together lemon juice, next 4 ingredients, and remaining 2 Tbsp. oil in a large bowl; stir in corn and butter beans. Serve immediately, or cover and chill up to 3 days. **Makes** 6 servings.

Per serving: Calories 239; Fat 8.2g (sat 0.6g, mono 4.4g, poly 2.5g); Protein 9.1g; Carb 35.5g; Fiber 8.7g; Chol 0mg; Iron 2.2mg; Sodium 112mg; Calc 30mg

Fresh Peach-Basil Vinaigrette
fast fixin's
PREP: 10 MIN.
Serve over a colorful variety of tomatoes from the local farmers market.

⅓ cup white balsamic vinegar
1 garlic clove, minced
2 Tbsp. brown sugar
¼ tsp. freshly ground pepper
⅛ tsp. salt
2 Tbsp. olive oil
1 large peach, chopped
1½ Tbsp. chopped fresh basil

1. Whisk together first 5 ingredients until sugar is dissolved. Whisk in olive oil. Stir in chopped peach and basil. Serve immediately. **Makes** about 1¼ cups.

Per Tbsp.: Calories 23; Fat 1.4g (sat 0.2g, mono 1g, poly 0.2g); Protein 0.1g; Carb 3g; Fiber 0.1g; Chol 0mg; Iron 0.1mg; Sodium 16mg; Calc 2mg

Cheesecake Tarts
family favorite
PREP: 30 MIN., BAKE: 20 MIN., COOL: 30 MIN
Red and golden raspberries, and slices of nectarine make the perfect topping for this summer dessert.

1 (8 oz.) package ⅓-less-fat cream cheese, softened
1 (8-oz.) package fat-free cream cheese, softened
¾ cup sugar
2 Tbsp. all-purpose flour
2 large eggs
½ tsp. vanilla extract
¼ tsp. almond extract
Vegetable cooking spray
⅔ cup gingersnap crumbs (12 to 16 gingersnaps)
3 cups assorted fresh fruit
Garnish: fresh mint sprigs

1. Beat cream cheeses at medium speed with an electric mixer until smooth; add sugar and flour, and beat well. Add eggs, 1 at a time, beating until blended after each addition. Stir in extracts.
2. Lightly coat 6 (4-inch) tart pans with removable bottoms with vegetable cooking spray; sprinkle pans evenly with gingersnap crumbs, shaking to coat bottom and sides of pans. (Let excess crumbs remain, evenly covering bottom of each tart pan.) Place tart pans on a baking sheet. Divide cheesecake batter evenly between tart pans.
3. Bake at 350° for 18 to 20 minutes or until set. Remove from oven, and let cool on a wire rack 30 minutes; remove from tart pans. (A pancake turner works great for removing the tarts from the bottom of the pans and transferring them to a serving platter.) Divide fruit evenly, and arrange decoratively over each cheesecake. Garnish, if desired. **Makes** 6 servings.

Per serving: Calories 356; Fat 12.1g (sat 6.6g, mono 1.6g, poly 0.6g); Protein 13.3g; Carb 49.5g; Fiber 2.7; Chol 101mg; Iron 1.7mg; Sodium 490mg; Calc 125mg

Healthy Benefits

■ Introducing a variety of fresh fruits and vegetables to children at an early age promotes healthful eating habits later in life.
■ Kids who play outside regularly are less likely to become overweight adults.

Simple Sides and Tasty Too

Add zip to your meals with these delicious sides. Not only do they complement most entrées, but they also deliver healthful benefits.

Crispy "Fried" Onion Rings

PREP: 20 MIN., COOK: 6 MIN., BAKE: 6 MIN.

1 large sweet onion
½ cup low-fat buttermilk
1 egg white
½ cup all-purpose flour
2 Tbsp. olive oil
Vegetable cooking spray
½ tsp. coarse kosher salt

1. Cut onion into ¼-inch-thick slices, and separate into rings. Select largest 12 rings, reserving remaining onion slices for another use.
2. Whisk together buttermilk and egg white in a small bowl until blended.
3. Dredge onion rings in flour; dip into buttermilk mixture, coating well. Dredge again in flour, and place on a baking sheet.
4. Heat 2 tsp. oil in a 10-inch skillet over medium-high heat. Tilt pan to coat bottom of skillet. Add 4 onion rings to skillet, and cook 1 minute on each side or until golden. Wipe skillet clean. Repeat procedure twice with remaining onion rings and oil. Place fried onion rings on an aluminum foil-lined baking sheet coated with vegetable cooking spray.
5. Bake at 400° for 3 minutes. Turn onion rings, and bake 3 more minutes. Remove from oven, and sprinkle with salt. Serve immediately. **Makes 3 servings.**

Per serving (4 onion rings): Calories 119; Fat 5.9g (sat 0.9g, mono 4.1g, poly 0.7g); Protein 3.1g; Carb 13.6g; Fiber 1g; Chol 1mg; Iron 0.6mg; Sodium 345mg; Calc 24mg

Beer-Battered "Fried" Onion Rings: Prepare recipe as directed through Step 1. Reduce buttermilk to ¼ cup, and whisk together with ¼ cup light beer and 1 egg white. Proceed with Steps 3, 4, and 5 as directed.

Per serving (4 onion rings): Calories 118; Fat 5.8g (sat 0.8g, mono 4.1g, poly 0.7g); Protein 3g; Carb 13.5g; Fiber 1g; Chol 0mg; Iron 0.6mg; Sodium 340mg; Calc 19mg

Orange-Ginger-Glazed Carrots

PREP: 15 MIN., COOK: 35 MIN.
Ground ginger is more potent than fresh, so if you opt for the substitution, 1 tsp. will be plenty.

1 (1-lb.) package baby carrots, thoroughly washed
1 tsp. grated orange rind
¼ cup fresh orange juice
2 tsp. butter
2 tsp. honey
1 to 3 tsp. freshly grated ginger✱
¼ tsp. salt
⅛ tsp. pepper

1. Stir together all ingredients and 1 cup water in a medium saucepan over medium heat, and bring to a boil. Reduce heat, and simmer, stirring occasionally, 30 to 35 minutes or until liquid evaporates and carrots are glazed. **Makes 6 servings.**

✱Substitute 1 tsp. ground ginger, if desired.

MILDRED HUFFMAN
LEXINGTON, VIRGINIA

Per serving: Calories 50; Fat 1.4g (sat 0.8g, mono 0.3g, poly 0.1g); Protein 0.6g; Carb 9.4g; Fiber 1.4g; Chol 3mg; Iron 0.7mg; Sodium 167mg; Calc 27mg

Onion Rings Step-by-Step

Follow these simple steps for fantastic "fried" onion rings.

1 Using a sharp knife, cut onion into thin slices, and separate into rings.

2 Dredge onion rings in flour, and dip into buttermilk mixture; dredge again in flour.

3 Cooking rings in oil for a short time gives them a fried flavor without the calories.

4 Finish up the rings by baking them at 400° for 3 minutes on each side.

Healthy Benefits

- Replacing saturated fats and trans fats with monounsaturated fats (such as those found in avocados) can help reduce the risk of heart disease and stroke.
- Carrots, the richest vegetable source of vitamin A, promote good vision while protecting against cancer and cardiovascular disease.

Mixed Green Salad With Cilantro-Lime Vinaigrette

fast fixin's

PREP: 15 MIN.

Add extra jicama to coleslaw for a crunchier texture, or serve jicama with other fresh vegetables for dipping in your favorite dressing.

1 (5-oz.) bag mixed salad greens, thoroughly washed
2 oranges, peeled and sectioned
1 avocado, sliced
¼ cup peeled, cubed jicama (about ½-inch cubes)
6 Tbsp. Cilantro-Lime Vinaigrette

1. Toss together first 4 ingredients in a large bowl. Serve immediately with Cilantro-Lime Vinaigrette. **Makes** 4 servings.

Per serving (includes vinaigrette): Calories 197; Fat 14.6g (sat 2.2g, mono 9.8g, poly 1.7g); Protein 2.2g; Carb 18.7g, Fiber 7.2g; Chol 0mg; Iron 1.3mg; Sodium 89mg; Calc 58mg

Cilantro-Lime Vinaigrette:

fast fixin's

PREP: 10 MIN.

Use extra vinaigrette on salads or as a poultry marinade.

½ cup cider vinegar
2 Tbsp. chopped fresh cilantro
1 tsp. grated lime rind
2 Tbsp. lime juice
1 Tbsp. honey
¼ tsp. salt
¼ cup olive oil

1. Whisk together first 6 ingredients; add oil in a slow, steady stream,

whisking constantly until smooth. Whisk well before serving. **Makes** ¾ cup.

AMANDA CLARK
SAN FRANCISCO, CALIFORNIA

Per (1½-Tbsp.) serving: Calories 72; Fat 6.8g (sat 0.9g, mono 4.9g, poly 0.7g); Protein 0g; Carb 2.7g; Fiber 0.1g; Chol 0mg; Iron 0.1mg; Sodium 75mg; Calc 2mg

Fresh Melon Sippers

Create sweet treats that offer powerful nutritional benefits. Seasonal fruits make these frozen beverages tasty. Enjoy these vitamin-rich quenchers as a midday snack, or make them for a healthy juice bar at your next gathering.

Watermelon Cooler

freezeable • make ahead

PREP: 30 MIN., FREEZE: 8 HR., STAND: 15 MIN.

Coat the glass rims in lime juice, and dip in lime zest or chopped mint. Add a colorful garnish with melon balls on wooden picks.

8 cups (½-inch) watermelon cubes
1½ cups ginger ale
⅓ cup water
1 (6-oz.) can frozen limeade concentrate

1. Place watermelon cubes in a single layer in an extra-large zip-top plastic

freezer bag, and freeze 8 hours. Let stand at room temperature 15 minutes.
2. Process half each of watermelon, ginger ale, water, and limeade concentrate in a blender until smooth; pour mixture into a pitcher. Repeat procedure with remaining half of ingredients; stir into pitcher, and serve immediately. **Makes** about 8 cups.

Per (1-cup) serving: Calories 102; Fat 0.2g (sat 0g, mono 0.1g, poly 0.1g); Protein 1g; Carb 25.9g; Fiber 0.7g; Chol 0mg; Iron 0.5mg; Sodium 7mg; Calc 15mg

Honeydew Cooler: Substitute 8 cups (½-inch) honeydew melon cubes for watermelon cubes and 1 (6-oz.) can frozen lemonade concentrate for limeade concentrate; proceed as directed.

Per (1-cup) serving: Calories 118; Fat 0.3g (sat 0.1g, mono 0g, poly 0.1g); Protein 1g; Carb 30g; Fiber 1.4g; Chol 0mg; Iron 0.4mg; Sodium 36mg; Calc 15mg

Cantaloupe Cooler: Substitute 8 cups (½-inch) cantaloupe cubes for watermelon, and add 2 tsp. grated fresh ginger to mixture in blender. Proceed as directed.

Per (1-cup) serving: Calories 117; Fat 0.3g (sat 0.1g, mono 0g, poly 0.1g); Protein 1.4g; Carb 29g; Fiber 0.1g; Chol 0mg; Iron 0.5mg; Sodium 32mg; Calc 19mg

Healthy Benefits

- Second to tomatoes, watermelon contains the highest levels of lycopene, an important antioxidant known to help protect against certain cancers and cardiovascular disease.
- Honeydew melon is an excellent source of folate, an essential nutrient for pregnant women.
- Vitamin C in melons boosts your immune system by fighting off infections.

from our kitchen

Marvelous Mason Jars

Of course you can transport iced tea or other beverages to an outdoor gathering in an insulated cooler, but what fun would that be? Use Mason jars as sealed individual servings. But don't fill them all the way to the top; make sure you leave plenty of room for ice. Your guests will be charmed by the rustic containers. The jars can also serve as low-tech cocktail shakers, for those times when you'd rather shake than stir.

Heck, don't limit yourself to drinks. These old-fashioned wonders are great for sauces, condiments, grape tomatoes, berries, lemon wedges, even croutons for salads. They're a fine way to contain anything that might spill or be crushed. You could even serve individual layered salads in them for a festive presentation. The possibilities are nearly limitless for these reusable and reliable containers.

Why We Love Kosher Salt

Though kosher salt and table salt are both sodium chloride, some table salt contains iodine and an anticaking agent, which lends a bitter flavor. Because of its coarse texture, kosher salt also has less sodium per teaspoon. It works well as a "finishing salt"; just sprinkle it on a dish right before serving. It is also great in rubs—it adds visual appeal, and the large grains distribute more evenly than fine ones.

Blueberry Everything

Now is the perfect time to enjoy the juicy splendor of these amazingly good-for-you berries. Though you can buy blueberries shipped from other parts of the world much of the year, the flavor just doesn't compare to those harvested locally in season. Senior Writer Donna Florio enjoys them in salads, on cereal, and in baked goods as often as possible. She also buys a couple of quarts to freeze for future use in recipes. Freeze them in a single layer in a pan; then store the frozen blueberries in plastic containers or zip-top plastic freezer bags for up to two months.

If you're baking with these beauties and the coffee cake or muffins start with a thick batter, tossing the berries in flour will help prevent them from sinking to the bottom. It will also keep them from releasing their vibrant color into the batter. But even flour won't help them stay evenly distributed in a thin batter.

Great Grilling Tip

Try this method to get a piece of fish off the grill without breaking it up. Slide a two-prong serving fork between the fish and the grill grate, and lift the fish enough to slide a spatula underneath.

july

Keep It Casual

Our friend Lanny Lancarte has tons of laid-back party tips. Join us for a visit to his Texas home.

Laid-Back Mexican Menu

Serves 8

Shrimp Mojo de Ajo

Pomegranate Margaritas

Lanny's Salad With Candied Pumpkin Seeds

Mixed Grill With Cilantro Pesto

Pasta Mexicana

Grilled Artichokes and Asparagus

Berries With Tequila Cream

"If you're hanging out with me, you're probably cooking," says Lanny Lancarte II. He's the cool, young chef/owner of Lanny's Alta Cocina Mexicana in Fort Worth and the great-grandson of Joe T. Garcia, whose landmark restaurant is where Lanny received his start. He keeps it casual at home, as you'll see with the easy, awesome recipes he shared with us.

On this evening, Lanny and his buddies grill chops and steaks, top 'em with Cilantro Pesto, add a side of Pasta Mexicana, and shake up a few Pomegranate Margaritas. He ends the party with Berries With Tequila Cream. No wonder our Foods staff loves Lanny's innovative style of Mexican cooking.

Shrimp Mojo de Ajo
chef recipe

PREP: 20 MIN., STAND/SOAK: 30 MIN., GRILL: 4 MIN.

This flavorful dish is marinated in a five-ingredient sauce of olive oil, garlic, chiles, lime juice, and salt.

24 unpeeled, large raw shrimp
½ cup Mojo de Ajo (at right)
24 (6-inch) wooden skewers
Garnishes: lime wedges, fresh cilantro sprigs, coarse sea salt

1. Peel shrimp, leaving tails on; devein, if desired. Combine shrimp and Mojo de Ajo, tossing to coat. Let stand 30 minutes.

2. Meanwhile, soak wooden skewers in water 30 minutes.

3. Remove shrimp from Mojo de Ajo, discarding marinade. Thread 1 shrimp onto each skewer.

4. Grill, covered with grill lid, over medium-high heat 1 to 2 minutes on each side or just until shrimp turn pink. Garnish, if desired. **Makes** 8 servings.

Mojo de Ajo
chef recipe • make ahead

PREP: 10 MIN., COOK: 5 MIN., COOL: 5 MIN., STAND: 5 MIN.

Guajillo (gwah-HEE-yoh) chiles are dried peppers with a bright tangy taste and kick of heat. Find them at grocery stores and supercenters alongside other Hispanic ingredients. Cook the chiles in hot oil for just seconds to mellow out the flavor and for easy crumbling. Don't let the ¾ cup minced garlic scare you away. The flavor smooths out as it cooks. Use this sauce in the Shrimp Mojo de Ajo (recipe at left) and the Pasta Mexicana (recipe on page 134).

¾ cup olive oil
3 whole guajillo chiles*
¾ cup bottled minced garlic
5 Tbsp. fresh lime juice
1½ tsp. salt

1. Heat oil in a 2-qt. saucepan over medium heat to 350°. Using tongs, submerge 1 chile into oil, and cook 5 seconds; remove and drain on paper towels. Let cool 5 minutes or until completely cool. Repeat with remaining 2 chiles. Remove and discard stems. Process remaining portion of chiles in food processor 30 seconds to 1 minute or until crumbled into small flakes.

2. Cook garlic in hot oil in same saucepan over medium heat, stirring occasionally, 3 to 4 minutes or until golden. Let stand 5 minutes.

3. Stir in chile flakes, lime juice, and salt. Store in an airtight container in refrigerator up to 5 days. Allow mixture to come to room temperature before using. **Makes** about 1½ cups.

*Substitute 2 Tbsp. sweet paprika, if desired. Omit Step 1; proceed with recipe as directed, stirring in paprika with lime juice and salt in Step 3.

Pomegranate Margaritas
chef recipe • fast fixin's
PREP: 10 MIN.

Chill batches of the margarita mixture ahead of time. Shake to order as friends arrive.

¼ cup sugar
¼ cup hot water
1½ cups pomegranate juice
¾ cup tequila
½ cup fresh lime juice (about 6 limes)
¼ cup orange liqueur
Ice cubes
Garnishes: orange and lime slices

1. Stir together sugar and hot water until sugar is dissolved. Stir in 1½ cups pomegranate juice and next 3 ingredients.
2. Pour desired amount of pomegranate juice mixture into a cocktail shaker filled with ice cubes. Cover with lid, and shake 30 seconds or until thoroughly chilled. Remove lid, and strain into chilled cocktail glasses. Repeat with remaining pomegranate mixture. Garnish, if desired. Serve immediately. **Makes** 4 servings.

Note: For testing purposes only, we used Triple Sec orange liqueur.

Lanny's Salad With Candied Pumpkin Seeds
chef recipe • fast fixin's
PREP: 5 MIN.

Use a fork to crumble queso fresco, which adds authentic flavor to this salad. It tastes and crumbles a little like feta cheese. It's the cheese often sprinkled on refried beans and enchiladas that doesn't melt. Find it at supercenters or Hispanic markets.

2 (5-oz.) bags sweet baby greens, thoroughly washed
Citrus-Cumin Dressing
1 cup crumbled queso fresco (about 4 oz.)
¾ cup Candied Pumpkin Seeds

1. Toss greens with Citrus-Cumin Dressing; arrange on a serving platter. Sprinkle evenly with queso fresco and Candied Pumpkin Seeds. Serve immediately. **Makes** 8 servings.

Note: For testing purposes only, we used Fresh Express Sweet Baby Greens.

Citrus-Cumin Dressing:
PREP: 10 MIN.

3 Tbsp. fresh orange juice
2 Tbsp. fresh lemon juice
½ tsp. sugar
½ tsp. ground cumin
¼ tsp. salt
¼ tsp. pepper
⅓ cup olive oil

1. Whisk together first 6 ingredients in a small bowl; add oil in a slow, steady stream, whisking constantly until smooth. Use immediately, or cover and chill up to 3 days. Whisk before serving. **Makes** ½ cup.

Candied Pumpkin Seeds:
PREP: 10 MIN., COOK: 10 MIN., BAKE: 6 MIN., COOL: 30 MIN.

Health food stores, Hispanic markets, and specialty grocery stores carry pumpkin seeds. Toast in a skillet until puffed, but watch them closely and don't brown or they'll taste burnt.

2 cups raw pumpkin seeds *****
½ cup granulated sugar
½ cup firmly packed light brown sugar
1 Tbsp. paprika
¾ tsp. salt
3 Tbsp. fresh orange juice

1. Cook pumpkin seeds in a medium nonstick skillet over medium heat, stirring often, 8 to 10 minutes or until puffed. (Do not brown.) Transfer to a medium bowl.
2. Combine granulated sugar and next 3 ingredients.
3. Toss pumpkin seeds with orange juice. Stir in sugar mixture, tossing to coat. Spread in a single layer on a parchment paper-lined jelly-roll pan.
4. Bake at 350° for 6 minutes, stirring once. Cool in pan on a wire rack 30 minutes. Store in an airtight container up to 2 days. **Makes** about 4¾ cups.

* Substitute 2 cups pecan halves, if desired. Cook as directed in Step 1 until lightly toasted. (Pecans will not puff.)

Mixed Grill With Cilantro Pesto
chef recipe • fast fixin's
PREP: 5 MIN., GRILL: 20 MIN., STAND: 5 MIN.

4 (1½-inch-thick) center-cut bone-in pork chops
4 (6-oz.) beef tenderloin fillets (about 2 inches thick)
Kosher salt
Pepper
Cilantro Pesto
Garnishes: fresh cilantro sprigs, rosemary sprigs, chives

1. Sprinkle pork chops and beef fillets evenly with desired amount of salt and pepper.
2. Grill chops and fillets, covered with grill lid, over medium-high heat (350° to 400°). Grill chops 8 to 10 minutes on each side or until done. Grill fillets 8 to 10 minutes. Turn fillets over, and cook 5 more minutes or to desired degree of doneness. Remove chops and fillets from grill, and let stand 5 minutes. Serve with Cilantro Pesto. Garnish, if desired. **Makes** 8 servings.

Cilantro Pesto:
chef recipe • make ahead
PREP: 10 MIN.

This pesto has a rougher, drier consistency than traditional ones. For a more saucy version, simply add more olive oil. Try it with grilled chicken, fish, or veggies.

½ cup loosely packed fresh cilantro leaves
½ cup loosely packed fresh flat-leaf parsley
2 garlic cloves
¼ cup (1 oz.) freshly grated Parmesan cheese
2 Tbsp. pumpkin seeds, toasted
¼ tsp. salt
¼ cup olive oil

1. Pulse first 6 ingredients in a food processor 10 times or just until chopped. Drizzle olive oil over mixture, and pulse 6 more times or until a coarse mixture forms. Cover pesto and chill until ready to serve. **Makes** about ¾ cup.

Pasta Mexicana
chef recipe • fast fixin's
PREP: 10 MIN., COOK: 10 MIN.
Use refrigerated pasta, not dried. It makes a big difference in taste.

2 (9-oz.) packages refrigerated angel hair pasta
¾ cup Mojo de Ajo (recipe on page 132)
Toppings: freshly grated Parmesan cheese, sliced fresh chives

1. Cook angel hair pasta according to package directions in a Dutch oven; drain. Return pasta to Dutch oven, and toss with ¾ cup Mojo de Ajo. Serve pasta immediately with desired toppings. **Makes** 8 servings.

Grilled Artichokes and Asparagus
chef recipe
PREP: 15 MIN., COOK: 30 MIN., GRILL: 15 MIN.
You can prep Steps 1 and 2 the day before and refrigerate artichokes in plastic bags. The choke is the inedible prickly center of the artichoke you scoop out after boiling. To eat artichokes, pull each leaf through your teeth to enjoy the tender bottom portion.

4 fresh artichokes
2 lb. fresh asparagus
½ cup olive oil
¼ cup fresh lemon juice
½ tsp. salt
½ tsp. fresh ground pepper

1. Wash artichokes by plunging up and down in cold water. Cut off stem ends, and trim about 1 inch from top of each artichoke. Remove and discard any loose bottom leaves. Trim and discard one-fourth off top of each outer leaf with scissors.
2. Bring artichokes and water to cover to a boil in a Dutch oven; cover, reduce heat, and simmer 25 minutes. Drain; pat dry with paper towels.
3. Cut artichokes in half lengthwise. Remove choke using a small spoon or melon baller. Snap off and discard tough ends of asparagus.
4. Stir together olive oil and next 3 ingredients. Brush cut sides of artichokes with one-third of oil mixture.

Brush asparagus evenly with one-third of olive oil mixture, reserving remaining olive oil mixture for later use.
5. Grill artichokes and asparagus, covered with grill lid, over medium-high heat (350° to 400°). Grill artichokes, cut sides down, 10 minutes; turn and grill 5 more minutes. Grill asparagus 1 to 2 minutes; turn and grill 2 more minutes or until tender. Drizzle with reserved olive oil mixture, if desired, and serve immediately. **Makes** 8 servings.

Berries With Tequila Cream
chef recipe • make ahead
PREP: 25 MIN., COOK: 15 MIN., STAND: 30 MIN.
For a smokier flavor, use mezcal, which is similar to tequila. You can make the sauce for this dessert a day ahead.

8 egg yolks
½ cup sugar
½ cup tequila or mezcal*
1 cup heavy cream
8 cups assorted fresh berries (such as blueberries, strawberries, blackberries, or raspberries)
Garnish: fresh mint sprigs

1. Whisk together egg yolks and sugar in a 2-qt. heavy saucepan; whisk in tequila.
2. Cook over medium-low heat, whisking constantly, 10 to 15 minutes or until mixture thickens and coats back of a spoon. (Do not boil.)
3. Fill a large bowl with ice. Place saucepan in ice. Let custard stand, stirring occasionally, until chilled (about 30 minutes).
4. Beat 1 cup heavy cream at high speed with an electric mixer until soft peaks form. Fold whipped cream gently into chilled tequila mixture just until blended.
5. Arrange assorted berries in 8 serving dishes, and top evenly with tequila cream. Garnish, if desired. Serve immediately. **Makes** 8 servings.

Note: To make ahead, cover and chill whipped cream and tequila mixture up to 24 hours.

*Substitute ½ cup orange juice, if desired.

Superfast dishes will help keep you and your kitchen cool. Put the water on to boil, chop the vegetables, open a jar or can, stir it all together, and cook until thoroughly heated.

Tuscan Pasta With Tomato-Basil Cream
fast fixin's
PREP: 10 MIN., COOK: 5 MIN.
This scrumptious dish features chopped tomatoes and basil that freshen up jarred sauce in 15 minutes.

1 (20-oz.) package refrigerated four-cheese ravioli*
1 (16-oz.) jar sun-dried tomato Alfredo sauce
2 Tbsp. white wine
2 medium-size fresh tomatoes, chopped**
½ cup chopped fresh basil
⅓ cup grated Parmesan cheese
Garnish: fresh basil strips

1. Prepare pasta according to package directions.
2. Meanwhile, pour sauce into a medium saucepan. Pour wine into sauce jar; cover tightly, and shake well. Stir wine mixture into saucepan. Stir in tomatoes and ½ cup chopped basil; cook over medium-low heat 5 minutes or until thoroughly heated. Toss with pasta; top with ⅓ cup grated Parmesan cheese. Garnish, if desired. **Makes** 4 to 6 servings.
MARGUERITE CLEVELAND
FORT LEAVENWORTH, KANSAS

Note: For testing purposes only, we used Buitoni Four Cheese Ravioli and Classico Sun-dried Tomato Alfredo Pasta Sauce.
*Substitute 1 (13-oz.) package three-cheese tortellini, if desired.
**Substitute 1 (14.5-oz.) can petite diced tomatoes, fully drained, if desired.

Summer Tortellini Salad

PREP: 10 MIN., COOK: 10 MIN., CHILL: 25 MIN.

This versatile and hearty dish makes a great one-bowl meal. You can also serve it as a side dish; just prepare the recipe without the meat.

1 (19-oz.) package frozen cheese tortellini
2 cups chopped cooked chicken
¼ cup sliced green olives
¼ cup sliced black olives
¼ cup diced red bell pepper
2 Tbsp. chopped sweet onion
2 Tbsp. chopped fresh parsley
2 Tbsp. mayonnaise
1 Tbsp. red wine vinegar
1 tsp. herbes de Provence ✱
¼ cup canola oil
Salt to taste
Garnish: fresh parsley sprigs

1. Cook tortellini according to package directions; drain. Plunge into ice water to stop the cooking process; drain and place in a large bowl. Stir in chicken and next 5 ingredients.
2. Whisk together mayonnaise, red wine vinegar, and herbes de Provence. Add oil in a slow, steady stream, whisking constantly until smooth. Pour over tortellini mixture, tossing to coat. Stir in salt to taste. Cover and chill 25 minutes. Garnish, if desired. **Makes** 4 servings.

Note: For testing purposes, we used Rosetto Cheese Tortellini.

✱Substitute 1 tsp. dried Italian seasoning, if desired.   SHIRLEY WOOD
                                                                                              SAN ANTONIO, TEXAS

Tuna Tortellini Salad: Substitute 1 (12-oz.) can albacore tuna, rinsed and drained well, for chicken. Prepare recipe as directed.

Summer's Best

If you like salt on your watermelon, you'll love this salad.

Watermelon and tomatoes may seem an unlikely combination, but when you put them together in a salad or sorbet you'll be amazed at how good they taste. There's a healthful bonus too. Both are high in lycopene, which helps prevent certain types of cancer.

Chef Bill Smith at Crook's Corner Cafe & Bar in Chapel Hill, North Carolina, first put his Tomato-and-Watermelon Salad on the menu about two years ago to rave reviews. "It sounds peculiar," he says, "But it's one of those things that once people taste it, they love it."

Even Bill was a little surprised at how well the two fruits married. "I think it was actually an accident," he says modestly. "We had lots of both items in the kitchen at one time, so I needed to find a use for them. I had enjoyed a watermelon gazpacho once before, and that kind of planted the seed for the salad."

We asked Bill to create another dish to share, and Tomato-Watermelon Sorbet (recipe on following page) is the result. Try a taste of one of the coolest concoctions we've seen in a while.

Test Kitchen Notebook

The unique combination of flavors and textures in this sorbet garnered our highest rating. Serve it as a palate cleanser between courses, or omit the coarse salt at the end and offer it as a marvelous seasonal dessert. It's best when the tomatoes are overripe.

Donna Florio
SENIOR WRITER

Tomato-and-Watermelon Salad
chef recipe

PREP: 20 MIN., STAND: 15 MIN., CHILL: 2 HR.

This refreshing dish is adapted from Seasoned in the South: Recipes From Crook's Corner and From Home (Algonquin Books, 2005) by Bill Smith, who has a passion for fresh, seasonal produce. One taste of this delicious recipe will tell you why it's so popular at Crook's Corner Cafe & Bar. The salad is juicy, so use a slotted spoon if placing on lettuce. If serving without lettuce, offer guests a fork and a spoon so they can enjoy the refreshing liquid.

5 cups (¾-inch) seeded watermelon cubes
1½ lb. ripe tomatoes, cut into ¾-inch cubes
3 tsp. sugar
½ tsp. salt
1 small red onion, quartered and thinly sliced
½ cup red wine vinegar
¼ cup extra virgin olive oil
Romaine lettuce leaves (optional)
Cracked pepper to taste

1. Combine watermelon and tomatoes in a large bowl; sprinkle with sugar and salt, tossing to coat. Let stand 15 minutes.
2. Stir in onion, vinegar, and oil. Cover and chill 2 hours. Serve chilled with lettuce leaves, if desired. Sprinkle with cracked pepper to taste. **Makes** 4 to 6 servings.

Tomato-Watermelon Sorbet
chef recipe

PREP: 20 MIN., STAND: 30 MIN.,
FREEZE: 25 MIN.

Colorful and delicious, this recipe consists of only five ingredients. (Pictured on page 7)

6 cups (1-inch) seeded ripe watermelon
    chunks
1 cup sugar
¼ tsp. salt
6 very ripe large tomatoes, quartered
    (about 3½ lb.)
2 Tbsp. fresh lemon juice
Coarse salt (optional)

1. Combine first 3 ingredients in a large bowl; stir well. Let stand 30 minutes.
2. Squeeze tomato quarters into a wire-mesh strainer over a 4-cup measuring cup. Place squeezed tomatoes into strainer, and firmly press with back of a spoon, pressing until liquid measures 3 cups. Discard tomato pulp in strainer.
3. Process half of tomato juice and half of watermelon mixture in a blender until smooth. Repeat with remaining tomato juice and watermelon. Stir in lemon juice. Pour mixture into freezer container of a 2½-qt. electric ice-cream maker, and freeze according to manufacturer's instructions. (Instructions and times will vary.) Sprinkle each serving with coarse salt, if desired. **Makes** about 2 qt.

Healthy Foods

Unexpected Flavor

Tea isn't just for sipping. Use it in some surprising dishes, and enjoy the many healthful benefits.

Create an exciting blend of flavors and add antioxidants to a variety of offerings with tea. These naturally healthful leaves lend subtle taste when used in cooking. Infuse tea flavor, such as mint, chai, or orange, when milk or water is called for in a recipe. Simply steep the designated amount of liquid with tea before preparing the dish. Go beyond the dainty teacup or pitcher of iced tea, and try one of these fragrantly delicious dishes.

Healthy Benefits

■ Tea consumption has been credited with helping decrease the risk of cancer and heart disease.
■ Steeping tea for three to five minutes actually enhances the antioxidant potency.

Mint Tea Custard
make ahead

PREP: 10 MIN., COOK: 3 MIN., STEEP: 20 MIN.,
BAKE: 50 MIN., STAND: 30 MIN.

Bruise mint sprigs by rolling them in your hands or pressing with the back of a spoon to release the flavorful oils. See tip box below before removing custard from oven.

1¼ cups low-fat evaporated
    milk
5 regular-size black tea bags
3 fresh mint sprigs, bruised
1 large lemon, quartered
½ cup sugar
4 large eggs
1 cup fat-free half-and-half
Garnishes: shaved chocolate, fresh
    mint sprigs

1. Cook milk in a small nonaluminum saucepan over medium-low heat, stirring once, 2 to 3 minutes or just

Cook's Tip

After custard cooks, siphon some of the hot water from pan with a turkey baster, and place in a large heat-resistant bowl or measuring cup. This prevents hot water from sloshing into the custard cups when lifting the pan out of the oven.

until bubbles appear (do not boil); remove from heat. Add next 3 ingredients. Cover and steep 20 minutes. Remove and discard tea bags, without squeezing; discard mint sprigs and lemon quarters. Reserve 1 cup tea mixture.

2. Whisk together sugar and eggs in a large bowl until mixture is thick and pale yellow. Gradually whisk in reserved 1 cup tea mixture and half-and-half until well blended. Pour mixture into 6 (4-oz.) custard cups or ramekins. Place custard cups in a roasting pan; add hot water to pan halfway up sides of cups.

3. Bake at 300° for 40 to 50 minutes or until a knife inserted in center of custard comes out clean. Carefully remove from oven, and let stand in pan in water bath 30 minutes. Remove from water bath. Serve immediately, or cover and chill 2 hours. Garnish, if desired. **Makes** 6 servings.

LORY MONTGOMERY
NASHVILLE, TENNESSEE

Per serving (does not include garnishes): Calories 183; Fat 4.2g (sat 1.9g, mono 1.3g, poly 0.5g); Protein 7.6g; Carb 26.2g; Fiber 0g; Chol 149mg; Iron 0.6mg; Sodium 145mg; Calc 179mg

Orange-Scented Couscous With Moroccan Dressing
fast fixin's

PREP: 5 MIN., COOK: 10 MIN., STEEP: 5 MIN., STAND: 5 MIN.

This versatile dish pairs well with poultry and can be served for special occasions and everyday meals.

¼ cup slivered almonds
4 regular-size orange-flavored
   tea bags
1 Tbsp. butter
½ tsp. salt
1 (12-oz.) box whole wheat
   couscous
½ cup golden raisins
Moroccan Dressing

1. Heat ¼ cup slivered almonds in a small nonstick skillet over medium-low heat, stirring often, 2 to 4 minutes or until toasted.

2. Bring 3 cups water to a boil in a medium saucepan; add tea bags, and remove from heat. Cover and steep 5 minutes. Remove and discard tea bags, without squeezing. Stir in butter and salt. Bring tea mixture to a boil; stir in couscous. Cover and cook 2 more minutes or until liquid is absorbed; remove from heat. Let stand, covered, 5 minutes.

3. Fluff couscous with a fork, and stir in almonds, raisins, and Moroccan Dressing until well blended. **Makes** 8 servings.

Note: For testing purposes only, we used Fantastic World Foods Organic Whole Wheat Couscous.

Per serving (includes dressing): Calories 308; Fat 10.8g (sat 2g, mono 6.4g, poly 1.2g); Protein 7.5g; Carb 49.6g; Fiber 6.5g; Chol 4mg; Iron 1.9mg; Sodium 308mg; Calc 35mg

Moroccan Dressing:
fast fixin's

PREP: 10 MIN.

½ cup chopped fresh cilantro
1 tsp. grated orange rind
¼ cup orange juice
1 Tbsp. honey
¾ tsp. ground cardamom
½ tsp. salt
½ tsp. white pepper
¼ cup olive oil

1. Whisk together first 7 ingredients in a bowl. Gradually add olive oil in a slow, steady stream, whisking until blended. **Makes** about ½ cup.

Per serving (1 Tbsp.): Calories 73; Fat 6.8g (sat 0.9g, mono 4.9g, poly 0.7g); Protein 0g; Carb 3.3g; Fiber 0.2g; Chol 0mg; Iron 0mg; Sodium 140mg; Calc 3mg

Chai Tea Mini Biscuits
freezeable • make ahead

PREP: 15 MIN., COOK: 3 MIN., STEEP: 5 MIN., BAKE: 7 MIN., STAND: 5 MIN.

1 cup 2% reduced-fat milk
3 regular-size chai tea bags
3 Tbsp. granulated sugar
¼ tsp. ground cinnamon
2 cups self-rising flour
¼ cup chilled butter, cut into small
   pieces
½ cup powdered sugar

1. Cook milk in a small nonaluminum saucepan over medium-low heat, stirring once, 2 to 3 minutes or just until bubbles appear (do not boil); remove from heat. Add tea bags; cover and steep 5 minutes. Remove and discard tea bags from milk, squeezing gently.

2. Stir together granulated sugar, cinnamon, and flour in a large bowl. Cut in butter with a pastry blender or a fork until crumbly. Add ¾ cup milk mixture, stirring just until dry ingredients are moistened. Reserve remaining milk mixture for later use.

3. Turn dough out onto a lightly floured surface; knead lightly 4 or 5 times with floured hands. Pat dough to ¾-inch thickness; cut with a 1½-inch round cutter. Place on a lightly greased baking sheet.

4. Bake at 400° for 6 to 7 minutes or until golden. Let stand 5 minutes. Whisk together reserved 1 Tbsp. milk mixture and powdered sugar until smooth. Drizzle over warm biscuits. **Makes** 2 dozen.

JAMIE KULOVITZ
BROOKLYN, NEW YORK

Per biscuit: Calories 74; Fat 2.2g (sat 1.3g, mono 0.6g, poly 0.1g); Protein 1.4g; Carb 12.3g; Fiber 0.3g; Chol 6mg; Iron 0.5mg; Sodium 151mg; Calc 48mg

Make-Ahead Chai Tea Mini Biscuits

Prepare biscuits, and freeze, without glaze, in a zip-top plastic freezer bag up to two weeks. To reheat, thaw biscuits on a lightly greased baking sheet 30 minutes. Bake at 350° for 4 to 5 minutes or until thoroughly heated. Whisk together 1 Tbsp. milk and ½ cup powdered sugar until smooth. Drizzle glaze evenly over biscuits, and serve immediately.

Summer Living.

*Celebrate the season with our creative menu ideas
and tips for outdoor entertaining.*

Pool Party

Chill out, and have fun with these
refreshing appetizers.

Splashy Gathering

Serves 16

Cucumber Dip

Italian Skewers

Mini Roast Beef Sandwiches

Brown Sugar Fruit Dip

Tropical White Chocolate Cookies

Beer and soft drinks

Go ahead—relax and spend time with your guests. Because the summer months are some of the busiest, we've put together a menu that will have you out of the kitchen in no time. Each of these recipes is make-ahead and requires 20 minutes or less of prep work. With the exception of fresh-baked Tropical White Chocolate Cookies, none requires cooking, and all feature the season's most flavorful ingredients. So dip your feet in the pool, and enjoy these tasty treats.

Cucumber Dip
make ahead
PREP: 20 MIN., CHILL: 9 HR.

5 small cucumbers, unpeeled
½ cup rice vinegar
1 tsp. kosher salt
1 tsp. garlic salt, divided
2 (8-oz.) packages cream cheese,
    softened
½ cup mayonnaise
2 tsp. chopped fresh chives
Garnish: fresh chives
Pita chips

1. Grate cucumbers into a medium bowl. Toss with rice vinegar, salt, and ½ tsp. garlic salt. Cover and chill 8 hours. Drain cucumber mixture well, pressing between paper towels.
2. Beat cream cheese, mayonnaise, and remaining ½ tsp. garlic salt at medium speed with an electric mixer 1 to 2 minutes or until smooth. Stir in cucumber mixture and 2 tsp. chopped chives. Cover and chill 1 hour. Garnish, if desired, and serve with pita chips. **Makes** 3 cups.

MARION HALL
KNOXVILLE, TENNESSEE

Italian Skewers
make ahead
PREP: 20 MIN., CHILL: 8 HR.

1 (8-oz.) block mozzarella cheese
16 (4-inch) Genoa salami slices
1 (14-oz.) can small artichoke hearts,
    drained and halved
1 pt. grape tomatoes
1 (6-oz.) jar large pitted Spanish olives,
    drained
16 (6-inch) wooden skewers
1 (16-oz.) bottle balsamic-basil
    vinaigrette
1 Tbsp. fresh lemon juice

1. Cut cheese evenly into 16 cubes. Wrap salami slices around cheese cubes. Thread cubes, artichoke hearts, tomatoes, and olives alternatively on skewers. Place skewers in a large plastic container or dish.
2. Stir together vinaigrette and lemon juice. Pour mixture over skewers; cover tightly, and chill 8 hours. Remove skewers from marinade, discarding marinade. **Makes** 16 servings.

Note: For testing purposes only, we used Ken's Steak House Balsamic & Basil Vinaigrette.

Give It a Hug

Help guests identify their beverages with a personalized hugger. Simply punch holes in sheets of foam core cut to fit the size of the bottle and lace up using string, ribbon, or raffia.

Mini Roast Beef Sandwiches
fast fixin's • make ahead
PREP: 20 MIN.

Prepare these up to 8 hours in advance, but don't add the avocado slices until ready to serve to prevent them from turning brown.

1 (8-oz.) container cream cheese spread
2 Tbsp. prepared horseradish
8 (4-inch) miniature pita rounds, cut in half
4 to 6 large green leaf lettuce leaves, torn
¾ lb. thinly sliced deli roast beef
½ small red onion, thinly sliced
1 avocado, peeled and thinly sliced

1. Stir together cream cheese and horse-radish until well blended.
2. Spread cream cheese mixture inside pita halves (about 2 tsp. each). Stuff pita halves with lettuce, roast beef, onion slices, and avocado slices. **Makes** 16 servings.

Brown Sugar Fruit Dip
make ahead
PREP: 10 MIN., CHILL: 4 HR.

We prefer strawberries, pineapple, and grapes with this creamy dip.

½ cup firmly packed brown sugar
1 (8-oz.) package cream cheese, softened
1 cup sour cream
1 tsp. vanilla extract
⅓ cup coffee liqueur (optional)
1 cup frozen whipped topping, thawed
Garnish: brown sugar
Assorted fruit

1. Beat ½ cup brown sugar and cream cheese at medium speed with an electric mixer until smooth. Add sour cream, vanilla, and, if desired, coffee liqueur, beating until blended and smooth; fold in whipped topping. Cover and chill 4 hours. Garnish, if desired. Serve with assorted fruit. **Makes** about 3½ cups.

Note: For testing purposes only, we used Kahlúa for coffee liqueur.

SAMI CAMERON
CORPUS CHRISTI, TEXAS

Tropical White Chocolate Cookies
freezeable • make ahead
PREP: 15 MIN., BAKE: 12 MIN. PER BATCH

To make the ultimate ice-cream sandwich, stuff about ¼ to ½ cup vanilla ice cream between two cookies. Seal in plastic wrap, and freeze until ready to serve. For an island twist, stuff with lime sherbet.

¾ cup butter, softened
¾ cup firmly packed brown sugar
¾ cup granulated sugar
1 tsp. vanilla extract
2 large eggs
1½ cups sweetened flaked coconut
3 tsp. grated lime rind
2 Tbsp. fresh lime juice
2½ cups all-purpose flour
1 tsp. baking soda
½ tsp. salt
1 (12-oz.) package white chocolate morsels
½ cup chopped macadamia nuts

1. Beat first 4 ingredients at medium speed with an electric mixer until creamy. Add eggs, beating until blended. Add coconut, lime rind, and lime juice, beating until blended.
2. Combine flour, baking soda, and salt in a small bowl; gradually add to butter mixture, beating well. Stir in white chocolate morsels and macadamia nuts. Drop by rounded tablespoonfuls onto ungreased baking sheets.
3. Bake at 375° for 10 to 12 minutes or until lightly brown. Cool on wire racks. **Makes** about 4 dozen.

CATHERINE GOLDSTEIN
ALPHARETTA, GEORGIA

Cool Cocktails

Slushy cocktails don't get better than those the Foods staff affectionately refers to as "Ernie's fruity drinks." Ernie Williams, of the *Southern Living* Consumer Marketing department, loves to gather on the patio with his pals and whip up a batch of daiquiri-like coolers. Omit the alcohol if you like, but paper umbrellas are a must.

Ernie's Fruity Drink
fast fixin's
PREP: 10 MIN.

1 (10-oz.) box frozen strawberries in syrup, thawed
3 cups "warm" ice (see box below)
1 cup frozen blueberries
1 very ripe medium banana
½ cup vodka
½ cup pineapple juice
¼ cup cream of coconut

1. Puree strawberries in a blender until smooth. Divide strawberry puree evenly among 4 tall glasses.
2. Place ice in blender; add blueberries and next 4 ingredients. Process until smooth. Pour blueberry mixture evenly over strawberry puree in glasses. **Makes** 4 servings.

Peach-Brandy Chiller: Substitute 1 cup fresh or frozen peaches for blueberries and banana and ½ cup brandy for vodka; proceed as directed.

Banana-Strawberry Daiquiri: Substitute 1 cup additional frozen strawberries, thawed, for blueberries and ½ cup rum for vodka; proceed as directed.

Watermelon Cooler: Substitute 1 cup watermelon cubes for blueberries and banana; proceed as directed.

Mango-Papaya Daiquiri: Substitute ½ cup each cubed mango and papaya for blueberries and banana and ½ cup coconut rum for vodka; proceed as directed.

"Warm" Ice

Slightly melted ice blends a better drink, Ernie says. He suggests letting the ice sit out at room temperature for about 30 minutes before using. "It should be wet to the touch without sticking to your fingers," he explains.

Breakfast on the Block

Host a neighborhood gathering in the morning.

A Bunch for Brunch

Serves 10

Tex-Mex Brunch Wraps

Buttermilk biscuits with
Boysenberry Butter

Honey-Nut Granola with yogurt

Peach Pie Quick Bread

Kick off Saturday with this clever get-together. Set up a coffee bar for the adults, or serve premixed, ready-to-drink cappuccinos. Have juice packs for the kids. Start at 9, finish by 10:30, and you will still have a full day ahead.

Tex-Mex Brunch Wraps
make ahead

PREP: 20 MIN., COOK: 10 MIN.,
COOL: 15 MIN., BAKE: 15 MIN.

Transfer the baked wraps to insulated or plastic foam coolers to keep warm. These handheld breakfast sandwiches are easy to eat—just peel away the foil.

2 Tbsp. butter
1 red bell pepper, finely chopped
6 green onions, thinly sliced
1 (1-lb.) ham steak, chopped
10 large eggs
½ tsp. coarsely ground pepper
1 (16-oz.) can refried beans
10 (8-inch) soft taco-size flour tortillas
1 (8-oz.) package shredded Cheddar-
   Jack cheese with peppers

1. Melt butter in a large skillet over medium-high heat. Add bell pepper and green onions, and sauté 2 minutes or until tender. Stir in ham, and cook 2 more minutes or until thoroughly heated.
2. Whisk together eggs and pepper. Pour egg mixture over ham mixture in skillet. Cook, without stirring, over medium heat until eggs begin to set on bottom. Gently stir to break up eggs. Cook, stirring occasionally, 2 to 3 minutes or until eggs are thickened and moist. (Do not overstir.) Spoon egg mixture into a large bowl; let cool 15 minutes.
3. Meanwhile, cut 10 (12-inch) aluminum foil squares.
4. Spread 2 Tbsp. beans down center of each tortilla; top each with ¼ cup egg mixture, and sprinkle with 2 Tbsp. cheese. Roll up tortillas; wrap each tightly in a piece of foil, and crimp edges under. Place wraps on a jelly-roll pan.
5. Bake at 350° for 15 minutes or until wraps are thoroughly heated. **Makes** 10 servings.

Note: To make ahead, prepare wraps as directed through Step 4. Store in refrigerator overnight. Bake at 350° for 25 minutes or until thoroughly heated.

Boysenberry Butter

PREP: 10 MIN.

You can substitute other preserves, such as strawberry or raspberry, in this flavored butter.

½ cup butter, softened
¼ cup boysenberry preserves
½ tsp. grated lime rind
Garnish: lime slices

1. Beat together first 3 ingredients at high speed with an electric mixer 1 minute or until combined. Garnish, if desired. Serve immediately, or cover and chill up to 1 week. (If chilled, let butter stand at room temperature 30 minutes before serving.) **Makes** ½ cup.

Note: For testing purposes only, we used Smucker's Boysenberry Preserves.

Honey-Nut Granola

PREP: 15 MIN., BAKE: 30 MIN.

1 (18-oz.) container uncooked regular
   oats (about 6 cups)
2½ cups coarsely chopped pecans
⅔ cup toasted wheat germ
¼ cup sesame seeds
2 cups sweetened flaked coconut
   (optional)
1 cup butter, melted
½ cup honey
¼ cup firmly packed light brown sugar
2 tsp. vanilla extract
¼ tsp. salt
1 (6-oz.) package sweetened dried
   cranberries

1. Stir together first 4 ingredients and, if desired, coconut in a large bowl.
2. Combine butter and next 4 ingredients in a medium bowl. Pour over oat mixture; stir until evenly coated. Divide mixture evenly between 2 lightly greased 15- x 10-inch jelly-roll pans.
3. Position 1 oven rack about 6 inches from top heating element in oven; place a second rack about 6 inches from bottom heating element. Place 1 pan on each rack.
4. Bake at 325° for 25 to 30 minutes or until toasted, stirring every 10 minutes and switching position of pans after first 15 minutes. Spread granola on wax paper to cool completely. Add dried cranberries. Store in an airtight container at room temperature up to 3 days, or freeze up to 6 months. **Makes** about 14 cups.

Note: For testing purposes only, we used Ocean Spray Craisins for sweetened dried cranberries.

Peach Pie Quick Bread

PREP: 10 MIN., COOK: 8 MIN., BAKE: 1 HR., COOL: 25 MIN.

Depending on the number of guests, you may need to double or triple this recipe. It's great served warm; expect a little crumbling when you slice it. It's also good at room temperature the next day and will slice beautifully.

1 cup chopped pecans
3 cups all-purpose flour
1 tsp. baking soda
1 tsp. salt
1 tsp. grated lemon rind
2 cups sugar
¾ cup canola oil
3 large eggs
1 tsp. vanilla extract
1 (21-oz.) can peach fruit filling
Cooking spray for baking

1. Heat chopped pecans in a small non-stick skillet over medium-low heat, stirring often, 5 to 8 minutes or until toasted.
2. Stir together flour and next 3 ingredients in a bowl of an electric mixer. Whisk together sugar, oil, and eggs. Gradually add sugar mixture to flour mixture, beating at low speed until blended. Stir in vanilla. Fold in fruit filling and pecans just until blended. Pour batter into 2 (8- x 4-inch) loaf pans coated with cooking spray for baking.
3. Bake at 350° for 45 minutes; shield with aluminum foil to prevent excessive browning, if necessary, and bake 15 more minutes or until a long wooden pick inserted in center comes out clean. Cool loaves in pan on a wire rack 10 minutes. Remove from pans to wire rack, and cool 15 minutes. **Makes** 2 loaves.

Note: For testing purposes only, we used Comstock More Fruit Peach Pie Filling or Topping. JANICE M. FRANCE DEPAUW, INDIANA

Enjoy a Picnic Lunch

Pack-and-Go Menu

Serves 4

Roasted Red Pepper Sandwiches
Rosemary-Parsley Hummus
Marinated Cucumbers
Blueberry-Pecan Shortbread Squares
Peach Lemonade

Make the most of the gorgeous weather with an invigorating hike and a delicious outdoor lunch. These recipes can be whipped up in a snap.

Roasted Red Pepper Sandwiches
make ahead
PREP: 20 MIN.

Prepare these sandwiches up to six hours ahead. For a heartier option, add turkey, chicken, or prosciutto.

1 (16.5-oz.) jar roasted red bell peppers, drained
1 garlic clove, minced
1 (9-inch) deli-loaf ciabatta or focaccia bread, sliced lengthwise
¼ cup refrigerated olive tapenade
1 (5.3-oz.) container goat cheese
1½ cups arugula

1. Toss together red peppers and garlic in a small bowl.
2. Spread cut side of top half of bread evenly with tapenade and cut side of bottom half with goat cheese. Layer red pepper mixture and arugula over goat cheese. Place top half of bread, tapenade side down, onto red pepper and arugula layers. Cut into 4 pieces. **Makes** 4 servings. CAROLINE W. KENNEDY COVINGTON, GEORGIA

Rosemary-Parsley Hummus
fast fixin's
PREP: 8 MIN.

Serve this delicious snack with sugar snap peas, carrots, or pita chips. It also doubles as a sandwich spread for grilled chicken, steak, and veggies.

2 (7-oz.) containers hummus
1 garlic clove, minced
2 Tbsp. fresh lime juice
2 tsp. chopped fresh parsley
1 tsp. chopped fresh rosemary
½ tsp. cracked black pepper
1 Tbsp. extra virgin olive oil
Ground red pepper to taste

1. Combine first 6 ingredients. Drizzle with olive oil, and sprinkle with red pepper to taste. **Makes** 1½ cups.

Marinated Cucumbers
make ahead
PREP: 25 MIN., COOK: 5 MIN., STAND: 3 HR., CHILL: 4 HR.

These also make the perfect summer veggie sandwich. Chill the vegetables with ice before marinating for extra crispness.

4 large cucumbers (about 2¾ lb.), thinly sliced
2 small onions, thinly sliced
½ green bell pepper, finely chopped
½ tsp. salt
Ice cubes
1¼ cups sugar
1¼ cups white vinegar
¼ tsp. ground turmeric
¼ tsp. ground cloves
¼ tsp. mustard seeds
¼ tsp. celery seeds

1. Spread vegetables in a 13- x 9-inch baking dish; sprinkle evenly with salt. Cover with ice; let stand 3 hours or until cool and crisp. Drain and return to dish.
2. Bring sugar and next 5 ingredients to a boil in a saucepan over medium-high heat. Let cool slightly. Pour mixture over vegetables. Cover and chill at least 4 hours or up to 5 days. Serve cold. **Makes** about 8 cups. BETTY DRENNEN BIRMINGHAM, ALABAMA

Blueberry-Pecan Shortbread Squares

family favorite

PREP: 20 MIN., BAKE: 58 MIN., COOL: 2 HR.

¾ cup chopped pecans
2¼ cups all-purpose flour
½ tsp. salt
1 cup butter, softened
1½ cups powdered sugar
¼ tsp. vanilla extract
3 (4.4-oz.) containers fresh blueberries (about 2½ cups)
2 Tbsp. granulated sugar
1 tsp. grated lime rind

1. Place pecans in a single layer in a shallow pan.
2. Bake at 350° for 8 minutes or until toasted.
3. Stir together pecans, flour, and salt in a bowl.
4. Beat 1 cup butter and 1½ cups powdered sugar at medium speed with a heavy-duty electric stand mixer 2 minutes or until pale and fluffy. Beat in ¼ tsp. vanilla extract. Gradually add flour mixture, beating at low speed 30 seconds after each addition until a dough forms and comes together to hold a shape.
5. Press 2 cups of dough in a thick layer onto bottom of a lightly greased 13- x 9-inch pan. Top evenly with fresh blueberries. Combine granulated sugar and lime rind, and sprinkle evenly over berries. Crumble remaining dough evenly over berries.
6. Bake at 350° for 45 to 50 minutes or until golden. Cool shortbread in pan on a wire rack 2 hours. Cut into squares before serving. **Makes** 2 dozen.

Peach Lemonade

family favorite • make ahead

PREP: 10 MIN., CHILL: 1 HR.

Freeze Peach Lemonade in sports bottles (leaving 2 inches from top for expansion) the night before your hike or picnic.

1 (3.2-oz.) container sugar-free lemonade drink mix
3 cups cold water
1 (33.8-oz.) bottle peach nectar

1. Remove 1 lemonade tub from container, reserving remaining tubs for another use.
2. Combine lemonade mix, water, and peach nectar in a pitcher. Cover and chill at least 1 hour. Serve over ice. **Makes** 7 cups.

Note: For testing purposes only, we used Crystal Light Lemonade Soft Drink Mix.

Have a Scoop

It's the iconic summer treat, and when you make your own, dessert becomes a family-friendly activity. Purchase an electric ice-cream maker (between $25 and $70 online or at a superstore), and start with these recipes. We personalized a basic vanilla ice cream by stirring in one of our fresh fruit blends.

Vanilla Ice Cream With Fruit Blend

PREP: 10 MIN., COOK: 20 MIN.,
COOL: 15 MIN., CHILL: 8 HR.

Serve this soft out of the ice-cream maker's container, or freeze it for a firmer consistency.

3 large eggs
1½ cups sugar
2 Tbsp. all-purpose flour
½ tsp. salt
4 cups 2% reduced-fat milk
1 cup whipping cream
1 Tbsp. vanilla extract
1 recipe desired fruit blend (See box on opposite page)

1. Beat eggs at medium speed with an electric mixer until frothy. Stir together sugar, flour, and salt until well blended. Gradually add sugar mixture to eggs, beating until thickened. Gradually add milk, beating until blended.
2. Cook egg mixture in a Dutch oven over medium-low heat, stirring constantly, 15 to 20 minutes or until a candy thermometer registers 170°. (Mixture should be thick enough to coat a spoon.)
3. Fill a large bowl or pan with ice; place Dutch oven in ice, and stir occasionally 10 to 15 minutes until custard is completely cool. Transfer mixture to an airtight container; cover and chill 8 hours. Stir in whipping cream, vanilla, and desired fruit blend.
4. Pour mixture into freezer container of a 1-gal. electric ice-cream maker, and freeze according to manufacturer's instructions. (Instructions and freezing times will vary.) **Makes** about ½ gal.

Play It Cool

Food needs to be kept colder than 40° to prevent bacteria from growing. Here are some tips for maintaining a proper temperature.
■ When it goes into the cooler, make sure all your food is cold and in containers with snug lids.
■ If any of the items you're transporting can be frozen, put them in the cooler that way. They'll help keep the other food cold.
■ As ice melts, it can seep into containers. Ice packs (in gel or hard plastic forms) are good alternatives.
■ Do not open your cooler until you're ready to unpack it. If you expect to drink lots of beverages on the way to your picnic, keep them in a separate cooler.

Choose Your Fruit Blend

Mixed Berry Blend
make ahead
PREP: 10 MIN., CHILL: 2 HR.

4 cups fresh strawberries,
  quartered
2 cups fresh raspberries
1 cup sugar

1. Process all ingredients in a food processor 30 to 45 seconds. Transfer mixture to a large bowl; cover and chill 2 hours. **Makes** 4 cups.

Nectarine-and-Toasted Almond Blend
make ahead
PREP: 15 MIN., CHILL: 2 HR.,
COOK: 6 MIN.
Like peaches, nectarines can be placed in a paper bag to speed ripening.

5 cups peeled nectarine slices,
  (about 2¾ lb.)
1 cup sugar
2 Tbsp. butter
¾ cup slivered almonds
¾ tsp. salt

1. Process nectarines and sugar in a food processor 30 to 45 seconds. Transfer to a large bowl; cover and chill 2 hours.
2. Melt butter over medium-low heat in a medium skillet; add almonds and salt. Cook almonds, stirring frequently, 3 to 5 minutes or until toasted and golden. Pour nut mixture through a fine wire-mesh strainer, shaking to remove excess butter and salt. Stir almonds into nectarine mixture; cover and chill until ready to use. **Makes** about 4 cups.

Movie Night

Our Test Kitchens supplied Lynlee and Kyle Hudlow with some recipe ideas for a Friday Night at the Movies party.

Gold-Dusted White Chocolate Popcorn
PREP: 10 MIN., STAND: 15 MIN.
We adapted this recipe from one on the Jolly Time Popcorn Web site (www.jollytime.com) called Glitterrazzi Popcorn.

1 (3.3-oz.) bag butter-flavored
  microwave popcorn, popped
1 cup salted mixed nuts
1 cup dried cranberries
1 (12-oz.) package white chocolate
  morsels
½ tsp. ground cinnamon
Edible gold dust

1. Place popcorn in a large bowl, discarding unpopped kernels. Stir in nuts and cranberries.
2. Microwave white chocolate morsels in a 2-cup glass measuring cup at HIGH 1½ minutes or until melted and smooth, stirring at 30-second intervals. Pour over popcorn mixture, stirring until evenly coated.
3. Spread mixture in a 15- x 10-inch jelly-roll pan. Sprinkle evenly with cinnamon. Let stand 15 minutes or until chocolate hardens. Sprinkle with gold dust. Break into pieces; serve immediately, or store in an airtight container up to 3 days. **Makes** 10 cups.

Note: Find the edible gold dust at cake or party supply stores.

Set Up a Popcorn Bar

■ If you're expecting a large crowd, shop for big bags of popped corn. For a group of six or fewer, you can probably keep up with the demand by making microwave popcorn.
■ If your gas grill has a side burner, pop corn the old-fashioned way with a pot, kernels, and oil. Do not pop directly on the grill, and read package instructions for how to pop corn on a gas heating element.
■ For a festive county fair atmosphere, rent a popcorn machine from your local party store. The cost is between $45 and $70 for a 24-hour rental, depending on the size. Popcorn and oil is sold separately. You'll need a minivan, SUV, or pickup truck to move a larger machine, and a heavy-duty extension cord is a must.
■ Offer guests a variety of fun sprinkle-ins, such as candies, tropical fruit mix, shredded cheeses, herbs, spice blends, and nuts. Fill the popcorn sack half full, add toppings, more popcorn, and a last sprinkle of good stuff.

Spicy Buffalo Chicken Sandwiches

fast fixin's

PREP: 10 MIN., BAKE: 10 MIN.

Our Foods staff rated the heat level of these sandwiches as mild. Let guests add more hot sauce to taste.

3 Tbsp. butter, melted
½ cup Buffalo-style hot sauce, divided
6 hoagie rolls, split
⅓ cup refrigerated blue cheese dressing
½ tsp. Creole seasoning
1½ cups matchstick-cut carrots
1½ cups diagonally sliced celery
¼ cup finely chopped onion (optional)
12 large deli-fried chicken strips (about 1¼ lb.)
1 (4-oz.) package crumbled blue cheese
Buffalo-style hot sauce (optional)

1. Stir together butter and 2 tsp. hot sauce. Brush cut sides of rolls evenly with mixture. Place, cut sides up, on a baking sheet.
2. Bake at 350° for 8 to 10 minutes or until toasted.
3. Stir together blue cheese dressing, 2 tsp. to 3 tsp. hot sauce, and Creole seasoning. Add carrots, celery, and, if desired, onion; toss to coat.
4. Arrange chicken on bottom halves of rolls; drizzle evenly with remaining hot sauce. Layer chicken evenly with carrot mixture and crumbled blue cheese. Top with remaining roll halves. Serve with additional hot sauce, if desired. **Makes** 6 servings.

Note: For testing purposes only, we used Frank's Original Buffalo Hot Wing Sauce, T. Marzetti's The Ultimate Blue Cheese refrigerated dressing, and Zatarain's Creole Seasoning.

Supper for a Crowd

Texan Summer Supper

Serves 8

Bacon-Wrapped Pork Medallions With Tomato-Corn Salsa

Grilled Lemon-Garlic Potatoes

Grilled Okra-and-Tomatillo Salad

Apple Slaw

Blond Texas Sheet Cake

Carolyn and Joe Bailey of Flatonia, Texas, serve up good times and one amazing feast from the grill.

Bacon-Wrapped Pork Medallions With Tomato-Corn Salsa

PREP: 20 MIN., CHILL: 2 HR., GRILL: 45 MIN., STAND: 10 MIN.

3 (¾-lb.) pork tenderloins
2 Tbsp. olive oil
1 Tbsp. white balsamic vinegar
1½ tsp. ancho chili powder
1 tsp. coarsely ground black pepper
8 thick-cut bacon slices
Tomato-Corn Salsa

1. Cut pork into 8 (3-inch-thick) slices. Place meat, cut sides up, between 2 sheets of heavy-duty plastic wrap, and flatten to 2-inch thickness, using a rolling pin or flat side of a meat mallet.
2. Whisk together olive oil and next 3 ingredients. Rub mixture evenly over pork; cover and chill 2 hours.
3. Microwave bacon at HIGH 2 minutes or until bacon is partially cooked. Wrap sides of each pork slice with 1 bacon slice, and secure with a wooden pick.
4. Light 1 side of grill, heating to medium-high heat (350° to 400°); leave other side unlit. Arrange pork over lit side; grill, covered with grill lid, 5 minutes on each side. Move pork to unlit side; grill, covered with grill lid, 30 to 35 minutes or until a meat thermometer registers 160°. Let stand 10 minutes. Serve with Tomato-Corn Salsa. **Makes** 8 servings.

Tomato-Corn Salsa:

PREP: 15 MIN., GRILL: 8 MIN., STAND: 10 MIN.

White balsamic vinegar instead of red balsamic has a milder flavor and won't darken the corn's color.

4 ears fresh corn, husks removed
2 tsp. olive oil
1 pt. grape tomatoes, halved
3 green onions, sliced
¼ cup chopped fresh basil
2 Tbsp. white balsamic vinegar
1 tsp. salt
½ tsp. pepper

1. Brush corn with oil. Grill, covered with grill lid, over medium-high heat (350° to 400°) 8 minutes, turning every 2 minutes or until done. Let stand 10 minutes. Cut kernels from cobs; discard cobs.
2. Combine corn, tomatoes, and next 5 ingredients; toss to coat. **Makes** 2 cups.

Grilled Lemon-Garlic Potatoes

make ahead

PREP: 10 MIN., COOK: 30 MIN., GRILL: 5 MIN.

Make the lemon mixture the day before; cover and chill. Remove from the fridge about 30 minutes before tossing with grilled potatoes.

4 lb. small red potatoes, halved
¼ cup olive oil, divided
1 Tbsp. grated lemon rind
¼ cup lemon juice
2 garlic cloves, pressed
1½ tsp. salt
½ tsp. coarsely ground pepper
⅓ cup chopped fresh parsley
Vegetable cooking spray

1. Bring potatoes and water to cover to a boil in a large Dutch oven over medium-high heat; cook 20 to 25 minutes or until tender. Drain and toss with 2 Tbsp. olive oil.

2. Stir together lemon rind, next 5 ingredients, and remaining 2 Tbsp. olive oil.
3. Coat a cold cooking grate with cooking spray; place on grill over medium-high heat (350° to 400°). Place potatoes on cooking grate, and grill, covered with grill lid, 5 minutes, turning occasionally. Gently toss hot potatoes with lemon mixture. Serve immediately or at room temperature. **Makes** 8 servings.

Grilled Okra-and-Tomatillo Salad
PREP: 15 MIN., GRILL: 18 MIN.

The tomatillo (tohm-ah-TEE-oh) is known as a Mexican green tomato. Its distinguishing feature is a paperlike husk, which, if fresh, will be tight-fitting around the fruit.

10 fresh tomatillos *
Vegetable cooking spray
1 large sweet onion, thinly sliced
2 tsp. olive oil, divided
1 lb. fresh okra, trimmed
1 tsp. grated lime rind
3 Tbsp. fresh lime juice
2 Tbsp. olive oil
1 garlic clove, pressed
¼ cup chopped fresh cilantro
1 tsp. salt
½ tsp. coarsely ground pepper

1. Remove husks from tomatillos; wash thoroughly, and thinly slice.
2. Coat a cold cooking grate with cooking spray; place on grill over medium-high heat (350° to 400°). Place tomatillos on cooking grate, and grill, covered with grill lid, 4 minutes on each side or until tender. Remove from grill; coarsely chop.
3. Toss onion with 1 tsp. olive oil. Grill onion in a grill wok or metal basket, covered with grill lid, over medium-high heat (350° to 400°) 5 minutes or until slightly charred, stirring occasionally. Remove from grill, and coarsely chop.
4. Cut okra in half lengthwise, and toss with remaining 1 tsp. oil. Grill okra in a grill wok or metal basket, covered with grill lid, over medium-high heat (350° to 400°) 5 minutes or until tender, stirring occasionally. Remove from grill.

5. Stir together lime rind and next 6 ingredients in a large bowl; add tomatillos, onion, and okra, tossing to coat. Serve at room temperature. **Makes** 8 servings.

* Substitute 2 large green tomatoes for tomatillos, if desired.

Apple Slaw
make ahead
PREP: 30 MIN., CHILL: 1 HR.

2 Granny Smith apples, thinly sliced
4 cups shredded green cabbage (about ½ head)
4 cups shredded red cabbage (about ½ head)
1 medium cucumber, seeded and sliced
2 large jalapeño peppers, seeded and minced
½ cup cider vinegar
⅓ cup honey
⅓ cup vegetable oil
2 tsp. salt
½ tsp. pepper

1. Combine first 5 ingredients in a large bowl.
2. Whisk together vinegar and next 4 ingredients. Toss with apple mixture. Cover and chill at least 1 hour or up to 4 hours. **Makes** 8 servings.

Blond Texas Sheet Cake
family favorite • make ahead
PREP: 15 MIN., BAKE: 20 MIN., COOL: 2 HR.
Here's a spin on the beloved chocolate Texas Sheet Cake. To serve as large triangles, cut cake into 5- x 5-inch squares, and then cut squares corner to corner.

1 (18.25-oz.) package white cake mix
1 cup buttermilk
⅓ cup butter, melted
4 egg whites
¼ tsp. almond extract
Caramel-Pecan Frosting

1. Beat together first 5 ingredients at low speed with an electric mixer 2 minutes or until blended. Pour batter into a greased 15- x 10-inch jelly-roll pan.
2. Bake at 350° for 15 to 20 minutes or until a wooden pick inserted in center comes out clean. Cool in pan on a wire rack 2 hours.
3. Prepare Caramel-Pecan Frosting. Pour immediately over cooled cake in pan, and spread quickly to cover cake. **Makes** 12 servings.

Note: For testing purposes only, we used Pillsbury Moist Supreme Premium Classic White Cake Mix.

Caramel-Pecan Frosting:
fast fixin's
PREP: 10 MIN., BAKE: 6 MIN., COOK: 10 MIN.

1 cup chopped pecans
½ cup butter
1 cup firmly packed light brown sugar
⅓ cup buttermilk
2 cups powdered sugar
½ tsp. vanilla extract
¼ tsp. almond extract

1. Place chopped pecans in a single layer in a shallow pan.
2. Bake at 350° for 6 minutes or until lightly toasted.
3. Bring butter and brown sugar to a boil in a 3½-qt. saucepan over medium heat, whisking constantly (about 2 minutes). Remove from heat, and slowly whisk in buttermilk.
4. Return mixture to heat, and bring to a boil. Pour into bowl of a heavy-duty electric stand mixer. Gradually add powdered sugar and vanilla and almond extracts, beating at medium-high speed until smooth (about 1 minute). Stir in pecans. Use immediately. **Makes** 3 cups.

Burgers Are a Hit

Fast Food Menu

Serves 4

Tasty Turkey Burgers
Herb-Grilled Onion Rings
Potato salad
Chocolate Cookie Bites

This quick supper beats the drive-through any day of the week. We made Tasty Turkey Burgers with ground turkey that included some dark meat. You can also use 100% turkey breast, which is lower in fat; just remember, it is the fat that helps keep the burgers moist. Add potato salad, and you're ready to serve.

Tasty Turkey Burgers
family favorite • fast fixin's
PREP: 15 MIN., GRILL: 14 MIN.

1 lb. ground turkey
½ cup Italian-seasoned breadcrumbs
1 large egg, beaten
¼ cup finely chopped green bell pepper
1 Tbsp. minced dried onion
½ tsp. salt
½ tsp. freshly ground pepper
2 Tbsp. Fresh Herb Marinade
4 hamburger buns
Herb-Grilled Onion Rings
Toppings: spicy mustard, shaved
   Parmesan cheese

1. Combine first 7 ingredients. Shape mixture into 4 equal-size patties.
2. Grill, covered with grill lid, over medium-high heat (350° to 400°) 5 to 6 minutes on each side or until no longer pink in center, basting each side occasionally with Fresh Herb Marinade.
3. Grill buns, cut sides down, 2 minutes or until toasted. Serve burgers on buns with Herb-Grilled Onion Rings and desired toppings. **Makes** 4 servings.

Classic Burgers: Substitute 1 lb. ground chuck for ground turkey. Prepare recipe as directed.
STEPHANIE NOLAN
BRADENTON, FLORIDA

Fresh Herb Marinade:
fast fixin's
PREP: 10 MIN.

¼ cup vegetable oil
2 Tbsp. balsamic vinegar
1½ Tbsp. chopped fresh cilantro
1 Tbsp. chopped fresh rosemary
½ tsp. kosher salt
Freshly ground pepper to taste

1. Stir together first 5 ingredients in a small bowl. Season with pepper to taste. **Makes** about ⅓ cup.

Herb-Grilled Onion Rings
fast fixin's
PREP: 5 MIN., GRILL: 12 MIN.

2 large Vidalia onions
4 Tbsp. Fresh Herb Marinade, divided

1. Cut each onion into ½-inch-thick slices. Brush slices evenly with 2½ Tbsp. Fresh Herb Marinade.
2. Grill, covered with grill lid, over medium-high heat (350° to 400°) 4 to 6 minutes on each side or until tender, basting once with remaining marinade. **Makes** 4 servings.

Chocolate Cookie Bites
family favorite
PREP: 10 MIN., BAKE: 21 MIN., COOL: 13 MIN.
Serve these bite-size treats with homemade Vanilla Ice Cream on page 142 or your favorite vanilla ice cream.

¾ cup chopped pecans
1¼ cups powdered sugar, divided
1 cup butter, softened
2 Tbsp. milk
1 tsp. vanilla extract
2 cups all-purpose flour
¼ cup unsweetened cocoa
¼ tsp. salt

1. Place pecans in a single layer in a shallow pan.
2. Bake at 350° for 6 to 8 minutes or until lightly toasted, stirring once after 3 minutes.
3. Beat 1 cup powdered sugar and butter at medium speed with an electric mixer until creamy. Add milk and vanilla, beating until blended.
4. Combine flour, cocoa, and salt; gradually add to butter mixture, beating until blended. Stir in pecans.
5. Shape dough into 1-inch balls, and place 1½ inches apart on lightly greased baking sheets.
6. Bake at 400° for 11 to 13 minutes or until tops of cookies just begin to crack. Cool on baking sheets 3 minutes. Remove to wire racks; dust with remaining ¼ cup powdered sugar. Cool 10 minutes. **Makes** 2½ dozen.
RICHARD JACK
GALENA, MISSOURI

Southern-Style Pickles

You won't believe how great these taste. Our Test Kitchens loved them, and you will too.

It takes a little time to wrap your mind around the idea of a fried pickle. Pickles + batter + hot grease seems an unlikely equation at first. But just imagine a salty pickle surrounded by a crunchy fried coating, and this tasty finger food takes on immediate appeal. Serve them at a casual party, using this terrific recipe. We sampled a variety of breadings and pickle flavors and shapes in our kitchens, but lengthwise-sliced dills with a light beer batter proved our favorites.

Test Kitchen *Notebook*

The decision is split as to who created fried pickles, but either way, they've been around since the 1960s. According to John T. Edge, author of *Southern Belly: The Ultimate Food Lover's Companion to the South,* (Algonquin Books, 2007), the Hollywood Cafe in Robinsonville, Mississippi, and the Duchess Drive Inn in Atkins, Arkansas, both claim the honor.

Who served them first might never be resolved, but there's no argument about the popularity of fried pickles. While often paired with fried catfish and hush puppies, they are also enjoyed as appetizers.

Donna Florio
SENIOR WRITER

Beer-Batter Fried Pickles

PREP: 15 MIN., FRY: 4 MIN. PER BATCH

We also tried and loved fried Wickles-brand sweet-hot sliced pickles in this recipe. These Alabama-bred pickles are sold nationwide, but you can also order them online from **www.wickles.com.**

2 (16-oz.) jars dill pickle sandwich slices, drained
1 large egg
1 (12-oz.) can beer
1 Tbsp. baking powder
1 tsp. seasoned salt
1½ cups all-purpose flour
Vegetable oil
Spicy Ranch Dipping Sauce

1. Pat pickles dry with paper towels.
2. Whisk together egg and next 3 ingredients in a large bowl; add 1½ cups flour, and whisk until smooth.
3. Pour oil to a depth of 1½ inches into a large heavy skillet or Dutch oven; heat over medium-high heat to 375°.
4. Dip pickle slices into batter, allowing excess batter to drip off. Fry pickles, in batches, 3 to 4 minutes or until golden. Drain and pat dry on paper towels; serve immediately with Spicy Ranch Dipping Sauce. **Makes** 8 to 10 servings.

Note: For testing purposes only, we used Vlasic Kosher Dill Stackers.

Spicy Ranch Dipping Sauce:

fast fixin's • make ahead
PREP: 10 MIN.

¾ cup buttermilk
½ cup mayonnaise
2 Tbsp. minced green onions
1 garlic clove, minced
1 tsp. hot sauce
½ tsp. seasoned salt
Garnish: seasoned salt

1. Whisk together first 6 ingredients. Garnish, if desired. Store in an airtight container in refrigerator up to 2 weeks. **Makes** about 1 cup.

Perfect Pickles

Follow these simple techniques for great results.

1 Pat the pickles dry before dipping in the batter so it will adhere evenly.

2 Keep the hot oil at a steady temperature by adding the pickles gradually.

New Take on Catfish

It's a staple of our region. With its firm flesh and mild, sweet flavor, catfish is versatile and delicious almost any way it is cooked. Both of these tempting recipes are sure to become menu favorites.

Catfish Beignets With Zesty Tartar Sauce

PREP: 20 MIN., BAKE: 25 MIN., COOK: 10 MIN., STAND: 5 MIN., RISE: 30 MIN.,
FRY: 4 MIN. PER BATCH

Beignets, time-tested New Orleans pastries, are usually sweet. We created a savory version that includes the diced onion, bell pepper, and celery that are considered the "holy trinity" in recipes with Louisiana roots.

1½ lb. catfish fillets
1 tsp. salt
1¼ tsp. Old Bay seasoning, divided
¾ cup frozen diced onion, red and green bell pepper, and celery
1½ Tbsp. vegetable oil, divided
⅓ cup beer (not dark)
¾ tsp. active dry yeast
½ cup 2% reduced-fat milk
1¾ cups all-purpose flour
2 dashes of hot sauce
3 egg whites
Vegetable oil
Zesty Tartar Sauce
Lemon wedges (optional)

1. Sprinkle fillets evenly with salt and ¼ tsp. Old Bay seasoning. Arrange fillets on a lightly greased rack in an aluminum foil-lined broiler pan.
2. Bake at 425° for 20 to 25 minutes or until fish flakes with a fork and is opaque throughout. Finely chop fish.
3. Cook diced onion, bell pepper, and celery in ½ Tbsp. hot oil in a small skillet over medium-high heat, stirring often, 3 to 4 minutes or until tender.
4. Cook beer in a small saucepan over medium-low heat 5 minutes or until a thermometer registers 105° to 115°. Remove from heat; add yeast, and let stand 5 minutes. Transfer yeast mixture to a large bowl; stir in vegetables, milk, flour, hot sauce, catfish, remaining 1 Tbsp. oil, and remaining 1 tsp. Old Bay seasoning.
5. Cover and let rise in a warm place (85°), free from drafts, 30 minutes.
6. Beat egg whites at medium speed with an electric mixer until soft peaks form. Fold into catfish mixture.
7. Pour vegetable oil to a depth of 2 inches into a Dutch oven or electric deep-fat fryer; heat to 360°. Drop batter, by heaping tablespoonfuls, into hot oil; fry, in batches, 3 to 4 minutes or until golden brown, turning once. Drain on a wire rack over paper towels. Serve with Zesty Tartar Sauce and, if desired, lemon wedges. **Makes** about 2 dozen.

Note: Keep beignets warm in a 225° oven for up to 30 minutes.

Zesty Tartar Sauce:
fast fixin's • make ahead
PREP: 5 MIN.

1 cup tartar sauce
1 tsp. grated lemon rind
1 Tbsp. fresh lemon juice
⅛ tsp. ground red pepper

1. Stir together all ingredients. Cover and chill until ready to serve. **Makes** about 1 cup.

Caribbean Catfish With Mango-Black Bean Salsa
make ahead
PREP: 5 MIN., COOK: 16 MIN.
The salsa can be made a day ahead. Or to save time, serve the fish with jarred salsa.

1½ lb. catfish fillets
2 tsp. Caribbean jerk seasoning
½ tsp. salt
1 Tbsp. butter
1 Tbsp. vegetable oil
Mango-Black Bean Salsa
Garnish: lime wedges

1. Sprinkle fillets evenly with jerk seasoning and salt.
2. Melt butter with oil in a large nonstick skillet over medium heat; add fillets, and cook 6 to 8 minutes on each side or until done. Serve immediately with salsa. Garnish, if desired. **Makes** 4 servings.

Mango-Black Bean Salsa:
fast fixin's
PREP: 10 MIN.

1 (15-oz.) can black beans, rinsed and drained
1 (8-oz.) can pineapple tidbits, drained ✱
1 small mango, diced
½ red bell pepper, finely chopped
1 jalapeño pepper, seeded and minced
1 tsp. grated lime rind
2 Tbsp. chopped fresh cilantro
2 Tbsp. fresh lime juice
1 Tbsp. honey
½ tsp. salt
⅓ cup diced jicama (optional)

1. Stir together first 10 ingredients and, if desired, jicama. Cover and chill until ready to serve. **Makes** 4 cups.

✱Substitute 1 cup diced fresh pineapple, if desired.

Fresh From the Garden

There is a magic way to inspire a family to eat fresh produce: Involve them in the growing, harvesting, and cooking of the food. Karen and Patrice Gros, of Eureka Springs, Arkansas, who sell their produce at the local farmers market, do just that. Try some of Karen's recipes to bring the pleasure of summer produce to your table.

Garlic Green Beans

PREP: 15 MIN., COOK: 8 MIN.

Blanch the green beans (Step 1) up to a day ahead. When you are ready to prepare supper, toss the green beans in the skillet and sauté.

1½ lb. tiny green beans (haricots verts), trimmed
1 Tbsp. butter
1 Tbsp. olive oil
3 garlic cloves, minced
1 tsp. kosher salt
1 tsp. freshly ground pepper

1. Cook green beans in boiling salted water to cover 3 minutes or until crisp-tender; drain. Plunge green beans into ice water to stop the cooking process, and drain.
2. Melt butter with oil in a medium skillet over medium-high heat; add green beans, garlic, salt, and pepper, and sauté 4 to 5 minutes or until thoroughly heated. **Makes** 6 to 8 servings.

Test Kitchen *Notebook*

How to Blanch
Retain the flavor, color, and texture of certain vegetables by boiling in water for about two minutes and then plunging into ice water until thoroughly chilled. This stops the cooking process and retains the bright color and crispness. Remove vegetables from ice water, wrap in paper towels, place in a zip-top plastic bag, and chill up to a day in advance. This process works extremely well with broccoli, green beans, and asparagus.

Holley Johnson
ASSOCIATE FOODS EDITOR

Garden Salad With Tarragon-Mustard Vinaigrette
fast fixin's
PREP: 15 MIN.

This quick side salad requires just a few staple ingredients and some fresh herbs. The dressing also tastes great tossed with diced roasted sweet potatoes.

8 cups torn green leaf and red leaf lettuce
2 Tbsp. fresh minced chives
1 Tbsp. fresh minced tarragon
Tarragon-Mustard Vinaigrette

1. Toss together lettuce, chives, and tarragon in a large bowl. Drizzle with Tarragon-Mustard Vinaigrette just before serving. **Makes** 6 servings.

Tarragon-Mustard Vinaigrette:
fast fixin's
PREP: 10 MIN.

1 Tbsp. fresh lemon juice
1 Tbsp. Dijon mustard
½ tsp. salt
3 Tbsp. extra virgin olive oil
2 tsp. finely chopped fresh tarragon*

1. Whisk together first 3 ingredients in a small bowl until blended. Add oil in a slow, steady stream, whisking vigorously until well blended. Stir in fresh tarragon. **Makes** about ¼ cup.

*Substitute fresh basil or flat-leaf parsley, if desired.

Good for You

Working in a garden offers a plethora of positive health implications. It has been known to help lower blood pressure, reduce muscle tension, and stimulate the brain. Because a sense of ownership is attached to watching something grow and develop, it can also boost self-confidence. Additionally, there is an increased awareness of and appreciation for nature.

Summer Squash Frittata

PREP: 20 MIN., COOK: 14 MIN., BAKE: 35 MIN.

This frittata is fantastic warm or cold and can be served with tomato sauce or salsa.

3 Tbsp. butter
2 small zucchini, chopped into ½-inch cubes (about 2 cups)
2 small summer squash, chopped into ½-inch cubes (about 2 cups)
1 small onion, coarsely chopped (½ cup)
12 large eggs, lightly beaten
½ cup sour cream
1 tsp. kosher salt
¾ tsp. freshly ground pepper
⅓ cup chopped fresh basil leaves

1. Melt 3 Tbsp. butter in a 10-inch ovenproof skillet over medium-high heat; add chopped zucchini, squash, and onion, and sauté 12 to 14 minutes or until onion is tender. Remove skillet from heat.
2. Whisk together eggs and next 3 ingredients until well blended. Pour over vegetable mixture in skillet.
3. Bake at 350° for 33 to 35 minutes or until edges are lightly browned and center is set. Sprinkle evenly with chopped fresh basil. **Makes** 6 to 8 servings.

from our kitchen

Make a Signature Sauce

Barbecue pit masters are often as well known for their sauces as they are for the slow-cooked meat on which they slather them. If you want to stir up your own claim to fame, you don't have to start from scratch—just add a little of your own personality to a bottled sauce. Whether you prefer vinegar-based, tomato-based, or mustard-based, find a brand you like, then stir in some jazzy ingredients to taste. Brown sugar, mustard, and lemon juice are must-haves, while garlic powder, minced onion, black pepper, crushed red pepper, soy sauce, and even ginger might suit your fancy.

If you like a touch of smoke, a few scant drops of liquid smoke will help provide the charcoal flavor missing from foods cooked over gas. Just be sure to use a light hand here to avoid an artificial taste.

Versatile Kitchen Shears

Once you own a pair of kitchen shears, you'll wonder how you ever got along without them. We use them for just about everything in the kitchen, including opening stubborn food packages. You can buy quality, inexpensive shears at discount and home goods stores, or purchase top-of-the-line versions at kitchen stores and Web sites. Here are some suggestions for using them.
- Cut up small amounts of fresh herbs. For larger amounts, put the herbs in a glass measuring cup, stick in the scissors, and snip away.
- Cut up whole canned tomatoes.
- Quarter quesadillas.
- Remove the excess skin from chicken.
- Cut pizza.
- Halve bacon slices for hors d'oeuvres.
- Use the center part of the handle to open bottles or cut the foil off wine bottles.

Potato Salad Made Easy

Even though you love potato salad, you likely aren't enthusiastic about having to peel and cube the potatoes that go in it. Fortunately, there's a better way. Test Kitchens Professional Vanessa McNeil Rocchio shares this tip: Cook scrubbed whole potatoes in their skins. Drain and set aside for 1 hour or until they're cool enough to handle but still warm. Use a clean dish towel to hold each potato, and gently squeeze until broken into bite-size pieces. The potato salad will have a creamy consistency similar to that of smashed potatoes.

Which type of potato do you prefer for potato salad? The Foods staff ranges across the board. Russet, Yukon gold, and red potatoes are favorites. Some people like to cook whole potatoes in the skins, while others prefer to cut them before cooking. Most start the cooking in cold water. Considering our combined years of cooking experience and love of potato salad, you can assume that pretty much any way you make it is fine—as long as you don't overcook the potatoes.

august

Backyard Favorite

Take a bite of these ribs, and you'll whisper "wow" in total respect for the amazing taste. We have new prep tricks too (see the box below). Is your mouth watering yet? Then start cooking—and eating.

Sweet-Hot Baby Back Ribs
family favorite

PREP: 30 MIN.; CHILL: 8 HR.; STAND: 40 MIN.; GRILL: 2 HR., 30 MIN.

An up-to-date cooking method makes these ribs easy to fix. Our directions are for a two-burner gas grill. If you have a three-burner grill, light both sides, and leave the center portion off. Potato salad makes a perfect pairing. Dress up your favorite potato salad recipe with new potatoes instead of Idaho.

2 Tbsp. ground ginger
1 tsp. salt
1 tsp. black pepper
½ tsp. dried crushed red pepper
3 slabs baby back pork ribs (about 5½ lb.)
2 limes, halved
Sweet-Hot 'Cue Sauce

1. Combine first 4 ingredients in a small bowl.
2. Rinse and pat ribs dry. If desired, remove thin membrane from back of ribs by slicing into it with a knife and then pulling it off. (This will make ribs more tender.)
3. Rub ribs with cut sides of limes, squeezing as you rub. Massage ginger mixture into meat, covering all sides. Wrap ribs tightly with plastic wrap, and place in zip-top plastic freezer bags or a 13- x 9-inch baking dish; seal or cover, and chill 8 hours. Let ribs stand at room temperature 30 minutes before grilling. Remove plastic wrap.
4. Light 1 side of grill, heating to medium-high heat (350° to 400°); leave other side unlit. Place rib slabs over unlit side, stacking 1 on top of the other.
5. Grill, covered with grill lid, 40 minutes. Reposition rib slabs, moving bottom slab to the top, and grill 40 minutes. Reposition 1 more time, moving bottom slab to the top; grill 40 minutes.
6. Lower grill temperature to medium heat (300° to 350°); unstack rib slabs, and place side by side over unlit side of grill. Cook ribs 30 more minutes, basting with half of Sweet-Hot 'Cue Sauce. Remove ribs from grill, and let stand 10 minutes. Cut ribs, slicing between bones. Serve ribs with remaining Sweet-Hot 'Cue Sauce. **Makes** 6 servings.

Sweet-Hot 'Cue Sauce:
PREP: 10 MIN., COOK: 35 MIN.

This sauce makes a large yield—it's so good, though, you won't mind having plenty left over for serving with grilled chicken or burgers.

2 (10-oz.) bottles sweet chili sauce
2 cups ketchup
⅓ cup firmly packed dark brown sugar
1 tsp. ground ginger
1 tsp. pepper
½ tsp. dried crushed red pepper flakes

1. Combine all ingredients in a saucepan over medium-high heat. Bring mixture to a boil; reduce heat, and simmer 30 minutes. **Makes** 4 cups.

Note: For testing purposes only, we used Maggi Taste of Asia Sweet Chili Sauce.

A New Way to Cook Ribs

This method comes from Test Kitchens Director Lyda Jones Burnette's father-in-law, who has cooked ribs this way for years.

Cook three rib slabs, stacked, 40 minutes. To rotate, lift the top slab off, and move to grill grate. Lift the other two slabs up, and stack on top of the one just moved to the grate; grill 40 more minutes. Reposition again,

and cook 40 more minutes. You're now ready to unstack and baste with Sweet-Hot 'Cue Sauce; then cook for a final 30 minutes.
Tip: Push the stack of slabs back into the center of the indirect heat grate after each rotation. Otherwise, the slabs will be too close to the heat source and could possibly overcook.

Grill Something New

Sizzling Supper

Serves 6

Honey Mustard Pork Kabobs or
Cajun Turkey Kabobs
or Caribbean Pork Kabobs or Spicy
Chicken Kabobs

Grilled Peaches Jezebel

Crusty French bread

Lemonade and tea

Get ready for some backyard fun. Reasonable prices on seasonal produce make these great-tasting kabobs and grilled peaches terrific choices for casual entertaining.

Honey Mustard Pork Kabobs

PREP: 20 MIN., SOAK: 30 MIN., GRILL: 16 MIN.
(Pictured on page 181)

6 (12-inch) wooden or metal skewers
1 (1.7-lb.) honey mustard pork loin,
   trimmed and cut into 1½-inch
   pieces
3 assorted bell peppers, cut into 1-inch
   pieces
3 small red onions, quartered
2 tsp. seasoned black pepper
Vegetable cooking spray
Garnish: fresh thyme sprigs

1. Soak wooden skewers in water 30 minutes to prevent burning.
2. Thread pork, peppers, and onions alternately onto skewers. Sprinkle kabobs evenly with seasoned pepper; lightly coat with cooking spray.
3. Grill kabobs, covered with grill lid, over medium heat (300° to 350°) 6 to 8 minutes on each side or until done. Garnish kabobs, if desired. **Makes** 6 servings.

Cajun Turkey Kabobs: Substitute 1½ lb. turkey tenderloin for pork loin and 2 Tbsp. Cajun seasoning for seasoned pepper. Proceed with recipe as directed.

Caribbean Pork Kabobs: Substitute 1½ lb. pork tenderloin for pork loin and 2 Tbsp. Caribbean Jerk seasoning for seasoned pepper. Proceed with recipe as directed. Squeeze juice from 1 large lime over kabobs just before serving.

Spicy Chicken Kabobs: Substitute 1½ lb. chicken tenderloin for pork loin. Whisk together ⅓ cup peanut butter, ⅓ cup water, ¼ cup soy sauce, 3 Tbsp. brown sugar, 3 minced garlic cloves, 1 Tbsp. grated lime rind, and 1 tsp. crushed red pepper flakes. Place chicken in a large zip-top plastic bag; pour peanut butter mixture over chicken. Seal bag, and chill at least 30 minutes or up to 4 hours. Remove chicken from marinade, discarding marinade. Proceed with recipe as directed.

Grilled Peaches Jezebel

fast fixin's

PREP: 5 MIN., GRILL: 6 MIN.
Horseradish adds a spicy bite to this simple and delicious side dish. (Pictured on page 181)

¼ cup honey
2 tsp. Dijon mustard
1 tsp. horseradish
6 firm, ripe peaches,
   halved
Vegetable cooking spray

1. Whisk together first 3 ingredients. Brush half of honey mixture evenly over cut sides of peaches.
2. Coat a cold cooking grate with cooking spray, and place on grill over medium heat (300° to 350°). Arrange peach halves, cut sides up, on grate; grill, covered with grill lid, 3 minutes on each side or until tender and golden. Remove from grill, and brush cut sides of peaches evenly with remaining honey mixture. **Makes** 6 servings.

Just-Right Iced Tea

You often tell us you turn to *Southern Living* for ideas on what to bring to church suppers or other events. For Vicky Sheridan of Fountain Inn, South Carolina, the just-right recipe from our pages turned out to be Southern Sweet Tea.

Southern Sweet Tea

fast fixin's

PREP: 5 MIN., COOK: 5 MIN., STEEP: 10 MIN.
We halved the original recipe to make it family-size, but it doubles easily. If you like tea that's really sweet, add the full cup of sugar.

3 cups water
2 family-size tea bags
½ to 1 cup sugar
7 cups cold water

1. Bring 3 cups water to a boil in a saucepan; add tea bags. Boil 1 minute; remove from heat. Cover and steep 10 minutes.
2. Remove and discard tea bags. Add desired amount of sugar, stirring until dissolved.
3. Pour into a 1-gal. container, and add 7 cups cold water. Serve over ice. **Makes** 2½ qt.
                        VICKY SHERIDAN
             FOUNTAIN INN, SOUTH CAROLINA

Peach Iced Tea: Stir together 1½ qt. Southern Sweet Tea made with ½ cup sugar; add 1 (33.8-oz.) bottle peach nectar and ¼ cup lemon juice. Stir well. Serve over ice. **Makes** about 2½ qt.

Tea 'n' Lemonade: Stir together 2 qt. Southern Sweet Tea made with ½ cup sugar; add 1 cup thawed lemonade concentrate, and stir well. Serve over ice. **Makes** 2¼ qt.

Melt-in-Your-Mouth Desserts

When it comes to desserts at Test Kitchens Professional Rebecca Kracke Gordon's house, sweeter is always better, and her mom's ooey-gooey Mississippi Mud Cake definitely fits the description. This dessert is simple to make, bake, and take and is the perfect crowd-pleaser.

Mississippi Mud Cake
PREP: 15 MIN., BAKE: 40 MIN.
This luscious dessert doesn't even require a mixer, and it's portable too. If you're really in a hurry, try our express version. (Pictured on page 7)

1 cup chopped pecans
1 cup butter
4 oz. semisweet chocolate, chopped
2 cups sugar
1½ cups all-purpose flour
½ cup unsweetened cocoa
4 large eggs
1 tsp. vanilla extract
¾ tsp. salt
1 (10.5-oz.) bag miniature
  marshmallows
Chocolate Frosting

1. Place pecans in a single layer on a baking sheet.
2. Bake at 350° for 8 to 10 minutes or until toasted.
3. Microwave 1 cup butter and semisweet chocolate in a large microwave-safe glass bowl at HIGH 1 minute or until melted and smooth, stirring every 30 seconds.
4. Whisk sugar and next 5 ingredients into chocolate mixture. Pour into a greased 15- x 10- x 1-inch jelly-roll pan.
5. Bake at 350° for 20 minutes. Remove from oven, and sprinkle evenly with miniature marshmallows; bake 8 to 10 more minutes or until golden brown. Drizzle warm cake with Chocolate Frosting, and sprinkle evenly with toasted pecans. **Makes** 15 servings.

Chocolate Frosting:
fast fixin's
PREP: 10 MIN., COOK: 5 MIN.

½ cup butter
⅓ cup unsweetened cocoa
⅓ cup milk
1 (16-oz.) package powdered sugar
1 tsp. vanilla extract

1. Stir together first 3 ingredients in a medium saucepan over medium heat until butter is melted. Cook, stirring constantly, 2 minutes or until slightly thickened; remove from heat. Beat in powdered sugar and 1 tsp. vanilla at medium-high speed with an electric mixer until smooth. **Makes** about 2 cups.

ANNE KRACKE
BIRMINGHAM, ALABAMA

Kitchen Express Mississippi Mud Cake: Prepare pecans as directed. Substitute 2 (17.6-oz.) packages fudge brownie mix for batter. Prepare mix according to package directions; pour batter into a greased 15- x 10- x 1-inch jelly-roll pan. Bake at 350° for 25 minutes. Remove from oven, and top with marshmallows; bake 8 to 10 more minutes. Proceed with recipe as directed.

Note: For testing purposes only, we used Duncan Hines Chocolate Lover's Double Fudge Brownie Mix.

Caramel-Peanut Mississippi Mud Cake: Omit pecans. Prepare and bake Mississippi Mud Cake as directed. Microwave ½ cup bottled caramel sauce at HIGH 15 seconds. Drizzle over browned marshmallows. Drizzle with Chocolate Frosting; sprinkle with 1 cup dry-roasted peanuts.

Mississippi Mud Cupcakes: *(Pictured on page 183)* Prepare pecans and Mississippi Mud Cake batter as directed. Spoon batter evenly into 24 paper-lined muffin cups. Bake at 350° for 20 minutes or until puffed. Sprinkle evenly with 2 cups miniature marshmallows, and bake 5 more minutes or until golden. Remove from oven, and cool cupcakes in muffin pans 5 minutes. Remove cupcakes from pans, and place on wire rack. Drizzle warm cakes evenly with 1¼ cups Chocolate Frosting, and sprinkle with toasted pecans. Reserve remaining ¾ cup frosting for another use.

Note: To serve remaining Chocolate Frosting over pound cake or ice cream, microwave reserved ¾ cup Chocolate Frosting in a medium-size microwave-safe glass bowl at HIGH 15 seconds or until warm.

Mississippi Mud Cookies
PREP: 25 MIN., BAKE: 12 MIN. PER BATCH
(Pictured on page 183)

1 cup semisweet chocolate
  morsels
½ cup butter, softened
1 cup sugar
2 large eggs
1 tsp. vanilla extract
1½ cups all-purpose flour
1 tsp. baking powder
½ tsp. salt
1 cup chopped pecans
½ cup milk chocolate morsels
1 cup plus 2 Tbsp. miniature
  marshmallows

1. Microwave semisweet chocolate morsels in a small microwave-safe glass

---

Test Kitchens Tips

■ Be sure to grease pans with shortening because butter may not release the cake from pan as easily.
■ Doughs containing sticky ingredients, such as marshmallows and toffee bits, are best baked on parchment paper-lined baking sheets.
■ When melting chocolate, allow the last bits of unmelted chocolate to stand briefly in the microwave-safe glass bowl before stirring until completely smooth.

bowl at HIGH 1 minute or until smooth, stirring every 30 seconds.

2. Beat butter and sugar at medium speed with an electric mixer until creamy; add eggs, 1 at a time, beating until blended after each addition. Beat in vanilla and melted chocolate.

3. Combine flour, baking powder, and salt; gradually add to chocolate mixture, beating until well blended. Stir in chopped pecans and ½ cup milk chocolate morsels.

4. Drop dough by heaping tablespoonfuls onto parchment paper-lined baking sheets. Press 3 marshmallows into each portion of dough.

5. Bake at 350° for 10 to 12 minutes or until set. Remove to wire racks to cool. **Makes** about 3 dozen.   MARY RUTH MASON
PEARSALL, TEXAS

healthy foods
Power-Packed Flavor

Enjoy these four tasty recipes, and improve your body's overall health with nutrition-dense foods. These recipes will show you simple ways to add healthful and wholesome foods to your diet.

Roasted Garlic-Rubbed Fillets
PREP: 5 MIN., BAKE: 40 MIN., STAND: 30 MIN., COOK: 10 MIN.

Try the roasted garlic rub on other cuts of meat such as pork chops or boneless, skinless chicken breasts.

2 large garlic bulbs
1¼ tsp. olive oil, divided
1 tsp. freshly ground pepper
½ tsp. kosher salt
4 (4-oz.) beef tenderloin
   fillets
1 tsp. butter

1. Cut off pointed ends of garlic; place on a piece of aluminum foil, and driz-

zle cut sides with ¼ tsp. olive oil. Fold foil to seal.

2. Bake at 400° for 40 minutes, and let stand 30 minutes. Squeeze pulp from cloves into a small bowl. Smash garlic, pressing with back of a spoon to make a paste.

3. Sprinkle pepper and salt evenly on beef fillets.

4. Melt butter with remaining 1 tsp. oil in an 8-inch nonstick skillet over medium heat. Add steaks; cook 4 to 5 minutes on each side or to desired degree of doneness. Top steaks evenly with garlic paste. **Makes** 4 servings.

Per serving: Calories 208; Fat 9.8g (sat 3.5g, mono 4.3g, poly 0.5g); Protein 25.7g; Carb 3.3g; Fiber 0.3g; Chol 78mg; Iron 2.1mg; Sodium 307mg; Calc 46mg

Tomato-Zucchini Tart
PREP: 20 MIN., BAKE: 26 MIN., COOK: 2 MIN.

½ (15-oz.) package refrigerated
   piecrusts
1 medium zucchini, thinly sliced (about
   ¾ lb.)
2 tsp. olive oil
3 medium plum tomatoes, sliced
½ cup fresh basil, chopped
⅓ cup (1½ oz.) freshly grated Parmesan
   cheese
⅓ cup light mayonnaise
½ tsp. freshly ground pepper

1. Fit piecrust into a 9-inch tart pan according to package directions; trim excess. Prick bottom and sides of piecrust using a fork.

2. Bake piecrust at 450° for 9 to 11 minutes or until lightly browned. Let cool.

3. Sauté zucchini in hot oil in a large skillet over medium-high heat 2 minutes or until tender. Arrange zucchini in bottom of prepared piecrust. Arrange tomatoes on top of zucchini.

4. Stir together basil, cheese, and mayonnaise. Drop by teaspoonfuls evenly on top of tomatoes, and spread gently. Sprinkle with pepper.

5. Bake at 425° for 10 to 15 minutes or until thoroughly heated and cheese mixture is slightly melted. **Makes** 8 servings.   JULIA RUTLAND
BIRMINGHAM, ALABAMA

Per serving: Calories 199; Fat 13g (sat 4.6g, mono 0.8g, poly 0.1g); Protein 3.8g; Carb 17.3g; Fiber 0.8g; Chol 13mg; Iron 0.4mg; Sodium 266mg; Calc 76mg

Basil-Balsamic Vinaigrette
fast fixin's
PREP: 5 MIN.

Serve over a mixed green salad, or toss with roasted potatoes or sweet potatoes for a tasty potato salad. Olive oil or another option low in saturated fat may be substituted for canola oil.

¼ cup white balsamic vinegar
2 Tbsp. chopped fresh basil *
2 Tbsp. fresh lemon juice
1 Tbsp. Dijon mustard
1 tsp. sugar
1 tsp. minced garlic
½ tsp. salt
½ tsp. pepper
⅓ cup canola oil

1. Whisk together first 8 ingredients in a small bowl; gradually add canola oil in a slow, steady stream, whisking until blended. **Makes** ¾ cup.

CAROLINE KENNEDY
COVINGTON, GEORGIA

*Substitute 2 Tbsp. chopped fresh oregano, if desired.

Per serving (2 Tbsp.): Calories 121; Fat 12.3g (sat 0.9g, mono 7.3g, poly 3.7g); Protein 0g; Carb 2.9g; Fiber 0g; Chol 0mg; Iron 0mg; Sodium 232mg; Calc 3mg

Corn, Avocado, and Black Bean Salsa
fast fixin's • make ahead
PREP: 15 MIN.

Serve with baked pita or tortilla chips, or top a grilled chicken sandwich or burger. Prepare salsa up to four hours ahead.

2 medium-size ripe avocados, cubed
1 (15.5-oz.) can black beans, rinsed and
   drained
1 (15¼-oz.) can whole kernel corn,
   rinsed and drained
1 fresh jalapeño pepper, seeded and
   diced
⅓ cup chopped red onion
3 Tbsp. fresh lime juice
½ tsp. salt
½ tsp. ground cumin
¼ tsp. ground red pepper

1. Gently stir together all ingredients in a large bowl. **Makes** 4⅔ cups.

Per serving (⅓ cup): Calories 78; Fat 4.6g (sat 0.7g, mono 2.8g, poly 0.6g); Protein 1.9g; Carb 9.1g; Fiber 3.2g; Chol 0mg; Iron 0.7mg; Sodium 154mg; Calc 12mg

Supper Solutions

Don't panic! Easy chicken recipes make mealtime a snap.

Busy families often must squeeze after-school activities, homework, and cooking into a small amount of time. We've created some recipes to help solve that time crunch by making a couple of meals from one main-dish ingredient. Start with Herb-Roasted Chickens at the beginning of the week, and use the second chicken to make another satisfying entrée for your family to enjoy later. We'll show you how.

Herb-Roasted Chickens
family favorite
PREP: 20 MIN.; BAKE: 1 HR., 25 MIN.; STAND: 15 MIN. *(Pictured on page 180)*

6 Tbsp. olive oil
½ cup poultry seasoning
¼ cup fresh rosemary leaves, finely chopped
¼ cup fresh thyme leaves, finely chopped
4 tsp. fresh minced garlic
2 tsp. salt
1 tsp. pepper
2 (3- to 4-lb.) whole chickens

1. Stir together first 7 ingredients until well blended.
2. If necessary, remove giblets and neck from chickens, and reserve for another use. Rinse chickens with cold water; pat dry.
3. Loosen and lift skin from chicken breasts with fingers (do not totally detach skin). Rub 2 Tbsp. olive oil mixture evenly underneath skin of each chicken. Carefully replace skin. Rub remaining olive oil mixture over both chickens, coating evenly. Place chickens, side by side, on a lightly greased wire rack in a pan.
4. Bake at 425° for 30 minutes; cover loosely with aluminum foil, and bake 45 to 55 minutes or until a meat thermometer inserted in thickest portion of breast registers 165°. Let stand 15 minutes before slicing. **Makes** 8 to 12 servings.

DENISE NICKERSON
LAWRENCEVILLE, GEORGIA

Note: Dried herbs and seasonings may be substituted for fresh. Substitute ½ tsp. garlic powder for minced, but use the same amounts for the other herbs and spices.

Pronto-Stuffed Pasta Shells
family favorite • make ahead
PREP: 30 MIN., BAKE: 45 MIN., STAND: 10 MIN.
We used half of one of the Herb-Roasted Chickens in this recipe.

18 jumbo pasta shells
2 (10-oz.) packages frozen chopped spinach, thawed
2 cups chopped cooked Herb-Roasted Chickens
1 Tbsp. chopped fresh basil
1 (16-oz.) container low-fat cottage cheese
1 large egg, lightly beaten
¼ cup grated Parmesan cheese
¼ tsp. ground nutmeg
1 (16-oz.) jar Alfredo sauce

1. Prepare pasta shells according to package directions.
2. Meanwhile, drain chopped spinach well, pressing between paper towels.
3. Stir together spinach, chicken, basil, and next 4 ingredients. Spoon mixture evenly into shells.
4. Spread half of jarred Alfredo sauce in a lightly greased 13- x 9-inch baking dish. Arrange stuffed pasta shells over sauce, and pour remaining sauce over shells.
5. Bake, covered, at 350° for 40 to 45 minutes or until filling is hot and sauce is bubbly. Remove from oven, and let stand 10 minutes. **Makes** 4 to 6 servings.

Note: To make ahead, prepare recipe as directed through Step 4. Cover and freeze up to 1 month. Thaw in refrigerator 24 hours. Let stand at room temperature 30 minutes. Bake, covered, for 1 hour and 20 minutes.

Mushroom-and-Fresh Parsley Noodles
fast fixin's
PREP: 10 MIN., COOK: 8 MIN.

1 (8-oz.) package medium egg noodles
3 chicken bouillon cubes
5 Tbsp. butter
1 (8-oz.) package sliced fresh button mushrooms *****
¼ cup finely chopped fresh parsley or basil
Freshly ground pepper to taste

1. Prepare pasta according to package directions, adding chicken bouillon cubes to water.
2. Meanwhile, melt 4 Tbsp. butter in a large skillet over medium heat. Add sliced mushrooms, and sauté 5 minutes or until liquid evaporates and mushrooms are golden brown. Remove from heat. Stir in chopped parsley, noodles, and remaining 1 Tbsp. butter. Stir in pepper to taste. **Makes** 6 servings.

LISA LUHRS
WAUKEGAN, ILLINOIS

*Substitute 1 (8-oz.) package assorted mushrooms, sliced, if desired.

Microwave Sides

The convenience of the microwave is often overlooked when cooking vegetables, but many choices steam beautifully due to their high moisture content.

Summer Squash Casserole
PREP: 20 MIN., COOK: 21 MIN.,
STAND: 10 MIN.

6 Tbsp. butter, divided
1 cup chopped onion
2½ lb. yellow squash, sliced
1 cup mayonnaise
2 large eggs, lightly beaten
1 Tbsp. all-purpose flour
2 tsp. sugar
½ tsp. salt
1 (10-oz.) block sharp Cheddar cheese, shredded
⅓ cup soft, fresh breadcrumbs

1. Microwave 4 Tbsp. butter in a large microwave-safe bowl at HIGH 1 minute or until melted. Add onion, and cover bowl tightly with plastic wrap, folding back a small edge to allow steam to escape. Microwave at HIGH 2 minutes.
2. Uncover, add squash, and cover bowl tightly with plastic wrap, folding back a small edge. Microwave at HIGH 5 minutes or until squash is tender. (Do not drain.)
3. Combine mayonnaise and next 4 ingredients in a large bowl. Stir in squash mixture and cheese.
4. Spoon mixture into a lightly greased 11- x 7-inch baking dish. Cover dish tightly with plastic wrap, folding back a small edge.
5. Microwave at HIGH 10 minutes or until casserole is set. Remove and let stand 10 minutes.
6. Microwave remaining 2 Tbsp. butter at HIGH 1 minute or until melted. Stir together melted butter and breadcrumbs; microwave at HIGH 2 minutes. Sprinkle over casserole. **Makes** 8 servings.

Note: The onion and squash release excess moisture when cooking; do not drain. The flour in the mayonnaise mixture will help absorb the moisture.

Brown Butter Green Beans
PREP: 10 MIN., COOK: 7 MIN.
Browning butter is a French technique that gives butter a rich and nutty flavor. We've simplified this process by preparing it in the microwave.

3 Tbsp. butter
1 garlic clove, minced
1 lb. fresh green beans, trimmed
½ small sweet onion, sliced
½ tsp. salt
¼ tsp. cracked pepper

1. Microwave butter in a 2-cup glass measuring cup at HIGH 1½ to 2 minutes or until butter is brown. Remove from microwave, and immediately add minced garlic.
2. Place green beans, onion, and 3 Tbsp. water in a microwave-safe bowl. Cover bowl tightly with plastic wrap, folding back a small edge to allow steam to escape.
3. Microwave at HIGH 4 to 5 minutes or until vegetables are tender; drain. Toss together hot beans and sliced onion, brown butter mixture, and salt; sprinkle with cracked pepper. **Makes** 4 servings.

CAROLYN NORMAN
OLD HICKORY, TENNESSEE

quick & easy
Salads Make a Meal

Enjoy a main-dish salad for supper. Just toss together a meat and a side dish with mouthwatering dressing.

Raspberry-Turkey Salad
PREP: 15 MIN., COOK: 24 MIN.
Raspberry-Turkey Salad starts with a simple dressing from raspberry preserves, wine, and mango chutney. You may substitute 1 lb. chicken cutlets for turkey.

½ tsp. seasoned salt
½ tsp. garlic powder
½ tsp. onion powder
1 lb. turkey breast cutlets
1 Tbsp. butter
1 Tbsp. olive oil
½ cup seedless raspberry preserves
½ cup chicken broth
½ cup white wine *
½ cup hot mango chutney
1 (7-oz.) package mixed salad greens, thoroughly washed

1. Stir together first 3 ingredients; rub evenly over turkey cutlets.
2. Melt butter with oil in a large skillet over medium-high heat; add cutlets, and cook 3 to 4 minutes on each side or until lightly browned. Remove from skillet, and keep warm.
3. Stir raspberry preserves and next 3 ingredients into skillet over medium-high heat, stirring until preserves melt and to loosen particles from bottom of skillet. Cook, stirring occasionally, 14 to 16 minutes or until mixture is reduced by half.
4. Toss salad greens with ¼ to ⅓ cup warm preserves mixture in a large salad bowl just until greens are thoroughly warmed and lightly coated with preserve mixture. Arrange on salad plates, and top with turkey cutlets. **Makes** 4 servings.

LYNDA SARKISIAN
SENECA, SOUTH CAROLINA

*Substitute ¼ cup chicken broth and ¼ cup fruit juice (such as white grape, orange, or apple), if desired.

Calypso Steak Salad

PREP: 20 MIN., GRILL: 10 MIN., STAND: 10 MIN.
To make the salsa mixture ahead, just cover and chill up to 8 hours. Let stand at room temperature about 20 minutes, while steaks marinate in lime juice mixture. (Pictured on page 181)

1½ lb. beef strip steaks
1½ tsp. grated lime rind, divided
3 Tbsp. fresh lime juice, divided
1 (8-oz.) can pineapple tidbits, drained
½ cup peach-mango salsa *
⅓ cup diced red onion
⅓ cup diced green bell pepper
¼ cup chopped fresh cilantro
½ tsp. salt
1 tsp. Jamaican jerk seasoning
1 head romaine lettuce
Garnish: chopped fresh cilantro

1. Place strip steaks in a shallow dish, and add 1 tsp. grated lime rind and 1½ Tbsp. lime juice, turning to coat.
2. Stir together pineapple, next 5 ingredients, remaining ½ tsp. grated lime rind, and remaining 1½ Tbsp. lime juice until blended.
3. Remove steaks from lime juice mixture, discarding juice. Sprinkle steaks evenly with 1 tsp. Jamaican jerk seasoning.
4. Grill steaks, covered with grill lid, over medium-high heat (350° to 400°) 4 to 5 minutes on each side or to desired degree of doneness. Let steaks stand 10 minutes, and cut into thin strips.
5. Arrange lettuce leaves on a serving platter, and top with sliced steak and salsa mixture. Garnish, if desired. **Makes** 4 servings.

DIANE SPARROW
OSAGE, IOWA

*Substitute ½ cup salsa, if desired.

Note: For testing purposes only, we used Desert Pepper Trading Company Peach Mango Salsa.

Breakfast Together

Rise and Shine Menu

Serves 8 to 10

Mini Sausage-and-Egg Casseroles

Honey-Ginger Fruit

Banana Breakfast Bread

Orange juice and coffee

Busy schedules often keep Julia Smeds Roth and her two teenage daughters from enjoying a meal together. This full-time working mom spends most of her afternoons and evenings at ball games, practices, and school functions, leaving little time to cook supper. So she and the girls make it a point to share breakfast and catch up each morning. It also gives Julia satisfaction to know the girls will begin their day with plenty of nourishment.

Mini Sausage-and-Egg Casseroles

freezeable • make ahead

PREP: 20 MIN., BAKE: 30 MIN.
Use 1 (16-oz.) package of crumbled pork sausage instead of the patties, if desired. Simply cook in a nonstick skillet until browned and crumbled. These little casseroles may be made ahead and frozen up to one month.

8 (1½-oz.) sourdough bread slices, cut into ½-inch cubes (about 8 cups)
Vegetable cooking spray
1 (12-oz.) package fully cooked pork sausage patties, chopped
2½ cups 2% reduced-fat milk
4 large eggs
1 Tbsp. Dijon mustard
½ cup buttermilk
1 (10¾-oz.) can cream of mushroom soup
1 cup (4 oz.) shredded sharp Cheddar cheese

1. Divide bread cubes evenly among 10 (8- to 10-oz.) ovenproof coffee mugs coated with cooking spray. Top evenly with sausage. Whisk together 2½ cups milk, eggs, and Dijon mustard. Pour evenly over bread mixture in mugs.
2. Whisk together buttermilk and cream of mushroom soup. Spoon over bread mixture in mugs; sprinkle with Cheddar cheese. Place coffee mugs on a baking sheet.
3. Bake at 350° for 25 to 30 minutes or until casseroles are set and puffed. Serve immediately. **Makes** 10 servings.

Note: Unbaked mugs of casserole can be covered with plastic wrap, then foil, and frozen up to 1 month. Thaw overnight in the refrigerator. Bake as directed.

Sausage-and-Egg Casserole: Omit coffee mugs. Arrange bread in 2 lightly greased 8-inch square baking dishes or 1 lightly greased 13- x 9-inch baking dish. Proceed as directed, increasing bake time to 1 hour or until casserole is set.

Note: An unbaked casserole can be covered with plastic wrap, then foil, and frozen up to 1 month. Thaw overnight in the refrigerator. Bake as directed.

Honey-Ginger Fruit

family favorite • fast fixin's

PREP: 20 MIN.
The combination of grape juice, honey, and ginger adds punch to whatever fruit you have on hand. Serve it alone or over yogurt or warm biscuits.

1 cup white grape juice
3 Tbsp. honey
1½ tsp. grated fresh ginger
1 pt. fresh strawberries, halved
3 oranges, sectioned
½ honeydew melon, chopped
1 cup seedless green grapes

1. Combine grape juice, honey, and ginger in a large bowl. Add remaining ingredients, tossing to coat. Serve immediately. **Makes** 7 cups.

Banana Breakfast Bread
family favorite

PREP: 15 MIN.; BAKE: 1 HR., 10 MIN.;
COOL: 2 HR., 10 MIN.

This can be doubled easily, so make two loaves to last all week. Try toasting slices and serving with cream cheese or peanut butter.

½ cup chopped pecans
1½ cups whole wheat flour
1 tsp. baking powder
1 tsp. baking soda
½ tsp. ground cinnamon
½ cup sugar
2 Tbsp. butter, melted
4 medium-size ripe bananas, mashed
1 egg, lightly beaten
1 (7-oz.) package dried fruit bits
Vegetable cooking spray

1. Place pecans in a single layer in a jelly-roll pan.
2. Bake at 350° for 8 to 10 minutes or until lightly browned.
3. Combine flour and next 3 ingredients in a large bowl. Combine sugar and next 3 ingredients in a small bowl; add to flour mixture, stirring just until dry ingredients are moistened. Stir in pecans and fruit bits. Pour mixture into an 8½- x 4½-inch loaf pan coated with cooking spray.
4. Bake at 350° for 55 to 60 minutes or until a wooden pick inserted in center of bread comes out clean. Cool in pan on wire rack 10 minutes; remove from pan, and cool on wire rack 2 hours or until completely cool. **Makes** 1 loaf.

Cool Soups

They are soothing, pretty, and easy on the palate. Make any of these soups up to three days ahead to keep on hand. Chilled Cucumber Soup and Cantaloupe Soup work best as first courses. Chilled Strawberry Soup and Tropical Fruit Medley are terrific not-too-sweet dessert choices. Serve in an assortment of glasses or teacups the next time you entertain.

Tropical Fruit Medley
make ahead

PREP: 25 MIN., CHILL: 30 MIN.

This is pretty served in a shallow, wide-rimmed bowl. Or, serve it in small glasses tucked inside a large, pretty bowl that's filled with ice and garnished with mint sprigs.

1 fresh pineapple, peeled, cored, and chopped
2 fresh mangoes, peeled and chopped
3 kiwifruit, peeled and chopped
¼ lb. green seedless grapes, halved (about 1 cup)
¼ tsp. ground cardamom
4 cups white grape juice
Garnish: fresh mint sprigs

1. Stir together first 4 ingredients in a large bowl. Sprinkle with cardamom.
2. Pour grape juice over fruit, stirring gently. Cover and chill 30 minutes. Garnish, if desired. **Makes** 12 cups.

Chilled Strawberry Soup
make ahead

PREP: 10 MIN., CHILL: 2 HR.

Garnish this creamy milk shake of a soup with chopped strawberries for added appeal.

1 (16-oz.) container fresh strawberries, sliced
2 cups half-and-half
1¼ cups sour cream
¾ cup powdered sugar
2 Tbsp. white balsamic vinegar

1. Process strawberries in a food processor until smooth, stopping to scrape down sides as needed; pour into a large bowl. Whisk in half-and-half and remaining ingredients. Cover and chill at least 2 hours or up to 3 days. Stir just before serving. **Makes** about 5 cups.

Lightened Chilled Strawberry Soup: Substitute 2 cups fat-free half-and-half and 1¼ cups light sour cream for regular. Proceed with recipe as directed.

Cantaloupe Soup
make ahead

PREP: 15 MIN., CHILL: 3 HR.

1 large cantaloupe, chopped
3 cups orange juice
1½ tsp. fresh lime juice
½ tsp. ground cinnamon
¼ tsp. salt

1. Process all ingredients, in batches, in a blender until smooth, stopping to scrape down sides as needed.
2. Transfer to a large bowl. Cover and chill at least 3 hours or up to 3 days. Stir just before serving. **Makes** about 8 cups.

BEBE MAY
PENSACOLA, FLORIDA

Chilled Cucumber Soup
make ahead

PREP: 20 MIN., CHILL: 2 HR.

4 cucumbers, peeled, seeded, and chopped (about 3 lb.)
3 cups buttermilk
1 (8-oz.) carton plain yogurt
2 green onions, chopped
¼ cup chopped fresh parsley
3 Tbsp. fresh lemon juice
2 Tbsp. chopped fresh dill
1½ tsp. salt
½ tsp. pepper

1. Process all ingredients, in batches, in a food processor until smooth, stopping to scrape down sides as needed. Transfer to a serving bowl; cover and chill 2 hours. **Makes** about 8 cups.

ADELYNE SMITH
DUNNVILLE, KENTUCKY

A Cajun Classic

You can serve it on fine china at formal gatherings or down-home style right from the pot on the stove.

Étouffée (ay-too-FAY) isn't just a fancy-sounding name—it's Cajun comfort food at its best. The thick, spicy mixture of crawfish, shrimp, or crab (or a combination of these) with onions and peppers is cooked in a light gravy and then served with rice. It's one of those classic recipes that's perfect just as it is, so there's no need to change anything.

These recipes call for fresh crawfish, crabmeat, and shrimp because they're readily available in Cajun country. Don't fret if you can't get your hands on the fresh seafood—frozen crawfish tails and frozen uncooked shrimp work very well. Whether you're hosting a fancy party or serving a weeknight dinner, bring étouffée to the table for a bowl of Cajun goodness.

Test Kitchen Notebook

Some étouffée experts share their thoughts on this classic dish.

"My dad made étouffée all the time when I was growing up," says cookbook author Marcelle Bienvenu, of St. Martinville, Louisiana. "He cooked it in a black iron pot over a wood-burning fire at our camp. Crawfish and shrimp were the most popular ingredients, but he used whatever we had—sometimes catfish, frog legs, or even chicken. It's such a simple dish to be so good."

For Ti Martin, co-owner of Commander's Palace in New Orleans, "the surroundings make étouffée elegant or casual. You can serve it on fine china with linen at formal gatherings or down-home style right from the pot on the stove."

Andria Scott Hurst
SENIOR WRITER

Crawfish Étouffée

PREP: 35 MIN., COOK: 22 MIN.
Louisiana, the self-proclaimed crawfish capital of the world, harvests much of our nation's supply from its nearby waters.

¼ cup butter
2 Tbsp. olive oil
⅓ cup all-purpose flour
1 medium onion, chopped
2 celery ribs, chopped
1 medium-size green bell pepper, chopped
4 garlic cloves, minced
1 large shallot, chopped
2 tsp. Cajun seasoning
½ tsp. ground red pepper
1 (14-oz.) can low-sodium chicken broth
¼ cup chopped fresh parsley
¼ cup chopped fresh chives
2 lb. cooked, peeled crawfish tails *
Hot cooked rice

1. Melt butter with oil in a large Dutch oven over medium-high heat; stir in flour, and cook, stirring constantly, 5 minutes or until caramel colored. Add onion and next 6 ingredients; sauté 5 minutes or until vegetables are tender.
2. Add chicken broth, parsley, and chives; cook, stirring constantly, 5 minutes or until mixture is thick and bubbly.
3. Stir in crawfish; cook 5 minutes or until thoroughly heated. Serve with hot cooked rice. **Makes** 4 to 6 servings.

*Substitute 2 lb. frozen cooked crawfish tails, thawed and drained, for fresh, if desired.

Crab-and-Shrimp Étouffée

PREP: 20 MIN., COOK: 27 MIN.
A combination of two favorites—fresh seafood and rice— tastes great in this one-dish meal.

2 lb. unpeeled, medium-size raw shrimp *
¼ cup butter
2 Tbsp. olive oil
⅓ cup all-purpose flour
⅔ cup chopped onion
¼ cup chopped green bell pepper
¼ cup chopped celery
3 garlic cloves, minced
1 (14-oz.) can chicken broth
⅓ cup dry white wine
¼ cup chopped green onions
1 Tbsp. low-sodium Creole seasoning
1 Tbsp. tomato paste
1 Tbsp. chopped fresh parsley
2 tsp. Worcestershire sauce
½ tsp. hot sauce
1 (16-oz.) container fresh crabmeat, drained and flaked
5 cups hot cooked long-grain rice
Garnish: chopped fresh flat-leaf parsley

1. Peel shrimp; devein, if desired.
2. Melt butter with oil in a large Dutch oven over medium-high heat; stir in flour, and cook, stirring constantly, 5 minutes or until caramel colored. Add chopped onion, green pepper, and celery; cook, stirring constantly, 4 minutes or until vegetables are tender. Add minced garlic, and sauté 1 minute.
3. Stir in chicken broth and next 7 ingredients, and cook, stirring occasionally, 10 minutes. Add shrimp. Cover, reduce heat, and simmer, stirring occasionally, 5 minutes.
4. Stir in crabmeat; cook, stirring often, until thoroughly heated.
5. Spoon shrimp mixture into individual serving bowls. Spoon hot cooked rice on top of shrimp mixture. Garnish, if desired. **Makes** 4 to 6 servings.

*Substitute 2 (16-oz.) packages frozen unpeeled, raw shrimp, thawed according to package directions, if desired.

Note: For testing purposes only, we used Tony Chachere's Lite Creole Seasoning.

30-Minute Chili, page 31

Chicken 'n' Spinach Pasta Bake , page 42

Stuffed Cherry Tomatoes, page 40

Chocolate Chimichangas With Raspberry
Sauce, page 41

Hot Fudge Sundae Shake, page 97

Chocolate-Mint
Cupcake, page 66

Coconut Cupcakes, page 66

Juiced-up Roast Pork, Edamame Succotash, and Cauliflower-Leek Puree, page 58

Apple-Pear Salad With Lemon-Poppy Seed Dressing, page 70

Honey Yeast Rolls, page 105

Turkey Cheeseburger With Rosemary
Onions, page 83

Veggie Fried Rice, page 84

Crispy Oven-Fried Drumsticks, page 84

Pepperoni Pizza, page 84

resh and HOT!

Bacon-Blue Cheese Salad With White Wine Vinaigrette, page 81

Lemon-Dill Chicken Salad-Stuffed Eggs, page 80

Cream Cheese-Olive Spread, page 80

Shrimp Shooters, page 117

Mediterranean Salmon With White Beans, page 55

Cha-Cha Chicken Salad, page 119

Minted Fruit Salsa over
angel food cake, page 99

Creamy Lemonade Pie, page 96

Cream-Filled Grilled Pound Cake,
page 119

Strip Steak With Rosemary Butter, Steak Fries, and Cucumber Salad page 118

Grilled Okra and Tomatoes, page 118

Herb-Roasted Chickens, page 156

Grilled Peaches Jezebel and
Honey Mustard Pork Kabobs,
page 153

Calypso Steak Salad, page 158

Chocolate-Ginger Pound Cake, page 211

Mississippi Mud Cookies, page 154

Mississippi Mud
Cupcakes, page 154

Corn-and-Crab Chowder, page 226

Sweet-and-Tangy Braised Greens With
Smoked Turkey, page 232

Porcini Mushroom Tortelloni With
Wilted Greens, page 264

Pan-Seared Flat Iron Steak, page 264; Creamed Turnip Greens, page 265

Bourbon-Cranberry Turkey Tenderloin,
page 260

Sweet-and-Sour Green Beans, page 260

Dark Chocolate Bundt Cake with
Wintry-White Icing, page 278

Vanilla Butter Cake with Wintry-White
Icing, page 278

Praline Bundt Cake, page 279

Tex-Mex Tonight

Spicy Supper

Serves 4

Easy Enchiladas

Mexican rice

Pronto Refried Beans

Margaritas and beer

Spice up a meal with savory Easy Enchiladas. In this recipe, we filled them with flavorful sausage, but if you'd like to make them with chicken, use about 2½ cups chopped or shredded meat from the Herb-Roasted Chickens on page 154.

Test Kitchen Notebook

To Make Easy Enchiladas Ahead: Prepare recipe as directed through Step 4. Cover baking dish with aluminum foil. Prepare sauce as directed in Step 6; place sauce in an airtight container. Freeze tortillas and sauce up to 2 months. Remove tortillas and frozen sauce from freezer; let stand at room temperature 15 minutes. Uncover tortillas; bake at 350° for 25 to 30 minutes or until thoroughly heated and tortillas are crisp. Cook sauce, covered, in a medium saucepan over medium-high heat, stirring occasionally, 10 minutes or until thoroughly heated. Pour sauce over tortillas; top with remaining cheese. Bake 5 more minutes or until cheese is melted. Let stand 5 minutes.

Kristi Michele Crowe
TEST KITCHENS PROFESSIONAL

Easy Enchiladas
make ahead

PREP: 20 MIN., COOK: 23 MIN., BAKE: 30 MIN., STAND: 5 MIN.

Look for fresh salsa in the refrigerated section or the deli counter at your supermarket, or feel free to use your favorite jar of tomato salsa.

1 lb. ground turkey sausage*
½ cup chopped onion
1 tsp. minced garlic
1 (7.76-oz.) can tomatillo salsa, divided
¼ cup chopped fresh cilantro
8 (6-inch) fajita-size corn tortillas**
2 cups (8 oz.) shredded Mexican four-cheese blend, divided
Vegetable cooking spray
2 cups refrigerated fresh medium-heat tomato salsa
½ cup low-sodium chicken broth
Garnish: chopped fresh cilantro

1. Brown sausage in a large skillet over medium-high heat, stirring occasionally, 11 to 14 minutes or until meat crumbles and is no longer pink. Remove sausage from skillet using a slotted spoon, and drain on paper towels.
2. Sauté onion and garlic in hot drippings over medium-high heat 2 to 3 minutes or until onion is tender. Remove from heat. Stir in sausage, ½ cup tomatillo salsa, and ¼ cup chopped cilantro.
3. Place 2 tortillas between damp paper towels. Microwave tortillas at HIGH 15 seconds. Repeat procedure with remaining tortillas.
4. Spoon about ⅓ cup sausage mixture evenly down center of each softened tortilla, and sprinkle each with 1 Tbsp. cheese; roll tortillas up, and place, seam sides down, in a lightly greased 13- x 9-inch baking dish. Lightly coat tops of tortillas with cooking spray.
5. Bake at 350° for 20 to 25 minutes or until tortillas are crisp.
6. Stir together 2 cups tomato salsa, ½ cup chicken broth, and remaining tomatillo salsa in a medium saucepan over medium-high heat; cook, stirring occasionally, 4 to 6 minutes or until thoroughly heated. Pour salsa mixture over tortillas, and top evenly with remaining cheese. Bake 5 more minutes or until cheese is melted. Let stand 5 minutes. Garnish, if desired. **Makes** 4 servings.

*Substitute ground pork sausage, if desired.

**Substitute 8 (6-inch) fajita-size flour tortillas, if desired, omitting Step 3.

Note: For testing purposes only, we used La Costeña Green Mexican Salsa for tomatillo salsa.

Pronto Refried Beans

PREP: 10 MIN., BAKE: 25 MIN., STAND: 5 MIN.

A sprinkle of queso fresco, a fresh white Mexican cheese, adds traditional flavor to this quick and easy side dish. You can buy it at your local supercenter or Hispanic market.

1. Stir together 1 (14½-oz.) can stewed Mexican-style tomatoes, undrained; 1 (31-oz.) can refried beans; 1 tsp. chili powder; and ½ tsp. cumin. Place bean mixture into a lightly greased 2-qt. baking dish. Sprinkle evenly with 1 cup (4 oz.) crumbled queso fresco. Bake at 350° for 25 minutes or until thoroughly heated. Let stand 5 minutes before serving. Garnish with cilantro sprigs, if desired. **Makes** 6 servings.

from our kitchen

Grill Toppers

Cooking vegetables, shrimp, chicken tenders, and other small things on the grill can be a challenge. Just as you go to flip asparagus, for example, it changes direction and slides between the grates into the fire. You can skewer items together, but if you're short on time and patience, a grill wok or topper is just the thing. These inexpensive devices are available at home goods stores, discount stores, and home-improvement stores during the spring and summer.

Grill woks work well for stir-frying on the grill, ensuring even cooking of the contents. The tall, flared sides allow them to easily accommodate a wok tool or spatula, and the small holes let in heat while corralling the food.

Grill toppers are flat, and you can cook more items on them. Use them for vegetables and small pieces of meat or seafood that don't need a lot of turning. If you want to sear onion slices, for example, coat the cold topper with cooking spray (we like the kind formulated for grilling), place it on the food grate, and then add the onions. Once they're the desired degree of doneness on one side, turn the slices with a pair of tongs or a spatula.

A Tender Tip

It's still prime okra season, which means there's a whole lot of fryin' going on in our region of the country. But full-size pods can be notoriously hard and chewy. So to be sure you're about to fry tender ones, try this trick from reader Pam Floyd (who also happens to be our Editor's wife). When you slice into the stem end of the okra with a sharp knife, it should cut "like butter," Pam says. If you encounter any resistance, put the pod aside for the soup pot or a batch of stewed okra and tomatoes.

Roast for Flavor

Tomato-based salsa and pico de gallo are delicious additions to all kinds of recipes. Try them as condiments for dipping, as healthful toppings, and as ingredients in the dish. Make them even more flavorful by roasting or broiling the tomato, onion, and pepper first. This enhances their sweetness by evaporating some of the moisture and caramelizing the natural sugars.

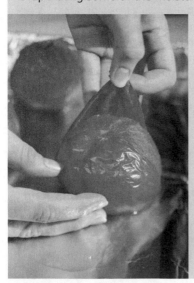

Once cooked, the tomatoes and peppers are really easy to peel—just wait until they're cool enough to handle. If using a hot variety of pepper, such as the serranos in Spicy Salsa Ranchera, wear rubber gloves so the oils don't burn your hands (and be sure not to touch your eyes).

Make this salsa several weeks ahead, and freeze. Thaw it in the refrigerator, and serve either warm or at room temperature. It's great with the Easy Enchiladas on page 193. Be warned: The serranos pack a punch, so this salsa lives up to its name. Scale back to two peppers if you want a milder flavor. You can also substitute other varieties—just adjust the level of heat to your taste.

Spicy Salsa Ranchera
PREP: 10 MIN., BROIL: 20 MIN., STAND: 15 MIN.

Broil 5 medium tomatoes (about 1¾ lb.); 3 serrano chile peppers; 2 garlic cloves, peeled; and 1 medium onion, sliced, on an aluminum foil-lined baking sheet 5 inches from heat 6 minutes on each side or until peppers are blistered. Remove tomatoes, chile peppers, and garlic from baking sheet; broil onions 4 more minutes on each side. Remove from oven; let stand 15 minutes. Remove peels and stem ends from tomatoes and chile peppers. Remove seeds from chile peppers. Pulse tomatoes, chile peppers, garlic, and onion in a blender 10 times or until chunky. Stir in 1 tsp. salt and ¼ cup chopped fresh cilantro. **Makes** about 2½ cups.

SUSAN POOLE
ALEXANDER, NORTH CAROLINA

september

Let's Tailgate

Follow our simple tips to kick off the season.

Game Day Get-Together

Serves 12

Turkey-Cheddar Kabobs With Honey Mustard Dipping Sauce

Mini Cajun Burgers With
Easy Rémoulade

Caramelized Onion Dip with potato chips

Lemony Spinach-Artichoke Dip with corn chips

Team Spirit Cupcakes

Cheer on your favorite high school, college, or pro team this football season by hosting a spirit-filled tailgate party.

Turkey-Cheddar Kabobs With Honey Mustard Dipping Sauce
make ahead
PREP: 20 MIN., CHILL: 30 MIN.
The dipping sauce can also be served with fried chicken breast strips from the deli.

1 lb. deli-smoked turkey, cut into
    1-inch cubes
1 (8-oz.) package Cheddar cheese cubes
1 pt. grape tomatoes
1 (16-oz.) jar dill gherkin pickles
27 (4-inch) wooden skewers
Honey Mustard Dipping Sauce

1. Thread 1 each of first 4 ingredients evenly onto wooden skewers. Cover and chill 30 minutes or up to 1 day. Serve kabobs with Honey Mustard Dipping Sauce. **Makes** 27 kabobs.

Honey Mustard Dipping Sauce: Stir together ¾ cup light mayonnaise, ¼ cup coarse grained Dijon mustard, and 2 Tbsp. honey. Cover and chill 20 minutes or up to 3 days. **Makes** about 1½ cups. Prep: 5 min., Chill: 20 min.

Mini Cajun Burgers With Easy Rémoulade
make ahead
PREP: 20 MIN., GRILL: 10 MIN.
Prepare patties the night before the game. Stack between sheets of wax paper, place in a disposable plastic container, cover with lid, and refrigerate overnight. Transport patties safely by packing in a cooler with ice. They'll be ready for the grill once you arrive at your destination.

1¼ lb. ground beef
½ lb. spicy Cajun sausage, finely
    chopped
2 tsp. Cajun seasoning
1 (14-oz.) package dinner rolls, split
Green leaf lettuce
Easy Rémoulade

1. Combine ground beef and sausage in a large bowl. Shape mixture into 12 (2½-inch) patties, and place on a large baking sheet. Sprinkle patties evenly with Cajun seasoning. Cover and chill up to 1 day, if desired.
2. Grill, covered with grill lid, over medium-high heat (350° to 400°) 5 minutes on each side or until no longer pink in center. Serve on split rolls with green leaf lettuce and Easy Rémoulade. **Makes** 12 appetizer servings.

Easy Rémoulade: Stir together ¾ cup light mayonnaise, 2 Tbsp. Creole mustard, and 2 Tbsp. chopped fresh parsley. Cover and chill 30 minutes or up to 3 days. **Makes** 1 cup. Prep: 5 min., Chill: 30 min.

Caramelized Onion Dip
make ahead
PREP: 10 MIN., COOK: 23 MIN.,
STAND: 30 MIN., CHILL: 30 MIN.

2 Tbsp. butter
2 medium-size yellow onions, chopped
1 tsp. salt, divided
½ tsp. freshly ground pepper, divided
1 (16-oz.) container sour cream
2 Tbsp. chopped fresh chives
Potato chips

1. Melt butter in a large nonstick skillet over medium-high heat; add onions, and cook, stirring occasionally, 20 minutes or until browned and tender. Sprinkle with ½ tsp. salt and ¼ tsp. pepper. Remove from heat, and let stand 30 minutes.
2. Stir together onions, sour cream, and chives in a medium bowl. Stir in remaining ½ tsp. salt and remaining ¼ tsp. pepper. Cover and chill 30 minutes or up to 2 days. Serve with potato chips. **Makes** 3 cups.

Note: Light sour cream may be substituted.

Lemony Spinach-Artichoke Dip
make ahead
PREP: 15 MIN., CHILL: 30 MIN.
Lemon juice adds fresh zip to this tasty dip.

1 (14-oz.) can artichoke hearts, drained
    and chopped
1 (8-oz.) container sour cream
1 cup mayonnaise
3 Tbsp. finely chopped onion
2 Tbsp. fresh lemon juice
1 (1.0-oz.) envelope dry vegetable
    soup mix
¼ tsp. freshly ground pepper
1 (10-oz.) package frozen chopped
    spinach, thawed
Assorted corn or tortilla chips

1. Stir together first 7 ingredients in a large bowl.

2. Drain thawed spinach well, pressing between paper towels; stir into artichoke mixture. Cover and chill 30 minutes or up to 2 days. Serve with assorted corn or tortilla chips. **Makes** 3½ cups.

Note: Light mayonnaise and sour cream may be substituted. For testing purposes only, we used Lipton Vegetable Soup & Dips Mix.

Roasted Red Bell Pepper-Spinach Dip: Substitute ½ (12-oz.) jar roasted red bell peppers, drained and chopped, for artichoke hearts. Proceed with recipe as directed.

Savory Appetizers

We used easy-to-find ingredients plus a little creativity for these new entertaining favorites. Each recipe can be made in advance to have on hand when the party starts. Whichever one you choose for your next gathering, you'll find them both equally delicious.

Creamy Crab Cheesecake
make ahead

PREP: 20 MIN.; BAKE: 50 MIN.; COOL: 1 HR., 15 MIN.; CHILL: 12 HR.; STAND: 30 MIN.

This recipe uses handy ingredients, such as canned crabmeat, that can be kept in the pantry. You can make it up to two days ahead; however, we don't recommend freezing it.

1 cup crushed cornbread-flavored crackers (about 14)
3 Tbsp. butter, melted
2 (8-oz.) packages cream cheese, softened
¾ cup sour cream, divided
3 large eggs
2 Tbsp. finely chopped onion
1 tsp. Old Bay seasoning
½ tsp. seasoned pepper blend
¼ tsp. garlic powder
½ tsp. grated lemon rind
2 Tbsp. lemon juice
1½ tsp. hot sauce
2 (6-oz.) cans fancy lump crabmeat, picked, rinsed, and drained
Garnishes: fresh parsley sprigs, chopped fresh parsley, lemon wedges
Assorted crackers

1. Combine cracker crumbs and melted butter, and press onto bottom of a lightly greased 9-inch springform pan.

2. Bake at 350° for 8 to 10 minutes or until lightly browned. Remove to a wire rack to cool 5 minutes. Reduce oven temperature to 325°.

3. Beat cream cheese and ¼ cup sour cream at medium speed with an electric mixer 1 to 2 minutes or until smooth. Add eggs, 1 at a time, beating until blended after each addition. Add onion and next 6 ingredients, beating just until blended. Fold in crabmeat. Pour mixture into prepared crust.

4. Bake at 325° for 40 minutes or until center is set. Let cool on a wire rack 10 minutes. Gently run a knife around edge of springform pan to loosen sides. Let cool 1 more hour.

5. Spread remaining ½ cup sour cream evenly over top of cheesecake; cover and chill at least 12 hours or up to 24 hours.

6. Let cheesecake stand at room temperature 30 minutes before serving. Remove sides of springform pan. Garnish, if desired. Slice cheesecake into wedges, and serve with assorted crackers. **Makes** 20 appetizer servings.

PEGGY SHARPE
MICHIGAN CITY, MISSISSIPPI

Sun-dried Tomato-and-Pesto Dip
make ahead

PREP: 10 MIN., BAKE: 7 MIN.

This is a great recipe for after-work entertaining; you can make it up to two days ahead.

2 Tbsp. pine nuts
1 (8-oz.) package cream cheese, softened
½ cup jarred refrigerated pesto
¼ cup coarsely chopped jarred roasted red bell peppers, drained
¼ cup coarsely chopped jarred sun-dried tomatoes in oil, drained
1 tsp. balsamic vinegar
1 tsp. capers, drained
Assorted vegetable crackers or pita chips

1. Place 2 Tbsp. pine nuts in a single layer in a shallow pan.

2. Bake at 350°, stirring occasionally, 5 to 7 minutes or until toasted. Remove from pan.

3. Process cream cheese and next 5 ingredients in a food processor until smooth. Transfer to a serving bowl. Top evenly with toasted pine nuts, and serve with assorted crackers or pita chips. **Makes** 1⅓ cups.

Grits Like You've Never Had 'em

Tasty toppings elevate this favorite to new heights.

Grits are hot. We've watched this humble breakfast side move to center stage in fabulous entrées. Simmer grits in your choice of water, broth, milk, or cream. Then have fun pairing them with toppings that go far beyond butter and brown gravy.

Creamy Grits Casserole

PREP: 10 MIN., COOK: 8 MIN., BAKE: 40 MIN., STAND: 5 MIN.

1¼ cups uncooked regular grits
2 cups chicken broth
2 cups milk
1 tsp. salt
¼ tsp. ground red pepper
½ cup butter, cut into cubes
1 (10-oz.) block sharp Cheddar cheese, shredded
1 (4-oz.) smoked Gouda cheese round, shredded
2 large eggs, lightly beaten

1. Bring first 5 ingredients to a boil in a medium saucepan over medium-high heat; reduce heat to low, and simmer, stirring occasionally, 4 to 5 minutes or until thickened. Stir in butter and cheeses until melted.
2. Gradually stir about one-fourth of hot grits mixture into eggs; add egg mixture to remaining hot grits mixture, stirring constantly. Pour grits mixture into a lightly greased 2½-qt. baking dish.
3. Bake at 350° for 35 to 40 minutes or until golden brown and bubbly around edges. Let stand 5 minutes before serving. **Makes** 8 servings.

Parmesan Grits

PREP: 10 MIN., COOK: 7 MIN., BAKE: 30 MIN.

1 cup uncooked regular grits
1¼ cups milk
1 (14-oz.) can chicken broth
1 (10¾-oz.) can cream of celery soup
1 cup grated Parmesan cheese
3 Tbsp. butter
2 Tbsp. chopped fresh basil
2 Tbsp. grated Parmesan cheese

1. Bring grits, milk, and broth to a boil in a medium saucepan over medium-high heat; reduce heat to low, and simmer, stirring occasionally, 4 to 5 minutes or until thickened. Remove from heat; stir in soup and next 3 ingredients. Pour mixture into a lightly greased 8-inch square baking dish.
2. Bake at 350° for 30 minutes. Top evenly with 2 Tbsp. grated Parmesan cheese. **Makes** 6 servings.

SUSANNAH JOHNSTON
ROME, GEORGIA

Shrimp-and-Tasso Gravy

PREP: 20 MIN., COOK: 25 MIN.

1 lb. peeled, medium-size raw shrimp
1 Tbsp. barbecue seasoning
3 Tbsp. olive oil
½ cup butter
½ cup chopped tasso ham *
⅓ cup all-purpose flour
1½ cups chicken broth
½ cup half-and-half
2 Tbsp. chopped fresh parsley

1. Devein shrimp, if desired. Rinse and pat dry with paper towels. Sprinkle barbecue seasoning evenly over shrimp.
2. Sauté shrimp in hot oil in a large skillet over high heat 3 to 4 minutes or just until shrimp turn pink. Remove shrimp from skillet.
3. Melt butter in skillet over medium heat; add tasso ham, and sauté 5 minutes. Gradually whisk in flour. Cook, whisking constantly, 1½ to 2 minutes or until mixture is golden brown. Whisk in chicken broth and half-and-half. Bring to a boil. Boil, whisking constantly, 6 to 8 minutes or until smooth and thickened. Stir in shrimp and parsley. **Makes** 4 servings.

* Smoked ham or hot smoked sausage may be substituted.

Note: For testing purposes only, we used McCormick Grill Mates Barbecue Seasoning.

Grits Bar

Feature grits the next time you entertain. Offer both plain and cheese, and keep them hot in slow cookers or chafing dishes. Choose quick-cooking, regular, or white or yellow stone-ground grits. (We don't recommend instant here.)

Serve several toppings, such as the ones listed below, so guests can mix in their favorite flavors.

- Gravies and pestos
- Shredded cheeses
- Roasted vegetables
- Crumbled bacon
- Grilled corn kernels

Tomato Gravy

PREP: 10 MIN., COOK: 30 MIN.

You'll love the flavor of this gravy. We tried it with canned tomatoes but prefer the flavor and texture of fresh. Pair it with hot grits for a winning combination.

2 garlic cloves, minced
1 medium onion, finely chopped
2 Tbsp. olive oil
4 large tomatoes, chopped
½ cup whipping cream
½ tsp. salt
½ tsp. ground red pepper
½ tsp. dried thyme

1. Sauté garlic and onion in hot oil in a medium skillet over medium heat 5 minutes or until tender. Stir in tomatoes; reduce heat to low, and simmer, stirring occasionally, 20 minutes.
2. Stir in whipping cream and remaining ingredients; simmer, stirring occasionally, 4 to 5 minutes or until slightly thickened. **Makes** 2½ cups.

Collard Green Pesto

fast fixin's • make ahead

PREP: 15 MIN., COOK: 4 MIN.

A twist on the classic basil version, this pesto tastes great stirred into plain grits. Refrigerate leftovers up to one week. Cover tightly with plastic wrap to keep pesto a vibrant green.

5 cups packaged fresh collard greens,
    washed, trimmed, and chopped
3 garlic cloves
¼ cup pecans
½ cup olive oil
⅓ cup grated Parmesan cheese
½ tsp. salt

1. Cook greens in boiling water to cover 3½ to 4 minutes or until tender; drain. Plunge into ice water to stop the cooking process; drain well.
2. Process garlic and pecans in a food processor until finely ground. Add greens, oil, cheese, salt, and ¼ cup water; process 2 to 3 seconds or until smooth, stopping to scrape down sides. (Mixture will be thick.) **Makes** 4 cups.

taste of the south
Best Boiled Peanuts

Most of us purchase them to enjoy on the way to the beach or at sporting events, but boiled peanuts are very easy to make at home. The basics are water, peanuts, and lots of salt, but you can add other flavors such as ham and Cajun seasoning. Purists might disapprove, but these variations can be wonderfully tasty.

Boiled Peanuts

PREP: 10 MIN.; SOAK: 8 HR.;

COOK: 6 HR., 15 MIN.; STAND: 1 HR.

You can find dried peanuts in the produce section of your local supermarket or at a farmers market. Store cooked peanuts in the refrigerator up to three days. If you prefer your peanuts warm, heat them in the microwave, covered, at 80% power for 3 to 5 minutes, stirring once.

2 lb. dried raw peanuts
½ to ⅔ cup salt

1. Soak peanuts in water to cover in a large stock pot at least 8 hours or up to 24 hours. (You may need to weigh down peanuts with a large plate or lid to ensure that they are fully submerged.) Drain and rinse.
2. Place peanuts and desired amount of salt in stock pot with 4½ qt. water; bring to a boil over high heat. Cover, reduce heat to medium-low, and cook 6 hours or until peanuts are tender, adding water as needed to keep peanuts covered; stir occasionally.
3. Remove from heat; let stand 1 hour. **Makes** 14 cups.

Cajun Boiled Peanuts: Proceed with Step 1, adding ½ cup Cajun seasoning to water. Proceed with Step 2, using ½ cup salt and 5 to 7 Tbsp. liquid Cajun crab boil before bringing to a boil. Proceed with recipe as directed.

Ham-Flavored Boiled Peanuts: Proceed with Step 1. Omit Step 2, and bring 6 qt. water and 2 smoked ham hocks to a boil in a large stock pot. Reduce heat, and simmer 3 hours. Remove and discard ham hocks. Cool broth; chill 8 hours. Skim fat from broth. Add peanuts and ½ cup salt to broth. Bring to a boil over high heat. Cover, reduce heat, and cook 6 hours or until tender, adding water as needed to keep peanuts covered; stir occasionally. Remove from heat; let stand 1 hour.

Hats Off to Hummus

We were delighted to discover this recipe created by chef Hugh Acheson of Five and Ten in Athens, Georgia.

Boiled Peanut Hummus

chef recipe • make ahead

PREP: 25 MIN.

While Hugh seasons his peanuts with Old Bay seasoning and star anise, we found that simply salting the water yields a fabulous product. You can make this ahead; it keeps in the refrigerator up to five days.

1 cup shelled boiled peanuts
2 Tbsp. tahini
2 Tbsp. fresh lemon juice
1 Tbsp. chopped fresh parsley
1 tsp. minced fresh garlic
¼ tsp. ground cumin
Pinch of ground red pepper
2 Tbsp. olive oil
Garnishes: olive oil, shelled boiled
    peanuts
Pita rounds or pita chips

1. Process first 7 ingredients in a food processor until coarsely chopped, stopping to scrape down sides. With processor running, pour olive oil through food chute in a slow, steady stream, processing until mixture is smooth. Stir in up to 5 Tbsp. water, 1 Tbsp. at a time, for desired spreading consistency. Garnish, if desired. Serve with pita rounds or pita chips. **Makes** 1 cup.

Stunning Apples

Enjoy this year-round fruit at its peak.

Take a bite out of any of these amazing recipes, and you'll never take apples for granted again. They're powerhouse ingredients. Change the flavor of a dish by switching the variety of the apple used or mixing several different types. A handy hint: Round-bottomed apples are for baking, while those with bumps at the base are eaten out of hand or tossed in salads. When shopping, remember the best apples are free from bruises, feel firm to a light squeeze, and are deeply colored. Store in the produce drawer of the refrigerator, and they'll stay fresh for a week.

Easy Cornbread-Sausage Stuffed Apples
family favorite

PREP: 25 MIN., COOK: 18 MIN., BAKE: 40 MIN.
Place crumbled foil around apple cups in baking dish to prevent them from tipping.

1 (6-oz.) package cornbread stuffing mix
½ (1-lb.) package ground pork sausage
1 Tbsp. lemon juice
5 Rome apples
1 medium-size sweet onion, chopped
1½ Tbsp. chopped fresh parsley
1 cup cider vinegar
Garnishes: apple peel strips, fresh
    parsley sprigs

1. Prepare stuffing mix according to package directions.
2. Cook sausage in a large skillet over medium-high heat, stirring often, 8 to 10 minutes or until meat crumbles and is no longer pink. Remove sausage from skillet with a slotted spoon, reserving drippings in skillet. Drain sausage on paper towels.
3. Stir together lemon juice and ¼ cup water.
4. Cut apples in half, cutting through stem and bottom ends. Carefully scoop out apple pulp and cores into a bowl, leaving a ¼-inch shell. Rub lemon juice mixture evenly onto cut sides of apple shells. Remove and discard seeds and cores from apple pulp; chop pulp.
5. Sauté onion and apple pulp in hot drippings over medium-high heat 6 to 8 minutes or until liquid evaporates and onion is tender.
6. Stir together stuffing, apple mixture, sausage, and parsley in a large bowl. Spoon stuffing mixture evenly in apple shells (about ½ cup stuffing per apple shell). Place apples in a 13- x 9-inch baking dish, and pour 1 cup cider vinegar around apples in dish.
7. Bake at 350° for 30 to 40 minutes or until apples are tender. Garnish, if desired. Serve immediately. **Makes** 10 servings.

Note: For testing purposes only, we used Stove Top Cornbread Stuffing Mix.

Cinnamon-Caramel Apple Dumplings With Golden Raisins
family favorite

PREP: 30 MIN., BAKE: 25 MIN.
We baked these in cast-iron skillets, but a 13- x 9-inch baking dish works just as well. See our directions at the end of the recipe.

1 (15-oz.) package refrigerated piecrusts
6 large Rome or Granny Smith apples,
    cored
6 Tbsp. golden raisins
1 large egg, beaten
½ cup butter, melted
1 cup firmly packed light brown sugar
¼ cup corn syrup
½ cup apple juice
1 tsp. ground cinnamon
6 cinnamon sticks
Garnish: golden raisins

1. Unroll piecrusts onto a lightly floured surface; cut dough into 12 (10- x 1-inch) strips, reserving dough scraps for later use. Crisscross 2 strips of dough on surface, forming an "X". Place 1 apple in center of "X". Spoon 1 Tbsp. raisins into apple core, pressing raisins to compact. Pull strips up and over apple, pressing dough into core; trim off excess, if necessary. Repeat with remaining piecrust strips, apples, and raisins.
2. Reroll remaining dough scraps. Cut leaf shapes from dough using a paring knife. Gently score designs in leaves using knife.
3. Stir together egg and 1 Tbsp. water; brush dough strips on apples with egg mixture. Gently press leaves onto dough strips at top of apples; brush leaves with egg mixture.
4. Whisk together melted butter and next 4 ingredients; pour mixture into 6 (6-inch) cast-iron skillets. Place 1 apple in center of each skillet.
5. Bake at 425° for 20 to 25 minutes or until pastry is golden brown, shielding apple tops with aluminum foil after 15 minutes to prevent excessive browning, if necessary. Remove from oven. Press 1 cinnamon stick into center of each apple to resemble a stem. Drizzle sauce in skillets over apples. Garnish, if desired. **Makes** 6 servings.

To bake in a 13- x 9-inch baking dish: Prepare recipe as directed through Step 3. Whisk together melted butter and next 4 ingredients; pour mixture into baking dish. Place apples in baking dish. Proceed with recipe as directed.

Here's a Trick

You can toss apple pieces in a mixture of ¼ cup water and 1 Tbsp. lemon juice to prevent pulp from turning brown. Or for an even simpler option, toss in lemon-lime soft drink. Remove apples from liquid; pat dry on paper towels.

Apple-Walnut Salad

family favorite • make ahead

PREP: 20 MIN., BAKE: 10 MIN., CHILL: 6 HR.

Reader Gwen Fox from Nokomis, Florida, gave us the idea to use lemon curd and mayonnaise in this salad.

1 cup chopped walnuts
⅔ cup mayonnaise
½ cup lemon curd
¼ tsp. ground cardamom
¼ tsp. ground nutmeg
⅛ tsp. ground cinnamon
1½ tsp. grated lemon rind
2 Gala apples, chopped
2 Granny Smith apples, chopped
2 Red Delicious apples, chopped
¾ cup thinly sliced celery
1 cup dried fruit mix

1. Place walnuts in a single layer in a shallow pan.

2. Bake at 350° for 8 to 10 minutes or until lightly toasted, stirring once after 5 minutes.

3. Stir together mayonnaise, next 4 ingredients, and ½ tsp. lemon rind in a large bowl. Add apples, celery, fruit mix, and ¾ cup walnuts; toss well. Cover and chill 6 hours. Sprinkle with remaining ¼ cup walnuts and 1 tsp. lemon rind. **Makes** 6 to 8 servings.

Note: For testing purposes only, we used Sun-Maid Fruit Bits.

Roast Beef, Two Ways

Imagine the aroma of a pot roast flowing through the house. We've provided two tasty options here—a traditional version and a Southwest variation. If you're lucky enough to have leftovers, these roasts make great sandwiches, tacos, or a base for a hearty soup.

Mom's Signature Roast Beef

PREP: 30 MIN.; CHILL: 8 HR.; COOK: 15 MIN.; BAKE: 4 HR., 30 MIN.

1 (12-oz.) bottle dark beer
1 medium onion, chopped
8 garlic cloves, minced
1 lemon, thinly sliced
1 cup soy sauce
3 Tbsp. vegetable oil, divided
1 (3- to 4-lb.) boneless chuck roast, trimmed
1 tsp. fresh coarsely ground pepper
8 carrots (about 1½ lb.), diagonally sliced
7 Yukon gold potatoes (3 lb.), peeled and cut into eighths
2 large onions, cut into eighths
2 Tbsp. cornstarch

1. Combine first 5 ingredients and 2 Tbsp. oil in a large zip-top plastic freezer bag. Add roast, turning to coat. Seal and chill at least 8 hours or up to 24 hours. Remove roast from marinade, reserving marinade. Sprinkle roast evenly with pepper.

2. Brown roast 4 minutes on each side in remaining 1 Tbsp. hot oil in a large heavy-duty roasting pan over medium-high heat. Add reserved marinade, stirring to loosen particles from bottom of pan. Bring to a boil. Remove from heat, and cover with heavy-duty aluminum foil.

3. Bake at 300° for 2½ hours. Turn roast, and stir in carrots, potatoes, and onions. Bake 2 more hours or until roast and vegetables are tender. Transfer roast and vegetables to a serving platter. Skim fat from juices in roasting pan.

4. Whisk together cornstarch and ½ cup water in a small bowl until smooth. Whisk cornstarch mixture into juices in pan; cook over medium-high heat 5 minutes or until thickened, whisking to loosen particles.

5. Drizzle ½ cup gravy over roast. Serve remaining gravy with meat and vegetables. **Makes** 6 to 8 servings.

CARMEN LAGARELLI
ELKTON, MARYLAND

Cola Pot Roast: Substitute 1 (12-oz.) can cola soft drink for beer, and proceed with recipe as directed.

Southwest Chuck Roast With Black Beans

PREP: 20 MIN.; CHILL: 8 HR.; COOK: 20 MIN.; BAKE: 3 HR., 30 MIN.

Serve with yellow rice and toasted Cuban bread.

1 (3- to 4-lb.) boneless chuck roast, trimmed
3 Tbsp. olive oil, divided
1 tsp. freshly ground pepper
2 medium onions, chopped
1 cup dry red wine
1½ tsp. salt
1 (14-oz.) can low-sodium chicken broth
1 (14½-oz.) can petite diced tomatoes, drained
1 (10-oz.) can diced tomatoes and green chiles, drained
2 Tbsp. dried parsley flakes
1 bay leaf
1 (15-oz.) can black beans, rinsed and drained

1. Rub roast evenly with 2 Tbsp. olive oil and 1 tsp. pepper. Place roast in a shallow dish or a large zip-top plastic freezer bag; add chopped onions and 1 cup red wine. Cover or seal, and chill at least 8 hours or up to 24 hours, turning once.

2. Remove roast from marinade, reserving marinade. Pat roast dry with paper towels, and sprinkle evenly with 1½ tsp. salt.

3. Brown roast 4 minutes on each side in remaining 1 Tbsp. hot oil in a large heavy-duty roasting pan over medium-high heat. Stir in chicken broth, next 4 ingredients, and reserved marinade; bring to a boil. Remove from heat, and cover with heavy-duty aluminum foil.

4. Bake at 300° for 1½ hours. Turn roast, and bake 1½ to 2 more hours or until meat shreds easily with a fork.

5. Remove and discard bay leaf. Stir in black beans, and cook, stirring occasionally, over medium-low heat 10 minutes or until thoroughly heated. **Makes** 6 to 8 servings.

WINONA COSTELLO
BRANDON, MISSISSIPPI

Enjoy the Harvest

Take advantage of what autumn has to offer. You won't believe how delicious these recipes are.

Assistant Foods Editor Marion McGahey always anticipates when the late-afternoon breeze carries the first smells of fall to her nose. She welcomes the comforts of the harvest into her kitchen. The vegetables lose the sun-warmed delicacy of summer squash and tomatoes, assuming sturdy textures and rich colors. Winter squash, root vegetables, Brussels sprouts, greens, pears, and apples are but a few of the flavors that grace our tables. These tasty recipes pay homage to the fresh produce that truly defines the season.

Roasted Root Vegetables With Horseradish Vinaigrette

PREP: 25 MIN., BAKE: 25 MIN., COOL: 15 MIN.
We decreased the baking time for this fall favorite by cutting the vegetables into smaller pieces.

2 large sweet potatoes
   (about 1½ lb.)
4 large parsnips (about 1 lb.)
6 medium beets (about 1½ lb.)
3 Tbsp. olive oil
1½ tsp. salt
1 tsp. pepper
Curly endive leaves
Horseradish Vinaigrette

1. Peel sweet potatoes, and cut into ¾-inch cubes. Peel parsnips; cut into ½-inch slices. Peel beets, and cut into ½-inch-thick wedges.
2. Toss parsnips and sweet potatoes with 2 Tbsp. olive oil in a large bowl; place in a single layer in an aluminum foil-lined 15- x 10-inch jelly-roll pan. Season with 1 tsp. salt and ½ tsp. pepper. Toss beets with remaining 1 Tbsp. olive oil; arrange beets in a single layer on a second aluminum foil-lined jelly-roll pan. Season with remaining ½ tsp. salt and ½ tsp. pepper.
3. Bake vegetables at 400° for 20 to 25 minutes or just until tender. Let cool 15 minutes or until completely cool.
4. Arrange curly endive leaves on a serving platter; top with vegetables, and drizzle evenly with Horseradish Vinaigrette. **Makes** 6 servings.

Horseradish Vinaigrette:
fast fixin's • make ahead
PREP: 10 MIN.

⅓ cup white wine vinegar
½ cup olive oil
2 Tbsp. prepared horseradish
1 Tbsp. chopped fresh flat-leaf
   parsley
1 Tbsp. chopped fresh tarragon
1 Tbsp. Dijon mustard
1 garlic clove, finely chopped
1½ tsp. honey
½ tsp. salt
½ tsp. pepper

1. Whisk together all ingredients. Serve immediately, or cover and chill up to 4 days. **Makes** about 1 cup.

Shredded Brussels Sprouts With Pecans and Prosciutto
PREP: 25 MIN., BAKE: 10 MIN., COOK: 15 MIN.

¾ cup chopped pecans
2 lb. fresh Brussels sprouts
2 Tbsp. butter
1 shallot, chopped
2 garlic cloves, minced
¼ lb. prosciutto, cut into thin strips
1 Tbsp. fresh lemon juice
½ tsp. pepper
½ tsp. salt
¼ cup freshly grated Parmesan
   cheese

1. Place pecans in a single layer in a shallow pan.
2. Bake at 350° for 8 to 10 minutes or until toasted, stirring after 5 minutes.
3. Remove discolored leaves from Brussels sprouts. Cut each sprout in half, and cut into shreds.
4. Melt butter in a large skillet over medium-high heat; add shallot and garlic, and sauté 1 to 2 minutes or until tender.
5. Add shredded Brussels sprouts to skillet; sauté 8 to 10 minutes or until just tender. Add prosciutto and next 3 ingredients; sauté 2 more minutes. Remove from heat, and sprinkle with cheese and toasted pecans. **Makes** 4 to 6 servings.

Butternut Squash Soufflé
family favorite
PREP: 20 MIN., COOK: 15 MIN.,
COOL: 25 MIN., BAKE: 1 HR.
This savory dish, with just a touch of sweetness, was well received at our tasting table. Try pairing it with roasted pork and a glass of Riesling or Pinot Noir.

1 large butternut squash (about 2 lb.)
3 large eggs
½ cup light sour cream
¼ cup sugar
¼ cup butter, softened
¼ cup all-purpose flour
1 Tbsp. finely chopped fresh
   sage ✱
1½ tsp. baking powder
½ tsp. salt
¼ tsp. ground nutmeg

1. Remove stem from squash. Cut squash lengthwise into 4 pieces; remove and discard seeds. Cook squash in boiling water to cover in a large saucepan over medium-high heat 10 to 15 minutes or until tender. Drain well; let cool for 25 minutes or until completely cool. Remove and discard peel.
2. Process squash and eggs in a food processor until smooth, stopping to scrape down sides. Add sour cream and remaining ingredients; process 20 to 30 seconds or until smooth. Pour mixture into a lightly greased 8-inch square baking dish.
3. Bake at 350° for 55 to 60 minutes or until set. **Makes** 6 servings.

*1 tsp. ground sage may be substituted.

Note: You can substitute 3 (12-oz.) packages frozen butternut squash puree for fresh squash. Omit Step 1, and prepare frozen squash according to package directions. Proceed with Steps 2 and 3, reducing butter to 2 Tbsp. and baking time to 45 to 50 minutes. For testing purposes only, we used McKenzie's Frozen Butternut Squash Puree.

Hot Off the Grill

The season is here for carefree suppers, and nothing could be easier than these time-saving recipes. Brush on the sauce, and Honey Mustard Grilled Chicken is ready for the grill. Jalapeño-Basil Pork Chops and Balsamic Flank Steak marinate at room temperature for just 30 minutes—about the time it takes to remove the chill for even cooking. Commercial herb and spice blends are also great to keep on hand for last-minute inspiration.

Jalapeño-Basil Pork Chops
PREP: 10 MIN., COOK: 5 MIN.,
STAND: 30 MIN., GRILL: 8 MIN.

1 (10-oz.) jar jalapeño pepper jelly
½ cup dry white wine
¼ cup chopped fresh basil
4 (1-inch-thick) bone-in pork loin chops
½ tsp. salt
¼ tsp. pepper

1. Cook first 3 ingredients in a small saucepan over low heat, stirring often, 5 minutes or until pepper jelly melts. Remove from heat, and let mixture cool completely.
2. Pour ¾ cup pepper jelly mixture into a large zip-top plastic freezer bag, reserving remaining mixture; add pork chops, turning to coat. Seal and let stand at room temperature 30 minutes, turning pork chops occasionally.
3. Remove chops from marinade, discarding marinade. Sprinkle evenly with salt and pepper.
4. Grill, covered with grill lid, over medium-high heat (350° to 400°) 3 to 4 minutes on each side or until a meat thermometer inserted into thickest portion registers 160°. Serve with remaining pepper jelly mixture. **Makes** 4 servings.
KAREN SHELBY
FLIPPIN, ARKANSAS

Jalapeño-Basil Chicken: Substitute 4 skinned and boned chicken breasts for pork chops. Prepare pepper jelly mixture, and marinate chicken as directed. Grill, covered with grill lid, over medium-high heat (350° to 400°) 4 minutes on each side or until done. Serve with remaining pepper jelly mixture.

Balsamic Flank Steak
PREP: 5 MIN., STAND: 40 MIN., GRILL: 14 MIN.

⅓ cup balsamic vinegar
4 garlic cloves, crushed
1 (1½-lb.) flank steak
1 tsp. fresh cracked pepper
¾ tsp. salt

1. Combine vinegar and garlic in a large zip-top plastic freezer bag; add steak, turning to coat. Seal and let stand at room temperature 30 minutes, turning steak occasionally.
2. Remove steak from marinade, discarding marinade. Sprinkle evenly with pepper and salt.
3. Grill, covered with grill lid, over medium-high heat (350° to 400°) 5 to 7 minutes on each side or to desired degree of doneness. Let stand 10 minutes; cut into thin slices diagonally across the grain. **Makes** 4 servings.
ANN RICHENBURG
ST. CHARLES, MISSOURI

Honey Mustard Grilled Chicken
family favorite • fast fixin's
PREP: 10 MIN., GRILL: 8 MIN.

4 skinned and boned chicken breasts
½ cup mayonnaise
2 Tbsp. spicy brown mustard
1 Tbsp. honey
1 tsp. apple cider vinegar
2 green onions, finely chopped
½ tsp. salt
¼ tsp. pepper

1. Place chicken between 2 sheets of heavy-duty plastic wrap; flatten to ½-inch thickness using the flat side of a meat mallet or rolling pin.
2. Stir together mayonnaise, brown mustard, and next 3 ingredients. Sprinkle chicken with salt and pepper; coat chicken with mayonnaise mixture.
3. Grill, covered with grill lid, over medium-high heat (350° to 400°) 4 minutes on each side or until done. **Makes** 4 servings.
MARIANNE HILGENBERG
ORLANDO, FLORIDA

Test Kitchen *Notebook*

If marinated meat is too wet, it won't sear properly, so make certain it's well drained before grilling. To allow marinade you've basted with to cook thoroughly, stop basting meat the last few minutes of grilling.

Mary Allen Perry
ASSOCIATE FOODS EDITOR

Try a New Steak

Fall Family Supper

Serves 6

Ham Steak With Orange Glaze

Roasted Vegetables

Bakery biscuits

Cinnamon-Caramel Apple Dumplings
With Golden Raisins (page 200)

Ham steak has been around for ages, but you might have never thought to put it on your grocery list. Well, add it to your cart, because it makes a great meal.

Ham Steak With Orange Glaze

family favorite • fast fixin's

PREP: 10 MIN., COOK: 12 MIN.

1 (2½-lb.) package fully cooked, bone-in (½-inch-thick) center-cut ham steak
1 cup orange juice
1 (8-oz.) can pineapple tidbits in juice
¼ cup golden raisins
1 Tbsp. Dijon mustard
1 tsp. cornstarch
1 Tbsp. cold water

1. Rinse ham, and pat dry.
2. Cook ham in a lightly greased skillet over medium-high heat 3 to 4 minutes on each side or until thoroughly heated. Remove ham, reserving drippings in skillet.
3. Stir in orange juice, and cook 2 minutes, stirring to loosen particles from bottom of skillet. Stir in pineapple, raisins, and mustard. Stir together cornstarch and 1 Tbsp. cold water; add to orange juice mixture. Bring to a boil; cook, stirring constantly, 1 minute. Serve sauce with ham. **Makes** 6 servings.

JOAN C. NORRIS
LILBURN, GEORGIA

Roasted Vegetables

PREP: 20 MIN., BAKE: 35 MIN.

This bounty of vegetables is the perfect accent for ham steak.

3 medium-size sweet potatoes (about 1½ lb.)
1 medium-size yellow bell pepper
1 medium-size sweet onion, coarsely chopped
2 Tbsp. olive oil
1 tsp. salt
1 tsp. ground cinnamon
¼ tsp. pepper

1. Peel sweet potatoes, and cut into ½-inch cubes. Cut yellow bell pepper into 1-inch pieces.
2. Combine sweet potatoes, bell pepper, onions, and remaining ingredients in a large zip-top plastic bag; seal bag, and turn until vegetables are evenly coated. Remove vegetable mixture from bag, and place in a single layer in a lightly greased 15- x 10-inch jelly-roll pan.
3. Bake at 450° for 30 to 35 minutes or until sweet potatoes are tender. **Makes** 6 servings.

Mealtime Secret

Waffles for supper has been a Southern restaurant secret for a long time. Our Foods staff has enjoyed everything from gravy-smothered fried chicken and waffles to decadent waffles Rockefeller. The honeycombed surface is just right for holding sauce, vegetables, and bite-size pieces of meat. Now you can serve a little bit of culinary magic with these highly rated recipes.

Corn Waffles With Cajun Vegetables and Shrimp

PREP: 10 MIN., COOK: 24 MIN.

1 (8½-oz.) package corn muffin mix
½ (8-oz.) block Monterey Jack cheese with peppers, shredded
1 large egg
¾ cup milk
2 Tbsp. olive oil
Cajun Vegetables and Shrimp

1. Stir together first 5 ingredients in a medium bowl.
2. Cook batter in a preheated, lightly greased waffle iron according to manufacturer's directions until golden. Remove waffles to a wire rack on a jelly-roll pan, and keep warm.
3. Place each waffle on a plate; top with ½ cup Cajun Vegetables and Shrimp. **Makes** 8 servings.

Cajun Vegetables and Shrimp:

PREP: 15 MIN., COOK: 25 MIN.

1 Tbsp. butter
1 cup diced Canadian bacon
1 cup diced Cajun sausage
1 red bell pepper, chopped
1 green bell pepper, chopped
2 celery ribs, sliced
1 (14½-oz.) can diced tomatoes
1 cup frozen peeled raw shrimp, thawed
1 tsp. Creole seasoning

1. Melt butter in a large nonstick skillet over medium-high heat; cook Canadian bacon and sausage in skillet 6 to 7 minutes or until lightly browned. Remove bacon and sausage from skillet, reserving drippings in skillet.
2. Sauté bell peppers and celery in pan drippings over medium-high heat 8 to 10 minutes or until tender. Stir in diced tomatoes, and cook, stirring occasionally, 2 to 3 minutes or until thoroughly heated.
3. Add bacon, sausage, shrimp, and Creole seasoning to skillet; cook, stirring occasionally, 5 minutes or just until shrimp turn pink. Serve warm over waffles. **Makes** 4 cups.

ANNE K. HALL
GREENWOOD, SOUTH CAROLINA

Note: For testing purposes only, we used Jiffy Corn Muffin Mix.

Waffles Benedict

PREP: 15 MIN., STAND: 5 MIN., COOK: 20 MIN.

Lemon juice and tarragon enhance packaged hollandaise sauce in this dish. You can substitute deli ham or country ham for the prosciutto.

2 cups all-purpose baking mix
1⅓ cups buttermilk
½ cup (2 oz.) shredded Parmesan cheese
2 Tbsp. vegetable oil
5 large eggs, divided
½ tsp. white vinegar
1 (0.9-oz.) envelope hollandaise sauce mix
1 Tbsp. lemon juice
¼ tsp. dried tarragon
8 thin prosciutto slices (about ¼ lb.)
Garnish: chopped fresh chives

1. Stir together first 4 ingredients and 1 egg in a medium bowl until blended. Let batter stand 5 minutes.
2. Meanwhile, add water to a depth of 3 inches in a large saucepan. Bring to a boil; reduce heat, and maintain a light simmer. Add vinegar. Break remaining 4 eggs, and slip into water, 1 at a time, as close as possible to surface. Simmer 3 to 5 minutes or to desired degree of doneness. Remove with a slotted spoon. Trim edges, if desired.
3. Cook batter in a preheated, lightly greased waffle iron according to manufacturer's directions until golden.
4. Prepare hollandaise sauce according to package directions, adding lemon juice and tarragon.
5. Stack 2 waffles, and top with 2 prosciutto slices, 1 poached egg, and desired amount of hollandaise sauce. Garnish, if desired. **Makes** 4 servings.

Note: For testing purposes only, we used Bisquick All-Purpose Baking Mix and Knorr Hollandaise Sauce Mix.

top-rated recipes
Salads We Love

A dinner based around a standout side takes only minutes to plan, but it dazzles guests. The flavors in our recipes are distinctive, so make the menu simple. Grilled steak or shrimp go with either salad. Round out your meal with a basket of sliced French bread or Italian ciabatta loaf.

Grilled Romaine Salad With Buttermilk-Chive Dressing
fast fixin's

PREP: 10 MIN., GRILL: 11 MIN.

4 romaine lettuce bunches
1 small red onion
2 Tbsp. olive oil
Vegetable cooking spray
Buttermilk-Chive Dressing
½ cup freshly shaved Parmesan cheese
Kosher salt and freshly ground pepper to taste

1. Pull off tough outer leaves of romaine bunches, and discard; cut bunches in half lengthwise, keeping leaves intact. Peel onion, and cut in half vertically, keeping core (root end and top) intact. Cut each half into 4 wedges. Brush lettuce and onion evenly with olive oil.
2. Coat cold cooking grate evenly with cooking spray, and place on grill over medium heat (300° to 350°). Place onion wedges on cooking grate, and grill, covered with grill lid, 3 to 4 minutes on each side or to desired degree of doneness. Remove onion wedges.
3. Place romaine halves, cut sides down, on cooking grate. Grill, without grill lid, 2 to 3 minutes or just until wilted.
4. Divide grilled lettuce, cut sides up, evenly among serving plates. Top each with 1 onion wedge (separate into slices, if desired), and drizzle with Buttermilk-Chive Dressing. Sprinkle evenly with shaved Parmesan cheese and salt and pepper to taste. Serve immediately. **Makes** 8 servings.

Buttermilk-Chive Dressing:
fast fixin's • make ahead

PREP: 10 MIN.

You can lighten this recipe by using nonfat buttermilk and light mayonnaise.

¾ cup buttermilk
½ cup mayonnaise
2 Tbsp. chopped fresh chives
1 Tbsp. minced green onions
1 garlic clove, minced
½ tsp. salt
¼ tsp. freshly ground pepper

1. Whisk together all ingredients. Cover and chill until ready to use. Dressing may be stored in an airtight container in the refrigerator up to 3 days. **Makes** 1¼ cups.

LAURA ZAPALOWSKI
BIRMINGHAM, ALABAMA

Warm Goat Cheese Salad

PREP: 20 MIN., CHILL: 2 HR., FRY: 8 MIN.

⅓ cup olive oil
⅓ cup lemon juice
1 Tbsp. thinly sliced green onions
1 Tbsp. honey
1 tsp. Dijon mustard
½ cup Italian-seasoned breadcrumbs
1½ Tbsp. grated Parmesan cheese
1½ Tbsp. sesame seeds
3 (4-oz.) goat cheese logs
1 large egg, lightly beaten
3 Tbsp. butter
1½ (5-oz.) packages sweet baby greens, thoroughly washed
12 pitted ripe olives, sliced

1. Whisk together first 5 ingredients.
2. Combine breadcrumbs, Parmesan cheese, and sesame seeds.
3. Cut each goat cheese log into 4 slices. Dip in egg, and dredge in breadcrumb mixture. Cover and chill 2 hours.
4. Melt butter in a medium skillet over medium-high heat. Fry goat cheese, in 2 batches, 1 to 2 minutes on each side or until browned; drain on paper towels.
5. Toss salad greens with olive oil mixture. Top with olives and warm goat cheese rounds. **Makes** 6 servings.

Skillet Sensations

It's a superfast cooking method associated with Asian food, but stir-frying works with all sorts of flavors.

Simple Stir-fry
fast fixin's

PREP: 5 MIN., COOK: 11 MIN.
For a heartier version, stir in 3 cups chopped cooked chicken, pork, or beef.

1 (14.5-oz.) can low-sodium fat-free
    chicken broth
¼ cup lite soy sauce
1 to 2 Tbsp. chili-garlic paste
2 Tbsp. cornstarch
1 Tbsp. brown sugar
1 tsp. ground ginger
2 Tbsp. dark sesame oil
1 (16-oz.) package frozen stir-fry
    vegetables

1. Whisk together first 6 ingredients.
2. Heat sesame oil in a large skillet or wok at medium-high heat 2 minutes. Add vegetables, and stir-fry 5 to 7 minutes. Add broth mixture, and stir-fry 1 to 2 minutes or until sauce thickens and vegetables are tender. **Makes** 4 to 6 servings.

Sausage Stir-fry

PREP: 15 MIN., COOK: 25 MIN.
This is a good-for-you meal with unexpected and delicious flavors.

1 (10-oz.) box plain couscous
¼ cup chopped pecans
1 lb. hot Italian sausage links
1 yellow bell pepper, thinly sliced
1 red bell pepper, thinly sliced
½ medium-size red onion, halved and
    thinly sliced
1 garlic clove, minced
½ (20-oz.) package bite-size dried
    plums
2 Granny Smith apples, chopped
1¼ cups chicken broth
2 Tbsp. brown sugar
1 Tbsp. cornstarch
1 tsp. grated orange rind
2 Tbsp. fresh orange juice
½ tsp. salt

1. Prepare couscous according to package directions. Keep warm.

2. Heat pecans in a large nonstick skillet over medium-low heat, stirring often, 3 to 4 minutes or until toasted. Remove from skillet.
3. Remove casing from sausage, and cut into ½-inch slices.
4. Heat skillet or wok at medium-high heat 1 minute. Add sausage, and stir-fry 7 to 8 minutes or until done and no longer pink.
5. Add bell peppers, onion, and garlic to skillet, and stir-fry 3 to 4 minutes or until tender. Add plums and apples, and stir-fry 1½ to 2 minutes. Stir together chicken broth and next 5 ingredients until cornstarch is dissolved. Add to sausage mixture, and bring to a boil. Boil 1 to 2 minutes or until thickened. Serve over couscous. Sprinkle with toasted pecans. **Makes** 6 to 8 servings.

LETHA BURDETTE
GREENVILLE, SOUTH CAROLINA

Yummy Quesadillas

We thought it would be fun to take the simple quesadilla in a different direction. So we layered flour tortillas with some well-known but unexpected flavors.

Swiss Cheese Club Quesadillas
family favorite

PREP: 10 MIN., COOK: 6 MIN., BAKE: 15 MIN.
These double-decker quesadillas stay true to the traditional club sandwich.

4 bacon slices
1 cup grape tomato halves
1 green onion, chopped
6 (8-inch) soft taco-size flour tortillas
2 Tbsp. melted butter
½ lb. deli-sliced smoked turkey
1½ cups (6 oz.) shredded Swiss cheese

1. Cook bacon slices in a skillet over medium-high heat 6 minutes or until crisp; drain on paper towels, and crumble. Stir together bacon, tomato halves, and green onion in a medium bowl.

Count On Couscous

It's pasta that looks like grits, except fluffier. Couscous is a fast substitute for rice, potatoes, noodles, or large-shaped pastas. Choose a whole wheat version for healthful benefits. Best of all, you don't have to cook it, and it's ready in minutes.
1. Pour boiling water or broth over couscous in large bowl.
2. Cover bowl, and let stand 5 minutes.
3. Uncover and fluff with a fork.

2. Brush 1 side of 2 tortillas with 1 Tbsp. melted butter, and place, buttered sides down, on a baking sheet. Layer buttered tortillas with half of bacon mixture, turkey, and cheese, leaving a ½-inch border. Top each with 1 tortilla, and layer evenly with remaining bacon mixture, turkey, and cheese, leaving a ½-inch border. Top with remaining tortillas, and gently press. Brush each with remaining 1 Tbsp. melted butter.
3. Bake at 425° for 12 to 15 minutes or until golden brown and cheese begins to melt. Gently press quesadillas with a spatula; cut in half, and serve immediately. **Makes** 4 servings.

BBQ Pork Quesadilla Torta
family favorite • fast fixin's
PREP: 10 MIN., BAKE: 20 MIN.

½ lb. chopped barbecued pork
   (about 2 cups)
1 (15-oz.) can black beans, rinsed
   and drained
½ cup barbecue sauce
4 (10-inch) burrito-size flour tortillas
1 cup seeded, diced plum tomatoes
   (about 2 large)
2 green onions, finely chopped
2 cups (8 oz.) shredded Mexican-style
   cheese blend
Avocado Mash
Toppings: sour cream, barbecue sauce
Garnish: fresh cilantro sprigs

1. Stir together barbecued pork, black beans, and ½ cup barbecue sauce in a medium bowl.
2. Place 1 tortilla in a lightly greased 10-inch springform pan, and spread with one-third pork mixture. Sprinkle with one-third each of tomatoes, green onions, and cheese. Repeat layers twice. Top with remaining tortilla; gently press. Cover pan with aluminum foil.
3. Bake at 400° for 15 to 20 minutes or until golden brown. Remove sides of pan, and cut into wedges. Serve with Avocado Mash and desired toppings. Garnish, if desired. **Makes** 4 to 6 servings.

BBQ Beef Quesadilla Torta: Substitute 2 cups chopped barbecued beef for pork, and proceed with recipe as directed.

BBQ Chicken Quesadilla Torta: Substitute 2 cups chopped barbecued chicken for pork, and proceed with recipe as directed.

Avocado Mash:
fast fixin's
PREP: 10 MIN.

2 medium-size ripe avocados, coarsely
   chopped
2 Tbsp. chopped fresh cilantro
1 Tbsp. fresh lime juice
½ tsp. pepper
¼ tsp. salt

1. Mash together all ingredients with a fork or potato masher just until mixture is chunky. **Makes** ¾ cup.

Spice Up Your Plate

Wake up your taste buds with these fine offerings, given to us by the Chile Pepper Institute at New Mexico State University.

New Mexico Spoon Bread
PREP: 15 MIN., BAKE: 1 HR., STAND: 5 MIN.

1 (14.75-oz.) can cream-style corn
2 cups milk
2 Tbsp. melted butter
1 cup yellow cornmeal
3 large eggs, lightly beaten
1 tsp. baking powder
1 tsp. salt
½ tsp. baking soda
1½ cups (6 oz.) grated Cheddar
   cheese
1 (4.5-oz.) can chopped green
   chiles

1. Stir together all ingredients in a large bowl. Pour batter into a lightly greased 9-inch square pan.
2. Bake at 350° for 55 to 60 minutes or until golden brown. Let stand 5 minutes before serving. **Makes** 6 to 8 servings.

Spicy Stuffed Peppers
PREP: 10 MIN., BROIL: 6 MIN., STAND: 10 MIN.,
COOK: 12 MIN.
These peppers combine a chile-cheese-corn filling with roasted Anaheim peppers for a burst of flavor.

8 Anaheim peppers, divided
2 Tbsp. butter
½ cup chopped green onions
1 (15-oz.) can stewed tomatoes, drained
½ tsp. salt
1 (15.5-oz.) can whole kernel corn,
   drained
1½ cups (6 oz.) shredded Cheddar
   cheese
Garnish: chopped green onions

1. Remove and discard seeds and membranes from 2 peppers. Chop peppers.
2. Broil remaining 6 peppers on an aluminum foil-lined baking sheet 5 inches from heat 2 to 3 minutes on each side or until peppers look blistered. Place peppers in a large zip-top plastic freezer bag; seal and let stand 10 minutes. Cut peppers lengthwise down 1 side, leaving other side intact; remove and discard seeds and membranes. Keep peppers warm.
3. Melt butter in a large skillet over medium heat. Add green onions, and sauté 1 minute. (Do not brown.) Stir in chopped peppers, tomatoes, and ½ tsp. salt; cook 4 to 5 minutes or until tender. Add corn, and cook, stirring occasionally, 6 minutes.
4. Remove from heat. Stir in cheese until melted. Spoon mixture evenly into cavity of each broiled pepper. Garnish, if desired, and serve immediately. **Makes** 4 to 6 servings.

Cookie Dough Fix-Ups

Tasty stir-ins add pizzazz to a grocery store favorite.

Forget the messy flour and eggs; thanks to refrigerated cookie dough, these terrific recipes cut your prep time in half. Kristi Michele Crowe of our Test Kitchens helped develop these delectable treats. One taste will have you believing you made them from scratch.

Peach-Pecan Bars
make ahead

PREP: 10 MIN., BAKE: 43 MIN., COOK: 3 MIN., COOL: 20 MIN.

These bars can be served right out of the oven, but we liked them better after they sat overnight. Store in an airtight container up to five days.

¾ cup chopped pecans
1 (16.5-oz.) package refrigerated sugar cookie dough
1 cup peach preserves
2 tsp. cornstarch
Powdered sugar

1. Place pecans in a single layer in a shallow pan.
2. Bake at 350° for 8 to 10 minutes or until lightly toasted, stirring once after 5 minutes.
3. Divide cookie dough into 3 equal pieces, and press evenly onto bottom of a lightly greased 11- x 7-inch baking dish. Sprinkle evenly with pecans, pressing into dough.
4. Bake at 350° for 25 minutes or until edges are golden brown.
5. Bring peach preserves and cornstarch to a boil in a small saucepan. Boil 1 minute, stirring constantly. Pour preserve mixture evenly over warm crust.

6. Bake at 350° for 8 minutes. Remove pan from oven, and cool on a wire rack 20 minutes. Sprinkle evenly with powdered sugar, and cut into bars. Serve immediately or at room temperature. **Makes** 15 bars.

Note: For testing purposes only, we used Pillsbury Create 'n Bake Sugar refrigerated cookie dough.

Carrot Cake Sandwich Cookies

PREP: 15 MIN., BAKE: 18 MIN., COOL: 15 MIN.

¾ cup grated carrots (about 2 medium carrots)
2 Tbsp. firmly packed dark brown sugar
½ tsp. ground ginger
½ tsp. ground cinnamon
⅓ cup raisins
1 (16.5-oz.) package refrigerated sugar cookie dough
Cream Cheese Icing

1. Toss together first 4 ingredients in a large bowl. Stir raisins into carrot mixture.
2. Tear cookie dough into pieces, and stir into carrot mixture until well combined.
3. Drop cookie dough mixture by tablespoonfuls, 2 inches apart, onto lightly greased baking sheets. (Dough should make 24 cookies.)
4. Bake at 350° for 15 to 18 minutes or until edges are crisp. Cool on baking sheets 5 minutes. Remove to wire racks, and cool 10 minutes or until completely cool.
5. Turn half of cookies over, bottom sides up. Spread each with 1 Tbsp. chilled Cream Cheese Icing. Top with remaining cookies, bottom sides down,

and press gently to spread filling to edges of cookies. **Makes** 1 dozen sandwiches.

Note: For testing purposes only, we used Pillsbury Create 'n Bake Sugar refrigerated cookie dough.

Cream Cheese Icing:
PREP: 10 MIN., CHILL: 30 MIN.

5 oz. cream cheese, softened
¼ cup unsalted butter, softened
1 cup powdered sugar
½ tsp. fresh lemon juice
¼ tsp. vanilla extract

1. Beat cream cheese and butter at medium speed with an electric mixer until creamy.
2. Add remaining ingredients, beating until smooth. Cover and chill 30 minutes or until spreading consistency. **Makes** about 1 cup.

Ginger-Molasses Biscotti
make ahead

PREP: 15 MIN.; BAKE: 1 HR., 16 MIN.; COOL: 45 MIN.

Turbinado sugar, found in supermarkets, is a raw sugar product with coarse, light brown crystals. We love it for its subtle molasses flavor. Store crunchy biscotti in an airtight container for up to one week.

1 (16.5-oz.) package refrigerated chocolate chip cookie dough
⅓ cup chopped crystallized ginger
2 Tbsp. molasses
1½ tsp. bourbon
½ tsp. ground cinnamon
¼ tsp. ground nutmeg
2 tsp. turbinado sugar *

1. Tear cookie dough into pieces in a large bowl. Stir in next 5 ingredients until well combined.
2. Press onto bottom of a lightly greased 1-qt. baking dish. Sprinkle evenly with turbinado sugar.
3. Bake at 350° for 40 minutes or until a wooden pick inserted in center comes out clean. Cool in baking dish on a wire

rack 20 minutes. Remove from baking dish to wire rack, and cool 10 more minutes. Reduce oven temperature to 300°.

4. Cut cookie into 14 (¾-inch-wide) strips with a serrated knife using a gentle sawing motion. Place strips on a baking sheet.

5. Bake at 300° for 18 minutes on each side. Remove to wire racks, and let cool 15 minutes or until completely cool. **Makes** 14 biscotti.

*2 tsp. granulated sugar may be substituted.

Note: For testing purposes only, we used Pillsbury Create 'n Bake Chocolate Chip refrigerated cookie dough.

healthy foods
Luscious Desserts

How can dessert be good for you? Easy—make it a part of your lifestyle by adding wholesome fruits, grains, and dairy. These tempting treats satisfy your sweet cravings and pack in powerful benefits. For a complete serving of fruit, enjoy warm Peach-Rhubarb Crisp; it has significantly less fat than you'd expect to find in such a delectable dish. With these fabulous recipes, you can have homemade comfort without the guilt.

Healthy Benefits

■ Peaches yield antioxidants and other phytochemicals that may inhibit tumor growth.
■ Fiber-rich oats lower the risk for a number of diseases, including diabetes, hypertension, cancer, and heart disease.

Peach-Rhubarb Crisp
PREP: 15 MIN., BAKE: 50 MIN.

Rhubarb adds fresh, tart flavor to compotes, crisps, and pies. Serve this dish warm with low-fat vanilla ice cream, vanilla yogurt, or low-fat whipped topping.

1 (20-oz.) bag frozen peaches, thawed
2 (16-oz.) packages frozen sliced
  rhubarb, thawed
1½ cups granulated sugar
3 Tbsp. lemon juice
1¼ cups all-purpose flour, divided
Vegetable cooking spray
⅓ cup uncooked quick-cooking oats
⅓ cup firmly packed brown sugar
⅓ cup cold butter, cut into small pieces

1. Combine first 4 ingredients in a medium bowl; add ¼ cup flour, stirring well. Pour mixture into a 13- x 9-inch baking dish coated with cooking spray.
2. Combine oats, brown sugar, and remaining 1 cup flour in a small bowl; cut in cold butter with a fork or pastry blender until mixture resembles coarse crumbs. Sprinkle mixture evenly over fruit filling.
3. Bake at 375° for 45 to 50 minutes or until bubbly. **Makes** 10 servings.

Per serving (does not include ice cream): Calories 308; Fat 6.4g (sat 3.9g, mono 1.6g, poly 0.4g); Protein 3g; Carb 61.4g; Fiber 2.7g; Chol 16mg; Iron 1.4mg; Sodium 48mg; Calc 188mg

Chocolate-Oatmeal Parfaits
make ahead
PREP: 15 MIN., COOK: 8 MIN., CHILL: 2 HR.

To save time, use instant chocolate pudding and store-bought granola. The pudding isn't as rich, but it's quick.

2 cups fat-free milk
⅔ cup sugar
⅓ cup unsweetened cocoa
3 Tbsp. cornstarch
⅛ tsp. salt
1 large egg, lightly beaten
½ (4-oz.) bar semisweet chocolate,
  chopped
1 tsp. vanilla extract
1½ cups Quick Oatmeal Granola
3 cups thawed reduced-fat whipped
  topping

1. Whisk together first 5 ingredients in a medium-size heavy saucepan over medium-high heat, and cook, whisking constantly, 5 minutes or until mixture is hot. Gradually whisk ⅓ cup hot milk mixture into egg in a small bowl. Whisk egg mixture into remaining hot milk mixture.
2. Cook, whisking constantly, 3 minutes or until mixture thickens. Remove from heat; add chopped chocolate, stirring until chocolate melts and mixture is smooth. Stir in vanilla. Pour mixture into a glass bowl. Place heavy-duty plastic wrap directly on warm mixture (to keep a film from forming), and chill 2 hours or until completely cool.
3. Layer 1½ Tbsp. Quick Oatmeal Granola, 3 Tbsp. chocolate mixture, and ¼ cup whipped topping into each of 6 (1½-cup) parfait glasses. Repeat layers once; sprinkle each parfait with 1 Tbsp. granola. **Makes** 6 servings.

Per serving (includes granola): Calories 380; Fat 11.4g (sat 7.2g, mono 1.6g, poly 0.7g); Protein 8.1g; Carb 67.5g; Fiber 3.5g; Chol 40mg; Iron 1.9mg; Sodium 162mg; Calc 126mg

Quick Oatmeal Granola:
fast fixin's
PREP: 10 MIN., BAKE: 20 MIN.

Be sure to use old-fashioned regular oats, not instant. Store granola in an airtight container up to one week.

¼ cup honey
2 Tbsp. light butter, melted
½ tsp. vanilla extract
1½ cups uncooked regular oats
½ cup whole wheat flour
⅓ cup sliced almonds
¼ tsp. salt

1. Stir together first 3 ingredients in a small bowl. Stir together oats, flour, sliced almonds, and salt in a large bowl. Add honey mixture to oatmeal mixture, stirring until combined. Spread oat mixture onto a lightly greased baking sheet.
2. Bake at 350° for 20 minutes, stirring often. **Makes** 3 cups.

BETH EATON
BIRMINGHAM, ALABAMA

Per serving (¼ cup): Calories 99; Fat 3.2g (sat 0.8g, mono 1.1g, poly 0.6g); Protein 2.6g; Carb 17g; Fiber 1.9g; Chol 3mg; Iron 0.8mg; Sodium 66mg; Calc 13mg

Italian Comfort Food

Make a big batch of sauce to enjoy now and freeze for later, or cook up a simple side.

Pasta lovers and others alike will want to try these terrific recipes. Beefy Slow-cooker Spaghetti Sauce is a tasty spin on a home-style Italian version, which uses a chuck roast for meaty flavor. It cooks all day in the slow cooker, yielding richly flavored sauce and melt-in-your-mouth tender beef. Italian Meatballs are also wonderful and very easy. You don't have to cook the meatballs before simmering them in the sauce, cutting out a time-consuming step. Serve seven-ingredient Spicy Spaghetti alongside roasted chicken and a green vegetable for a hearty, simple supper. This recipe doesn't freeze well, but you can refrigerate leftovers to enjoy the next day.

Spicy Spaghetti
fast fixin's
PREP: 5 MIN., COOK: 18 MIN.

1. Prepare 1 (12-oz.) package spaghetti according to package directions; drain. Sauté 1 large onion, chopped, in 2 Tbsp. hot olive oil in a medium skillet over medium-high heat 8 minutes or until tender. Stir in 1 (10-oz.) can mild diced tomatoes with green chiles and ⅛ tsp. salt. Cook 5 minutes or until liquid has almost fully evaporated. Whisk together 1 cup half-and-half and 1 Tbsp. all-purpose flour in a small bowl. Stir half-and-half mixture into tomatoes, and cook, stirring often, 5 minutes or until slightly thickened and bubbly. Serve sauce over hot cooked spaghetti. **Makes** 4 servings.

DIANE P. WADDILL
COLUMBIA, SOUTH CAROLINA

Italian Meatballs
freezeable • make ahead
PREP: 20 MIN., COOK: 35 MIN.

We adapted and scaled down this recipe from Barbara Jean's Cookbook (Barbara Jeans LLC, 2005) by Barbara Jean Barta, owner of the Barbara Jean's restaurant chain. Make a large batch of these, and freeze them in meal-size portions to cook during the week.

½ lb. mild Italian sausage, casings removed
¾ lb. ground turkey
1 cup fine, dry breadcrumbs
¾ cup minced onion
4 large eggs, lightly beaten
¾ cup grated Parmesan cheese
1 Tbsp. minced garlic
½ tsp. salt
½ tsp. pepper
2 tsp. dried Italian seasoning
Marinara Sauce
Hot cooked spaghetti
Freshly grated Parmesan cheese (optional)

1. Combine first 10 ingredients in a large bowl until well blended.
2. Gently shape meat mixture into 30 (1½-inch) balls.
3. Bring Marinara Sauce to a boil in a Dutch oven over medium heat, stirring occasionally; reduce heat, and simmer. Add 10 meatballs, and cook 6 to 8 minutes or until meatballs are done. Remove meatballs from sauce, and keep warm; repeat procedure with remaining meatballs.

4. Return all cooked meatballs to sauce, reduce heat to low, and cook 10 more minutes. Serve over hot cooked spaghetti, and, if desired, sprinkle with Parmesan cheese. **Makes** 30 meatballs (6 to 8 servings).

Marinara Sauce:
fast fixin's
PREP: 5 MIN., COOK: 10 MIN.

1. Stir together 1 cup beef broth; ½ cup dry red wine; ½ cup water; 1 (26-oz.) jar marinara sauce; and 1 (8-oz.) can tomato sauce with basil, garlic, and oregano. Cook over medium heat, stirring occasionally, 10 minutes or until thoroughly heated. **Makes** about 6 cups.

Beefy Slow-cooker Spaghetti Sauce
freezeable • make ahead
PREP: 20 MIN., COOK: 6 HR.

This makes enough sauce for several meals, so serve some today and freeze the rest. You can also cook this on top of the stove over very low heat, stirring often, for several hours or until the meat is tender.

1 (3- to 3½-lb.) boneless chuck roast, trimmed
2 tsp. salt, divided
2 Tbsp. olive oil
2 garlic cloves, minced
1 large onion, chopped
4 (14.5-oz.) cans Italian-style diced tomatoes, undrained
1 (15-oz.) can tomato sauce
1 (12-oz.) can tomato paste
1 Tbsp. sugar
2 tsp. dried basil
2 tsp. dried oregano
1 tsp. dried crushed red pepper
Hot cooked spaghetti (optional)

1. Sprinkle roast evenly with 1 tsp. salt. Cook roast in hot oil in a large skillet over medium-high heat 3 minutes on each side or until browned.
2. Combine minced garlic, remaining 1 tsp. salt, and next 8 ingredients in a 6-qt. slow cooker; gently add roast.
3. Cook, covered, on HIGH 6 hours or until roast is very tender. Remove roast

from slow cooker, and shred using 2 forks. Skim off any fat from tomato sauce, if desired, and return shredded meat to sauce. Serve over hot cooked spaghetti, if desired. **Makes** about 3 qt.

MENT FLORIO
WADMALAW ISLAND, SOUTH CAROLINA

Note: Freeze spaghetti sauce in airtight containers for up to 6 weeks, if desired.

Freeze Now, Serve Later

Here are the recipes you've been looking for. Put on your favorite tunes, and spend a day cooking and packaging. You'll be on your way to having a terrific meal on hand.

Chocolate-Ginger Pound Cake
freezeable • make ahead
PREP: 20 MIN.; BAKE: 1 HR., 10 MIN.;
COOL: 1 HR., 10 MIN. *(Pictured on page 182)*

1 (12-oz.) package semisweet chocolate
   morsels
1¼ cups butter, softened
2 cups sugar
5 large eggs
3 cups all-purpose flour
1 tsp. baking powder
1 tsp. ground ginger
⅛ tsp. salt
1 cup buttermilk
½ cup crystallized ginger, finely
   chopped
1 tsp. vanilla extract

1. Place chocolate morsels in a small microwave-safe glass bowl. Microwave at HIGH 1½ to 2 minutes or until melted and smooth, stirring at 30-second intervals.
2. Beat butter at medium speed with a heavy-duty electric stand mixer until creamy. Gradually add sugar, beating at medium speed until light and fluffy.

Add eggs, 1 at a time, beating just until yellow disappears. Add melted chocolate, beating just until blended.
3. Sift together flour and next 3 ingredients. Stir together buttermilk and crystallized ginger. Add flour mixture to butter mixture alternately with buttermilk mixture, beginning and ending with flour mixture. Beat at low speed just until blended after each addition. Stir in vanilla. Pour into a greased and floured 10-inch tube pan.
4. Bake at 325° for 1 hour and 10 minutes or until a long wooden pick inserted in center comes out clean. Cool in pan on a wire rack 10 minutes. Remove cake from pan to wire rack, and cool 1 hour or until completely cool. **Makes** 12 servings.

To freeze: Wrap cooled cake tightly with plastic wrap. Wrap cake loosely with aluminum foil. Freeze up to 1 month.

Italian Chicken Casserole
freezeable • make ahead
PREP: 20 MIN., COOK: 20 MIN., BAKE: 30 MIN.

2 (3.5-oz.) bags quick-cooking rice
1 lb. chicken breast, cut into cubes
½ tsp. salt
¼ tsp. pepper
3 Tbsp. olive oil, divided
1 small onion, finely chopped
1 (8-oz.) package sliced fresh
   mushrooms
1 (10¾-oz.) can reduced-fat cream of
   chicken soup
½ (8-oz.) container sour cream
½ tsp. dried Italian seasoning
1 (28-oz.) can diced tomatoes with basil,
   garlic, and oregano, undrained

1. Cook rice according to package directions.
2. Sprinkle chicken evenly with salt and pepper. Sauté, in 2 batches, in 2 Tbsp. hot oil in a large skillet over medium-high heat 5 to 7 minutes or until lightly browned. Remove from skillet.
3. Add remaining 1 Tbsp. oil to skillet, and sauté onion 2 to 3 minutes or until tender. Stir in mushrooms, and cook 2

to 3 minutes or until liquid evaporates. Remove skillet from heat.
4. Stir together soup, sour cream, and Italian seasoning in a medium bowl until well blended. Stir soup mixture into onion mixture in skillet; stir in rice. Gently stir in tomatoes and chicken just until combined. Spoon mixture into a lightly greased 13- x 9-inch baking dish.
5. Bake at 350° for 25 to 30 minutes. **Makes** 6 servings.

To make ahead: Line a 13- x 9-inch baking dish with heavy-duty aluminum foil, allowing several inches of foil to extend over sides. Prepare recipe as directed through Step 4; spoon mixture into dish. Freeze 2 hours or until firm. Lift casserole from dish using foil sides; fold foil over casserole. Wrap in additional foil, or place in a large zip-top plastic freezer bag. Freeze up to 3 months. Remove casserole from foil or freezer bag. Place in a lightly greased 13- x 9-inch baking dish. Thaw in refrigerator 24 hours. Bake at 350° for 1 hour to 1 hour and 10 minutes or until bubbly.

Test Kitchen *Notebook*

Freezer Facts

■ Use freezer bags rather than storage bags when freezing. The thicker bags keep food fresher longer.
■ Set freezer temperature to 0° or lower, and monitor with freezer thermometer.
■ Most chocolate desserts freeze well because of their fat content.
■ Stack frozen foods close together to maximize freezer efficiency.

Mary Allen Perry
ASSOCIATE FOODS EDITOR

Top It and Toast It

We've taken garlic bread up a notch. These tasty toasts make perfect entertaining starters. For a light meal, serve them with a salad and glass of wine. Mix spreads the day before, and refrigerate overnight.

Caramelized Onion-and-Goat Cheese Bread

PREP: 15 MIN., BAKE: 27 MIN., COOK: 27 MIN., STAND: 30 MIN.

½ cup chopped pecans
1 Tbsp. butter
1 medium-size sweet onion, halved and thinly sliced
½ tsp. sugar
1 large garlic clove, minced
1 (10.5-oz.) goat cheese log
⅛ tsp. salt
⅛ tsp. pepper
1 (8.5-oz.) loaf French bread baguette, cut in half lengthwise
½ cup honey

1. Place pecans in a single layer in a baking sheet.
2. Bake at 350° for 10 to 12 minutes or until lightly toasted.
3. Melt butter in a 10-inch skillet over medium-high heat. Stir in onion and sugar. Cook, stirring often, 20 to 25 minutes or until onions are caramel colored. Add garlic, and cook 2 more minutes. Remove from heat, and let stand 30 minutes.
4. Process onion mixture, goat cheese, salt, and pepper in a blender or food processor 30 to 45 seconds or until ingredients are well blended and smooth. Spread mixture evenly onto cut sides of bread. Place on a baking sheet.
5. Bake at 375° for 15 minutes or until thoroughly heated and edges are lightly browned. Cut into 1-inch slices. Drizzle evenly with honey, and sprinkle with toasted pecans. **Makes** 10 to 12 servings.

Tomato Bruschetta

PREP: 15 MIN., BAKE: 15 MIN., BROIL: 5 MIN.

Scooping out the soft center of the loaf makes this bruschetta easier to bite into.

1 (12-oz.) French bread loaf, cut in half lengthwise
1 Tbsp. olive oil
4 small fresh tomatoes, seeded and diced
⅔ cup fresh basil leaves, cut into thin strips
2 Tbsp. balsamic vinaigrette
¼ tsp. pepper
¼ tsp. salt
⅔ cup (3 oz.) shredded Parmesan cheese
6 cooked bacon slices, crumbled

1. Cut French bread halves into 4 equal pieces. Scoop out and reserve soft centers of bread, leaving shells intact with ½-inch-thick sides and 1½-inch-thick bottoms.
2. Cut reserved soft centers of bread halves into small cubes. Place on a baking sheet.
3. Bake at 350° for 14 to 15 minutes or until toasted and lightly browned. Remove from oven; place toasted bread cubes in a large bowl. Place bread shells, cut sides up, on baking sheet. Brush cut sides evenly with olive oil. Increase oven temperature to broil.
4. Broil bread shells 5 inches from heat 2 to 3 minutes or until lightly brown. Remove from oven.
5. Place tomatoes in a small mixing bowl, and gently crush with a fork. Add toasted bread cubes, basil, and next 3 ingredients, tossing to coat.
6. Using a slotted spoon, fill each toasted bread shell evenly with tomato mixture. Sprinkle evenly with ⅔ cup Parmesan cheese.
7. Broil 1 to 2 minutes or until cheese is melted. Top each portion evenly with crumbled bacon. **Makes** 8 servings.

HELEN KEE
GREENVILLE, SOUTH CAROLINA

Fantastic Fish Sandwich

You don't need to go to Florida to enjoy one of its signature dishes. Start with fresh white fish fillets, and coat them in this easy beer batter.

Fried Fish Sandwiches

PREP: 20 MIN., FRY: 4 MIN. PER BATCH

This superb sandwich is inspired by the Black Grouper Sandwich served at Dockside Dave's in St. Pete Beach, Florida.

2 lb. grouper, mahi mahi, cod, or halibut fillets
2 tsp. Greek seasoning, divided
1½ tsp. salt, divided
1 tsp. freshly ground pepper, divided
2¼ cups all-purpose flour
¼ cup yellow cornmeal
2 tsp. baking powder
2 cups cold beer
1 large egg, lightly beaten
Vegetable oil
4 sesame seed hamburger buns
Tartar sauce or mayonnaise
4 green leaf lettuce leaves
4 tomato slices

1. Cut fish into 3-inch strips. Sprinkle evenly with 1 tsp. Greek seasoning, 1 tsp. salt, and ½ tsp. pepper.
2. Combine flour, cornmeal, baking powder, remaining 1 tsp. Greek seasoning, ½ tsp. salt, and ½ tsp. pepper; stir well. Add 2 cups cold beer and egg, stirring until thoroughly blended and smooth.
3. Pour oil to a depth of 2 to 3 inches into a Dutch oven; heat to 375°.
4. Dip fish strips into batter, coating both sides well; shake off excess. Fry fish, in batches, 2 minutes on each side or until golden (do not crowd pan). Drain on paper towels.
5. Spread top half of each bun evenly with tartar sauce. Place 1 lettuce leaf and 1 tomato slice on bottom half of each bun; top each with 2 fried fish strips and top halves of buns. **Makes** 4 servings.

Southern Living Cooking School

Sweet and Savory Treats.

Sample this trio of flavorful recipes.

When you have the urge to nibble, try one of these tasty creations. Easy Tropical Banana Dessert, wholesome Oatmeal Scones, and Tortilla-Lime Crackers will earn kudos for the cook. They're simple, delicious, and almost guilt-free.

Oatmeal Scones
family favorite
PREP: 10 MIN., STAND: 10 MIN., COOL: 25 MIN., BAKE: 30 MIN.

⅓ cup raisins
½ cup hot water
2 Tbsp. chopped pecans
¾ cup uncooked quick-cooking oats
⅓ cup granulated sugar
1¾ cups all-purpose flour
2 tsp. baking powder
½ tsp. baking soda
¼ tsp. salt
⅓ cup PROMISE BUTTERY SPREAD
¾ cup nonfat buttermilk
1 large egg
Vegetable cooking spray
1 Tbsp. PROMISE BUTTERY SPREAD
½ cup powdered sugar
2 Tbsp. nonfat buttermilk

1. Combine raisins and hot water in a 1-cup glass measuring cup. Let stand 10 minutes. Drain well.
2. Place pecans in a single layer in a 15- x 10-inch jelly-roll pan. Bake at 350° for 4 to 6 minutes or until lightly toasted, stirring occasionally. Remove from pan.
3. Place oats in jelly-roll pan.
4. Bake at 400° for 5 to 6 minutes or until lightly browned. Cool 15 minutes.
5. Combine pecans, oats, granulated sugar, and next 4 ingredients.
6. Cut ⅓ cup buttery spread into oats mixture with a pastry blender or fork until crumbly. Stir together raisins, ¾ cup buttermilk, and egg. Add to flour mixture, stirring just until dry ingredients are moistened.
7. Coat jelly-roll pan with cooking spray. Turn dough out onto pan. Shape dough into a 7-inch circle.
8. Bake at 400° for 15 to 18 minutes or until a wooden pick inserted in center comes out clean. Brush with 1 Tbsp. buttery spread. Let cool 10 minutes.
9. Stir together powdered sugar and 2 Tbsp. buttermilk until smooth; drizzle over scone. Cut into 8 wedges. **Makes** 8 servings.

Easy Tropical Banana Dessert
family favorite
PREP: 10 MIN., COOK: 21 MIN.

1 cup orange juice
1 cup pineapple juice
2 Tbsp. PROMISE BUTTERY SPREAD
2 Tbsp. dark brown sugar
3 bananas, each cut into 8 pieces
½ tsp. vanilla extract
¼ tsp. ground cinnamon
Vanilla low-fat frozen yogurt
¼ cup chopped macadamia nuts

1. Cook juices in a medium-size non-stick skillet over medium heat, stirring occasionally, 14 to 16 minutes or until mixture is reduced to ¾ cup. Remove from skillet.
2. Melt buttery spread in skillet over medium-high heat; add brown sugar, and cook, stirring often, 2 minutes. Add bananas; cook, stirring occasionally, 2 minutes. Stir in vanilla and cinnamon. Add juice mixture, and cook, stirring occasionally, 1 minute. Serve over frozen yogurt, and top with chopped nuts. **Makes** 4 servings.

Test Kitchen Notebook

If you want your bananas to ripen faster, place them in a paper bag with an apple, close the bag, and store it on the countertop overnight.

Tortilla-Lime Crackers
fast fixin's
PREP: 10 MIN., BAKE: 16 MIN.
Serve with your favorite queso dip or salsa as an appetizer, or top with shredded pork or cooked ground beef for hearty nachos.

2 Tbsp. PROMISE BUTTERY SPREAD, melted
1 Tbsp. lime juice
½ tsp. Creole seasoning
4 (8-inch) soft taco-size flour or whole wheat tortillas

1. Combine buttery spread, lime juice, and seasoning.
2. Cut each tortilla into 8 wedges. Place in a single layer on a baking sheet. Brush top of wedges evenly with buttery spread mixture.
3. Bake at 375° for 14 to 16 minutes or until lightly browned. **Makes** about 3 dozen.

Weeknight Wonders

These yummy offerings are simple enough for a great casual supper.

Herb Dill Dip
PREP: 10 MIN., CHILL: 1 HR.

1 (12-oz.) container whipped cream cheese
½ cup chopped CLAUSSEN Dill Pickle Halves
3 Tbsp. chopped fresh parsley
3 Tbsp. chopped fresh basil
2 Tbsp. pickle juice
1 garlic clove, minced
1 tsp. grated lemon rind
Assorted fresh vegetables

1. Stir together first 7 ingredients. Cover and chill at least 1 hour or up to 2 days. Serve with vegetables. **Makes** about 1¾ cups.

Shaping Tuna Cakes

Use a 3-inch plastic snap-on lid as a mold to easily shape Tuna Cakes.

A 3-inch biscuit cutter is another option to evenly shape the cakes.

Tuna Cakes
make ahead
PREP: 20 MIN., COOK: 6 MIN. PER BATCH
Tuna Cakes start with tuna from foil pouches (which our Test Kitchens Professionals just love). You can make the cakes up to eight hours ahead, store them in the refrigerator, and then cook them when you're ready.

2 (7-oz.) foil pouches solid white tuna in water, flaked
1⅓ cups fine, dry breadcrumbs
2 large eggs, lightly beaten
2 CLAUSSEN Kosher Dill Pickle Spears, finely chopped
1 celery rib, finely chopped
¼ cup finely chopped red onion
¼ tsp. salt
½ tsp. freshly ground pepper
2 Tbsp. olive oil
Bibb lettuce leaves
Tomato slices
Dill pickle spears

1. Stir together tuna, ⅓ cup breadcrumbs, and next 6 ingredients in a large bowl just until blended. Shape tuna mixture into 8 equal patties (about ⅓ cup each). Dredge patties in remaining 1 cup breadcrumbs.
2. Cook 4 patties in 1 Tbsp. hot olive oil in a large nonstick skillet over medium heat 3 minutes on each side or until golden. Remove from skillet. Repeat with remaining 1 Tbsp. oil and 4 patties. Place Tuna Cakes on top of Bibb lettuce leaves and tomato slices; serve with dill pickle spears. **Makes** 4 servings.

Open-Faced Monte Cristo Sandwiches
PREP: 10 MIN., COOK: 12 MIN., BROIL: 5 MIN.

2 large eggs
½ cup milk
1 Tbsp. honey mustard
6 whole wheat or whole grain white bread slices
2 Tbsp. butter
1 lb. thinly sliced smoked deli ham
12 Havarti cheese slices (about ½ lb.)
6 CLAUSSEN Kosher Dill Pickle Spears

1. Whisk together first 3 ingredients in a shallow dish. Dip both sides of each bread slice into egg mixture.
2. Melt 1 Tbsp. butter in a large nonstick skillet over medium heat; add 3 bread slices, and cook 2 to 3 minutes on each side or until golden brown. Remove from skillet. Repeat with remaining 1 Tbsp. butter and 3 bread slices.
3. Place bread slices on a baking sheet. Top each bread slice with ham and cheese.
4. Broil 5½ inches from heat 3 to 5 minutes or until cheese is melted. Serve immediately with dill pickle spears. **Makes** 6 servings.

Delicious and Healthful

Take a new look at the idea of a meal without meat. The recipes featured here will win you over. Be sure to try Creole Breakfast Crostinis, which doubles as a brunch or dinnertime favorite.

Creole Breakfast Crostinis

fast fixin's

PREP: 20 MIN., BAKE: 5 MIN.

We tried this breakfast eye-opener with both traditional eggs and egg substitute—it is delicious with either one.

1 (11-oz.) package MORNINGSTAR
    FARMS Breakfast Starters Classic
    Scramble
4 large eggs
¾ tsp. Creole seasoning
½ (8-oz.) French bread baguette
4 (1-oz.) slices Monterey Jack cheese
    with peppers
Creole Sauce
Garnish: chopped fresh parsley

1. Prepare breakfast starters with eggs according to package directions, adding ¾ tsp. Creole seasoning.
2. Cut bread diagonally into 4 (1¼-inch-thick) slices. Top bread slices with cheese, and place on a baking sheet.

The key to perfect scrambled eggs is to avoid high heat and let the uncooked portion flow underneath the cooked eggs.

3. Bake at 400° for 5 minutes or until cheese is melted and bread is lightly toasted.
4. Top bread slices evenly with scrambled egg mixture. Drizzle evenly with Creole Sauce. Garnish, if desired. Serve immediately. **Makes** 4 servings.

Creole Sauce:

fast fixin's • make ahead

PREP: 5 MIN.

Serve extra sauce with fresh tomato slices or over blanched asparagus and green beans. This can be stored in the refrigerator for up to a week.

1 (1.25-oz.) envelope hollandaise
    sauce mix
1 Tbsp. Creole mustard
1 Tbsp. chopped fresh parsley
¼ tsp. ground red pepper

1. Prepare hollandaise sauce mix according to package directions. Stir in remaining ingredients. **Makes** 1 cup.

Philly Cheese "Steak"

PREP: 15 MIN., COOK: 16 MIN., BAKE: 8 MIN.

1 Tbsp. butter
1 medium onion, thinly sliced
½ large red bell pepper, cut into
    thin strips
1½ cups sliced fresh mushrooms
1 (8-oz.) package MORNINGSTAR FARMS
    Meal Starters Steak Strips
1 garlic clove, minced
3 Tbsp. Italian dressing
¼ tsp. dried crushed red pepper
    (optional)
Salt and black pepper to taste
4 (2.5-oz.) hoagie rolls, split
4 (1-oz.) provolone cheese slices

1. Melt butter in a large skillet over medium-high heat; add onion, bell pepper, and mushrooms, and sauté 13 minutes or until onions are golden brown. Add strips and garlic; sauté 3 minutes or until thoroughly heated. Stir in dressing, and, if desired, crushed red pepper. Season with salt and black pepper to taste.
2. Arrange strips mixture evenly on bottom roll halves; top with cheese and remaining roll halves. Arrange on a baking sheet. Bake at 400° for 8 minutes or until buns are toasted and cheese is melted. **Makes** 4 servings.

Sticky Noodle Bowl

PREP: 15 MIN., COOK: 15 MIN.

Shorten your time in the kitchen by accomplishing two things at once: While the pasta cooks, sauté the vegetables and steak strips.

1 (11-oz.) box Asian-style noodles with
    soy-ginger sauce
1 (6-oz.) package fresh snow peas
1 small red bell pepper, thinly sliced
½ medium onion, thinly sliced
2 Tbsp. freshly grated ginger
1 Tbsp. olive oil
1 (8-oz.) package MORNINGSTAR FARMS
    Meal Starters Steak Strips
1 tsp. minced garlic
⅓ cup vegetable broth
1 Tbsp. creamy peanut butter
Toppings: chopped peanuts, chopped
    fresh cilantro, bean sprouts, lime
    wedges

1. Remove and reserve sauce and sesame seed topping packets from box of noodles. Cook noodles according to package directions, stirring in snow peas during last minute of cooking; drain and rinse.
2. Sauté bell pepper, onion, and ginger in hot oil in a large skillet over medium-high heat 3 minutes or until crisp-tender. Stir in strips and garlic; sauté 3 minutes or until thoroughly heated. Stir in cooked noodles, reserved sauce packet, vegetable broth, and peanut butter, tossing to coat. Cook, stirring constantly, 2 minutes or until peanut butter is melted and mixture is thoroughly heated.
3. Transfer noodle mixture to a large serving platter; serve with desired toppings. Top with reserved sesame seed topping, if desired. **Makes** 4 servings.

Pass the Pasta

Jazz up meals for family and friends with these crowd-pleasing recipes. These three Italian-inspired dishes—filled with flavorful vegetables, cheeses, and seasonings—are sure to earn rave reviews.

Marinated Vegetable Platter
make ahead

PREP: 30 MIN., COOK: 14 MIN., GRILL: 12 MIN., STAND: 10 MIN., CHILL: 2 HR.

1 (16-oz.) box BARILLA Penne
1 red bell pepper
2 medium zucchini
3 medium-size yellow squash
1 small red onion
2 cups chopped tomatoes (2 medium)
1 (16-oz.) package fresh mozzarella cheese in water, cubed
½ cup red wine vinegar
¼ cup olive oil
½ tsp. finely chopped fresh rosemary
½ tsp. grated lemon rind
½ tsp. salt
½ tsp. pepper

1. Cook pasta according to package directions; drain well.
2. Cut bell pepper into 1-inch-wide strips. Cut off ends of zucchini and yellow squash; cut each lengthwise into 4 equal slices. Cut onion into ¾-inch-thick rounds.
3. Grill bell pepper, zucchini, yellow squash, and onion, covered with grill lid, over medium-high heat (350° to 400°) 4 to 6 minutes on each side until tender. Let stand 10 minutes, and coarsely chop.
4. Place pasta in a large bowl, and stir in grilled vegetables, tomatoes, and cheese.
5. Whisk together red wine vinegar and remaining ingredients; add to pasta mixture, tossing to coat. Cover and chill at least 2 hours or up to 6 hours. **Makes** 8 servings.

Fettuccine With Wilted Greens

PREP: 20 MIN., COOK: 40 MIN.
This impressive entrée is ready to serve in an hour. Try a sprinkle of red pepper flakes to add a kick to this dish.

1 (16-oz.) box BARILLA Fettuccine
8 chicken cutlets (about 2½ lb.)
1 tsp. salt
½ tsp. pepper
1 cup all-purpose flour
½ cup extra virgin olive oil
2 sweet onions, thinly sliced
2 (8-oz.) packages sliced fresh mushrooms
2 tsp. minced garlic
½ cup chicken broth
1 cup white wine
1 tsp. salt
1 tsp. pepper
2 (9-oz.) packages fresh spinach, thoroughly washed
Freshly grated Parmesan cheese

1. Cook pasta in a Dutch oven according to package directions. Drain, return to Dutch oven, and keep warm.
2. Sprinkle chicken with 1 tsp. salt and ½ tsp. pepper. Dredge in flour.
3. Sauté chicken, in batches, in hot oil in a large skillet over medium-high heat 3 to 5 minutes on each side or until chicken is browned. Remove and keep warm.
4. Add onions, mushrooms, and garlic to skillet; sauté 5 to 7 minutes or until mushrooms are lightly browned. Stir in chicken broth and next 3 ingredients, and cook 3 to 5 minutes or until liquid is reduced by half, stirring to loosen particles from bottom of skillet.
5. Add mushroom mixture and spinach to pasta in Dutch oven, tossing to coat. Cook, covered, over medium-low heat 4 to 6 minutes or until greens are wilted. Spoon into a serving dish, and top evenly with chicken and Parmesan cheese. **Makes** 8 servings.

You can make large shreds of Parmesan cheese with a vegetable peeler.

Classic-Style Lasagne
freezeable • make ahead

PREP: 15 MIN., COOK: 12 MIN., BAKE: 50 MIN., STAND: 10 MIN.
Use 2 (8-inch) square baking dishes so you have the option of baking both for a large gathering or baking one and freezing one for later.

1¼ lb. Italian pork sausage, casings removed
1 (8-oz.) package sliced fresh mushrooms
2 (24-oz.) jars tomato-and-basil pasta sauce
1 (10-oz.) package frozen chopped spinach, thawed
1 (32-oz.) container low-fat ricotta cheese
1 large egg, lightly beaten
½ cup grated Parmesan cheese
1 (9-oz.) box BARILLA Oven Ready Lasagne
1 (16-oz.) package shredded mozzarella-provolone cheese blend

1. Cook sausage and mushrooms in a lightly greased large Dutch oven over medium-high heat, stirring occasionally, 10 to 12 minutes or until meat crumbles and is no longer pink. Drain and return to Dutch oven. Stir in pasta sauce.
2. Drain spinach well, pressing between paper towels. Stir together spinach, ricotta cheese, egg, and Parmesan cheese in a large bowl until blended.
3. Arrange 2 lasagne noodles in a single layer in a lightly greased 8-inch square baking dish; layer evenly with

¾ cup spinach mixture, 1 cup sausage mixture, and ½ cup cheese blend. Repeat layers twice, gently pressing layers to compact. Top with 2 noodles, 1 cup sausage mixture, and ½ cup cheese blend. (Dish will be full.) Repeat procedure with remaining ingredients in another lightly greased 8-inch square baking dish. Place both dishes on an aluminum foil-lined baking sheet.

4. Bake, covered, at 350° for 40 minutes; uncover and bake 8 to 10 more minutes or until bubbly. Let stand 10 minutes before serving. **Makes** 12 servings.

Note: To freeze, prepare as directed through Step 3. Cover baking dishes tightly with aluminum foil. Freeze up to 1 month. Thaw overnight in the refrigerator. Let stand at room temperature 30 minutes. Bake, covered, at 350° for 1 hour. Uncover and bake 15 more minutes or until bubbly.

Bold Flavor in a Flash

Enjoy the beginning of fall with these hearty, better-for-you recipes. Prep times of only 10 minutes get you to the supper table faster.

Roasted Steak Fries
family favorite
PREP: 10 MIN., BAKE: 30 MIN.

2 lb. red potatoes
2 Tbsp. vegetable oil
1 Tbsp. MCCORMICK Grill Mates Montreal Steak Seasoning

1. Cut potatoes into 1- to 1½-inch wedges. Combine potatoes, oil, and seasoning, tossing to coat. Place potato mixture in a single layer on a lightly greased 17- x 12-inch jelly-roll pan.
2. Bake at 450° for 25 to 30 minutes or until potatoes are tender and lightly browned. **Makes** 4 to 6 servings.

Garlic Herb Tilapia With Fruit Salsa
PREP: 10 MIN., COOK: 10 MIN.
We prefer to use mango-peach salsa in this recipe, but your favorite flavor will work just fine. You can substitute catfish for the tilapia.

1½ lb. tilapia fillets (about 4 fillets)
1 Tbsp. MCCORMICK Grill Mates Roasted Garlic and Herb Seasoning
1 cup refrigerated fruit salsa
½ cup seeded and chopped cucumber
2 Tbsp. butter
Lime wedges

1. Rub tilapia fillets evenly with seasoning. Stir together salsa and cucumber in a small bowl.
2. Melt butter in a large nonstick skillet over medium-high heat; add tilapia, and cook 3 to 4 minutes on each side or until well browned and done. Serve immediately with salsa mixture and lime wedges. **Makes** 4 servings.

Mushroom Gravy
fast fixin's
PREP: 10 MIN., COOK: 15 MIN.

1 medium onion, minced
2 garlic cloves, minced
1 Tbsp. olive oil
1 (8-oz.) package sliced fresh mushrooms
1 (0.87-oz.) package MCCORMICK Homestyle Gravy Mix
1 (14-oz.) can beef broth
1 Tbsp. soy sauce
½ tsp. pepper

1. Sauté minced onion and garlic in hot oil in a medium saucepan over medium-high heat 4 to 5 minutes until tender; add sliced fresh mushrooms, and sauté 5 minutes.
2. Stir together gravy mix, beef broth, and soy sauce. Stir into mushroom mixture, stirring to loosen particles from bottom of skillet. Bring to a boil over medium-high heat, stirring constantly. Reduce heat to medium, and cook, stirring occasionally, 4 to 5 minutes or until slightly thickened. Stir in pepper. **Makes** 3 cups.

Versatile Side Dishes

Rice is the star attraction in these savory recipes. With the aid of ready-to-use products from the grocery shelf, we've trimmed preparation time, which makes them excellent choices for weekday meals.

Hands-off Risotto With Zucchini
family favorite
PREP: 15 MIN., COOK: 40 MIN.,
STAND: 12 MIN.
Add shrimp, ham, or additional vegetables for more flavor.

1 lb. zucchini
5¼ cups chicken broth
2 Tbsp. butter
1 small onion, chopped (about ½ cup)
1¼ cups MAHATMA Extra Long Grain Enriched White Rice
3 carrots, shredded
¼ cup freshly grated Parmesan cheese
2 Tbsp. finely chopped fresh oregano
1 tsp. grated lemon rind
2 Tbsp. lemon juice
Garnishes: oregano sprig, grated lemon rind

1. Cut zucchini in half lengthwise; cut each half into ¼ inch slices.
2. Microwave broth in a 2-qt. microwave-safe bowl at HIGH 6 to 7 minutes or until very hot.
3. Melt butter in a large Dutch oven over medium heat; add onion, and sauté 4 to 5 minutes or until tender. Stir in rice, and cook, stirring constantly, 2 minutes. Stir in hot broth, and bring to a boil over medium-high heat. Cover, reduce heat to low, and simmer 10 minutes. Stir in zucchini and carrots. Cover and cook 10 to 12 more minutes or until rice is tender. Stir in cheese and next 3 ingredients, stirring until cheese is melted. Remove from heat; cover and let stand 10 to 12 minutes or until liquid is absorbed. Garnish, if desired. **Makes** 8 (1-cup) servings.

Hoppin' John Rice Bowl
family favorite
PREP: 15 MIN., COOK: 20 MIN.

2 (3.5-oz.) bags SUCCESS White Rice, uncooked
1 Tbsp. butter
1 (8-oz.) package diced smoked ham
½ medium onion, diced
1 tsp. minced garlic
2 (15½-oz.) cans seasoned black-eyed peas
1 Tbsp. cider vinegar
3 green onions, chopped
⅓ cup chopped fresh parsley
1 large tomato, chopped

1. Prepare rice according to package directions.
2. Melt butter in a large skillet over medium-high heat; add ham, onion, and garlic, and sauté 6 to 7 minutes or until onion is tender. Stir in black-eyed peas and ½ cup water. Bring to a boil; reduce heat, and simmer 10 minutes. Stir in vinegar.
3. Place hot cooked rice in a serving dish; spoon ham mixture over rice. Sprinkle with green onions, parsley, and tomato. **Makes** 4 servings.

Rice Croquettes
family favorite
PREP: 5 MIN., COOK: 20 MIN., COOL: 10 MIN., FRY: 5 MIN. PER BATCH
Serve these crisp rice bites with your favorite rémoulade sauce.

1⅓ cups MAHATMA Extra Long Grain Enriched White Rice
½ tsp. salt
1½ cups Japanese breadcrumbs (panko), divided
3 large eggs
1 cup shredded Parmesan cheese
2 Tbsp. chopped fresh basil
1 tsp. minced garlic
½ tsp. freshly ground pepper
Vegetable oil

1. Bring 2⅔ cups water to a boil over medium-high heat; add rice and salt.

Cover, reduce heat to low, and simmer 20 minutes or until liquid is absorbed and rice is tender. Let cool 10 minutes.
2. Stir together rice, ½ cup breadcrumbs, and next 5 ingredients.
3. Shape rice mixture into 18 (¼-cup) balls. Dredge in remaining 1 cup breadcrumbs.
4. Pour oil to a depth of 3 inches into a Dutch oven. Heat oil to 350° over medium-high heat. Fry rice balls, in batches, 2 to 2½ minutes on each side or until golden brown. Drain. **Makes** about 1½ dozen.

Add a Tasty Twist to All-Star Dishes

Quick Catfish Supper

Serves 6

Catfish Nuggets With
Honey Dipping Sauce

Florentine Potato Salad

Chocolate-Almond Bars

Catfish and potato salad are top picks for almost any occasion. We've created recipes that will spice up your repertoire.

Use a handheld microplane grater to make grating lemon rind extra easy. Turn the sharp side down to capture all the flavor in the grated rind and lemon oil.

Catfish Nuggets With Honey Dipping Sauce
PREP: 15 MIN., BAKE: 15 MIN.

1 cup HELLMANN'S Real Mayonnaise
3 Tbsp. yellow mustard
3 Tbsp. honey
1 Tbsp. milk
Dash of liquid from hot peppers in vinegar
1½ cups crushed cornflakes cereal
1½ tsp. garlic powder
½ tsp. seasoned salt
1½ lb. farm-raised catfish fillets, cut into 1½- to 2-inch pieces
Lemon wedges

1. Whisk together first 5 ingredients. Spoon ½ cup mayonnaise mixture into a shallow bowl or pie plate. Cover and chill remaining mayonnaise mixture.
2. Stir together cereal, garlic powder, and salt until blended.
3. Dip fish into ½ cup mayonnaise mixture in pie plate, coating both sides; dredge in cereal mixture. Place fish on a lightly greased wire rack in a jelly-roll pan.
4. Bake at 450° for 14 to 15 minutes or until fish flakes with a fork. Serve with remaining mayonnaise mixture and lemon wedges. **Makes** 6 servings.

Florentine Potato Salad
make ahead
PREP: 10 MIN., COOK: 25 MIN., CHILL: 1 HR.

3 lb. small red potatoes, quartered
1¼ tsp. salt, divided
1½ cups shredded fresh baby spinach
¾ cup HELLMANN'S Real Mayonnaise
¼ cup chopped fresh flat-leaf parsley
2 cooked bacon slices, crumbled
2 Tbsp. chopped green onions
1 tsp. grated lemon rind
¼ tsp. freshly ground pepper
1 cup celery slices

1. Bring potatoes, 1 tsp. salt, and water to cover to a boil in a large Dutch oven over high heat; cook 20 to 25 minutes or until potatoes are tender. Drain and toss with spinach.

2. Stir together mayonnaise, next 5 ingredients, and remaining ¼ tsp. salt. Place potato mixture in a large mixing bowl; add celery and mayonnaise mixture, stirring gently until blended. Cover and chill at least 1 hour or until ready to serve. **Makes** 6 to 8 servings.

Chocolate-Almond Bars
family favorite
PREP: 10 MIN., BAKE: 17 MIN., STAND: 5 MIN., COOL: 2 HR.

1 cup firmly packed light brown sugar
¾ cup HELLMANN'S Real Mayonnaise
1 large egg
1 tsp. vanilla extract
2 cups all-purpose flour
½ tsp. baking powder
½ tsp. salt
1 (12-oz.) package milk chocolate
   morsels
1½ cups sliced almonds

1. Beat brown sugar and mayonnaise at medium speed with an electric mixer until creamy. Add egg and vanilla, beating until blended.
2. Stir together flour, baking powder, and salt; gradually add to mayonnaise mixture, beating until blended.
3. Press dough into an ungreased 15-x 10-inch jelly-roll pan.
4. Bake at 350° for 15 to 17 minutes or until golden. Place pan on a wire rack. Sprinkle chocolate morsels over warm cookie. Let stand 5 minutes; spread chocolate evenly over top. Sprinkle with almonds. Cool in pan on a wire rack 1½ to 2 hours or until completely cool. Cut into bars. **Makes** 3 dozen.

Family Favorites

These stick-to-your-ribs recipes are sure to please the entire family. All use ingredients you likely have on hand.

Pan-Seared Chicken Breasts
family favorite
PREP: 10 MIN., COOK: 35 MIN.
A few pantry herbs and spices dress up this healthful chicken breast entrée. Try serving the chicken and light pan sauce over creamy mashed potatoes.

2 tsp. dried Italian seasoning
1½ tsp. paprika
1 tsp. dried marjoram
½ tsp. salt
¼ tsp. pepper
6 (6- to 8-oz.) PILGRIM'S PRIDE
   Boneless, Skinless Chicken Breasts
2 Tbsp. olive oil
1 garlic clove, minced
⅔ cup chicken broth

1. Stir together first 5 ingredients. Sprinkle evenly on both sides of chicken.
2. Cook 3 chicken breasts in 1 Tbsp. hot oil over medium heat 6 to 8 minutes on each side or until done. Remove chicken from pan. Repeat with remaining 3 chicken breasts and 1 Tbsp. oil.
3. Sauté garlic in hot skillet 1 minute. Add chicken broth, and cook 2 minutes, stirring to loosen particles from bottom of skillet. Serve sauce over chicken. **Makes** 6 servings.

White Bean Chili
family favorite
PREP: 10 MIN., COOK: 30 MIN.

1½ lb. PILGRIM'S PRIDE Boneless,
   Skinless Chicken Breasts, chopped
2 Tbsp. olive oil
4 (16-oz.) cans navy beans, undrained
4 (4.5-oz.) cans chopped green chiles,
   undrained
1 cup chicken broth
1 (1.25-oz.) envelope white chicken chili
   seasoning mix
Toppings: chopped fresh cilantro,
   shredded Monterey Jack cheese,
   chopped tomatoes, chopped avocado

1. Sauté chicken in hot oil in a large Dutch oven over medium-high heat 8 minutes or until done.
2. Stir in beans and next 3 ingredients; bring to a boil over medium-high heat, stirring occasionally. Cover, reduce heat to low, and simmer, stirring occasionally, 15 minutes. Serve with desired toppings. **Makes** 8 servings.

Chicken Fajita Salad
PREP: 10 MIN., COOK: 20 MIN.

½ (24-oz.) package frozen PILGRIM'S
   PRIDE Grilled Chicken Breast Strips
1 large onion, sliced
1 large red bell pepper, sliced
1 tsp. chili powder
½ tsp. ground cumin
¼ tsp. salt
1 Tbsp. olive oil
4 (10-inch) burrito-size flour tortillas
1 medium head iceberg lettuce, torn
   (about 6 cups)
1 cup (4 oz.) shredded Monterey Jack
   cheese with peppers
Toppings: sour cream, salsa, guacamole,
   Ranch dressing, lime wedges,
   chopped fresh cilantro

1. Prepare chicken strips according to stovetop package directions. Remove chicken from skillet.
2. Sauté onion, bell pepper, and next 3 ingredients in hot oil in skillet over medium-high heat 6 to 8 minutes or until vegetables are lightly browned. Stir in chicken strips and 2 Tbsp. water, and cook 2 to 3 minutes or until mixture is thoroughly heated.
3. Arrange tortillas in 4 individual serving bowls. Divide lettuce and cheese evenly in tortilla-lined bowls. Top with hot chicken mixture. Serve with desired toppings. **Makes** 4 servings.

from our kitchen

Bloody Mary Bar

Create a Bloody Mary bar at your next tailgate or party. Our staff agrees that the quality of the mixer is far more important than the caliber of vodka in making a delicious cocktail. We tasted quite a few Bloody Mary mixes and chose Major Peters' (Original or Hot & Spicy), Zing Zang, Mr. & Mrs. T's Bold & Spicy, and Whiskey Willy's (all available at **www.hotshoppe.com**) as our favorites. Offer guests an array of festive garnishes such as celery sticks, carrot sticks, pickled okra, assorted olives, pepperoncini salad peppers, and lemon and lime slices to add pizzazz. The drinks will look as good as they taste. Cheers.

Start With Flattened Chicken

Consumers love chicken breasts, so much so that birds are bred to have plenty of white meat. The breasts are often so large that they don't cook easily. And one end is thinner than the other, causing uneven cooking. Here's an easy fix. Place boneless chicken breasts between pieces of plastic wrap, and pound them with a meat mallet or rolling pin until they're a uniform thickness.

Flattened breasts are used in Chicken With White Wine and Mushrooms. It has fine-dining flavor and appearance with down-home goodness and ease.

Chicken With White Wine and Mushrooms

PREP: 15 MIN., COOK: 30 MIN.

4 skinned and boned chicken breasts
1½ tsp. kosher salt
½ tsp. pepper
¼ cup butter, divided
1 (16-oz.) package linguine
1 (8-oz.) package sliced fresh mushrooms
1 cup dry white wine
1 (10¾-oz.) can cream of chicken soup
Garnish: fresh parsley sprig

1. Place chicken between sheets of plastic wrap; flatten to ¼-inch thickness, using a meat mallet or rolling pin. Sprinkle chicken with salt and pepper.
2. Melt 1 Tbsp. butter in a skillet over medium-high heat; cook 2 breasts 4 to 5 minutes on each side or until done. Remove chicken; cover and keep warm. Repeat with remaining chicken and 1 Tbsp. butter; reserve drippings in skillet.
3. Prepare pasta according to package directions.
4. Melt remaining 2 Tbsp. butter in skillet over medium-high heat; add mushrooms, and sauté 8 minutes. Add wine, and stir to loosen particles from bottom of skillet; bring to a boil. Remove from heat; add soup, and whisk vigorously until smooth.
5. Arrange pasta on serving plate; top with chicken and sauce. Garnish, if desired.
Makes 4 servings.

DIANNA HUTTS ASTON
BUDA, TEXAS

myrecipes.com

Check out our dazzling new Web portal, **myrecipes.com.** You'll have instant access to more than 20,000 recipes from *Southern Living* and her sister publications—*Cooking Light, Sunset, Coastal Living, Cottage Living,* and *Health.* Use this advanced recipe search tool to find the perfect recipe by ingredient, cuisine, course, occasion, dietary considerations, or to search *Southern Living* recipes alone. You can also save shopping lists, add personal recipes, view informative how-to videos, read cookbook and kitchen gadget reviews, and create menus. There will be exciting daily updates and opportunities to share your thoughts. So give **myrecipes.com** a try—we think you'll really like it.

october

New Look For Pizza

Sink your teeth into these restaurant-style recipes. They're faster than delivery and taste incredible grilled.

Get ready for a flavor experience that's so melt in your mouth, you'll wish you had tried this clever cooking technique sooner. We discovered that the grill yields irresistible brick-oven flavor and crispy-tender crust, similar to the fire-baked flat bread you find in fancy Italian restaurants. Better still, it's ready quicker than you can say "delivery."

All you do is put the store-bought dough or crust directly on the hot grate, add your toppings, and let the grill do the work. We make the prep even more convenient by offering bottled sauces and other shortcut ingredients. Follow our simple steps, and see for yourself how easy it is.

Test Kitchen Notebook

Easiest Pizza Ever

It's a breeze to cook a pizza on the grill. Here's our secret when working with fresh dough: First make sure your cutting board or other surface is well floured and sprinkled with cornmeal to keep the dough from sticking. Then, roll out the dough. Next, use your cutting board to slide the crust onto the hot cooking grate; add your toppings, and grill as directed.

Shannon Sliter Satterwhite
FOODS EDITOR

Grilled Pizza With Steak, Pear, and Arugula

PREP: 10 MIN., GRILL: 30 MIN., STAND: 10 MIN.

Vegetable cooking spray
½ lb. flank steak
Salt and pepper
1 Tbsp. olive oil
1½ tsp. white balsamic vinegar
1 (12-inch) prebaked pizza crust
1 red Bartlett pear, peeled and sliced
1½ cups fresh arugula, divided
¼ cup crumbled Gorgonzola cheese
Freshly cracked pepper

1. Coat cold cooking grate of grill with cooking spray, and place on grill. Preheat grill to 350° (medium heat).
2. Season flank steak with salt and pepper.
3. Grill steak, covered with grill lid, at 350° (medium heat) 8 to 10 minutes on each side or to desired degree of doneness. Cover and let stand 10 minutes.
4. Meanwhile, whisk together oil and vinegar in a small bowl.

5. Cut steak diagonally across grain into thin strips. Cut strips into bite-size pieces (about 1 cup).
6. Place pizza crust directly on hot cooking grate. Brush top of crust with oil mixture; layer with pear slices, 1 cup arugula, cheese, and beef strips.
7. Grill, covered with grill lid, 4 minutes. Rotate pizza one-quarter turn; grill, covered with grill lid, 5 to 6 more minutes or until thoroughly heated. Remove pizza from grill, and sprinkle with remaining ½ cup arugula and freshly cracked pepper. **Makes 4 servings.**

Note: For testing purposes only, we used ½ (16-oz.) package Mama Mary's Thin & Crispy Pizza Crusts.

Oven-Baked Pizza With Steak, Pear, and Arugula: Assemble pizza as directed, and bake according to package directions for pizza crust.

Buffalo Chicken Pizza

fast fixin's
PREP: 10 MIN., GRILL: 10 MIN.

Vegetable cooking spray
½ cup Buffalo-style hot sauce
1 (16-oz.) package prebaked Italian pizza crust
2 cups chopped deli-roasted whole chicken
1 cup (4 oz.) shredded provolone cheese
¼ cup crumbled blue cheese

1. Coat cold cooking grate of grill with cooking spray, and place on grill. Preheat grill to 350° (medium heat).
2. Spread hot sauce over crust, and layer with next 3 ingredients.

Take Your Temperature

It's important to keep your grill near 350° for these recipes. If your grill doesn't have a built-in thermometer, purchase an oven thermometer for about $2.50 at your local superstore. Simply preheat the grill at a medium setting, place the thermometer on the grill grate, and close the lid. Check the temperature periodically, and adjust the heat as needed.

3. Place crust directly on cooking grate. Grill, covered with grill lid, at 350° (medium heat) 4 minutes. Rotate pizza one-quarter turn, and grill, covered with grill lid, 5 to 6 more minutes or until thoroughly heated. Serve immediately. **Makes** 3 to 4 servings.

Note: For testing purposes only, we used Boboli prebaked pizza crust.

Oven-Baked Buffalo Chicken Pizza: Assemble pizza as directed, and bake according to package directions for pizza crust.

Shortcut Crust

- We found fresh pizza dough at our local supermarket bakery for about $2. Ask if your grocery store offers the same.
- Use a 10-oz. can of refrigerated dough, such as Pillsbury, if you can't find it fresh.
- Don't want to deal with dough? Purchase a prebaked Italian crust, such as Boboli or Mama Mary's instead.

Shrimp-Pesto Pizza

PREP: 20 MIN., COOK: 8 MIN., GRILL: 10 MIN.

Preheat the grill while you roll out the dough and sauté the vegetable mixture for this pizza. To save even more time, purchase peeled and cooked shrimp.

Vegetable cooking spray
½ lb. unpeeled, large raw shrimp
1 large yellow onion, chopped
1 red bell pepper, chopped
¼ tsp. salt
¼ tsp. pepper
2 Tbsp. olive oil
All-purpose flour
Yellow cornmeal
1 lb. bakery pizza dough
⅓ cup refrigerated pesto
½ cup freshly grated Parmesan cheese

1. Coat cold cooking grate of grill with cooking spray, and place on grill. Preheat grill to 350° (medium heat).
2. Peel shrimp, and slice in half lengthwise; devein, if desired.
3. Sauté onion, bell pepper, salt, and pepper in 1 Tbsp. hot oil in a large skillet over medium-high heat 5 minutes or until tender. Transfer onion mixture to a large bowl. Sauté shrimp in remaining 1 Tbsp. hot oil 3 minutes or just until shrimp turn pink. Add shrimp to onion mixture, and toss.
4. Lightly sprinkle flour and cornmeal on a large surface. Place dough on surface, and roll to a ¼-inch thickness. Carefully transfer pizza dough to a cutting board or baking sheet lightly sprinkled with flour and cornmeal.
5. Slide pizza dough from cutting board or baking sheet onto cooking grate (photos 1 and 2); spread ⅓ cup refrigerated pesto evenly over crust (photo 3), and top with shrimp mixture (photo 4). Sprinkle with ½ cup Parmesan cheese (photo 5).
6. Grill, covered with grill lid, at 350° (medium heat) 4 minutes. Rotate pizza one-quarter turn, and grill, covered with grill lid, 5 to 6 more minutes or until pizza crust is cooked. Serve immediately. **Makes** 2 to 3 servings.

STACEY ANGEL
CHARLESTON, WEST VIRGINIA

Shrimp-Pesto Pizza Step-by-Step

Pop the Top on Flavor

You won't believe where we found the secret ingredient to these fabulous recipes.

Most folks define "cooking with beer" as enjoying a cold one while barbecuing or grilling. Truth is, beer is one of the most versatile ingredients in the kitchen. Its flavor flexibility adds richness to meats, helps create super-moist cakes, and makes a tasty substitute for chicken or beef broth. With Oktoberfest celebrations cropping up all over the region, now's the perfect time to add some fun to your menu.

Many tried-and-true Southern dishes only get better with this secret ingredient. So don't miss the Beer-Kissed Cheese Grits or hearty Pork-and-Greens Stew. The possibilities are endless, so let your imagination run wild.

Beer for Beginners

The rule for cooking with beer is the same one that applies to wine: Choose something you like to drink. There are, of course, a couple of things to remember to help the process along. First, the same style of beer (i.e. pilsner, ale, pale ale) from two different breweries may taste nothing alike. So give it a taste before adding it to a recipe.

Second, looks can be deceiving. Unlike wine, the color of a beer doesn't always confirm its body or flavor. In other words, light-colored beers (often thought to be more mild) may explode with flavorful hops, fruit, or even chile peppers. Darker beers, such as brown ale and bock, have a richer, deeper flavor while still being surprisingly refreshing and easy to drink. The exceptions are full-bodied stout and porter. These opaque gems are full of character and even taste great when served with dessert.

Gingerbread Cake With Stout Buttercream

PREP: 15 MIN.; BAKE: 35 MIN.;
COOL: 1 HR., 10 MIN.
You'll need about 2 (12-oz.) bottles stout beer for this recipe. (Pictured on page 8)

2 (14.5-oz.) packages gingerbread cake mix
2 large eggs
2¾ cups stout beer, at room temperature, divided
½ cup butter, softened
1 (16-oz.) package powdered sugar
Garnishes: toasted pecans, rosemary sprigs

1. Stir together cake mix, eggs, and 2½ cups stout beer in a large bowl until combined. Pour batter evenly into 2 lightly greased 8-inch square pans.

2. Bake at 350° for 35 minutes or until a wooden pick inserted in center comes out clean. Cool in pans on a wire rack 10 minutes. Remove from pans, and let cool on wire rack 1 hour or until completely cool.

3. Beat softened butter at medium speed with an electric mixer until creamy. Gradually add powdered sugar and remaining ¼ cup stout beer, beating until blended after each addition. Beat 1 minute or until light and fluffy.

4. Spread stout buttercream between layers and on top of cake. Garnish, if desired. **Makes** 12 servings.

Note: For testing purposes only, we used Betty Crocker Gingerbread Cake & Cookie Mix. We used Terrapin Wake-n-Bake Coffee Oatmeal Imperial Stout at one testing and Guinness Extra Stout beer at another.

Black Velvet

Combine sparkling wine and full-bodied stout beer into one delicious cocktail.
Pour chilled sparkling wine into Champagne flutes, filling half full. Top with an equal amount of chilled stout beer (such as Guinness Extra Stout). Serve immediately.

Pork-and-Greens Stew

PREP: 20 MIN.; COOK: 2 HR., 30 MIN.

1 (3½- to 4-lb.) boneless pork shoulder roast, trimmed
1 tsp. salt
1 tsp. pepper
2 (12-oz.) bottles Oktoberfest beer
2 (10.75-oz.) cans condensed chicken broth, undiluted
1 large sweet onion, chopped
1 (16-oz.) package frozen chopped turnip greens, thawed
1 (15-oz.) can white hominy, rinsed and drained

1. Cut pork into 3-inch pieces; sprinkle evenly with salt and pepper, and place in a large Dutch oven. Stir in beer, broth, and onion. Bring to a boil over medium-high heat; cover, reduce heat to low, and simmer 1½ to 2 hours or until pork shreds easily with a fork.

2. Remove pork, and shred with 2 forks. Skim fat from surface of broth in Dutch oven.

3. Return pork to Dutch oven, and stir in greens and hominy. Bring to a boil; reduce heat, and simmer 20 minutes or until greens are tender. **Makes** 6 to 8 servings.

SHAWN CARLETON
EVERETT, WASHINGTON

Note: For testing purposes only, we used Saint Arnold Oktoberfest beer.

Kitchen Express Pork-and-Greens Stew: Omit salt. Substitute 2 (17-oz.) packages fully cooked pork roast au jus for pork shoulder roast. Rinse pork roast, and shred. Combine pork, pepper, beer, broth, and onion in Dutch oven. Bring to a boil; reduce heat, and simmer, uncovered, 20 minutes. Stir in greens and hominy. Bring to a boil; reduce heat, and simmer 20 minutes or until greens are tender.

Note: For testing purposes only, we used Hormel Pork Roast Au Jus.

Beer-Kissed Cheese Grits

Bring 1 (12-oz.) bottle of mild beer (such as Budweiser) and 3 cups water to a boil in a medium saucepan over medium-high heat. Gradually whisk in 1 cup uncooked quick-cooking grits and 1¼ tsp. salt. Cover, reduce heat to low, and simmer, stirring occasionally, 10 minutes or until thickened. Add 1½ cups (6 oz.) shredded smoked Gouda, whisking until cheese melts.

Beer-Cheese Spread
freezeable • make ahead
PREP: 15 MIN., CHILL: 2 HR.

This easy spread is a tasty cousin of pimiento cheese. The recipe makes a lot, but it can be frozen up to a month. It fits perfectly into 4 (10-oz.) ramekins. Try it over French fries, hot dogs, chili, and the Ale Biscuits too.

1 (2-lb.) block sharp Cheddar cheese, shredded
1 small onion, minced
2 garlic cloves, minced
½ tsp. hot sauce
¼ tsp. ground red pepper
1 (12-oz.) bottle amber beer, at room temperature
Salt and pepper to taste
Garnish: thyme sprig

1. Beat together first 5 ingredients at low speed with a heavy-duty electric stand mixer until blended. Gradually add beer, beating until blended after each addition. Beat at medium-high speed 1 minute or until blended and creamy. Season with salt and pepper to taste. Cover and chill 2 hours. Garnish, if desired. Store in an airtight container in refrigerator up to 2 weeks. **Makes** 5 cups.

THERESE HALASKA
PORTAGE, WISCONSIN

Note: For testing purposes only, we used Abita Amber Beer. This spread can be frozen up to 1 month; thaw overnight in refrigerator.

Grilled Beer-Cheese Sandwich: Spread 1 tsp. softened butter evenly on 1 side of 2 bread slices. Place bread slices, buttered sides down, on wax paper. Spread ¼ cup Beer-Cheese Spread onto 1 side of 1 bread slice. Top with remaining bread slice, buttered side up. Cook sandwich in a nonstick skillet or griddle over medium heat 3 to 5 minutes on each side or until golden brown and cheese is melted.

Ale Biscuits
fast fixin's
PREP: 10 MIN., BAKE: 10 MIN.

⅓ cup butter, frozen
2½ cups all-purpose baking mix
⅔ cup lager beer

1. Grate ⅓ cup frozen butter through large holes of a cheese grater into 2½ cups baking mix, and toss to combine. Stir in ⅔ cup lager beer just until dry ingredients are moistened. (Dough will be thick.)

2. Spoon dough evenly into lightly greased miniature muffin pans, filling completely full.

3. Bake at 450° for 8 to 10 minutes or until biscuits are golden brown. **Makes** about 2 dozen.

SARAH JOSEPH
GRAND RAPIDS, MICHIGAN

Note: For testing purposes only, we used Shiner Bock Beer.

Porter Float
Pour creamy porter or stout beer over ice cream for an extraordinary adult float.

Top premium vanilla ice cream with a few tablespoonfuls of a creamy porter or stout (such as Samuel Smith Oatmeal Stout). Add a sprinkle of fresh raspberries and a fresh mint sprig for a quick and creative dessert.

Our Favorite Southern Brews

■ **Abita Brewing Company:** These handcrafted beers are still made in small batches in Abita Springs, Louisiana.

■ **Saint Arnold Brewing Company:** This is Texas's oldest craft brewer. Their Oktoberfest beer is only available for a short time and shouldn't be missed.

■ **Terrapin Beer Co.:** We fell in love with Wake-n-Bake Coffee Oatmeal Imperial Stout from this Athens, Georgia, brewer. A full-bodied beer, it hits the spot when the weather turns cool.

Share the Warmth

Celebrate friendship over hearty bowls of homemade goodness.

Homemade soup soothes both body and soul. But it's hard to make just a little if you're cooking for one or two people, and you're tired of eating it long before it's all gone. Here's the perfect solution. Get a group of friends to each make a large pot of their favorite recipe and gather at one house to sip and share.

Share any of these tasty recipes with some friends, and accompany them with hot corn muffins, whole grain breads, or assorted crackers. Before everyone leaves, fill freezer containers with leftovers, and label each soup. You'll go home with clean pots and a bounty of comfort food. Store tightly sealed containers in the freezer up to one month so you can savor a different soup each week. Repeat the swap as often as you want to replenish your supply.

Chicken-Cabbage Soup
freezeable • make ahead
PREP: 20 MIN.; COOK: 1 HR., 10 MIN.

1 large onion, chopped
2 celery ribs, chopped
1½ Tbsp. vegetable oil
½ cup white wine
1 (32-oz.) can tomato juice
1 (16-oz.) can tomato sauce
1 extra-large chicken bouillon cube
½ tsp. garlic powder
1 head cabbage (about 2 lb.), shredded
2 cups chopped cooked chicken
½ tsp. salt
½ tsp. pepper

1. Sauté onion and celery in hot oil in a large Dutch oven over medium-high heat 5 minutes. Stir in wine, next 4 ingredients, and 4 cups water; bring to a boil.
2. Stir in cabbage. Cover, reduce heat to low, and simmer 45 minutes. Add chicken, salt, and pepper. Simmer, covered, 15 minutes. **Makes** 15 cups.

JOYCE WARE LANE
BIRMINGHAM, ALABAMA

Corn-and-Crab Chowder
freezeable • make ahead
PREP: 20 MIN., COOK: 55 MIN.
It's worth the splurge to buy fresh crabmeat, but it's just as good with fresh shrimp. (Pictured on page 184)

6 bacon slices
2 celery ribs, diced
1 medium-size green bell pepper, diced
1 medium onion, diced
1 jalapeño pepper, seeded and diced
1 (32-oz.) container chicken broth
3 Tbsp. all-purpose flour
3 cups fresh corn kernels (6 ears)
1 lb. fresh lump crabmeat, drained and picked *
1 cup whipping cream
¼ cup chopped fresh cilantro
½ tsp. salt
¼ tsp. pepper
Oyster crackers
Garnish: chopped fresh cilantro

1. Cook bacon in a Dutch oven over medium heat 8 to 10 minutes or until crisp; remove bacon, and drain on paper towels, reserving 2 Tbsp. drippings in Dutch oven. Crumble bacon.
2. Sauté celery and next 3 ingredients in hot drippings 5 to 6 minutes or until tender.
3. Whisk together broth and flour until smooth. Add to celery mixture. Stir in corn. Bring to a boil; reduce heat, and simmer, stirring occasionally, 30 minutes. Gently stir in crabmeat and next 4 ingredients; cook 4 to 5 minutes or until thoroughly heated. Serve warm with crumbled bacon and oyster crackers. Garnish, if desired. **Makes** 10 cups.

*1 lb. peeled cooked shrimp or chopped cooked chicken may be substituted.

Store It Right

- Select heavy-duty freezer containers to pack and store soups.
- Fill container to recommended capacity to preserve freshness.
- Chill soups completely in refrigerator before freezing, but be sure to cool it first—learn how we do it in "From Our Kitchen" on page 238. You can also quickly chill it by placing frozen water bottles directly in the soup.
- If you don't plan to freeze the soup, you can store most of these recipes in airtight containers in the coldest part of your refrigerator up to three days. (Store Corn-and-Crab Chowder up to 24 hours.)

Beef Vegetable Soup

freezeable • make ahead
PREP: 15 MIN.; COOK: 1 HR., 15 MIN.

Canned tomatoes and frozen mixed vegetables rush the prep time on this recipe. An extra-large bouillon cube adds more flavor. If you don't have this size, you can use two regular cubes.

1½ lb. beef stew meat
1 Tbsp. olive oil
1 (32-oz.) bag frozen mixed vegetables (peas, carrots, green beans, and lima beans)
1 (15-oz.) can tomato sauce
1 (14.5-oz.) can diced Italian-style tomatoes
1 medium-size baking potato, peeled and diced
1 celery rib, chopped
1 medium onion, chopped
2 garlic cloves, minced
½ cup ketchup
1 extra-large chicken bouillon cube
½ tsp. pepper

1. Cook meat in hot oil over medium-high heat in a large Dutch oven 6 to 8 minutes or until browned.
2. Stir in frozen mixed vegetables, next 9 ingredients, and 1½ qt. water, stirring to loosen particles from bottom of Dutch oven. Bring mixture to a boil over medium-high heat; cover, reduce heat to low, and simmer, stirring occasionally, 55 to 60 minutes or until potatoes are tender. **Makes** 18 cups.

BETTY W. BROWN
BIRMINGHAM, ALABAMA

Note: For testing purposes only, we used Knorr Chicken Bouillon cube.

Fill Up the Lunchbox

School's in, but you're fresh out of lunch ideas. Try our kid-friendly recipes to banish the daily lunchbox blues. Add some unexpected variety to the usual fare, and everyone in the class will want to trade lunch with your child.

Back-to-School Fun

Serves 6

Festive Turkey Rollups

Crunchy-Munchy Mix

Individual packs of yogurt

S'more Cupcakes

Juice boxes

Festive Turkey Rollups

family favorite • make ahead
PREP: 10 MIN., CHILL: 8 HR.

Make a batch of these tasty little sandwiches the night before and place them into everyone's lunchbox—including your own. They're wrapped in plastic wrap, which makes them an easy take-along treat.

6 (8-inch) flour tortillas *
½ cup hot pepper jelly with red jalapeño peppers
½ cup red raspberry preserves
¾ cup Ranch vegetable dip
12 thinly sliced turkey breast slices, halved
1 bunch green leaf lettuce
1½ cups (6 oz.) shredded Cheddar cheese **

1. Microwave tortillas on HIGH 10 to 15 seconds, and set aside.
2. Stir together jelly and preserves.
3. Spread 2 Tbsp. Ranch dip on 1 side of each tortilla. Top each tortilla with 4 turkey slice halves, and spread with 2½ Tbsp. jelly mixture. Top

tortillas evenly with lettuce and cheese.
4. Roll up tortillas; wrap with plastic wrap. Chill up to 8 hours. **Makes** 6 servings.

MAUDE GRIFFITH
STOW, OHIO

* 6 pita rounds may be substituted.

* * Shredded Monterey Jack cheese with peppers may be substituted.

Crunchy-Munchy Mix

family favorite • make ahead
PREP: 5 MIN., BAKE: 30 MIN.

This makes a big batch so you'll have some left over for an after-school snack.

1 (16-oz.) jar dry-roasted peanuts
1 (10-oz.) package pretzel pieces *
1 (7-oz.) can potato sticks
1 (6-oz.) can fried onions
1 (6-oz.) package bite-size bagel chips **
⅓ cup butter, melted ***
1 (1.25-oz.) package taco seasoning

1. Combine first 5 ingredients in a large roasting pan. Drizzle with butter, gently stirring to coat. Stir in taco seasoning.
2. Bake at 250° for 30 minutes, stirring occasionally. Cool on paper towels. Store in an airtight container. **Makes** 12 cups.

KATHY HUNT
DALLAS, TEXAS

* 1 (7-oz.) can potato sticks may be substituted.

* * 1 (6-oz.) can fried onions may be substituted.

* * * Butter-flavored cooking spray may be substituted.

S'more Cupcakes
family favorite • fast fixin's
PREP: 10 MIN., BAKE: 18 MIN.

Kids love these cupcakes with graham crackers, marshmallows, and chocolate.

⅔ cup shortening
1½ cups sugar
3 large eggs
1½ cups all-purpose flour
1½ cups graham cracker crumbs
2 tsp. baking powder
1 tsp. salt
1¼ cups milk
1 tsp. vanilla extract
24 chocolate nuggets
4 cups miniature marshmallows
1 cup chopped pecans (optional)

1. Beat shortening at medium speed with an electric mixer until fluffy. Gradually add sugar, beating well. Add eggs, 1 at a time, beating until blended after each addition.
2. Combine flour and next 3 ingredients; add to egg mixture alternately with milk, beginning and ending with flour mixture. Beat until blended after each addition. Stir in vanilla.
3. Place paper baking cups in muffin pans, and spoon ¼ cup batter into each cup.
4. Bake at 350° for 18 minutes or until done. Quickly insert a chocolate nugget into center of each warm cupcake; top each with 4 to 5 marshmallows, gently pressing into melted chocolate. Sprinkle with pecans, if desired. **Makes** 2 dozen.
TERRYANN MOORE
OAKLYN, NEW JERSEY

Note: For testing purposes only, we used Hershey's Nuggets.

Try These Smothered Sandwiches

Bite into amazing melted layers with these heavenly hot browns, which are heavy on flavor, not on fat.

Grab a knife and fork, and dig in. There's no guilt behind these hot browns—they're lightened and full of flavor. Typically, this open-faced Kentucky classic is made with a heavy cheese sauce that would have your arteries begging for mercy, but we found a way to deliver the same richness without all the saturated fat. See how we did it, and taste a piece of heaven for yourself.

Lightened Hot Browns
fast fixin's
PREP: 15 MIN., BROIL: 6 MIN.

8 (1-oz.) rye, wheat, or white bread slices, toasted
¾ lb. sliced deli-roasted turkey breast
Parmesan Cheese Sauce (see box on opposite page)
¼ cup freshly shredded Parmesan cheese
4 cooked reduced-fat bacon slices, crumbled
3 plum tomatoes, sliced

1. Arrange desired bread slices on an aluminum foil-lined 15- x 10-inch jelly-roll pan. Top evenly with turkey and Parmesan Cheese Sauce, and sprinkle with Parmesan cheese.
2. Broil 6 inches from heat 4 to 6 minutes or until bubbly and lightly browned; remove from oven. Top with crumbled bacon and tomato slices; serve immediately. **Makes** 4 servings.

Club-Style Lightened Hot Browns With Caramelized Onions: Melt 2 Tbsp. butter in a medium skillet over medium heat. Add 1 large sweet onion, sliced, and ¼ tsp. salt. Cook, stirring often, 15 to 20 minutes or until onions are caramel colored. Place desired bread slices on jelly-roll pan, and layer with ¼ lb. each of sliced deli-roasted turkey, roast beef, and ham. Top with Parmesan Cheese Sauce and onions; sprinkle with Parmesan cheese. Broil as directed. Top with crumbled bacon and tomato slices; serve immediately.

Southwestern Lightened Hot Browns: Substitute 4 (2-inch-thick) square cornbread slices, halved and toasted, for bread. Place on jelly-roll pan, and top with turkey, Spicy Cheese Sauce (recipe at right), and 1 (4.5-oz) can chopped green chiles, drained. Substitute shredded Mexican four-cheese blend for Parmesan cheese, and sprinkle over sandwiches; broil as directed. Top with crumbled bacon and tomato slices; serve immediately.

Parmesan Cheese Sauce
fast fixin's

PREP: 5 MIN., COOK: 5 MIN.
This creamy sauce is also great over steamed veggies and multi-grain pasta.

1. Melt 1½ Tbsp. butter in a medium skillet over medium-high heat. Sprinkle 2 Tbsp. flour into melted butter, whisk-

ing constantly. Cook, whisking constantly, 30 seconds to 1 minute or until mixture is golden and lumpy.
2. Gradually whisk in 1 cup 1% low-fat milk, and bring to a boil. Cook, whisking constantly, 1 to 2 minutes, or until thickened.
3. Add ½ cup freshly shred-ded Parme-san cheese, ¼ tsp. each salt and pepper, and a pinch of paprika, whisking

until smooth. Remove from heat, and use immediately. **Makes** about 1¼ cups.

Spicy Cheese Sauce: Prepare Parmesan Cheese Sauce as direct-ed, and whisk in 1 tsp. hot sauce.

No-Fuss Breads

You'll love that we made baking bread simple with these offerings. Our recipes are easy by nature: One uses a cake mix, the other a store-bought loaf of French bread. You'll breeze through the preparation and get to the sampling in a hurry.

Easy Zucchini Bread
family favorite

PREP: 25 MIN., BAKE: 47 MIN., COOL: 25 MIN.
A spice cake mix, shredded zucchini, and a few basic ingredients are all you need to make two loaves of this ultra-tender bread. For best results, shred zucchini using the large holes on a box grater.

1 cup chopped pecans, divided
1 (18.25-oz.) package spice cake mix
1¼ cups milk
½ cup canola oil
3 large eggs
2 cups shredded zucchini (1 medium zucchini)

1. Place ⅔ cup pecans in a single layer in a shallow pan.
2. Bake at 350° for 6 to 7 minutes or until pecans are lightly toasted, stirring occasionally.
3. Beat cake mix and next 3 ingredients at low speed with an electric mixer 30 seconds. Increase speed to medium, and beat 1 minute, stopping to scrape bottom and down sides of bowl as needed. Stir in zucchini and ⅔ cup toasted pecans. Pour batter evenly into 2 (9- x 5-inch) lightly greased loaf pans. Sprinkle remaining ⅓ cup pecans evenly over batter.
4. Bake at 350° for 35 to 40 minutes or until a long wooden pick inserted in center comes out clean. Cool in pans on a wire rack 10 minutes. Remove from pans to wire rack, and let cool 15 min-utes before slicing. **Makes** 2 loaves.

Note: For testing purposes only, we used Duncan Hines Moist Deluxe Spice Cake Mix.

Cajun-Style French Bread
freezeable • make ahead

PREP: 20 MIN., BAKE: 20 MIN., STAND: 5 MIN.
Serve this bold and rich bread as an appe-tizer. It also pairs well with vinaigrette-dressed salad or your favorite grilled meat.

1 (14-oz.) French bread loaf
¼ cup butter, melted
1 medium onion, finely chopped
1 small jalapeño pepper, seeded and finely minced
1 garlic clove, minced
⅔ cup mayonnaise
½ cup (2 oz.) shredded Parmesan cheese
1 Tbsp. lemon juice
½ tsp. Worcestershire sauce
1½ tsp. Creole seasoning

1. Cut bread loaf in half lengthwise. Brush melted butter evenly onto cut sides of bread halves.
2. Stir together onion, jalapeño pepper, and next 5 ingredients, and spread mix-ture evenly over buttered sides of bread halves. Place bread halves, buttered sides up, on a baking sheet, and sprinkle evenly with 1½ tsp. Creole seasoning.
3. Bake at 350° for 18 to 20 minutes or until brown and bubbly. Let stand 5 minutes; cut crosswise into 1-inch-thick slices, and serve immediately. **Makes** 8 servings.
WENDI ALLEN
BRANDON, MISSISSIPPI

Note: To make ahead, wrap prepared unbaked bread halves in aluminum foil, place in a large zip-top plastic freezer bag, and freeze up to 1 month. To bake frozen, remove bread halves from freez-er bag, and place foil-wrapped bread on a baking sheet. Bake at 350° for 10 min-utes or until thawed. Remove foil, return to baking sheet, buttered sides up, and bake 8 to 10 minutes or until brown and bubbly. Let stand 5 minutes, and cut bread halves as directed.

Tasty Spin on Lasagna

Make your next meal a fun family affair with this twist on a classic.

Tex-Mex Family Supper

Serves 8

Tex-Mex Lasagna

Fiesta Salad

Ice-cream sandwiches

Do a little bonding in the kitchen by cooking with teenagers. We think they'll enjoy making this recipe for Tex-Mex Lasagna. Simply layer the mildly spiced ground beef mixture, corn tortillas, and cheese in four two-serving dishes or one large baking dish. Add quick-to-fix Fiesta Salad and ice-cream sandwiches for a complete meal. With these delicious offerings your young chef will dish up a wonderful supper and pick up valuable tips and secrets from mom and dad.

Test Kitchen *Notebook*

Tips for Teen Chefs

1. Read your recipe first.

2. Wash and dry your hands, and make sure your work area and utensils are clean before you start cooking.

3. Make sure your cooking coach has shown you how to use a knife properly. When working with sharp knives, make sure they are visible and not hidden by a dish towel or soapy water.

4. Practice food safety by keeping hot foods hot and cold foods cold.

Charla Draper
ASSOCIATE FOODS EDITOR

Tex-Mex Lasagna
family favorite

PREP: 20 MIN., COOK: 22 MIN., BAKE: 35 MIN., STAND: 10 MIN.

1 lb. lean ground beef
1 cup frozen diced onion, red and green bell pepper, and celery
3 garlic cloves, minced
1 Tbsp. chili powder
1 tsp. salt-free chipotle seasoning blend
1 (24-oz.) jar mild salsa
1 (15-oz.) can dark red kidney beans, drained
1 (10-oz.) can enchilada sauce
1 (10-oz.) package frozen whole kernel corn, thawed
16 (6-inch) fajita-size corn tortillas
4 cups (16 oz.) shredded Mexican four-cheese blend
Toppings: sour cream, chopped tomatoes

1. Cook first 5 ingredients in a large nonstick skillet over medium-high heat, stirring often, 10 to 12 minutes or until vegetables are tender and beef crumbles and is no longer pink.

2. Stir in salsa and next 3 ingredients. Cook 5 to 10 minutes or until thoroughly heated.

3. Layer 1 cup beef mixture, 2 tortillas (overlapping edges), and ½ cup cheese in a lightly greased 7- x 5- x 1½-inch baking dish. Repeat layers once. Repeat procedure with 3 additional 7- x 5- x 1½-inch baking dishes. Cover dishes with nonstick aluminum foil.

4. Bake, covered, at 350° for 30 minutes; uncover and bake 5 more minutes or until bubbly. Let stand 10 minutes before serving. Serve with desired toppings. **Makes** 8 servings.

ERICA SHARP
MEBANE, NORTH CAROLINA

Note: To use a lightly greased 13- x 9-inch baking dish, prepare recipe as directed through Step 2. Omit 4 corn tortillas. Layer one-third beef mixture, 6 tortillas (overlapping edges), and 2 cups cheese in baking dish. Repeat layers with one-third beef mixture, remaining 6 tortillas, remaining beef mixture, and ending with remaining 2 cups cheese. Bake, covered, at 350° for 40 minutes; uncover and bake 10 more minutes or until bubbly. Let stand 10 minutes before serving.

Fiesta Salad

family favorite • fast fixin's

PREP: 15 MIN.

Prepare Salsa Balsamic Dressing for this salad by stirring together ½ cup balsamic vinaigrette, ¼ cup medium salsa, 2 Tbsp. fresh lemon juice, and 2 Tbsp. chopped fresh cilantro.

10 cups torn romaine lettuce leaves
   (1 large head)
1½ cups chopped tomato or cherry
   tomato halves
2 avocados, diced
2 green onions, chopped
1 cup tortilla chips, crushed

1. Toss together first 4 ingredients in a large bowl. Top with crushed tortilla chips. **Makes** 8 servings.

Great Stuffed Spuds

These updated tubers are family-friendly additions to any menu.

Apple-Pecan-Stuffed Sweet Potatoes

family favorite

PREP: 20 MIN.; BAKE: 1 HR., 35 MIN.; COOK: 12 MIN.

4 medium-size sweet potatoes (3½ lb.)
¾ cup coarsely chopped pecans
¼ cup butter
1 large Rome Beauty apple, chopped
¼ cup golden raisins
½ cup firmly packed brown sugar
½ tsp. ground cinnamon
¼ tsp. ground nutmeg

1. Place potatoes on an aluminum foil-lined baking sheet. Bake at 425° for 1 hour and 15 minutes or until tender.
2. Heat nuts in a nonstick skillet over medium-low heat, stirring often, 5 to 7 minutes or until toasted. Remove from skillet.
3. Melt butter in skillet over medium-high heat. Add apple and raisins; sauté

2 to 3 minutes or until apple is tender. Stir in brown sugar, cinnamon, and nutmeg. Remove from heat.
4. Cut potatoes in half lengthwise; scoop pulp into a large bowl, leaving shells intact. Add apple mixture to pulp in bowl; stir until blended. Spoon into shells. Place on baking sheet.
5. Bake at 350° for 15 to 20 minutes or until thoroughly heated. Top with nuts. **Makes** 8 servings.

Chicken-Club-Stuffed Potatoes

PREP: 20 MIN.; BAKE: 1 HR., 25 MIN.; COOK: 10 MIN.

4 (8-oz.) baking potatoes (2 lb.)
1½ tsp. olive oil
2 tsp. salt
8 bacon slices
1 cup diced cooked chicken
1 cup (4 oz.) shredded Cheddar cheese,
   divided
1 cup (4 oz.) shredded Swiss cheese,
   divided
½ cup mayonnaise
⅓ cup sun-dried tomatoes in oil,
   drained and chopped
2 Tbsp. minced onion
1 Tbsp. Dijon mustard

1. Rub potatoes evenly with oil; sprinkle with salt. Bake at 425° directly on top oven rack for 55 minutes or until potatoes are tender and skin is crisp.
2. Cook bacon in a skillet over medium-high heat 7 to 10 minutes or until crisp; drain on paper towels. Crumble bacon.
3. Cut potatoes in half lengthwise; scoop pulp into a large bowl, leaving shells intact. Stir together pulp, bacon, chicken, ¾ cup each Cheddar and Swiss cheese, and next 4 ingredients.
4. Spoon mixture into shells; sprinkle with remaining cheeses. Place on an aluminum foil-lined baking sheet.
5. Bake at 400° for 25 to 30 minutes or until thoroughly heated. **Makes** 8 servings.

Our Easiest Pecan Pie

This Southern classic is a basic necessity this time of year. We found an eight-ingredient gem that stirs together in a jiffy. It even uses a frozen pie shell for added ease. Top a slice with a scoop of vanilla ice cream, and you'll see why it's our no-fuss favorite.

Mom's Pecan Pie

family favorite

PREP: 10 MIN.; BAKE: 1 HR., 5 MIN.

For a richer flavor, try using dark corn syrup. Both variations received high marks in our Test Kitchens.

1½ cups pecan pieces
3 large eggs
1 cup sugar
¾ cup light or dark corn syrup
2 Tbsp. melted butter
2 tsp. vanilla extract
½ tsp. salt
1 (9-inch) deep-dish frozen unbaked
   pie shell

1. Spread pecans in a single layer on a baking sheet.
2. Bake at 350° for 8 to 10 minutes or until toasted.
3. Stir together eggs and next 5 ingredients; stir in pecans. Pour filling into pie shell.
4. Bake at 350° for 55 minutes or until set, shielding pie with aluminum foil after 20 minutes to prevent excessive browning. Serve warm or cold. **Makes** 8 servings.

LINDA SCHEND
KENOSHA, WISCONSIN

Note: For testing purposes only, we used Mrs. Smith's Deep Dish Frozen Pie Shell.

Great-Tasting Greens

Fall is the peak season to select fresh greens. These powerhouse vegetables are low in calories and packed with vitamins.

Sweet-and-Tangy Braised Greens With Smoked Turkey

PREP: 15 MIN., COOK: 1 HR.
(Pictured on page 185)

1 (16-oz.) package fresh collard greens, stems removed
1 (0.75-lb.) smoked turkey leg
5 garlic cloves, chopped
2 Tbsp. oil
½ cup cider vinegar
⅓ cup low-sodium chicken broth
½ tsp. pepper
2 Tbsp. maple syrup

1. Thoroughly wash greens. Pat dry with paper towels.
2. Remove skin and meat from turkey leg, discarding skin and bone. Coarsely chop meat.
3. Sauté chopped turkey and garlic in hot oil in a large skillet over medium-high heat 2 to 3 minutes. Add vinegar, chicken broth, and pepper; bring to a boil. Add greens, reduce heat to low, and simmer, stirring occasionally, 25 minutes. Stir in 2 Tbsp. maple syrup; simmer, stirring occasionally, 20 to 30 minutes or until greens are tender. Serve immediately. **Makes** 4 servings.

Note: For a milder flavor, reduce cider vinegar to ⅓ cup and maple syrup to 1 Tbsp.; increase chicken broth to ½ cup. Proceed with recipe as directed.

Sweet-and-Tangy Braised Kale With Smoked Turkey: Substitute 1 (16-oz.) package fresh kale for collard greens. Prepare recipe as directed.

Tips for Cleaning Greens

- Submerge in cold water, and rinse several times to remove dirt and sand.
- Place greens in colander; rinse thoroughly until clean.

Vegetable & Fruit Wash: Commercial wash treatments used to clean produce are available at your local grocery store. You could also mix up a batch of our homemade, budget-friendly wash for an effective method of removing residual pesticides. Combine 2⅔ cups distilled water with 1⅓ cups 3% hydrogen peroxide in a 1-liter spray bottle; you can use it for up to seven days. Spray the greens well before rinsing.

---

quick & easy
Start With Rotisserie Chicken

Rotisserie chicken rates as one of our favorite shortcuts, and it's also the focus of the cookbook *Rotisserie Chickens to the Rescue* (Hyperion Books, 2003). Written by Atlanta native Carla Fitzgerald Williams, this book features loads of family-friendly meals, including Snappy Smothered Chicken. We devoured every morsel of this recipe during testing.

Snappy Smothered Chicken
family favorite

PREP: 10 MIN., COOK: 30 MIN.
We added a little white wine to this recipe to dress it up a bit. If you prefer not to use wine, increase the milk to 1⅓ cups.

1 (8-oz.) package wide egg noodles
1 tsp. paprika
1 tsp. dried thyme leaves, crumbled
½ tsp. salt
¼ tsp. pepper
3 Tbsp. butter
1 large onion, chopped
1 (16-oz.) package mushrooms, sliced
2 tsp. jarred minced garlic
1 (10¾-oz.) can cream of mushroom soup
1 cup milk
⅓ cup dry white wine (optional)
1 rotisserie chicken, cut into serving pieces
2 Tbsp. chopped fresh parsley

1. Prepare noodles according to package directions. Keep warm.
2. Meanwhile, stir together paprika, dried thyme, salt, and pepper in a small bowl.
3. Melt butter in a large skillet over medium-high heat; add onion and mushrooms, and sauté 8 to 10 minutes or until onion is tender. Stir in garlic and paprika mixture; sauté 2 minutes. Add soup, milk, and, if desired, wine,

and bring to a boil, stirring frequently. Add chicken pieces; spoon sauce over top of chicken. Reduce heat to low, and cook, covered, 10 to 15 minutes or until chicken is thoroughly heated. Stir in 1 Tbsp. parsley. Serve over hot cooked noodles. Sprinkle with remaining parsley. **Makes** 4 servings.

Fast Pork Chops

Don't overlook this affordable cut of meat for a satisfying supper.

An excellent meal is just minutes away. Whether broiled, grilled, or sautéed, these recipes have cook times of 10 minutes or less.

Pork Chops With Herb-Mustard Butter
PREP: 10 MIN., BROIL: 10 MIN.

4 (½-inch-thick) bone-in pork loin chops
1 tsp. salt
½ tsp. pepper
¼ cup butter, softened
¼ cup chopped fresh parsley
2 Tbsp. honey mustard
1 tsp. chopped fresh sage

1. Sprinkle chops evenly with salt and pepper, and place on a wire rack in an aluminum foil-lined broiler pan.
2. Stir together butter and next 3 ingredients in a small bowl until blended. Top each chop with 1 rounded Tbsp. butter mixture.
3. Broil 5 inches from heat 8 to 10 minutes or until a meat thermometer inserted into thickest portion registers 155°. **Makes** 4 servings.

Lemon-Thyme-Crusted Pork Chops
PREP: 10 MIN., COOK: 8 MIN.

4 (6-oz.) boneless center-cut pork chops
1 tsp. salt
½ tsp. pepper
½ cup fine, dry breadcrumbs
¼ cup freshly grated Parmesan cheese
1 Tbsp. grated lemon rind
1 tsp. chopped fresh thyme
¼ cup vegetable oil

1. Sprinkle pork chops evenly with salt and pepper.
2. Stir together ½ cup breadcrumbs and next 3 ingredients in a large shallow baking dish.
3. Dredge pork chops in breadcrumb mixture.
4. Cook chops in hot oil in a large skillet over medium heat 3 to 4 minutes on each side or until done. **Makes** 4 servings.

Asian Pork Chops
family favorite
PREP: 10 MIN., CHILL: 4 HR., COOK: 8 MIN.

½ cup hoisin sauce
3 Tbsp. cider vinegar
1 Tbsp. Asian sweet chili sauce
¼ tsp. garlic powder
4 (½-inch-thick) boneless pork chops
1 tsp. salt
½ tsp. pepper

1. Stir together first 4 ingredients in a large shallow dish or zip-top plastic freezer bag; remove and reserve ¼ cup marinade. Add chops to remaining marinade in dish. Cover or seal, and chill 2 to 4 hours. Remove chops from marinade, discarding marinade. Sprinkle chops evenly with salt and pepper.
2. Heat a grill pan over medium-high heat; cook chops 3 to 4 minutes on each side or until done. Brush with reserved ¼ cup marinade. **Makes** 4 servings.

PAMELA BROWN
BIRMINGHAM, ALABAMA

Note: For testing purposes only, we used Maggi Taste of Asia Sweet Chili Sauce.

Halloween Party Starters

Ghoulish Gathering

Serves 6

Green Dip With Spooky Chips

Monster Eyes

Purchased sub sandwiches or chicken wings

Candy

Lemonade

Pull off a casual get-together before trick-or-treating or after a fall carnival. Our planning tip (apply this to your next non-themed gathering as well): Offer a dip (served with chips, crackers, and veggies) and a festive nibble such as Monster Eyes. Then, add a hearty option by picking up sub sandwiches or hot wings. Dessert? Candy, of course.

Green Dip With Spooky Chips

family favorite

PREP: 10 MIN., COOK: 5 MIN., COOL: 15 MIN.,
CHILL: 1 HR.

Keep this recipe on hand for spring and summer; just change its name to Creamy Pesto Dip, and serve it with chips or fried chicken tenders.

3 Tbsp. pine nuts
3 (1-oz.) packages fresh basil (about
   3 cups)
1 (16-oz.) container sour cream
¾ cup grated Parmesan cheese
1 garlic clove, chopped
2 Tbsp. fresh lemon juice
1 tsp. sugar
¼ tsp. salt
Garnish: shredded fresh basil
Spooky Chips

1. Heat pine nuts in a small nonstick skillet over medium-low heat, stirring often, 3 to 5 minutes or until toasted. Cool 15 minutes.
2. Process pine nuts, basil, and next 6 ingredients in a food processor until smooth, stopping to scrape down sides. Transfer to a serving bowl. Cover and chill 1 hour. Store in refrigerator up to 2 days. Garnish, if desired. Serve with Spooky Chips. **Makes** about 2½ cups.

Spooky Chips:

PREP: 20 MIN., BAKE: 10 MIN. PER BATCH,
COOL: 15 MIN.

Short on time? Skip the bone-shaped cookie cutter, and cut wheat wraps into about 2-inch-wide strips using kitchen shears.

¼ cup butter, melted
½ tsp. coarsely ground
   pepper
½ tsp. kosher salt
5 (9-inch) wheat wraps

1. Stir together first 3 ingredients.
2. Cut wheat wraps with a 3-inch bone-shaped cutter, and place on baking sheets. Brush evenly with butter mixture.
3. Bake at 350° for 8 to 10 minutes or until crispy. Remove to wire racks, and cool 15 minutes or until completely cool. **Makes** 45 chips.

Note: For testing purposes only, we used Toufayan Bakeries Wheat Wraps.

Updated Pickup Food

A switch from traditional Cheddar cheese to Muenster gives a new look, er, taste to sausage balls.

Monster Eyes

family favorite

PREP: 20 MIN., BAKE: 18 MIN. PER BATCH

1. Combine 3 cups all-purpose baking mix; 1 lb. ground hot pork sausage; and 1 (8-oz.) block Muenster cheese, shredded, in a large bowl until blended. Shape sausage mixture into 1¼-inch balls, and place on lightly greased baking sheets. Press 1 pimiento-stuffed Spanish olive (you'll need 1 [7-oz.] jar) deeply into center of each ball. Bake at 400° for 15 to 18 minutes or until lightly browned. **Makes** about 4½ dozen.

Note: For testing purposes only, we used Bisquick for all-purpose baking mix and Jimmy Dean Hot Ground Pork Sausage.

Healthy Living.

Let the season cast its spell on you. Take advantage of beautiful days and crisp evenings with these delicious recipes.

Slim Down With Dairy

Make these calorie-burning recipes part of your daily regimen.

We all know that calcium-rich milk and other dairy foods are good for strong bones and prevention of osteoporosis. Reduced- or low-fat dairy is also good for your waistline. At least three servings a day can help you burn more calories and fat than just exercising alone. Start with these tasty and good-for-you dishes. All contain low-fat products that promise great flavor without all the calories.

Easy Greek Dip

make ahead

PREP: 10 MIN., STAND: 15 MIN., CHILL: 1 HR.

½ (32-oz.) container plain low-fat yogurt
1 (12-oz.) jar roasted red bell peppers, drained and chopped
¼ cup crumbled feta cheese
2 Tbsp. chopped fresh dill
1 tsp. Greek seasoning
1 small garlic clove, pressed
Pita chips

1. Line a fine wire-mesh strainer with a coffee filter. Place strainer over a bowl. Spoon yogurt into strainer. Let stand 15 minutes. Spoon yogurt into a medium bowl, and discard strained liquid.
2. Pat bell peppers dry with paper towels. Stir peppers, feta cheese, chopped fresh dill, Greek seasoning, and garlic into yogurt. Cover and chill at least 1 hour. Store in an airtight container in refrigerator up to 3 days. Serve with pita chips. **Makes** 2½ cups.

MELODY LEE
DOTHAN, ALABAMA

Per ¼-cup serving (not including chips): Calories 44; Fat 1.5g (sat 1g, mono 0.4g, poly 0g); Protein 2.9g; Carb 4.6g; Fiber 0g; Chol 6mg; Iron 0.1mg; Sodium 267mg; Calc 102mg

Dairy Does a Body Good

It's no secret that diet and exercise are the key factors in maintaining a healthy weight, but eating low-fat dairy can help you reach your goal more effectively.
■ Include low-fat foods such as part-skim mozzarella, low-fat ricotta or cottage cheese, and ⅓-less fat cream cheese in your diet.
■ Top whole grain crackers with reduced-fat spreadable cheese for a snack.
■ Use plain yogurt, light sour cream, and 2% cheese as toppings for chili and baked potatoes.
■ Whip up a quick smoothie or shake with low-fat ice cream or frozen yogurt.
■ Make vegetable dips, sandwich spreads, and picnic salads with light sour cream or low-fat yogurt.

Spiced Apple-Pecan Oatmeal
PREP: 10 MIN., COOK: 35 MIN., STAND: 10 MIN.

2 Tbsp. chopped pecans
3 cups apple juice
3 cups fat-free milk
2 cups uncooked regular oats (not quick-cooking)
½ cup coarsely chopped dried apples
½ tsp. salt
2 Tbsp. cinnamon sugar
¼ tsp. vanilla extract

1. Cook pecans in a Dutch oven over medium-high heat, stirring constantly, 5 to 6 minutes or until toasted. Remove pecans, and wipe Dutch oven clean.
2. Bring juice, milk, and next 3 ingredients to a boil in Dutch oven over high heat; reduce heat to medium-low, and simmer, stirring occasionally, 20 minutes or until thickened. Remove from heat. Cover and let stand 10 minutes. Stir in cinnamon sugar, vanilla, and toasted pecans. Serve immediately. **Makes** 6 cups.

JOANNA L. SMITH
MAYLENE, ALABAMA

Per 1-cup serving: Calories 275; Fat 3.6g (sat 0.4g, mono 1.5g, poly 1.1g); Protein 9.2g; Carb 51.5g; Fiber 3.8g; Chol 2mg; Iron 1.3mg; Sodium 364mg; Calc 141mg

Healthy Benefits

■ Research suggests that adequate calcium from dairy can reduce the risk of colorectal cancer and hypertension.
■ Probiotics in yogurt can help suppress pathogenic bacteria in the gastrointestinal tract, improve lactose tolerance, and strengthen your immune system.

Goodness From the Grill

Share a hearty (but not heavy) meal with family anytime.

Steak-and-Potatoes Menu
Serves 6

Spice-Rubbed Flank Steak
Grilled Sweet Potatoes With Creamy Basil Vinaigrette
Green Beans With Bacon
Whole Grain Marshmallow Crispy Bars

Cooler weather invites you to get out and grill. Entice everyone to the table with lean Spice-Rubbed Flank Steak and Green Beans With Bacon. Add a side of power-packed Grilled Sweet Potatoes With Creamy Basil Vinaigrette.

You can even prepare some of these great-tasting recipes in advance, which makes this menu practical enough to serve at any weeknight or weekend gathering. Don't forget dessert: Whole Grain Marshmallow Crispy Bars are sweetly nutritious.

Spice-Rubbed Flank Steak
family favorite
PREP: 10 MIN., STAND: 25 MIN., GRILL: 16 MIN.

3 Tbsp. brown sugar
2 tsp. ground cumin
2 tsp. ground oregano
2 tsp. garlic powder
½ tsp. salt
¼ tsp. ground allspice
1½ Tbsp. olive oil
1 (2-lb.) flank steak, trimmed
Vegetable cooking spray

1. Combine first 6 ingredients in a shallow bowl. Stir in olive oil until combined. Gently rub olive oil mixture evenly on steak. Let stand 20 minutes.
2. Coat cold cooking grate with cooking spray, and place on grill over medium-high heat (350° to 400°). Place steak on cooking grate, and grill, covered with grill lid, 8 minutes on

each side or to desired degree of doneness. Let stand 5 minutes; cut steak diagonally across the grain into thin slices. **Makes** 6 servings.

Per serving: Calories 245; Fat 10.4g (sat 3.9g, mono 4.4g, poly 0.6g); Protein 30.4g; Carb 5.9g; Fiber 0.7g; Chol 60mg; Iron 2.6mg; Sodium 258mg; Calc 36mg

Grilled Sweet Potatoes With Creamy Basil Vinaigrette

family favorite

PREP: 10 MIN., COOK: 15 MIN., STAND: 10 MIN., GRILL: 14 MIN.

3 lb. sweet potatoes (about 4 to 5)
Vegetable cooking spray
Creamy Basil Vinaigrette

1. Bring potatoes and water to cover to a boil in a Dutch oven over high heat; reduce heat to medium-high, and cook 12 to 15 minutes or just until slightly tender. Drain. Plunge potatoes into ice water to stop the cooking process. Drain well. Let stand 10 minutes. Peel and cut into wedges.
2. Coat cold cooking grate with cooking spray, and place on grill over medium-high heat (350° to 400°). Place potatoes on cooking grate, and grill, covered with grill lid, 6 to 7 minutes on each side or until grill marks appear. Drizzle potato wedges with Creamy Basil Vinaigrette, and serve immediately. **Makes** 6 servings.

Per serving (including about 2½ Tbsp. vinaigrette): Calories 201; Fat 1g (sat 0.2g, mono 0g, poly 0.2g); Protein 4.8g; Carb 44.6g; Fiber 6g; Chol 0mg; Iron 1.3mg; Sodium 352mg; Calc 111mg

Healthy Benefits

■ Grilling is a tasty and heart-healthy cooking method because you don't add fat to boost flavor.
■ Sweet potatoes have anti-inflammatory effects and can help reduce the severity of osteoarthritis and asthma.

Creamy Basil Vinaigrette:

fast fixin's

PREP: 10 MIN.

½ cup plain fat-free yogurt
2 Tbsp. chopped fresh basil
2 Tbsp. balsamic vinaigrette
2 Tbsp. honey
¼ cup red wine vinegar
½ tsp. salt
¼ tsp. pepper

1. Whisk together all ingredients. Serve immediately, or cover and chill up to 8 hours. If chilling, let stand at room temperature 30 minutes before serving. **Makes** about 1 cup.

Note: For testing purposes only, we used Newman's Own Balsamic Vinaigrette.

Per serving (about 2½ Tbsp.): Calories 42; Fat 0.7g (sat 0.1g, mono 0g, poly 0g); Protein 1.3g; Carb 7.9g; Fiber 0.1g; Chol 0mg; Iron 0.1mg; Sodium 288mg; Calc 44mg

Green Beans With Bacon

family favorite

PREP: 10 MIN., COOK: 21 MIN.

3 reduced-fat bacon slices
1 cup chopped sweet onion
2 (12-oz.) packages frozen green beans, thawed
1 cup low-sodium fat-free chicken broth
2 Tbsp. Dijon mustard
Salt and pepper to taste

1. Cook bacon in a large nonstick skillet over medium-high heat 6 to 8 minutes or until crisp; remove bacon, and drain on paper towels, reserving 2 tsp. drippings in skillet. Crumble bacon.
2. Sauté onion in hot drippings in skillet over medium-high heat 2 to 3 minutes or until golden. Add green beans, broth, and mustard, tossing to coat. Reduce heat to medium; cover and cook 5 minutes. Uncover and cook, stirring occasionally, 3 to 5 more minutes or until liquid thickens and is reduced by half. Add salt and pepper to taste. Top with crumbled bacon. Serve immediately. **Makes** 6 servings.

Per serving (not including salt and pepper to taste): Calories 62; Fat 1g (sat 0.3g, mono 0g, poly 0.1g); Protein 3.7g; Carb 11.3g; Fiber 3.6g; Chol 3mg; Iron 1.1mg; Sodium 217mg; Calc 53mg

Whole Grain Marshmallow Crispy Bars

family favorite

PREP: 15 MIN., COOK: 5 MIN., STAND: 15 MIN.

3 Tbsp. butter
1 (10.5-oz.) bag miniature marshmallows
1 (15-oz.) box multi-grain cluster cereal
1¼ cups dried cranberries, divided
Vegetable cooking spray

1. Melt butter in a large saucepan over low heat. Add marshmallows, and cook, stirring constantly, 4 to 5 minutes or until melted and smooth. Remove from heat.
2. Stir in cereal and 1 cup cranberries until well coated.
3. Press mixture into a 13- x 9-inch baking dish coated with cooking spray. Chop remaining ¼ cup cranberries, and sprinkle on top. Let stand 10 to 15 minutes or until firm. Cut into 24 bars. **Makes** 24 bars.

Note: For testing purposes only, we used Kashi GOLEAN Crunch! cereal.

Per bar: Calories 132; Fat 1.9g (sat 0.9g, mono 0.4g, poly 0.1g); Protein 2.6g; Carb 27.6g; Fiber 1.7g; Chol 4mg; Iron 0.6mg; Sodium 22mg; Calc 8mg

Cinnamon-Pecan Crispy Bars: Place ⅓ cup pecan halves, chopped, in a single layer on a shallow pan. Bake at 350° for 8 to 9 minutes or until toasted, stirring once after 5 minutes. Prepare Whole Grain Marshmallow Crispy Bars as directed through Step 2. Press mixture as directed into baking dish coated with cooking spray. Sprinkle with toasted pecans and 1 tsp. ground cinnamon. Proceed with recipe as directed.

Per bar: Calories 142; Fat 2.9g (sat 1g, mono 0.9g, poly 0.4g); Protein 2.7g; Carb 27.9g; Fiber 1.9g; Chol 4mg; Iron 0.7mg; Sodium 22mg; Calc 10mg

from our kitchen

Fresh Take on Salsa

Orange and avocado pair wonderfully together with their pleasing contrast of textures. Serve this marvelous relish with grilled, baked, or sautéed fish.

Orange-Avocado Salsa

PREP: 15 MIN., STAND: 30 MIN.
Soaking the onion in ice water takes away some of the sting.

¼ cup thinly sliced red onion
2 cups ice water
3 navel oranges
2 avocados, chopped
2 Tbsp. lime juice
¼ tsp. salt

1. Combine onion and water in a bowl; let stand 30 minutes. Drain well.
2. Peel and section oranges; cut orange sections in half crosswise. Place in a medium bowl. Add onion and avocado; sprinkle with lime juice and salt, tossing gently to combine. **Makes** about 3½ cups.

Storing Soup

Large batches of soup, such as those on pages 226-227, can take quite a while to cool down, so don't put them in the fridge while still hot. Hot foods must be cooled to at least 45° within two hours to be safe. To speed things up, put the pot in a sink full of ice water for about 30 minutes, stirring often to help release some of the heat. Ladle the soup into small containers, and refrigerate, uncovered, for 30 to 45 minutes. Cover, label, and chill for up to three days or freeze up to one month.

All About Avocados

Buttery avocados are available year-round, thanks to complementary growing seasons in California, Chile, and Mexico. Though you may have enjoyed them mainly in Southwestern cuisine, avocados work well in a variety of dishes. They're a staple in sushi, taste wonderful in salads, and tame fiery curries. Mash avocado slices on a piece of toast, and sprinkle with salt and pepper for a healthful snack or light breakfast.

Avocados do have a high fat content, but it's monounsaturated, which is excellent for heart health. And they're packed with fiber and vitamin C.

- To pick a ripe avocado, don't squeeze the sides. Instead, gently grasp the top and bottom; the stem end should yield to gentle pressure.

- Use the tip of a spoon to lift out the seed. Or gently squeeze the sides of the avocado, and lift the seed out with your fingers.

- Coax an avocado out of its shell by gently sliding a spatula or a large spoon between the flesh and the skin.

home for the holidays

Dinner Is Served

Timing is everything: Follow our detailed timeline to host a memorable party.

Celebrate With Friends

Serves 6 to 8

Pink Lemonade Cocktail

Marinated Mozzarella (page 246)

Mushroom, Apple, and Goat Cheese Salad

Mustard-and-Wine Pork Tenderloin

Browned Butter Mashed Potatoes

Green Bean-and-Red Bell Pepper Toss

Brandy-Vanilla Cheesecake Dip with fruit and cookies (page 258)

You have to try this menu. It's one sit-down dinner that's dressy enough to impress yet comfortable to enjoy. Pull it off by following our timeline and make-ahead tips, such as freezing pork tenderloin in marinade up to one month before the party and making Browned Butter Mashed Potatoes two days ahead. Budget watchers, we give you less expensive ingredient and decoration options. Dress the table with grocery store flowers, votive candles, and big glass bowls for huge impact without the fuss. Ask a guest or two to come early to light candles, make the Pink Lemonade Cocktail, and toss the salad. You'll be relaxed and ready for fun.

Pink Lemonade Cocktail
fast fixin's
PREP: 5 MIN.

1 (12-oz.) can frozen pink lemonade concentrate, thawed
3 (12-oz.) bottles beer (not dark), chilled
¾ cup vodka, chilled
Ice
Garnishes: fresh cranberries, citrus slices

1. Stir together first 3 ingredients. Serve over ice. Garnish, if desired. **Makes** 6 to 8 servings.
CAMI PERRY
BIRMINGHAM, ALABAMA

Mushroom, Apple, and Goat Cheese Salad
PREP: 20 MIN., BAKE: 10 MIN., COOK: 8 MIN., COOL: 15 MIN.
If you receive candied or spiced nuts as a holiday gift, try them on this salad for a special touch. To splurge, use a variety of mushrooms such as shiitake, portobello, oyster, or enoki. Often grocers carry a gourmet mushroom mix. Standard white mushrooms will yield tasty results too.

½ cup walnut halves
1 Tbsp. butter
1 lb. assorted mushrooms, trimmed and coarsely chopped
Honey-Balsamic Vinaigrette, divided
1 (4-oz.) package arugula, thoroughly washed
1 large Cameo apple, thinly sliced
3 oz. goat cheese, crumbled

1. Place walnuts in a single layer on a baking sheet.
2. Bake at 350° for 8 to 10 minutes or until toasted.
3. Melt butter in a large skillet over medium-high heat; add mushrooms, and sauté 6 minutes or until tender. Stir in 2 Tbsp. Honey-Balsamic Vinaigrette. Remove from heat, and let cool 15 minutes.
4. Toss together arugula, apple, mushrooms, and desired amount of Honey-Balsamic Vinaigrette. Transfer to a serving dish, and sprinkle with toasted walnuts and goat cheese. **Makes** 6 to 8 servings.

Honey-Balsamic Vinaigrette:
PREP: 10 MIN.
Make this up to two days ahead, and refrigerate in an airtight container. Let it to come to room temperature, and whisk before serving.

½ cup olive oil
⅓ cup balsamic vinegar
1 Tbsp. chopped fresh parsley
1 Tbsp. chopped fresh thyme
2 Tbsp. honey
Salt and pepper to taste

1. Whisk together first 5 ingredients until blended. Whisk in salt and pepper to taste. **Makes** about 1 cup.
SHELLEY JOHNSON
GILBERT, ARIZONA

Mustard-and-Wine Pork Tenderloin
freezeable • make ahead
PREP: 15 MIN., CHILL: 24 HR., BROIL: 30 MIN., STAND: 10 MIN.
Oven broilers will vary depending on your model so you may not need to turn the tenderloin as it broils to produce even browning. Coating the pork with flour adds rich flavor and visual appeal.

2¼ lb. pork tenderloin
1¼ cups dry white wine
1 cup chicken broth
2 Tbsp. coarse-grained mustard
1 Tbsp. chopped fresh thyme
1 tsp. minced garlic
1 tsp. pepper, divided
1½ tsp. kosher salt
½ cup all-purpose flour
Vegetable cooking spray

1. Remove silver skin from tenderloin, leaving a thin layer of fat covering the tenderloin.

2. Combine wine and next 4 ingredients in a zip-top plastic freezer bag; add pork and ½ tsp. pepper. Seal freezer bag and chill 24 hours, turning occasionally.

3. Remove pork tenderloin from marinade, discarding marinade. Pat dry, and sprinkle evenly with salt and remaining ½ tsp. pepper. Dredge in flour. Place pork on a lightly greased rack in a broiler pan; coat pork evenly with cooking spray.

4. Broil 5½ inches from heat 27 to 30 minutes or until pork is browned and a meat thermometer inserted in thickest portion registers 150°, turning pork occasionally. Let stand 10 minutes. **Makes** 6 to 8 servings.

Note: Pork tenderloin may be frozen raw in marinade up to 1 month. Thaw in refrigerator 2 days or until completely thawed. Proceed as directed.

Browned Butter Mashed Potatoes

make ahead

PREP: 15 MIN., COOK: 35 MIN.

Browned butter enhances many dishes by adding a rich nutty flavor. The key is making sure the butter turns a deep caramel color. In addition to stirring browned butter into mashed potatoes, try tossing browned butter with steamed vegetables, or drizzle it over warm, crusty French bread.

¾ cup butter
4 lb. Yukon gold potatoes, peeled and
    cut into 2-inch pieces
1 Tbsp. salt, divided
¾ cup buttermilk
½ cup milk
¼ tsp. pepper
Garnishes: fresh parsley, rosemary, and
    thyme sprigs

1. Cook butter in a 2-qt. heavy saucepan over medium heat, stirring constantly, 6 to 8 minutes or just until butter begins to turn golden brown. Immediately remove pan from heat, and pour butter into a small bowl. (Butter will continue to darken if left in saucepan.) Remove and reserve 1 to 2 Tbsp. browned butter.

2. Bring potatoes, 2 tsp. salt, and water to cover to a boil in a large Dutch oven over medium-high heat; boil 20 minutes or until tender. Drain. Reduce heat to low. Return potatoes to Dutch oven, and cook, stirring occasionally, 3 to 5 minutes or until potatoes are dry.

3. Mash potatoes with a potato masher to desired consistency. Stir in remaining browned butter, buttermilk, milk, pepper, and remaining 1 tsp. salt, stirring just until blended.

4. Transfer to a serving dish. Drizzle with reserved 1 to 2 Tbsp. browned butter. Garnish, if desired. **Makes** 6 to 8 servings.

Note: To make ahead, prepare recipe as directed through Step 3. Place in a lightly greased 2½-qt. ovenproof serving dish; cover and chill up to 2 days. Let stand at room temperature 30 minutes. Bake, uncovered, at 350° for 35 to 40 minutes or until thoroughly heated. Drizzle with reserved brown butter, and garnish, if desired.

Schedule for Success

1 Month Before:
▪ Freeze pork in prepared marinade.

2 Days Before:
▪ Prepare vinaigrette, and toast walnuts for salad.
▪ Prepare mashed potatoes, and refrigerate.
▪ Defrost pork in the refrigerator.

1 Day Before:
▪ Cut peppers, shallots, and garlic for green bean recipe, and place in a zip-top plastic bag in the refrigerator.
▪ Wash salad greens, and store in a damp paper towel in a zip-top plastic bag in the refrigerator.
▪ Prepare Marinated Mozzarella (page 246).
▪ Mix together Brandy-Vanilla Cheesecake Dip (page 258). Ask guests to bring fruit and cookies to serve with this dessert dip.

1½ Hours Before:
▪ Reheat potatoes. Remove from oven, and cover with foil to keep warm. Turn oven to broil.
▪ Sauté mushrooms for salad. Slice apples, and toss with lemon-lime soda to prevent darkening.
▪ Stir together ingredients for Pink Lemonade Cocktail in pitcher.

50 Minutes Before:
▪ Remove pork from marinade, coat with flour, and season as directed. Broil. Remove from oven; turn oven off. Return potatoes to oven until serving time.
▪ Transfer Marinated Mozzarella to serving dish.

20 Minutes Before:
▪ Cook Green Bean-and-Red Bell Pepper Toss.
▪ Assemble salad. Enjoy!

Green Bean-and-Red Bell Pepper Toss
fast fixin's
PREP: 10 MIN., COOK: 10 MIN.
This side cooks up quickly and complements pork, beef, or chicken. Substitute 1 lb. trimmed green beans for the slender French beans.

2 Tbsp. butter
2 (8-oz.) packages French green
    beans
1 red bell pepper, cut into thin
    strips
3 shallots, sliced
2 garlic cloves, minced
½ tsp. salt
⅛ tsp. ground red pepper

1. Melt butter in a large Dutch oven over medium-high heat. Add green beans, bell pepper strips, and remaining ingredients, tossing to coat. Add ¼ cup water.
2. Cook, covered, 4 to 6 minutes; uncover and cook, stirring often, 1 to 2 more minutes or until water is evaporated and beans are crisp-tender. **Makes** 6 to 8 servings.
MEGAN NATTER
SLIDELL, LOUISIANA

Sugar Snap Peas-and-Red Bell Pepper Toss: Substitute 1 lb. trimmed sugar snap peas for green beans. Proceed as directed.

Barbecue on the Spot

Attention, spur-of-the-moment hosts: Our Assemble-Your-Own Barbecue Stacks are right up your alley. They're a spin on a fancy appetizer called blini, in which caviar and sour cream top buckwheat pancakes. Give assembly instructions (see Step 2 in recipe) after meet-and-greet time, then turn your friends loose to enjoy making their own.

Assemble-Your-Own Barbecue Stacks
fast fixin's
PREP: 15 MIN.
Inspired by a recipe from Teresa Todd of Dickson, Tennessee, we came up with our version. Expand toppings to include pickled okra or sliced jalapeño peppers.

2 lb. warm shredded barbecued chicken
    without sauce *
⅓ cup red barbecue sauce
Cornbread Griddle Cakes
Red barbecue sauce to taste
30 plum tomato slices (about
    5 tomatoes)
White Barbecue Sauce Slaw
1 cup White Barbecue Sauce
Toppings: red onion slices, cracked
    pepper

1. Toss chicken in ⅓ cup red barbecue sauce.
2. Spoon barbecued chicken mixture evenly onto Cornbread Griddle Cakes. Drizzle each with red barbecue sauce to taste. Top each with 1 tomato slice. Spoon White Barbecue Sauce Slaw onto each tomato slice. Serve with White Barbecue Sauce and desired toppings. **Makes** 6 to 8 servings.

*2 lb. shredded barbecued beef or pork without sauce may be substituted.

Note: For testing purposes only, we used Stubb's Original Bar-B-Q Sauce.

Cornbread Griddle Cakes:
make ahead
PREP: 5 MIN., COOK: 5 MIN. PER BATCH
Don't get confused and buy a cornbread mix; it won't work in this recipe. If you're out of time, buy cornbread muffins from the deli. Split them in half from top to bottom; use each half in place of one cake.

2 cups yellow self-rising cornmeal
1 cup all-purpose flour
1½ cups milk
⅓ cup butter, melted
2 large eggs, lightly beaten
1 Tbsp. sugar
¼ tsp. ground red pepper

1. Stir together all ingredients just until moistened. Pour 2 Tbsp. batter for each cake onto a hot, greased griddle or large nonstick skillet. Cook cakes 2 to 3 minutes or until tops are covered with bubbles and edges look dry and cooked; turn and cook other side (about 2 minutes). **Makes** 30 (2-inch) cakes.

Note: To make ahead, place cooked griddle cakes on baking sheets. Cover and chill up to 24 hours. To reheat, bake at 300° for 8 to 10 minutes or until thoroughly heated. Serve immediately.

White Barbecue Sauce:
make ahead
PREP: 15 MIN., CHILL: 1 HR.
This makes 1½ cups sauce. Reserve 1 cup for guests to drizzle over their assembled stacks. Use the remaining ½ cup to make the White Barbecue Sauce Slaw.

1¼ cups mayonnaise
¼ cup horseradish
3 Tbsp. cider vinegar
1 Tbsp. lemon juice
1 tsp. coarsely ground pepper
¼ tsp. salt

1. Stir together all ingredients in a small bowl. Cover and chill at least 1 hour until ready to serve. **Makes** 1½ cups.

White Barbecue Sauce Slaw: Combine 1 (16-oz.) package shredded coleslaw mix with carrots, ½ cup White Barbecue Sauce, ¼ cup chopped red onion, and ½ tsp. salt. Toss gently; cover and chill 1 hour. **Makes** 6 to 8 servings.

Peppered Caramel Corn

fast fixin's

PREP: 5 MIN , COOL: 10 MIN.

We tried this recipe with several buttery toffee popcorn brands with mixed results. To equal our Test Kitchens results, buy the one suggested at the end of our recipe. Heating the purchased mix in the microwave allows the pepper to stick.

1 (12-oz.) package buttery toffee
  popcorn with peanuts
¼ tsp. pepper

1. Microwave popcorn with peanuts in a large microwave-safe bowl at HIGH 2 minutes, stirring at 30-second intervals. Stir in pepper. Spread mixture in an even layer in a lightly greased jelly-roll pan. Let cool 10 minutes; break into pieces. Store in an airtight container up to 1 week. **Makes** 4 cups.

Note: For testing purposes only, we used Crunch 'n Munch Buttery Toffee Popcorn With Peanuts.

Freeze Your Favorite Dressing

Avoid an eleventh hour rush during the holidays by putting some of the recipes you plan to serve in the freezer. Sage Cornbread Dressing is a great choice to prep and freeze unbaked because this seasonal favorite requires very little last-minute preparation.

Sage Cornbread Dressing

freezeable • make ahead

PREP: 35 MIN., COOL: 30 MIN.,
COOK: 12 MIN., BAKE: 50 MIN.

Use all 3 cups of broth if you like a really moist dressing.

2 (6-oz.) packages buttermilk
  cornbread mix
⅓ cup butter
1 cup chopped celery
½ cup chopped onion
1 Tbsp. chopped fresh or
  1½ tsp. dried sage
½ tsp. pepper
¼ tsp. salt
4 white bread slices, cut into
  ½-inch cubes (about 2 cups)
2½ to 3 cups chicken broth
2 large eggs, lightly beaten
Garnish: fresh sage leaves

1. Prepare cornbread according to package directions for a double recipe. Let cool 30 minutes; crumble into a large bowl.
2. Melt ⅓ cup butter in a large skillet over medium heat; add chopped celery and onion, and sauté 10 to 12 minutes or until tender. Stir in sage, pepper, and salt. Stir celery mixture and bread cubes into crumbled cornbread in bowl, stirring gently until blended. Add chicken broth and eggs, and gently stir until moistened. Spoon mixture into a lightly greased 11- x 7-inch baking dish.
3. Bake at 350° for 45 to 50 minutes or until golden brown. Garnish, if desired. **Makes** 8 to 10 servings.

ADELYNE SMITH
DUNNVILLE, KENTUCKY

Note: For testing purposes only, we used Martha White Cotton Country Cornbread Mix. To make ahead, prepare recipe as directed through Step 2. Cover with plastic wrap; cover with heavy-duty aluminum foil or container lid. Freeze unbaked dressing up to 3 months, if desired. Thaw in refrigerator 24 hours. Let stand at room temperature 30 minutes. Bake, uncovered, at 350° for 1 hour and 10 minutes to 1 hour and 15 minutes or until golden.

Sausage Dressing: Prepare recipe as directed through Step 1. Omit ⅓ cup butter. Cook 1 (16-oz.) package pork sausage in a large skillet over medium-high heat, stirring often, 10 to 12 minutes or until meat crumbles and is no longer pink. Remove cooked sausage from skillet using a slotted spoon, and drain, reserving 2 tsp. drippings in skillet. Add chopped celery and onion, and sauté 10 to 12 minutes or until vegetables are tender; stir in sage, pepper, and salt. Stir in cooked sausage. Proceed with recipe as directed. Follow make-ahead directions, if desired.

Oyster Dressing: Prepare recipe as directed through Step 2, stirring 1 (12-oz.) container fresh oysters, drained, into cornbread mixture. Proceed with recipe as directed, increasing bake time to 50 to 55 minutes or until golden. Follow make-ahead directions, if desired.

Chili and Friends

Let guests help themselves to a laid-back menu with all the fixin's.

L ife's busy, especially during the holidays, so it's smart to go with recipes that are make ahead, freezeable, and easy to finish off at the last minute. This anything-but-ordinary chili party is just the ticket. It's perfect for the night before Thanksgiving or Christmas Eve, a dinner club gathering, or tree-trimming party.

Smoky Chicken Chili

PREP: 15 MIN.; COOK: 1 HR., 15 MIN.
Pick up smoked chicken from your favorite barbecue restaurant to use in this dish, or use a barbecue-flavored rotisserie chicken from your local supermarket.

2 poblano chile peppers, chopped
1 large red bell pepper, chopped
1 medium-size sweet onion, chopped
3 garlic cloves, minced
2 Tbsp. olive oil
2 (14½-oz.) cans zesty chili-style diced tomatoes
3 cups shredded or chopped smoked chicken (about 1 lb.)
1 (16-oz.) can navy beans
1 (15-oz.) can black beans, rinsed and drained
1 (12-oz.) can beer *
1 (1.25-oz.) envelope white chicken chili seasoning mix
Toppings: shredded Cheddar cheese, chopped fresh cilantro, sour cream, lime wedges, baby corn, sliced black olives, chopped red onion, tortilla chips

1. Sauté first 4 ingredients in hot oil in a large Dutch oven over medium-high heat 8 minutes or until vegetables are tender. Stir in diced tomatoes and next 5 ingredients. Bring to a boil over medium-high heat. Reduce heat to low, and simmer, stirring occasionally, 1 hour. Serve with desired toppings. **Makes** 9 cups.

* 1½ cups low-sodium chicken broth may be substituted.

Note: For testing purposes only, we used Del Monte Diced Tomatoes Zesty Chili Style and McCormick White Chicken Chili Seasoning Mix.

Citrus-Avocado Salad With Tex-Mex Vinaigrette
fast fixin's
PREP: 10 MIN.
Two bags of your favorite lettuce blend can be substituted for Bibb lettuce. Pomegranate seeds are a unique crunchy addition to this salad. See the box below on how to remove seeds from the whole fruit.

3 heads Bibb lettuce, torn
2 avocados, sliced
1 (24-oz.) jar refrigerated orange and grapefruit sections, drained
Tex-Mex Vinaigrette
Garnishes: pomegranate seeds, fresh cilantro sprigs

How to Remove Pomegranate Seeds

Cut off crown of pomegranate. Using a small paring knife, score the outer layer of skin into sections. Working with pomegranate fully submerged in a large bowl of water, break apart sections along scored lines. Roll out seeds with your fingers. (The seeds will sink to the bottom, while the white membrane will float to the top.) Remove and discard membrane with a slotted spoon. Pour seed mixture through a fine wire-mesh strainer. Pat seeds dry with paper towels.

1. Combine first 3 ingredients in a salad bowl. Toss with Tex-Mex Vinaigrette. Garnish, if desired. Serve immediately. **Makes** 8 servings.

Note: For testing purposes only, we used Del Monte Sunfresh Citrus Salad for orange and grapefruit sections.

Tex-Mex Vinaigrette:
fast fixin's • make ahead
PREP: 10 MIN.

½ cup fresh orange juice
¼ cup fresh lime juice
1 tsp. brown sugar
½ tsp. ground cumin
½ tsp. salt
½ tsp. pepper
⅓ cup olive oil

1. Combine first 6 ingredients in a small bowl. Whisk in oil in a slow, steady stream, whisking until smooth. Use immediately, or cover and chill up to 3 days. Whisk before serving. **Makes** ⅔ cup.

Cornbread Muffin Trees
fast fixin's
PREP: 10 MIN., BAKE: 17 MIN.
Jump-start this recipe by preparing and refrigerating dry and wet ingredients separately. Stir together as directed, and bake while guests enjoy salad.

2 (6-oz.) packages buttermilk
  cornbread mix
1 cup (4 oz.) shredded sharp Cheddar
  cheese
2 jalapeño peppers, seeded and finely
  chopped
1 tsp. ground cumin
2 (7-oz.) cans Mexican-style corn,
  drained
1½ cups buttermilk

1. Stir together buttermilk cornbread mix and next 3 ingredients in a large bowl; make a well in center of mixture. Stir together corn and 1½ cups buttermilk; add to cornbread mixture, stirring just until dry ingredients are moistened.
2. Spoon into well-greased Christmas tree-shaped silicone muffin pans, filling three-fourths full.
3. Bake at 425° for 15 to 17 minutes or until lightly browned. **Makes** 2 dozen.

Note: For testing purposes only, we used Martha White Cotton Country Cornbread mix. To use regular muffin pans, prepare recipe as directed through Step 2, filling muffin cups two-thirds full. Bake as directed. **Makes** 18 muffins.

Pound Cake With Caramel Icing and Apricot-Ginger Sprinkles
freezeable • make ahead
PREP: 20 MIN.; BAKE: 1 HR., 10 MIN.;
COOL: 2 HR., 10 MIN.; STAND: 30 MIN.
Bake the cake ahead of time. Store at room temperature up to three days, or place it in a large zip-top plastic freezer bag, and store in the freezer up to one month. Let thaw; then top with icing and sprinkles.

1½ cups butter, softened
2½ cups granulated sugar
½ cup firmly packed light brown sugar
6 large eggs
3 cups all-purpose flour
½ tsp. salt
¼ tsp. baking soda
1 (8-oz.) container sour cream
2 tsp. vanilla extract
Caramel Icing
Apricot-Ginger Sprinkles

1. Beat butter at medium speed with an electric mixer until creamy. Gradually add sugars, beating at medium speed until light and fluffy. Add eggs, 1 at a time, beating just until yellow disappears after each addition.
2. Stir together flour, salt, and baking soda. Add to butter mixture alternately with sour cream, beginning and ending with flour mixture. Beat at low speed just until blended after each addition. Stir in vanilla. Pour into 2 greased and floured 9- x 5-inch loaf pans.

3. Bake at 325° for 1 hour to 1 hour and 10 minutes or until a wooden pick inserted in center comes out clean. Cool in pans on a wire rack 10 minutes. Remove cakes from pans, and let cool 2 hours or until completely cool.
4. Prepare Caramel Icing, and pour over cake, allowing it to drip down sides of cake. Top with Apricot-Ginger Sprinkles; let stand 30 minutes or until icing is firm. **Makes** 16 servings.

Caramel Icing:
fast fixin's
PREP: 10 MIN., COOK: 5 MIN.

1¼ cups firmly packed light brown
  sugar
5 Tbsp. heavy cream
¼ cup butter
Dash of salt
½ tsp. vanilla extract

1. Bring first 4 ingredients to a full rolling boil in a medium saucepan over medium heat, stirring often. Boil, stirring constantly, 1 minute. Remove from heat; stir in vanilla.
2. Beat at medium speed with an electric mixer 2 to 4 minutes or until thickened. Use immediately. **Makes** 1⅓ cups.

Apricot-Ginger Sprinkles:
fast fixin's
PREP: 10 MIN.
Toss together, and top pound cake no more than one hour before serving.

½ cup salted cashews
⅓ cup finely chopped dried
  apricots
3 Tbsp. minced crystallized ginger

1. Stir together all ingredients. **Makes** about 1 cup.

Appetizers for Any Crowd

Tasty tidbits perfect to serve 2, 12, 20, or more.

Prepare each one of these recipes the number of times necessary to serve the number of people you're entertaining. But watch out if you decide to multiply—strong flavors such as black pepper, garlic, and jalapeño peppers can be very overwhelming. Trust your judgment, taste as you go, and the results will be delicious.

Three-Cheese Pimiento Cheese
PREP: 15 MIN.

1 (8-oz.) package cream cheese
1 (4-oz.) jar diced pimiento, drained
1 (5-oz.) jar pimiento cheese spread
½ cup mayonnaise
¼ tsp. garlic powder
¼ tsp. ground chipotle chile pepper
¼ tsp. salt
Freshly ground pepper to taste
3 cups (12 oz.) shredded sharp
  Cheddar cheese

1. Microwave cream cheese in a microwave-safe bowl at HIGH 1 to 1½ minutes or until melted and smooth, stirring at 30-second intervals. Stir in diced pimiento and next 6 ingredients.
2. Stir in Cheddar cheese. Serve immediately, or cover and chill up to 4 hours. Store in the refrigerator in an airtight container up to 4 days. **Makes** 3½ cups.

KAREN ISBELL
CORINTH, MISSISSIPPI

Note: For testing purposes only, we used Kraft Pimento Spread.

Marinated Mozzarella
make ahead
PREP: 20 MIN., CHILL: 8 HR.

3 (8-oz.) blocks mozzarella cheese
1 (8.5-oz.) jar sun-dried tomatoes,
  drained and halved
½ cup olive oil
3 Tbsp. finely chopped fresh
  flat-leaf parsley
1 tsp. garlic powder
1 tsp. onion powder
½ tsp. dried oregano
½ tsp. dried Italian seasoning
¼ tsp. salt
¼ tsp. freshly ground pepper
Garnish: flat-leaf parsley sprigs or
  fresh rosemary stems

1. Cut blocks of cheese into 1-inch cubes. Arrange cheese cubes and tomato halves in an 8-inch square baking dish.
2. Whisk together ½ cup olive oil, chopped parsley, and next 6 ingredients; pour evenly over cheese cubes. Cover and chill at least 8 hours or up to 24 hours. Transfer mixture to a serving plate. Garnish with fresh flat-leaf parsley sprigs, or spear tomato halves and cheese cubes with short rosemary stems, if desired. Drizzle with marinade, if desired. **Makes** about 4 cups.

Serve Marinated Mozzarella Three Ways

Thread cheese cubes and sun-dried tomatoes onto short rosemary skewers for a striking presentation.

For a large crowd, arrange the appetizer and flat-leaf parsley on a platter; serve with festive picks.

Cocktail or fondue forks are just right for popping Marinated Mozzarella into your mouth.

Warm Turnip Green Dip

PREP: 15 MIN., COOK: 20 MIN., BROIL: 5 MIN.

This is a yummy Southern version of artichoke dip. Transfer the dip to a 1- or 2-qt. slow cooker set on WARM so guests can enjoy this creamy dip throughout your party. To make it spicier, serve your favorite brand of hot sauce on the side.

5 bacon slices, chopped
½ sweet onion, chopped
2 garlic cloves, chopped
¼ cup dry white wine
1 (16-oz.) package frozen chopped
    turnip greens, thawed
12 oz. cream cheese, cut into pieces
1 (8-oz.) container sour cream
½ tsp. dried crushed red pepper
¼ tsp. salt
¾ cup freshly grated Parmesan

1. Cook bacon in a Dutch oven over medium-high heat 5 to 6 minutes or until crisp; remove bacon, and drain on paper towels, reserving 1 Tbsp. drippings in Dutch oven.
2. Sauté onion and garlic in hot drippings 3 to 4 minutes. Add wine, and cook 1 to 2 minutes, stirring to loosen particles from bottom of Dutch oven. Stir in turnip greens, next 4 ingredients, and ½ cup Parmesan cheese. Cook, stirring often, 6 to 8 minutes or until cream cheese is melted and mixture is thoroughly heated. Transfer to a lightly greased 1½-qt. baking dish. Sprinkle evenly with remaining ¼ cup Parmesan cheese.
3. Broil 6 inches from heat 4 to 5 minutes or until cheese is lightly browned. Sprinkle evenly with bacon. **Makes** 4 cups.

Dressed-up Salsa

fast fixin's • make ahead

PREP: 10 MIN.

No one will guess this dish took just 10 minutes to make. It tastes like you chopped, peeled, and worked all day long.

1 (24-oz.) jar chunky medium salsa
2½ Tbsp. fresh lime juice
3 Tbsp. chopped fresh cilantro
2 garlic cloves, minced
1 jalapeño pepper, seeded and
    chopped

1. Pulse all ingredients in a food processor or blender 3 to 4 times or until mixture is thoroughly combined. **Makes** 2 cups.

Note: For testing purposes only, we used Pace Chunky Medium Salsa.

Baked Pita Chips

fast fixin's

PREP: 10 MIN., BAKE: 15 MIN.

1 (8-oz.) package 4-inch pita rounds
Olive oil cooking spray
1½ tsp. coarsely ground kosher salt

1. Separate each pita into 2 rounds. Cut each round into 4 wedges. Arrange in a single layer on ungreased baking sheets. Coat with olive oil cooking spray, and sprinkle evenly with 1½ tsp. kosher salt.
2. Bake at 350° for 12 to 15 minutes or until golden and crisp. **Makes** about 5 dozen.

Note: For testing purposes only, we use Toufayan Mini Pitettes.

Relax With a Snack

Kick back a little during the holidays. Our Test Kitchens did a super makeover on a traditional salad dressing-seasoned snack mix, adding dried cherries, mixing up the types of cereals used, and, of course, including chocolate.

Microwave Snack Mix

make ahead

PREP: 15 MIN., COOL: 30 MIN.

Use a glass bowl when you zap this in the microwave. (Don't use a plastic bowl; we tried it, and the mixture got too hot and could possibly burn.)

2 (1-oz.) envelopes Ranch dressing mix
½ cup vegetable oil
3 cups crisp oatmeal cereal squares
3 cups corn-and-rice cereal
3 cups crisp wheat cereal squares
2 cups pretzel sticks
1 cup dried cherries
1 cup candy-coated chocolate pieces

1. Whisk together Ranch dressing mix and ½ cup vegetable oil in a large microwave-safe glass bowl. Stir in oatmeal cereal squares and next 3 ingredients.
2. Microwave mixture at HIGH 2 minutes, and stir well. Microwave at HIGH 2 more minutes, and stir well. Spread mixture in a single layer on wax paper, and let cool 30 minutes. Add cherries and candy pieces. Store in an airtight container up to 5 days. **Makes** 13 cups.

Note: For testing purposes only, we used Quaker Essentials Oatmeal Squares for crisp oatmeal cereal squares, Crispix for corn-and-rice cereal, and Wheat Chex for wheat cereal squares.

Super-Easy Sweets

Everyone will want to come to your house when you serve these decadent treats.

You'll have guests begging for the recipes of these irresistible sweets. Package them in festive tins or cellophane bags as gifts, and you'll be more popular than Santa Claus.

Reindeer Gingersnaps
family favorite
PREP: 45 MIN., BAKE: 10 MIN. PER BATCH, COOL: 30 MIN.

1 (14.5-oz.) package gingerbread mix
1 tsp. meringue powder
½ tsp. hot water
1 (12-oz.) container ready-to-spread fluffy white frosting
Decorations: 32 miniature candy canes, 32 licorice candies, 16 sour cherry candies

1. Prepare gingerbread dough according to package instructions for gingersnap cookies.
2. Roll dough out on a lightly floured surface, and cut into 3½-inch ovals, using an egg-shaped or oval cookie cutter. Place 2 inches apart on parchment paper-lined baking sheets.
3. Bake at 375° for 8 to 10 minutes or until edges are lightly browned. Remove to wire racks, and let cool 30 minutes.
4. Stir together meringue powder and ½ tsp. hot water until combined; stir in frosting. Spoon frosting mixture into a zip-top plastic freezer bag; snip 1 corner of bag to make a small hole. Pipe 1 dot of frosting mixture

at top of 1 cookie; press straight ends of 2 candy canes into piped dot to form antlers. Pipe 2 dots in center of cookie; press 1 licorice candy in each dot to form eyes. Pipe 1 dot at bottom of cookie; press 1 cherry candy in dot to form a nose. Repeat procedure with remaining cookies, frosting mixture, and candies. Let stand 24 hours to dry, if desired. **Makes** 16 cookies.

Note: For testing purposes only, we used Betty Crocker Gingerbread Cake & Cookie Mix and Betty Crocker Fluffy White Whipped Frosting.

Salty Chocolate-Pecan Candy
make ahead
PREP: 10 MIN., BAKE: 15 MIN., CHILL: 1 HR.
This candy will soften slightly while at room temperature.

1 cup pecans, coarsely chopped
3 (4-oz.) bittersweet chocolate baking bars
3 (4-oz.) white chocolate baking bars
1 tsp. coarse sea salt *****

1. Place pecans in a single layer on a baking sheet.
2. Bake at 350° for 8 to 10 minutes or until toasted. Reduce oven temperature to 225°.
3. Line a 17- x 12-inch jelly-roll pan with parchment paper. Break each chocolate bar into 8 equal pieces. (You will have 48 pieces total.) Arrange in a checkerboard pattern in jelly-roll pan, alternating white and dark chocolate. (Pieces will touch.)

4. Bake at 225° for 5 minutes or just until chocolate is melted. Remove pan to a wire rack. Swirl chocolates into a marble pattern using a wooden pick. Sprinkle

evenly with toasted pecans and salt.
5. Chill 1 hour or until firm. Break into pieces. Store in an airtight container in refrigerator up to 1 month. **Makes** 1¾ lb.

* ¾ tsp. kosher salt may be substituted.

Note: For testing purposes only, we used Ghirardelli 60% Cacao Bittersweet Chocolate Baking Bars and Ghirardelli White Chocolate Baking Bars.

Our Most Showstopping Cakes Ever

Try one of these creations to make your holidays special.

The December issue of *Southern Living* is renowned for the fabulous "big white cake," as our staff knows it, that always adorns its cover. Whether it's a lavish extravaganza, such as 1998's Red Velvet-Peppermint Cake, or a one-pan wonder, such as 2004's Cream Cheese-Coconut-Pecan Pound Cake, these recipes represent the very best of the season.

1995 Coconut-Lemon Cake
PREP: 45 MIN., BAKE: 20 MIN.

This is a classic in every way with three golden yellow layers and a fluffy, light-as-meringue seven-minute frosting. The flavor profile pairs two seasonal Southern favorites—fresh lemon and coconut. The Lemon Filling is a quick and easy stovetop stir-together that can also be used to fill tart shells.

1 cup unsalted butter, softened
2 cups sugar
4 large eggs, separated
3 cups all-purpose flour
1 Tbsp. baking powder
1 cup milk
1 tsp. vanilla extract
⅛ tsp. salt
Lemon Filling
Fluffy White Frosting
1 cup flaked coconut
Garnish: fresh cranberries

1. Beat butter at medium speed with an electric mixer until fluffy; gradually add sugar, beating well. Add egg yolks, 1 at a time, beating after each addition.
2. Combine flour and baking powder; add to butter mixture alternately with milk, beginning and ending with flour mixture. Beat at low speed until blended after each addition. Stir in 1 tsp. vanilla.
3. Beat egg whites and salt at high speed with an electric mixer until stiff peaks form. Stir about one-third of egg whites into batter; fold in remaining egg whites. Spoon batter into 3 greased and floured 9-inch round cake pans.
4. Bake at 350° for 18 to 20 minutes or until a wooden pick inserted in center comes out clean. Cool in pans on wire racks 10 minutes; remove from pans, and cool completely on wire racks.
5. Spread Lemon Filling between layers. Spread Fluffy White Frosting on top and sides of cake. Sprinkle top and sides with coconut; garnish, if desired. **Makes** 1 (3-layer) cake.

Lemon Filling:
PREP: 10 MIN., COOK: 5 MIN.

1 cup sugar
¼ cup cornstarch
1 cup boiling water
4 egg yolks, lightly beaten
⅓ cup fresh lemon juice
2 Tbsp. butter

1. Combine sugar and cornstarch in a medium saucepan; stir in 1 cup boiling water. Cook over medium heat, stirring constantly, until sugar and cornstarch dissolve (about 3 minutes). Gradually stir about one-fourth of hot mixture into yolks; add to remaining hot mixture, stirring constantly with a wire whisk. Stir in lemon juice.
2. Cook, stirring constantly, until thickened. Remove from heat; stir in butter. Cool, stirring occasionally. **Makes** 1⅔ cups.

Fluffy White Frosting:
PREP: 10 MIN., COOK: 15 MIN.

1 cup sugar
1½ cups water
2 Tbsp. light corn syrup
4 egg whites
¼ tsp. cream of tartar

1. Combine first 3 ingredients in a small heavy saucepan; cook over medium heat, stirring constantly, until clear. Cook, without stirring, until mixture reaches soft-ball stage or candy thermometer registers 240°.
2. Beat egg whites and cream of tartar at high speed with an electric mixer until soft peaks form; slowly add syrup, beating constantly. Beat until stiff peaks form. **Makes** 7 cups.

1996 Gift Box Cake

PREP: 45 MIN., BAKE: 20 MIN., STAND: 15 MIN.

This is a fun cake for the whole family—perfect not only for the holidays, but for year-round celebrations. It's an impressively moist three-layered white cake with a fine crumb texture.

½ cup butter, softened
½ cup shortening
2 cups sugar
⅔ cup milk
3 cups all-purpose flour
1 Tbsp. baking powder
1 tsp. salt
2 Tbsp. vanilla extract
1 tsp. almond extract
6 egg whites
Powdered Sugar Frosting
3 (4.5-oz.) packages chewy fruit rolls by the foot
⅓ cup white sparkling sugar or edible glitter
8 gingerbread men cookies (3 to 3½ inches tall)

1. Beat butter and shortening at medium speed with an electric mixer 2 minutes or until creamy; gradually add sugar, beating well.

2. Combine ⅔ cup water and milk. Combine flour, baking powder, and salt; add to sugar mixture alternately with milk mixture, beginning and ending with flour mixture. Beat at low speed until blended after each addition. Stir in vanilla and almond extracts.

3. Beat egg whites at high speed until stiff peaks form; fold into batter. Pour into 3 greased and floured 8-inch square pans.

4. Bake at 350° for 20 minutes or until a wooden pick inserted in center comes out clean. Cool in pans on wire racks 10 minutes; remove from pans, and cool completely on wire racks.

5. Reserve 2 cups Powdered Sugar Frosting. Spread ½ cup frosting into an 8-inch square on cake plate.

6. Spread remaining frosting between layers and on top and sides of cake.

7. Unroll fruit rolls (do not remove paper backing), and brush with water.

Sprinkle with sparkling sugar; let stand 15 minutes.

8. Cut four (12-inch-long) strips from fruit rolls. Remove paper backing, and arrange on top and sides of cake, pressing gently into frosting, to resemble a ribbon.

9. Spoon ½ cup reserved frosting onto center of cake, forming a 3-inch mound.

10. Cut remaining fruit rolls into 4-inch pieces; remove paper backing. Fold each piece in half, resembling the loop of a bow; press cut ends into frosting mound, creating a large bow on top of cake. Place 2 gingerbread men cookies on each side of cake.

11. Spoon 1½ cups reserved frosting into a decorating bag fitted with a large star tip. Pipe a border around bottom edge of cake. **Makes** 1 (8-inch) cake.

Note: You can also make this cake with 2 (18.25-oz.) packages white cake mix and 4 (16-oz.) containers ready-to-spread frosting. Make the gingerbread men using your favorite recipe or a gingerbread mix, or buy the cookies from your local bakery.

Powdered Sugar Frosting:

PREP: 10 MIN.

2 cups shortening
1 tsp. salt
1 tsp. almond extract
1 tsp. vanilla extract
3 (16-oz.) packages powdered sugar, sifted
1 cup evaporated milk

1. Beat first 4 ingredients at medium speed with a heavy-duty electric mixer until blended. Add powdered sugar alternately with evaporated milk, beating at low speed until blended after each addition. Beat at medium speed 8 minutes or until light and fluffy. **Makes** 7 cups.

Note: Frosting may be stored in refrigerator up to 2 weeks. If using a handheld mixer, prepare frosting in 2 batches.

1998 Red Velvet-Peppermint Cake

PREP: 15 MIN., BAKE: 25 MIN.

This is a great holiday twist on those chocolate-swirled marbled cake batters we've loved for years. It's a super-quick recipe that starts with two mixes; stirs in a few clever ingredients, such as buttermilk, cocoa, and cider vinegar; and yields a terrific cake with made-from-scratch red velvet flavor.

1 (18.25-oz.) package white cake mix
3 egg whites
1⅓ cups buttermilk
2 Tbsp. vegetable oil
1 (9-oz.) package yellow cake mix
½ cup buttermilk
1 large egg
1½ Tbsp. cocoa
½ tsp. baking soda
2 Tbsp. liquid red food coloring
1 tsp. cider vinegar
Peppermint-Cream Cheese Frosting
Garnishes: Holiday Trees; 6 (5-inch) red-and-white candy canes, crushed; 12 (5-inch) green candy canes, broken; 12 round peppermint candies

1. Beat white cake mix and next 3 ingredients according to package directions.

2. Beat yellow cake mix and next 6 ingredients according to package directions. Spoon red batter alternately with white batter into 3 greased and floured 9-inch round cake pans. Swirl batter gently with a knife.

3. Bake at 350° for 22 to 25 minutes or until a wooden pick inserted in center comes out clean. Cool in pans on wire racks 10 minutes. Remove from pans, and cool completely on wire racks.

4. Spread Peppermint-Cream Cheese Frosting between layers and on top and sides of cake. Garnish, if desired. Serve within 2 hours. **Makes** 1 (3-layer) cake.

Note: For testing purposes only, we used Duncan Hines Moist Deluxe Classic White Cake Mix, Jiffy Golden Yellow Cake Mix, and McCormick Red Food Color. Cake may be chilled up to 2 days or frozen up to 1 month. If cake is frozen, thaw completely before garnishing to prevent crushed candy from running. Do not refrigerate after garnishing.

Peppermint-Cream Cheese Frosting:
PREP: 10 MIN.

1 (8-oz.) package cream cheese, softened
1 cup butter, softened
1 (2-lb.) package powdered sugar
2 tsp. peppermint extract *

1. Beat cream cheese and butter at medium speed with an electric mixer until creamy. Gradually add sugar, beating at low speed until smooth. Add peppermint extract, beating until blended. **Makes** about 5 cups.

*2 tsp. vanilla extract may be substituted.

Quick Peppermint-Cream Cheese Frosting: Stir together 3 (16-oz.) containers ready-to-spread cream cheese frosting and 2 tsp. peppermint extract.

Holiday Trees:
PREP: 35 MIN., STAND: 8 HR.

1 (16-oz.) package powdered sugar
3 Tbsp. meringue powder
6 Tbsp. warm water
6 (4-inch) sugar ice-cream cones
12 (5-inch) red-and-white candy canes, coarsely crushed
12 (5-inch) green candy canes, coarsely crushed
Edible glitter or sparkling sugar (optional)

1. Beat powdered sugar, meringue powder, and 6 Tbsp. warm water at low speed with an electric mixer until blended. Beat at high speed 4 to 5 minutes or until stiff peaks form. If icing is too stiff, add additional warm water, ¼ tsp. at a time, until desired consistency.

2. Spoon icing into a zip-top plastic bag; seal. Snip a ¼-inch hole in 1 corner of bag. Pipe 2 rows of points around 1 ice-cream cone, beginning at large end and working upward, to resemble a tree. Sprinkle with crushed candy canes and, if desired, edible glitter or sparkling sugar. Invert 2 ice-cream cones, stacking one on top of the other; repeat decorating procedure. Invert remaining 3 ice-cream cones, stacking one on top of the other; repeat decorating procedure. Let stand 8 hours. Store in a cool, dry place up to 1 month. **Makes** 3 trees.

Note: For fuller trees, double icing recipe, and repeat piping procedure before adding crushed candy canes.

1999 **Holiday Lane Cake**
PREP: 20 MIN., BAKE: 20 MIN.
A deliciously easy version of the bourbon-laced original, this cake is perfect for the beginning baker who wants to make a big impression. The traditional raisin filling is updated with a colorful mixture of candied cherries and sweetened dried cranberries; it's then trimmed with a candy bow and holly leaves, creating a dazzling centerpiece.

1 (18.25-oz.) package white cake mix
3 large eggs
1¼ cups buttermilk
¼ cup vegetable oil
Nutty Fruit Filling
1 (7.2-oz.) package home-style fluffy white frosting mix
½ cup boiling water
Holly Leaves (following page)
Assorted red candies
Candy Bow (following page)
White sugar crystals

1. Beat first 4 ingredients at medium speed with an electric mixer 2 minutes. Pour into 3 greased and floured 8-inch square or round cake pans.
2. Bake at 350° for 15 to 20 minutes or until a wooden pick inserted in center comes out clean. Cool in pans on wire racks 10 minutes. Remove from pans,

and cool completely on wire racks.
3. Spread Nutty Fruit Filling between layers.
4. Beat frosting mix and ½ cup boiling water at low speed 30 seconds. Beat at high speed 5 to 7 minutes or until stiff peaks form.
5. Spread frosting on top and sides of cake. Arrange Holly Leaves around top of cake to resemble a wreath. Arrange candies for berries, and place Candy Bow on wreath. Sprinkle cake with sugar crystals. Arrange additional Holly Leaves and red candies around bottom edge of cake. **Makes** 1 (3-layer) cake.

Note: For testing purposes only, we used Betty Crocker Home Style Fluffy White Frosting Mix. We used M&Ms and Skittles for assorted red candies.

Nutty Fruit Filling:
PREP: 15 MIN., COOK: 15 MIN.

½ cup butter
8 egg yolks
1 cup sugar
1 cup chopped pecans, toasted
1 cup chopped sweetened dried cranberries or dried cherries
1 cup flaked coconut
½ cup diced red or green candied cherries
⅓ cup orange juice

1. Melt butter in a heavy saucepan over low heat. Whisk in egg yolks and sugar; cook, whisking constantly, 11 minutes or until mixture thickens. Stir in remaining ingredients. Cool. **Makes** 3½ cups.

Note: For testing purposes only, we used Craisins for sweetened dried cranberries.

Holly Leaves:

PREP: 20 MIN., STAND: 12 HR.

1 (14-oz.) package green candy melts
⅓ cup light corn syrup
Powdered sugar

1. Microwave candy melts in a glass bowl at MEDIUM (50% power), stirring once, 1 minute or until melted. Stir in corn syrup. Place in a zip-top plastic bag; seal and let stand 8 hours.
2. Knead 2 to 3 minutes or until soft (about 12 times). Turn out onto a surface dusted with powdered sugar. Roll to ¹⁄₁₆-inch thickness. Cut with 1- and 2-inch holly leaf-shaped cutters. Score leaves with a knife. Place on wax paper over sides of an inverted cake pan for a curved shape. Let stand 3 to 4 hours. Store in an airtight container up to 3 days, if desired. **Makes** 8 dozen.

Candy Bow:

PREP: 25 MIN.; STAND: 8 HR., 30 MIN.

1 (14-oz.) package red candy melts
⅓ cup light corn syrup
Powdered sugar

1. Microwave candy melts in a glass bowl at MEDIUM (50% power), stirring once, 1 minute or until melted. Stir in corn syrup. Place in a zip-top plastic bag; seal and let stand 8 hours.
2. Knead 2 to 3 minutes or until soft (about 12 times). Turn out onto a surface dusted with powdered sugar. Roll to ¹⁄₁₆-inch thickness. Cut into 6 (6- x ½-inch) strips and 1 (½-inch) square using a fluted pastry cutter.
3. Pinch ends of each strip together to form loops. Pinch ends of loops together to form a bow. Wrap ½-inch square around center of bow. Place bow on side of an inverted cake pan, and let stand until firm. Cut 2 (12- x ½-inch) strips; shape strips into streamers. Place streamers on sides of inverted cake pan, and let stand until firm. Store in an airtight container up to 3 days. Attach bow and streamers on outer edge of cake. **Makes** 1 bow.

2001 Pecan Divinity Cake

PREP: 45 MIN.

This multilayered sour cream cake is shelf magic at its best. The cake, the frosting, and the candy all begin with a mix and end with one incredible layer cake. Enjoy it the day you make it; the Divinity Frosting won't hold up for longer storage.

Divinity Frosting
Sour Cream Cake Layers
Toasted pecan halves
Divinity Candy
Sugared Maraschino Cherries and Mint
  Sprigs
Small candy canes

1. Spread ½ cup Divinity Frosting between each cake layer; spread remaining frosting on top and sides of cake.
2. Arrange pecan halves and Divinity Candy on top of cake. Arrange Sugared Maraschino Cherries and Mint Sprigs and candy canes around bottom edge of cake. Store at room temperature. **Makes** 1 (4-layer) cake.

Divinity Frosting:

PREP: 10 MIN.

1 (7.2-oz.) package home-style fluffy
  white frosting mix
½ cup boiling water
⅓ cup light corn syrup
2 tsp. vanilla extract
1 (16-oz.) package powdered sugar
1½ cups chopped pecans, toasted

1. Place first 4 ingredients in a 4-qt. mixing bowl. Beat at low speed with a heavy-duty electric mixer 1 minute or until blended. Beat mixture at high speed 3 to 5 minutes or until stiff peaks form. Gradually add powdered sugar, beating at low speed until blended. Stir in toasted pecans. Spread frosting immediately on cake. **Makes** about 4½ cups.

Note: For testing purposes only, we used Betty Crocker Home Style Fluffy White Frosting Mix.

Sour Cream Cake Layers:

PREP: 10 MIN., BAKE: 17 MIN.

1 (18.25-oz.) package white cake mix
2 large eggs
1 (8-oz.) container sour cream
⅓ cup vegetable oil

1. Beat all ingredients and ½ cup water at low speed with an electric mixer 30 seconds or just until moistened; beat at medium speed 2 minutes. Pour batter evenly into 4 greased and floured 8-inch round cake pans.
2. Bake at 350° for 15 to 17 minutes or until a wooden pick inserted in center comes out clean. Cool in pans on wire racks 10 minutes. Remove from pans, and cool completely on wire racks. Wrap layers in plastic wrap, and freeze 2 hours or up to 1 month, if desired. **Makes** 4 (8-inch) layers.

Divinity Candy:

PREP: 30 MIN., STAND: 16 HR.

1 (7.2-oz.) package home-style fluffy
  white frosting mix
½ cup boiling water
⅓ cup light corn syrup
2 tsp. vanilla extract
1 (16-oz.) package powdered sugar
1½ cups chopped pecans, toasted
Toasted pecan halves

1. Place first 4 ingredients in a 4-qt. mixing bowl. Beat at low speed with a heavy-duty electric mixer 1 minute or until mixture is blended. Beat mixture at high speed 3 to 5 minutes or until stiff peaks form. Gradually add powdered sugar, beating at low speed until blended. Stir in chopped pecans.
2. Drop mixture by rounded tablespoonfuls onto wax paper. Gently press a toasted pecan half into center of each candy. Let stand 8 hours; remove to wire racks, and let stand 8 more hours or until bottom of candy is firm. Store in airtight containers. **Makes** 5 dozen.

Divinity Candy With Sugared Maraschino Cherries: Substitute Sugared Maraschino Cherries for toasted pecan halves. Drop mixture by rounded tablespoonfuls onto wax paper. Press tip of a lightly greased wooden spoon handle into center of each candy, making an indentation. Let stand as directed. Place 1 cherry in each indentation just before serving.

Sugared Maraschino Cherries and Mint Sprigs:

PREP: 45 MIN., STAND: 3 HR.

20 maraschino cherries with stems, rinsed and well drained
16 fresh mint sprigs, rinsed
1⅓ cups powdered sugar
1 Tbsp. meringue powder
½ cup sugar

1. Place cherries and mint on paper towels; let stand until dry.
2. Beat powdered sugar, ⅓ cup water, and meringue powder at medium speed with an electric mixer 2 to 3 minutes or until smooth and creamy.
3. Brush cherries and mint sprigs with meringue mixture, using a small paintbrush; sprinkle with ½ cup sugar, and place on a wire rack. Let stand 2 to 3 hours or until dry. **Makes** 20 cherries and 16 mint sprigs.

2002 Fresh Orange Italian Cream Cake

PREP: 45 MIN., BAKE: 25 MIN., CHILL: 8 HR.

Italian Cream Cake is irresistible any time of day, but the fresh citrus filling makes this the perfect surprise for a holiday brunch. You'll need to start this cake a day ahead because the cake and Fresh Orange Curd must both chill for 8 hours.

½ cup butter, softened
½ cup shortening
2 cups sugar
5 large eggs, separated
1 Tbsp. vanilla extract
2 cups all-purpose flour
1 tsp. baking soda
1 cup buttermilk
1 cup sweetened flaked coconut
Fresh Orange Curd
3 cups Pecan-Cream Cheese Frosting (following page)
½ cup sweetened flaked coconut, lightly toasted
Glazed Pecan Halves (following page)
Garnishes: sour cherry candy, orange rind curl
Glazed Tangerine Segments (following page)
Sugared Fruit Ribbons (following page)

1. Beat butter and shortening at medium speed with an electric mixer until fluffy; gradually add sugar, beating well. Add egg yolks, 1 at a time, beating until blended after each addition. Add vanilla; beat until blended.
2. Combine flour and baking soda; add to sugar mixture alternately with buttermilk, beginning and ending with flour mixture. Beat at low speed until blended after each addition. Stir in 1 cup flaked coconut.
3. Beat egg whites until stiff peaks form; fold into batter. Pour batter into 3 greased and floured 9-inch round cake pans.
4. Bake at 350° for 25 minutes or until a wooden pick inserted in center comes out clean. Cool in pans on wire racks 10 minutes; remove from pans, and cool completely on wire racks.
5. Spread ¾ cup chilled Fresh Orange Curd between layers; spread remaining Fresh Orange Curd on top of cake. (The Fresh Orange Curd layer on top of cake will be very thick.) Loosely cover cake; chill 8 hours. (Chilling the cake with the curd between layers keeps layers in place and makes it easier to spread the frosting.)
6. Spread 3 cups Pecan-Cream Cheese Frosting on sides of cake, reserving remaining frosting for another use. Sprinkle ½ cup toasted coconut over top of cake. Arrange Glazed Pecan Halves around top edge of cake. Store in refrigerator until ready to serve. Garnish, if desired. **Makes** 12 to 16 servings.

Note: Cake may be frosted with Pecan-Cream Cheese Frosting immediately after adding the Fresh Orange Curd, but the cake layers will not be as steady.

Fresh Orange Curd:

PREP: 20 MIN., COOK: 10 MIN., CHILL: 8 HR.

You can substitute refrigerated orange juice for fresh; however, squeezing navel oranges only takes about 15 minutes and makes all the difference in this cake's fresh flavor.

1 cup sugar
¼ cup cornstarch
2 cups fresh orange juice (about 4 lb. navel oranges)
3 large eggs, lightly beaten
¼ cup butter
1 Tbsp. grated orange rind

1. Combine sugar and cornstarch in a 3-qt. saucepan; gradually whisk in juice. Whisk in lightly beaten eggs. Bring to a boil over medium heat, whisking constantly. Cook, whisking constantly, 1 to 2 minutes or until mixture reaches a pudding-like thickness. Remove from heat; whisk in butter and orange rind. Cover, placing plastic wrap directly on curd; chill 8 hours. **Makes** about 3 cups.

Pecan-Cream Cheese Frosting:
PREP: 10 MIN.

1 (8-oz.) package cream cheese, softened
½ cup butter, softened
1 Tbsp. vanilla extract
1 (16-oz.) package powdered sugar
1 cup chopped pecans, toasted

1. Beat first 3 ingredients at medium speed with an electric mixer until creamy. Gradually add powdered sugar, beating at low speed until blended. Beat at high speed until smooth; stir in pecans. **Makes** about 4 cups.

Glazed Pecan Halves:
PREP: 5 MIN., BAKE: 20 MIN.

2 cups pecan halves
⅓ cup light corn syrup
Vegetable cooking spray

1. Combine pecan halves and corn syrup, stirring to coat pecans. Line a 15- x 10-inch jelly-roll pan with parchment paper or aluminum foil; coat with cooking spray. Arrange pecans in an even layer in pan.
2. Bake at 350° for 12 minutes; stir using a rubber spatula. Bake 8 more minutes. Remove from oven, and stir. Arrange in an even layer on wax paper; cool completely. **Makes** 2 cups.

Glazed Tangerine Segments: Separate a peeled tangerine into individual segments, and brush lightly with corn syrup to create the appearance of glazed fruit.

Sugared Fruit Ribbons: Create ribbons from strawberry-flavored chewy fruit rolls by the foot. (They come in a 4.5-oz. package. One roll will provide enough ribbon for the garland.) Unroll fruit roll, and remove paper backing. Using scissors, cut roll in half lengthwise to form 2 narrow ribbons. Brush both sides of each ribbon lightly with water, and sprinkle evenly with granulated sugar. Let stand 15 minutes on wire rack or until dry. Cut into desired lengths, and arrange as desired in the garland.

2004 Cream Cheese-Coconut-Pecan Pound Cake
PREP: 20 MIN.; BAKE: 1 HR., 35 MIN.
There really is nothing better than a good pound cake, and this is one of the best.

1½ cups butter, softened
1 (8-oz.) package cream cheese, softened
3 cups sugar
6 large eggs
3 cups all-purpose flour
½ tsp. salt
¼ cup bourbon
1½ tsp. vanilla extract
1 cup chopped toasted pecans
½ cup shredded coconut

1. Beat butter and cream cheese at medium speed with an electric mixer until creamy. Gradually add sugar, beating at medium speed until light and fluffy. Add eggs, 1 at a time, beating just until yellow disappears.
2. Sift together 3 cups flour and ½ tsp. salt; add to butter mixture alternately with bourbon, beginning and ending with flour mixture. Beat batter at low speed until blended after each addition. Stir in 1½ tsp. vanilla, toasted pecans, and shredded coconut. Pour

batter into a greased and floured 12-cup tube pan.
3. Bake at 325° for 1 hour and 30 minutes to 1 hour and 35 minutes or until a long wooden pick inserted in center of cake comes out clean. Cool in pan on a wire rack 10 to 15 minutes. Remove from pan, and cool completely on wire rack. **Makes** 10 to 12 servings.

Puttin' on the Glitz

Any flavor of pound cake that pairs well with coconut can be decorated like our Cream Cheese-Coconut-Pecan Pound Cake using these easy instructions:
• Place completely cooled pound cake on serving plate or cake stand; spoon Powdered Sugar Glaze (below) evenly over cake.
• Toss together ¾ cup each of coconut chips and sweetened flaked coconut, and sprinkle evenly over cake. Sprinkle coconut mixture with 2 Tbsp. white edible glitter.
• Arrange Sugared Rosemary, Sugared Cranberries (opposite page), and pecan halves around bottom edge of cake.
Note: Coconut chips can be found in the produce section of many supermarkets or ordered online ($4.99 for 8 oz.) from **www.kalustyans.com.**

Powdered Sugar Glaze: Stir together 2 cups powdered sugar, 3 Tbsp. milk, and 1 tsp. vanilla extract until smooth, adding another 1 Tbsp. milk, if necessary, for desired consistency. **Makes** about 1 cup.

Sugared Rosemary: Microwave ½ cup corn syrup at HIGH 10 seconds or until warm. Brush 10 to 12 rosemary sprigs lightly with corn syrup; sprinkle evenly with granulated sugar. Arrange in a single layer on wax paper. Use immediately, or let stand at room temperature, uncovered, for up to 24 hours.

Sugared Cranberries: Bring ½ cup sugar, ½ cup water, and 1 cup fresh cranberries to a boil in a small saucepan, stirring often, over medium-high heat. (Do not overcook; cranberries should swell and just begin to pop.) Remove from heat, and drain. Toss cranberries with ¼ cup granulated sugar, and arrange in a single layer on wax paper. Use immediately, or let stand at room temperature, uncovered, for 24 hours.

2005 Chocolate-Red Velvet Layer Cake

PREP: 30 MIN., BAKE: 20 MIN.
Both of these festive cakes get their inspiration from one easy-to-make sour cream cake batter.

1 recipe Chocolate-Red Velvet Cake
   Batter
1½ recipes Cream Cheese Frosting
Garnishes: fresh mint sprigs, raspberry
   candies

1. Spoon Chocolate-Red Velvet Cake Batter evenly into 6 greased and floured 8-inch round foil cake pans.
2. Bake at 350° for 18 to 20 minutes or until a wooden pick inserted in center comes out clean.
3. Cool in pans on wire racks 10 minutes; remove from pans, and cool completely on wire racks.
4. Spread Cream Cheese Frosting between layers and on top and sides of cake. Garnish, if desired. **Makes** 16 servings.

Note: We baked our cake layers in 6 (8-inch) disposable foil cake pans, so we could fill all the pans at once. This way, if you need to bake the cake layers in

batches, the second batch will be ready to put in the oven as soon as the first one is done. To allow the heat to circulate for even baking, space pans at least 2 inches apart from one another and away from the inside walls of the oven. Although the pans are disposable, they can be washed and reused.

Chocolate-Red Velvet Cake Batter:

PREP: 15 MIN.

1 cup butter, softened
2½ cups sugar
6 large eggs
3 cups all-purpose flour
3 Tbsp. unsweetened cocoa
¼ tsp. baking soda
1 (8-oz.) container sour cream
2 tsp. vanilla extract
2 (1-oz.) bottles red food coloring

1. Beat butter at medium speed with an electric mixer until creamy. Gradually add sugar, beating until light and fluffy. Add eggs, 1 at a time, beating just until blended after each addition.
2. Stir together flour, cocoa, and baking soda. Add to butter mixture alternately with sour cream, beginning and ending with flour mixture. Beat at low speed until blended after each addition. Stir in vanilla and red food coloring. Use batter immediately. **Makes** about 7 cups.

Cream Cheese Frosting:

PREP: 15 MIN.

2 (8-oz.) packages cream cheese,
   softened
½ cup butter, softened
2 (16-oz.) packages powdered sugar
2 tsp. vanilla extract

1. Beat cream cheese and butter at medium speed with an electric mixer until creamy. Gradually add powdered sugar, beating until light and fluffy. Stir in 2 tsp. vanilla. **Makes** about 5 cups.

Fluted Chocolate-Red Velvet Cakes

PREP: 30 MIN., BAKE: 50 MIN.

1 recipe Chocolate-Red Velvet Cake
   Batter
1 recipe Vanilla Glaze
Garnishes: fresh mint sprigs, raspberry
   candies

1. Spoon Chocolate-Red Velvet Cake Batter evenly into 3 greased and floured 8-inch brioche pans.
2. Bake at 325° for 50 minutes or until a wooden pick inserted in center comes out clean.
3. Cool in pans on wire racks 10 minutes; remove from pans, and cool completely on wire racks.
4. Spoon Vanilla Glaze evenly over top of cakes. Garnish, if desired. **Makes** 3 cakes.

Vanilla Glaze: Stir together 1 (16-oz.) package powdered sugar, 5 Tbsp. milk, and 2 tsp. vanilla extract just until powdered sugar is moistened and mixture is smooth. Add an additional 1 Tbsp. milk, if necessary, for desired consistency. Use immediately.

Note: We kept this glaze very thick so it wouldn't drip all the way down the sides of the Fluted Chocolate-Red Velvet Cakes, but feel free to make it a little thinner if you'd like to drizzle it over other cakes.

Praline-Pecan Cakes

PREP: 30 MIN., BAKE: 35 MIN.

4 cups finely chopped Praline
    Pecans
1 recipe Sour Cream-Pecan Cake
    Batter

1. Sprinkle chopped Praline Pecans evenly into 9 buttered 5- x 3-inch disposable foil loaf pans; shake to coat bottoms and sides of pans. Spoon Sour Cream-Pecan Cake Batter evenly into prepared pans (a little less than 1 cup batter per pan).
2. Bake at 325° for 28 to 35 minutes or until a wooden pick inserted in center comes out clean. Cool in pans on wire racks 15 minutes; remove from pans, and cool completely on wire racks. **Makes** 9 (5-inch) loaves.

Praline Pecans:

PREP: 5 MIN., COOK: 15 MIN., STAND: 20 MIN.
Pralines are best made when the weather is dry; humidity tends to make them grainy. Be sure to use a heavy saucepan in this recipe, and work quickly when spooning the pecan mixture onto the wax paper.

1½ cups granulated sugar
¾ cup firmly packed brown sugar
½ cup butter
½ cup milk
2 Tbsp. corn syrup
5 cups pecan halves, toasted

1. Stir together 1½ cups granulated sugar and next 4 ingredients in a heavy 3-qt. saucepan. Bring to a boil over medium heat, stirring constantly. Boil, stirring constantly, 7 to 8 minutes or until a candy thermometer registers 234°.
2. Remove from heat, and vigorously stir in pecans. Spoon pecan mixture onto wax paper, spreading in an even layer. Let stand 20 minutes or until firm. Break praline-coated pecans apart into pieces. Store in an airtight container at room temperature up to 1 week. Freeze in an airtight container or zip-top plastic freezer bag up to 1 month. **Makes** about 8 cups.

Sour Cream-Pecan Cake Batter:

PREP: 15 MIN.

1 cup butter, softened
1¼ cups firmly packed brown
    sugar
1¼ cups granulated sugar
6 large eggs
3 cups all-purpose flour
¼ tsp. baking soda
1 (8-oz.) container sour cream
2 tsp. vanilla extract
1½ cups pecans, chopped and toasted

1. Beat butter at medium speed with an electric mixer until creamy. Gradually add sugars, beating until light and fluffy. Add eggs, 1 at a time, beating just until blended after each addition. Stir together flour and baking soda. Add to butter mixture alternately with sour cream, beginning and ending with flour mixture. Beat at low speed until blended after each addition. Stir in vanilla and pecans. Use batter immediately. **Makes** about 7 cups.

2006 Lemon-Coconut Cake

PREP: 30 MIN., BAKE: 20 MIN.
With our 2006 cake, we circle back around to 1995, the year the "big white cake" all began. We couldn't resist updating the original version (see page 249) with a cream cheese frosting.

1 cup butter, softened
2 cups sugar
4 large eggs, separated
3 cups all-purpose flour
1 Tbsp. baking powder
1 cup milk
1 tsp. vanilla extract
Lemon Filling
Cream Cheese Frosting
2 cups sweetened flaked coconut
Garnishes: fresh rosemary sprigs,
    gumdrops

1. Beat butter at medium speed with an electric mixer until fluffy; gradually add sugar, beating well. Add egg yolks, 1 at a time, beating until blended after each addition.
2. Combine flour and baking powder; add to butter mixture alternately with milk, beginning and ending with flour mixture. Beat at low speed until blended after each addition. Stir in vanilla.
3. Beat egg whites at high speed with electric mixer until stiff peaks form; fold one-third of egg whites into batter. Gently fold in remaining beaten egg whites just until blended. Spoon batter into 3 greased and floured 9-inch round cake pans.
4. Bake at 350° for 18 to 20 minutes or until a wooden pick inserted in center comes out clean. Cool in pans on wire racks 10 minutes; remove from pans, and cool completely on wire racks.
5. Spread Lemon Filling between layers. Spread Cream Cheese Frosting on top and sides of cake. Sprinkle top and sides with coconut. Garnish, if desired. **Makes** 12 servings.

Lemon Filling:

PREP: 10 MIN., COOK: 5 MIN.

1 cup sugar
¼ cup cornstarch
1 cup boiling water
4 egg yolks, lightly beaten
2 tsp. grated lemon rind
⅓ cup fresh lemon juice
2 Tbsp. butter

1. Combine sugar and cornstarch in a medium saucepan; whisk in 1 cup boiling water. Cook over medium heat, whisking constantly, until sugar and cornstarch dissolve (about 2 minutes). Gradually whisk about one-fourth of hot sugar mixture into egg yolks; add to remaining hot sugar mixture in pan, whisking constantly. Whisk in lemon rind and juice.
2. Cook, whisking constantly, until mixture is thickened (about 2 to 3 minutes). Remove from heat. Whisk in butter; let cool completely, stirring occasionally. **Makes** about 1⅔ cups.

Cream Cheese Frosting:
PREP: 10 MIN.

½ cup butter, softened
1 (8-oz.) package cream cheese,
    softened
1 (16-oz.) package powdered sugar
1 tsp. vanilla extract

1. Beat butter and cream cheese at medium speed with an electric mixer until creamy. Gradually add powdered sugar, beating at low speed until blended; stir in vanilla. **Makes** about 3 cups.

Get Ready to Celebrate!

Cooking and hosting guests can be one of the great joys of the season. We gathered some of our great party recipes plus some of our best ideas and other reminders and practical hints that we couldn't resist sharing with you. Let this be your guide to your most memorable holiday ever.

Smart Planning

Involve your family in the fun of preparing for a party. For big gatherings, shop two weeks before the event for nonperishable and frozen items. Keep ingredients all together in bags in one area of your pantry or freezer, instead of storing them with your everyday items. Shop three to five days ahead for perishables, and try to keep the day-before-the-party shopping list to fewer than 10 items.

Greet your guests with a signature drink

Cranberry-rosemary stir sticks are fun garnishes for Frozen Cranberry Margaritos, iced tea, or water. Choose hearty 6-inch-long rosemary sprigs; remove leaves from bottom 4 inches, and use for cooking. Thread cranberries on the rosemary stem. Offer tie-on gift tags as wine charms to mark each person's glass.

Frozen Cranberry Margaritos
fast fixin's
PREP: 5 MIN.
A mojito traditionally uses rum; here we use tequila instead, hence the fun title. Dip rims of glasses in lime juice and a mixture of equal parts kosher salt and sugar for a twist on salt-rimmed glasses.

1 (10-oz.) can frozen mojito mix
¾ cup tequila
¼ cup whole-berry cranberry sauce
2 Tbsp. orange liqueur
2 Tbsp. fresh lime juice
Ice

1. Combine first 5 ingredients in a blender. Fill blender with ice to 5-cup level, and process until smooth. Serve immediately. **Makes** 5 cups.

Note: For testing purposes only, we used Triple Sec for orange liqueur.

Southern Shrimp Cocktails
fast fixin's
PREP: 15 MIN.
Have the seafood market steam shrimp to save time, or follow our easy instructions at right. Serve the shrimp, okra, and breadsticks on a platter around a bowl of the sauce, or make individual cocktails. Use 4-oz. votive candleholders, shot glasses, cordial glasses, or mini-martini glasses.

12 unpeeled, jumbo cooked shrimp
Rémoulade Sauce
12 whole pickled okra
12 very thin crispy breadsticks, broken
    in half
Garnish: grape tomato slices

1. Peel shrimp, leaving tails on; devein, if desired.
2. Spoon 1 heaping Tbsp. of Rémoulade Sauce evenly into each of 12 individual serving glasses. Place 1 shrimp, 1 whole pickled okra, and 2 breadstick halves in each glass. Garnish, if desired. Serve immediately. **Makes** 12 servings.

Note: To cook shrimp at home, bring 3 qt. water to a boil in a large Dutch oven. Cut 2 lemons in half, and squeeze juice into boiling water; add squeezed lemon halves to water. Add 1 tsp. pepper, 1 tsp. salt, and 2 bay leaves. Return to a boil over medium-high heat. Add 1 to 2 lb. unpeeled, jumbo raw shrimp, and cook 3 minutes or just until shrimp turn pink; drain. Plunge shrimp into ice water to stop the cooking process; drain. Cover and chill.

Rémoulade Sauce:
make ahead
PREP: 10 MIN., CHILL: 1 HR.
You can make this sauce three days ahead.

1½ cups mayonnaise
4 green onions, sliced
3 Tbsp. chopped fresh parsley
3 Tbsp. Creole mustard
1½ Tbsp. lemon juice
1 garlic clove, pressed
1½ tsp. horseradish
1 tsp. paprika

1. Stir together all ingredients; cover and chill 1 hour. **Makes** 2 cups.

Start the Party With Style

Don't eat Ham-and-Cheese Skewers a piece at a time. Enjoy all the pieces at once to fully experience the smoky-sweet flavor and creamy-crisp texture of these appetizers. Ask a guest or two to serve, or place on a coffee or sofa table.

Stash a few recipes of Hot Roast Beef Party Sandwiches in the freezer for tree-trimming nibbles, unexpected guests, or an open house. Max freezing time is one month, so stock the freezer early in November for Thanksgiving entertaining and early in December for Christmas and New Year's parties.

Hot Roast Beef Party Sandwiches

freezeable • make ahead

PREP: 20 MIN., COOK: 6 MIN., BAKE: 25 MIN.

This is an updated version of a recipe that used ham, cheese, and mustard. Eyes lit up at our tasting table when these came out of the oven.

½ cup finely chopped walnuts
2 (9.25-oz.) packages dinner rolls
⅔ cup peach preserves
½ cup mustard-mayonnaise blend
¾ lb. thinly sliced deli roast beef, chopped
½ lb. thinly sliced Havarti cheese
Salt and pepper to taste (optional)

1. Heat walnuts in a small nonstick skillet over medium-low heat, stirring occasionally, 5 to 6 minutes or until lightly toasted.
2. Remove rolls from packages. (Do not separate rolls.) Cut rolls in half horizontally, creating 1 top and 1 bottom per package. Spread preserves on cut sides of top of rolls; sprinkle with walnuts. Spread mustard-mayonnaise blend on cut sides of bottom of rolls; top with beef and cheese. Sprinkle with salt and pepper to taste, if desired. Cover with top halves of rolls, preserves sides down, and wrap in aluminum foil.
3. Bake at 325° for 20 to 25 minutes or until cheese is melted. Slice into

individual sandwiches. **Makes** 12 to 16 servings.

Note: To make ahead, prepare recipe as directed through Step 2, and freeze up to 1 month. Thaw overnight in refrigerator, and bake as directed in Step 3. For testing purposes only, we used Rainbo Dinner Time Rolls, Hellmann's Dijonnaise Mustard, and Boar's Head Londonport Top Round Seasoned Roast Beef.

Ham-and-Cheese Skewers

fast fixin's • make ahead

PREP: 25 MIN.

Assemble up to one hour ahead, cover with damp paper towels, and chill. Serve coarse-grain mustard or chutney alongside the skewers.

½ lb. (¾-inch-thick) sliced smoked Virginia deli ham
1 (5-oz.) blue cheese wedge
1 large Gala apple, sliced
1 bunch fresh watercress
60 (4-inch) wood or metal skewers

1. Cut ham into ¾-inch cubes. Carefully break cheese into 60 small pieces. Cut apple slices into thirds.
2. Thread cheese, apple, watercress leaves, and ham onto skewers. Stand skewers upright, ham ends down, on a serving plate. **Makes** about 60 skewers.

Bubbly on a Budget

Take time to toast the season. Good quality sparkling wines are available for less than $15. Executive Editor and wine expert Scott Jones recommends the following.
■ Blanc de Blancs, Domaine Ste. Michelle, Washington
■ Brut, Reserva, Cava Jaume Serra, Spain
■ Prosecco di Valdobbiadene, Mionetto, Italy

Gather for Sweets

When you pick one theme, it's easy to entertain. In our dining room, we whipped up a dessert party with cookies, dip, and fruit. That's right—no silverware required. If your table looks a little lonely once the chairs are pulled away, just slide a few back in place. Fill space under the table with a large poinsettia.

Brandy-Vanilla Cheesecake Dip

fast fixin's • make ahead

PREP: 5 MIN.

Refrigerated cheesecake filling is sold in a tub near the cream cheese. It is fully cooked and ready to use. Serve this incredibly easy but equally impressive dessert dip with sliced pears, apricots, cherries, strawberries, and assorted cookies.

1 (24.2-oz.) container ready-to-eat cheesecake filling
5 Tbsp. brandy
1 tsp. vanilla extract

1. Stir together all ingredients. Cover and chill until ready to serve. **Makes** 3 cups.

Note: For testing purposes only, we used Philadelphia Ready-To-Eat Cheesecake Filling.

Orange Cheesecake Dip: Prepare recipe as directed, substituting ¼ cup orange marmalade, melted, and 2 tsp. grated orange rind for brandy and vanilla.

Rum-Almond Cheesecake Dip: Prepare recipe as directed, substituting 3 to 5 tsp. spiced rum and ½ tsp. almond extract for brandy and vanilla.

november

Fresh Flavors for Thanksgiving

Whether you're a novice or a pro, you'll breeze through this menu of updated favorites.

You can take the girl out of the South, but you can't take the South out of the girl. Just ask Tennessee-born Lauren Wilson, who moved her Memphis roots to San Jose, California, with husband Brian. "I brought my love of entertaining to the West Coast," says Lauren. "Needless to say, we made instant friends by inviting neighbors over for some home cooking."

Ever since, the Wilsons have entertained their California cronies with casseroles, pies, you name it—and the holidays are no exception. Lauren updated some of her family recipes. Mix-and-match your family favorites with some of these wonderful dishes.

Bourbon-Cranberry Turkey Tenderloin

PREP: 15 MIN.; COOK: 15 MIN.;
STAND: 1 HR., 15 MIN.; GRILL: 24 MIN.
Throw some orange slices on the grill for a colorful accompaniment. (Pictured on page 188)

1 (16-oz.) can whole-berry cranberry sauce
⅓ cup firmly packed brown sugar
⅔ cup bourbon
2 Tbsp. grated orange rind
4 lb. turkey tenderloins
1½ tsp. salt
1 Tbsp. coarsely ground pepper
Garnish: grilled orange slices

1. Bring first 4 ingredients to a boil in a saucepan over medium-high heat; reduce heat to medium-low, and simmer 10 minutes or until mixture thickens slightly. Remove from heat, and let stand 30 minutes or to room temperature. Remove ½ cup cranberry mixture; reserve remaining mixture.
2. Rinse tenderloins, and pat dry with paper towels. Brush with ¼ cup cranberry mixture, and let stand at room temperature 30 minutes. Sprinkle with salt and pepper.
3. Grill over medium-high heat (350° to 400°) 10 to 12 minutes on each side or until a meat thermometer inserted in thickest portion registers 165°, basting occasionally with ¼ cup cranberry mixture. Remove from heat, and let stand 15 minutes before slicing. Serve with reserved cranberry mixture. Garnish, if desired. **Makes** 8 to 10 servings.

LAUREN WILSON
SAN JOSE, CALIFORNIA

Bourbon-Cranberry Roasted Turkey: Substitute 1 (14-lb.) whole fresh turkey for tenderloins. Remove giblets and neck, and rinse turkey with cold water. Drain cavity well; pat dry. Let turkey stand at room temperature 30 minutes. Meanwhile, prepare cranberry mixture as directed in Step 1. Place turkey, breast side up, on a lightly greased wire rack in a roasting pan. If desired, tie ends of legs together with kitchen string; tuck wing tips under. Brush with 2 Tbsp. melted butter, and sprinkle with salt and pepper. Bake at 325° for 3½ hours or until meat thermometer inserted in thickest portion of thigh registers 170°, brushing with ½ cup cranberry mixture during the last 30 minutes of roasting. (If turkey starts to brown too much, cover loosely with aluminum foil.) Let turkey stand 15 minutes before carving. Serve with reserved cranberry mixture. **Makes** 8 to 10 servings. Prep: 20 min.; Cook: 15 min.; Stand: 1 hr., 15 min.; Bake: 3 hr., 30 min.

Sweet-and-Sour Green Beans

PREP: 30 MIN., COOK: 22 MIN.
We loved the finely chopped look of this dish. (Pictured on page 189)

2 lb. fresh green beans, trimmed
6 bacon slices, chopped
½ cup sugar
½ cup red wine vinegar

1. Cook beans in boiling salted water to cover 9 minutes or until crisp-tender; drain. Plunge into salted ice water to stop the cooking process; drain. Cut beans into ⅛- to 1-inch-long pieces.
2. Cook bacon in a large skillet over medium-high heat 5 to 6 minutes or until crisp; remove bacon, and drain on paper towels, reserving 1 Tbsp. drippings in skillet. Stir in sugar and vinegar; cook, stirring occasionally, 5 minutes or until sugar dissolves.
3. Add beans and bacon to skillet, tossing to coat; cook 2 minutes or until thoroughly heated. **Makes** 8 servings.

DANNIE LORENTZ
MEMPHIS, TENNESSEE

Lemon Rice

PREP: 10 MIN., COOK: 25 MIN.

We used basmati rice for its fine texture, but you can use long-grain rice if you wish.

1 garlic clove
2 cups chicken broth
2 Tbsp. butter
½ tsp. salt
1 cup basmati rice
1 Tbsp. grated lemon rind

1. Slightly smash garlic clove using flat side of a knife. Stir together garlic, broth, butter, and salt in a large saucepan; bring to a boil over high heat. Stir in rice; reduce heat to low, and cook, covered, 20 minutes or until broth mixture is absorbed and rice is tender.
2. Remove and discard garlic; stir in lemon rind using a fork. **Makes** 8 servings.

LORA KRUG
BARRINGTON HILLS, ILLINOIS

Lemon-Dill Rice: Proceed with recipe as directed, stirring 1 tsp. dried dill into cooked rice with lemon rind.

Thanksgiving Sparkler

PREP: 5 MIN., COOK: 25 MIN , COOL: 30 MIN.

2 cups sugar
2 Tbsp. mulling spices
Chilled sparkling wine, sparkling water, or club soda

1. Stir together sugar, spices, and 1 cup water in a large saucepan; bring to a boil over medium-high heat. Reduce heat to low, and simmer 20 minutes. Remove from heat, and let cool 30 minutes or until completely cool. Pour through a wire-mesh strainer into a bowl; discard spices.
2. Stir 1 to 2 Tbsp. spiced syrup into a glass of sparkling wine, sparkling water, or club soda. Repeat procedure with remaining syrup. **Makes** 1½ cups.

LAUREN WILSON
SAN JOSE, CALIFORNIA

Offer a No-Fuss Appetizer

A fruit-and-cheese platter is about as easy as it gets. Purchase favorite cheeses, preserves, dried fruits, breads, and crackers, and arrange them on a serving tray or cutting board. Complete your presentation by adding roasted garlic—it spreads well and melts in your mouth. Follow these simple steps for roasting garlic.

1. Cut off pointed end of desired number of garlic bulbs; place bulbs on a piece of aluminum foil, and drizzle with olive oil. Fold foil to seal.
2. Bake at 425° for 30 minutes; let cool.

Pour on the Flavor

It's time for turkey gravy, and we have two recipes sure to accommodate. One calls for pan drippings and one doesn't, so use the one that works with your menu.

Roasted Turkey Gravy

fast fixin's

PREP: 5 MIN., COOK: 12 MIN.

¼ cup butter
¼ cup all-purpose flour
2½ cups chicken broth
½ cup pan drippings
¼ tsp. poultry seasoning
⅛ tsp. freshly ground pepper

1. Melt butter in a large skillet over medium heat; whisk in flour, and cook, whisking constantly, 1 to 2 minutes or until golden and smooth. Gradually whisk in chicken broth and pan drippings; increase heat to medium-high, and bring to a boil. Reduce heat to medium, and simmer, stirring occasionally, 5 minutes or to desired thickness. Stir in remaining ingredients. **Makes** about 3 cups.

Anytime Turkey Gravy

PREP: 15 MIN.; COOK: 1 HR., 20 MIN.

No roasted turkey drippings? No problem. This gravy uses canned chicken broth that's doctored up for flavor similar to pan drippings.

2½ lb. dark meat turkey pieces (wings and necks)
2 Tbsp. vegetable oil
1 medium onion, chopped
2 celery ribs, chopped
1 (49.5-oz.) can chicken broth
½ cup chopped fresh parsley
⅓ cup butter
⅓ cup all-purpose flour
½ tsp. freshly ground pepper
½ tsp. poultry seasoning
¼ tsp. rubbed sage

1. Cook turkey pieces in hot oil in a Dutch oven over medium-high heat 6 to 8 minutes on each side or until lightly browned. Add onion and celery, and sauté 4 minutes. Gradually stir in chicken broth, stirring to loosen particles from bottom of skillet; stir in parsley. Bring to a boil; cover, reduce heat to medium-low, and simmer, stirring occasionally, 30 minutes. Pour mixture through a wire-mesh strainer into a large bowl, discarding solids.
2. Melt butter in Dutch oven over medium heat; whisk in flour, and cook, whisking constantly, 1 to 2 minutes or until mixture is golden and smooth. Gradually whisk in broth mixture; increase heat to medium-high, and bring to a boil. Reduce heat to medium, and simmer, stirring occasionally, 15 to 20 minutes or to desired thickness. Stir in remaining ingredients. **Makes** about 2½ cups.

5 Sensational Takes on Pecan Pie

This Southern favorite never tasted so good.

The hardest part of making these desserts will be deciding which one to try first. They all won rave reviews at our tasting table, but the fresh combination of texture and flavor found in Caramel-Pecan Tart created the biggest sensation. If you don't have a tart pan handy, you can still make a grand presentation using an aluminum foil-lined baking pan.

Chocolate-Bourbon-Pecan Pie

PREP: 15 MIN., BAKE: 55 MIN., COOL: 1 HR.

½ (15-oz.) package refrigerated
  piecrusts
4 large eggs
1 cup light corn syrup
6 Tbsp. butter, melted
½ cup sugar
¼ cup firmly packed light brown sugar
3 Tbsp. bourbon
1 Tbsp. all-purpose flour
1 Tbsp. vanilla extract
1 cup coarsely chopped pecans
1 cup semisweet chocolate morsels

1. Fit piecrust into a 9-inch pie plate according to package directions. Fold edges under, and crimp.
2. Whisk together eggs and next 7 ingredients until thoroughly blended. Stir in pecans and morsels. Pour mixture into piecrust; place pie on a baking sheet.
3. Bake at 350° on lowest oven rack 55 minutes or until set. Cool on a wire rack 1 hour or until completely cool. **Makes** 8 servings.

Caramel-Pecan Tart

PREP: 20 MIN., BAKE: 57 MIN., COOL: 1 HR.,
COOK: 5 MIN.
This tart pairs the cookie-like crispness of shortbread with a buttery-rich brown sugar - and-honey topping. (Pictured on page 9)

3½ cups coarsely chopped pecans
2 cups all-purpose flour
⅔ cup powdered sugar
¾ cup butter, cubed
½ cup firmly packed brown sugar
½ cup honey
⅔ cup butter
3 Tbsp. whipping cream

1. Arrange pecans in a single layer on a baking sheet. Bake at 350° for 5 to 7 minutes or until lightly toasted. Cool on a wire rack 15 minutes or until completely cool.
2. Pulse flour, powdered sugar, and ¾ cup butter in a food processor 5 to 6 times or until mixture resembles coarse meal. Pat mixture evenly on bottom and up sides of a lightly greased 11-inch tart pan with removable bottom.
3. Bake at 350° for 20 minutes or until edges are lightly browned. Cool on a wire rack 15 minutes or until completely cool.
4. Bring brown sugar, honey, ⅔ cup butter, and whipping cream to a boil in a 3-qt. saucepan over medium-high heat. Stir in toasted pecans, and spoon hot filling into prepared crust.
5. Bake at 350° for 25 to 30 minutes or until golden and bubbly. Cool on a wire rack 30 minutes or until completely cool. **Makes** 12 servings.

Caramel-Pecan Bars: Prepare Caramel-Pecan Tart recipe as directed, pressing crumb mixture evenly on bottom and ¾ inch up sides of a lightly greased heavy-duty aluminum foil-lined 13- x 9-inch pan. When completely cool, using the aluminum foil as handles, carefully lift the tart from the pan, and transfer to a serving tray. Cut into bars.

German Chocolate-Pecan Pie

PREP: 15 MIN., BAKE: 50 MIN., COOL: 1 HR.

½ (15-oz.) package refrigerated
  piecrusts
3 large eggs
¾ cup sugar
¾ cup dark corn syrup
¼ cup butter, melted
1 Tbsp. cocoa
1 tsp. vanilla extract
⅛ tsp. salt
2 cups coarsely chopped pecans
½ cup sweetened flaked coconut

1. Fit piecrust into a 9-inch pie plate according to package directions. Fold edges under, and crimp.
2. Whisk together eggs and next 6 ingredients until thoroughly blended. Stir in pecans and coconut. Pour mixture into piecrust; place pie on a baking sheet.
3. Bake at 350° on lowest oven rack 50 minutes or until pie is set. Cool on a wire rack 1 hour or until completely cool. **Makes** 8 servings.

Pecan Tassies

PREP: 45 MIN., CHILL: 1 HR.,
BAKE: 20 MIN., COOL: 30 MIN.
If you don't have four mini muffin pans, you can bake these in batches. Keep the extra dough chilled until you're ready to use it.

1 cup butter, softened
1 (8-oz.) package cream cheese, softened
2½ cups all-purpose flour
1½ cups firmly packed brown sugar
1½ cups chopped pecans
2 large eggs
2 Tbsp. butter, melted
2 tsp. vanilla extract
⅛ tsp. salt

1. Beat 1 cup butter and cream cheese at medium speed with an electric mixer until creamy. Gradually add flour to butter mixture, beating at low speed. Shape mixture into 48 balls, and place on a baking sheet; cover and chill 1 hour.

2. Place 1 dough ball into each lightly greased muffin cup in mini muffin pans, shaping each into a shell.

3. Whisk together brown sugar and next 5 ingredients. Spoon into tart shells.

4. Bake at 350° for 20 minutes or until filling is set. Cool in pans on wire racks 10 minutes. Remove from pans; cool on wire racks 20 minutes or until completely cool. **Makes** 4 dozen.

Pecan Cheesecake Pie
make ahead

PREP: 15 MIN., BAKE: 55 MIN., COOL: 1 HR.
This pie starts with a creamy bottom layer of batter that rises to the top of the crust during baking. (Pictured on page 2 and page 10)

⅓ (15-oz.) package refrigerated
   piecrusts
1 (8-oz.) package cream cheese,
   softened
4 large eggs, divided
¾ cup sugar, divided
2 tsp. vanilla extract, divided
¼ tsp. salt
1¼ cups chopped pecans
1 cup light corn syrup

1. Fit piecrust into a 9-inch pie plate according to package directions. Fold edges under, and crimp.

2. Beat cream cheese, 1 egg, ½ cup sugar, 1 tsp. vanilla, and salt at medium speed with an electric mixer until smooth. Pour cream cheese mixture into piecrust; sprinkle evenly with chopped pecans.

3. Whisk together corn syrup, remaining 3 eggs, ¼ cup sugar, and 1 tsp. vanilla; pour mixture over pecans. Place pie on a baking sheet.

4. Bake at 350° on lowest oven rack 50 to 55 minutes or until pie is set. Cool on a wire rack 1 hour or until completely cool. Serve immediately, or cover and chill up to 2 days. **Makes** 8 servings.

Our Best Buttermilk Biscuits

The trick to these biscuits is in the unique dough-folding method, the same one used to make puff pastries and croissants. Folding creates multiple layers of dough and fat, giving rise to a tender, puffy biscuit.

Buttermilk Biscuits

PREP: 20 MIN., CHILL: 10 MIN., BAKE: 15 MIN.
(Pictured on page 10)

½ cup cold butter
2¼ cups self-rising soft-wheat flour
1¼ cups buttermilk
Self-rising soft-wheat flour
2 Tbsp. melted butter

1. Cut butter with a sharp knife or pastry blender into ¼-inch-thick slices. Sprinkle butter slices over flour in a large bowl. Toss butter with flour. Cut butter into flour with a pastry blender until crumbly and mixture resembles small peas. Cover and chill 10 minutes. Add buttermilk, stirring just until dry ingredients are moistened.

2. Turn dough out onto a lightly floured surface; knead 3 or 4 times, gradually adding additional flour as needed. With floured hands, press or pat dough into a ¾-inch-thick rectangle (about 9 x 5 inches). Sprinkle top of dough with additional flour. Fold dough over onto itself in 3 sections, starting with 1 short end. (Fold dough rectangle as if folding a letter-size piece of paper.) Repeat entire process 2 more times, beginning with pressing into a ¾-inch-thick dough rectangle (about 9 x 5 inches).

3. Press or pat dough to ½-inch thickness on a lightly floured surface; cut with a 2-inch round cutter, and place, side by side, on a parchment paper-lined or lightly greased jelly-roll pan. (Dough rounds should touch.)

4. Bake at 450° for 13 to 15 minutes or until lightly browned. Remove from oven; brush with 2 Tbsp. melted butter. **Makes** 2 dozen.

Note: For testing purposes only, we used White Lily Self-Rising Soft Wheat Flour.

Divinely Delicious

These variations are simple to make and all received our Test Kitchens' highest rating.

Cinnamon-Raisin Biscuits: Omit 2 Tbsp. melted butter. Combine ½ cup golden raisins, ½ tsp. ground cinnamon, and ⅓ cup chopped pecans with flour in a large bowl. Proceed with recipe as directed. Stir together ½ cup powdered sugar and 2 Tbsp. buttermilk until smooth. Drizzle over warm biscuits. **Makes** 2½ dozen.

Black Pepper-Bacon Biscuits: Combine ⅓ cup cooked and crumbled bacon slices (about 5 slices) and 1 tsp. black pepper with flour in a large bowl. Proceed with recipe as directed. **Makes** 2½ dozen.

Feta-Oregano Biscuits: Combine 1 (4-oz.) package crumbled feta cheese and ½ tsp. dried oregano with flour in a large bowl. Proceed with recipe as directed. **Makes** 2½ dozen.

Pimiento Cheese Biscuits: Combine 1 cup (4 oz.) shredded sharp Cheddar cheese with flour in a large bowl. Reduce buttermilk to 1 cup. Stir together buttermilk and 1 (4-oz.) jar diced pimiento, undrained. Proceed with recipe as directed. **Makes** 2½ dozen.

30-Minute Meals

These recipes get us through the busy season. We bet you'll make them as often as we do.

Start supper with this collection of speedy recipes from *Southern Living* staffers. Associate Foods Editor Vicki Poellnitz sent one quick e-mail to her colleagues, and the ideas poured in immediately. They prepare these time-tested favorites for family and friends all the time, so passing along ingredients and techniques is almost second nature. We consider you family, so we're sharing these scrumptious offerings in hopes you'll make them over and over again, too.

Black Bean Chili

fast fixin's

PREP: 10 MIN., COOK: 20 MIN.

3 (15-oz.) cans black beans
1 large sweet onion, chopped
1 (12-oz.) package meatless burger crumbles
2 Tbsp. vegetable oil
4 tsp. chili powder
1 tsp. ground cumin
½ tsp. pepper
¼ tsp. salt
1 (14-oz.) can low-sodium fat-free chicken broth
2 (14.5-oz.) cans petite diced tomatoes with jalapeños
Toppings: sour cream, shredded Cheddar cheese, lime wedges, sliced jalapeño peppers, chopped fresh cilantro, chopped tomatoes, corn chips

1. Rinse and drain 2 cans black beans. (Do not drain third can.)
2. Sauté chopped onion and burger crumbles in hot oil in a large Dutch oven over medium heat 6 minutes.

Stir in chili powder and next 3 ingredients; sauté 1 minute. Stir in drained and undrained beans, chicken broth, and diced tomatoes. Bring to a boil over medium-high heat; cover, reduce heat to low, and simmer 10 minutes. Serve chili with desired toppings. **Makes** 8 servings.

Note: For testing purposes only, we used Boca Meatless Ground Burger for meatless burger crumbles.

Meaty Black Bean Chili: Substitute 1 lb. ground round for meatless burger crumbles, sautéing ground round with onion 10 minutes or until meat is no longer pink. Omit vegetable oil. Proceed as directed.

KATE NICHOLSON
BIRMINGHAM, ALABAMA

Pan-Seared Flat Iron Steak

fast fixin's

PREP: 5 MIN., COOK: 10 MIN., STAND: 5 MIN.

The trick to a great crust is to use a very hot skillet; a large cast-iron or heavy stainless steel skillet works best. Have your hood fan on high—there will be some smoke. If you can't find flat iron steak in your local market, a top blade chuck or sirloin steak will work just fine. (Pictured on page 187)

1 (1-lb.) flat iron steak
2 tsp. Montreal steak seasoning
¼ tsp. kosher salt
1 Tbsp. vegetable oil

1. Rub steak evenly with steak seasoning and salt.

2. Cook in hot oil in a large skillet over medium-high heat 4 to 5 minutes on each side or to desired degree of doneness. Let stand 5 minutes. Cut diagonally across the grain into thin strips. **Makes** 4 servings.

MARIAN COOPER CAIRNS
BIRMINGHAM, ALABAMA

Note: For testing purposes only, we used McCormick Grill Mates Montreal Steak Seasoning.

Porcini Mushroom Tortelloni With Wilted Greens

PREP: 15 MIN., COOK: 17 MIN.
(Pictured on page 186)

1 (8-oz.) package porcini mushroom tortelloni
4 bacon slices, chopped
1 small onion, chopped
1 garlic clove, minced
¼ cup dry white wine
1 to 2 Tbsp. balsamic vinegar
½ cup chicken broth
½ cup frozen peas
2 plum tomatoes, chopped
½ (5.5-oz.) package baby spinach-and-spring greens mix, thoroughly washed
½ cup freshly shaved Parmesan cheese

1. Prepare tortelloni according to package directions. Keep warm.
2. Meanwhile, cook bacon in a large skillet over medium-high heat 6 to 8 minutes or until crisp; remove bacon, reserving 2 Tbsp. drippings in skillet. Add onion, and sauté 3 minutes or until tender. Stir in garlic, and sauté 1 minute. Stir in wine and vinegar, and cook 2 minutes, stirring to loosen particles from bottom of skillet.
3. Stir in chicken broth, peas, tomatoes, and tortelloni, and cook 2 to 3 minutes or until thoroughly heated. Serve over salad greens, and sprinkle evenly with Parmesan cheese. **Makes** 4 servings.

MARIAN COOPER CAIRNS
BIRMINGHAM, ALABAMA

Note: For testing purposes only, we used Barilla Porcini Mushroom Tortelloni and Fresh Express 50/50 Mix.

Bourbon-Marinated Salmon

fast fixin's

PREP: 10 MIN., STAND: 10 MIN.,
BROIL: 10 MIN.

¼ cup firmly packed brown sugar
¼ cup bourbon
¼ cup spicy brown mustard
1 tsp. ground chipotle chile
    pepper
4 (6-oz.) salmon fillets
½ tsp. salt
¼ tsp. pepper

1. Stir together first 4 ingredients in a shallow dish. Add salmon, gently turning to coat, and let stand 10 minutes. Place salmon on a lightly greased aluminum foil-lined broiler pan, reserving marinade. Sprinkle evenly with salt and pepper. Pour marinade over salmon.
2. Broil 5 inches from heat 8 to 10 minutes or until fish flakes with a fork. **Makes** 4 servings.

LYDA JONES BURNETTE
HOMEWOOD, ALABAMA

Note: For testing purposes only, we used McCormick Gourmet Collection Chipotle Chile Pepper.

Barbecue Chicken

fast fixin's

PREP: 8 MIN., COOK: 20 MIN.

Serve over a baked potato, mashed potatoes, or roasted red potato wedges. Sprinkle with toppings such as shredded Cheddar cheese, sour cream, green onions, and chopped fresh parsley.

3 skinned and boned chicken breasts
    (about 1½ lb.)
Barbecue Sauce

1. Place chicken and Barbecue Sauce in a medium saucepan, and cook, covered, over low heat 15 to 20 minutes or until chicken is done. Remove chicken, and shred with two forks. Return chicken to sauce until ready to serve. **Makes** 5 servings.

Barbecue Sauce:

fast fixin's

PREP: 5 MIN., COOK: 5 MIN.

Deputy Editor Kenner Patton uses both versions of this sauce on chicken and all cuts of pork.

1 (18-oz.) jar barbecue sauce
¾ cup apple juice
½ cup honey

1. Stir together all ingredients in a medium saucepan over medium-high heat until thoroughly heated. **Makes** 3 cups.

Note: For testing purposes only, we used Stubb's Original Bar-B-Q Sauce.

Chipotle Barbecue Sauce: Stir 3 Tbsp. chipotle hot sauce and 3 Tbsp. molasses into barbecue sauce mixture. Proceed with recipe as directed.

KENNER PATTON
BRIERFIELD, ALABAMA

Note: For testing purposes only, we used Tabasco brand Chipotle Pepper Sauce.

Creamed Turnip Greens

fast fixin's

PREP: 10 MIN., COOK: 15 MIN.

Don't miss this Southern spin on a steak house favorite. (Pictured on page 187)

1 Tbsp. butter
½ sweet onion, chopped
2 garlic cloves, minced
1 (16-oz.) bag frozen turnip greens,
    thawed
½ cup chicken broth
½ tsp. dried crushed red pepper
    (optional)
2 Tbsp. all-purpose flour
1 cup milk
5 oz. cream cheese, cut into pieces
Salt to taste
Garnish: freshly shaved Parmesan
    cheese

1. Melt butter in a large nonstick skillet over medium-high heat. Stir in onion and garlic, and sauté 3 minutes or until tender. Stir in turnip greens, chicken broth, and, if desired, red pepper; cook 4 to 5 minutes or until liquid evaporates.

2. Sprinkle turnip green mixture with flour, and sauté 2 minutes. Gradually stir in milk, and cook, stirring occasionally, 3 minutes. Add cream cheese, stirring until melted. Season with salt to taste. Garnish, if desired. **Makes** 4 servings.

Lightened Creamed Turnip Greens: Substitute 2% milk and ⅓-less-fat cream cheese for milk and cream cheese. Proceed with recipe as directed.

MARIAN COOPER CAIRNS
BIRMINGHAM, ALABAMA

Try These Side Dishes

Here are two great recipes to jazz up your holiday table.

Cranberry Sweet Potatoes

PREP: 15 MIN., BAKE: 40 MIN.

The secret to the full flavor of this four-ingredient dish is the crushed fruit or cranberry sauce stirred in for a zesty finish. This recipe easily doubles. Just bake as directed in two separate pans. (Pictured on page 2)

1. Peel 2 lb. fresh sweet potatoes, and cut into 1-inch cubes. Arrange cubes in a single layer in a jelly-roll pan coated with cooking spray. Sprinkle with ½ tsp. salt and ¼ tsp. pepper, and toss. Bake at 375° for 35 to 40 minutes or until tender, stirring once after 20 minutes. Transfer potatoes to a large serving bowl; add ½ cup cranberry-orange crushed fruit or whole-berry cranberry sauce, and toss to combine. **Makes** 6 servings.

Note: For testing purposes only, we used Ocean Spray Cranberry Orange Cran-Fruit.

Kitchen Express: Substitute 2 (16-oz.) packages fresh, cubed sweet potatoes (such as Glory Foods brand) for whole sweet potatoes. Proceed with recipe as directed.

Pecan-Buttermilk Dressing Cakes
family favorite

PREP: 15 MIN., BAKE: 5 MIN.,
COOK: 15 MIN. PLUS 4 MIN. PER BATCH

This holiday favorite makes a tasty alternative to traditional dressing. Dried cranberries add a touch of sweetness.

1 cup pecan halves
½ cup finely chopped onion
1½ tsp. to 1 Tbsp. rubbed sage
1½ tsp. olive oil
½ cup sweetened dried cranberries, chopped
2¼ cups all-purpose flour
1 tsp. salt
¾ tsp. baking soda
¼ tsp. pepper
3 large eggs
2 cups buttermilk

1. Place pecans in a single layer in a shallow pan. Bake at 350° for 5 minutes or until toasted, stirring occasionally. Coarsely chop.
2. Sauté onion and sage in hot oil in a large skillet 5 minutes or until onion is tender. Add cranberries and ½ cup water; bring to a boil, and cook 10 minutes or until water evaporates. Remove from heat.
3. Combine flour and next 3 ingredients. Whisk together eggs and buttermilk; stir in flour mixture, onion mixture, and chopped pecans just until combined.
4. Drop batter by tablespoonfuls into a hot greased skillet. Cook, in batches, over medium-high heat 1 to 2 minutes on each side or until golden. Serve immediately. **Makes** 8 servings.

"GRAN BETTY" LORENTZ
ROLLING MEADOWS, ILLINOIS

healthy foods
Lean and Light

One of the leanest—and tastiest—meats around, pork tenderloin makes busy weeknights a breeze. There are many ways to cook with this low-fat protein.

Pork Pot Pies With Corn Pudding Crust
family favorite

PREP: 25 MIN., COOK: 25 MIN., BAKE: 20 MIN.
Serve this one-dish meal with your favorite salsa.

2 lb. pork tenderloin *
½ tsp. salt
¼ cup all-purpose flour
1 Tbsp. olive oil
1 large sweet onion, diced
2 poblano chile peppers, seeded and diced **
3 garlic cloves, minced
1 tsp. dried oregano
½ tsp. ground cumin
1 cup low-sodium fat-free chicken broth
1 (15-oz.) can black beans, rinsed and drained
Corn Pudding Crust Batter
Garnish: fresh cilantro sprigs

1. Remove silver skin from pork tenderloin, leaving a thin layer of fat covering meat. Cut pork into 1-inch cubes.
2. Sprinkle pork with salt; dredge in flour. Sauté pork, in batches, in hot oil in a large nonstick skillet over medium-high heat 5 minutes or until browned.
3. Return pork to skillet. Stir in onion and next 4 ingredients, and sauté 3 minutes.
4. Gradually stir in broth, stirring to loosen particles from bottom of skillet. Cook, stirring constantly, 3 minutes or until mixture begins to thicken. Bring to a boil, and stir in black beans. Remove from heat.
5. Spoon mixture into 8 lightly greased 8-oz. ramekins. Spoon Corn Pudding Crust Batter evenly over pork mixture.
6. Bake at 425° for 20 minutes or until set and golden. Garnish, if desired. **Makes** 8 servings.

* 2 lb. skinned and boned chicken breasts may be substituted.

* * 1 green bell pepper and 1 seeded and minced jalapeño pepper may be substituted.

Note: To make pot pie in a 13- x 9-inch baking dish, prepare recipe as directed through Step 4. Spoon pork mixture into a lightly greased baking dish. Proceed with recipe as directed.

Per serving: Calories 318; Fat 8.6g (sat 2.2g, mono 3.3g, poly 0.7g); Protein 28.9g; Carb 32.5g; Fiber 4.2g; Chol 117.2mg; Iron 2.6mg; Sodium 752mg; Calc 62mg

Corn Pudding Crust Batter:
fast fixin's

PREP: 5 MIN.

2 (10-oz.) packages frozen cream-style corn, thawed
2 large eggs, lightly beaten
½ cup reduced-fat baking mix
½ cup 2% reduced-fat milk

1. Stir together all ingredients until combined. **Makes** enough dough for 1 (13- x 9-inch) baking dish or 8 (8-oz.) ramekins.

Note: For testing purposes only, we used Heart Smart Bisquick All-Purpose Baking Mix.

Healthy Benefits

■ Trimming fat from meats before you cook them greatly reduces the amount of saturated fat, which can lower the risk of cardiovascular disease.

■ Using a nonstick skillet to brown meats and sauté vegetables requires only a small amount of heart-healthy cooking oil, such as olive oil, keeping the calorie count low.

Sage-and-Pecan Pork Tenderloin Cutlets

family favorite

PREP: 15 MIN., COOK: 30 MIN.

Pork tenderloin frequently goes on sale, so look for deals and stock up on this versatile meat. It's important to turn the cutlets every two minutes for even browning.

1 cup red wine vinegar
5 Tbsp. seedless blackberry preserves
½ tsp. salt
1 lb. pork tenderloin
¾ cup fine, dry breadcrumbs
½ cup finely chopped pecans
2 tsp. rubbed sage
2 large eggs, beaten
4 tsp. olive oil, divided
Fresh spinach leaves (optional)
Garnish: fresh blackberries

1. Bring vinegar to a boil in a small saucepan over medium-high heat. Reduce heat to medium, and cook 6 minutes or until reduced by half. Stir in blackberry preserves, and cook 5 minutes. Stir in salt.
2. Remove silver skin from pork tenderloin, leaving a thin layer of fat covering meat. Cut pork into 8 slices. Place pork between 2 sheets of plastic wrap, and flatten to a ¼-inch thickness, using a rolling pin or flat side of a meat mallet.
3. Stir together breadcrumbs, pecans, and sage in a shallow bowl.
4. Dredge pork in breadcrumb mixture, dip in beaten eggs, and dredge again in breadcrumb mixture.
5. Cook 4 pork slices in 2 tsp. hot oil in a large nonstick skillet over medium heat 8 minutes or until done, turning every 2 minutes. Repeat procedure with remaining pork and oil. Serve pork over fresh spinach, if desired. Drizzle with vinegar mixture; garnish, if desired. **Makes** 4 servings.

CAMILLA SAULSBURY
BLOOMINGTON, INDIANA

Per serving (not including spinach or garnish): Calories 452; Fat 22.4g (sat 3.9g, mono 11.1g, poly 4.4g); Protein 29.6g; Carb 33.6g; Fiber 2.5g; Chol 171mg; Iron 3mg; Sodium 516mg; Calc 68mg

what's for supper?
Serve Chowder Tonight

Soup for Supper

Serves 6 to 8

Doc's Corn-and-Potato Chowder

Mixed salad greens

Garlic-Herb Bread

Doc's Corn-and-Potato Chowder

PREP: 25 MIN., COOK: 45 MIN., STAND: 10 MIN.

2 cups peeled, diced Yukon gold potatoes (about 2 lb.)
2 Tbsp. butter
1 (10-oz.) package frozen diced onion, red and green bell pepper, and celery
1 cup chopped yellow onion
2 cups milk
1 (12-oz.) can evaporated milk
1 (11-oz.) can yellow-and-white whole kernel corn, drained
1 (10¾-oz.) can cream of mushroom soup with roasted garlic
½ cup thinly sliced green onions
1 Tbsp. chopped fresh parsley
1 to 2 tsp. hot sauce
Salt and pepper to taste
Garnish: thinly sliced green onions

1. Bring potatoes and water to cover to a boil in a Dutch oven over medium-high heat. Cook potatoes 10 to 15 minutes or until tender. Drain and place in a large bowl.
2. Melt butter in Dutch oven over medium-high heat. Stir in frozen vegetables and chopped yellow onion; sauté onion mixture 6 to 8 minutes or until tender.
3. Add 2 cups milk, next 6 ingredients, and potatoes. Reduce heat to medium, and bring to a boil; reduce heat to low, and simmer, stirring occasionally, 15 minutes or until thoroughly heated. Season with salt and pepper to taste. Let stand 10 minutes before serving. Garnish, if desired. **Makes** 6 to 8 servings (about 8 cups).

DAVID CROWE
TRUSSVILLE, ALABAMA

Note: For testing purposes only, we used McKenzie's Seasoning Blend for diced onion, red and green bell pepper, and celery and Campbell's Cream of Mushroom with Roasted Garlic Soup.

Corn-and-Potato Seafood Chowder: Prepare recipe as directed through Step 2. Omit 2 cups milk in Step 3, and add 1 lb. fresh crabmeat, drained, and 2 (6½-oz.) cans minced clams, undrained, with evaporated milk, next 5 ingredients, and potatoes. Proceed with recipe as directed.

Garlic-Herb Bread

PREP: 10 MIN., BAKE: 15 MIN.

3 garlic cloves, minced
2 Tbsp. extra virgin olive oil
2 Tbsp. butter, melted
1 Tbsp. chopped fresh chives
½ tsp. dried crushed red pepper
1 (16-oz.) French bread loaf

1. Stir together first 5 ingredients in a small bowl.
2. Cut bread in half lengthwise. Brush cut sides with garlic mixture; place on a baking sheet.
3. Bake at 350° for 13 to 15 minutes or until golden brown. Cut each bread half into 8 slices. **Makes** 8 servings.

What's in a Name?

Chowder is traditionally the name given to a thick, rich, chunky soup. Potato and corn are popular vegetable chowders. Seafood varieties are probably the most well-known and may include clams, oysters, shrimp, cod, conch, or a combination of several. Manhattan-style chowder is made with tomatoes, while New England-style chowder is prepared with milk or cream.

Holiday Dinners.

Get ready for an all-star collection of recipes that is sure to be a hit this season and into next year. From festive celebrations to easy family suppers, these menu options meet all your entertaining needs.

Tradition With a Twist

Bold flavors and a great look are the hallmarks of this updated Hanukkah feast.

Hanukkah Feast

Serves 8

Roasted Paprika Chicken

Warm Frisée Salad With Crispy Kosher Salami

Mini Latkes With Salmon-Olive Relish

Pomegranate-Cider Baked Apples WIth Sugared Piecrust Strips

"Family tradition evolves, and your menus can too," says David Poran, culinary director of Balducci's Food Lover's Market in Washington, D.C. David pulls from his Eastern European Jewish heritage, French culinary training, and an understanding of doable recipes to come up with these gems. He and his wife, Leslie, truly gave their friends a treat with this meal.

Roasted Paprika Chicken
PREP: 20 MIN., BAKE: 40 MIN., STAND: 5 MIN.
A five-ingredient paprika rub and lemon slices give this entrée its rich flavor. Choose a mixture of everyone's favorite chicken pieces, such as drumsticks, bone-in breasts, and thighs.

¼ cup smoked paprika
2 Tbsp. chopped fresh thyme leaves
3 Tbsp. extra virgin olive oil
2 tsp. kosher salt
1 tsp. coarsely ground pepper
5 lb. assorted chicken pieces
2 lemons, thinly sliced
Garnishes: lemon slices, fresh thyme sprigs

1. Stir together first 5 ingredients to form a paste.
2. Spread half of paprika mixture evenly underneath skin of chicken pieces. Place 1 to 2 lemon slices underneath skin on top of paprika mixture. Arrange chicken pieces in a single layer on a wire rack in an aluminum foil-lined broiler pan or 17- x 12-inch jelly-roll pan. Rub remaining paprika mixture evenly over skin.
3. Bake at 425° for 35 to 40 minutes or until a meat thermometer inserted into thickest portions registers 165°. Let chicken stand 5 minutes; lightly brush with pan juices just before serving. Garnish, if desired. **Makes** 6 to 8 servings.

Warm Frisée Salad With Crispy Kosher Salami
PREP: 20 MIN., COOK: 13 MIN.
Frisée is a member of the chicory family often used in mesclun salad mixes. Buy bunches with crisp leaves and no signs of wilting. Use all of the leaves except the core.

½ (12-oz.) package kosher beef salami slices
¼ cup extra virgin olive oil
½ medium-size red onion, sliced
1 garlic clove, minced
⅓ cup plus 1 Tbsp. sherry vinegar
2 tsp. whole grain mustard
½ tsp. kosher salt
¼ tsp. coarsely ground pepper
4 bunches frisée, torn *
1 pt. grape tomatoes, halved

1. Cut kosher beef salami slices into ¼-inch strips.
2. Cook salami strips in hot olive oil in a medium skillet over medium heat

5 to 10 minutes or until crispy. Remove salami with a slotted spoon, reserving remaining oil in skillet. Drain salami pieces on paper towels.

3. Sauté onion and garlic in reserved hot oil 2 minutes. Stir in vinegar, mustard, salt, and pepper; cook 1 minute.

4. Place frisée and grape tomato halves in a large bowl, and drizzle with vinegar mixture; toss to coat. Sprinkle with crispy salami pieces, and serve immediately. **Makes** 8 servings.

* 2 bunches curly endive may be substituted for frisée.

Note: For testing purposes only, we used Hebrew National Kosher Beef Salami.

Mini Latkes With Salmon-Olive Relish

PREP: 20 MIN., COOK: 8 MIN. PER BATCH

The key to the best latkes is patting the potato-and-onion mixture very dry on paper towels before adding eggs and matzo meal. David adds, "Get everything ready, including the salt for sprinkling on the cooked latkes, before you grate the potatoes and onion."

2 baking potatoes (about 1½ lb.), peeled
1 small sweet onion
2 large eggs, lightly beaten
⅓ cup unsalted matzo meal
1 tsp. kosher salt
1 tsp. coarsely ground pepper
¾ cup canola oil
Kosher salt to taste (optional)
Salmon-Olive Relish
Garnish: green onion curls

1. Grate potatoes and onion through large holes on a box grater. Pat grated potatoes and onion dry with paper towels.

2. Place potatoes and onion in a large bowl. Stir in lightly beaten eggs and next 3 ingredients.

3. Drop potato mixture by heaping tablespoonfuls into hot canola oil in a large, deep skillet over medium-high heat; cook 2 to 4 minutes on each side or until golden brown. Drain latkes on paper towels, and sprinkle with kosher salt to taste, if desired. Top each latke with 1 tsp. Salmon-Olive Relish. Garnish, if desired. Serve immediately. **Makes** 8 servings.

Note: To keep latkes warm before topping with relish, place on a wire rack on a baking sheet. Place in a 250° oven up to 30 minutes.

Salmon-Olive Relish:
fast fixin's • make ahead
PREP: 10 MIN.
You can make this up to one day ahead; cover and refrigerate until ready to use.

1 (4-oz.) package smoked salmon, diced
1 green onion, minced
3 oil-cured black olives, minced
1 tsp. extra virgin olive oil
1 tsp. fresh lemon juice

1. Stir together all ingredients. **Makes** ¾ cup.

Pomegranate-Cider Baked Apples With Sugared Piecrust Strips

PREP: 15 MIN., COOK: 20 MIN., BAKE: 42 MIN., STAND: 10 MIN.

Granny Smith apples work beautifully in this recipe. Pomegranate juice is reduced when the consistency changes from liquid to a syrup-like thickness.

¾ cup chopped pecans
1 (16-oz.) bottle pomegranate juice
¾ cup apple cider
½ cup firmly packed light brown sugar
½ tsp. ground cinnamon
¼ tsp. kosher salt
¼ tsp. black pepper
8 small Granny Smith apples, cored
¼ cup butter, cut into pieces
Sugared Piecrust Strips

1. Place pecans in a single layer on a baking sheet. Bake at 350° for 10 to 12 minutes or until nuts are toasted.

2. Cook pomegranate juice in a large saucepan over medium-high heat, stirring often, 18 to 20 minutes or until reduced to ⅓ cup. Remove from heat, and carefully stir in apple cider. Pour cider mixture into a lightly greased 8-inch square baking dish.

3. Stir together brown sugar, next 3 ingredients, and toasted pecans.

4. Cut ½ inch from top of each apple. Place about 3 Tbsp. of pecan mixture into each apple cavity, pressing down and mounding on top. Arrange apples in baking dish with cider mixture. Top apples evenly with butter.

5. Bake apples at 400° for 30 minutes or until apples are tender and sauce is slightly thickened. Let stand 10 minutes. Place apples in serving bowls; spoon sauce from baking dish over apples, and serve with Sugared Piecrust Strips. **Makes** 8 servings.

Sugared Piecrust Strips:
fast fixin's
PREP: 10 MIN., BAKE: 8 MIN., COOL: 10 MIN.

½ (15-oz.) package refrigerated piecrusts
1 Tbsp. sugar

1. Cut piecrust into ¾- to 1-inch-wide strips. Place on a lightly greased baking sheet; sprinkle with sugar.

2. Bake at 450° for 5 to 8 minutes or until golden brown. Let cool on baking sheet 10 minutes. **Makes** about 16.

Appetizer Party With Style

Throwing a holiday shindig is easy when friends pitch in.

Invite friends over for the most creative gathering of the season—a cook-together appetizer party. It's the idea of Sheri Castle, a cooking-school teacher in Chapel Hill, North Carolina (**www.sheri-castle.com**). "This brings guests into their favorite party room—the kitchen—to cook and catch up," she says. "Assign two recipes for each couple, and have a no-cleanup policy for your guest chefs."

Beef-and-Asparagus Bundles
fast fixin's
PREP: 20 MIN., COOK: 2 MIN.

16 asparagus spears
1 (4-oz.) package garlic-and-herb spreadable cheese
2 heads Bibb lettuce, leaves separated
8 thin slices deli roast beef, halved
1 red bell pepper, cut into 16 strips
16 fresh chives (optional)

1. Snap off and discard tough ends of asparagus. Cut asparagus tips into 3½-inch pieces, reserving any remaining end portions for another use.
2. Cook asparagus in boiling water to cover 1 to 2 minutes or until crisp-tender; drain. Plunge into ice water to stop the cooking process; drain and pat dry with paper towels.
3. Spoon cheese into a 1-qt. zip-top plastic freezer bag. (Do not seal.) Snip 1 corner of bag to make a small hole, and pipe cheese down center of each lettuce leaf. Arrange 1 roast beef slice,

1 asparagus spear, and 1 red bell pepper strip in each lettuce leaf. If desired, wrap sides of lettuce around roast beef and vegetables, and tie bundles with chives. **Makes** 16 bundles (8 appetizer servings).

Note: For testing purposes only, we used Alouette Garlic & Herbs for garlic-and-herb spreadable cheese and Boar's Head Londonport Seasoned Roast Beef for deli roast beef.

Brie Tartlets With Grape Relish
PREP: 30 MIN., BAKE: 23 MIN., COOL: 15 MIN.

¼ cup chopped walnuts
½ (15-oz.) package refrigerated piecrusts
½ (8-oz.) Brie round, rind removed
¾ cup seedless red grapes, chopped
1 green onion, minced
1½ tsp. balsamic vinegar
1 tsp. chopped fresh rosemary
¼ tsp. freshly ground pepper
Garnish: fresh rosemary sprigs

1. Place walnuts in a single layer on a baking sheet. Bake at 350° for 8 to 10 minutes or until lightly toasted and fragrant. Increase oven temperature to 425°.
2. Unroll piecrust on a flat surface. Cut into 24 rounds using a 2-inch round cutter. Press rounds into bottoms of ungreased miniature muffin cups (dough will come slightly up sides,

forming a cup). Prick bottom of dough with a fork.
3. Bake at 425° for 6 to 7 minutes or until golden. Remove from pans, and cool on a wire rack 15 minutes. Reduce oven temperature to 300°.
4. Meanwhile, cut Brie round into 24 pieces. Stir together grapes and next 4 ingredients.
5. Arrange pastry shells on a baking sheet. Place 1 Brie piece in each pastry cup; sprinkle Brie pieces evenly with toasted walnuts.
6. Bake at 300° for 4 to 6 minutes or just until cheese begins to melt. Top tarts evenly with grape mixture. Garnish, if desired. Serve immediately. **Makes** 8 appetizer servings.

Pancetta Crisps With Goat Cheese and Pear
PREP: 15 MIN., BAKE: 10 MIN., STAND: 10 MIN.
Save the final step of drizzling honey over these appetizer snacks for each guest to do.

12 thin slices pancetta (about ⅓ lb.)
1 Bartlett pear
½ (4-oz.) package goat cheese, crumbled
Freshly cracked pepper
Honey
Garnish: fresh thyme sprigs

1. Arrange pancetta slices in a single layer on an aluminum foil-lined baking sheet.
2. Bake at 450° for 8 to 10 minutes or until golden. Transfer to a paper towel-lined wire rack using a spatula. Let stand 10 minutes or until crisp.
3. Core pear with an apple corer. Cut pear crosswise into 12 thin rings. Arrange on a serving platter. Top evenly with pancetta and goat cheese; sprinkle with pepper. Drizzle with honey just before serving. Garnish, if desired. **Makes** 6 servings.

Blue Cheese Shortbread Leaves

PREP: 20 MIN., BAKE: 28 MIN., COOL: 45 MIN., CHILL: 1 HR.

Nibble while you work. Provide Blue Cheese Shortbread Leaves and bubbly for your guests to enjoy.

⅓ cup chopped pecans
4 oz. blue cheese, crumbled
3 Tbsp. butter, softened
½ cup all-purpose flour
¼ cup cornstarch
¼ tsp. salt
¼ tsp. pepper

1. Place chopped pecans in a single layer on a baking sheet. Bake at 350° for 8 to 10 minutes or until lightly toasted. Cool 30 minutes. Reduce oven temperature to 325°.
2. Process blue cheese and butter in a food processor 10 to 15 seconds or until creamy, stopping to scrape down sides as needed. Add flour and next 3 ingredients; pulse 9 to 10 times or until the mixture is crumbly. Add toasted pecans; pulse 9 to 10 times or until mixture forms moist clumps.
3. Transfer mixture onto plastic wrap on a flat surface, and gather dough into a ball shape; flatten into a 1-inch-thick disk. Wrap in plastic wrap, and chill 1 hour or until firm.
4. Turn dough out onto a lightly floured surface. Pat or roll to ⅛- to ¼-inch thickness. Cut with 1½- and 2-inch leaf-shaped cutters. Place on a parchment paper-lined baking sheet.
5. Bake at 325° for 16 to 18 minutes or until light golden brown. Transfer to a wire rack; cool 15 minutes. **Makes** about 40.

Cozy Up to the Season

Nothing is more comforting on a chilly winter day than sitting by the fireplace with your hands wrapped around a toasty warm mug. We offer a few more ways to enjoy traditional coffee and hot cocoa. Pair them with your favorite cookie recipes for a casual evening of entertaining friends.

Orange-Scented Mocha

fast fixin's • make ahead
PREP: 10 MIN., COOK: 9 MIN.

3 cups milk
6 oz. semisweet chocolate morsels
4 (2-inch) orange rind strips
½ tsp. instant espresso or ¾ tsp. instant coffee granules
⅛ tsp. ground nutmeg
Sweetened whipped cream
Garnishes: orange rind strips and curls, ground nutmeg

1. Combine first 5 ingredients in heavy medium saucepan. Cook over medium heat, whisking often, 3 to 4 minutes or until chocolate is melted. Increase heat to medium-high, and cook, whisking often, 4 to 5 minutes or just until mixture begins to boil. Remove from heat; discard orange rind strips. Serve immediately with sweetened whipped cream. Garnish, if desired. **Makes** about 3½ cups (about 4 servings).

Orange-Scented Mocha Sipping Dessert: Prepare recipe as directed, decreasing milk to 2 cups and stirring in 1 cup half-and-half with milk and remaining ingredients.

Note: Both of these recipes can be prepared up to 2 hours ahead. Let stand at room temperature. Before serving, bring to a light boil, whisking occasionally; remove from heat, and serve immediately.

Minted Hot Chocolate Mix

fast fixin's • make ahead
PREP: 10 MIN.

3 (4½-inch) soft peppermint candy sticks
1 cup sugar
¾ cup instant nonfat dry milk
¾ cup powdered nondairy coffee creamer
½ cup unsweetened cocoa

1. Place peppermint sticks in a zip-top plastic freezer bag; seal bag, and crush candy with a mallet.
2. Combine crushed candy and remaining ingredients in an airtight container, and store at room temperature up to 1 month. **Makes** 3 cups dry mix (about 16 servings).

Note: For testing purposes only, we used King Leo Peppermint Sticks.

Minted Hot Chocolate: Stir about 2½ to 3 Tbsp. Minted Hot Chocolate Mix into 1 cup hot milk, stirring until dissolved. Top with marshmallows, if desired. **Makes** 1 serving.

Bring Your Own Mug

Add interesting conversation to your next holiday gathering by having your guests bring their own mugs for hot drinks. It's a fun ice breaker to ask people what they're drinking from, whether it's an antique teacup passed down from a relative or a kitschy souvenir picked up on their latest travels.

Their First Christmas

These newlyweds toast friends with a casual gathering.

If you're newly married, deciding where to spend Christmas dinner can be a challenge. Tim and Elizabeth Griffin solved the matter by inviting over a few couples for a laid-back get-together at their home in Little Rock, Arkansas.

Christmas Dinner

Serves 6

Holiday Pork Loin Roast

Holiday Roast With Gravy

Sautéed Brussels Sprouts With Apples

Buttermilk Mashed Potatoes

White Chocolate-Cranberry Crème Brûlée

Holiday Pork Loin Roast
PREP: 15 MIN.; BAKE: 1 HR., 25 MIN.; STAND: 10 MIN. *(Pictured on page 2)*

1. Tie 1 (4-lb.) boneless pork loin roast at 2-inch intervals with kitchen string; sprinkle with ½ tsp. each of salt and pepper; place in an aluminum foil-lined jelly-roll pan. Bake at 375° for 1 hour or until a meat thermometer inserted into thickest portion registers 150°. Stir together 6 shallots, peeled and thinly sliced, and ⅓ cup pepper relish; spoon evenly over top of roast, and bake 10 to 15 more minutes or until shallots are tender. Let stand 10 minutes before slicing. **Makes** 8 to 10 servings.

Holiday Roast With Gravy
make ahead
PREP: 35 MIN.; CHILL: 8 HR.; STAND: 30 MIN.; COOK: 26 MIN.; BAKE: 1 HR., 35 MIN.
Elizabeth recommends preparing this the day before. "Once the roast cools, I cut it into slices and then pour the gravy over the meat," she says. "I cover it with foil and refrigerate it overnight. The next day, I pop it in the oven for about 45 minutes to reheat."

1 (4½- to 5-lb.) eye-of-round roast
2 Tbsp. minced garlic
1 Tbsp. plus 1½ tsp. chopped fresh rosemary
2 tsp. pepper
2 tsp. dried oregano
3 Tbsp. vegetable oil, divided
1 (15-oz.) can tomato sauce
½ cup dry red wine
1 large onion, chopped
2 Tbsp. Greek seasoning
3 Tbsp. all-purpose flour
1 cup low-sodium beef broth

1. Cut 12 (1-inch-deep) slits in top and bottom of roast.
2. Stir together garlic, next 3 ingredients, and 1 Tbsp. vegetable oil to form a paste. Rub mixture into slits. Cover and chill at least 8 hours or up to 12 hours. Let roast stand at room temperature 30 minutes.
3. Brown roast on all sides in remaining 2 Tbsp. hot oil in a heavy-duty roasting pan over medium-high heat 5 to 6 minutes.
4. Stir together tomato sauce and next 3 ingredients; pour over roast in roasting pan.
5. Bake, covered, at 325° for 1 hour and 35 minutes or until a meat thermometer inserted into thickest portion registers 135°. Remove roast, reserving sauce in roasting pan. Keep roast warm.
6. Whisk together flour and beef broth until smooth; whisk into sauce mixture in pan. Cook mixture, whisking frequently, over medium heat 15 to 20 minutes or until thickened. Serve gravy with roast. **Makes** 8 to 10 servings.

Sautéed Brussels Sprouts With Apples
PREP: 20 MIN., COOK: 30 MIN.
This dish elevates this often overlooked veggie to new and delicious heights. Even the skeptics on our Foods staff agreed that Brussels sprouts never looked or tasted so good.

1½ lb. Brussels sprouts, trimmed
4 bacon slices
1 Braeburn apple, peeled and diced
2 Tbsp. minced shallots
1 garlic clove, minced
¼ cup dry white wine
¼ cup low-sodium fat-free chicken broth
1 tsp. salt
½ tsp. pepper
¼ cup freshly shaved Parmesan cheese

1. Cut Brussels sprouts in half, and cut into shreds.
2. Cook bacon in a large skillet over medium heat 8 to 10 minutes or until crisp; remove bacon, and drain on paper towels, reserving 3 Tbsp. drippings in skillet. Crumble bacon.
3. Sauté apple, shallots, and garlic in hot drippings over medium-high heat 3 minutes. Stir in wine and next 3 ingredients, stirring to loosen particles from bottom of skillet. Bring to a boil; reduce heat, and simmer 5 minutes. Add Brussels sprouts; sauté 8 to 10 minutes or until sprouts are crisp-tender. Top with shaved Parmesan cheese and crumbled bacon. Serve immediately. **Makes** 6 servings.

Buttermilk Mashed Potatoes
family favorite
PREP: 25 MIN., COOK: 30 MIN.

3 garlic cloves, minced
1 Tbsp. olive oil
2 cups low-sodium chicken broth
3½ lb. Yukon gold potatoes, peeled
  and cubed
1¼ tsp. salt, divided
1½ cups warm buttermilk
⅓ cup butter, melted
¾ tsp. pepper
4 Tbsp. chopped fresh chives

1. Sauté garlic in hot oil in a Dutch oven over medium heat 3 minutes. Add 8 cups water, chicken broth, potatoes, and ¼ tsp. salt; bring to a boil. Cover, reduce heat, and cook 15 to 20 minutes or until potatoes are tender.
2. Drain potatoes, and return to Dutch oven. Add buttermilk, butter, pepper, and remaining 1 tsp. salt. Mash potatoes with a large fork or potato masher to desired consistency. Sprinkle evenly with chives; serve immediately. **Makes** 6 servings.

White Chocolate-Cranberry Crème Brûlée
PREP: 15 MIN., COOK: 3 MIN., BAKE: 55 MIN., COOL: 25 MIN., CHILL: 8 HR., BROIL: 5 MIN., STAND: 5 MIN.
Whole-berry cranberry sauce adds an unexpected layer of flavor to this decadent dessert.

2 cups whipping cream, divided
4 oz. white chocolate
1 tsp. vanilla extract
5 egg yolks
½ cup sugar, divided
½ (15-oz.) can whole-berry cranberry
  sauce
Ice cubes
Garnish: Sugared Cranberries and Mint
  (at right)

1. Combine ½ cup cream and white chocolate in a heavy saucepan; cook over low heat, stirring constantly, 2 to 3 minutes or until chocolate is melted. Remove from heat, and stir in vanilla and remaining 1½ cups cream.
2. Whisk together egg yolks and ¼ cup sugar until sugar is dissolved and mixture is thick and pale yellow. Add cream mixture, whisking until well blended. Pour mixture through a fine wire-mesh strainer into a large bowl.
3. Spoon 1½ Tbsp. cranberry sauce into each of 6 (4-oz.) ramekins. Pour cream-and-egg mixture evenly into ramekins; place ramekins in a large roasting pan. Add water to pan to depth of ½ inch.
4. Bake at 300° for 45 to 55 minutes or until edges are set. Cool custards in pan on a wire rack 25 minutes. Remove ramekins from water bath; cover and chill 8 hours.
5. Sprinkle 1½ to 2 tsp. remaining sugar evenly over each ramekin. Fill a large roasting pan or 15- x 10- x 1-inch jelly-roll pan with ice; arrange ramekins in pan.
6. Broil 5 inches from heat 3 to 5 minutes or until sugar is melted and caramelized. Let stand 5 minutes. Garnish, if desired. **Makes** 6 servings.

White Chocolate-Banana Crème Brûlée: Prepare recipe as directed through Step 2. Slice 2 bananas into ¼-inch-thick slices; toss bananas with ⅓ cup sugar. Melt 2 Tbsp. butter in a large nonstick skillet over medium-high heat. Add bananas, and cook 1 to 2 minutes on each side or until lightly browned. Line bottoms of 6 (4-oz.) ramekins evenly with banana slices. Pour cream mixture evenly into ramekins; place ramekins in a large roasting pan. Add water to pan to depth of ½ inch. Proceed with recipe as directed.

Garnish With Style
Create a sensational look on the White Chocolate-Cranberry Crème Brûlée with this simple idea.

Sugared Cranberries and Mint
PREP: 15 MIN., STAND. 5 MIN.

¼ cup corn syrup
¼ cup dried cranberries
1 bunch fresh mint sprigs
¼ cup sugar

1. Using a clean paintbrush, gently brush ¼ cup corn syrup onto the top side of dried cranberries and mint sprigs (photo 1).
2. Sprinkle sugar over cranberries and mint (photo 2). Let stand 5 minutes; sprinkle remaining sugar over cranberries and mint, gently shaking off excess.

Thanksgiving at the Firehouse

Join these guys as they cook up a festive celebration.

Firehouse Feast

Serves 8

Two-Alarm Deep-Fried Turkey

Cornbread Dressing

Classic Parmesan Scalloped Potatoes

Cranberry Compote

Sweet Potato-Pecan Cupcakes With Cream Cheese Frosting

Sometimes duty calls even on the holidays, but it doesn't stop these firefighters in Birmingham, Alabama, from cooking up a scrumptious Thanksgiving spread. Fireman Andrew Lewis shares his down-home recipes with us, and you'll want to add them to your files. Wherever you celebrate this year, make it special with good food and great companions.

Two-Alarm Deep-Fried Turkey

PREP: 15 MIN., FRY: 45 MIN., STAND: 15 MIN.
You'll need about 3 to 4 gallons of oil to completely submerge your turkey. Make sure you don't overfill your turkey fryer.

2 Tbsp. kosher salt
1 Tbsp. salt-free spicy seasoning blend
1 tsp. garlic powder
1 tsp. onion powder
1 tsp. dried crushed red pepper
1 (12- to 14-lb.) whole frozen turkey, thawed
2 Tbsp. vegetable oil
Peanut oil

1. Stir together first 5 ingredients.
2. Remove giblets and neck from turkey, and, if desired, reserve for another use. Rinse turkey with cold water. Drain cavity well; pat dry. Rub turkey evenly with 2 Tbsp. vegetable oil. Loosen and lift skin from turkey breasts with fingers without totally detaching skin; spread one-fourth salt mixture evenly underneath. Carefully replace skin. Sprinkle additional one-fourth salt mixture inside cavity; rub into cavity. Sprinkle remaining salt mixture evenly on skin; rub into skin. Place turkey on fryer rod.
3. Pour peanut oil into a deep propane turkey fryer, pouring 10 to 12 inches below top of fryer. Heat to 300° over a medium-low flame according to manufacturer's instructions. Carefully lower turkey into hot oil with rod attachment.
4. Fry 45 minutes or until a meat thermometer inserted in thickest portion of thigh registers 165°. (Keep oil temperature between 300° to 325°.) Remove turkey from oil; drain and let stand 15 minutes before slicing. **Makes** 10 to 12 servings.

Cornbread Dressing
family favorite
PREP: 20 MIN., COOK: 10 MIN., BAKE: 30 MIN.

2 Tbsp. butter
2 Tbsp. olive oil
1 (8-oz.) package sliced fresh mushrooms
1 cup chopped celery
½ cup chopped green bell pepper
Andrew's Cornbread
1 cup half-and-half
¼ cup firmly packed fresh flat-leaf parsley, chopped
½ cup melted butter
2 Tbsp. fresh sage, chopped
1 tsp. salt
½ tsp. pepper
2 large eggs, lightly beaten
½ tsp. chopped fresh rosemary (optional)
1½ cups chicken broth

1. Melt 2 Tbsp. butter with oil in a large skillet over medium heat; add mushrooms, celery, and bell pepper, and sauté 8 to 10 minutes or until vegetables are tender.
2. Crumble cornbread into a large mixing bowl. Stir in mushroom mixture, half-and-half, and next 6 ingredients, and, if desired, rosemary. Add chicken broth, and gently stir until moistened. Spoon into a lightly greased 13- x 9-inch baking dish.
3. Bake, covered, at 350° for 25 to 30 minutes or until golden. **Makes** 8 to 10 servings.

Andrew's Cornbread:
PREP: 10 MIN., BAKE: 25 MIN., COOL: 5 MIN.

1 tsp. vegetable oil
2 cups self-rising yellow cornmeal
2 Tbsp. sugar
1 Tbsp. self-rising flour
½ tsp. salt
1 cup buttermilk
2 large eggs, lightly beaten
1 Tbsp. mayonnaise

1. Brush a 10-inch cast-iron skillet with oil, and heat in a 425° oven 5 minutes.
2. Stir together cornmeal and next 3 ingredients in a large mixing bowl. Stir in buttermilk, eggs, and mayonnaise, stirring just until blended. Pour batter into hot skillet.
3. Bake at 425° for 18 to 20 minutes or until golden brown and cornbread pulls away from sides of skillet. Remove to a wire rack, and cool 5 minutes. **Makes** 6 servings.

Classic Parmesan Scalloped Potatoes
family favorite
PREP: 15 MIN., COOK: 20 MIN.,
BAKE: 30 MIN., STAND: 10 MIN.

¼ cup butter
2 lb. Yukon gold potatoes, peeled and
    thinly sliced
3 cups whipping cream
2 garlic cloves, chopped
1½ tsp. salt
¼ tsp. freshly ground pepper
¼ cup fresh flat-leaf parsley, chopped
½ cup (2 oz.) grated Parmesan cheese

1. Melt butter in a large Dutch oven over medium-high heat. Stir in potatoes and next 5 ingredients, and bring to a boil. Reduce heat to medium-low, and cook, stirring gently, 15 minutes or until potatoes are tender.
2. Spoon mixture into a lightly greased 13- x 9-inch baking dish; sprinkle with cheese.
3. Bake at 400° for 25 to 30 minutes or until bubbly and golden brown. Remove to a wire rack, and let stand 10 minutes before serving. **Makes** 6 to 8 servings.

Cranberry Compote
make ahead
PREP: 10 MIN., COOK: 12 MIN., COOL: 15 MIN.

2 (12-oz.) packages fresh cranberries
1¾ cups sugar
1 Tbsp. grated orange rind
¼ cup orange juice
2 Tbsp. orange liqueur
1 cinnamon stick
1 tsp. grated lemon rind
1 tsp. vanilla extract
½ tsp. freshly grated nutmeg

1. Stir together all ingredients in a heavy saucepan over medium-high heat; cook, stirring often, 5 to 7 minutes or until cranberry skins begin to split. Reduce heat to medium-low, and cook, stirring occasionally, 5 minutes or until thickened. Remove from heat, and let cool 15 minutes. Remove and discard cinnamon stick. Store mixture in an airtight container in refrigerator up to 1 week. **Makes** 3½ cups.

Sweet Potato-Pecan Cupcakes With Cream Cheese Frosting
family favorite
PREP: 15 MIN., BAKE: 40 MIN., COOL: 1 HR.

1 cup coarsely chopped pecans
2 cups sugar
1 cup butter, softened
4 large eggs
1 (16-oz.) can mashed sweet potatoes
⅔ cup orange juice
1 tsp. vanilla extract
3 cups all-purpose flour
1 tsp. baking powder
1 tsp. ground cinnamon
½ tsp. baking soda
½ tsp. ground nutmeg
¼ tsp. salt
Cream Cheese Frosting
Garnish: coarsely chopped pecans

1. Place pecans in a single layer in a shallow pan.
2. Bake at 350° for 8 to 10 minutes or until toasted, stirring once after 4 minutes.

3. Beat sugar and butter at medium speed with an electric mixer until blended. Add eggs, 1 at a time, beating until blended after each addition.
4. Whisk together mashed sweet potatoes, orange juice, and vanilla extract. Combine flour and next 5 ingredients. Add flour mixture to sugar mixture alternately with sweet potato mixture, beginning and ending with flour mixture. Beat at low speed just until blended after each addition. Fold in toasted pecans. Place foil baking cups in muffin pans, and coat with vegetable cooking spray; spoon batter into cups, filling two-thirds full.
5. Bake at 350° for 28 to 30 minutes or until a wooden pick inserted into center comes out clean. Remove immediately from pans, and cool 50 minutes to 1 hour or until completely cool. Spread cupcakes evenly with Cream Cheese Frosting. Garnish, if desired. **Makes** 2 dozen.

Cream Cheese Frosting:
fast fixin's
PREP: 10 MIN.

½ cup butter, softened
1 (8-oz.) package cream cheese,
    softened
1 (16-oz.) package powdered sugar
1 tsp. vanilla extract

1. Beat butter and cream cheese at medium speed with an electric mixer until creamy. Gradually add powdered sugar, beating at low speed just until blended; stir in vanilla. **Makes** about 2 cups.

from our kitchen

Extra-Easy Tart

We all love dishes that are actually very simple to prepare but appear to take lots of time and skill, such as Lemon-Coconut Tart. This variation on the ever-popular lemon squares is a stylish addition to a holiday buffet when served whole on a pretty platter. Let guests cut their own pieces with a pie server, or serve them generous squares on small plates.

Lemon-Coconut Tart

PREP: 10 MIN.; COOK: 7 MIN.; BAKE: 1 HR.;
COOL: 1 HR., 30 MIN.

½ cup chopped slivered almonds
2 cups all-purpose flour
1 cup powdered sugar, divided
1 cup butter, softened
Lemon Chess Pie Filling
1 cup sweetened flaked coconut
Garnishes: lemon thyme sprigs, fresh
    raspberries

1. Heat almonds in a small nonstick skillet over medium-low heat, stirring often, 5 to 7 minutes or until toasted.
2. Combine flour and ½ cup powdered sugar. Cut butter into mixture with a pastry blender until crumbly; stir in almonds. Firmly press mixture on bottom and 1 inch up sides of a lightly greased, heavy-duty aluminum foil-lined 13- x 9-inch pan.
3. Bake at 350° for 20 to 25 minutes or until lightly golden brown. Stir together Lemon Chess Pie Filling and coconut; pour over baked crust.

4. Bake at 350° for 30 to 35 minutes or until set. Cool in pan on a wire rack 30 minutes or until completely cool. Carefully lift tart from pan, and transfer to a serving platter, using foil sides as handles; remove foil. Cool 1 hour; sprinkle with remaining ½ cup powdered sugar. Garnish, if desired. **Makes** 16 servings.

Lemon Chess Pie Filling:

PREP: 10 MIN.

2 cups sugar
4 large eggs
¼ cup butter, melted
¼ cup milk
1 Tbsp. grated lemon rind
¼ cup fresh lemon juice
1 Tbsp. all-purpose flour
1 Tbsp. white or yellow cornmeal
¼ tsp. salt

1. Whisk together all ingredients. Use filling immediately. **Makes** about 3 cups.

Make the Most of Leftovers

This is the season when food is plentiful, so use a vacuum-packaging system to make your own frozen dinners from leftovers. Foods Executive Editor Scott Jones has been using the Food-Saver for years and convinced us that it's the best thing since, well, frozen dinners. The heavy plastic bag and vacuum seal prevent freezer burn. We tried several and like the FoodSaver brand best.

Package your leftover meat, whether it's short ribs, turkey, slices of roast, or another holiday favorite, with creamy mashed potatoes. And by all means, save some turkey and dressing for the chilly days of February.

Tricks to Perfect Turkey

In her 14 years with the Butterball Turkey Talk-Line, Renee Ferguson heard it all. She shares delightful anecdotes as well as every possible way to thaw and cook that favorite Thanksgiving entrée in *Talk Turkey To Me* (Wishbone Press and Promotions; 2006). Whether you favor cooking your bird breast up, breast down, on the grill, in an oven bag, or in the deep fryer, you'll find more than 20 methods and techniques in this informative and comprehensive book. Renee also shares recipes for delicious appetizers, sides, and desserts, so you have a fabulous turkey plus all the trimmings. Available at **www.amazon.com** or through your local bookstore.

december

One-Pan Wonders

Amaze your guests with these simply beautiful Bundt cakes. They're so easy—but only you will know.

Forget the mix! These fabulous cakes are so simple to make you won't believe you started from scratch. Good to the last crumb, a Bundt cake is just as grand as a layer cake, but far less fussy. A gentle tap sends them tumbling from the pan, perfectly fluted and party ready.

Dark Chocolate Bundt Cake

PREP: 20 MIN.; BAKE: 1 HR., 20 MIN.; COOL: 45 MIN. *(Pictured on page 190)*

8 oz. semisweet chocolate, coarsely chopped
1 (16-oz.) can chocolate syrup
1 cup butter, softened
2 cups sugar
4 large eggs
2½ cups all-purpose flour
½ tsp. baking soda
¼ tsp. salt
1 cup buttermilk
1 tsp. vanilla extract
Garnishes: Wintry-White Icing (see Festive Trims at right), strawberry slices

1. Melt chocolate in a microwave-safe bowl at HIGH for 30-second intervals until melted (about 1½ minutes total). Stir in chocolate syrup until smooth.
2. Beat butter at medium speed with an electric mixer until creamy. Gradually add sugar, beating at medium speed until light and fluffy. Add eggs, 1 at a time, beating just until blended after each addition.
3. Sift together flour, baking soda, and salt. Add to butter mixture alternately with buttermilk, beginning and ending with flour mixture. Beat at low speed just until blended after each addition. Stir in vanilla and melted chocolate just until blended. Pour batter into a greased and floured 14-cup Bundt pan.
4. Bake at 325° for 1 hour and 20 minutes or until a long wooden pick inserted in center comes out clean. Cool in pan on a wire rack 15 minutes; remove from pan to wire rack, and let cool 30 minutes or until completely cool. Garnish, if desired. **Makes** 12 servings.

JERRY MILLS
BIRMINGHAM, ALABAMA

Vanilla Butter Cake

PREP: 20 MIN.; BAKE: 1 HR., 10 MIN.; COOL: 45 MIN.
(Pictured on cover and page 191)

1 cup butter, softened
2½ cups sugar
5 large eggs
3 cups all-purpose flour
1 tsp. baking powder
¼ tsp. salt
¾ cup half-and-half
1 Tbsp. vanilla extract
Garnishes: See Festive Trims box below or Sparkling Peppermint Candy (page 280)

1. Beat butter at medium speed with an electric mixer until creamy. Gradually add sugar, beating at medium speed until light and fluffy. Add eggs, 1 at a time, beating just until blended after each addition.
2. Sift together flour, baking powder, and salt. Add to butter mixture alternately with half-and-half, beginning and ending with flour mixture. Beat at low speed just until blended after each

---

Festive Trims

A dusting of powdered sugar or a drizzle of Wintry-White Icing brings unexpected elegance to the fluted lines of a Bundt cake. One of our favorite seasonal garnishes, a wreath of Sugared Rosemary scattered with Christmas-red cranberries, adds a merry touch. Sliced strawberries and mint sprigs are pretty too.

Wintry-White Icing: Stir together 2 cups powdered sugar, 3 to 4 Tbsp. milk, and 1 tsp. vanilla extract until smooth.

Fluffy Wintry-White Icing: Beat 2 cups powdered sugar, 3 to 4 Tbsp. milk, 1 tsp. vanilla extract, and 1 tsp. meringue powder with an electric mixer until light and fluffy.

Sugared Rosemary: Microwave ½ cup corn syrup at HIGH 10 seconds or until warm. Brush 10 to 12 rosemary sprigs lightly with corn syrup; sprinkle evenly with sugar. Arrange in a single layer on wax paper. Use immediately, or let stand at room temperature, uncovered, up to 24 hours.

Sugared Cranberries: Bring ½ cup sugar, ½ cup water, and 1 cup fresh cranberries to a boil in a small saucepan over medium-high heat, stirring often. (Do not overcook—cranberries should swell and just begin to pop.) Remove from heat immediately, and drain well. Toss cranberries with ¼ cup sugar, and arrange in a single layer on wax paper. Use immediately, or let stand at room temperature, uncovered, up to 24 hours.

addition. Stir in vanilla. Pour batter into a greased and floured 12-cup Bundt pan.
3. Bake at 325° for 1 hour to 1 hour and 10 minutes or until a long wooden pick inserted in center of cake comes out clean. Cool in pan on a wire rack 15 minutes. Remove from pan to wire rack; cool 30 minutes or until completely cool. Garnish, if desired. **Makes** 12 servings.

Praline Bundt Cake

PREP: 30 MIN.; BAKE: 1 HR., 22 MIN.; COOL: 1 HR. *(Pictured on page 192)*

1 cup chopped pecans
1 cup butter, softened
1 (8-oz.) package cream cheese, softened
1 (16-oz.) package dark brown sugar
4 large eggs
2½ cups all-purpose flour
1 tsp. baking powder
½ tsp. baking soda
¼ tsp. salt
1 (8-oz.) container sour cream
2 tsp. vanilla extract
Praline Icing
Sugared Pecans

1. Arrange 1 cup pecans in a single layer on a baking sheet.
2. Bake at 350° for 5 to 7 minutes or until toasted. Cool on a wire rack 15 minutes or until completely cool. Reduce oven temperature to 325°.
3. Beat butter and cream cheese at medium speed with an electric mixer until creamy. Gradually add brown sugar, beating until well blended. Add eggs, 1 at a time, beating just until blended after each addition.
4. Sift together flour and next 3 ingredients. Add to butter mixture alternately with sour cream, beginning and ending with flour mixture. Beat batter at low speed just until blended after each addition. Stir in toasted pecans and vanilla. Spoon batter into a greased and floured 12-cup Bundt pan.
5. Bake at 325° for 1 hour and 15 minutes or until a long wooden pick inserted in center comes out clean. Cool in pan on a wire rack 15 minutes; remove

from pan to wire rack, and let cool 30 minutes or until completely cool.
6. Prepare Praline Icing, and spoon immediately over cake. Sprinkle top of cake with Sugared Pecans. **Makes** 12 servings.

Praline Icing:

PREP: 10 MIN., COOK: 5 MIN.

1 cup firmly packed light brown sugar
½ cup butter
¼ cup milk
1 cup powdered sugar, sifted
1 tsp. vanilla extract

1. Bring first 3 ingredients to a boil in a 2-qt. saucepan over medium heat, whisking constantly; boil 1 minute. Remove from heat; whisk in powdered sugar and vanilla until smooth. Stir gently 3 to 5 minutes or until mixture begins to cool and thickens slightly. Use immediately. **Makes** about 1½ cups.

Measured Success

■ Cake recipes often yield different amounts of batter, so it's a good idea to double check the size of your Bundt pan by filling it to the rim with cups of water. Depending on the brand, a 10-inch pan may hold 10, 12, or 14 cups. If you use a smaller pan than is called for in a recipe, fill the pan no more than one-half to two-thirds full. Refrigerate the remaining batter up to 1½ hours, return to room temperature, and bake as cupcakes or miniature loaf cakes. (For more information on baking with different size pans, see "From Our Kitchen" on page 296.)

■ Beware of the bright-colored silicone Bundt pans. Results vary, but many buckle when heated, and bake unevenly, producing lopsided cakes that stick to the pan.

■ To ensure a Bundt cake releases easily from the pan, use a pastry brush to generously coat the inside with solid vegetable shortening. Then sprinkle with flour, tilting and tapping the pan to evenly cover all the narrow crevices. If the pan has a nonstick coating, a vegetable cooking spray made especially for baking, such as Pam with Flour or Crisco with Flour, works equally well.

Sugared Pecans:

freezeable • make ahead

PREP: 10 MIN., BAKE: 20 MIN., COOL: 30 MIN.

1 egg white
4 cups pecan halves (about 1 lb.)
⅓ cup granulated sugar
⅓ cup firmly packed light brown sugar

1. Whisk egg white in a large bowl until foamy; add pecans, and stir until evenly coated.
2. Stir together sugars until blended; sprinkle sugar mixture over pecans. Stir gently until pecans are evenly coated. Spread pecans in a single layer in a lightly greased aluminum foil-lined 15- x 10-inch jelly-roll pan.
3. Bake at 350° for 18 to 20 minutes or until pecans are toasted and dry, stirring once after 10 minutes. Remove from oven, and let cool 30 minutes or until completely cool. **Makes** about 5 cups.

Note: Store pecans in a zip-top plastic freezer bag at room temperature up to 3 days or freeze up to 3 weeks.

Sparkling Peppermint Candy

PREP: 15 MIN., COOK: 20 MIN., COOL: 45 MIN.

This glittery candy makes a spectacular finish for Vanilla Butter Cake. For a simpler adornment, just drizzle with your choice of icing (page 278) and crush your favorite holiday candy to decorate the cake.

Vegetable oil
2 cups granulated sugar
¾ cup light corn syrup, divided
1 tsp. peppermint flavoring
½ tsp. red food coloring paste
Clear sparkling sugar

1. Generously oil bottom and sides of a 15- x 11-inch jelly-roll pan. Stir together granulated sugar, ½ cup corn syrup, and ½ cup water in a medium saucepan over medium heat until a candy thermometer registers 300° to 310° (hard-crack stage, about 15 to 20 minutes).
2. Remove from heat, and stir in peppermint flavoring and food coloring paste until well blended; quickly pour mixture onto prepared jelly-roll pan. Cool 45 minutes or until completely cool. Break into pieces.
3. Carefully brush or dip edges (some edges will be jagged and sharp) of candy pieces with remaining corn syrup allowing excess syrup to drip off, and sprinkle with clear sparkling sugar. **Makes** about 1 lb.

Clear Sparkling Peppermint Candy: Omit red food coloring. Proceed with recipe as directed.

Beef Three Ways

Beef is probably the most diverse of all meats. Multiple cuts can be selected to fit any budget and are ideal for stewing, roasting, grilling, braising, or broiling.

Slow-cooker Burgundy Beef Tips

PREP: 10 MIN., COOK: 4 HR.

This recipe calls for baby portobellos, but your favorite sliced mushrooms will work fine. Serve the beef tips over hot cooked egg noodles or rice tossed with parsley.

2 lb. beef sirloin tips, cut into 1-inch pieces
1 (8-oz.) package sliced fresh baby portobello mushrooms
1 (10¾-oz.) can cream of mushroom soup
½ cup dry red wine
1 (1.0-oz.) envelope dry onion soup mix
⅛ tsp. pepper

1. Stir together all ingredients in a lightly greased 5-qt. slow cooker.
2. Cover and cook on HIGH 4 hours or until beef is tender, stirring once after 2 hours. **Makes** 6 servings.

TRICIA MALMUT
CONCORD, NORTH CAROLINA

Note: Though we love the hands-off advantage of the slow cooker, this recipe works better when you can stay close by to stir it after two hours. Stirring prevents sticking and distributes ingredients evenly.

Beef Gorgonzola

PREP: 10 MIN., COOK: 40 MIN.,
GRILL: 16 MIN., STAND: 10 MIN.

2 Tbsp. butter
1 medium onion, thinly sliced
1 (8-oz.) package sliced fresh mushrooms
1 pt. whipping cream
4 oz. crumbled Gorgonzola cheese
6 (6-oz.) beef tenderloin fillets
¾ tsp. salt
¼ tsp. pepper
Garnish: crumbled Gorgonzola cheese

1. Melt butter in a large skillet over medium-high heat; add onion, and cook, stirring often, 6 to 8 minutes or until tender. Add mushrooms, and cook, stirring often, 5 minutes. Reduce heat to medium, and cook 5 more minutes or until mushrooms are tender.
2. Bring whipping cream to a boil in a medium saucepan over medium heat.

Reduce heat to low, and simmer, stirring often, 15 minutes or until slightly thickened.
3. Whisk cheese into whipping cream, and cook, whisking often, over medium heat 4 minutes or until cheese is melted. Stir in onion mixture. Keep warm.
4. Sprinkle fillets with salt and pepper. Grill fillets, covered with grill lid, over medium-high heat (350° to 400°) 5 to 8 minutes on each side or to desired degree of doneness. Remove from grill, and let stand 10 minutes. Serve with warm cheese sauce. Garnish, if desired. **Makes** 6 servings.

JEFFREY CARUANA
TRINITY, FLORIDA

Note: To make recipe on an indoor grill pan, prepare recipe as directed through Step 3. Heat a nonstick grill pan over medium-high heat. Sprinkle fillets with salt and pepper. Cook 4 to 5 minutes on each side or to desired degree of doneness. Proceed with recipe as directed.

Beef With Roasted Poblano Chile Peppers

PREP: 20 MIN.; BROIL: 16 MIN.;
STAND: 10 MIN.; COOK: 1 HR., 20 MIN.

3 poblano chile peppers
1½ lb. beef stew meat, cut into 1-inch cubes
2 Tbsp. olive oil
1 large onion, diced (about 2 cups)
1 (14-oz.) can beef broth
2 medium-size red potatoes, peeled and diced (about 2 cups)
1 tsp. salt
½ tsp. pepper
Corn Tortilla Strips

1. Broil peppers on an aluminum foil-lined baking sheet 5 inches from heat 7 to 8 minutes on each side or until peppers look blistered. Place peppers in a large zip-top plastic freezer bag; seal and let stand 10 minutes to loosen skins. Peel peppers; remove and discard seeds. Chop peppers.
2. Cook beef in hot oil in a large Dutch oven over medium-high heat, stirring occasionally, 8 minutes or until browned. Stir in onion, and cook 8 minutes or until tender.

3. Stir in beef broth, chopped peppers, and 1½ cups water, stirring to loosen particles from bottom of Dutch oven. Bring mixture to a boil over high heat. Cover, reduce heat to low, and cook 40 minutes. Stir in potatoes; cover and cook 20 minutes or until potatoes and meat are tender. Season with salt and pepper. Serve with Corn Tortilla Strips. **Makes** 6 servings.　　GREG FONTENOT
THE WOODLANDS, TEXAS

Corn Tortilla Strips:
fast fixin's
PREP: 10 MIN., BAKE. 18 MIN.

10 (5½-inch) fajita-size corn tortillas, cut into ¼-inch strips
Vegetable cooking spray
1 tsp. coarse salt

1. Place strips in a single layer on a lightly greased 15- x 11- inch jelly-roll pan. Coat with cooking spray. Sprinkle with salt.
2. Bake at 375° for 16 to 18 minutes or until lightly browned and crisp, turning once after 8 minutes. Remove from oven, and let cool. **Makes** 6 servings.

Scrumptious Southwestern Suppers

Slow-cooker Black Beans
PREP: 15 MIN.; SOAK: 8 HR.;
COOK: 5 HR., 20 MIN.

1 (16-oz.) package dried black beans
2 bacon slices
1 large sweet onion, diced (about 2 cups)
2 celery ribs, diced (about ½ cup)
3 garlic cloves, chopped
2 cups diced cooked ham
½ tsp. ground cumin
¼ tsp. coarsely ground black pepper
¼ tsp. ground red pepper
1 (32-oz.) container low-sodium fat-free chicken broth

1. Rinse and sort beans according to package directions. Place beans in a 6-qt. slow cooker. Add water 2 inches above beans; let soak 8 hours. Drain and rinse. Return beans to slow cooker.
2. Cook bacon in a large skillet over medium-high heat 4 to 5 minutes or until crisp; remove bacon, and drain on paper towels, reserving 2 Tbsp. drippings in skillet. Crumble bacon, and add to slow cooker.
3. Sauté onion, celery, and garlic in hot drippings 7 to 8 minutes or until tender. Reduce heat to medium, and stir in ham, cumin, and ground peppers. Sauté 5 minutes or until thoroughly heated. Stir in ½ cup chicken broth, and cook 2 minutes, stirring to loosen particles from bottom of skillet; add mixture to slow cooker. Stir in remaining chicken broth and 1 cup water.
4. Cover and cook on HIGH 5 hours or LOW 8 hours or until beans are tender. **Makes** 8 cups.

Creamy Black Bean Soup
PREP: 15 MIN., COOK: 30 MIN.

1 medium onion, diced (about 1 cup)
1 tsp. minced garlic
1 Tbsp. olive oil
4 cups undrained Slow-cooker Black Beans *
1 (32-oz.) container chicken broth
2 (4.5-oz.) cans chopped green chiles, undrained
1 (14.5-oz.) can Mexican-style stewed tomatoes, undrained
1 (14.5-oz.) can diced tomatoes, undrained
1 (11-oz.) can whole kernel corn, rinsed and drained
2 Tbsp. chili powder
1 tsp. ground cumin
Toppings: sour cream, shredded Cheddar cheese, diced tomatoes, chopped fresh cilantro

1. Sauté onion and garlic in hot oil in a Dutch oven over medium-high heat 6 minutes or until tender. Stir in next 8 ingredients, stirring to loosen particles from bottom of Dutch oven; cover and bring to a boil. Uncover, reduce heat to medium-low, and simmer, stirring occasionally, 15 minutes.
2. Process 2 cups of soup in blender or food processor 30 seconds or until smooth. Return to Dutch oven, and stir until blended. Serve with desired toppings. **Makes** 16 cups.

＊2 (15-oz.) cans black beans, rinsed and drained, may be substituted.

Black Bean Chimichangas
make ahead
PREP: 15 MIN., BAKE: 18 MIN.

1 (8.8-oz.) pouch ready-to-serve Mexican-style rice and pasta mix
2 cups drained Slow-cooker Black Beans ＊
1 cup chunky medium salsa
1 cup (4 oz.) shredded Mexican four-cheese blend
2 cups shredded deli-roasted chicken (optional)
10 (8-inch) soft taco-size flour tortillas
¼ cup butter, melted
Toppings: shredded lettuce, diced tomatoes, sour cream, guacamole, olives

1. Heat rice according to package directions.
2. Stir together rice, next 3 ingredients, and if desired, chicken. Spread ½ cup rice mixture just below center of each tortilla. Fold bottom third up and over filling of each tortilla, just until covered. Fold left and right sides of tortillas over and roll up. Place, seams side down, on a lightly greased jelly-roll pan. Brush tops of tortillas with melted butter.
3. Bake at 400° for 15 to 18 minutes or until golden brown. Serve with desired toppings. **Makes** 5 servings.

＊1 (15-oz.) can black beans, rinsed and drained, may be substituted.

Note: For testing purposes only, we used Rice-A-Roni Express Mexican.

To make ahead: Prepare chimichangas as directed through Step 2; cover and chill 8 hours. Let stand at room temperature 30 minutes; bake as directed.

Super Doable Sides

Six-ingredient recipes deliver big taste.

These easy but impressive vegetable recipes are just right to add a breath of fresh air to your meal planning. Try the Sweet Potato Pockets with baked ham or pork roast. Thyme-Scented Mushrooms and Potatoes Baked in Sea Salt are perfect alongside grilled steaks or beef tenderloin. With these highly rated dishes, change is a good thing.

Sweet Potato Pockets
family favorite
PREP: 20 MIN., COOK: 25 MIN.

½ (16-oz.) package won ton wrappers
1 (15-oz.) can sweetened mashed sweet potatoes*
2 Tbsp. olive oil
½ cup butter
1 Tbsp. chopped fresh sage
Salt to taste

1. Arrange 1 won ton wrapper on a clean, flat surface (Cover remaining wrappers with plastic wrap or a damp towel to prevent drying out.) Lightly moisten wrapper with water. Place about 1 Tbsp. mashed sweet potatoes in center of wrapper; fold 2 opposite corners together over mashed sweet potatoes, forming a triangle. Press edges together to seal, removing any air pockets. Cover with plastic wrap or a damp cloth. Repeat procedure with remaining wrappers and mashed sweet potatoes.
2. Cook pockets, in 2 batches, in boiling water to cover in a large Dutch oven over medium-high heat 3 minutes. Remove with a slotted spoon, and drain well.
3. Sauté pockets, in batches, in hot oil in a large nonstick skillet over medium-high heat 2 to 3 minutes on each side or until golden brown. Drain well. Arrange pockets on a serving platter.
4. Melt butter in skillet over medium heat; stir in sage. Cook, stirring occasionally, 4 minutes or until butter is lightly browned. Pour butter mixture over pockets, add salt to taste, and serve immediately. **Makes** 4 to 5 servings.

BEN STOVER
GRANGER, INDIANA

*1 (15-oz.) can cut sweet potatoes in syrup, mashed, may be substituted.

Note: For testing purposes only, we used Glory Foods Sweet Potato Casserole.

Potatoes Baked in Sea Salt
family favorite
PREP: 15 MIN., BAKE: 20 MIN.

6 large red potatoes (about 4 lb.)*
3 Tbsp. olive oil
6 Tbsp. sea salt**
Butter
Pepper

1. Rinse potatoes, and pierce several times with tines of a fork. Place on a microwave-safe plate; cover with damp paper towels. Microwave at HIGH 8 to 10 minutes. Place potatoes in a large ovenproof skillet or 15- x 10-inch jelly-roll pan. Drizzle with oil, and sprinkle evenly with sea salt, turning to coat.

Pockets of Flavor

Lightly mist won ton wrapper with water. You may also use your fingertips to moisten the wrapper.

Spoon 1 Tbsp. of mashed sweet potatoes in center of each wrapper.

Fold 2 opposite corners together, forming a triangle. Press edges together to seal, removing any air pockets.

2. Bake at 450° for 20 minutes or until tender, turning after 10 minutes. Serve with butter and pepper. **Makes** 6 servings.
DIANE LEWIS
OCEAN CITY, MARYLAND

*4 lb. petite red potatoes may be substituted.

**6 Tbsp. table salt may be substituted.

Thyme-Scented Mushrooms
fast fixin's
PREP: 5 MIN., COOK: 12 MIN.

4 Tbsp. butter
1½ tsp. olive oil
2 (8-oz.) packages fresh mushrooms
2 to 3 tsp. dried thyme leaves, crushed
Salt and pepper to taste

1. Melt butter with oil in a large non-stick skillet over medium-high heat; add mushrooms and thyme, and sauté 10 minutes or until golden brown. Add salt and pepper to taste. **Makes** 4 servings.
JAN KIMBELL
VESTAVIA HILLS, ALABAMA

Thyme-Scented Sliced Mushrooms: Substitute 2 (8-oz.) packages sliced fresh mushrooms. Proceed with recipe as directed.

Cranberry-Filled Acorn Squash
fast fixin's • make ahead
PREP: 20 MIN., COOK: 8 MIN.
Serve extra cranberry filling over waffles or pancakes.

1 large orange
1 (12-oz.) package fresh
   cranberries
1 cup sugar
2 acorn squash, halved and seeded
   (about 2 lb.)
½ tsp. salt
¼ tsp. pepper

1. Grate orange rind from orange, avoiding pale bitter pith, into a medium saucepan to equal 1 Tbsp.; squeeze orange juice into pan to equal 5 Tbsp.
2. Stir in cranberries, sugar, and 1 cup water; cover and bring to a boil over medium-high heat. Uncover and cook, stirring occasionally, 5 minutes. Remove from heat.
3. Place squash, cut sides down, and ½ cup water in an 8-inch square microwave-safe dish. Cover tightly with heavy-duty plastic wrap; fold back a small edge to allow steam to escape. Microwave squash, in 2 batches, at HIGH 7 minutes or until tender. Carefully remove squash, and place on a serving platter.
4. Sprinkle squash with salt and pepper. Fill each squash with ¼ cup cranberry mixture. Store remaining mixture in refrigerator in an airtight container up to 1 week. **Makes** 4 servings.
MELANIE WANDERS
CHAPEL HILL, NORTH CAROLINA

Fresh Take on Chicken Tenders

It's time to give chicken tenders a new try—without a deep fryer. You see, what makes them perfect for frying (their consistent size resulting in even cooking) makes them the ideal choice for other dishes.

Artichoke 'n' Chicken Alfredo Over Wilted Spinach
PREP: 15 MIN., BAKE: 40 MIN., COOK: 3 MIN.

2 lb. chicken tenders
¼ tsp. pepper
½ (16-oz.) jar sun-dried tomato Alfredo
   sauce
2 Tbsp. dry white wine
1 (12-oz.) jar quartered marinated
   artichoke hearts, drained
½ cup grated Asiago cheese, divided
2 (6-oz.) bags fresh baby spinach
2 tsp. fresh lemon juice
2 Tbsp. chopped fresh parsley

1. Sprinkle chicken tenders with pepper, and place in a lightly greased 13- x 9-inch baking dish. Stir together Alfredo sauce and white wine, and spoon evenly over chicken. Cut artichoke quarters in half, and arrange over chicken; sprinkle with ¼ cup cheese.
2. Bake at 350° for 35 to 40 minutes or until sauce is bubbly and chicken is done.
3. Meanwhile, thoroughly wash spinach. Cook spinach in a lightly greased skillet over medium-high heat 2 to 3 minutes or just until wilted; sprinkle with lemon juice. Place spinach on a serving platter, and top with chicken tenders. Spoon artichokes and sauce over chicken, and sprinkle with parsley and remaining ¼ cup cheese. **Makes** 6 to 8 servings.
EARLYNE SALAZAR
ALPHARETTA, GEORGIA

Note: For testing purposes only, we used Classico Sun-Dried Tomato Alfredo sauce.

Easy Skillet Cordon Bleu
family favorite
PREP: 10 MIN., COOK: 8 MIN., BROIL: 2 MIN.

½ cup Italian-seasoned breadcrumbs
1 tsp. pepper
½ tsp. salt
8 chicken tenders (about 1 lb.)
1 Tbsp. butter
1 Tbsp. olive oil
8 Canadian bacon slices, cut into thin
   strips
4 Swiss cheese slices, halved

1. Combine first 3 ingredients in a large zip-top plastic freezer bag. Rinse chicken tenders, and add to freezer bag. Seal bag, and shake to coat.
2. Melt butter with oil in an oven-proof skillet over medium heat. Cook chicken 3½ to 4 minutes on each side or until done. Arrange Canadian bacon strips over chicken in skillet, and top each with 1 cheese slice. Broil 5½ inches from heat 2 minutes or until cheese is melted. **Makes** 4 to 6 servings.
CARLY HERBERT
MECHANICSVILLE, VIRGINIA

Dill Pickle-Marinated Chicken Tenders With Dilly Dipping Sauce

PREP: 10 MIN., CHILL: 2 HR., GRILL: 10 MIN.
Often discarded after the pickles are eaten, humble dill pickle juice becomes a star ingredient in this recipe.

1 lb. chicken tenders
¾ cup dill pickle juice
½ tsp. seasoned salt
¼ tsp. pepper
Vegetable cooking spray
Dilly Dipping Sauce

1. Place chicken tenders and ¾ cup pickle juice in a shallow dish or zip-top plastic freezer bag. Cover or seal, and chill 2 hours.
2. Remove chicken from marinade, discarding marinade. Sprinkle chicken with salt and pepper.
3. Coat a cold cooking grate with cooking spray, and place on grill over medium-high heat (350° to 400°). Place chicken tenders on cooking grate, and grill, covered with grill lid, 4 to 5 minutes on each side or until done. Serve with Dilly Dipping Sauce. **Makes** 4 servings.

Note: To broil, proceed with Steps 1 and 2 as directed. Omit Step 3, and place chicken tenders on an aluminum foil-lined baking sheet. Broil 5½ inches from heat 4 to 5 minutes on each side or until done. Serve with Dilly Dipping Sauce.

Dilly Dipping Sauce:

PREP: 10 MIN.

1 cup mayonnaise
¼ cup Ranch dressing
1 large dill pickle, diced (about ½ cup)
1 Tbsp. country-style Dijon mustard
1 Tbsp. dill pickle juice

1. Stir together all ingredients until blended. Cover and chill until ready to serve. Store in refrigerator in an airtight container up to 1 week. **Makes** about 1½ cups.

Note: For testing purposes only, we used Grey Poupon Country Dijon mustard.

healthy foods
Creative Ways With Cranberries

Cranberries aren't just a condiment for your holiday turkey. You're in for a scrumptious surprise when you taste what these readers shared with us. They reinvented ways to use fresh, frozen, and dried cranberries, offering everyday recipes loaded with good-for-you flavor. Stock up now when fresh cranberries are abundant, and enjoy these appetizers, main dishes, and desserts year-round. Purchase them in bulk, and freeze them up to a year. If you don't have fresh or frozen on hand, try Cranberry-Orange Bread. It calls for dried cranberries, which are just as nutritious.

Cranberry-Orange Bread
family favorite • make ahead
PREP: 15 MIN., BAKE: 32 MIN., COOL: 25 MIN.
Crispy cereal adds a light crunch to this moist breakfast bread. The slices are also great toasted with light butter spread or cream cheese.

1 cup nutlike cereal nuggets
1 cup uncooked regular oats
½ cup whole wheat flour
⅓ cup sugar
½ tsp. baking soda
½ tsp. salt
½ cup nonfat buttermilk
¼ cup vegetable oil
2 large eggs
1 tsp. grated orange rind
½ cup low-sugar orange marmalade
½ cup sweetened dried cranberries
Light Cranberry Butter Spread

1. Combine first 6 ingredients in a large bowl; make a well in center of mixture.
2. Whisk together buttermilk, oil, and eggs; add to dry mixture, stirring just until moistened. Gently fold in grated orange rind, marmalade, and cranberries. Spoon into a lightly greased 8½- x 4½-inch loaf pan.
3. Bake at 375° for 28 to 32 minutes or until a wooden pick inserted in center comes out clean. Cool in pan on wire rack 5 minutes. Remove from pan to wire rack, and let cool 20 minutes or until completely cool. Serve with Light Cranberry Butter Spread. **Makes** 12 servings.

LUANNE SMITH
ELON, NORTH CAROLINA

Note: For testing purposes only, we used Post Grape-Nuts cereal. To make ahead, store bread loaf or muffins in a zip-top plastic freezer bag, and freeze up to 1 month or refrigerate up to 3 days. Reheat at 350° for 8 to 10 minutes or until warmed.

Cranberry-Orange Muffins: Prepare recipe as directed through Step 2, spooning batter into a lightly greased muffin pan, filling two-thirds full. Bake at 375° for 16 to 18 minutes or until golden brown. Cool in pan on wire rack 5 minutes; remove from pan to wire rack, and cool 10 minutes or until completely cool. **Makes** 1 dozen. Prep: 15 min., Bake: 18 min., Cool: 15 min.

Per bread slice or muffin (not including light butter spread): Calories 186; Fat 6.2g (sat 0.7g, mono 1.5g, poly 3.3g); Protein 4.1g; Carb 30.4g; Fiber 2.4g; Chol 35mg; Iron 3.4mg; Sodium 231mg; Calc 26mg

Light Cranberry Butter Spread:
fast fixin's • make ahead
PREP: 10 MIN.

½ cup light whipped butter
⅓ cup sweetened dried cranberries
1 Tbsp. honey

1. Stir together all ingredients in a medium bowl. Store in an airtight container in refrigerator up to 1 week. **Makes** about ⅔ cup.

Note: For testing purposes only, we used Land O'Lakes Whipped Light Butter at one testing and Fleischmann's Made With Olive Oil at another.

Per Tbsp.: Calories 54; Fat 3.7g (sat 1.5g, mono 0g, poly 0g); Protein 0g; Carb 4.6g; Fiber 0.2g; Chol 4mg; Iron 0mg; Sodium 69mg; Calc 0mg

Caramelized Onion-Cranberry Compote
make ahead

PREP: 10 MIN., COOK: 22 MIN.

You can make this a day ahead, and store it in an airtight container in the fridge. Let stand at room temperature 30 minutes before serving.

1 Tbsp. butter
2 cups thinly sliced sweet onions
¼ cup balsamic vinegar
½ cup fresh or frozen cranberries (thawed), coarsely chopped *
1 Tbsp. sugar
½ tsp. salt
½ tsp. grated orange rind

1. Melt 1 Tbsp. butter in a large skillet over medium heat; add onions, and sauté 15 to 18 minutes or until golden and tender. Stir in vinegar and remaining ingredients, and cook, stirring occasionally, 2 to 4 minutes or until liquid is reduced to about 2 Tbsp. **Makes** 1 cup.

***** ½ cup coarsely chopped sweetened dried cranberries may be substituted.

Per Tbsp.: Calories 20; Fat 0.7g (sat 0.5g, mono 0.2g, poly 0g); Protein 0.2g; Carb 3.2g; Fiber 0.4g; Chol 2mg; Iron 0.1mg; Sodium 79mg; Calc 5mg

Bistro Steaks With Caramelized Onion-Cranberry Compote: Combine ½ cup dry red wine, 2 Tbsp. olive oil, and 2 tsp. herbes de Provence in a shallow dish or large zip-top plastic freezer bag; add 1 (1-lb.) flank steak. Cover or seal, and chill 8 hours. Remove steak from marinade, discarding marinade. Grill steak, covered with grill lid, over medium-high heat (350° to 400°) 8 to 10 minutes on each side or to desired degree of doneness. Let stand 10 minutes. Cut diagonally across the grain into thin strips, and divide among 4 plates. Top each with ¼ cup Caramelized Onion-Cranberry Compote and 1 Tbsp. crumbled blue cheese. **Makes** 4 servings. Prep: 10 min., Grill: 20 min., Stand: 10 min.

LORI WELANDER
RICHMOND, VIRGINIA

Per serving: Calories 307; Fat 15.2g (sat 6.4g, mono 5.9g, poly 0.9g); Protein 24.8g; Carb 13.8g; Fiber 1.6g; Chol 58mg; Iron 1.7mg; Sodium 457mg; Calc 72mg

Caramelized Onion-Cranberry-Cream Cheese Bites: Spread 16 whole grain crackers each with 1½ tsp. ⅓-less-fat cream cheese; top each with 1 Tbsp. Caramelized Onion-Cranberry Compote. Garnish with fresh parsley or cilantro leaves. **Makes** 16 appetizer servings. Prep: 10 min.

Per serving: Calories 56; Fat 2.9g (sat 1.6g, mono 0.6g, poly 0.1g); Protein 1.3g; Carb 6.2g; Fiber 0.8g; Chol 7mg; Iron 0.2mg; Sodium 137mg; Calc 12mg

Blue Cheese-Cranberry Salad
fast fixin's

PREP: 10 MIN., BAKE: 10 MIN.

⅓ cup walnut pieces
4 cups mixed greens
½ cup blue cheese
½ cup grape tomatoes, halved
⅓ cup sweetened dried cranberries
½ cup light raspberry vinaigrette

1. Place walnuts in a single layer in a shallow pan. Bake at 350° for 8 to 10 minutes or until toasted, stirring after 5 minutes.
2. Arrange greens on 6 salad plates. Sprinkle each with blue cheese, tomatoes, cranberries, and toasted walnuts. Drizzle each with 4 tsp. vinaigrette. **Makes** 6 servings.

KATHLEEN SCHIRF
BOWIE, MARYLAND

Note: For testing purposes only, we used Ken's Lite Raspberry Walnut Vinaigrette.

Per serving: Calories 159; Fat 11.1g (sat 2.8g, mono 0.6g, poly 3.2g); Protein 3.7g; Carb 13.1g; Fiber 1.8g; Chol 8mg; Iron 0.8mg; Sodium 221mg; Calc 78mg

Ice Cream With Warm Cranberry Sauce
fast fixin's • make ahead

PREP: 5 MIN., COOK: 12 MIN., COOL: 10 MIN.

Store the sauce in an airtight container in the refrigerator up to three days, and reheat in a microwave-safe glass bowl on high 1½ to 2 minutes or until warmed.

1 (12-oz.) package fresh cranberries *
1¼ cups sugar
1 cup light white cranberry juice
2 Tbsp. brandy (optional)
3 cups low-fat vanilla ice cream

1. Stir together first 3 ingredients and, if desired, brandy, in a heavy saucepan. Cook over medium heat, stirring often, 10 to 12 minutes or until cranberry skins begin to split. Remove from heat, and cool 10 minutes. Spoon ½ cup ice cream into 6 bowls; top each with ⅓ cup cranberry sauce. **Makes** 6 servings (about 2½ cups topping).

ANGELA JOHNSON
ATLANTA, GEORGIA

***** 1 (12-oz.) package frozen cranberries, thawed, may be substituted.

Note: For testing purposes only, we used Ocean Spray Light White Cranberry Juice Drink.

Per serving (including brandy): Calories 327; Fat 2.1g (sat 1g, mono 0g, poly 0.1g); Protein 3.4g; Carb 72.7g; Fiber 3.7g; Chol 5mg; Iron 0.3mg; Sodium 47mg; Calc 108mg

Splurge-Worthy Seafood

We tend to splurge a little more on ingredients this time of year, especially when cooking for those we love. These recipes are surprisingly easy to make and will certainly impress.

Crab Cakes

PREP: 20 MIN., CHILL: 1 HR.,
COOK: 6 MIN. PER BATCH

Work gently when handling fresh crabmeat to preserve the delicate lumps. Make patties up to six hours in advance, keep chilled, and cook at the last minute.

1 lb. fresh lump crabmeat, drained
2 green onions, thinly sliced
1 red bell pepper, finely chopped
2 garlic cloves, minced
1 large egg, lightly beaten
3 Tbsp. heavy cream
1 Tbsp. chopped fresh parsley
1 Tbsp. Dijon mustard
¼ tsp. ground red pepper
1½ cups multigrain rectangular-shaped crackers, finely crushed
¼ cup freshly grated Parmigiano-Reggiano cheese *
4 Tbsp. butter
Watercress
Lemon-Caper Mayonnaise
Lemon wedges

1. Gently pick crabmeat, removing any bits of shell.
2. Stir together green onions, next 7 ingredients, and ½ cup crushed crackers; gently fold crabmeat into mixture. Shape into 8 equal patties. Combine remaining cracker crumbs and cheese in a shallow dish. Dredge patties in breadcrumb mixture. Cover and chill 1 hour.
3. Melt 2 Tbsp. butter in a large nonstick skillet over medium-high heat. Add 4 patties, and cook 3 minutes on each side or until golden brown; drain on paper towels. Repeat procedure with remaining 2 Tbsp. butter and patties.

Serve crab cakes over watercress with Lemon-Caper Mayonnaise and lemon wedges. **Makes** 4 servings.

ROYAL S. DELLINGER
ROCKVILLE, MARYLAND

* ¼ cup grated Parmesan cheese may be substituted.

Note: For testing purposes only, we used Keebler Club Multi-Grain crackers.

Lemon-Caper Mayonnaise:
fast fixin's
PREP: 5 MIN.

¾ cup mayonnaise
2 tsp. capers, drained
1 tsp. grated lemon rind
1 tsp. chopped fresh parsley
1 tsp. fresh lemon juice

1. Stir together all ingredients. Cover and chill until ready to serve. **Makes** about ¾ cup.

Oven-Roasted Shrimp With Romesco Sauce

PREP: 20 MIN., COOK: 4 MIN., BAKE: 8 MIN.

2½ lb. unpeeled, large raw shrimp
3 Tbsp. olive oil
Romesco Sauce

1. Peel shrimp; devein, if desired.
2. Sauté shrimp in hot oil in a large ovenproof skillet over medium-high heat 3 to 4 minutes or just until barely pink. Remove from heat; add 2 cups Romesco Sauce, and toss to coat.
3. Bake at 450° for 6 to 8 minutes. Serve shrimp with remaining sauce. **Makes** 4 servings.

Note: To make this recipe in a baking dish, prepare recipe as directed through Step 1. Stir together shrimp and 2 cups Romesco Sauce. Place shrimp mixture in a lightly greased 13-x 9-inch baking dish. Bake at 450° for 20 to 25 minutes, stirring and turning shrimp after 15 minutes. Serve with remaining sauce.

Romesco Sauce:
PREP: 15 MIN., BAKE: 10 MIN.

Romesco is a classic Spanish sauce made of finely ground almonds, bread, bell peppers, garlic, and tomatoes. We added pecans to give it a little Southern flavor.

½ cup slivered almonds
⅓ cup pecan halves
2 white bread slices, toasted
6 garlic cloves
1 (14½-oz.) can diced tomatoes, drained
1 cup fire-roasted red bell peppers, chopped
1 Tbsp. chopped fresh oregano
1 Tbsp. chopped fresh parsley
1 tsp. sugar
1 tsp. salt
¼ tsp. pepper
1 tsp. smoked Spanish paprika
2 Tbsp. white wine vinegar
⅓ cup olive oil

1. Place almonds and pecans in a single layer in a shallow pan. Bake at 350° for 8 to 10 minutes or until lightly toasted, stirring once after 5 minutes.
2. Process almonds, pecans, bread slices, and next 9 ingredients in a food processor until smooth, stopping to scrape down sides. With processor running, pour vinegar and oil through food chute in a slow, steady stream, processing until blended. **Makes** 3 cups.

SHERI CASTLE
CHAPEL HILL, NORTH CAROLINA

New Orleans Barbecue Shrimp

PREP: 30 MIN., COOK: 10 MIN.

2 lb. unpeeled, large raw shrimp
6 Tbsp. butter
1 Tbsp. olive oil
4 garlic cloves, minced
¼ cup chili sauce
¼ cup Worcestershire sauce
1½ Tbsp. Creole seasoning *
1 Tbsp. chopped fresh parsley
1 tsp. dried oregano
½ tsp. paprika
½ tsp. hot sauce
¼ tsp. ground red pepper
⅓ cup beer (not dark)
2 small lemons, seeded and sliced
1 (16-oz.) French bread baguette, sliced

1. Peel shrimp, leaving tails on; devein, if desired.

2. Melt butter with oil in a large skillet over medium-high heat. Add garlic; sauté 1 minute or until garlic begins to turn golden. Stir in chili sauce and next 7 ingredients; cook 1 minute. Stir in beer, lemons, and shrimp; cook 6 to 8 minutes, stirring occasionally, or just until shrimp turn pink. Serve with French bread slices. **Makes** 6 servings.

*1 ½ Tbsp. salt-free Creole seasoning may be substituted.

Heavenly Cinnamon Rolls

One taste of our perfectly tender cinnamon rolls and you'll never want store-bought again. If you have never made homemade, this is the place to start.

Cinnamon Rolls With Cream Cheese Icing

PREP: 30 MIN., STAND: 5 MIN., RISE: 3 HR., BAKE: 32 MIN., COOL: 2 MIN.
Be sure the butter you spread on the rolled-out dough is very soft.

1 (¼-oz.) envelope active dry yeast
¼ cup warm water (100° to 110°)
1 tsp. granulated sugar
½ cup butter, softened
1 cup granulated sugar, divided
1 tsp. salt
2 large eggs, lightly beaten
1 cup milk
1 Tbsp. fresh lemon juice
4½ cups bread flour
¼ tsp. ground nutmeg
¼ to ½ cup bread flour
1 cup chopped pecans
½ cup butter, very softened
½ cup firmly packed light brown sugar
1 Tbsp. ground cinnamon
Cream Cheese Icing

1. Combine first 3 ingredients in a 1-cup glass measuring cup; let stand 5 minutes.

2. Beat ½ cup softened butter at medium speed with a heavy-duty electric stand mixer, using paddle attachment, until creamy. Gradually add ½ cup granulated sugar and 1 tsp. salt, beating at medium speed until light and fluffy. Add eggs, milk, and lemon juice, beating until blended. Stir in yeast mixture.

3. Combine 4½ cups bread flour and ¼ tsp. nutmeg. Gradually add to butter mixture, beating at low speed 1 to 2 minutes or until well blended.

4. Sprinkle about ¼ cup bread flour onto work surface; turn dough out, and knead 5 minutes, adding additional bread flour as needed (to prevent dough from sticking to hands and work surface). Place dough in a lightly greased large bowl, turning to grease top of dough. Cover and let rise in a warm place (85°), free from drafts, 1½ to 2 hours or until doubled in bulk.

5. Meanwhile, place chopped pecans in a single layer in a shallow pan. Bake at 350° for 8 to 10 minutes or until toasted.

6. Punch dough down; turn out onto a lightly floured surface. Roll into a 16-x 12-inch rectangle. Spread with ½ cup very soft butter, leaving a 1-inch border. Stir together brown sugar, cinnamon, and remaining ½ cup granulated sugar, and sprinkle evenly over butter. Sprinkle with pecans.

7. Roll up, starting at long end; cut into 16 equal (about 1-inch-thick) slices. Place rolls into 2 lightly greased 10-inch round pans.

8. Cover and let rise in a warm place (85°), free from drafts, 1 hour or until doubled in bulk.

9. Bake at 350° for 20 to 22 minutes or until rolls are lightly browned. Cool in pans 2 minutes. Brush warm rolls with Cream Cheese Icing. Serve warm. **Makes** 16 rolls.

Apple-Cinnamon Rolls: Prepare recipe as directed through Step 5. Peel and chop 2 Granny Smith apples (about 3 cups chopped). Place apples in a small microwave-safe bowl, and pour 1 cup apple cider or apple juice over apples. Microwave at HIGH 5 minutes or until tender. Drain and cool 15 minutes. Proceed with recipe as directed, sprinkling apples over brown sugar mixture and topping with pecans.

Chocolate-Cinnamon Rolls: Prepare recipe as directed through Step 5. Chop 2 (4-oz.) bittersweet chocolate baking bars. Proceed with recipe as directed, sprinkling chocolate over brown sugar mixture and topping with pecans.

Cranberry-Cinnamon Rolls: Prepare recipe as directed through Step 5. Pour 1 cup boiling water over 1 cup dried cranberries; let stand 15 minutes. Drain cranberries. Proceed with recipe as directed, sprinkling cranberries over brown sugar mixture and topping with pecans.

Cream Cheese Icing:
fast fixin's
PREP: 10 MIN.

2 Tbsp. butter, softened
1 (3-oz.) package cream cheese, softened
2¼ cups powdered sugar
1 tsp. vanilla extract
2 Tbsp. milk

1. Beat butter and cream cheese at medium speed with an electric mixer until creamy. Gradually add powdered sugar, beating at low speed until blended. Stir in vanilla and 1 Tbsp. milk. Add remaining 1 Tbsp. milk, 1 tsp. at a time as needed, until icing is smooth and creamy. **Makes** 1½ cups.

Charleston Cheer

Fun is in full swing when the Lee brothers throw an easygoing Christmas dinner that's oh-so Southern.

Dashing Christmas Dinner

Serves 6

Spiced Pecans

Cheese Straws

New Ambrosia With Buttermilk-Coconut Dressing

Squash-and-Mushroom Hominy

Hot Slaw à la Greyhound Grill

Pork Loin Chops With Pear-and-Vidalia Pan Gravy

Sweet Potato-Buttermilk Pie

Hot-Spiced Bourbon Balls

"Meeerry Christmas. Come on in," encourages Matt Lee while greeting guests with warm hugs and a cheerful smile. Inside, Matt's younger brother, Ted, pops a bottle of bubbly for a quick toast while folks nibble on crunchy Spiced Pecans and peppery Cheese Straws. It's shortly after noon and the house is filled with an amazing combination of holiday aromas and the jazzy sounds of Sinatra's "Jingle Bells."

There's something delightfully laid-back about a party hosted by the Lees. But don't let their easygoing style fool you—food is serious business for these guys. In fact, the Charleston natives adapted this tempting holiday menu from *The Lee Bros. Southern Cookbook* (W.W. Norton, 2006), their critically acclaimed collection of regional recipes and witty commentary. From the cleverly delicious New Ambrosia salad to vinegary Hot Slaw to rich, sorghum-infused Hot-Spiced Bourbon Balls, this merry menu reflects Ted and Matt's knack for updating Southern classics without losing a lick of their delectable essence.

Spiced Pecans
freezeable • make ahead
PREP: 10 MIN., COOK: 3 MIN., BAKE: 50 MIN., COOL: 1 HR.

1 Tbsp. sugar
1 tsp. ground cinnamon
1 tsp. ground red pepper
1 tsp. kosher salt
1 tsp. sweet paprika
½ tsp. ground ginger
½ tsp. ground nutmeg
¼ to ½ tsp. ground cumin
¼ cup unsalted butter
1 Tbsp. honey
3 cups pecan halves

1. Stir together first 8 ingredients; remove and reserve 1 tsp. sugar mixture.
2. Melt butter in a 3½-qt. saucepan over low heat. Remove from heat, and stir in sugar mixture and honey, stirring until blended. Add pecans, and stir until well blended.
3. Spread pecans in a single layer on an ungreased 15- x 10-inch jelly-roll pan.

4. Bake at 250° for 50 minutes or until pecans are dark brown and syrup is slightly dry. Remove from oven, and sprinkle with reserved 1 tsp. sugar mixture. Cool in pan 1 hour. Store in an airtight container up to 1 week. **Makes 3 cups.**

Note: Baked pecans may be stored in a zip-top plastic freezer bag up to 3 months.

Cheese Straws
freezeable • make ahead
PREP: 30 MIN., BAKE: 12 MIN. PER BATCH, COOL: 30 MIN.
These tasty treats pack a pretty good kick. If you like yours less spicy, use the smaller amount of red pepper flakes.

1½ cups (6 oz.) shredded extra-sharp Cheddar cheese
¾ cup all-purpose flour
¼ cup unsalted butter, cut into 4 pieces and softened
½ tsp. kosher salt
¼ to ½ tsp. dried crushed red pepper
1 Tbsp. half-and-half

1. Combine first 5 ingredients in a food processor; pulse in 5-second intervals until mixture resembles coarse crumbs. Add half-and-half, and process 10 seconds or until dough forms a ball.
2. Turn dough out onto a well-floured surface, and roll into an 8- x 10-inch rectangle (about ⅛ inch thick). Cut dough with a sharp knife into ¼- to ½-inch-wide strips, dipping knife in flour after each cut to ensure clean cuts. Place on ungreased baking sheets.
3. Bake at 350° for 12 minutes or until ends are slightly browned. Cool on baking sheets on a wire rack 30 minutes. Break into desired lengths. **Makes about 2 dozen.**

Note: To make cheese rounds, roll dough to ⅛-inch thickness, and cut with a 1½-inch round cutter. Place on ungreased baking sheets. Bake and cool as directed. Freeze baked cheese straws and rounds in a heavy-duty zip-top plastic freezer bag up to 3 months. Let thaw at room temperature 30 minutes before serving.

New Ambrosia With Buttermilk-Coconut Dressing
make ahead
PREP: 30 MIN., CHILL: 1 HR.

2 large ruby red grapefruit, peeled and sectioned
2 large navel oranges, peeled and sectioned
3 celery ribs, chopped (about ¾ cup)
2 large avocados, cut into 1-inch cubes
1 large cucumber, peeled, seeded, and chopped (about 1½ cups)
1 jalapeño pepper, seeded and minced
½ cup chopped fresh basil
Buttermilk-Coconut Dressing
1 (5-oz.) package arugula, thoroughly washed
Garnish: toasted sweetened flaked coconut

1. Combine first 7 ingredients in a large bowl. Pour Buttermilk-Coconut Dressing over grapefruit mixture, tossing to coat. Cover and chill 1 hour.
2. Arrange arugula evenly on 6 salad plates. Toss grapefruit mixture, and place on arugula using a slotted spoon. Garnish, if desired. **Makes** 6 servings.

Buttermilk-Coconut Dressing:
make ahead
PREP: 10 MIN.
Prepare this versatile dressing and store in the refrigerator up to 3 days ahead.

1 garlic clove
1 tsp. kosher salt
⅔ cup buttermilk
2 Tbsp. fresh lime juice
1 Tbsp. plus 1 tsp. finely chopped fresh tarragon
1 Tbsp. plus 1 tsp. sweetened shredded coconut
1 Tbsp. extra virgin olive oil
½ tsp. freshly ground pepper

1. Place peeled garlic clove on a cutting board with salt. Smash garlic and salt together using flat side of a knife to make a paste.
2. Whisk together smashed garlic and remaining ingredients. Cover and chill until ready to use. **Makes** about 1 cup.

Squash-and-Mushroom Hominy
PREP: 25 MIN., COOK: 36 MIN.

3 small yellow squash (about 10 oz.)
4 thick-cut bacon slices, diced
1 cup chopped onion
1 Tbsp. olive oil
1 (29-oz.) can hominy, drained
4 cups chopped fresh mushrooms
1 cup chicken broth
½ tsp. freshly ground pepper
1 tsp. grated lemon rind
2 Tbsp. lemon juice
½ cup chopped fresh parsley
Salt to taste

1. Slice squash lengthwise, and cut into ¼-inch slices.
2. Cook bacon in a skillet over medium-low heat 8 minutes or just until crisp; remove bacon, and drain on paper towels, reserving 2 Tbsp. drippings in skillet.
3. Sauté onion in hot drippings with olive oil over medium-high heat 8 minutes or until tender. Stir in hominy, and sauté 5 minutes or until most of liquid is absorbed. Add mushrooms, broth, and pepper; cover, reduce heat to medium-low, and cook 5 minutes or until mushrooms darken. Add squash; cover and cook, stirring occasionally, 5 minutes or until tender. Stir in lemon rind and juice. Cook, uncovered, 3 to 5 minutes or until liquid thickens slightly. Remove from heat, and stir in parsley and bacon. Season with salt to taste. **Makes** 6 servings.

Note: If preferred, omit bacon and add 2 Tbsp. olive oil in place of drippings.

Hot Slaw à la Greyhound Grill
PREP: 15 MIN., COOK: 40 MIN.
This recipe is an ode to the Greyhound Tavern in Fort Mitchell, Kentucky, which, according to Matt and Ted, serves some of the finest fried chicken anywhere. It's here where they were first introduced to hot slaw.

½ large red cabbage (about 1½ lb.), shredded
½ large green cabbage (about 1½ lb.), shredded
4 thick-cut bacon slices, diced
½ cup cider vinegar
½ tsp. celery seeds
¼ tsp. dried crushed red pepper
2 tsp. salt
1 tsp. freshly ground black pepper
Pepper vinegar to taste (optional)

1. Bring 3½ qt. water to a boil in a large stockpot. Cook cabbage in boiling water 4 minutes or just until it turns a dull gray purple. Remove from heat, and drain well.
2. Cook bacon in a skillet over medium-low heat 8 minutes or just until crisp; remove bacon, and drain on paper towels, reserving drippings in skillet. Stir in cider vinegar, celery seeds, and crushed red pepper, stirring to loosen particles from bottom of skillet. Stir in cabbage, salt, black pepper, and bacon; cook, stirring occasionally, 4 minutes or until cabbage is tender and turns a bright magenta color. Place cabbage mixture in a serving dish, and, if desired, sprinkle with pepper vinegar to taste. **Makes** 6 servings.

Pork Loin Chops With Pear-and-Vidalia Pan Gravy

PREP: 25 MIN., COOK: 32 MIN., BAKE: 7 MIN.

1 Tbsp. all-purpose flour
2 tsp. kosher salt
1½ tsp. freshly ground pepper
6 (1-inch-thick) bone-in pork loin chops
    (about 4 lb.)
1 Tbsp. peanut oil
2 Tbsp. unsalted butter
1 large Vidalia onion, thinly sliced
    (about 1½ cups)
2 Bartlett pears, peeled and diced
    (about 2 cups), divided
¾ cup chicken broth
1 tsp. all-purpose flour
1 Tbsp. dry sherry *
1 tsp. sherry vinegar * *
Salt and pepper to taste
Garnish: sliced green onions

1. Combine 1 Tbsp. flour, kosher salt, and pepper in a small bowl. Sprinkle half of flour mixture on 1 side of each pork loin chop.

2. Cook chops, in batches, flour mixture sides down, in hot oil in a large skillet over medium-high heat 5 minutes or until browned. (Do not turn.) Sprinkle remaining flour mixture on top of each chop; turn chops over, and cook 5 minutes or until browned. Transfer to an aluminum foil-lined broiler pan.

3. Bake chops at 425° for 7 minutes or until a meat thermometer inserted into thickest portion registers 150°. Transfer chops to a platter, and keep warm. Reserve juices in broiler pan for later use.

4. Add butter, onion, and half of pears to skillet; cook over medium-low heat 8 minutes or until onion is tender, stirring to loosen particles from bottom of skillet.

5. Stir together broth and 1 tsp. flour in a small bowl. Stir broth mixture, sherry, vinegar, and reserved juices from chops into skillet; cook, stirring occasionally, 4 minutes or until liquid is reduced by half. Remove from heat, and stir in remaining pears. Season with salt and pepper to taste. Spoon gravy over chops. Garnish, if desired. **Makes** 6 servings.

* 1 Tbsp. port may be substituted.

** 1 tsp. cider vinegar may be substituted.

Sweet Potato-Buttermilk Pie
family favorite

PREP: 25 MIN.; BAKE: 1 HR., 51 MIN.;
COOL: 1 HR., 40 MIN.

2 medium-size sweet potatoes
    (about 1½ lb.)
½ (15-oz.) package refrigerated
    piecrusts
4 Tbsp. unsalted butter, melted
2 Tbsp. fresh lemon juice
½ tsp. freshly grated ground nutmeg
½ tsp. ground cinnamon
½ tsp. kosher salt
3 large eggs, separated
½ cup sugar
2 Tbsp. all-purpose flour
¾ cup buttermilk
Toppings: whipped cream, fresh mint
    sprigs

1. Bake potatoes at 400° for 1 hour or until tender; cool 10 minutes. Increase oven temperature to 450°.

2. Fit piecrust into a 9-inch pie plate according to package directions; fold edges under, and crimp. Prick bottom and sides of piecrust with a fork.

3. Bake at 450° for 9 to 11 minutes or until lightly browned. Reduce oven temperature to 375°.

4. Cut potatoes in half lengthwise. Scoop out pulp into a medium bowl; mash until smooth. Stir in butter and next 4 ingredients until well combined.

5. Whisk egg yolks until thick and pale. Add sugar, and whisk 1½ minutes or until lemon-yellow color. Stir egg yolk mixture into sweet potato mixture until well blended. Add flour, 1 tsp. at a time, stirring until blended after each addition. Add buttermilk, and stir until combined.

6. Whisk egg whites in a bowl until soft peaks form. Gently fold egg whites into sweet potato mixture just until blended. Spoon sweet potato mixture into prepared piecrust.

7. Bake at 375° for 35 to 40 minutes or until center is set. Let cool on a wire rack 1½ hours or until completely cool. Serve at room temperature, or cover with plastic wrap, and chill 8 hours. Serve with desired toppings. **Makes** 6 servings.

Hot-Spiced Bourbon Balls
make ahead

PREP: 35 MIN., BAKE: 10 MIN., CHILL: 1 HR.

1 cup coarsely chopped pecans
1¼ cups powdered sugar, divided
2 Tbsp. unsweetened cocoa
½ tsp. salt
¼ tsp. ground cinnamon
¼ tsp. ground nutmeg
½ tsp. ground red pepper (optional)
¼ cup bourbon
2 Tbsp. sorghum *
60 vanilla wafers, finely crushed (about
    2 cups plus 2 Tbsp.)

1. Place pecans in a single layer in a shallow pan. Bake at 350° for 8 to 10 minutes or until toasted.

2. Sift together 1 cup powdered sugar, next 4 ingredients, and, if desired, ground red pepper. Stir together bourbon and sorghum. Gradually add powdered sugar mixture to bourbon mixture, stirring until blended. Stir in vanilla wafers and toasted pecans; stir 1 minute. (Place a small amount of mixture in palm of hand, and make a fist around mixture, testing to be sure dough will hold its shape. If not, continue to stir in 20-second intervals.)

3. Shape mixture into 1-inch balls. Roll balls in remaining ¼ cup powdered sugar, and place on a wax paper-lined baking sheet.

4. Chill 1 hour or until slightly firm. Store in an airtight container in refrigerator up to 1 week. **Makes** 30 balls.

* Molasses, honey, or cane syrup may be substituted.

Note: For testing purposes only, we used Hershey's Dutch Processed Cocoa at one tasting and Hershey's Unsweetened Cocoa at another.

Christmas All Through the House®

*Celebrate the season with our creative menu ideas
and tips for festive entertaining.*

Easy Ways to Entertain

The best parties are those where the host and hostess are relaxed and make their guests feel at home too. So follow our lead in putting together an evening with dishes that are a breeze to prepare and taste fantastic.

Plan-Ahead Party for 12

Shrimp with Basic Cocktail Sauce, Curry Mayonnaise, and Spicy Rémoulade

Beef Tidbits With Horseradish Sauce

Black-eyed Pea Dip

Vegetable tray With Curry Mayonnaise

Savory Deviled Eggs

Southwest Fondue

Jingle Juice

Basic Cocktail Sauce
fast fixin's • make ahead
PREP: 5 MIN.
This makes enough sauce for 2 pounds of shrimp.

½ cup ketchup
2 Tbsp. prepared horseradish
1 Tbsp. lemon juice
Dash of hot sauce

1. Stir together all ingredients in a small bowl. Store in an airtight container in refrigerator up to 2 weeks. **Makes** about ¾ cup.
WILL LACEY
COLUMBIA, SOUTH CAROLINA

Curry Mayonnaise
fast fixin's • make ahead
PREP: 10 MIN., CHILL: 30 MIN.
This dip does double duty, served both with boiled shrimp and raw vegetables.

1 cup regular or light mayonnaise
¼ cup sour cream
1 Tbsp. lemon juice
1 green onion, minced
½ tsp. curry powder
Garnish: sliced green onion

1. Stir together first 5 ingredients. Cover and chill 30 minutes. Garnish, if desired. **Makes** about 1¼ cups.

Spicy Rémoulade
fast fixin's • make ahead
PREP: 10 MIN.
This classic mayonnaise-based sauce, created by Associate Foods Editor Mary Allen Perry, is also terrific on sandwiches. If you don't have sweet Hungarian paprika, regular paprika will work just fine.

2 cups mayonnaise
¼ cup Creole mustard
2 Tbsp. chopped fresh parsley
1 Tbsp. fresh lemon juice
2 tsp. sweet Hungarian paprika
1 garlic clove, pressed
¾ tsp. ground red pepper

1. Stir together all ingredients until blended. Cover and chill until ready to serve. **Makes** 2⅓ cups.

Note: For testing purposes only, we used Zatarain's Creole Mustard.

Beef Tidbits With Horseradish Sauce

PREP: 10 MIN., CHILL: 2 HR., STAND: 40 MIN., BAKE: 1 HR.

1 cup soy sauce
½ cup vegetable oil
¼ cup bourbon *
3 garlic cloves, pressed
1 (3-lb.) eye-of-round
    roast
48 small dinner rolls
Horseradish Sauce

1. Combine first 4 ingredients in a 1-gal. zip-top plastic bag; add roast, turning to coat. Seal and chill 2 hours or up to 24 hours, turning occasionally.
2. Let roast stand at room temperature 30 minutes. Remove roast from marinade, discarding marinade. Place roast on a lightly greased wire rack in a roasting pan.
3. Bake at 500° for 10 minutes; reduce oven temperature to 375°, and bake 50 minutes or until a meat thermometer inserted into thickest portion registers 135°. Cover loosely with foil, and let stand 10 minutes.
4. Cut roast into thin slices; serve with rolls and Horseradish Sauce. **Makes** 10 to 12 servings.

*** ¼ cup apple juice may be substituted for bourbon.

Horseradish Sauce:

fast fixin's • make ahead
PREP: 10 MIN.

1 cup whipping cream
1 cup mayonnaise
⅛ tsp. salt
¼ cup prepared horseradish
1 tsp. grated lemon rind
1 tsp. fresh lemon juice

1. Beat whipping cream at medium speed with an electric mixer until soft peaks form. Add mayonnaise and salt, beating until blended; stir in horseradish, lemon rind, and lemon juice. **Makes** 3 cups.

Black-eyed Pea Dip

fast fixin's • make ahead
PREP: 15 MIN.
This also makes a nice relish for grilled or broiled catfish.

1 (15-oz.) can black-eyed peas seasoned
    with pork, rinsed and drained
½ cup diced red bell pepper
⅓ cup finely chopped sweet onion
3 Tbsp. garlic Ranch dressing
1 tsp. cider vinegar
¼ tsp. pepper
Cornbread crackers or corn chips

1. Stir together first 6 ingredients. Serve with cornbread crackers or corn chips. Store in an airtight container up to 3 days. **Makes** 1¾ cups.

Note: For testing purposes only, we used Hidden Valley Garlic Ranch.

Savory Deviled Eggs

make ahead
PREP: 20 MIN.
Serve these tasty snacks as soon as you make them, or refrigerate them up to 24 hours.

1 dozen large hard-cooked eggs, peeled
2 garlic cloves, minced
3 Tbsp. chopped black olives
1 tsp. grated lemon rind
½ cup olive oil
Salt and pepper to taste
Hot sauce to taste
Garnish: chopped fresh parsley

1. Slice eggs in half lengthwise; carefully remove yolks, keeping egg white halves intact. Process yolks, garlic, olives, and lemon rind in a food processor until combined, stopping to scrape down sides. With food processor running, gradually pour olive oil through food chute in a slow, steady stream, processing until mixture thickens. Stir in salt, pepper, and hot sauce to taste.
2. Spoon yolk mixture evenly into egg white halves. Garnish, if desired. **Makes** 24 deviled eggs.   ELIZABETH WILLIAMS
NEW ORLEANS, LOUISIANA

Countdown to Good Times

Two weeks before party:
■ Select serving pieces, and mark each with a sticky note to indicate which dish will be served in it.
■ Pick out table linens, and iron if necessary. Choose vases, candles, and table decorations.

One week before party:
■ Make sauces to accompany shrimp; cover tightly and refrigerate.

Two days before party:
■ Make Black-eyed Pea Dip, Horseradish Sauce, and Jingle Juice.
■ Pick up prepared vegetable tray from the deli.

One day before the party:
■ Make Savory Deviled Eggs.
■ Place shrimp in refrigerator to thaw.
■ Marinate eye-of-round roast.
■ Place linens on table. Arrange serving dishes and flowers.

Day of party:
■ Roast and slice beef.
■ Assemble fondue; microwave just before guests are to arrive. Serve in a fondue pot or in a small slow cooker.

Southwest Fondue

fast fixin's
PREP: 18 MIN.

1 (16-oz.) package pepper Jack
    pasteurized prepared cheese
    product, cubed
1 lb. white American deli cheese slices,
    torn
1¼ cups milk
2 to 3 plum tomatoes, seeded and diced
¼ cup chopped fresh cilantro
Assorted dippers: toasted bread cubes,
    corn chips, pretzels, thin breadsticks,
    pita chips

1. Combine first 3 ingredients in a large microwave-safe bowl. Microwave at HIGH 8 minutes or until cheese is melted, stirring every 2 minutes. Stir in tomatoes and cilantro. Serve with desired dippers. **Makes** 6 cups.

Note: For testing purposes only, we used Velveeta Pepper Jack for pasteurized prepared cheese product.

Southwest Fondue With Chorizo: Prepare recipe as directed. Stir in 9 oz. finely chopped, fully cooked chorizo. **Makes** 7 cups. Prep: 12 min.

Jingle Juice
fast fixin's
PREP: 10 MIN.
If you don't have orange liqueur, such as Triple Sec, substitute an equal amount of orange juice.

5 cups orange juice
1 cup vodka
⅓ cup orange liqueur
¼ cup fresh lemon juice
½ cup maraschino cherry juice
Garnishes: fruit-flavored candy cane sticks, cherries with stems, orange and lemon slices, lime wedges

1. Stir together first 5 ingredients; serve over ice. Garnish, if desired. **Makes** 1½ qt.

Rudolph's Spritzer: Omit vodka and orange liqueur. Add 2 cups chilled lemon-lime soft drink. Proceed as directed.

Panini Party

Try this no-fuss idea for a Christmas Eve gathering—invite friends in for a panini-and-soup party. Panini, or pressed sandwiches, are the rage and are really easy to prepare.

Stop by for Supper
Serves 8

Hot Brown Panini or
Muffuletta Panini or
Peppery Turkey-and-Brie Panini

Southern Tortellini Minestrone

Mint Hot Fudge-Brownie Sundaes

Hot Brown Panini
PREP: 20 MIN., COOK: 3 MIN. PER BATCH
This richly delicious sandwich was inspired by reader Julie Morgan's recipe for a Kentucky classic.

2 Tbsp. melted butter
16 (½-inch-thick) Italian bread slices
1 cup (4 oz.) shredded Swiss cheese, divided
3 cups chopped cooked chicken or turkey
4 plum tomatoes, sliced
3 cups warm White Cheese Sauce, divided
13 cooked bacon slices, crumbled

1. Brush melted butter evenly on outsides of bread halves. Place, butter sides down, on wax paper.
2. Sprinkle 1 Tbsp. Swiss cheese on 1 side of each of 8 bread slices; top evenly with chicken, tomato slices, and 1 cup warm White Cheese Sauce. Sprinkle with bacon and remaining cheese; top with remaining bread slices, butter sides up.
3. Cook sandwiches, in batches, in a preheated panini press 2 to 3 minutes or until golden brown. Serve with remaining 2 cups warm White Cheese Sauce for dipping. **Makes** 8 servings.

JULIE MORGAN
DANBURY, NORTH CAROLINA

Note: Sandwiches may be prepared in a preheated grill pan over medium-high heat. Cook 2 to 3 minutes on each side or until golden.

White Cheese Sauce:
PREP: 10 MIN., COOK: 10 MIN.

¼ cup butter
¼ cup all-purpose flour
3½ cups milk
1 cup (4 oz.) shredded Swiss cheese
1 cup grated Parmesan cheese
½ tsp. salt
¼ tsp. ground red pepper

1. Melt butter in a heavy saucepan over low heat; whisk in flour until smooth. Cook 1 minute, whisking constantly. Gradually whisk in milk; cook over medium heat, whisking constantly, until mixture is thickened and bubbly. Whisk in cheeses, salt, and red pepper, whisking until cheeses are melted and sauce is smooth. **Makes** 3 cups.

Muffuletta Panini
PREP: 15 MIN., COOK: 3 MIN. PER BATCH

2 Tbsp. melted butter
8 crusty deli rolls, split
1 cup olive salad
½ lb. hard salami slices
1 lb. thinly sliced deli ham slices
¾ lb. thinly sliced Swiss cheese (about 24 slices)
¾ lb. thinly sliced provolone cheese (about 24 slices)

1. Brush melted butter evenly on outsides of bread halves. Place, butter sides down, on wax paper.
2. Spoon 1 Tbsp. olive salad onto cut side of each bottom bread half; top evenly with salami, ham, cheeses, and remaining olive salad. Cover with bread tops.
3. Cook sandwiches, in batches, in a preheated panini press 2 to 3 minutes or until golden brown. **Makes** 8 servings.

ELIZABETH PEARCE
NEW ORLEANS, LOUISIANA

Note: For testing purposes only, we used Boscoli Family Italian Olive Salad. Sandwiches may be prepared in a preheated grill pan over medium-high heat. Cook 2 to 3 minutes on each side or until golden.

Peppery Turkey-and-Brie Panini

fast fixin's

PREP: 10 MIN., COOK: 3 MIN. PER BATCH

1 (15-oz.) Brie round
16 multigrain sourdough bread slices
2 lb. thinly sliced smoked turkey
½ cup red pepper jelly
2 Tbsp. melted butter

1. Trim and discard rind from Brie. Cut Brie into ½-inch-thick slices. Layer 8 bread slices evenly with turkey and Brie.
2. Spread 1 Tbsp. pepper jelly on 1 side of remaining bread slices; place, jelly sides down, onto Brie. Brush sandwiches with melted butter.
3. Cook sandwiches, in batches, in a preheated panini press 2 to 3 minutes or until golden brown. **Makes** 8 servings.

AMY WESTMORELAND
SCOTTSBORO, ALABAMA

Note: For testing purposes only, we used Braswell's Red Pepper Jelly. Sandwiches may be prepared in a preheated grill pan over medium-high heat. Cook 2 to 3 minutes on each side or until golden.

Southern Tortellini Minestrone

PREP: 20 MIN., COOK: 42 MIN.
This soup, which features collards and green beans, is warm and wonderful alongside a sandwich or on its own. Use your favorite frozen greens in this soup, or substitute a bag of thoroughly washed fresh spinach.

1 medium onion, chopped
1 Tbsp. olive oil
3 garlic cloves, chopped
2 (32-oz.) containers chicken broth
¾ cup dry white wine
2 (14.5-oz.) cans Italian-seasoned diced
  tomatoes
1 (16-oz.) package frozen green beans
1 (16-oz.) package chopped frozen
  collard greens
3 Tbsp. chopped fresh parsley
1 Tbsp. chopped fresh rosemary
½ tsp. dried crushed red pepper
1 (16-oz.) package frozen cheese
  tortellini

1. Sauté onion in hot oil in a large Dutch oven over medium heat 8 minutes or until onion is tender. Add garlic, and cook 1 minute. Stir in chicken broth, white wine, and tomatoes; bring to a boil over medium-high heat. Add green beans and next 4 ingredients. Reduce heat to medium, and simmer, stirring occasionally, 15 minutes. Add pasta, and cook 10 to 12 minutes or until pasta is done. **Makes** 8 to 10 servings.

NIKI GASCON SHERROD
LOS ANGELES, CALIFORNIA

Mint Hot Fudge-Brownie Sundaes

family favorite • fast fixin's

PREP: 10 MIN
Ice cream never goes out of season, especially when it's part of a Mint Hot Fudge-Brownie Sundae.
Place 1 (2-inch) brownie in each of 8 sundae dishes; top each with 2 scoops vanilla ice cream and ¼ cup Mint Hot Fudge Sauce. Garnish with crushed hard peppermint candies, if desired. **Makes** 8 servings.

Mint Hot Fudge Sauce:

fast fixin's

PREP: 10 MIN., COOK: 10 MIN.
To crush the candies, unwrap them, place in a large zip-top plastic bag, and seal. Bash the candies with a rolling pin until coarse.
Microwave 1 (12-oz.) can evaporated milk in a microwave-safe bowl at HIGH 2 minutes or until hot. Stir in 8 oz. crushed hard peppermint candies (about 45 candies), stirring constantly until candies dissolve. Melt 4 (1-oz.) unsweetened chocolate squares and ½ cup butter in a large heavy saucepan over low heat, stirring constantly. Gradually stir in evaporated milk mixture. Gradually whisk in ½ cup sugar. Cook, whisking constantly, over low heat 3 minutes or until smooth. Remove from heat, and whisk in ⅛ tsp. salt. **Makes** about 3½ cups.

Christmas Morning

Serves 8

Breakfast Tortillas

Baby PB&J Bagel Panini

Cornmeal-Cranberry Muffins

Holiday Cream Cheese
Coffee Cake

Fruit Dippers

Santa's Cider

Excitement rules on Christmas morning. Food that everyone can nibble while simultaneously opening gifts and playing is a must.

Breakfast Tortillas

PREP: 5 MIN., BAKE: 10 MIN., COOK: 13 MIN.
Wrap these individually in foil or parchment for a portable breakfast. Little hands will wrap happily around these hearty little sandwiches filled with egg and sausage.

10 (6-inch) fajita-size flour
  tortillas
½ (16-oz.) package ground pork
  sausage
6 large eggs
Vegetable cooking spray
½ cup shredded colby-Jack cheese
  blend
Salsa (optional)
Sour cream (optional)

1. Wrap tortillas loosely with aluminum foil, and place in a 250° oven for 10 minutes.
2. Meanwhile, cook sausage in a large skillet over medium-high heat, stirring often, 8 minutes or until sausage crumbles and is no longer pink; drain,

remove sausage from skillet, and pat dry with paper towels. Wipe skillet clean. Reduce heat to medium.

3. Whisk together eggs and 2 Tbsp. water. Coat same skillet with vegetable cooking spray; add egg mixture, and cook, without stirring, 2 to 3 minutes or until eggs begin to set on bottom. Gently draw cooked edges away from sides of pan to form large pieces. Cook, stirring occasionally, 2 minutes or until eggs are thickened but still moist. (Do not overstir.)

4. Spoon sausage and eggs evenly onto tortillas, and sprinkle with cheese; roll up tortillas. Serve with salsa and sour cream, if desired. **Makes** 10 servings.

LOUISE HORN
MADISON, MISSISSIPPI

Note: To lighten, substitute 1½ cups egg substitute for eggs and reduced-fat pork sausage for sausage.

Baby PB&J Bagel Panini

family favorite • fast fixin's
PREP: 10 MIN., COOK: 2 MIN.
Press gently on the lid of the panini grill so you won't squeeze the filling out.

6 Tbsp. creamy peanut butter
6 mini bagels, split
6 tsp. strawberry or grape
    jelly
1 Tbsp. butter, melted

1. Spread peanut butter evenly on cut sides of bottom halves of bagels; spread jelly evenly on cut sides of top halves of bagels. Place top halves of bagels on bottom halves, jelly side down.

2. Brush bagels lightly with melted butter; cook in a preheated panini press 2 minutes or until lightly browned and grill marks appear. Serve immediately. **Makes** 6 servings.

Note: Panini may also be cooked in a grill pan. Cook 2 minutes on each side or until lightly browned and grill marks appear.

Cornmeal-Cranberry Muffins

freezeable • make ahead
PREP: 15 MIN., BAKE: 20 MIN., COOL: 15 MIN.
You can freeze these muffins in zip-top plastic freezer bags. Thaw at room temperature, or microwave frozen muffins at HIGH 15 to 30 seconds.

1⅓ cups all-purpose flour
¾ cup sugar
½ cup yellow cornmeal
2 tsp. baking powder
¾ cup buttermilk
¼ cup orange juice
3 Tbsp. butter, melted
1 egg, lightly beaten
1 cup cranberries

1. Stir together first 4 ingredients in a large bowl; make a well in center of mixture. Add buttermilk and next 3 ingredients, and stir just until dry ingredients are moistened. Fold in cranberries.

2. Spoon batter evenly into 12 paper-lined muffin cups, filling two-thirds full.

3. Bake at 425° for 20 minutes or until lightly browned and a wooden pick inserted in center comes out clean. Remove muffins from pans to wire racks, and let cool 15 minutes. Serve warm or at room temperature. **Makes** 1 dozen.

CHARLOTTE BRYANT
GREENSBURG, KENTUCKY

Holiday Cream Cheese Coffee Cake

family favorite
PREP: 5 MIN., BAKE: 20 MIN., COOL: 10 MIN.
Get the enjoyment of a cream cheese Danish the easy way in this clever confection.

1 (11.5-oz.) frozen pecan coffee cake,
    thawed
4 oz. cream cheese, softened
¼ cup firmly packed dark brown sugar

1. Remove coffee cake from package; remove and discard plastic overwrap.

2. Slice coffee cake in half horizontally. Spread softened cream cheese on bottom

half of coffee cake; sprinkle with brown sugar. Place top layer of coffee cake right side up on bottom layer.

3. Bake at 350° for 15 to 20 minutes. Let cool on a wire rack 10 minutes. **Makes** 8 servings.

BRENDA ORBELL
NORTH WALES, PENNSYLVANIA

Fruit Dippers

family favorite • fast fixin's
PREP: 20 MIN.

1 (1¼-lb.) peeled and cored pineapple
1 Red Delicious apple
2 oranges
1 (8-oz.) container plain or vanilla
    nonfat yogurt
2 Tbsp. honey
½ tsp. lime rind
2 tsp. lime juice

1. Reserve juice from pineapple; cut pineapple lengthwise into spears, then in half.

2. Core apple, and cut into 16 slices; toss with pineapple juice.

3. Peel and section oranges.

4. Stir together yogurt and next 3 ingredients. Serve with fruit slices. **Makes** 8 servings.

Santa's Cider

family favorite • fast fixin's
PREP: 5 MIN., COOK: 10 MIN.

1 tsp. whole cloves
1 orange, cut into ¼-inch-thick slices
1 (46-oz.) jar apple juice
1 (12-oz.) bottle pomegranate juice
1 cup orange juice
Cinnamon sticks (optional)

1. Insert 4 cloves into white pith of each orange slice.

2. Stir together orange slices and juices in a Dutch oven over medium-high heat; cook 10 minutes or until thoroughly heated. (Do not boil.) Serve with cinnamon sticks, if desired. **Makes** 9 cups.

Plan a Simple, Special Dinner

Impress your guests and enjoy a new level of kitchen confidence with this deliciously doable menu.

Festive Menu

Serves 6

Roast Pork Loin With Crumb Crust

Loaded Baked Potato Casserole

Honey Glazed Carrots

Steamed broccoli (or asparagus)

Double Coffee Tiramisù

Roast Pork Loin With Crumb Crust

family favorite

PREP: 30 MIN.; BAKE: 1 HR., 30 MIN.; STAND: 10 MIN.

1 (4½-lb.) boneless pork loin, trimmed
2 tsp. salt
1 tsp. pepper
1 cup fine, dry breadcrumbs
¼ cup olive oil
2 Tbsp. finely chopped fresh parsley
2 Tbsp. chopped garlic
2 Tbsp. coarse-grained Dijon mustard

1. Sprinkle pork loin with salt and pepper. Place pork loin on an aluminum foil-lined broiler pan.
2. Stir together breadcrumbs and next 4 ingredients; press breadcrumb mixture onto top of pork loin.
3. Bake at 425° for 15 minutes; cover loosely with aluminum foil. Bake 1 hour to 1 hour and 15 minutes or until a meat thermometer inserted in thickest portion registers 155°. Let stand 10 minutes before slicing. **Makes** 6 servings.

BROOKS HART
RIVERDALE, NEW YORK

Loaded Baked Potato Casserole

PREP: 15 MIN., COOK: 5 MIN., BAKE: 30 MIN.

1 (22-oz.) package frozen mashed potatoes
1 (6.5-oz.) container garlic-and-herb spreadable cheese
½ cup milk
4 cooked bacon slices, crumbled
1 tsp. salt
½ tsp. pepper
1 cup (4 oz.) shredded Cheddar cheese
Garnish: chopped fresh chives

1. Prepare potatoes according to package directions.
2. Stir in spreadable cheese and next 4 ingredients; stir until blended. Spread mixture on bottom of a lightly greased 11- x 7-inch baking dish; top with Cheddar cheese.
3. Bake at 350° for 25 to 30 minutes or until thoroughly heated. Garnish, if desired. **Makes** 6 servings.

CADY BRITTEN
HUNTERSVILLE, NORTH CAROLINA

Note: For testing purposes only, we used frozen Ore-Ida Mashed Potatoes and Alouette Garlic & Herbs Spreadable Cheese.

Honey Glazed Carrots

family favorite

PREP: 5 MIN., COOK: 33 MIN.

1 (2-lb.) bag baby carrots
2 Tbsp. butter
1 Tbsp. brown sugar
2 Tbsp. honey
1 tsp. salt
1 Tbsp. chopped fresh mint
Freshly ground pepper to taste

1. Bring carrots and water to cover to a boil in a 3 qt. saucepan over high heat; reduce heat to medium, and cook 15 to 20 minutes or just until carrots are tender. Drain.
2. Melt butter in a large skillet over low heat; stir in sugar, honey, and salt. Add carrots, and cook, stirring constantly, 5 to 8 minutes or until carrots are glazed. Sprinkle with mint and pepper to taste. **Makes** 6 servings.

CHARLOTTE BRYANT
GREENSBURG, KENTUCKY

Double Coffee Tiramisù

PREP: 25 MIN., CHILL: 2 HR.

Lavish Double Coffee Tiramisù looks complicated but is an easy dessert you can make a day ahead. Enjoy the two extra servings the next day. Find ladyfingers in the bakery section of supermarkets.

1 (8-oz.) package cream cheese
½ cup sugar
2 cups whipping cream
½ cup hot water
1 Tbsp. instant coffee granules
¼ cup coffee liqueur
2 (3-oz.) packages ladyfingers
½ cup grated semisweet or dark chocolate

1. Beat cheese and sugar at medium speed with an electric mixer until creamy.
2. Beat whipping cream with an electric mixer until soft peaks form. Fold into cream cheese mixture.
3. Stir together ½ cup hot water and coffee granules until dissolved. Stir in liqueur.

---

4. Arrange ladyfingers evenly around sides of 8 (6-oz.) ramekins or coffee cups. Drizzle ladyfingers with coffee mixture. Spoon or pipe cheese mixture into center of ramekins. Sprinkle with grated chocolate. Cover, and chill 2 hours. **Makes** 8 servings.

LAURI HUSS
FOLLY BEACH, SOUTH CAROLINA

Note: To serve the tiramisù in a single dish, prepare recipe as directed through Step 3. Arrange half of ladyfingers in bottom and up sides of a 2-qt. serving bowl. Drizzle evenly with half of coffee mixture. Top with half of cream cheese mixture. Repeat layers once. Sprinkle with grated chocolate. Cover and chill 2 hours.

A Send-off for Santa

Chicken-Tasso-Andouille Sausage Gumbo

PREP: 45 MIN.; COOK: 4 HR., 15 MIN.

Tasso is a spicy smoked cut of pork or beef popular in many Cajun dishes.

4 lb. skinned and boned chicken thighs
1 lb. andouille or smoked sausage
1 lb. tasso or smoked ham
1 cup vegetable oil
1 cup all-purpose flour
4 medium onions, chopped
2 large green bell peppers, chopped
2 large celery ribs, chopped
4 large garlic cloves, minced
4 (32-oz.) boxes chicken broth
1½ tsp. dried thyme
1 tsp. black pepper
½ tsp. ground red pepper
⅓ cup chopped fresh parsley
Hot cooked rice
Garnishes: sliced green onions, filé powder

1. Cut first 3 ingredients into bite-size pieces. Place in a large Dutch oven over medium heat, and cook, stirring often, 20 minutes or until browned. Drain on paper towels. Wipe out Dutch oven with paper towels.
2. Heat oil in Dutch oven over medium heat; gradually whisk in flour, and cook, whisking constantly 25 minutes or until mixture is a dark mahogany.
3. Stir in onions and next 3 ingredients; cook, stirring often, 18 to 20 minutes or until tender. Gradually add broth. Stir in chicken, sausage, tasso, thyme, and black and red ground peppers.
4. Bring mixture to a boil over medium-high heat. Reduce heat to medium-low, and simmer, stirring occasionally, 2½ to 3 hours. Stir in parsley. Remove from heat; serve over hot cooked rice. Garnish, if desired. **Makes** 5 qt. (about 20 servings).

PHILIP ELLIOTT
BATON ROUGE, LOUISIANA

Shrimp-Tasso-Andouille Sausage Gumbo: Omit chicken thighs and proceed with Steps 1, 2, and 3. Proceed with Step 4, stirring in 4 lb. medium-size raw shrimp, peeled and, if desired, deveined, the last 15 minutes of cooking.

Easy Mini Muffulettas

PREP: 15 MIN., BAKE: 16 MIN.

1 (32-oz.) jar Italian olive salad
12 small deli rolls, cut in half
12 thin Swiss cheese slices
12 thin deli ham slices
12 thin provolone cheese slices
12 Genoa salami slices

1. Spread 1 Tbsp. olive salad evenly over each cut side of roll bottoms. Top each with 1 Swiss cheese slice, 1 ham slice, 1 Tbsp. olive salad, 1 provolone cheese slice, 1 salami slice, and 1 Tbsp. olive salad. Cover with roll tops, and wrap sandwiches together in a large piece of aluminum foil. Place on a baking sheet.
2. Bake at 350° for 14 to 16 minutes or until cheeses are melted. **Makes** 12 servings.

Note: For testing purposes only, we used Boscoli Italian Olive Salad.

Rudolph's Christmas Sugar Cookies

PREP: 30 MIN., FREEZE: 15 MIN.,
BAKE: 12 MIN. PER BATCH, COOL: 21 MIN.

1 (16.5-oz.) package refrigerated sugar cookie dough
36 pretzel twists
36 semisweet chocolate mini morsels
18 red cinnamon candies

1. Freeze dough 15 minutes.
2. Roll dough to a ¼-inch thickness on a floured surface. Cut dough with a 3-inch round cutter, and place 2 inches apart on ungreased baking sheets. Using thumb and forefinger, pinch opposite sides of each slice about two-thirds of the way down to shape face.
3. Break curved sides away from center of each pretzel twist to form antlers. Press bottom of 1 set of antlers on each side at top of each reindeer face.
4. Bake at 350° according to package directions or until lightly browned. Remove from oven; press in 2 chocolate mini morsels for eyes and 1 red cinnamon candy for nose. Let cool 1 minute on baking sheets. Remove to wire racks, and cool 20 minutes or until completely cool. **Makes** 1½ dozen.

Note: Store baked cookies in an airtight container up to 3 days, or freeze baked and decorated cookies in an airtight container up to 1 month.

Christmas Tree Sugar Cookies: Omit pretzels, chocolate mini morsels, and cinnamon candies. Freeze dough 15 minutes. Roll dough to a ¼-inch thickness on a floured surface, and cut with a 3-inch Christmas tree-shaped cookie cutter. Place 2 inches apart on ungreased baking sheets. Bake at 350° according to package directions or until lightly browned. Remove from oven, and cool as directed. Frost tops of cookies with ready-to-spread vanilla frosting, and sprinkle with red and green colored sugars and sprinkles.

Note: You can use any 3-inch cookie cutter that goes with the Christmas theme.

from our kitchen

Sizable Offerings

Bundt cakes always make a welcome gift. Decorative pans are available in an amazing array of shapes and sizes. You'll find baking instructions included on the packaging with most specialty pans, but because the same cake batter rises and bakes differently in each pan, keep these helpful tips in mind when trying new options.

■ It's important to fill pans with the correct amount of batter. If you use a smaller pan than is called for in a recipe, fill the pan no more than one-half to two-thirds full, and reduce the bake time. Too much batter will overflow and cause the cake to collapse back into the pan. Too little batter will leave the sides of the pan exposed and shield the cake from baking evenly.

■ Even when using the same size pans, bake times can vary according to the density of the batter. Depending on the recipe, a cake may take as little as 45 minutes or as long as 1½ hours to bake in a 12-cup Bundt pan.

■ One Bundt cake recipe fills 6 to 8 small (5- x 3-inch) loaf pans and usually bakes in 30 to 40 minutes. Each pan holds a little over a cup of batter, leaving just the right amount of room to add a frosting or glaze and some fun toppings when the cakes are cool. Larger (8- x 4-inch) loaf pans require 50 to 60 minutes of bake time.

On the Rise

To the disappointment of many, beaten biscuits have all but disappeared from the linen-lined breadbaskets of holiday tables. Their unique and somewhat mystifying texture is created by beating the dough for an incredibly long amount of time rather than by adding leavening. Traditionally served with slivers of country ham, these cream-colored little biscuits can now be had with the click of a mouse. At $2.50 a dozen (plus shipping from **www.jacksonbiscuit.com**), they're a bargain, and every bit as good as you remember.

Make It Snappy

When it comes to stocking the pantry with ingredients for fast party food and speedy weeknight suppers, our favorite products are always versatile and full of fresh flavor. The best finds, such as this new Pepper Marmalade ($5.99 from **notyomamasgourmet.com**), deliver big dividends in time-saving shortcuts.

Used straight from the jar, Pepper Marmalade adds a spark of sweetness to almost any entrée—from roast chicken to pan-fried pork chops. A bold blend of diced bell peppers and serranos, spiked with bits of mango and orange zest, it's surprisingly delicious served alongside baked cheese grits, black-eyed peas, or greens as well.

Pepper Marmalade also makes a quick start for this colorful Holiday Salsa, as well as dozens of other terrific recipes. Inspired by the classic cream cheese-and-pepper jelly combo, we created this festive pairing. Spoon Holiday Salsa over White Cheddar Spread, and serve with assorted crackers.

Holiday Salsa: Stir together 1 (10-oz.) jar pepper marmalade, 2 cups diced mango (fresh or refrigerated), and ¼ cup chopped fresh cilantro. Serve immediately, or cover and chill up to 3 days. **Makes** about 3 cups. Prep: 5 min.

White Cheddar Spread: Stir together 1 (8-oz.) package softened cream cheese, 2 cups shredded white Cheddar cheese, and 2 pressed garlic cloves. Serve immediately, or shape, if desired, and cover and chill up to 1 week. **Makes** 10 to 12 servings. Prep: 10 min.

2007 cook-off winners

2007
Cook-Off Winners

Everybody wins in our cook-off—the finalists get cash,
our readers get amazing recipes.

Would $100,000 change your life? Ask Lindsay Weiss of Overland Park, Kansas, winner of the 2007 *Southern Living* Cook-Off, and we think the answer will be a resounding "yes!"

Lindsay credits her idea with being pregnant and having food cravings as she was working on her submissions. "I entered about 10 different recipes," she says with a laugh. "And all of them contained peanut butter and banana." The combination appealed to our judges, too, and Lindsay's Roasted Banana Ice Cream With Warm Peanut Butter Sauce took top honors.

The Road to Riches

Becoming a finalist takes creativity, competitive spirit, and a fair amount of luck. But most of all, it takes an unimpeachable recipe that is accurately written, so that when we test it, it turns out perfectly. We sifted through many thousands of entries to find a few hundred that sound delicious and creative. Our Test Kitchen staff prepared some 650 of the best for our Foods Staff to taste. Once we arrived at the final 15, the call went out for the contestants to come to Birmingham to prepare their recipes for the judges and be honored at a celebratory dinner.

As for what she'll do with the prize money, Lindsay says, "I haven't got a clue! But we're not big spenders, so we'll likely put it in the bank to use later for our children."

We hope we'll see you in Birmingham as one of our 15 finalists, so be sure to enter the 2008 Cook-Off. Look for information in upcoming issues of *Southern Living* magazines, with monthly updates of sponsors, or get details at **www.southernlivingcookoff.com.**

Sweet Endings

$100,000 Grand Prize Winner

SWEET ENDINGS
Category Winner

Roasted Banana Ice Cream With Warm Peanut Butter Sauce

PREP: 30 MIN., BAKE: 40 MIN., CHILL: 4 HR.,
FREEZE: 4 HR.

Only freeze the ice cream about an hour-and-a-half after it's finished churning for the best texture. If you make it ahead, take it out of the freezer 20 minutes before serving to soften.

3 medium-size ripe bananas, cut into
½-inch slices
⅓ cup firmly packed DOMINO Light
Brown Sugar
1 Tbsp. butter, cut into pieces
1 cup milk
½ cup heavy cream
2 Tbsp. DOMINO Granulated Sugar
1 MCCORMICK Gourmet Collection
Madagascar Vanilla Bean, cut into
2-inch pieces
¼ tsp. salt
⅛ tsp. MCCORMICK Gourmet Collection
Ground Nutmeg
½ cup Salted USA-GROWN PEANUTS,
coarsely chopped
Warm Peanut Butter Sauce
Garnish: chopped Salted USA-GROWN
PEANUTS

1. Preheat oven to 400°.

2. Toss together first 3 ingredients in a 2-qt. baking dish, and bake at 400° for 40 minutes or until bananas are browned and softened, stirring once after 20 minutes.

3. Spoon bananas and all of syrup in baking dish in a blender or food processor; add milk and next 5 ingredients to blender, and process 1 minute or until smooth. Pour mixture into an airtight container, and chill at least 4 hours or up to 24 hours.

4. Pour mixture into freezer container of a ½-gal. electric ice-cream maker, and freeze according to manufacturer's instructions. (Instructions and times may vary.) Stir in chopped peanuts during last 1 minute of freezing, or add according to manufacturer's instructions.

5. Divide ice cream between 4 chilled sundae bowls, and top with desired amount of Warm Peanut Butter Sauce. Garnish, if desired. **Makes** 4 to 6 servings.

Note: If ice cream is too thin and runny after freezing, transfer ice cream mixture to an airtight container, and freeze 1 to 2 hours or to desired consistency.

Warm Peanut Butter Sauce:

PREP: 10 MIN., COOK: 5 MIN.

1 cup DOMINO Granulated Sugar
¾ cup milk
1 Tbsp. light corn syrup
¼ tsp. salt
6 Tbsp. Creamy USA-GROWN PEANUT
    Butter
½ tsp. vanilla extract

1. Stir together first 4 ingredients in a small saucepan. Cook over low heat, stirring constantly, 5 minutes or until thickened and sugar is dissolved. Stir in peanut butter until smooth. Remove from heat, and stir in vanilla. Whisk before serving. **Makes** 1½ cups.

LINDSAY WEISS
OVERLAND PARK, KANSAS

FLORIDA'S NATURAL Orange Juice
Brand Winner

Tequila-Flambéed Bananas With Coconut Ice Cream

PREP: 15 MIN., COOK: 8 MIN.

4 Tbsp. butter
¼ cup firmly packed DOMINO Light or
    Dark Brown Sugar
¼ cup FLORIDA'S NATURAL Brand
    Premium Orange Juice
½ tsp. grated lime rind
1 Tbsp. fresh lime juice
½ tsp. ground cinnamon
4 unpeeled bananas with green
    tips
4 Tbsp. tequila
2 pt. coconut ice cream

1. Melt butter with next 5 ingredients in a medium skillet over medium-high heat, stirring until blended. Reduce heat to medium, and cook 3 minutes or until sugar is dissolved. Peel bananas, and cut in half lengthwise. Add bananas, and cook 1 minute.
2. Remove skillet from heat; stir in tequila, and carefully ignite the fumes just above mixture with a long match

or long multipurpose lighter. Let flames die down.
3. Return skillet to heat, and cook 3 to 4 minutes or until bananas are soft and liquid is caramelized, spooning sauce over bananas. Serve immediately over coconut ice cream. **Makes** 4 servings.

Note: For testing purposes only, we used All Natural Boulder Brand Island Coconut Ice Cream.   CHRIS MILANO
SAN FRANCISCO, CALIFORNIA

DOMINO SUGAR *Brand Winner*

Coconut-Cream Bread Pudding

PREP: 20 MIN., STAND: 5 MIN., BAKE: 43 MIN.,
COOK: 6 MIN.
Coconuts, pecans, and melted butter make a crunchy, crisp topping for this melt-in-your-mouth dessert.

1 (8-oz.) package PHILADELPHIA Cream
    Cheese, softened
1½ cups DOMINO Granulated Sugar,
    divided
4 large eggs
2½ cups milk, at room temperature and
    divided
1 (15-oz.) can cream of coconut, divided
8 Tbsp. butter, melted and divided
1 (8-oz.) French bread loaf, cut into
    1-inch cubes
Vegetable cooking spray
½ cup sweetened flaked
    coconut
½ cup chopped pecans

1. Preheat oven to 350°.
2. Beat cream cheese at low speed with an electric mixer until creamy and smooth. Add 1 cup sugar and eggs, and beat at medium speed 2 minutes or until sugar is dissolved. Stir in 2 cups milk, 1 cup cream of coconut, and 3 Tbsp. melted butter. Stir in bread cubes. Let stand 5 minutes.
3. Coat a 13- x 9-inch baking dish with cooking spray. Pour bread mixture into dish.
4. Bake at 350° for 35 minutes or until set.
5. Stir together flaked coconut, pecans, and 3 Tbsp. melted butter. Sprinkle coconut mixture over baked pudding, and bake 5 to 8 more minutes or until browned.
6. Stir together remaining ½ cup milk and ½ cup cream of coconut.
7. Cook remaining ½ cup sugar in a medium-size heavy saucepan over low heat, stirring constantly, 3 minutes or until sugar is caramelized and mixture becomes a light brown syrup. Stir in milk mixture, and cook, stirring occasionally, 3 minutes or until sauce is thickened slightly and sugar is dissolved. Stir in remaining 2 Tbsp. melted butter.
8. Cut bread pudding into 8 to 10 servings, and serve with caramelized sugar sauce. **Makes** 8 to 10 servings.

ANN TAYLOR
HARVEST, ALABAMA

Judges' Notes

Associate Foods Editor and Judge Mary Allen Perry says the popularity of banana bread recipes in the magazine proves our grand prize winner Roasted Banana Ice Cream With Warm Peanut Butter Sauce has a flavor profile our readers love. "The peanut butter sauce makes this dessert a great choice for Saturday night suppers or for entertaining. You could even stir the roasted bananas into purchased vanilla ice cream for an express version." Winner Lindsay Weiss recalls making the sauce recipe some 25 times after she learned that she was a finalist.

Party Starters

Coconut Macadamia Shrimp With Warm Tropical Salsa

PREP: 20 MIN., FRY: 2 MIN. PER BATCH

The fresh, fruity flavor of the Warm Tropical Salsa makes a spectacular pairing with the crusty shrimp.

1 lb. unpeeled, uncooked fresh or frozen large CERTIFIED WILD AMERICAN Shrimp
½ cup all-purpose flour
¼ tsp. coarsely ground MCCORMICK Gourmet Collection Black Pepper
¼ tsp. MCCORMICK Gourmet Collection Ground Cayenne Red Pepper
¼ tsp. MCCORMICK Gourmet Collection Cajun Seasoning
¾ tsp. salt, divided
2 egg whites
1 cup unsweetened frozen shredded coconut, thawed
1 cup finely chopped macadamia nuts
½ cup Japanese breadcrumbs (panko)
6 cups vegetable oil
Warm Tropical Salsa

1. If frozen, thaw shrimp according to package directions. Peel shrimp, leaving tails on; devein, if desired.
2. Stir together flour, next 3 ingredients, and ¼ tsp. salt in a medium-size shallow dish or pie plate. Whisk egg whites in a small bowl until slightly foamy. Stir together coconut, macadamia nuts, and breadcrumbs in another medium-size shallow dish or pie plate.
3. Dredge shrimp in flour mixture; dip in egg whites. Dredge in coconut mixture, pressing coconut mixture onto shrimp. Place shrimp on a large baking sheet.
4. Pour oil to a depth of 1 inch in a large 6-qt. Dutch oven; heat over medium-high heat to 350°. Fry shrimp, 5 to 6 at a time, 1 to 2 minutes or until golden brown. Drain on a paper towel-lined baking sheet. Sprinkle hot shrimp with remaining salt.
5. Place Warm Tropical Salsa in a serving bowl, and place bowl in center of a serving dish. Arrange shrimp around salsa. Serve warm. **Makes** 6 servings.

Warm Tropical Salsa:

PREP: 10 MIN., COOK: 3 MIN.

¾ cup orange marmalade
1 Tbsp. fresh lime juice
1 Tbsp. FLORIDA'S NATURAL Brand Premium Orange Juice
1½ tsp. horseradish
1½ tsp. Dijon mustard
1 cup finely diced fresh mango
¼ cup canned crushed pineapple, drained
1½ Tbsp. finely chopped fresh cilantro

1. Stir together first 5 ingredients in a small saucepan; cook over medium-low heat 3 minutes or until thoroughly heated. Transfer mixture to a food processor, and pulse 5 to 6 times or until smooth. Return mixture to saucepan, and stir in mango, pineapple, and cilantro. Keep warm over low heat until ready to serve. **Makes** about 2 cups.

JENNY FLAKE
GILBERT, ARIZONA

California Sushi Bites

PREP: 40 MIN., COOK: 40 MIN.,
COOL: 15 MIN., CHILL: 2 HR.

⅓ cup rice vinegar
¼ cup DOMINO Granulated Sugar
1 tsp. salt
2¼ cups MAHATMA Valencia White Rice
¼ cup rice wine or dry sherry
8 oz. unpeeled, uncooked, fresh or frozen medium-size CERTIFIED WILD AMERICAN Shrimp
1 (7-oz.) jar roasted red bell peppers, drained
Vegetable cooking spray
4 large eggs, beaten
3 to 4 Tbsp. drained small capers, rinsed and drained
3 Tbsp. toasted sesame seeds
4 oz. thinly sliced Nova smoked salmon
2 to 3 cups fresh spinach leaves
½ cup thinly sliced green onions
2 ripe Haas avocados, thinly sliced
Fresh or bottled lime juice
Toppings: pickled ginger, lite soy sauce, prepared wasabi

1. Bring first 3 ingredients and 4½ cups water to a boil in a medium saucepan over high heat. Stir in rice. Cover, reduce heat to medium-low, and simmer 15 to 20 minutes or until rice is tender and liquid is absorbed. Stir in rice wine using a fork.
2. If frozen, thaw shrimp according to package directions. Peel shrimp; devein, if desired.
3. Cook shrimp in boiling water to cover 2 to 3 minutes or just until shrimp turn pink. Drain, and let cool 15 minutes. Coarsely chop shrimp.
4. Cut bell peppers into ¼- to ½-inch-wide strips.
5. Coat a griddle with cooking spray, and heat over medium heat. Pour a thin layer of beaten eggs onto griddle to make a thin omelet. Cook, without stirring, 1 minute or until egg is cooked and dry. Transfer omelet to a clean

kitchen towel. Repeat procedure with remaining eggs. (Do not stack or over-lap omelets on towel.)

6. Arrange omelets in a single layer in a plastic wrap-lined 13- x 9-inch pan, overlapping edges and piecing together as needed to cover bottom of pan. Sprinkle capers and toasted sesame seeds over egg layer. Arrange salmon over half of mixture in pan; arrange shrimp over other half. Using wet hands, top with 2½ cups rice mixture, pressing into an even layer and pack-ing down firmly.

7. Arrange spinach over rice, overlap-ping edges. Top with green onions. Using wet hands, top with 2½ cups rice mixture, pressing into an even layer and packing down firmly.

8. Remove and reserve 1 bell pepper strip. Arrange remaining bell pepper strips over rice. Top with avocado. Sprinkle with lime juice (about 1 Tbsp.). Using wet hands, top with remaining rice mixture, pressing into an even layer and packing down firmly. Cover with plastic wrap, and place a second 13- x 9-inch pan, right-side up, directly on filled pan, pressing down firmly on topmost pan to compact lay-ers. Chill at least 2 hours or up to 8 hours.

9. Remove top pan; remove and dis-card plastic wrap. Invert sushi onto a cutting board, and remove and discard plastic wrap. Using a thin sharp knife, cut sushi into 1- to 1½-inch pieces, cutting straight down through sushi. (Do not use a sawing motion when cutting.)

10. Cut reserved bell pepper strip into tiny diamond shapes or pieces; top each sushi bite with a bell pepper piece. Serve with desired toppings. **Makes** 50 to 60 bites.

LILLIAN JULOW
GAINESVILLE, FLORIDA

MCCORMICK Gourmet Collection
Brand Winner

Curried Beef Kabobs With Jade Sauce

PREP: 15 MIN., SOAK: 30 MIN., GRILL: 6 MIN.

12 (6-inch) wooden skewers
2 Tbsp. peanut oil
1¼ tsp. MCCORMICK Gourmet Collection Garam Masala
1¼ tsp. freshly ground MCCORMICK Gourmet Collection Roasted Garlic And Sea Salt
¾ tsp. MCCORMICK Gourmet Collection Indian Curry Powder
½ tsp. freshly ground MCCORMICK Gourmet Collection Peppercorn Mélange
¼ tsp. MCCORMICK Gourmet Collection Ground Cumin
1½ lb. flat iron steak, cut into 1-inch pieces
Jade Sauce
½ cup sweetened flaked coconut, toasted
Garnishes: fresh cilantro sprigs, fresh mint sprigs

1. Soak wooden skewers in water 30 minutes.
2. Preheat grill to 350° to 400° (medium-high). Whisk together peanut oil and next 5 ingredients in a large bowl until blended. Add steak pieces, and toss to coat. Thread beef onto skewers.
3. Grill beef, covered with grill lid, over 350° to 400° (medium-high) heat, 3 minutes on each side or to desired degree of doneness.
4. Place skewers on a serving platter, and drizzle with Jade Sauce. Sprinkle with toasted coconut. Garnish, if desired. **Makes** 12 servings.

Jade Sauce:

PREP: 10 MIN.

½ cup chopped fresh cilantro
¼ cup chopped fresh mint
2 Tbsp. chopped green onions
¼ cup extra virgin olive oil
1 tsp. grated lime rind
1 Tbsp. fresh lime juice
2 tsp. seeded and minced jalapeño pepper
2 tsp. honey
1 tsp. minced garlic
¼ tsp. salt

1. Process all ingredients in a food processor 10 seconds or until thor-oughly blended, stopping to scrape down sides as needed. **Makes** ⅔ cup.

JAMIE MILLER
MAPLE GROVE, MINNESOTA

Judges' Notes

Associate Foods Editor and Judge Mary Allen Perry describes the salsa on the Coconut Macadamia Shrimp With Warm Tropical Salsa as "a twist on Jezebel sauce but with a very contemporary feel." Test Kitchens Director and Judge Lyda Jones Burnette says, "This is a fun take-off on traditional coconut shrimp. The sauce is pretty, with nice, bright color and flavor."

Quick Weeknight Favorites

Tuscan Catfish With Sun-dried Tomato Aïoli

PREP: 15 MIN., FRY: 10 MIN. PER BATCH

6 (6-oz.) catfish fillets
½ tsp. salt
½ tsp. freshly ground pepper
2 cups firmly packed STACY'S Pesto and Sun-Dried Tomato Pita Chips
2 cups all-purpose flour
1 Tbsp. freshly ground MCCORMICK Gourmet Collection Italian Herb Blend Grinder
2 large eggs, lightly beaten
Vegetable oil
Sun-dried Tomato Aïoli
Garnishes: fresh basil leaves, lemon slices

1. Sprinkle catfish with salt and pepper.
2. Pulse pita chips in a food processor 6 to 8 times or until coarsely chopped. Place in a shallow dish or pie plate.
3. Stir together flour and Italian herb blend in another shallow dish or pie plate. Stir together eggs and ⅓ cup water in a third shallow dish or pie plate.
4. Dredge catfish in flour mixture, shaking off excess. Dip catfish in egg mixture, shaking off excess. Dredge in pita chips, pressing mixture into catfish to coat thoroughly.
5. Pour oil to depth of 1 inch into a large deep skillet; heat to 350°. Fry catfish, in batches, 4 to 5 minutes on each side or until golden brown. Drain on paper towels. Serve with Sun-dried Tomato Aïoli. Garnish, if desired. **Makes** 6 servings.

Sun-dried Tomato Aïoli:

PREP: 10 MIN.

¼ cup sun-dried tomatoes in oil
2 garlic cloves, finely minced
1 Tbsp. minced fresh basil leaves
1 Tbsp. lemon juice
1 Tbsp. Dijon mustard
1 cup mayonnaise

1. Process first 5 ingredients in a food processor 30 seconds or until combined. Add mayonnaise, and process 15 seconds or until smooth. Cover and chill until ready to serve. **Makes** about 1½ cups.

MICHAEL COHEN
LOS ANGELES, CALIFORNIA

Pork Pad Thai

PREP: 30 MIN., COOK: 11 MIN.

1½ lb. pork tenderloin, trimmed
2 Tbsp. canola oil
3 large eggs, lightly beaten
1 bunch green onions, cut into 2-inch pieces
Spicy Peanut Butter Sauce
1 (1-lb.) package rice noodles, cooked
2 cups matchstick carrots
2 cups bean sprouts
½ cup finely chopped Dry-Roasted USA-GROWN PEANUTS

1. Cut pork into very thin pieces.
2. Stir-fry pork in hot oil in a large wok over medium heat 5 to 8 minutes or until done. Place pork in a bowl.
3. Add eggs to wok, and cook, stirring constantly, 1 minute or until set. Add pork and green onions to wok, and sauté 1 to 2 minutes. Stir in Spicy Peanut Butter Sauce and hot cooked noodles.
4. Divide pork mixture evenly between 8 plates. Place ¼ cup carrots onto left side of each plate and ¼ cup bean sprouts onto right side of each plate. Sprinkle each serving with 1 Tbsp. chopped peanuts. Serve immediately. **Makes** 8 servings.

Spicy Peanut Butter Sauce:

PREP: 10 MIN.

½ cup creamy USA-GROWN PEANUT Butter
½ cup soy sauce
4 garlic cloves, chopped
¼ cup honey
2 Tbsp. rice wine vinegar
2 Tbsp. sesame oil
2 Tbsp. Asian sriracha hot chili sauce
1 Tbsp. chopped fresh ginger
¼ tsp. MCCORMICK Gourmet Collection Ground Cayenne Red Pepper

1. Process all ingredients and ½ cup cold water in a food processor 10 to 12 seconds or until well blended. **Makes** about 2 cups.

STEPHANIE SAWYER
VIRGINIA BEACH, VIRGINIA

Judges' Notes

Head Judge Lyda Jones Burnette says of the Quick Weeknight Favorites winner, "The pita chips provide a creative and really crisp crust for the catfish. And the aïoli is a cool and colorful twist on tartar sauce. This is a dish you'd be proud to serve at a casual gathering."

Good for You

Szechwan Burgers With Cilantro Slaw

PREP: 20 MIN., CHILL: 30 MIN., GRILL: 10 MIN.

⅓ cup KRAFT Cucumber Ranch Dressing
2 Tbsp. minced fresh cilantro
2 tsp. FLORIDA'S NATURAL Brand Premium Orange Juice
1 tsp. kosher salt, divided
1½ cups loosely packed shredded coleslaw mix
½ cup diced green onions
1 Tbsp. MCCORMICK Gourmet Collection Black Sesame Seeds
Vegetable cooking spray for grilling
1½ lb. ground chicken breast
¼ cup KRAFT Asian Toasted Sesame Dressing
2 tsp. minced garlic
1½ tsp. MCCORMICK Gourmet Collection Szechwan Seasoning
6 sesame seed hamburger buns

1. Whisk together first 3 ingredients and ¼ tsp. salt in a large bowl. Stir in coleslaw mix, green onions, and sesame seeds. Cover and chill at least 30 minutes or up to 2 hours.
2. Coat a cold cooking grate with cooking spray, and place on grill. Preheat grill to 300° to 350° (medium).
3. Combine ground chicken, next 3 ingredients, and remaining ¾ tsp. salt in a large bowl until blended. Shape mixture into 6 (¾-inch-thick) patties.
4. Grill patties, covered with grill lid, over 300° to 350° (medium) heat 5 minutes on each side or until done. Grill hamburger buns, cut sides down, 1 to 2 minutes or until lightly toasted.
5. Place 1 burger on top of each bottom bun; top evenly with coleslaw mixture and tops of buns. **Makes** 6 servings.

DEBORAH BIGGS
OMAHA, NEBRASKA

Peanut Shrimp Salad With Basil-Lime Dressing

PREP: 20 MIN., COOK: 6 MIN. PER BATCH
Using Japanese breadcrumbs in this recipe ensures that the shrimp stay crispy on the outside.

3 green onions, white and light green parts only
20 unpeeled, uncooked, fresh or frozen jumbo CERTIFIED WILD AMERICAN Shrimp
1 cup Japanese breadcrumbs (panko)
½ cup Dry-Roasted Salted USA-GROWN PEANUTS
1 Tbsp. cornstarch
1 tsp. MCCORMICK Gourmet Collection Red Curry Powder
1 large egg, lightly beaten
2 Tbsp. peanut oil
3 cups mixed baby salad greens
1 cup diced English cucumber
1 cup peeled, diced mango
½ cup mung bean sprouts
¼ cup loosely packed fresh mint leaves
Basil-Lime Dressing
¼ cup Dry-Roasted Salted USA-GROWN PEANUTS, chopped

1. Cut green onions into 2-inch-long thin strips.
2. If frozen, thaw shrimp according to package directions. Peel shrimp; devein, if desired.
3. Pulse breadcrumbs and next 3 ingredients in a food processor 5 times or until mixture resembles fine crumbs. Transfer mixture to a shallow dish or pie plate.
4. Dip shrimp in egg; dredge in breadcrumb mixture.

5. Cook shrimp in hot oil in a large nonstick skillet over medium-high heat 3 minutes on each side or until golden.
6. Gently toss together green onions, salad greens, next 4 ingredients, and 2 Tbsp. Basil-Lime Dressing in a large bowl. Arrange salad on 4 individual plates; top each with 5 shrimp. Sprinkle with ¼ cup peanuts, and drizzle with remaining dressing. Serve immediately. **Makes** 4 servings

Basil-Lime Dressing:
PREP: 10 MIN.

½ cup loosely packed fresh basil leaves
¼ cup fresh lime juice
2 Tbsp. peanut oil
1 Tbsp. fish sauce
1 Tbsp. DOMINO Granulated Sugar
1 tsp. Asian garlic-chili sauce
1 tsp. grated fresh ginger
1 garlic clove, minced

1. Process all ingredients in a food processor 20 seconds or until blended. **Makes** ½ cup.

KAREN TEDESCO
WEBSTER GROVES, MISSOURI

Mole Rubbed Chicken With Confetti Corn Relish
PREP: 10 MIN., GRILL: 12 MIN.

Vegetable cooking spray
2 Tbsp. DOMINO Light Brown Sugar
1½ tsp. MCCORMICK Gourmet Collection Chili Powder
1½ tsp. MCCORMICK Gourmet Collection Garlic Powder
1½ tsp. unsweetened cocoa
½ tsp. coarse-grain salt
½ tsp. MCCORMICK Gourmet Collection Cracked Black Pepper
¼ tsp. MCCORMICK Gourmet Collection Saigon Cinnamon
4 (5-oz.) skinned and boned chicken breasts
Confetti Corn Relish
Garnish: fresh cilantro sprigs

1. Coat cold cooking grate with cooking spray, and place on grill. Preheat grill to 350° to 400° (medium-high).
2. Stir together brown sugar and next 6 ingredients in a small bowl until well blended. Place chicken in a shallow dish; add brown sugar mixture, and turn chicken to coat, pressing mixture into chicken.
3. Place chicken on cooking grate, and grill, covered with grill lid, over 350° to 400° (medium-high) heat 5 to 6 minutes on each side or until done. (Meat thermometer should read 165° when inserted into thickest portion of breast.)
4. Place chicken on a serving platter. Spoon Confetti Corn Relish over top of and around chicken. Garnish, if desired. **Makes** 4 servings.

Confetti Corn Relish:
PREP: 15 MIN., COOK: 5 MIN.

1 Tbsp. unsalted butter
½ cup diced sweet onion
1 cup fresh corn kernels
1 cup diced red bell pepper
1 jalapeño pepper, seeded and minced
½ tsp. salt
¼ tsp. MCCORMICK Gourmet Collection Cracked Black Pepper
2 Tbsp. chopped fresh cilantro

1. Melt butter in a large skillet over medium heat. Add onion, and sauté 2 to 3 minutes or just until onion begins to turn golden. Stir in corn and next 4 ingredients; sauté 1 to 2 minutes or until vegetables are crisp-tender. Remove from heat, and stir in cilantro. **Makes** about 2½ cups.

TERESA RALSTON
NEW ALBANY, OHIO

Chili-and-Lime Grilled Shrimp With Seasoned White Beans and Rice
PREP: 25 MIN., SOAK: 30 MIN., GRILL: 8 MIN.

6 (12-inch) wooden skewers
1 lb. unpeeled, uncooked fresh or frozen large CERTIFIED WILD AMERICAN Shrimp
2 tsp. chili with lime seasoning
2 tsp. MCCORMICK Gourmet Collection Ground Mustard
1 tsp. MCCORMICK Gourmet Collection Garlic Powder
1 lime
2 Tbsp. extra virgin olive oil
Seasoned White Beans and Rice
Garnish: 6 lime wedges

1. Soak wooden skewers in water 30 minutes.
2. If frozen, thaw shrimp according to package directions. Peel shrimp, leaving tails on; devein, if desired. Place shrimp in a medium bowl.
3. Stir together chili with lime seasoning, ground mustard, and garlic powder in a small bowl. Sprinkle mixture over shrimp, tossing to coat.
4. Grate rind from 1 lime, and add to shrimp mixture in bowl. Cut lime in half, and squeeze juice into bowl. Stir in olive oil. Thread 4 to 5 shrimp onto each skewer, and place skewers on a plate. Cover and chill.
5. Preheat grill to 300° to 350° (medium).
6. Prepare Seasoned White Beans and Rice.
7. Meanwhile, grill shrimp skewers, covered with grill lid, over 300° to 350° (medium) heat 3 to 4 minutes on each side or just until shrimp turn pink. Spoon Seasoned White Beans and Rice onto a serving platter, and top with shrimp skewers. Garnish, if desired. **Makes** 6 servings.

Note: For testing purposes only, we used McCormick Chili With Lime Seasoning.

Judges' Notes

"This salad is bright and refreshing and makes a cool all-in-one dish," says Associate Foods Editor and Judge Mary Allen Perry of the Peanut Shrimp Salad With Basil Lime Dressing (page 305). "It's very colorful and would be a great salad for a luncheon. And the shrimp would be great as an appetizer by itself."

Your Best Recipe

Seasoned White Beans and Rice:
PREP: 30 MIN.

1½ cups MAHATMA Brown Rice
Pinch of salt and pepper
1 lime
1 cup loosely packed fresh cilantro
   leaves
1 cup loosely packed fresh parsley
   leaves
1 cup loosely packed baby arugula
   leaves
2 garlic cloves
⅔ cup extra virgin olive oil
¼ tsp. salt
¼ tsp. pepper
2 (15½-oz.) cans cannellini beans,
   drained

1. Prepare rice according to package directions with a pinch of salt and pepper.
2. Meanwhile, grate rind from lime into a small bowl. Cut lime in half, and squeeze juice into bowl.
3. Pulse cilantro, next 3 ingredients, lime rind, and lime juice in a blender until combined. Gradually add olive oil, salt, and pepper, and process just until blended, stopping to scrape down sides.
4. Microwave cannellini beans in a large microwave-safe bowl at HIGH 1½ minutes or until thoroughly heated. Stir in hot cooked rice. Add cilantro mixture, and toss to combine. Serve warm. **Makes** 4 cups.

DIANE BARTOLOMEO
PORT ST. LUCIE, FLORIDA

YOUR BEST RECIPE
Category Winner

Decadent S'mores Tiramisù
PREP: 40 MIN.; COOK: 7 MIN.;
CHILL: 6 HR., 15 MIN.; BROIL: 1 MIN.;
COOL: 10 MIN.
Graham crackers make a delicious substitute for the ladyfingers traditionally found in this classic dessert.

14 graham cracker sheets
½ cup cold whipping cream
1 tsp. MCCORMICK Gourmet Collection
   Pure Madagascar Organic Vanilla
   Extract
3 egg yolks
½ cup DOMINO Granulated Sugar
1 (8-oz.) package PHILADELPHIA Cream
   Cheese, softened
2 Tbsp. orange liqueur *****
1 cup brewed espresso or double-
   strength coffee, at room
   temperature
2 (1.55-oz.) milk chocolate candy bars,
   chopped
2 cups miniature marshmallows
1 tsp. unsweetened cocoa
Garnish: 6 fresh mint sprigs

1. Break each graham cracker sheet into 4 equal pieces along perforations. Remove and reserve 2 graham cracker pieces.
2. Beat whipping cream and vanilla at high speed with an electric mixer until soft peaks form. Cover and chill.
3. Meanwhile, bring a small amount of water to a boil in a medium saucepan over medium heat. Whisk together egg yolks and sugar in a medium-size stainless steel bowl. Place metal bowl with egg mixture over boiling water in saucepan, making sure bottom of bowl does not touch boiling water. Whisk egg mixture constantly, over boiling water, 6 to 7 minutes or until a candy thermometer registers 165°. (Mixture should be thick, pale, and hot to the touch.) Transfer to a small bowl; cover and chill 15 minutes or until cool.
4. Beat cream cheese at medium speed 30 seconds or until creamy. Gradually add cooled egg mixture and orange liqueur, beating until smooth. Gently fold in whipped cream mixture.
5. Place espresso in a shallow dish or bowl. Quickly dip 18 graham cracker pieces, 1 at a time, into espresso, and place in an 8-inch square baking dish to cover bottom. (Make certain that you use a broiler-proof baking dish.) Spread one-third of cream cheese mixture evenly over crackers. Repeat layers twice. Sprinkle with chopped chocolate, and top with marshmallows.
6. Broil 5 inches from heat 30 seconds to 1 minute or until marshmallows are puffed and golden. Let cool 10 minutes. Dust with cocoa. Cover and chill at least 6 hours or up to 24 hours.
7. Break each reserved graham cracker piece into thirds. Insert 1 corner of 1 graham cracker piece into top of each serving. Garnish, if desired. Serve cold. **Makes** 6 servings.

*2 Tbsp. milk may be substituted.

BEV JONES
BRUNSWICK, MISSOURI

Judges' Notes

"This dish is very creative," Test Kitchens Director and Head Judge Lyda Jones Burnette says of the Your Best Recipe winner, and Associate Foods Editor and Judge Mary Allen Perry concurs. "This would be the star of a potluck party," she says. "It's like a tiramisù moon pie. And it offers a very clever use of graham crackers—no one would figure out that they're used in place of ladyfingers in this dessert."

Hazelnut-Chocolate Biscotti

PREP: 20 MIN., BAKE: 25 MIN., STAND: 1 HR.

2½ cups all-purpose flour
¾ cup white cornmeal
2 tsp. baking powder
¼ tsp. salt
2 (1.4-oz.) milk chocolate-covered
    buttery toffee candy bars, cut into
    small chunks
1 (5-oz.) milk chocolate candy bar, cut
    into small chunks
½ cup butter, softened
1 cup DOMINO Granulated Sugar
2 large eggs
3 Tbsp. hazelnut liqueur

1. Preheat oven to 350°. Stir together first 4 ingredients in a bowl. Stir in chocolate chunks.
2. Beat butter at medium speed with an electric mixer until creamy. Gradually add sugar, beating until blended and stopping to scrape down sides as needed. Add eggs, 1 at a time, beating until blended after each addition. Add flour mixture (1 cup at a time) alternately with liqueur (1 Tbsp. at a time). Beat until blended after each addition.
3. Divide dough in half. Roll each dough half into a 16-inch-long log, and place on a greased baking sheet. Flatten each log to ¾-inch thickness. (Dough will be soft and sticky.)
4. Bake at 350° for 20 to 25 minutes or just until golden.
5. Cut each log crosswise into 3 equal sections. Transfer each section to a cutting board, and cut into ½-inch-thick slices, wiping knife clean after every 2 cuts. Transfer biscotti to baking sheet, cut sides up.
6. Turn oven off. Let biscotti stand in oven, with door closed, 1 hour. **Makes** about 2½ dozen.

Note: For testing purposes only, we used Hershey's Skor Bars for milk chocolate-covered buttery toffee candy bars, Hershey's Symphony Bars for milk chocolate candy bars, and Frangelico for hazelnut liqueur.

MARY SHERMAN
ARVADA, COLORADO

Apple Jack Pork Burgers With Apple-Fennel Marmalade

PREP: 25 MIN., COOK: 15 MIN.,
STAND: 25 MIN., GRILL: 10 MIN.

1 large Granny Smith apple,
    peeled
¼ cup mayonnaise
1 tsp. DOMINO Granulated Sugar
1 tsp. cider vinegar
Salt to taste
1 Tbsp. butter
1 Tbsp. canola oil
1 tsp. MCCORMICK Gourmet Collection
    Fennel Seed, divided
Pinch of MCCORMICK Gourmet
    Collection Crushed Red Pepper
2 Tbsp. DOMINO Light or Dark Brown
    Sugar
2 Tbsp. whiskey
3 Tbsp. cider vinegar
¾ tsp. salt, divided
⅓ cup boiling water
½ tsp. MCCORMICK Gourmet Collection
    Garlic Powder
½ tsp. MCCORMICK Gourmet Collection
    Onion Powder
¼ tsp. MCCORMICK Gourmet Collection
    Rubbed Sage
1 lb. lean ground pork
5 (½-oz.) Monterey Jack cheese slices
5 soft hamburger buns

1. Cut apple into fourths. Cut core away from each slice. Grate 1 slice into a small bowl; add mayonnaise, granulated sugar, and vinegar, and stir until blended. Season with salt to taste. Finely chop remaining 3 apple slices.
2. Melt butter with oil in a 10-inch skillet over medium-high heat. Add chopped apples, ½ tsp. fennel seed, and crushed red pepper, and cook, stirring often, 10 to 12 minutes or until apples turn golden brown. Reduce heat to medium low, and add brown sugar, whiskey, vinegar, and ¼ tsp. salt. Cook 2 to 3 minutes or until mixture is thickened. (Mixture will be a syrup consistency.) Remove from heat, and keep warm.
3. Combine ⅓ cup boiling water, next 3 ingredients, remaining ½ tsp. fennel seed, and remaining ½ tsp. salt in a 1-cup glass measuring cup. Let stand 10 to 15 minutes or to room temperature.
4. Preheat grill to 350° to 400° (medium-high). Combine pork and water mixture in a large bowl until blended and liquid is absorbed. (Do not overwork meat mixture.) Shape mixture into 5 thin patties. (Patties should be no more than ½ inch thick.)
5. Grill patties, covered with grill lid, over 350° to 400° (medium-high) heat 4 to 5 minutes on each side or until done. Top each patty with 1 cheese slice during last 1 minute of grilling. Remove from grill, and let stand 5 to 10 minutes.
6. Spread mayonnaise mixture evenly on cut sides of bottom hamburger buns. Top with burgers. Spoon apple mixture evenly over burgers; cover with tops of buns. **Makes** 5 servings.

ERIN BRAY
KNOXVILLE, TENNESSEE

Brand Winners

BORDEN *Brand Winner*

Tamale-Stuffed Roasted Poblano Peppers

PREP: 25 MIN., COOL: 5 MIN., BAKE: 58 MIN.

1 (28-oz.) can mild enchilada sauce
1 (17-oz.) package fully cooked pork roast au jus
1 (6-oz.) package buttermilk cornbread mix
2 Tbsp. butter, melted
1 tsp. MCCORMICK Gourmet Collection Ground Cumin
4 poblano chile peppers (about 1½ lb.)
1 cup BORDEN Shred Medleys Southwestern Style Shredded Cheese
1 cup sour cream
3 Tbsp. refrigerated cilantro paste
1 cup diced plum tomatoes
1 (2¼-oz.) can sliced ripe black olives, drained

1. Preheat oven to 375°. Pour enchilada sauce in a 13- x 9-inch baking dish.
2. Remove outer packaging (sleeve) from pork roast. Microwave pork in vacuum-sealed tray at HIGH 2 to 3 minutes. Remove from microwave, and let cool 5 minutes. Drain au jus in tray into a medium bowl. Shred pork.
3. Add cornbread mix, butter, and cumin to au jus in bowl, and stir until blended. Stir in shredded pork.
4. Cut stems from top of each pepper. Cut each pepper lengthwise down 1 flat side, leaving other side intact; remove seeds and membranes. Spoon pork mixture evenly into cavity of each pepper. Place stuffed peppers in baking dish, stuffed sides up. Cover dish with aluminum foil.
5. Bake at 375° for 40 to 50 minutes or until peppers are tender. Uncover and sprinkle each pepper with ¼ cup cheese. Bake, uncovered, 6 to 8 minutes or until cheese is melted.
6. Stir together sour cream and cilantro paste in a small bowl.
7. Spoon about ½ cup enchilada sauce onto a plate; top with 1 stuffed pepper. Drizzle one-fourth of sour cream mixture over pepper. Arrange ¼ cup tomatoes on 1 side of pepper; arrange one-fourth of olives on other side. Repeat procedure with remaining enchilada sauce, stuffed peppers, sour cream mixture, tomatoes, and olives. Serve immediately with remaining enchilada sauce. **Makes** 4 servings.

Note: For testing purposes only, we used Gourmet Garden Cilantro Herb Blend for refrigerated cilantro paste.

ANGELA BUCHANAN
LONGMONT, COLORADO

CRISCO *Brand Winner*

Blue Cheese Biscuits With Buffalo Shrimp Salad

PREP: 25 MIN., BAKE: 12 MIN., COOL: 10 MIN.

2 cups all-purpose flour
3 tsp. baking powder
½ tsp. baking soda
¼ tsp. salt
¼ cup CRISCO Shortening
1 Tbsp. cold butter
½ cup crumbled blue cheese
1 cup buttermilk
Buffalo Shrimp Salad

1. Preheat oven to 450°. Stir together first 4 ingredients in a large bowl. Cut shortening and butter into dry ingredients using a pastry blender until mixture resembles coarse crumbs. Stir in blue cheese.
2. Make a well in center of mixture. Add buttermilk to dry mixture, and stir until dry ingredients are moistened. Turn dough out onto a floured surface, and knead 4 to 5 times. Pat dough to ½-inch thickness; cut with a 1¾-inch round cutter, and place on ungreased baking sheets.
3. Bake at 450° for 10 to 12 minutes or until light golden brown. Let cool on baking sheets 10 minutes.
4. Cut each biscuit in half lengthwise. Spoon 1 Tbsp. Buffalo Shrimp Salad onto bottom half of each biscuit; cover with top halves of each biscuit. Reserve remaining Buffalo Shrimp Salad for another use. Serve immediately. **Makes** 18 to 20 appetizer servings.

Buffalo Shrimp Salad:
PREP: 20 MIN., COOK: 4 MIN.

1 lb. peeled, uncooked, fresh or frozen medium-size CERTIFIED WILD AMERICAN Shrimp
½ tsp. salt, divided
½ tsp. pepper, divided
2 Tbsp. liquid from hot peppers in vinegar
2 Tbsp. extra virgin olive oil
½ cup mayonnaise
2 tsp. liquid from hot peppers in vinegar
½ cup chopped celery
½ cup chopped red onion

1. If frozen, thaw shrimp according to package directions. Devein shrimp, if desired.
2. Toss together shrimp, ¼ tsp. salt, and ¼ tsp. pepper in a bowl. Add 2 Tbsp. liquid from hot peppers in vinegar, and toss to coat.
3. Cook shrimp in hot oil in a large nonstick skillet over medium heat 1½ to 2 minutes on each side or just until shrimp turn pink. Coarsely chop shrimp.
4. Whisk together mayonnaise, 2 tsp. liquid from hot peppers in vinegar, and remaining ¼ tsp. salt and pepper in a medium bowl. Stir in shrimp, celery, and onion until well blended. Mixture may be covered and chilled until ready to use. If chilled, let stand at room temperature 15 minutes before serving.
Makes 2½ cups.

LORIE ROACH
BUCKATUNNA, MISSISSIPPI

Pecan-Crusted Custard With Peaches and Berries

PREP: 15 MIN., COOK: 3 MIN., COOL: 55 MIN., CHILL: 2 HR., BROIL: 3 MIN., STAND: 5 MIN.

2¼ cups milk
⅓ cup pure maple syrup
1 (4.6-oz.) package JELL-O Brand Vanilla Flavor Cook-And-Serve Pudding & Pie Filling
3 fresh peaches
1 cup pecan halves
2 Tbsp. pure maple syrup
¾ cup heavy cream
6 Tbsp. DOMINO Light Brown Sugar
2 to 3 cups assorted fresh berries
Garnish: fresh mint leaves

1. Stir together milk and ⅓ cup maple syrup in a medium saucepan. Stir in pudding and pie filling. Bring to a boil over medium heat, stirring constantly. Pour mixture into a medium bowl, and let cool 45 minutes.
2. Meanwhile, peel peaches, if desired. Cut peaches into slices.
3. Heat pecans in a skillet over medium heat, stirring constantly, 3 minutes or until lightly toasted and fragrant. Let cool 10 minutes. Finely chop pecans.
4. Place 4 tsp. chopped pecans in each of 6 (6-oz.) ramekins. Drizzle 1 tsp. maple syrup over pecans in each ramekin.
5. Beat heavy cream at medium speed with an electric mixer until stiff peaks form. Fold into cooled milk mixture. Spoon custard mixture evenly into ramekins. Chill 2 hours or until set.
6. Place brown sugar in a small fine wire-mesh strainer. Using the back of a spoon, press sugar through strainer onto tops of chilled custards. Arrange ramekins in a shallow roasting or broiler pan filled with ice.
7. Broil 5 inches from heat 2 to 3 minutes or until sugar is melted. Let stand 5 minutes (to allow sugar to harden). Place ramekins on individual serving plates; arrange peach slices and assorted berries around ramekins. Sprinkle tops of custards with remaining pecans (about 4 tsp. each). Garnish, if desired. **Makes** 6 servings.

ROSEMARIE BERGER
JAMESTOWN, NORTH CAROLINA

Savory Cajun Shrimp Cheesecake

PREP: 25 MIN.; BAKE: 1 HR.; COOK: 6 MIN.; COOL: 1 HR., 15 MIN.; STAND: 1 HR.

1 lb. unpeeled, uncooked fresh or frozen medium-size CERTIFIED WILD AMERICAN Shrimp
1 (8-oz.) package ZATARAIN'S Jambalaya Mix
2 Tbsp. butter
1 small onion, diced
3 garlic cloves, chopped
1 red bell pepper, diced
½ (16-oz.) package smoked sausage, diced
1 Tbsp. ZATARAIN'S Creole Seasoning
½ tsp. ZATARAIN'S Cayenne Pepper
3 (8-oz.) packages PHILADELPHIA Cream Cheese, softened
½ (8-oz.) container sour cream
2 Tbsp. cornstarch
3 large eggs

1. If frozen, thaw shrimp according to package directions. Peel shrimp; devein, if desired.
2. Preheat oven to 350°. Grease a 9-inch springform pan with butter.
3. Prepare jambalaya mix according to package directions, omitting meats. Press jambalaya mixture in bottom and up sides of prepared pan.
4. Bake at 350° for 10 minutes. Remove from oven, and let cool.
5. Melt 2 Tbsp. butter in a large skillet over medium heat; add onion and garlic, and sauté 3 minutes or until tender. Stir in red bell pepper, next 3 ingredients, and shrimp. Cook, stirring often, 3 minutes or just until shrimp turn pink. Remove from heat, and let cool 15 minutes. (Do not drain mixture.)
6. Meanwhile, beat cream cheese, sour cream, and cornstarch at low speed with a heavy-duty electric stand mixer, using paddle attachment, until blended and smooth. Add eggs, 1 at a time, beating until blended after each addition. Fold in cooled shrimp mixture. Pour batter into prepared crust, and smooth top of batter using a spatula. Place pan on an aluminum foil-lined jelly-roll pan.
7. Bake at 350° for 50 minutes or until set. Turn off oven; let cheesecake stand in oven 1 hour. Remove cheesecake from oven. Let cool on a wire rack 1 hour or until completely cool. Remove sides of springform pan. Cut cheesecake into 12 to 16 wedges. Serve at room temperature. **Makes** 12 to 16 servings.

CYNTHIA COX
NEW ORLEANS, LOUISIANA

Peanut Butter-and-Chocolate Cheesecake

PREP: 1 HR., 45 MIN.; BAKE: 1 HR., 28 MIN.; COOL: 2 HR.; CHILL: 6 HR.

CRISCO Vegetable Shortening
4 Tbsp. unsalted butter
14 peanut butter sandwich cookies
3 Tbsp. USA-Grown Dry-Roasted Salted Peanuts
1 cup milk chocolate morsels
4 (8-oz.) packages PHILADELPHIA Cream Cheese, at room temperature
½ tsp. salt
1¼ cups DOMINO Granulated Sugar
1 (8-oz.) container sour cream
4 large eggs, at room temperature
1¼ tsp. vanilla extract, divided
1 cup 60% cocoa bittersweet chocolate morsels
⅔ cup USA-Grown Creamy Peanut Butter
Milk Chocolate Ganache
1 cup heavy cream
3 Tbsp. DOMINO 10X Confectioners Sugar
Virginia Peanut Candy Crunch

1. Preheat oven to 350°. Grease bottom of a 10-inch springform pan with shortening, and line with parchment paper. Wrap outside of pan with 2 sheets of heavy-duty aluminum foil.

2. Melt butter in a small saucepan over low heat.

3. Process cookies and peanuts in a food processor 25 seconds or until finely ground. Transfer mixture to a medium bowl; add butter, and stir until blended. Press mixture on bottom of prepared pan.

4. Bake at 350° for 12 minutes. Remove from oven, and sprinkle with milk chocolate morsels. Bake 1 more minute. Remove from oven to a wire rack, and spread melted morsels over bottom of crust using a small offset spatula.

5. Beat cream cheese and salt at medium-high speed with a heavy-duty electric stand mixer, using the paddle attachment, 3 minutes or until creamy and smooth, stopping to scrape bottom and down sides of bowl. Gradually add granulated sugar, and beat 3 to 4 minutes or until smooth, stopping to scrape bottom and down sides of bowl. Add sour cream, and beat at medium speed just until combined, stopping to scrape bottom and down sides of bowl. Add eggs, 1 at a time, beating at medium speed just until blended after each addition. Stop to scrape down bottom and sides of bowl. Beat in 1 tsp. vanilla at low speed until blended. Stop and scrape down bottom and sides of bowl until mixture is well blended.

6. Lightly grease remaining portion of inside of springform pan (just above prepared crust) with shortening.

7. Microwave bittersweet chocolate morsels in a 1-cup microwave-safe glass measuring cup at MEDIUM HIGH (70% power) 2 minutes or until melted and smooth, stirring at 30-second intervals.

8. Pour half of cheesecake batter into a medium bowl. Stir in melted bittersweet morsels until blended. Add peanut butter to remaining half of batter, and whisk until blended.

9. Slowly pour peanut butter batter evenly over prepared crust; level top of batter using a spatula. Slowly pour chocolate batter over peanut butter batter, and level with a spatula. Place springform pan in a 12-inch round cake pan or a large roasting pan; add hot water to pan to depth of 1¼ inch.

10. Bake at 350° for 1 hour and 15 minutes or until tiny cracks appear around edges. Remove from oven. Carefully remove cheesecake from water bath, and place on a wire rack. Remove foil. Let cool at room temperature 2 hours. (Center will set as cheesecake cools.)

11. Prepare Milk Chocolate Ganache. Spread top of cheesecake evenly with ganache. Cover and chill at least 6 hours or up to 24 hours. Release and remove sides of pan. Run a knife between parchment paper and pan bottom. Carefully tilt cheesecake upward, and remove parchment paper. Transfer cheesecake to a serving platter. Chill until ready to serve.

12. Beat heavy cream, confectioners sugar, and remaining ¼ tsp. vanilla at medium-high speed with an electric mixer until stiff peaks form.

13. Serve cheesecake slices with a dollop of sweetened whipped cream, and sprinkle with a generous amount of Virginia Peanut Candy Crunch. **Makes** 12 to 14 servings.

Note: For testing purposes only, we used Nabisco Brand Nutter Butter Cookies for peanut butter cookies.

Milk Chocolate Ganache:
PREP: 5 MIN., COOK: 5 MIN., STAND: 1 MIN.

¼ cup plus 1 Tbsp. heavy cream
1½ tsp. light corn syrup
⅔ cup milk chocolate morsels

1. Bring heavy cream and corn syrup to a boil in a small saucepan over medium heat, whisking occasionally.

2. Place chocolate morsels in a bowl. Pour hot cream over chocolate, and let stand 1 minute. Stir until chocolate is melted and mixture is smooth. Use immediately. **Makes** ⅔ cup.

Virginia Peanut Candy Crunch:
PREP: 10 MIN., BAKE: 30 MIN., COOL: 15 MIN.

¼ cup DOMINO Granulated Sugar
3 Tbsp. DOMINO Light Brown Sugar
½ tsp. ground cinnamon
1 egg white, at room temperature
1¾ cups USA-Grown Dry-Roasted Salted Peanuts

1. Preheat oven to 300°. Whisk together first 3 ingredients in a small bowl.

2. Whisk egg white in a medium bowl until frothy; add peanuts, tossing to coat. Sprinkle sugar mixture over peanuts in bowl, and toss to coat. Spread peanut mixture in a single layer on a parchment paper-lined baking sheet.

3. Bake at 300° for 15 minutes; turn peanuts, and bake 15 more minutes or until nuts are toasted and caramelized. Cool in pan on a wire rack 15 minutes, separating peanuts as they cool.

4. Pulse peanuts in a food processor 5 to 6 times or until coarsely chopped. Store in an airtight container 7 to 10 days. **Makes** 2 cups.

CONNIE WEIS
VIRGINIA BEACH, VIRGINIA

More Brand-Winning Recipes

Certified Wild American Shrimp: Coconut Macadamia Shrimp With Warm Tropical Salsa, page 302

Domino Sugar: Coconut-Cream Bread Pudding, page 301

Florida's Natural Orange Juice: Tequila-Flambéed Bananas With Coconut Ice Cream, page 301

Kraft Dressing: Szechwan Burgers With Cilantro Slaw, page 305

Mahatma Rice : California Sushi Bites, page 302

McCormick Gourmet Collection: Curried Beef Kabobs With Jade Sauce, page 303

Stacy's Chips: Tuscan Catfish With Sun-dried Tomato Aïoli, page 304

USA-Grown Peanuts: Peanut Shrimp Salad With Basil-Lime Dressing, page 305

1. Stir together first 8 ingredients in a large bowl.
2. Whisk together olive oil, sugar, and vinegar until blended. Pour over tomato mixture in bowl, and toss to coat. Cover and let stand at room temperature 1 hour. Season with salt and pepper to taste. **Makes** 1¾ cups.

GLORIA BRADLEY
NAPERVILLE, ILLINOIS

Category Descriptions

In our cook-off contest this year, each contestant had to use at least one sponsor product and submit recipes in the following categories:

■**Your Best Recipe:** Your signature recipe—the favorite someone is always asking for.

■**Quick Weeknight Favorites:** Entrées and side dishes with short ingredient lists and super-easy hands-on prep of less than 30 minutes. Entries may also include slow cooker recipes.

■**Sweet Endings:** Any sweet creation that is the perfect ending to your casual or elegant gathering.

■**Good for You:** Recipes using fresh flavors reflecting your healthy lifestyle.

■**Party Starters**: Appetizers and beverages for your next get-together.

RIVIANA *Brand Winner*

Grilled Swordfish With Olive-Basil Relish

PREP: 30 MIN., GRILL: 10 MIN., COOK: 10 MIN.

4 (1-inch-thick) swordfish steaks (about 24 oz.)
Extra virgin olive oil
½ tsp. salt
½ tsp. MCCORMICK Gourmet Collection Ground White Pepper
1 (3.5-oz.) bag SUCCESS Whole Grain Brown Rice
Olive-Basil Relish
½ cup mixed baby greens
Garnishes: fresh basil sprigs, orange slices

1. Preheat grill to 350° to 400° (medium-high). Brush swordfish evenly with olive oil; sprinkle with salt and pepper.
2. Grill swordfish, covered with grill lid, over 350° to 400° (medium-high) heat 4 to 5 minutes on each side or to desired degree of doneness. Keep warm.
3. Prepare rice according to package directions. Place rice in a medium skillet, and stir in ⅔ cup Olive-Basil Relish. Cook over medium heat 1 minute or until thoroughly heated.

4. Divide rice mixture between 4 plates; top each with 1 swordfish fillet. Spoon remaining Olive-Basil Relish over swordfish fillets and rice mixture. Top fillets evenly with mixed baby greens. Garnish, if desired. **Makes** 4 servings.

Olive-Basil Relish:
PREP: 20 MIN., STAND: 1 HR.

2 plum tomatoes, seeded and finely diced
½ cup finely diced yellow bell pepper
¼ cup pitted kalamata olives, finely diced
¼ cup pitted green olives, finely diced
¼ cup finely diced red onion
2 Tbsp. drained small capers
1 Tbsp. MCCORMICK Gourmet Collection Basil Leaves
1 garlic clove, minced
¼ cup extra virgin olive oil
2 tsp. DOMINO Granulated Sugar
1 tsp. red wine vinegar
Salt and MCCORMICK Gourmet Collection Coarse Grind Pepper to taste

inspirations

in season

Take a break from January's chill to enjoy this refreshing—and healthy—fruit.

Winter's sweetest blessing comes in the form of citrus, and our favorite pick hails from the Lone Star State. We're not alone either. An Internet search for Texas Ruby Red grapefruit yields thousands of sites, but it's really not the numbers that set the Texas fruit apart. Credit the rich color and unforgettable flavor for that. Also, it delivers beyond the glorious taste. A grapefruit boasts more vitamin C than an orange; provides a great source of fiber; and has no fat, sodium, or cholesterol. All the more reason to enjoy!

dressed up and good for you

Sweet potatoes make the ultimate weeknight dish. Try our easy serving idea for great taste.

Delicious, Healthful Sweet Potatoes

1. Pierce 4 to 6 small sweet potatoes with a fork, place on an aluminum foil-lined jelly-roll pan, and bake at 450° for 50 minutes or until tender. Cool slightly; then cut ends off potatoes. Stand each potato on larger end in a small bowl or ramekin; squeeze potato, pushing pulp upward, and fluff with a fork. Add desired toppings. **Makes** 4 to 6 servings. Prep: 20 min., Bake: 50 min.

Sprinkle on a flavorful spice blend, tasty toppings, etc., but use them sparingly to avoid excess calories. Here are some of our favorite combinations.

- Dried cranberries, grated orange rind, ground cinnamon, salt, and pepper
- Cooked-and-crumbled turkey bacon, light butter, sliced green onions, reduced-fat sour cream, and pepper
- Brown sugar, light butter, and toasted pecans
- Roasted chicken, chopped fresh rosemary, reduced-fat sour cream, salt, and pepper
- Honey, yogurt, and toasted pecans
- Cilantro, reduced-fat sour cream, chives, salt, and pepper

these onions won't make you cry

May is one of the sweetest months, courtesy of a special Southern veggie. In honor of the harvest of the legendary Vidalia, here's a mouthwatering microwave side that can be ready in minutes.

Vidalia Onion Side Dish

1. Peel 2 medium onions, and cut a thin slice from bottom and top of each one. Scoop out a 1-inch-deep hole from the top of each onion. Place onions, top sides up, in a 2-qt. microwave-safe dish with a lid. Add 1 beef bouillon cube and ½ Tbsp. butter to shallow hole in each onion; cover with lid. Microwave, covered, at HIGH for 8 to 10 minutes or until onion is tender. Garnish each serving with fresh parsley sprig and pepper, if desired. **Makes** 2 servings. Prep: 5 min., Cook: 10 min.

- We recommend only Vidalia or Texas Sweets for this recipe.
- Be sure to use a microwave-safe lid only; plastic wrap will melt.
- If you'd rather grill, wrap each filled-and-topped onion in heavy-duty aluminum foil (or a double layer of regular aluminum foil). Grill over high heat (400° to 450°) 15 to 20 minutes or until tender. Let stand 10 minutes.

tea with a twist

For those who believe that iced tea is the house wine of the South, we've created a very special vintage just for you. Cheers!

Blueberry-Lemon Iced Tea

1. Bring 1 (16-oz.) package frozen blueberries and ½ cup fresh lemon juice to a boil in a large saucepan over medium heat. Cook, stirring occasionally, 5 minutes. Remove from heat, and pour through a fine wire-mesh strainer into a bowl, using back of a spoon to squeeze out juice. Discard solids. Wipe saucepan clean.
2. Bring 4 cups water to a boil in same saucepan; add 3 family-size tea bags, and let stand 5 minutes. Remove and discard tea bags. Stir in ¾ cup sugar and blueberry juice mixture. Pour into a pitcher; cover and chill 1 hour. Serve over ice.
Makes 5 cups. Prep: 5 min., Cook: 10 min., Stand: 5 min., Chill: 1 hr.

good and healthy

We asked our staff health expert Shannon Sliter Satterwhite, M.S., R.D., to recommend a great-tasting alternative to the office snack machines. She whipped up a dandy one that satisfies longer and provides a quick boost of energy.

Healthful Fruit-and-Nut Mix
1. Combine 1 (9.5-oz.) container mixed nuts, 1 (6-oz.) container smoked almonds, 1 cup quartered dried apricots, and ¾ cup dried cranberries in a large bowl. Store in an airtight container. **Makes** about 4½ cups. Prep: 5 min.

■ Indulge a little more: Add a few morsels of delicious antioxidant-rich dark chocolate.
■ For testing purposes only, we used Planters Select Cashews With Almonds and Pecans and Blue Diamond Smokehouse Almonds.

the best corn ever

Nothing—repeat, nothing—tastes better in mid-summer than fresh corn on the cob. Just cook up your favorite variety, and then flavor it with one of our tasty butters. Start each recipe with ½ cup softened butter, and add our suggested stir-ins.

Lemon-Basil Butter:
2 tsp. finely chopped fresh basil, 2 tsp. grated lemon rind, salt and pepper to taste
Prep: 5 min.

Chili-Lime Butter:
2 tsp. grated lime rind, ½ tsp. chili powder, salt and pepper to taste
Prep: 5 min.

Parmesan-Parsley Butter:
½ cup freshly grated Parmesan cheese, 2 Tbsp. chopped fresh parsley, salt and pepper to taste
Prep: 8 min.

sweet and tart

This refreshing treat comes from Baltimore's Flower Mart, held in the Mount Vernon neighborhood. One of the event's most popular traditions, lemon sticks are a zippy combination of half a lemon served with a porous peppermint candy stick to use as a straw. Try our version. The tart juice and the sweet candy cane will bring some zing to your taste buds.

Peppermint Citrus Cooler

1. Roll 1 chilled lemon, lime, or orange on countertop 3 or 4 times, pressing gently with palm of your hand. Cut a small "X" into top of fruit with a paring knife. Insert 1 soft peppermint candy stick into "X." Sip fruit juice through candy stick. Prep: 5 min.

■ For testing purposes only, we used Bobs Mint Sticks®, available from Cracker Barrel Old Country Store.
■ You can also use King Leo Soft Peppermint Sticks, available at **www.candycrate.com.**

easy as ABC

Personalized brownies make the perfect treat to take to a party—especially if you start with a mix.

Monogrammed Jumbo Brownies

1. Prepare and bake 1 (21-oz.) package fudge brownie mix according to directions for a 13- x 9-inch pan. Let cool in pan on a wire rack for 45 minutes.
2. Stir together ½ cup butter, ⅓ cup milk, and 5 Tbsp. unsweetened cocoa over low heat, stirring constantly, 5 minutes or until butter melts and mixture is blended. Remove from heat, and beat in 1 (16-oz.) package powdered sugar at low speed with an electric mixer until smooth; spread frosting evenly over prepared brownies. Let stand 45 minutes or until frosting is firm. Cut into 12 equal squares.
3. Tint ½ (16-oz.) container ready-to-spread vanilla frosting with desired shade of food coloring gel. Spoon frosting mixture into a small zip-top plastic freezer bag. Snip a hole in 1 corner of the bag. Pipe desired monogram on each brownie. **Makes** 1 dozen. Prep: 20 min., Bake: 30 min., Cool: 45 min., Stand: 45 min.

■ You can find small letter-shaped cookie cutters at crafts stores to use as templates. Simply imprint letter on iced surface; then pipe over the imprint.
■ If you don't have time to monogram, pick up a box of alphabet-shaped cookies to use as a topping.

dressed-up tomato soup

Steaming tomato soup rates high among fall's popular comfort foods, but we decided to take this seasonal favorite to another flavor level. Try our suggestions to turn your next bowl of soup into the best you've ever had.

1. Pulse 1 (28-oz.) can Italian-seasoned diced tomatoes in a food processor 3 to 4 times or until finely diced. Stir together tomatoes; 1 (26-oz.) can tomato soup, undiluted; 1 (32-oz.) container chicken broth; and ½ tsp. freshly ground pepper in a Dutch oven. Cook over medium heat, stirring occasionally, 10 minutes or until thoroughly heated. **Makes** about 11 cups. Prep: 5 min., Cook: 10 min.

■ To serve, we topped the soup with a dollop of sour cream and sprinkled it with chopped fresh parsley. Other tasty additions include chopped fresh basil, chopped fresh chives, chopped fresh rosemary, croutons, freshly grated Parmesan cheese, and grated lemon rind.

■ For testing purposes only, we used Progresso Diced Tomatoes With Italian Herbs.

serve a surprise

Try our easy but elegant nut course to impress dinner guests. The duo draws rave reviews no matter when you serve them—before the meal as an appetizer or after, as a dessert.

Decked-Out Dates

1. Cut a lengthwise slit down the center of 24 seedless dates, forming a pocket. Stuff with toasted walnut halves and thin shavings of manchego cheese.
Makes 24 servings. Prep: 15 min.

UpTown Figs

1. Cut a slit in large side of 24 dried figs, cutting to, but not through, stem end. Stir together 1 (3-oz.) package softened cream cheese, 2 tsp. powdered sugar, and 2 tsp. orange liqueur; fill each fig evenly with cream cheese mixture and 1 roasted, salted almond. Press figs to secure filling. **Makes** 24 servings. Prep: 20 min.

■ You can make both recipes ahead of time and store them in the refrigerator. Before serving, let stand at room temperature for 30 minutes.

serving pot

Most people only think about garden projects when they see a strawberry jar. These versatile pots, though, can fill a host of uses. We wowed guests by turning one into a serving piece for crisp veggies with a great dip. Try it this weekend.

Fresh Buttermilk-Herb Dip

1. Whisk together 1¼ cups mayonnaise, 6 Tbsp. buttermilk, 2 Tbsp. fresh lemon juice, 1 Tbsp. chopped fresh chives, 1 Tbsp. chopped fresh parsley, ¼ tsp. salt, and freshly ground pepper to taste in a medium bowl. Cover and chill 30 minutes. Place a 2-gallon zip-top plastic bag in the center of an 18-inch-tall, glazed strawberry jar; fill to top with ice and seal. Nestle a ramekin on ice in top opening of jar. Fill ramekin with dip. Arrange assorted vegetable sticks, such as carrots, celery, and bell peppers, in side pockets of jar, and serve. **Makes** about 1½ cups. Prep: 10 min., Chill: 30 min.

herb art

Welcome your new neighbor—or just surprise a friend—with this easy gift from the kitchen.

Herb-Topped Bread

1. Purchase a French baguette or some other type of artisan bread from a local bakery. Stir together 1 egg white and 1 Tbsp. water. Brush egg white mixture on top of bread; press fresh herbs onto dampened bread. Secure the herbs by gently brushing additional egg mixture on top. Bake at 350° for 5 minutes or until bread surface is dry. Prep: 5 min., Bake: 5 min.

■ The best fresh herb choices include dill weed, flat-leaf parsley sprigs, chives, and thyme leaves.

"big easy" appetizers

You don't have to go to New Orleans to enjoy its trademark flavors. Our Test Kitchens wizards have transformed the Crescent City's popular muffuletta into a can't-miss appetizer for your next party.

Muffuletta on a Stick

1. Layer 1 slice each of deli-style smoked ham, provolone cheese, and Genoa salami; tightly roll up, and slice into 4 equal pieces. Repeat procedure 5 times.

2. Thread 24 (4-inch) wooden skewers with 1 of each: pepperoncini salad pepper, meat-and-cheese roll, 1½-inch-long roasted red bell pepper, large pitted ripe black olive, another 1½-inch-long roasted red bell pepper, and pimiento-stuffed Spanish olive. Place in a 13- x 9-inch baking dish. Whisk together 1 (8-oz.) bottle olive oil-and-vinegar dressing and ½ tsp. Italian seasoning; pour over skewers, and chill 30 minutes. **Makes** 24 servings. Prep: 30 min., Chill: 30 min.

■ Don't bother roasting the peppers yourself. Look for a jar of roasted red bell peppers at your grocery.

carve a cooler

You don't have to light a candle in a pumpkin to make it the center of attention. This idea will transform that seasonal icon into the hit of your next party.

Pumpkin Cooler

1. Cut top from a large, wide pumpkin using a serrated knife. Scoop out seeds and pulp. Line bottom and sides with a 2-gal. zip-top plastic bag. Fill bag with ice and assorted beverages. **Makes** 1 cooler. Prep: 15 min

■ One large pumpkin yields about 1 cup of seeds, but don't throw them out. Season them instead. Rinse 1 cup fresh pumpkin seeds; pat dry with paper towels. Toss seeds with 1 Tbsp. olive oil, 1 Tbsp. dried ground thyme, and 1½ tsp. kosher salt; place in a single layer on a lightly greased baking sheet. Bake at 350° for 20 to 25 minutes or until toasted. Serve on top of a salad, or just enjoy them as a yummy snack. **Makes** 1 cup. Prep: 10 min., Bake: 25 min.

granola on the go

Foods Executive Editor Scott Jones tasted our treats and promptly exclaimed, "These are so good!" Believe us, he is not given to easy praise. So when you need a great snack that's a snap to transport, whip up a batch of these.

Cranberry-Almond Chewy Granola Bars
1. Melt 3 Tbsp. butter in a buttered Dutch oven over low heat. Add 1 (10½-oz.) package miniature marshmallows, and cook, stirring occasionally, until melted. Remove from heat. Meanwhile, process 1 (15-oz.) box honey-almond-flax multi-grain cluster cereal, in batches, in a food processor until finely ground; combine with 3 cups crisp rice cereal, 1 (6-oz.) package sweetened dried cranberries, and 1 tsp. salt. Stir into marshmallow mixture. Press cereal mixture into a buttered 15- x 10-inch jelly-roll pan. Let stand 1 hour. Cut into 40 (1¼- x 3-inch) bars.
Makes 40 bars. Prep: 10 min., Cook: 10 min., Stand: 1 hr.

■ For easy travel, layer bars with parchment paper in disposable plastic containers with lids.
■ For testing purposes only, we used Kashi GOLEAN Crunch honey-almond-flax cereal.

a tasty toast

Whether you're hosting an after-caroling party or just entertaining neighbors and friends at a casual gathering, this dessert-like drink will delight your guests. We predict it will become your newest holiday tradition.

Ultimate Alexander
1. Process ¼ cup cold brewed coffee, 2 pts. coffee ice cream, ½ cup brandy, and ½ cup chocolate syrup in a blender until smooth, stopping to scrape down sides. Pour mixture into glasses, and garnish with sweetened whipped cream, chocolate curls, and milk chocolate sticks, if desired. Serve immediately.
Makes 5 cups. Prep: 5 min.

■ For testing purposes only, we used Häagen-Dazs Coffee ice cream and Hershey's Milk Chocolate Sticks.

leftovers you'll love

Don't settle for just turkey sandwiches when it comes to after-the-holiday lunches. This salad, which tastes as good as it looks, makes great use of those leftovers.

Thanksgiving Salad

1. Cut cold cornbread dressing into 1-inch cubes; place on a lightly greased aluminum foil-lined baking sheet. Broil dressing cubes 6 inches from heat 3 to 4 minutes or until golden. Remove from oven, and turn dressing cubes onto other side; broil 2 to 3 more minutes or until golden. Serve these croutons over a bed of mixed baby greens with leftover turkey and cranberry sauce. Drizzle with bottled olive oil-and-vinegar dressing, and sprinkle with salt and pepper to taste. Prep: 10 min., Broil: 7 min.

special weekend breakfast

You always want a morning meal on a Saturday or Sunday to taste special, but this flavorful, low-fat dish makes the end of the week more than memorable. It jump-starts the day in a healthful way.

Buttermilk-Pear Pancakes

1. Whisk together 2 cups reduced-fat, all-purpose baking mix; 2 cups nonfat buttermilk; and 1 egg in a bowl. Pour ¼ cup batter for each pancake onto a hot, lightly greased griddle or large nonstick skillet. Cook pancakes 3 to 4 minutes or until tops are covered with bubbles and edges look dry and cooked; turn and cook other side. Spoon on Fresh Pear-Cinnamon Topping, and serve immediately. **Makes** about 14 pancakes. Prep: 10 min., Cook: 8 min. per batch

Fresh Pear-Cinnamon Topping:

1. Toss 4 peeled, cored, and sliced pears with 1 Tbsp. fresh lemon juice, 1 Tbsp. honey, and ¼ tsp. ground cinnamon in a medium bowl. Melt ½ Tbsp. butter in a nonstick skillet over medium-high heat; sauté pear mixture, stirring occasionally, 8 to 10 minutes or until slightly thickened. **Makes** about 1¼ cups. Prep: 10 min., Cook: 10 min.

■ We recommend Pioneer Low-Fat Biscuit & Baking Mix or Bisquick Heart Smart Pancake and Baking Mix; we used Comice pears.

slow-cooker favorites

Slow-Cooker Favorites

This collection of kitchen-tested one-dish meals, savory sides, and even tempting desserts will spark your slow-cooking desire.

Sensational Starts

Surprise family and friends with tempting snacks from the slow cooker.

Hot Parmesan-Artichoke Dip

family favorite
PREP: 18 MIN., COOK: 4 HR.
Freshly shredded Parmesan cheese melts more smoothly than preshredded options.

1½ cups mayonnaise
2 (12-oz.) jars marinated quartered artichoke hearts, drained and chopped
2 (4.5-oz.) cans chopped green chiles, drained
1 (7-oz.) jar roasted red bell peppers, drained and chopped
2 cups freshly shredded Parmesan cheese
4 garlic cloves, minced
Toasted baguette slices or assorted crackers

1. Stir together first 6 ingredients. Spoon into a 3-qt. slow cooker.
2. Cover and cook on LOW 4 hours. Stir well before serving. Serve with baguette slices or assorted crackers. **Makes** 6 cups.

Slow-Cooker Queso Blanco

family favorite • freezeable
PREP: 22 MIN., COOK: 2 HR.
This queso dip freezes well. Spoon into serving-size freezer containers, and freeze up to one month. Thaw overnight in refrigerator. Reheat in microwave on MEDIUM.

1 small onion, diced
3 garlic cloves, minced
1 (14½-oz.) can petite cut diced tomatoes, drained
1 cup milk
¾ cup pickled jalapeño slices, minced
1 Tbsp. juice from jalapeño slices
1 (4.5-oz.) can chopped green chiles, undrained
1 tsp. ground cumin
½ tsp. dried oregano
½ tsp. coarsely ground pepper
2 lb. deli white American cheese, sliced

1. Place onion in a microwave-safe bowl; cover loosely with heavy-duty plastic wrap. Microwave at HIGH 2 minutes. Stir in garlic and next 8 ingredients.
2. Roughly tear cheese; place in a 4-qt. slow cooker. Pour onion mixture over cheese.
3. Cover and cook on LOW 2 hours. Stir gently to blend ingredients. Serve with tortilla chips. **Makes** 6½ cups.

Note: For testing purposes only, we used DiLusso deli white American cheese. Buy it by the pound at the deli counter and have it sliced so you can forgo shredding; just roughly tear the slices, and place them in the cooker.

Baked Pimiento Cheese Dip

PREP: 17 MIN., COOK: 3 HR.
This dip is great with celery sticks or crackers.

1 (10-oz.) block sharp Cheddar cheese, shredded
1 (10-oz.) block extra-sharp Cheddar cheese, shredded
1 Tbsp. cornstarch
8 bacon slices, cooked and crumbled
½ small onion, finely grated (about 3 Tbsp.)
1 cup mayonnaise
2 (4-oz.) jars diced pimiento, drained
2 tsp. Worcestershire sauce
¼ tsp. pepper

1. Toss together cheeses and cornstarch in a medium bowl. Add half of bacon and all of remaining ingredients; stir well to blend. Spoon mixture into a lightly greased 3-qt. slow cooker. Sprinkle with remaining bacon.
2. Cover and cook on LOW 2 to 3 hours or until melted and bubbly. Serve warm with crackers. **Makes** 5 cups.

Note: For testing purposes only, we used Cracker Barrel Sharp Cheddar cheese.

Soups and Stews

Warm heart and soul with these savory soups and chunky stews.

Texas Stew

PREP: 10 MIN., COOK: 5 HR.

Is mild picante sauce not spicy enough for you? Kick it up a notch with hot picante sauce. If you like it really hot, add chopped jalapeño.

2 lb. beef tips, cut into 1-inch cubes
1 (14½-oz.) can Mexican-style stewed
    tomatoes, undrained
1 (10½-oz.) can condensed beef broth,
    undiluted
1 (8-oz.) jar mild picante sauce
1 (10-oz.) package frozen whole kernel
    corn, thawed
3 carrots, cut into ½-inch pieces
1 onion, cut into thin wedges
2 garlic cloves, pressed
½ tsp. ground cumin
½ tsp. salt
¼ cup all-purpose flour

1. Combine first 10 ingredients in a 5-qt. slow cooker.
2. Cover and cook on HIGH 3 to 4 hours or until meat is tender.
3. Stir together ½ cup water and flour. Stir into meat mixture; cover and cook on HIGH 1 more hour or until thickened. **Makes** 12 cups.

"Baked" Potato Soup

family favorite
PREP: 21 MIN.; COOK: 4 HR. OR 8 HR.
Reduce the fat in this soup by using fat-free half-and-half along with reduced-fat cheese and sour cream.

6 large russet potatoes, peeled and cut
    into ½-inch cubes (about 3¾ lbs.)
1 large onion, chopped (about
    1½ cups)
3 (14-oz.) cans chicken broth with
    roasted garlic
¼ cup butter
2½ tsp. salt
1¼ tsp. freshly ground pepper
1 cup whipping cream or half-and-half
1 cup (4 oz.) sharp Cheddar cheese,
    shredded
3 Tbsp. chopped fresh chives
1 (8-oz.) container sour cream (optional)
4 bacon slices, cooked and crumbled
Shredded Cheddar cheese

1. Combine first 6 ingredients in a 5-qt. slow cooker.
2. Cover and cook on HIGH 4 hours or on LOW 8 hours or until potato is tender.
3. Mash mixture until potatoes are coarsely chopped and soup is slightly thickened; stir in whipping cream, cheese, and chives. Top with sour cream, if desired, and sprinkle with bacon and Cheddar cheese before serving. **Makes** 12 cups.

Taco Soup

family favorite
PREP: 15 MIN., COOK: 6 HR.
Use alcohol-free beer instead of regular, if you prefer.

1½ lb. ground beef
1 cup chopped red onion
1 (1.25-oz.) package taco seasoning mix
1 (1-oz.) envelope Ranch dressing mix
2 (15.25-oz.) cans whole kernel corn,
    undrained
1 (16-oz.) can pinto beans, undrained
1 (15-oz.) can black beans, undrained
2 (10-oz.) cans chili-style diced
    tomatoes with green chiles,
    undrained
1 (12-oz.) can light beer
Toppings: shredded Cheddar cheese,
    sour cream, tortilla chips, cilantro

1. Cook beef and onion in a large skillet over medium-high heat, stirring until meat crumbles and is no longer pink; drain.
2. Combine meat mixture, 1½ cups water, taco seasoning mix, and next 6 ingredients in a 5½-qt. slow cooker.
3. Cover and cook on LOW 5 to 6 hours. Serve with desired toppings. **Makes** 16 cups.

Note: For testing purposes only, we used Rotel Chili Fixin's diced tomatoes.

Slow-Cooker Safety

■ When cooking raw meats and poultry, the USDA recommends using HIGH heat for the first hour to make sure ingredients reach a safe temperature quickly. Then you can reduce the heat to LOW for the remainder of cooking.
■ You can omit the HIGH heat for the first hour in recipes that brown the meat first, since precooking jump-starts the initial temperature of ingredients.
■ Defrost any frozen foods before cooking to make sure the contents of the crock reach a safe temperature quickly.
■ Always fill a slow cooker at least halfway full and no more than two-thirds full in order for food to reach a safe temperature.

Main-Dish Marvels

Choose an entrée guests and family will love—from beef and pork classics to chicken.

Beef Brisket With Fall Vegetables
make ahead
PREP: 18 MIN., COOK: 12 HR.

2 (2-lb.) beef briskets, trimmed
2 tsp. salt
1 tsp. pepper
1 Tbsp. vegetable oil
4 carrots, cut into 2-inch pieces
3 parsnips, sliced
2 celery ribs, sliced
1 large onion, sliced
1 fennel bulb, quartered
12 fresh thyme sprigs
1 (1-oz.) envelope dry onion soup mix
1 (14-oz.) can low-sodium beef broth
¾ cup dry red wine
½ cup ketchup
2 Tbsp. Beau Monde seasoning
8 garlic cloves
¾ cup chopped fresh parsley
Garnish: fresh thyme sprigs

1. Sprinkle beef with salt and pepper.
2. Heat oil over medium-high heat in a large nonstick skillet. Add beef; cook 4 minutes on each side or until browned. Transfer beef to a 6-qt. slow cooker. Add carrot and next 5 ingredients.
3. Whisk together soup mix and next 6 ingredients. Pour mixture evenly over beef.
4. Cover and cook on LOW 12 hours or until tender. Transfer beef to a serving platter. Pour remaining vegetable mixture through a wire-mesh strainer, reserving juices, carrot, and onion; discard remaining vegetable mixture. Serve beef and vegetables with juices. Garnish, if desired. **Makes** 8 servings.

Creamy Beef and Spinach Over Noodles
family favorite
PREP: 9 MIN., COOK: 4 HR.
This one-dish-meal pairs nicely with a fresh fruit salad and yeast rolls.

1 lb. ground chuck
1 medium onion, chopped
1 (8-oz.) package sliced fresh mushrooms
1 (10-oz.) package frozen chopped spinach, thawed
1 (14-oz.) can low-sodium, fat-free beef broth
1 (10¾-oz.) can cream of mushroom soup
1 (8-oz.) container sour cream
½ tsp. salt
¼ tsp. pepper
1 (8-oz.) block Monterey Jack cheese with peppers, shredded
Hot cooked egg noodles

1. Cook first 3 ingredients in a large skillet over medium heat, stirring until beef crumbles and is no longer pink; drain.
2. Drain spinach well, pressing between paper towels. Combine beef mixture, spinach, broth, and next 5 ingredients in a large bowl. Spoon into a lightly greased 4-qt. slow cooker. Cover and cook on LOW 4 hours. Serve over egg noodles. **Makes** 4 to 6 servings.

Open-Faced Meatball Sandwiches
PREP: 5 MIN., COOK: 6 HR.

24 frozen cooked Italian-style meatballs, thawed
1 (26-oz.) jar super chunky mushroom pasta sauce
1 (15-oz.) can Italian-style tomato sauce
1 (5.5-oz.) can spicy tomato juice
6 (6-inch) hoagie rolls, split but not cut through and toasted
1½ cups (6 oz.) shredded mozzarella cheese

1. Combine first 4 ingredients in a 3-quart slow cooker.
2. Cover and cook on HIGH 1 hour. Reduce heat to LOW, and cook 4½ to 5 hours or until slightly thickened. Spoon meatball mixture evenly into rolls. Sprinkle with cheese. **Makes** 6 servings.

Note: For testing purposes only, we used Mama Mia Italian-style Meatballs, Ragu Chunky Garden Mushroom Pasta Sauce, Hunt's Family Favorites Italian-style Tomato Sauce, and V8 Spicy Tomato Juice.

Saucy Chipotle Barbecue Pork
PREP: 15 MIN., COOK: 7 HR.

2 tsp. dry mustard
1 tsp. salt
½ tsp. ground red pepper
1 (4- to 5-lb.) boneless pork butt roast, cut in half
2 Tbsp. butter
1 large onion, chopped (about 2½ cups)
1 (18-oz.) bottle spicy original barbecue sauce
1 (12-oz.) bottle Baja chipotle marinade
Garnish: sliced green onions

1. Rub first 3 ingredients evenly over pork. Melt butter in a large nonstick skillet over medium-high heat. Add pork; cook 10 minutes or until browned on all sides.
2. Place onion and pork in a 5-qt. slow cooker. Add barbecue sauce and marinade.
3. Cover and cook on HIGH 7 hours or until pork is tender and shreds easily.
4. Remove pork to a large bowl, reserving sauce; shred pork. Stir shredded pork into sauce. Serve as is, over a cheese-topped baked potato, in a sandwich, or over a green salad. Garnish, if desired. **Makes** 8 servings.

Note: For testing purposes only, we used KC Masterpiece Spicy Original Barbecue Sauce and Lawry's Baja Chipotle Marinade.

Country Pork and Corn on the Cob
make ahead
PREP: 14 MIN., COOK: 4 HR.

½ cup all-purpose flour
1½ tsp. salt, divided
1 tsp. pepper, divided
6 (5-oz.) bone-in center-cut pork chops
    (about ½ inch thick)
2 to 3 Tbsp. olive oil, divided
4 large garlic cloves, pressed
3 ears fresh corn, cut in half
1 (18-oz.) bottle honey barbecue sauce
1 cup chicken broth

1. Combine flour, 1 teaspoon salt, and ½ teaspoon pepper in a large zip-top plastic freezer bag; add pork, tossing to coat.
2. Heat 1 Tbsp. oil in a large nonstick skillet over medium-high heat. Cook pork, in 2 batches, 2 minutes on each side or until browned, adding additional 1 tablespoon oil if needed.
3. Place in a lightly greased 4½-qt. slow cooker. Rub remaining 1 Tbsp. oil and garlic evenly over corn. Sprinkle with remaining ½ tsp. each salt and pepper; add to slow cooker. Combine barbecue sauce and broth; add to slow cooker.
4. Cover and cook on LOW 4 hours or until meat is tender. **Makes** 6 servings.

Note: For testing purposes only, we used KC Masterpiece Honey Barbecue Sauce.

Shredded Barbecue Chicken
make ahead
PREP: 22 MIN., COOK: 7 HR.

1½ lb. skinned and boned chicken
    thighs
1 Tbsp. olive oil
1 cup ketchup
¼ cup dark brown sugar
1 Tbsp. Worcestershire sauce
1 Tbsp. cider vinegar
1 Tbsp. yellow mustard
1 tsp. ground red pepper
½ tsp. garlic salt
6 hamburger buns
Dill pickle slices

1. Brown chicken 4 minutes on each side in 1 tablespoon hot oil in a large skillet over medium-high heat. Remove from heat, and place in a 4-qt. slow cooker.
2. Combine ketchup and next 6 ingredients. Pour over chicken.
3. Cover and cook on HIGH 1 hour. Reduce heat to LOW, and cook 5 to 6 hours. Remove chicken from sauce; shred chicken. Stir shredded chicken into sauce. Spoon mixture evenly onto buns, and top with pickle slices. **Makes** 6 servings.

Mu Shu Chicken Wraps
make ahead
PREP: 11 MIN., COOK: 6 HR.
Wrap the spicy chicken mixture in lettuce or cabbage leaves to serve as appetizers.

1 medium onion, diced
2 lb. skinned and boned chicken thighs
¼ tsp. salt
¼ tsp. pepper
1 Tbsp. sesame or vegetable oil
¾ cup hoisin sauce
1 Tbsp. soy sauce
1 Tbsp. honey
2 tsp. rice wine
¼ tsp. ground ginger
8 (6-inch) flour tortillas
3 cups shredded napa cabbage
½ cup thinly sliced green onions

1. Place diced onion in a 3- or 4-qt. slow cooker.
2. Sprinkle chicken evenly with salt and pepper.
3. Brown chicken 2 to 3 minutes on each side in hot oil in a large skillet over medium-high heat. Remove skillet from heat, and place chicken on top of onion in slow cooker.
4. Whisk together hoisin sauce and next 4 ingredients; pour over chicken. Cover and cook on HIGH 1 hour. Reduce heat to LOW, and cook 5 hours. Shred chicken in cooker with a fork.
5. Top each tortilla evenly with cabbage, chicken, and green onions. Fold

bottom edge of each tortilla in to hold filling; roll tortillas crosswise, and, if desired, secure with wooden picks or in parchment paper. **Makes** 8 servings.

Chicken-and-Wild Rice Hot Dish
make ahead
PREP: 15 MIN., COOK: 4 HR.

4 skinned and boned chicken breasts
    (about 2 lb.)
1 cup chopped onion
1 cup chopped celery
5 garlic cloves, pressed
2 (6-oz.) packages uncooked long-grain
    and wild rice mix
2 (14-oz.) cans chicken broth with
    roasted garlic
2 (10¾-oz.) cans cream of mushroom soup
1 (8-oz.) package sliced fresh mushrooms
1 (8-oz.) can sliced water chestnuts,
    drained
1 cup chopped walnuts, toasted
2 Tbsp. butter

1. Brown chicken in a lightly greased large nonstick skillet over medium-high heat; remove from pan, and cut into ½-inch pieces. Add onion, celery, and garlic to pan; sauté 3 to 4 minutes or until tender.
2. Combine rice mix and remaining 6 ingredients in a 5-qt. slow cooker. Stir in chicken and vegetables.
3. Cover and cook on LOW 4 hours or until rice is tender and liquid is absorbed. **Makes** 6 servings.

Note: For testing purposes only, we used Uncle Ben's Long-Grain and Wild Rice Mix.

Loaded Jambalaya

PREP: 25 MIN., COOK: 5 HR., 15 MIN.

¾ lb. skinned and boned chicken
    thighs, cut into 1-inch pieces
¾ lb. skinned and boned chicken
    breasts, cut into 1-inch pieces
1 tsp. salt
⅛ tsp. black pepper
⅛ tsp. ground red pepper
2 Tbsp. vegetable oil
1 large onion, chopped (about 2 cups)
1 large green bell pepper, chopped
2 celery ribs, chopped
4 garlic cloves, minced
1 (14½-oz.) can diced tomatoes,
    undrained
½ lb. fully cooked ham, cut into ½-inch
    pieces
1 (14-oz.) can chicken broth
2 (3.5-oz.) bags boil-in-bag rice
1 lb. unpeeled, medium-size raw shrimp
½ cup chopped green onions
2 Tbsp. chopped fresh parsley
1 Tbsp. hot sauce

1. Sprinkle chicken with salt, black pepper, and red pepper.
2. Heat oil in a large skillet over high heat. Add chicken; cook 4 to 5 minutes, stirring occasionally, or until browned. Spoon into a 5-qt. slow cooker.
3. Add large chopped onion and next 3 ingredients to skillet; sauté 4 minutes or until tender. Transfer to slow cooker. Add tomatoes, ham, and broth to slow cooker.
4. Cover and cook on LOW 5 hours. Meanwhile, cook rice according to package directions. Set aside.
5. Peel shrimp, and devein, if desired. Stir shrimp, cooked rice, and remaining ingredients into slow cooker. Cover and cook on HIGH 15 minutes or until shrimp turn pink. **Makes** 4 to 6 servings.

Note: For testing purposes only, we used Frank's Hot Sauce.

Slow-Cooker Tips and Techniques

■ Removing the cooker lid during cooking releases a great deal of heat, so resist the urge to lift the lid and peek. Each time you remove it when not required, you'll need to increase the cooking time by 20 to 30 minutes.
■ There's no need to stir ingredients unless a recipe specifically calls for it. Always layer ingredients as the recipe directs.
■ Remember that 1 hour on HIGH equals approximately 2 hours on LOW. A bonus to cooking on LOW is that recipes can generally cook a little longer than the recipe states without becoming overdone.
■ Trim excess fats from meats. If desired, brown meat in a skillet or broiler to remove fat and then drain the fat before adding the meat to the cooker.
■ You can thicken juices and make gravy by removing the lid and cooking on HIGH for the last 20 or 30 minutes.

Chicken Enchiladas

family favorite

PREP: 18 MIN.; COOK: 4 HR., 45 MIN.

3 cups chopped cooked chicken
2 cups (8 oz.) shredded Monterey Jack
    cheese with peppers
1 (4.5-oz.) can chopped green
    chiles
½ cup sour cream
⅓ cup chopped fresh cilantro
8 (8-inch) flour tortillas
1 (8-oz.) container sour cream
1 (8-oz.) bottle green taco sauce
1 cup (4 oz.) shredded Monterey Jack
    cheese with peppers
Toppings: chopped tomato, chopped
    avocado, sliced green onions,
    sliced ripe olives, chopped fresh
    cilantro

1. Stir together first 5 ingredients. Spoon chicken mixture evenly down center of tortillas, and roll up. Arrange, seam sides down, in a lightly greased 6-qt. slow cooker, stacking tortillas, if needed.
2. Stir together sour cream and taco sauce; spoon over enchiladas. Cover and cook on LOW 4½ hours. Remove lid, and sprinkle enchiladas with 1 cup cheese.
3. Cover and cook on LOW 15 more minutes or until cheese melts. Serve enchiladas with desired toppings. **Makes** 8 enchiladas.

Sausage-and-White Bean Cassoulet

PREP: 10 MIN., COOK: 8 HR.

Serve this dish with a tossed green salad drizzled with vinaigrette.

2 (16-oz.) cans great Northern beans,
    undrained
1 (28-oz.) can diced tomatoes,
    undrained
1 (14-oz.) package smoked turkey
    sausage, sliced
¾ cup vegetable broth
3 medium carrots, sliced
1 cup frozen chopped onion, minced
2 garlic cloves, minced
½ tsp. salt
½ tsp. dried thyme
¼ tsp. pepper
1 bay leaf
½ cup fine, dry breadcrumbs
¼ cup freshly grated Parmesan cheese

1. Combine first 11 ingredients in a 5- qt. slow cooker.
2. Cover and cook on LOW 8 hours or until vegetables are tender. Remove and discard bay leaf.
3. Stir in breadcrumbs. Sprinkle each serving with Parmesan cheese before serving. **Makes** 6 servings.

Slow-Cooked Sides

Rounding out a meal is easy with these veggie, pasta, and rice choices.

Barbecue Baked Beans
family favorite
PREP: 20 MIN., COOK: 12 HR., STAND: 1 HR.
This recipe's 12-hour cook time allows you the flexibility to go to work, come home, fire up the grill, and entertain guests—the beans will be done just in time for dinner to be served.

1 (20-oz.) package dried Cajun 15-bean soup mix
1 (12-oz.) package diced cooked ham
2 cups chicken broth
1 cup chopped onion
1 (18-oz.) bottle hickory smoke barbecue sauce
¼ cup firmly packed light brown sugar
¼ cup molasses
½ tsp. salt
¼ tsp. ground red pepper

1. Reserve spice packet in soup mix for other uses. Place beans in a large glass bowl; add water 2 inches above beans. Microwave at HIGH 15 minutes; cover and let stand 1 hour. Drain.
2. Combine beans, ham, broth, and onion in a 4-qt. slow cooker. Combine barbecue sauce and remaining 4 ingredients; stir into bean mixture.
3. Cover and cook on LOW 12 hours or until beans are tender and sauce is slightly thickened. **Makes** 9 servings.

Note: For testing purposes only, we used Hurst's HamBeens Cajun 15-Bean Soup Mix, Hormel Diced Cooked Ham, and KC Masterpiece Hickory Barbecue Sauce.

Hot-and-Spicy Black-Eyed Peas
PREP: 20 MIN.; COOK: 8 HR., 30 MIN.; STAND: 8 HR.
Jalapeño pepper and Mexican-style stewed tomatoes spice up these black-eyed peas.

1 (16-oz.) package dried black-eyed peas
4 green onions, chopped
1 red bell pepper, chopped
1 jalapeño pepper, diced
1 (3-oz.) package pepperoni slices, diced
2 cups hot water
1 chicken bouillon cube
½ tsp. salt
¼ tsp. ground red pepper
1 (14½-oz.) can Mexican-style stewed tomatoes
¾ cup uncooked quick rice

1. Place peas in a 5-qt. slow cooker. Cover with water 2 inches above peas; let stand 8 hours. Drain.
2. Combine peas and next 8 ingredients in slow cooker.
3. Cover and cook on LOW 8 hours or until beans are tender. Stir in tomatoes and rice. Cover and cook on LOW 30 more minutes or until rice is tender. **Makes** 12 cups.

Spinach-Artichoke Casserole
PREP: 20 MIN., COOK: 2 HR. OR 4 HR.
Choose to serve this casserole as a side dish or as an appetizer. Toasted Melba rounds make sturdy dippers for serving this dish straight out of the pot.

1 Tbsp. butter or margarine
1 (8-oz.) package sliced fresh mushrooms
2 garlic cloves, pressed
1 Tbsp. lemon juice
½ tsp. pepper
2 (10-oz.) packages frozen chopped spinach, thawed
1 (14-oz.) can quartered artichoke hearts, drained and chopped
1 (10¾-oz.) can reduced-fat, reduced-sodium cream of mushroom soup
1 (8-oz.) container reduced-fat sour cream
3 green onions, chopped
2 Tbsp. all-purpose flour
1 Tbsp. chopped fresh parsley
¼ tsp. Worcestershire sauce
2 cups (8 oz.) shredded Monterey Jack cheese with peppers

1. Melt butter in a large skillet over medium-high heat. Add mushrooms and next 3 ingredients, and sauté 5 minutes.
2. Meanwhile, drain spinach well, pressing between paper towels. Stir together spinach and next 7 ingredients in a bowl.
3. Stir mushroom mixture into spinach mixture. Add 1 cup cheese, stirring well. Spoon into a 4-qt. slow cooker. Sprinkle with remaining 1 cup cheese.
4. Cover and cook on HIGH 2 hours or on LOW 4 hours. **Makes** 8 to 10 servings.

Cleanup Secret

Always allow the slow cooker insert to cool completely before washing it. Cold water poured over a hot insert can cause cracking.

Slow-Cooked Collard Greens

PREP: 5 MIN., COOK: 9 HR.

1 smoked turkey wing (about 1¼ lb.)
2 (14-oz.) cans seasoned chicken
   broth
2 (1-lb.) packages chopped fresh collard
   greens
5 green onions, chopped
1 green bell pepper, seeded and
   coarsely chopped
¾ tsp. salt
½ tsp. black pepper
Pepper sauce

1. Remove skin and meat from turkey wing, discarding skin and bone. Coarsely chop meat.
2. Combine chopped turkey and next 6 ingredients in a 6-qt. slow cooker.
3. Cover and cook on LOW 9 hours or until greens are tender. Serve with pepper sauce. **Makes** 10 to 12 servings.

Sweet Potato Casserole With Pecan Topping

family favorite
PREP: 14 MIN., COOK: 4 HR.
This holiday side cooks on the countertop while your turkey and dressing fill your oven.

2 (29-oz.) cans sweet potatoes in syrup,
   drained and mashed (about 4 cups
   mashed)
⅓ cup butter, melted
½ cup granulated sugar
3 Tbsp. light brown sugar
2 large eggs, lightly beaten
1 tsp. vanilla extract
½ tsp. ground cinnamon
¼ tsp. ground nutmeg
⅓ cup heavy whipping cream
¾ cup chopped pecans
¾ cup firmly packed light brown sugar
¼ cup all-purpose flour
2 Tbsp. butter, melted

1. Combine first 8 ingredients in a large bowl; beat at medium speed with an electric mixer until smooth. Add whipping cream; stir well. Pour into a lightly greased 3-qt. slow cooker.
2. Combine pecans and remaining 3 ingredients in a small bowl. Sprinkle over sweet potatoes.
3. Cover and cook on HIGH 3 to 4 hours. **Makes** 8 servings.;

Mexican Macaroni

family favorite
PREP: 7 MIN., COOK: 4 HR., 30 MIN.
This dish is an interesting spin on the typical mac-and-cheese recipe. Green chiles give this comforting dish just enough kick to make it spicy.

1 (8-oz.) package elbow macaroni,
   uncooked
1 (10-oz.) can diced tomatoes and green
   chiles, undrained
1 (10¾-oz.) can cream of mushroom
   soup, undiluted
1 cup water
1 (8-oz.) container sour cream
1 (4.5-oz.) can chopped green
   chiles
2 cups (8 oz.) shredded Mexican four-
   cheese blend

1. Stir together first 6 ingredients in a bowl; stir in 1½ cups cheese. Pour mixture into a lightly greased 3-qt. slow cooker; top with remaining ½ cup cheese.
2. Cover and cook on LOW 4½ hours or until macaroni is done. **Makes** 6 servings.

Toasted Herb Rice

PREP: 7 MIN., COOK: 2 HR.

3 Tbsp. butter or margarine
1¾ cups uncooked converted long-grain
   rice
2 (14-oz.) cans chicken broth
¼ tsp. salt
6 green onions, chopped
1 tsp. dried basil
⅓ cup pine nuts, toasted
Garnish: fresh basil sprig

1. Melt butter in a large skillet over medium-high heat; add rice, and sauté 4 minutes or until golden brown. Combine sautéed rice, broth, and next 3 ingredients in a 4-qt. slow cooker.
2. Cover and cook on HIGH 2 hours or until liquid is absorbed and rice is tender. Stir in pine nuts. Garnish, if desired. **Makes** 6 servings.

Note: For testing purposes only, we used Uncle Ben's Converted Long-Grain Rice.

Sweet Endings

Create a dessert bonanza with unexpected finales from your slow cooker.

Triple Chocolate-Covered Peanut Clusters

make ahead • freezeable
PREP: 15 MIN., COOK: 2 HR.
Clusters may be frozen up to 1 month.

1 (16-oz.) jar dry-roasted peanuts
1 (16-oz.) jar unsalted dry-roasted
   peanuts
18 (2-oz.) chocolate candy coating
   squares, cut in half
2 cups (12-oz. package) semisweet
   chocolate morsels
1 (4-oz.) package German chocolate
   baking squares, broken into pieces
1 (9.75-oz.) can salted whole cashews
1 tsp. vanilla extract

1. Combine first 5 ingredients in a 3½- or 4-qt. slow cooker.
2. Cover and cook on LOW 2 hours or until melted. Stir chocolate mixture. Add cashews and vanilla, stirring well to coat cashews.
3. Drop nut mixture by heaping tablespoonfuls onto wax paper. Let stand until firm. Store in an airtight container. **Makes** 5 pounds or about 60 clusters.

Cinnamon-Raisin Bread Pudding

PREP: 13 MIN., COOK: 3 HR., CHILL: 1 HR.

3 large eggs, beaten
½ cup sugar
1 tsp. ground cinnamon
¼ tsp. ground nutmeg
1 cup milk
1 cup whipping cream
1 tsp. vanilla extract
2 Tbsp. butter or margarine, melted
1 (1-lb.) cinnamon-raisin bread loaf, cut into 1-inch cubes
½ cup chopped pecans, toasted
Whipped cream (optional)

1. Whisk together first 4 ingredients in a large bowl; stir in milk, cream, vanilla, and butter. Add bread cubes and pecans, stirring gently just until bread is moistened. Cover and chill 1 hour.
2. Pour bread mixture into a lightly greased 2½-qt. soufflé dish; cover with aluminum foil. Pour 1 cup water into a 6-qt. round slow cooker; place a wire rack to fit cooker on bottom. Set soufflé dish on rack.
3. Cover and cook on HIGH 3 hours or until a sharp knife comes out clean. Cool slightly before serving. Serve warm with whipped cream, if desired. **Makes** 8 servings.

Cinnamon Apples

family favorite

PREP: 16 MIN., COOK: 6 HR.

Serve these sweet apples alone or over ice cream or pound cake.

6 medium Granny Smith apples, peeled and cut into eighths
1 Tbsp. lemon juice
½ cup firmly packed dark brown sugar
½ cup chopped walnuts
½ cup maple syrup
¼ cup sweetened dried cranberries (we tested with Craisins)
¼ cup butter, melted
2 tsp. ground cinnamon
2 Tbsp. water
1 Tbsp. cornstarch

1. Combine apples and lemon juice in a 4-qt. slow cooker; toss well to coat. Add brown sugar and next 5 ingredients, combining well.
2. Cover and cook on LOW 3 hours.
3. Stir together water and cornstarch in a small bowl; stir into apples.
4. Cover and cook on LOW 3 more hours or until apples are tender. **Makes** 6 to 8 servings.

Apple Crisp

PREP: 30 MIN., COOK: 7 HR., 30 MIN.

The type of apples used in an apple crisp or pie can make or break the dessert. Use an all-purpose or cooking apple, such as Granny Smith, Fuji, Braeburn, or other handpicked apples straight from a local orchard.

8 large Granny Smith apples, peeled and sliced (about 4 lb.)
1½ cups all-purpose baking mix, divided
1 cup firmly packed light brown sugar, divided
2 tsp. lemon juice
2 tsp. vanilla extract
1 tsp. ground cinnamon
¼ tsp. ground nutmeg
5 Tbsp. butter, cut into pieces and divided
Vanilla ice cream

1. Combine apples, ½ cup baking mix, ½ cup brown sugar, lemon juice, and next 3 ingredients, tossing to coat. Add 3 tablespoons butter. Spoon into a lightly greased 5-qt. slow cooker.
2. Combine remaining 1 cup baking mix and remaining ½ cup brown sugar; cut in remaining 2 tablespoons butter with a pastry blender until crumbly. Sprinkle evenly over apple mixture.
3. Cover and cook on LOW 7½ hours or until apples are tender and topping is golden. Serve with ice cream. **Makes** 6 servings.

Cookie-Crusted Rhubarb Cherry Dessert

PREP: 5 MIN., COOK: 5 HR.

We used plain shortbread cookies, but you can use the variety with pecans if you'd like.

1½ cups firmly packed light brown sugar
⅓ cup all-purpose flour
2 (16-oz.) packages frozen cut rhubarb
2 (14.5-oz.) cans pitted tart cherries, drained
1 Tbsp. lemon juice
1 Tbsp. butter
2 tsp. vanilla extract
2 cups coarsely chopped shortbread cookies

1. Stir together sugar and flour in a 4-quart slow cooker. Add rhubarb, cherries, and lemon juice, tossing to coat.
2. Cover and cook on LOW 5 hours. Stir in butter and vanilla. Sprinkle each serving with coarsely chopped cookies. **Makes** 8 servings.

Caramel Fondue

make ahead

PREP: 12 MIN.; COOK: 3 HR., 30 MIN.

Keep this fondue warm in the slow cooker for easy dipping. Reheat any leftovers in the microwave, stirring at one-minute intervals until heated through.

2 (14-oz.) packages caramels
2 (14-oz.) cans sweetened condensed milk
Apple slices
Pound cake squares

1. Place caramels in a 3-qt. slow cooker; stir in condensed milk.
2. Cover and cook on LOW 3½ hours, stirring occasionally, until caramels melt and mixture is smooth. Serve with apple slices and pound cake squares. **Makes** 4½ cups or 18 servings.

appendices

handy substitutions

ingredient	substitution
baking products	
Baking powder, 1 teaspoon	• ½ teaspoon cream of tartar plus ¼ teaspoon baking soda
Chocolate	
semisweet, 1 ounce	• 1 ounce unsweetened chocolate plus 1 tablespoon sugar
unsweetened, 1 ounce or square	• 3 tablespoons cocoa plus 1 tablespoon fat
chips, semisweet, 6-ounce package, melted	• 2 ounces unsweetened chocolate, 2 tablespoons shortening plus ½ cup sugar
Cocoa, ¼ cup	• 1 ounce unsweetened chocolate (decrease fat in recipe by ½ tablespoon)
Corn syrup, light, 1 cup	• 1 cup sugar plus ¼ cup water • 1 cup honey
Cornstarch, 1 tablespoon	• 2 tablespoons all-purpose flour or granular tapioca
Flour	
all-purpose, 1 tablespoon	• 1½ teaspoons cornstarch, potato starch, or rice starch • 1 tablespoon rice flour or corn flour • 1½ tablespoons whole wheat flour
all-purpose, 1 cup sifted	• 1 cup plus 2 tablespoons sifted cake flour
cake, 1 cup sifted	• 1 cup minus 2 tablespoons all-purpose flour
self-rising, 1 cup	• 1 cup all-purpose flour, 1 teaspoon baking powder plus ½ teaspoon salt
Shortening	
melted, 1 cup	• 1 cup cooking oil (don't use cooking oil unless recipe calls for melted shortening)
solid, 1 cup (used in baking)	• 1⅛ cups butter or margarine (decrease salt called for in recipe by ½ teaspoon)
Sugar	
brown, 1 cup firmly packed	• 1 cup granulated white sugar
powdered, 1 cup	• 1 cup sugar plus 1 tablespoon cornstarch (processed in food processor)
granulated white, 1 teaspoon	• ⅛ teaspoon noncaloric sweetener solution or follow manufacturer's directions
granulated white, 1 cup	• 1 cup corn syrup (decrease liquid called for in recipe by ¼ cup) • 1 cup honey (decrease liquid called for in recipe by ¼ cup)
Tapioca, granular, 1 tablespoon	• 1½ teaspoons cornstarch or 1 tablespoon all-purpose flour
dairy products	
Butter, 1 cup	• ⅞ to 1 cup shortening or lard plus ½ teaspoon salt • 1 cup margarine (2 sticks; do not substitute whipped or low-fat margarine)
Cream	
heavy (30% to 40% fat), 1 cup	• ¾ cup milk plus ⅓ cup butter or margarine (for cooking and baking; will not whip)
light (15% to 20% fat), 1 cup	• ¾ cup milk plus 3 tablespoons butter or margarine (for cooking and baking) • 1 cup evaporated milk, undiluted
half-and-half, 1 cup	• ⅞ cup milk plus ½ tablespoon butter or margarine (for cooking and baking) • 1 cup evaporated milk, undiluted
whipped, 1 cup	• 1 cup frozen whipped topping, thawed
Egg	
1 large	• ¼ cup egg substitute
2 large	• 3 small eggs or ½ cup egg substitute • 1 large egg plus 2 egg whites
1 egg white (2 tablespoons)	• 2 tablespoons egg substitute
Milk	
buttermilk, 1 cup	• 1 tablespoon vinegar or lemon juice plus whole milk to make 1 cup (let stand 10 minutes) • 1 cup plain yogurt • 1 cup whole milk plus 1¾ teaspoons cream of tartar
fat free, 1 cup	• 4 to 5 tablespoons nonfat dry milk powder plus enough water to make 1 cup • ½ cup evaporated skim milk plus ½ cup water
whole, 1 cup	• 4 to 5 tablespoons nonfat dry milk powder plus enough water to make 1 cup • ½ cup evaporated milk plus ½ cup water

handy substitutions, continued

ingredient	substitution

Milk (continued)
sweetened condensed,
1 (14-ounce) can (about 1¼ cups)
	• Heat the following ingredients until sugar and butter dissolve: ⅓ cup plus
	  2 tablespoons evaporated milk, 1 cup sugar, 3 tablespoons butter or margarine.
	• Add 1 cup plus 2 tablespoons nonfat dry milk powder to ½ cup warm water.
	  Mix well. Add ¾ cup sugar, and stir until smooth.

Sour cream, 1 cup	• 1 cup plain yogurt plus 3 tablespoons melted butter or 1 tablespoon cornstarch • 1 tablespoon lemon juice plus evaporated milk to equal 1 cup
Yogurt, 1 cup (plain)	• 1 cup buttermilk

miscellaneous

ingredient	substitution
Broth, beef or chicken canned broth, 1 cup	• 1 bouillon cube or 1 teaspoon bouillon granules dissolved in 1 cup boiling water
Garlic 1 small clove garlic salt, 1 teaspoon	 • ⅛ teaspoon garlic powder or minced dried garlic • ⅛ teaspoon garlic powder plus ⅞ teaspoon salt
Gelatin, flavored, 3-ounce package	• 1 tablespoon unflavored gelatin plus 2 cups fruit juice
Herbs, fresh, chopped, 1 tablespoon	• 1 teaspoon dried herbs or ¼ teaspoon ground herbs
Honey, 1 cup	• 1¼ cups sugar plus ¼ cup water
Mustard, dried, 1 teaspoon	• 1 tablespoon prepared mustard
Tomatoes, fresh, chopped, 2 cups	• 1 (16-ounce) can (may need to drain)
Tomato sauce, 2 cups	• ¾ cup tomato paste plus 1 cup water

alcohol substitutions

alcohol	substitution
Amaretto, 2 tablespoons	• ¼ to ½ teaspoon almond extract*
Bourbon or Sherry, 2 tablespoons	• 1 to 2 teaspoons vanilla extract*
Brandy, fruit-flavored liqueur, port wine, rum, or sweet sherry: ¼ cup or more	• Equal amount of unsweetened orange or apple juice plus 1 teaspoon vanilla extract or corresponding flavor
Brandy or rum, 2 tablespoons	• ½ to 1 teaspoon brandy or rum extract*
Grand Marnier or other orange liqueur, 2 tablespoons	• 2 tablespoons unsweetened orange juice concentrate or 2 tablespoons orange juice and ½ teaspoon orange extract
Kahlúa or other coffee or chocolate liqueur, 2 tablespoons	• ½ to 1 teaspoon chocolate extract plus ½ to 1 teaspoon instant coffee dissolved in 2 tablespoons water
Marsala, ¼ cup	• ¼ cup white grape juice or ¼ cup dry white wine plus 1 teaspoon brandy
Wine red, ¼ cup or more white, ¼ cup or more	 • Equal measure of red grape juice or cranberry juice • Equal measure of white grape juice or nonalcoholic white wine

Add water, white grape juice, or apple juice to get the specified amount of liquid (when the liquid amount is crucial).

equivalent measures

3 teaspoons	= 1 tablespoon	2 tablespoons (liquid)	= 1 ounce	⅛ cup	= 2 tablespoons
4 tablespoons	= ¼ cup	1 cup	= 8 fluid ounces	⅓ cup	= 5 tablespoons plus 1 teaspoon
5⅓ tablespoons	= ⅓ cup	2 cups	= 1 pint (16 fluid ounces)		
8 tablespoons	= ½ cup			⅔ cup	= 10 tablespoons plus 2 teaspoons
16 tablespoons	= 1 cup	4 cups	= 1 quart		
		4 quarts	= 1 gallon	¾ cup	= 12 tablespoons

ground rules for grilling

meat	cooking time	method	instructions
Beef			
Ground beef patties	8 to 12 minutes	Direct	Cook, without grill lid, until no longer pink.
Steaks (1 to 1½ inches thick)	8 to 12 minutes	Direct	Cook, without grill lid, to at least 145°.
Steaks (2 inches thick)	8 to 10 minutes	Direct	Cook, covered with grill lid, to at least 145°.
Tenderloin	30 to 45 minutes	Indirect	Cook, covered with grill lid, to at least 145°.
Brisket (6 pounds)	3 to 4 hours	Indirect	Cook, covered with grill lid, to at least 145°.
Fish			
Whole fish (per inch of thickness)	10 to 12 minutes	Direct	Cook, covered with grill lid.
Fish fillets (per inch of thickness)	10 minutes	Direct	Cook, without grill lid.
Lamb			
Chops or steaks (1 inch thick)	10 to 12 minutes	Direct	Cook, without grill lid, to at least 145°.
Leg of lamb (boneless or butterflied)	40 to 50 minutes	Indirect	Cook, covered with grill lid, to at least 145°.
Pork			
Pork chops (½ inch thick)	7 to 11 minutes	Direct	Cook, covered with grill lid, to 160°.
Pork chops (¾ inch thick)	10 to 12 minutes	Direct	Cook, covered with grill lid, to 160°.
Pork chops (1½ inches thick)	16 to 22 minutes	Direct	Cook, covered with grill lid, to 160°.
Kabobs (1-inch cubes)	9 to 13 minutes	Direct	Cook, covered with grill lid, to 160°.
Pork tenderloin (½ to 1½ pounds)	16 to 21 minutes	Indirect	Cook, covered with grill lid, to 160°.
Ribs	1½ to 2 hours	Indirect	Cook, covered with grill lid, to 160°.
Poultry			
Chicken (whole, halves, quarters, and thighs)	45 to 55 minutes	Indirect	Cook, covered with grill lid, to 165° or until desired doneness.
Chicken (bone-in breast)	25 to 30 minutes	Indirect	Cook, covered with grill lid, to 165°.
Chicken (boneless breast)	10 to 12 minutes	Direct	Cook, without grill lid.
Turkey (bone-in breast, cut lengthwise in half	40 to 45 minutes	Indirect	Cook, covered with grill lid, to 165°.

metric equivilants

The recipes that appear in this cookbook use the standard United States method for measuring liquid and dry or solid ingredients (teaspoons, tablespoons, and cups). The information on this chart is provided to help cooks outside the U.S. successfully use these recipes. All equivalents are approximate.

METRIC EQUIVALENTS FOR DIFFERENT TYPES OF INGREDIENTS

A standard cup measure of a dry or solid ingredient will vary in weight depending on the type of ingredient. A standard cup of liquid is the same volume for any type of liquid. Use the following chart when converting standard cup measures to grams (weight) or milliliters (volume).

Standard Cup	Fine Powder	Grain	Granular	Liquid Solids	Liquid
	(ex. flour)	(ex. rice)	(ex. sugar)	(ex. butter)	(ex. milk)
1	140 g	150 g	190 g	200 g	240 ml
¾	105 g	113 g	143 g	150 g	180 ml
⅔	93 g	100 g	125 g	133 g	160 ml
½	70 g	75 g	95 g	100 g	120 ml
⅓	47 g	50 g	63 g	67 g	80 ml
¼	35 g	38 g	48 g	50 g	60 ml
⅛	18 g	19 g	24 g	25 g	30 ml

USEFUL EQUIVALENTS FOR DRY INGREDIENTS BY WEIGHT

(To convert ounces to grams, multiply the number of ounces by 30.)

1 oz	=	1/16 lb	=	30 g
4 oz	=	¼ lb	=	120 g
8 oz	=	½ lb	=	240 g
12 oz	=	¾ lb	=	360 g
16 oz	=	1 lb	=	480 g

USEFUL EQUIVALENTS FOR LENGTH

(To convert inches to centimeters, multiply the number of inches by 2.5.)

1 in				=	2.5 cm		
6 in	=	½ ft	=	=	15 cm		
12 in	=	1 ft		=	30 cm		
36 in	=	3 ft	=	1 yd	=	90 cm	
40 in				=	100 cm	=	1 m

USEFUL EQUIVALENTS FOR LIQUID INGREDIENTS BY VOLUME

¼ tsp	=						1 ml
½ tsp	=						2 ml
1 tsp	=						5 ml
3 tsp	=	1 tbls		=	½ fl oz	=	15 ml
	=	2 tbls	= ⅛ cup	=	1 fl oz	=	30 ml
	=	4 tbls	= ¼ cup	=	2 fl oz	=	60 ml
	=	5⅓ tbls	= ⅓ cup	=	3 fl oz	=	80 ml
	=	8 tbls	= ½ cup	=	4 fl oz	=	120 ml
	=	10⅔ tbls	= ⅔ cup	=	5 fl oz	=	160 ml
	=	12 tbls	= ¾ cup	=	6 fl oz	=	180 ml
	=	16 tbls	= 1 cup	=	8 fl oz	=	240 ml
	=	1 pt	= 2 cups	=	16 fl oz	=	480 ml
	=	1 qt	= 4 cups	=	32 fl oz	=	960 ml
					33 fl oz	=	1000 ml = 1 l

USEFUL EQUIVALENTS FOR COOKING/OVEN TEMPERATURES

	Fahrenheit	Celsius	Gas Mark
Freeze Water	32° F	0° C	
Room Temperature	68° F	20° C	
Boil Water	212° F	100° C	
Bake	325° F	160° C	3
	350° F	180° C	4
	375° F	190° C	5
	400° F	200° C	6
	425° F	220° C	7
	450° F	230° C	8
Broil			Grill

menu index

This index lists every menu by suggested occasion. Recipes in bold type are provided with the menu and accompaniments are in regular type.

≫ menus with local flavor

Healthy Southern Supper
Serves 4
(page 32)
Oven-fried Chicken
Creamy Macaroni and Cheese
Green Beans, Corn, and Pea Salad
Ham-and-Broccoli Muffins

Fill Your Plate With Flavor
Serves 4 to 6
(page 88)
Ham-and-Tomato Pie
Caesar-Style Salad or Caesar salad kit
French bread or crescent rolls
S'more Puffs

Spanish Supper
Serves 4
(page 104)
Cuban-Style Shredded Pork over Black Beans 'n' Spuds
Weeknight Fondue

Laid-Back Mexican Menu
Serves 8
(page 132)
Shrimp Mojo de Ajo
Pomegranate Margaritas
Lanny's Salad With Candied Pumpkin Seeds
Mixed Grill With Cilantro Pesto
Pasta Mexicana
Grilled Artichokes and Asparagus
Berries With Tequila Cream

Spicy Supper
Serves 4
(page 193)
Easy Enchiladas
Mexican rice
Pronto Refried Beans
Margaritas and beer

Quick Catfish Supper
Serves 6
(page 218)
Catfish Nuggets With Honey Dipping Sauce
Florentine Potato Salad
Chocolate-Almond Bars

Tex-Mex Family Supper
Serves 8
(page 230)
Tex-Mex Lasagna
Fiesta Salad
Ice-cream sandwiches

Southwestern-Style Gathering
Serves 8
(page 244)
Frozen Cranberry Margaritos (page 257)
Salsas, guacamole, and chips: Buy fresh salsas in the deli or produce department. Add a little chopped fresh cilantro to brighten the flavor. Buy frozen guacamole, and add fresh lime juice to perk it up.
Smoky Chicken Chili
Citrus-Avocado Salad With Tex-Mex Vinaigrette
Cornbread Muffin Trees
Pound Cake With Caramel Icing and Apricot-Ginger Sprinkles

≫ menus for special occasions

New Year's Day Meal
Serves 4 to 6
(page 28)
Classic Barbecue Ribs
Hearty Black-eyed Peas
Turnip Greens Stew
Cornbread

Festive Food
Serves 24
(page 108)
Dressed-Up Burger Wraps (make 4 recipes)
Horseradish-Dijon Potato Salad (make 4 recipes)
Store-bought baked beans
Graduation Cake With Cream Cheese Frosting or
Memorial Day Cupcakes With Cream Cheese Frosting

A Bunch for Brunch
Serves 10
(page 140)
Tex-Mex Brunch Wraps
Buttermilk biscuits with **Boysenberry Butter**
Honey-Nut Granola with yogurt
Peach Pie Quick Bread

Rise and Shine Menu
Serves 8 to 10
(page 158)
Mini Sausage-and-Egg Casseroles
Honey-Ginger Fruit
Banana Breakfast Bread
Orange juice and coffee

Game Day Get-Together
Serves 12
(page 196)
Turkey-Cheddar Kabobs With Honey Mustard Dipping Sauce
Mini Cajun Burgers With Easy Rémoulade
Caramelized Onion Dip with potato chips
Lemony Spinach-Artichoke Dip with corn chips
Team Spirit Cupcakes

A Casual Feast
Serves 8
(page 260)
Bourbon-Cranberry Turkey Tenderloin
Gravy (page 261)
Pecan-Buttermilk Dressing Cakes (page 264)
Sweet-and-Sour Green Beans (page 264)
Cranberry Sweet Potatoes (page 263)
Lemon Rice
Pecan Cheesecake Pie (page 261)
Thanksgiving Sparkler

Hanukkah Feast
Serves 8
(page 268)
Roasted Paprika Chicken
Warm Frisée Salad With Crispy Kosher Salami
Mini Latkes With Salmon-Olive Relish
Pomegranate-Cider Baked Apples With Sugared Piecrust Strips

Christmas Dinner
Serves 6
(page 272)
Holiday Pork Loin Roast
Holiday Roast With Gravy
Sautéed Brussels Sprouts With Apples
Buttermilk Mashed Potatoes
White Chocolate-Cranberry Crème Brûlée

Firehouse Feast
Serves 8
(page 274)
Two-Alarm Deep-Fried Turkey
Cornbread Dressing
Classic Parmesan Scalloped Potatoes
Cranberry Compote
Sweet Potato-Pecan Cupcakes With Cream Cheese Frosting

Dashing Christmas Dinner
Serves 6
(page 288)
Spiced Pecans
Cheese Straws
New Ambrosia With Buttermilk-Coconut Dressing
Squash-and-Mushroom Hominy
Hot Slaw à la Greyhound Grill
Pork Loin Chops With Pear-and-Vidalia Pan Gravy
Sweet Potato-Buttermilk Pie
Hot-Spiced Bourbon Balls

>> menus for family

A Comfy Busy-Day Dinner
Serves 6
(page 38)
Slow-cooker Roast and Gravy
Noodles, mashed potatoes, or
   rice
Sautéed Broccoli Spears
Italian-seasoned cloverleaf rolls
   (Tip: Find these rolls among
   other frozen bread products.)
Blackberry Dumpling Cobbler
   (page 30)

One Swift Dinner
Serves 4
(page 45)
**Smoked Chops-and-Cheese
   Omelets**
Tangelo segments dipped in
   vanilla yogurt or a green
   salad with Ranch dressing
Sparkly Cranberry Scones
Frozen biscuits with raspberry
   jam, or garlic toast
Iced coffee or tea

Family Friendly Dinner
Serves 8
(page 58)
Juiced-up Roast Pork
Edamame Succotash
Cauliflower-Leek Puree
Tomato Florentine
Berry Cobbler (double recipe)

A Chicken-and-Two Plate
Serves 6
(page 63)
Sun-dried Tomato Chicken or
Crispy Seasoned Chicken Cutlets
Hash browns or rice
**Apple-Pear Salad With Lemon-
   Poppy Seed Dressing**
   (page 70)
Vanilla Ice Milk

Sloppy Joe Supper
Serves 8
(page 90)
Slow-cooker Sloppy Joes
Chive 'n' Onion Potato Chips
Easy Coleslaw
Ice-cream sandwiches

Laid-Back Menu
Serves 4
(page 121)
**Turkey, Bacon, and Havarti
   Sandwich**
Sour Cream Coleslaw
Fresh-Squeezed Lemonade

Meal With Pizzazz
Serves 4
(page 122)
Peanut-Baked Chicken
Sesame-Ginger Rice
Steamed broccoli
Orange sherbet

Pack-and-Go Menu
Serves 4
(page 141)
Roasted Red Pepper Sandwiches
Rosemary-Parsley Hummus
Marinated Cucumbers
**Blueberry-Pecan Shortbread
   Squares**
Peach Lemonade

Fast Food Menu
Serves 4
(page 146)
Tasty Turkey Burgers
Herb-Grilled Onion Rings
Potato salad
Chocolate Cookie Bites

Homestyle Chicken Dinner
Serves 4 to 6
(page 156)
Herb-Roasted Chicken
**Mushroom-and-Fresh Parsley
   Noodles**
Sautéed zucchini
Ice cream

Pronto Pasta Supper
Serves 4 to 6
(page 156)
Pronto-Stuffed Pasta Shells
Mixed salad greens with Italian
   dressing
Garlic bread
Fresh fruit or **Honey-Ginger
   Fruit** (page 158)

Fall Family Supper
Serves 6
(page 204)
Ham Steak With Orange Glaze
Roasted Vegetables
Bakery biscuits
**Cinnamon-Caramel Apple
   Dumplings With Golden
   Raisins** (page 202)

Back-to-School Fun
Serves 6
(page 227)
Festive Turkey Rollups
Crunchy-Munchy Mix
Individual packs of yogurt
S'more Cupcakes
Juice boxes

Soup for Supper
Serves 6 to 8
(page 267)
Doc's Corn-and-Potato Chowder
Mixed salad greens
Garlic-Herb Bread

>> menus for mornings

Start With Tex-Mex
Serves 8
(page 67)
Southwest Eggs Benedict with
   Chipotle Hollandaise Sauce
Creamy grits
Pineapple-Grapefruit Spritzer

Midmorning Menu
Serves 8 to 10
(page 123)
Blushing Mimosas
Brie-and-Veggie Breakfast Strata
Sweet 'n' Spicy Sausage
Minted Mixed Fruit
Heart-Shaped Cookies

A Bunch for Brunch
Serves 10
(page 140)
Tex-Mex Brunch Wraps
Buttermilk biscuits with
   Boysenberry Butter
Honey-Nut Granola with yogurt
Peach Pie Quick Bread

Rise and Shine Menu
Serves 8 to 10
(page 158)
Mini Sausage-and-Egg
   Casseroles
Honey-Ginger Fruit
Banana Breakfast Bread
Orange juice and coffee

Christmas Morning
Serves 8
(page 294)
Breakfast Tortillias
Baby PB&J Bagel Panini
Cornmeal-Cranberry Muffins
Holiday Cream Cheese Coffee
   Cake
Fruit Dippers
Santa's Cider

>> menus for grilling

Surefire Meal
Serves 4
(page 113)
Garlic Flank Steak
Dill Rice
Grilled Vegetables With Pesto
Creamy Lemonade Pie (page 96)

Steak Dinner
Serves 4
(page 118)
Strip Steak With Rosemary Butter
Steak Fries
Grilled Okra and Tomatoes
Cucumber Salad
Cream-Filled Grilled Pound Cake

Summertime Feast
Serves 6
(page 126)
Grilled Pork Tenderloin
   Sandwiches
Grilled Summer Veggies
Succotash Salad
Fresh Peach-Basil Vinaigrette
   over tomatoes
Cheesecake Tarts

Texan Summer Supper
Serves 8
(page 144)
Bacon-Wrapped Pork
   Medallions With Tomato-
   Corn Salsa
Grilled Lemon-Garlic Potatoes
Grilled Okra-and-Tomatillo
   Salad
Apple Slaw
Blond Texas Sheet Cake

Sizzling Supper
Serves 6
(page 153)
Honey Mustard Pork Kabobs or
   Cajun Turkey Kabobs or
   Caribbean Pork Kabobs or
   Spicy Chicken Kabobs
Grilled Peaches Jezebel
Crusty French bread
Lemonade and tea

Steak-and-Potatoes Menu
Serves 6
(page 236)
Spice-Rubbed Flank Steak
Grilled Sweet Potatoes With
   Creamy Basil Vinaigrette
Green Beans With Bacon
Whole Grain Marshmallow
   Crispy Bars

>> menus for company

Memorable Menu
Serves 6
(page 40)
Stuffed Cherry Tomatoes
Mixed Greens Salad With Apple
   Cider Vinaigrette
Marinated Flank Steak
Roasted Garlic Smashed
   Potatoes
Spinach-and-Red Pepper Sauté
Chocolate Chimichangas With
   Raspberry Sauce

Easygoing Entertaining Menu
Serves 8
(page 116)
Delta Tamales
Dixie Caviar
Shrimp Shooters
Lemon Squares
Beer, wine, and soft drinks

Splashy Gathering
Serves 16
(page 138)
Cucumber Dip
Italian Skewers
Mini Roast Beef Sandwiches
Brown Sugar Fruit Dip
Tropical White Chocolate
   Cookies
Beer and soft drinks

Ghoulish Gathering
Serves 6
(page 234)
Green Dip With Spooky Chips
Monster Eyes
Purchased sub sandwiches or
   chicken wings
Candy
Lemonade

Celebrate With Friends
Serves 6 to 8
(page 240)
Pink Lemonade Cocktail
Marinated Mozzarella (page
   246)
Mushroom, Apple, and Goat
   Cheese Salad
Mustard-and-Wine Pork
   Tenderloin
Browned Butter Mashed
   Potatoes
Green Bean-and-Red Bell Pepper
   Toss
Brandy-Vanilla Cheesecake Dip
   with fruit and cookies (page
   258)

Plan-Ahead Party for 12
Serves 12
(page 291)
Shrimp with Basic Cocktail
   Sauce, Curry Mayonnaise, and
   Spicy Rémoulade
Beef Tidbits With Horseradish
   Sauce
Black-eyed Pea Dip
Vegetable tray With Curry
   Mayonnaise
Savory Deviled Eggs
Southwest Fondue
Jingle Juice

Stop by for Supper
Serves 8
(page 293)
Hot Brown Panini or Muffuletta
   Panini or Peppery Turkey-and-
   Brie Panini
Southern Tortellini Minestrone
Mint Hot Fudge-Brownie
   Sundaes

Festive Menu
Serves 6
(page 296)
Roast Pork Loin With Crumb
   Crust
Loaded Baked Potato Casserole
Honey-Glazed Carrots
Steamed broccoli (or asparagus)
Double Coffee Tiramisù

recipe title index

This index lists every recipe by food category and/or major ingredient.
All microwave recipe page numbers are preceded by an "M."

month-by-month index

This index alphabetically lists every food article and accompanying recipes by month. All microwave recipe page numbers are preceded by an "M."

home for the holidays

general recipe index

This index lists every recipe by food category and/or major ingredient.
All microwave recipe page numbers are preceded by an "M."

favorite recipes journal

Jot down your family's and your favorite recipes for quick and handy reference. And don't forget to include the dishes that drew rave reviews when company came for dinner.

RECIPE	SOURCE/PAGE	REMARKS